Charles Handfield

Clinical observations on functional nervous disorders

Second American Edition

Charles Handfield

Clinical observations on functional nervous disorders
Second American Edition

ISBN/EAN: 9783337713676

Printed in Europe, USA, Canada, Australia, Japan

Cover: Foto ©ninafisch / pixelio.de

More available books at **www.hansebooks.com**

CLINICAL OBSERVATIONS

ON

FUNCTIONAL NERVOUS DISORDERS.

BY

C. HANDFIELD JONES,
M.B. CANTAB.; F.R.C.P. LOND.; F.R.S.; PHYSICIAN TO ST. MARY'S HOSPITAL.

SECOND AMERICAN EDITION.

PHILADELPHIA:
HENRY C. LEA.
1868.

TO

SIR JAMES RANALD MARTIN, C.B., F.R.S.,

PHYSICIAN TO THE COUNCIL OF INDIA,

MEMBER OF THE ROYAL ASIATIC SOCIETY OF GREAT BRITAIN

AND IRELAND, ETC. ETC.,

This Work is Dedicated,

AS A TRIBUTE OF RESPECT AND ADMIRATION DUE TO HIS MANLY

VIRTUES, HIS PROFESSIONAL ATTAINMENTS,

AND

THE EMINENT SERVICES HE HAS RENDERED TO HIS COUNTRY,

BY HIS SINCERE AND OBLIGED FRIEND,

THE AUTHOR.

PREFACE.

This work professes to contain little more than a truthful record of experience and an endeavour to view that experience in the light of scientific research. Though I have cast it in the form of a treatise on nervous disorders, I regard it, of course, as a mere and very imperfect contribution to the literature of so great a subject. I have only touched on those points which seemed to me to have most bearing on practice, but have endeavoured as far as possible to indicate general principles both in pathology and treatment. I am not without hope that the reviewing of a number of cognate affections may be of advantage to the reader, as showing how close a family resemblance prevails among them, and how the phenomena of one often elucidate those of another disorder. I have necessarily been led to set much value on the results of treatment as indications of the essential nature of disease, in which I am supported by no less a name than Gooch, and this will explain why I have recorded few cases except those in which some definite conclusion can be drawn from the actions of remedies. Having myself generally derived most profit from the records of cases, I have used this method of illustration freely, and I trust not unprofitably. There is this value in authentic histories of disease that they represent actual occurrences, and are always available for any future inquirer as evidence of the writer's views, which can hardly be said of abstract descriptions. I do not think it so necessary, as some consider it, to be accurately acquainted with the natural history of disease, for the reason that I believe it impossible in most cases to ascertain it. The attempt recently made by Flint to determine the duration of acute rheumatism, no real treatment being adopted, gives in thirteen cases the sufficiently wide variation of from twelve to fifty-six days. I believe with most diseases except the exanthemata it would be nearly the same. In fact I am more and more convinced that we ought not to think of diseases as uniform entities, but as very varying and inconstant pathological conditions.

The points which I would indicate as most worthy of attention are the recognition of primary paresis of nervous centres, and its distinction from reflex paralysis, the numerous illustrations of vasomotor nerve disorder, the theory of inhibitory action, the remarkable affinity between paralysis, spasm, anæsthesia, and neuralgia, the different quality of nervous disorder apparently of the same kind in different instances, the intimate relation of neuralgia in most instances to debility, and the importance of an accurate adjustment of remedies to each individual case.

While I fully agree with my master, Arnold, in having an unfeigned respect for all kinds of work, I yet think that we have clear indications at the present day what kind of work is most needed, and most likely to bear fruit. While duly estimating morbid anatomy and minute physical diagnosis, I cannot but reiterate the wish I have several years ago expressed, that we were more earnest in inquiring into the working of our means of cure, and gaining a more thorough mastery over them. Some united mode of action might surely be devised, I care little about the particular plan, which might in the course of years give us much more certain knowledge about many things in therapeutics than we at present possess. What is the real value of colchicum in gouty disease? Is digitalis to be specially relied on as a safe stimulant to a weak and failing heart? Have mercury and antimony a positive control over sthenic inflammatory action, or have they none? Should the treatment of acute disease differ materially in town and country folk? What is the real action of opium? These and such questions as these I would fain have answered as the profession could answer them if the means at their disposal were effectually employed.

I must not conclude without expressing my thanks to many gentlemen who have worked with me as clinical assistants during the past thirteen years at St. Mary's, and whose help has often aided me very greatly in studying the cases which have come before me.

49 GREEN STREET,
    PARK LANE.

CONTENTS.

			PAGE
CHAPTER	I.	INTRODUCTORY	17
"	II.	GENERAL PATHOLOGY	20
"	III.	CEREBRAL ANÆMIA	48
"	IV.	ANÆMIA OF THE SPINAL CORD	61
"	V.	HYPERÆMIA OF THE BRAIN	63
"	VI.	SPINAL HYPERÆMIA	71
"	VII.	CEREBRAL PARESIS	74
"	VIII.	SPINAL PARESIS	88
"	IX.	CEREBRAL EXCITEMENT	100
"	X.	DELIRIUM TREMENS	112
"	XI.	TETANUS	123
"	XII.	CATALEPSY	131
"	XIII.	EPILEPSY	134
"	XIV.	HEADACHE	153
"	XV.	VERTIGO	157
"	XVI.	CHOREA	160
"	XVII.	PARALYSIS AGITANS	165
"	XVIII.	SPASMODIC AFFECTIONS	169
"	XIX.	SLEEPLESSNESS	174
"	XX.	FACIAL NEURALGIA	181
"	XXI.	FACIAL PARALYSIS	188
"	XXII.	RETINAL HYPERÆSTHESIA	190
"	XXIII.	THROAT DYSÆSTHESIA	193
"	XXIV.	LINGUAL NEURALGIA	194
"	XXV.	BRACHIAL NEURALGIA	197
"	XXVI.	SCIATICA	204
"	XXVII.	ANGINA PECTORIS	210

CONTENTS.

		PAGE
Chapter XXVIII.	Respiratory Neuroses	231
" XXIX.	Myalgia	248
" XXX.	Abdominal Neuralgia	249
" XXXI.	Neuroses of the Urinary Organs	261
" XXXII.	Neuroses of the Lower Intestine	268
" XXXIII.	Uterine Neuroses	271
" XXXIV.	Cutaneous Neuroses	274
" XXXV.	Malarioid Disorder	287
" XXXVI.	Secretion Fluxes	305
" XXXVII.	Hysteria	307
" XXXVIII.	Syphilitic and Rheumatic Nerve Affections	310
" XXXIX.	Remedies	315
Appendix		337
Vindemiatio		343

CLINICAL OBSERVATIONS

ON

FUNCTIONAL NERVOUS DISORDERS.

CHAPTER I.

INTRODUCTORY.

OF all the parts which go to make up the wonderful whole of the human body, there is none to which a deeper and more mysterious interest is attached than to the nervous system. By this we think, and move, and have our conscious being; in this, if anywhere, inhabits our "divinæ particula auræ;" by this we are linked with the outer world, and are capable of affecting and being again affected by the persons and things around us. By this, our immaterial acts upon and sways our material part; and by the higher development of this, and its capability for higher actions, man is especially distinguished from the lower creation. All the passions and emotions, all the intellectual efforts, all the perceptions and recollections, operate through and on this system. If this be so, is it any wonder that exhaustion should frequently befall this delicate and complex machinery, or that its disorders should be amongst the most frequent that our fallen nature is doomed to bear? Even under favourable circumstances, the nervous system must often be hardly taxed: how much more, then, will this be the case when sorrow, toil, and anxiety predominate in the lot assigned?

It is difficult to form a decided opinion on the matter; but there seems, I think, reason to entertain the belief that failure of nervous power is much more characteristic of disease of the present day, than of that which prevailed thirty years ago. For this there may be various causes: the greater confinement of large numbers of the population within doors, and often in unhealthy rooms or workshops; the harder struggle to be maintained in the battle of life, the greater amount of the *commoda vitæ*—may all tend to increase the susceptibility of the nervous system, and to impair its resisting power. Further, in the two following instances we have, it seems to me, considerable evidence of the altered character of morbid action, depending, in all probability, on still more general causes than those just mentioned. (1). Sir Ranald Martin informs me, that whereas invalids returning from India used to take leave of their agues when they arrived in this country, this is no longer the case, relapses being of frequent occurrence. Practitioners of long experience, also, tell us that aguish disorder prevails of late years in places where it was previously unknown, without there being any change in the state of the soil to account for it. (2). There seems no question that puerperal fever is a disease of very different character in different epidemics. As Dr. Ferguson writes, "under this test," viz., of therapeutic action, "Gooch discovered that puerperal fevers were many, requiring various modes of treatment." I believe this statement cannot be denied; and if not, it seems a legitimate inference that other diseases may vary also at different times. I may add that my own experience certainly indicates that cholera has a modifying influence on disease. I have not met with nearly so many peculiar neuroses of depression the last few years, as I did for three or four after the last epidemic. Dr. Prout gives testimony to the same effect, v. p. 67.

However the exact truth may be, whether the type of disease is altered or not, I hold it to be abundantly clear that the great majority of disorders we have to treat at the present time show more or less marked indications of failure of nervous power; and I believe it to be a matter of great practical moment to keep this steadily in view. While, however, believing this, I also think that our current pictures of disease are taken far too exclusively from the sick field of large towns; and I am much inclined to think that if our rural brethren wrote as much as their urban fellows do, they would give a somewhat different account.

The course I propose to pursue is, first, to consider the behaviour of the nerves and nervous centres in certain well-marked simple morbid states, and subsequently to notice the more important features of several classic diseases, and of some other less commonly recognized disorders. I do not intend to deal with the results of manifest organic lesion, but to confine my attention chiefly to such disorders as are termed functional. It seems to me a vain dispute, whether in strict accuracy there are, or are not, any such disorders. The probability is that there are not—that in all morbid action the cells and the fibres of the organs undergo some molecular change from their perfectly normal condition. It is, however, perfectly certain that there are very grave disorders in which the most careful scrutiny fails to detect any actual change, in which complete recovery is perfectly possible, and in which the "juvantia" are such as operate more in modifying the power of the organs than their texture. To take an example: a man may have paralysis of some muscle or group of muscles which yields to the use of strychnia or galvanism. Now, these agents can scarcely be thought to act otherwise than by exciting and increasing the vital power of the affected nerve or nervous centre; or, to put it shortly, as nerve tonics. Cod-liver oil, iron, and phosphorus might be given without effecting the same beneficial change—at least, as speedily, because they are rather analeptics than tonics. They may improve the nutrition of the nervous tissue, but they do not directly arouse it. Now, between such a case of functional paralysis as we have supposed, and paralysis from organic lesion, there is a wide interval. Strychnia and galvanism will, in all probability, make the latter worse; certainly, will not cure it. Something more is needed in this case than to arouse defective nervous energy. Between the typical cases which we have taken of functional and organic disease, there intervene numerous instances of more or less mixed character. Inflammatory disease is from one point of view organic, from another functional. It commences essentially as the latter, it ends as the former.

The arrangement I shall adopt is merely topographical, but will, I hope, be found practically convenient. Commencing with the encephalon, including the cerebral hemispheres, mesocephale, cerebellum, and medulla oblongata, we shall proceed to the spinal cord, and thence to the several nerves or nervous districts, which are found by experience to be most prone to disorder. Under the term cerebral hemispheres is comprised all the convoluted gray exterior of the brain, with its basal ganglia, the corpora striata and thalami optici, and the various longitudinal and transverse commissural fibres. The functions of these parts are eminently mental: they minister to conscious sensation, memory, reflection, judgment, and volition. Their structure is essentially similar to that of other nervous centres, but has this peculiarity—that the gray matter contains a very considerable quantity of loose granular material, and is by no means chiefly made up of nervous cells. This seems to have relation to the rapid nutritional change required by the active function of the tissue. The perfect cell indicates a greater degree of permanency, and slower change than the nucleus with diffused granular material. The very copious supply of blood sent to the hemispheres is also in harmony with this view. The cerebellum is probably concerned in regulating the motor nervous actions, and is, perhaps, the special seat of the muscular sense. The mesocephale is connected with the two chief nerves of special sense, and is, we know from experiment, capable of producing general convulsions when directly irritated. The medulla oblongata is the chief centre of the respiratory nervous actions, and is capable of influencing very materially the cardiac movements: with it are connected all the cranial nerves from the sixth to the ninth. The spinal cord constitutes by its gray matter an independent centre for the nerves which are implanted in it, but is naturally associated by its longitudinal commissural fibres with the superior nervous centres in sensation and volition. The cervical and upper dorsal regions of the cord constitute, according to Bezold, a special motor centre to the heart, furnishing three-fourths of its entire propulsive force. The sympathetic is partly an independent system, partly an offset from the cerebro-spinal; as, indeed, its anatomy indicates.

CHAPTER II.

GENERAL PATHOLOGY.

BEFORE entering on the special study of disease, it seems desirable to allude briefly to some well-established points in neuro-physiology and pathology, and to discuss, in a general manner, some questions which are as yet unsolved. The subjects thus elucidated will be convenient for future reference.

(I.) It is certain that the nervous cords, whether motor or sensory, in the whole of their course, from their origin to their peripheral distribution, allow of no communication of the active state from one fibre to another. A single point of the skin when touched is distinguished by the sensorium from the adjacent, the size of the district thus represented in the brain varying inversely with the abundance of nervous supply; and a single muscle can be put into action without exciting others receiving nerves from the same trunk. It is remarkable how the stimulus of the will can be limited to certain groups of nerve-cells at some distance from each other without affecting others in close proximity. We can call into action the triceps extensor cubiti without moving any other muscle. Yet, the filaments animating this nerve must come, in all probability, from various points of the spinal cord between the fifth cervical and first dorsal nerves; and the cells of these points alone are excited, while others close by remain inactive.

(II.) While the above, which Romberg terms the law of isolated conduction, holds in the peripheral tracts, we find another of a very different kind to come into play in the nervous centres. In them we have—(*a*.) What is termed excito-motory or reflex action, viz., an impression from a centripetal nerve, producing an active state of a motor through the intermedium of certain multipolar cells. Sensation almost invariably ensues at the same time, but is not an essential part of the chain of actions. Volition is quite unconcerned in the act, and is often quite incapable of controlling it. (*b*.) The impression arriving at the centre is communicated, not to a motor, but to a sensory nerve-root, perhaps to several adjacent, or to another more remote. In this way, sensations are produced which continue as long as the original impression is maintained by its existing cause. In certain states of great excitability of the nervous centres, the range over which the primary stimulus may extend, especially in the case where motor nerves are affected, is very considerable. In dealing with neuralgic disorders, this point, viz., the irradiation, as it is called, of sensation, is of capital importance, and may often lead to the discovery of the cause of suffering, which would otherwise have remained quite obscure.

Pfluger lays down the following laws: (1.) That when reflex action occurs on one side, it is always on that where the sensitive nerve has been excited; and if it occurs on both sides, it is strongest on the side stimulated. (2.) When reflex action occurs on both sides from excitation of one, it affects parts symmetrically situated. (3.) Reflex excitation in cerebral nerves extends from before backwards, in spinal nerves from behind forwards. (Vide *Brit. & For. Med.-Chir. Rev.*, Jan. 1864, p. 9.)

(III.) The law of eccentric phenomena affirms that every sensation, as it becomes perceptible to consciousness, is referred to the periphery of a sensitive fibre, no matter at what part of the whole length of the fibre the impression is made. This law is to a certain extent true, but admits, as I shall point out subsequently, of numerous exceptions.

(IV.) It seems to be well ascertained that an *unfelt irritation* may give rise to very various morbid phenomena affecting both the motor and sensory nervous organs. Dr. Brown-Séquard maintains that various forms of insanity, of vertigo, epilepsy, of hallucinations and illusions, and also extasis, catalepsy, hysteria, chorea, hydrophobia, tetanus, &c., may be due to irritations starting from a centripetal nerve, and frequently slightly felt, or unfelt, and that the suppression of these irritations may promptly cure the patient. Graves records a case (Vide *Clin. Med.*, p. 244) where an extremely severe cough, which had resisted all treatment directed to relieve bronchitis, ceased at once on the expulsion of a mass of tapeworm by a dose of turpentine. It does not appear that any symptoms had existed in this case to announce the presence of the intestinal parasite. Perhaps the following instance is still more proving, inasmuch as the seat of the irritation was in a much more sensitive part. A married lady had suffered for a considerable time from a spasmodic pain in the womb, which ceased completely on the extraction of a tooth that had not caused any material annoyance.

(V.) Attention has lately been directed by Pfluger and Lister to certain nerve phenomena, which the former terms inhibitory (*hemmungs*), and supposes to belong to a certain set or system of nerve-fibres whose sole function is to arrest or diminish action. Lister, on the contrary, concludes, from his inquiries,[1] "that one and the same afferent nerve may, according as it is operating mildly or energetically, either exalt or depress the functions of the nervous centre on which it acts. It is, I believe (he says), upon this that all inhibitory influence depends; and I suspect that the principle will be found to admit of a very general application in physiology." The following are instances of inhibitory action: The poles of a galvanic apparatus being fixed to the spinous processes of the ninth

---

[1] Proceedings of the Royal Society, No. 82, p. 367.

and twelfth dorsal vertebræ of a rabbit, currents were passed through the spine (of course, affecting the cord), with the effect of inducing "complete relaxation and quiescence of the small intestines, which had been previously in considerable movement, while the muscles of the limbs were thrown into spasmodic action; but on the discontinuance of the galvanism the previous intestinal motion returned." Weaker currents were then passed, and markedly increased the action of the intestines in every instance during the first twenty-five minutes. In the next half-hour the increase of action from the galvanism though still distinct, was less strongly marked, and at the end of that period, with stronger currents, the inhibitory influence was also found to be much less complete than before, indicating that the parts of the nervous apparatus concerned were in a less active condition, no doubt in consequence of exhaustion. Increased movements of the intestine were produced by direct irritation of the cord with a fine needle. It was very worthy of remark, that violent struggling of the rabbit, when the intestines were in pretty free movement, was followed by absolute and universal quiescence of those organs for several seconds. This showed that an inhibitory action was capable of being produced naturally as well as artificially. The recent observations of Hufschmidt and Moleschott,[1] as to the effect of mechanical irritation of the medulla oblongata and spinal cord on the frequency of the pulse, accord very much with those of Lister. They found[1] that slight electric irritation of the medulla oblongata augmented, while more powerful diminished the frequency of the heart's action, or even arrested it. (2.) Powerful mechanical irritation of the medulla oblongata diminished the frequency of the heart's action. (3.) Slight irritation of the spinal cord increases, powerful irritation diminishes the frequency of the heart's action. Weber and Bernard[2] had long before demonstrated the possibility of arresting or slowing the action of the heart by galvanizing the medulla oblongata or the pneumogastric nerve.

In a paper on Inhibitory Influence[3] I have endeavoured to show that pathological phenomena are not infrequent which seem to be of this nature. I modify, however, the statement of Mr. Lister, so far as to believe that it is not the energetic operation of an afferent nerve that causes inhibitory action, but its being injuriously affected by some impression made upon it. The enfeebled state of the nerve itself, or of the centre to which it proceeds, or the severity or malignity of the impression, may give rise to the peculiar effect. The following instances may be cited as fair examples: O. J.,[4] æt. 37, got a whitlow on the last phalanx of left thumb; the lymphatics were inflamed, and the axillary glands swollen; the whole arm was

[1] Moleschott's Untersuch, vol. viii. part 6, 1862. Syd. Soc. Year-book, 1863, p. 17.
[2] Leçons sur le Système Nerveux, tome ii. p. 392.
[3] British Medical Journal, February 5, 1859.
[4] Medical Times and Gazette, January 29, 1859.

very painful. While the limb was in this state, one morning he found that he saw double, and had a squint in the left eye. At the Ophthalmic Hospital, it was found that the external rectus muscle was completely paralyzed, and he had circumorbital pain. It was supposed that there was periosteal inflammation about the orbit, and pot. iodid. was given; the whitlow was poulticed, and the arm fomented. After a month of this treatment, there was no improvement of the eye, but the arm inflammation had quite subsided. A piece of dead bone was now removed from the seat of the whitlow; soon after which the squint disappeared, as well as the pain in the arm and about the orbit. The external rectus had quite recovered its power. In this instance, pain in sensory nerves about the orbit and paralysis of a single motor nerve were co-results of the morbid impression conveyed from the diseased finger to the centre. Dr. Watson refers to the production of amaurosis without visible change in the eye, in consequence, apparently, of irritation of the dental nerves, the blindness ceasing after the extraction of some teeth which had grown irregularly.[1] He quotes from Mr. Lawrence an interesting case, in which the extraction of a carious tooth, with a splinter of wood projecting from one of its fangs, procured the restoration of the sight of the eye of the same side, which had been entirely lost for thirteen months. In such cases, the paralysis of the retina or of the optic tubercles may fairly be designated inhibitory. Two cases of amaurosis and one of ptosis are recorded by Mr. Hancock[2] as cured by the removal of decayed or overcrowded teeth. Mr. Fleischmann[3] gives a case in which an obstinate muco-purulent discharge from the right nostril, which had resisted other treatments, yielded to extraction of the right upper canine. Plucking the large vibrissæ at the entrance of the nostrils, will, at least in some persons, cause a notable secretion of mucus, evidently dependent on the pain excited. Some while ago, I had a gentleman under my care with acute rosacea of the face and head, and chronic corneitis, with vascular development on the cornea. I applied on one occasion some liq. plumbi diacet., diluted with an equal amount of water, to the upper lids (everted), which I found very red. This caused excessive irritation; the eyes became greatly congested, watered extremely, and were very painful; while the skin of the face, the nose especially, became of a deep red, and all the vessels of the face much congested. There was extreme photophobia. It was half an hour before the hyperæmia began to subside. The irritation in this case evidently was reflected from the branches of the first division of the fifth nerve supplying the lids, on to the vasomotor nerves of the arteries, supplying the skin of the face, which, in consequence of the *morbid* impression, became *dilated*—not contracted, as they normally should, according to the law of reflex

[1] Watson's Lectures, vol. i. p. 336.   [2] Lancet, January 22, 1859.
[3] British Medical Journal, April 9, 1859.

action. This was a marked example of inhibitory action. Dr. Brinton informs me that he has long held and taught a view almost identical with the above, under the name of "reflex relaxation." The pathology of these cases is, no doubt, the same; a nerve of special sense, a musculo-motor or a vaso-motor being paralyzed according to the direction which the irritation happens to take. To the same class belong, I think, instances of paralysis produced by exposure to cold and wet, though the paralysis often continues long after the morbid impression has ceased. In Mr. Hancock's communication, a case of lockjaw and of extreme wryneck are mentioned as having been cured by removal of dental irritation. This shows that it depends very much on the condition of the nervous centre which is affected, what the result of a nervous stimulus shall be, whether paralyzing or exciting. So, in some persons opium causes marked powerlessness (a degree of paralysis); to others it tones and prevents fatigue.

The only objection which can be made, I conceive, to the above evidence is, that in the instances cited the paralysis depended, not on a direct morbid influence exerted on the tissue of the nervous centre, but on anæmia of the part, produced by the reflection of the original irritation on the vaso-motor nerves supplying its arteries. This is what Dr. Brown-Séquard supposes to occur in reflex paralysis—a form which appears to me to be similar to inhibitory. In reflex paralysis, the loss of motor power appears to depend on an actually existing irritation, with which it increases or diminishes, and with the removal of which it ceases. This is evidently almost identical with what we have described above. The only difference is, that in some instances of inhibitory action the paretic state of the centre persists for an indefinite time after the cessation of the cause which has morbidly affected it. The grounds which led me to believe that Brown-Séquard's view is incorrect are—(1st). It is difficult to suppose that a spasm of reflex origin should be limited to such a very small extent of vessels as would be involved in some instances, *e g.*, palsy of one sixth nerve, ptosis of one eye. (2d). It is almost impossible to believe that a contraction of vessels should be so persistent as the hypothesis requires. Can we suppose, in the case of amaurosis above cited, that the arteria centralis retinæ was spasmodically occluded for thirteen months? (3d). It has been found by Gull that irritation of the renal nerves does not cause contraction of the vessels of the spinal cord, nor paralysis of the lower limbs, as Brown-Séquard stated in explanation of the paraplegia from renal disease. (4th). In some cases of paralysis from exposure to cold and wet—*v.* one related by Dr. Copland (*Dict. of Pract. Med.*, art. Paralysis, 76), the paralysis continues long after the exciting cause has ceased, and is removed by stimuli applied to the sensory cutaneous surface. Here the paralysis must be non-organic; and yet it can scarcely be supposed to depend on anæmia of the centres resulting from arterial spasm. On the other hand, it is intelligible that the nerve-cells might be thrown into a state of enfeebled action by the cold, &c., from which they could not easily recover. These cases, though not typically inhibitory, seem to me very illustrative of the nature of the morbid action.

(VI.) It is, I think, a matter of certainty, that a nervous centre may be more or less completely paralyzed without having undergone organic change, in consequence of some enfeebling morbid influence, as the influenzal or malarious miasms, &c. Dr. Gull[1] has published a most interesting instance of complete paraplegia induced by sexual excess, in which nothing abnormal could be detected in the cord even by careful microscopy. This was paralysis from simple exhaustion. Such paralysis may be distinguished as simple or neurolytic. I think it is certain that this does not depend on local anæmia; which adds to the probability that inhibitory paralysis does not either.

(VII.) Anatomically regarded, it is very remarkable how closely the different nervous centres, or parts of a nervous centre, are connected by commissural fibres; and from a pathological point of view, the same connection is often very manifest. The general exhaustion induced by excess in venery, the reproduction of neuralgia in weakly persons by bodily exercise, the effect of muscular exertion in producing drowsiness, are examples which show how excessive consumption of the nerve-force in one part weakens it also in others: and this can only be adequately explained by the intimate commissural connection between the various centres. Tetanus is a good instance of the diffusion of a state of excitement from one part of the cord throughout its whole extent.

(VIII.) The remarkable influence of the nervous system over the bloodvessels requires some particular notice. Our knowledge on this head has been chiefly the result of Bernard's labours; and it is difficult to overestimate the importance of the study of these phenomena to every physician who desires either to comprehend aright the varying and manifold phases of disease, or to attempt the control of morbid actions by remedies in a rational and satisfactory manner. It is well known that in paralysis from disease of the brain or spinal cord, the temperature of the paralyzed parts, as a rule, is lowered. This was found to occur when the anterior or posterior roots of the spinal nerves, or the root of the fifth pair, or that of the facial, were divided. The loss was not very considerable, varying from about 3° to 7° F. When the sympathetic nerve in the neck was divided, or the superior cervical ganglion extirpated, the following phenomena were observed: the temperature of the operated side increased rapidly, and in a quarter of an hour had risen 11° F.; the arteries and small vessels dilated, and became much more full of blood than those of the opposite side; the pupil contracted, as well as the palpebral opening, while the globe of the eye appeared depressed in the orbit. The hyperæmia, which is the immediate result of the

---

[1] Guy's Hospital Reports, 1858, Case xvii.

operation, subsides considerably in a day or two; but the elevation of the temperature is much more persistent, lasting in rabbits 16 to 18 days; in dogs 6 weeks to 2 months. Not only the superficial parts, but the deep-seated, and even the blood returning by the jugular vein can be shown to be hotter than the corresponding parts of the healthy side, or than they themselves were previously. It is an important circumstance, observed by Bernard and Brown-Séquard, that the temperature on the sound side falls below its previous figure, the difference in one experiment amounting to $5\frac{1}{2}°$ F. The phenomena now described are more prominently marked in healthy and vigorous animals than in those that are weakly, and in those that are digesting food than in those that are fasting. When an animal whose cervical sympathetic has been divided on one side is exposed to a temperature above that of its own body, the side where the nerve is entire gains heat, while the other remains almost unchanged, and, before long, no difference can be detected between them. On the other hand, when an animal similarly circumstanced is placed in a medium considerably colder than its own body, the difference between the normal and the operated side becomes more prominently marked. The former loses heat much faster than the latter, and the thermometer shows it may become as much as 21° F. colder than its fellow. If the upper end of the divided sympathetic is galvanized, all the effects produced by the previous operation disappear, and are replaced by their converse. The pupil dilates, as well as the palpebral opening, and the eyeball projects from the orbit. Instead of being active, the circulation becomes weak; the conjunctivæ, nostrils, and ears, which were red, become pale. The temperature falls below the normal figure, while, curiously enough, that of the opposite side increases notably. According to Brown-Séquard, the effects produced by a transverse lateral section of the semi-cord in the dorsal region, on the posterior limb of the same side, are exactly similar to those we have been considering. The condition also of the opposite sides in both cases is quite similar; " both receive less blood than usual, their temperature diminishes, their nutrition is less active, and their vital properties also diminish." By recent investigations, Bernard has found that there are two sets of nerves in the cervical sympathetic—one oculo-pupillary, arising in the dog from the anterior roots of the two first dorsal; and the other vascular and calorific, arising from the sympathetic ganglia. He also states that division of the anterior and posterior roots of the nerves proceeding to the posterior extremity in dogs causes paralysis of motion and sensation, but no change of temperature or vascularity. Division of the sciatic nerve, however, raises the temperature 6° to 8° C. (11° to 14° F.), and increases the vascularity. Division of the sympathetic nerves has the same effect, but causes no paralysis. Bernard's observations thus go to attribute more importance to the proper fibres of the sympathetic system than to those which it receives from the spinal nerve in controlling the local circulation. They demonstrate, certainly, the partial independence of the sympathetic system. Bernard remarks that though he has watched for a length of time animals who had undergone division of the cervical sympathetic, he has never seen any œdema or inflammatory action supervene in the abnormally hot parts so long as the animals continued in good health; but if they fell sick, either spontaneously or from the effects of other operations, the mucous membranes of the eye and nose on the operated side *only* became very red, swelled, and poured out purulent matter abundantly. If the animal's health improved, these inflammatory phenomena ceased. This highly important observation I can quite confirm from my own experience. A cat on which I operated had severe purulent ophthalmia of the left eye for five or six days; after which it spontaneously declined. Sixteen days after the operation, the left ear was 15° F. hotter than the right. She had been debilitated by an unsuccessful attempt to divide the renal nerves on one side.

The cause of the elevated temperature of the parts lying in the range of the divided sympathetic is attributed by Brown-Séquard and Waller to the increased afflux of blood to the local hyperæmia. Bernard, however, opposes this view, because the temperature does not vary when the hyperæmia declines; because hyperæmia occurs when the fifth nerve is divided, but is attended with diminished temperature; and because ligature of the veins of each ear, and consequent gorging of the vessels with blood, lowers the temperature of the parts, which again rises on the side on which the sympathetic is subsequently divided. It is true, that if the carotid be tied, and the sympathetic afterwards divided on the same side, no calorification takes place; but if the sympathetic be first divided, and calorification have come on, ligature of the carotid does not lower the temperature to that of the sound side. Another argument which may be used, in support of Bernard's opinion, is that the temperature in the paralyzed parts exceeds, in some cases, by 2° or 3° the normal temperature of internal parts, as the rectum. On the whole, it seems to me decidedly most probable that the increase of heat is not solely due to hyperæmic afflux, but that accelerated tissue change also plays a considerable part in its causation. It is a very important point, which is well illustrated by Brown-Séquard,[1] that the vital properties of the tissues in the range of the divided sympathetic are increased. He states that sensibility is augmented and persists longer; the sense of hearing seems to be more acute; the secretions of cerumen, tears, and perspiration are increased; chloroform anæsthesia occurs later in these parts than in others; the first convulsions in strychnia poisoning take place there; a galvanic current, too weak to act on the other side, produces contractions there; after death, the muscles and the iris remain contractile longer than usual; the

[1] Phys. of Central Nervous System, p. 141.

galvanic current of the muscles, detected with the galvanoscopic frog, is stronger than in those of the other side; cadaveric rigidity comes later and lasts longer, and putrefaction ensues later. Bernard doubts that the effect of dividing the sympathetic is to paralyze the arteries, and so cause their dilatation; he seems to regard it as an anomaly that arterial paralysis should promote greater activity of the circulation. This, however, seems only natural, when we reflect that arterial contraction would necessarily have the opposite effect, and would diminish the afflux of blood to the part. This is well seen when the arteries in the frog's web are made to contract by the application of cold; whole tracts of capillaries appear empty, and deprived of red corpuscles. On warming the web, the arteries immediately pour in blood abundantly. The old and oft-used phrase, "great arterial action," descriptive of a large and bounding pulse, when translated into correct physiological language means, of course, great *cardiac* action with *a want* of arterial. Some recent observations by Bernard[1] show very clearly how paralysis of the sympathetic nerves increases and accelerates the arterial current. When a manometer was inserted into the right coronary artery of the lip of a horse, and another into the left, both instruments showed a pressure of 160 to 180 millim. The pressure of the blood increased 40 millim. on the left side after division of the corresponding cervical sympathetic. In the coronary veins of the lip, the instrument showed a pressure of 30 to 40 millim., which increased to 50 or 60 after section of the sympathetic, while the pressure again fell 20 millim. when the nerve was galvanized. As other results of division of the same nerve, were noticed pulsation of the veins, and a brighter colour of the venous blood.

Analogous experiments made by other observers strongly corroborate Bernard's statements. Jaschkowitz shows that section of the sympathetic plexus of the splenic artery causes congestion of blood, softening and distension of the capsule. If part only of the plexus is divided, the corresponding part only of the spleen is affected. Samuel, in experiments upon rabbits, dogs, and cats, found that the hyperæmia of the intestinal mucous membrane produced by the extirpation of the cœliac plexus was so great that it exceeded all pathological hyperæmias hitherto known. The secretion of the mucous membrane is increased by the operation, but not to the same degree as in violent diarrhœa. Wharton Jones finds that after removal of the lower part of the spinal cord and the roots of the nerves in a frog, the arteries of the webs retain all their contractility, or are even more than usually disposed to be constricted. If now the ischiatic nerve be divided on one side, "the result is, that the skin of the extremity subjected to the experiment becomes, even to the naked eye, redder from vascular congestion than that of the opposite extremity; and, on examination of the web under the

---

[1] La Clin. Europ. 1859, No. 29, p. 282. Syd. Soc. Year-book, 1861, p. 29.

microscope, the arteries are found considerably dilated. In the web of the opposite extremity, on the contrary, the arteries are seen still much contracted, some even to closure." Instances have been observed in man where like results have ensued. A man cut his leg with a hay-knife; profuse bleeding ensued, and nearly proved fatal. Ever after he observes that the wounded leg is hot and moist, while the other is apt to be cold. A patient of my own cut the inner side of the index finger deeply; and after the wound had quite healed I found the distal part of the finger 2° hotter than the corresponding part of the middle. Algide fever, where the surface is icy cold, affords an example of the opposite state.

The above statements show, in the clearest manner, how considerable a control the sympathetic nerves accompanying the arteries have over the circulation, and the nutritive actions in a part. It is, therefore, certain that the influence of those vaso-motor nerves must rank very high in the pathology of all disorders attended with alterations of the circulation. But, we have now to inquire whether these are the only nervous organs which act on the circulation, or whether there exist others also. The answer to this last question must be in the affirmative. Ludwig's and Bernard's experiments show convincingly that stimulation of the third division of the fifth pair, and of the facial produces a greatly increased flow of saliva, while at the same time the circulation in the gland is accelerated. It is not known so certainly whether this is the case with other glands; but with regard to muscles it seems sufficiently evident that their voluntary exercise coincides with increased blood-flow. The darker colour, increased bulk, firmness, and strength of a muscle that has been well exercised contrasted with the paleness, flaccidity, and wasted condition of one that has been long unused, can be accounted for in no other way than by admitting that the former has received a much larger supply of blood. If any further evidence were required, it would be found in the observations of Becquerel and Breschet, as to the increase of temperature which is produced by muscular exercise, amounting sometimes to 2° F. The phenomenon of erection of the penis is, beyond doubt, dependent on a state of active innervation of the part causing increased afflux of blood. At certain times its occurrence can be perceived to be distinctly voluntary, and can be induced or prevented at the will of the individual. Samuel[1] contends for the existence of fibres, distinct from the motor of muscles and vessels, as well as from the sensory, whose office is to preside over nutrition, and which are divisible into a centrifugal and centripetal set. The former, when excited, increase nutrition, when paralyzed decrease it. Paralysis of the centripetal fibres Samuel regards as the cause of the diminished resisting power of anæsthetic parts to injuries, &c. Fever and inflammation he

---

[1] Die trophische Nerven, Leipzig, Wigand, 1860. Canst. Jahresb., vol. ii. pp. 53–57, 1861.

explains as states of excitement of the trophic nerves. He records various experiments in which irritation of sensory and of compound nerves caused intense inflammation of the parts to which they were distributed. Thus irritation of the auriculo-temporal in the rabbit produces acute inflammation of the whole auricle, issuing in puriform effusion, and inducing death by exhaustion. This inflammation did not begin until from three to six days after the operation, and most evidently was not traumatic. Irritation of the gangliform plexus of the vagus on one or both sides caused general and intense pneumonia. From these statements, I think we cannot doubt that certain nerves, when stimulated, do exert a very considerable influence in the districts to which they are distributed, in the way of increasing the amount of blood circulating through the tissues. Herein they exactly antagonize the ordinary vaso-motor nerves accompanying the arteries, whose activity induces the opposite condition. For the present it must remain doubtful whether these so-called trophic nerves are indeed a special set, or whether the same effects may not be produced through ordinary motor and sensory nerves. The latter view seems the most probable, and is strongly corroborated by the atrophy of the hands and feet, which occurs as the result of the anæsthesia of Indian leprosy.

(IX.) Some common facts, of daily occurrence, are worth considering in reference to the above doctrines. It seems that there exists a kind of alternation between the action of the vaso-motor and cerebro-spinal nerves, the period of activity of the one corresponding to that of quietude in the other. Thus, while we remain at rest, the temperature of the surface of the body generally, and especially that of the limbs, is decidedly lower than when we are in active exercise, and the cutaneous bloodvessels are comparatively contracted and small. This condition, when it is somewhat excessive, produces the cold hands and feet from which not a few persons suffer. On the other hand, there are instances, though less frequent, where the reverse seems to be the case, and the hands and feet are prone to be hot and bedewed with excess of secretion. In the former it is clear that the cutaneous arteries are habitually contracted, in the latter relaxed. Now, it is certainly remarkable that voluntary exercise of the muscles should so speedily effect the distribution of blood to the cutaneous surface. We might have expected that it would have caused an increased flow to the muscles, according to the function assigned to the trophic nerves; but we should scarcely have surmised *à priori* that an active state of the musculo-motor would coincide with a paretic of the vaso-motor nerves of the integument of the same limb. The fact, however, is unquestionable, and it is worth inquiring how it comes to pass. There seems no other explanation than that the *vis nervosa* of the centres, which while the muscles are at rest can act only on the vaso-motor nerves, is withdrawn from the latter to a great extent when these great organs are put into action, and, consequently, the cutaneous and other arteries become dilated and permit free access to the blood. That this is really the case is tolerably clear, I think, from the circumstance that not only the vessels of the integument of the working muscles are relaxed, but those also of distant parts, as the head, which are not specially active. A rower, or a pedestrian wending his way up a mountain pass, finds the toil-drops fall thick and fast from his brow, though his brain is far less active than it was when he was engaged in his study. The influence of cold also goes far to prove that the relation of the phenomena to each other is such as I have suggested. It is certain that in cold weather we are capable of much more muscular exertion than in hot. On a cold day we can walk briskly with a weight of clothing which would be intolerable on a warm; the cold evidently increases our muscular force. At the same time, we find that our limbs do not warm nearly so readily, though they may be well wrapped up, and sensible perspiration is with difficulty induced. This is because the greater amount of *vis nervosa* not being so soon expended on the voluntary muscles, keeps the arteries longer contracted. Again, it is well known that horses, who are in good training, will do their work with much less sweating than those who are out of condition. Patients suffering with neurolytic disorder often complain that the least exertion causes them to break out into perspiration, while, as they improve, this tendency diminishes. Here, again, we see a positive relation between nerve-power and vascular dilatation. The increased secretion from the cutaneous surface may be reasonably supposed in a state of health to be the result of an increased supply of blood to the perspiratory glands, and we have already seen that such has actually been found to result from the hyperæmia induced by dividing the vaso-motor nerves. We may, therefore, I think, fairly surmise that what takes place on the cutaneous expansion and glands takes place also in internal lining membranes and glands, and that thus by means of the free flow of blood to all parts the general nutrition is more perfectly carried on.

One chief cause of arterial dilatation, when the muscular coat is relaxed, is of course the pressure of the column of blood driven by the heart. Now, during exercise the action of the heart is increased; and it is interesting to inquire how this occurs. Moleschott's experiments show that a weak stimulus applied to the vagi increases the frequency of the pulse; yet it is also almost the universal testimony of all observers that division of these nerves greatly accelerates it. In one experiment of my own, the rate was nearly doubled. It seems, therefore, that paresis of the vagi may be looked upon as a probable cause of acceleration of the heart's action; and this paresis would be produced in the same way as that of the arterial nerves. Moleschott asserts that the sympathetic has the same influence on the heart as the vagus, so that all the cardiac nerves would be affected in the same way. Moreover, paresis, of the coronary plexuses would have the effect of admitting a larger supply of blood through these arteries to the muscular tissue of the heart. This would certainly favour, if it did not set up, increased action of the organ. There exists evidence to show that heat has a stimulating effect on the movements of the heart; and it is probable that the increased temperature of the blood in febrile states is concerned in causing the rapid pulse. But the acceleration of the heart's movements by muscular exertion ensues too rapidly to be ascribable in any great degree to this cause. In feeble persons, palpitation and quickening of the pulse on any slight muscular effort are familiar occurrences; and it may be said generally, that the greater the debility, the more readily does the change in the cardiac rhythm occur. There can be little question that the two phenomena are really related to each other, and it is difficult to see any more probable connection between them than that which I have suggested. It is evidently in accordance with the plan of the circulation, that dilatation of the arteries should concur with increased action of the heart. If the reverse was the case, we should have the heart's energy wasted in endeavouring to overcome the undue resistance of the vessels. As it is, however, the central impelling organ puts forth its activity at the time when it can be really effective. Some of the phenomena of disease accord remarkably with the above views. The rapidly-acting heart of the patient prostrated by low fever is often greatly quieted by wine. The quick, feeble, irregular pulse of cardiac dilatation is not unfrequently made steadier, slower, and stronger by digitalis, which is certainly a cardiac stimulant. The degree of acceleration of the pulse produced by sitting up in bed is a good indication of the extent to which a patient is exhausted by fever, or any other asthenic disease.[1] In the affection termed "goitre exophthalmique," the heart's action is often remarkably excited, the carotid and thyroid arteries uncontracted, while the general condition is mostly one of great, perhaps extreme, debility.

The application of cold to the cutaneous surface exerts, as is well known, a striking influence on its contractile tissue, producing the so-called goose-flesh. This is not (at least necessarily) the result of direct stimulus, as it is equally produced when the cold is applied to another part of the surface. Thus, a cold wet towel flapped on the back immediately causes contraction of the cutaneous muscles on the anterior part of the trunk, which, of course, can only take place in a reflex manner, the stimulus of the cold to the sensory nerves being reflected on the vaso-motor, and those which influenue the cutaneous fibres. This contraction, it may be remarked, is precisely the same to all appearance as that which results from direct stimulation of the tissue by the interrupted current. It seems highly probable that the same contraction of organic muscular fibre takes place in internal parts when cold affusion is applied to the surface, since there is no reason why we should suppose the stimu-

---

[1] Graves, Dublin Hospital Reports, 1830, v. p. 469.

lant impression to be reflected on the nerves of the skin alone. Indeed, there is actual proof that such is the case; for we find that the heart's action is notably influenced by the cold shower-bath. Dr. Sieveking states that when the bath was taken after the pulse had been increased by exercise, the average depression in twenty observations amounted to 8.05 beats. When the bath was taken immediately after rising, the average depression in thirty observations was 6.14, and this was not counteracted by subsequent exercise, which only increased the pulse on the average by 3.21 beats. These results were obtained upon a person in good health, and in whom sufficient reaction occurred; but it is probable that in a less vigorous subject the depression would have been still greater. In fact, what happens when reaction is insufficient seems to be this—that the heart's action continues depressed, and the arteries generally contracted, so that free flow of the blood-current is prevented. The depressing action of the bath should be but temporary, and should be succeeded by the opposite condition. Dr. Brown-Séquard avails himself of this natural tendency of the vaso-motor nerves in his recommendation of the alternate application of cold and heat to procure the healing of bed-sores arising from defective circulation. Dr. Bence Jones's observations as to the effect of prolonged cold affusion show that it has a most powerful sedative effect on the heart, reducing the pulse thirty to fifty beats in a minute, and often rendering it quite imperceptible. When the water was cooled down to 50° F., the effect was much more rapid.

In the treatment of acute mania, the cold douche has long been recognized as a most efficient sedative to an excited nervous system; and, indeed, much judgment may be requisite so to employ it as not to induce serious, or even fatal depression. A patient of Dr. Currie's, who had derived benefit from cold effusion during the hot stage of an ague-fit, nearly died from the alarming depression which resulted from the same application while he was in the cold stage. The facts now referred to set in a clear light the great influence which the state of the nervous centres has on the results produced by the impressions conveyed to them. The latter may remain the same, but the effects will vary greatly, according to the condition of the recipient centre. Thus the shock of cold speedily causes in one person activity of the circulation and vigorous action of the heart; while in another the primary depression persists, and is never succeeded by the opposite state. It is a point well worth remarking, that when the arteries are contracted by cold, the capillaries and veins are often filled with stagnant venous blood. This condition may sometimes be well seen in the frog's web; and we may then observe how speedily the congestion is dissipated by warming the web and relaxing the arteries, so as to allow free blood-flow to take place. A good example of this kind of congestion was presented to me the other day in a man suffering from a small abdominal aneurism. An ice-bag had been applied over the tumour, and all the area of integument where it lay was of a dusky venous red, while the surrounding skin was quite pale. On laying my warm finger on the chilled skin, the venous hue quickly disappeared from that part. The foregoing remarks illustrate the converse occurrence to that first examined; they show how depression of the heart's action, the result of a stimulus, coincides with constriction of the arteries. The observations of Drs. Bence Jones and Dickinson[1] are very interesting as to the effect of a very hot vapour-bath taken just before the cold douche. They found that the increased action of the pulse produced by the exposure of the body to hot steam prevented that depression which would otherwise have arisen from the cold water. The action of heat is certainly relaxing to the muscles of the skin and the arteries; so that it is quite intelligible how in the above experiment it should have obviated the over-stimulating effects of the cold—rendering both the coronary arteries of the heart, as well as those of the body generally, less prone to constriction.

(X.) The relation which the febrile state bears to disorder of the nervous system is a topic of high interest. It did not escape the notice of Hippocrates, as shown by his aphorism, Πυρετος λυει σπασμους. The essential phenomena of fever seem to be increased temperature, more or less prostration, and derangement of the nervous functions; disorder of the secretions, and impairment of nutrition generally. The intention of the following remarks is not, of course, to notice any particular kind of fever, but to endeavor to trace the extent in which the phenomena of fever in general can be explained in reference to neuro-pathology. Debility of the cerebro-spinal system does not seem, *per se*, capable of producing fever. We see patients continually who are extremely weak, with a small and languid pulse, yet quite without fever. On the other hand, mere exhaustion from muscular exercise does seem sometimes to set up fever. I know myself two individuals in whom this has occurred. Again, all the phenomena of the earlier periods of fever are indicative of depression; and in the prevailing fevers of our day, the stamp of debility is apparent throughout. There is much in the facts above stated as to the influence of the vaso-motor nerves to suggest that paralysis or weakening of their power may be an essential condition in fever. If we suppose the effects produced by dividing the sympathetic in the neck to be general, to occur all over the body—which is quite conceivable—there would ensue general pyrexia. In fact, we are sure that elevation of temperature and relaxation of arteries cannot exist with any other than a paretic condition of the sympathetic. Taking first for consideration the ordinary low or asthenic fevers, with which we are familiar, let us see how far we can account for their phenomena on the assumption that the poisonous miasma has weakened the vaso-motor system, as well as all the others. The increased temperature—the quick, but soft and weak pulse—the

---

[1] Vid. Proc. of Med.-Chir. Soc., vol. i. p. 77, 1857.

hyperæmias of various viscera, may all, according to the foregoing views, be regarded as natural results. The increased secretion of urea may be accounted for partly by the augmented chemical changes which take place in the mass of the blood (considered for the time as a solid tissue) uncontrolled by the sympathetic nerves, and partly by the increased amount of renal action, depending on the same cause.[1] The hypertrophy which affects the glandulæ solitariæ and agminatæ in typhoid may be also traced to the same nervous paresis, and may be regarded as analogous to the enlarged spleen of ague, or the goître of Swiss malaria. To regard this hypertrophy as an attempt at elimination seems to me quite a mistake. It is no more to be considered such than the enlargement of the correlated mesenteric glands is, which takes place at the same time. Both are similar structures, and both hypertrophy under the same conditions, viz., hyperæmia and loss of nerve influence. The condition of the other systems in low fever quite corroborates our assumption as to the condition of the sympathetic. The quiet muttering delirium, the unconsciousness or half consciousness, testify how the brain is enfeebled; while the down-sunken posture in bed and the subsultus reveal the extreme muscular debility. The feebleness of the heart's action and the softening of its texture prove how its vital energy is depressed. The readiness of the skin to slough shows how its nutritive power is impaired. In certain cases, it seems as if the sympathetic system was but little affected, and the main stress of disease fell upon the cerebro-spinal. This one may conclude to have been the condition in the instances mentioned by Graves[2] (*v. loc. cit..*), where he says, "It was very curious to see a patient with a skin of a natural temperature, a perfectly natural pulse, tranquil respiration, clear eyes, no headache, a soft and fallen abdomen, incoherent, or with a low muttering delirium, excessive subsultus, extreme debility."

Let us now turn to the opposite type of fever, the sthenic, marked by strong, frequent, full or hard pulse, dry hot skin, intense headache, active delirium, laboured respiration, diminished or suppressed secretions, in which bloodletting is not only tolerated, but may be essential to the preservation of life. It is evident that in such cases the greater part of the organs must be in a very different vital state to that which exists in low fever, where stimulants are for the most part of prime necessity. Let it be assumed that the poison acts primarily upon the sympathetic system, limiting its action to it, as woorara does to the motor nerves: increased heat will be developed, and subsequently a tendency to local congestion, varying in situation according to the part where the paralysis is greatest. The increased temperature of the blood will act as a stimulus to the heart, whose

[1] Oppler has shown that the kidneys actually form a considerable proportion of the urea secreted. Virch. Archiv., vol. xxi. part 3. Syd. Soc. Year-book, p. 219, 1862.
[2] Clin. Med., p. 157.

tissue is vigorous (not debilitated, as in asthenic fever), and capable of responding energetically. The heart's action will thus be increased, and thus the character of the pulse is explained, except as relates to its hardness—a point we shall presently notice. The very interesting experiments of M. Calliburcès, mentioned in Bernard's *Leçons* (vol. ii. pp. 395—403), corroborate the opinion advanced above, that the increased heat of the blood is the cause of increased cardiac action. He found that when the leg of a frog was dipped into warm water, the heart constantly contracted more frequently. Thus, the number of pulsations in three separate trials being 52, 32, 42 at the commencement, a temperature of 51°, 50°, 55° raised (respectively) the number of the beats to 90, 64, 100. Similar results were obtained when the heat was applied directly to the heart. Ligature of the vessels and section of the crural nerve did not prevent the increase of cardiac action from the application of heat to the leg. He concludes that the acceleration of the heart's action by heat is owing to the direct action of this agent upon the circulatory centre. That a high external temperature, which notably raises that of the body, quickens the pulse, is certain. Blagden,[1] on exposing himself for eight minutes to a temperature of about 260° F., found his pulse rise to 144; and Constantine James,[2] in hot moist air of about 100° F., found his pulse to reach 120, while his temporal arteries beat forcibly. The acceleration of the pulse may be owing in part to the enfeebling influence of the poison affecting the vagi nerves; but the increased strength of the heart's contractions must depend on the dilatation of the coronary arteries and the free circulation of blood through its muscular tissues, whose vital power is thus temporarily increased. The hardness of the pulse in certain (sthenic) fevers and inflammations, implies a contracted state of the arterial coats. This, if general, is an opposite condition to that which is produced by section of the sympathetic, and, therefore, demands explanation in an hypothesis which is based on a presumed palsy of the system. It is to be remembered that arterial dilatation is by no means inseparably connected with increased blood heat; that the latter persists when the hyperæmia, which the former occasions, has materially subsided. In sthenic fevers, it may fairly be presumed that the arterial coats, like the heart, retain for a time excitability, and contract, therefore, moderately under the direct stimulus of the rapid blood-current which traverses them. The pulse is, therefore, hard. In low fever, on the contrary, the pulse is soft, because the poison impairs at once the vital power of the arterial coats, as well as that of their vaso-motor nerves.

Pyrexia, or the fever of inflammation, may next be considered. It is, probably, excited by a morbid impression conveyed from the inflamed part to the sympathetic centres; in consequence of which by a reflex inhibitory action, the vaso-motor nerves generally are

---

[1] Brewster's Nat. Magic, p. 311.   [2] Gaz. Médic., April 27, 1844.

enfeebled, and so, as in other cases, fever results, with increased cardiac action. The production of pyrexia is the ordinary case; the exceptional is that already mentioned (*vide* p. 22), where irritation in some organ occasions paralysis of musculo-motor nerves. On the view just proposed, it is intelligible why the administration of tonic and nervine medicines is injurious in the pyrexia of sthenic inflammation, while it is beneficial in that of asthenic. The inflamed tissue being highly sensitive and impressionable, becomes further irritated by the tonic remedy; and so the morbid impression conveyed to the centres, and reflected on the vaso-motor nerves, becomes intensified. By the employment of tissue sedatives, on the other hand, the morbid stimulus is annulled, and the fever movement subsides. This view assumes as certain a point which, though admitted by most of our best authorities, seems to be often ignored in the present day. I mean the existence of forms of disease which, though affecting the same part, and called by the same name, are as essentially different in their nature and tendencies as can possibly be—and this, too, independently of the original vital power of the patient. The distinction between sthenic and asthenic forms and phases of disease seems to me to be one of the leading truths in medicine; and I cannot conceive how any one with the evidence of his daily experience before him, can think lightly of it. To take but one instance. It is unquestionably true that cases of erysipelas do occur, mostly among the rural population, where free venesection is positively beneficial, as well as purging and other lowering means. On the other hand, we frequently have to treat cases of the same disease where the only indication, and that an urgent one, is to stimulate very freely. The outside show of these cases is very similar, but how different are they in reality! *Sthenic* disease is by no means synonymous with *acute;* the latter term has reference chiefly to the rate of progress, and may belong quite as well to asthenic as to the opposite class. One highly important character of sthenic disease is the state of the tissues with respect to their tolerance of any matters conveyed to them which are at all of an exciting quality. Let the skin be sthenically inflamed, as in eczema impetiginodes, and the arsenic or citrine ointment, which would benefit another case of a different temper, will grievously aggravate the disorder. On the other hand, when, in suitable cases of this kind, leeches, lead-lotion, salines, and antimonials have done their work, the same remedies which before were injurious prove healing. This is so because the vital condition of the tissue is now changed. Much of the "tactus eruditus" of the physician consists in being able to determine what cases belong more to the sthenic and what to the asthenic class, and in adjusting his remedies accordingly.

The cause of the rigors of fever is a question of some interest. The phenomenon clearly belongs to the nervous system, and must be regarded as a kind of minor convulsion.[1] It can be produced by various morbid impressions made on sensitive surfaces, as when a catheter is passed along a hyperæsthetic urethra, or, as in the case mentioned by Dr. Watson, where immersion of a recently-scalded arm in cold water brought on severe rigors. The forcing of a gallstone along the narrow duct may have the same effect; and so may a descending renal calculus. I have found, in my own person, very extensive irritation of the skin from harvest bugs produce even during very warm weather distinct though slight shivering. Similar shivering was observed in the early part of catarrhal fever, evidently connected with cutaneous hyperæsthesia; the sensation of coolness, which in health would have been very agreeable, being then actually repugnant. In malarious and other fevers the initial rigor is probably dependent on the action of the poison on the spinal cord, throwing it into a state of undue excitability, so that the nerves issuing from it keep the muscles in a state of clonic contraction, while the vaso-motor nerves maintain the organic muscles in a state of tonic. The same influence thus produces varying effects, according to the structures on which it acts. The rigors of pyæmia and of suppurating foci I should ascribe to the operation of contaminated blood on the nervous centres, and regard them, therefore, as having a similar causation to those of ague. On the other hand, those of hectic fever are most probably essentially dependent on nervous exhaustion, the centres falling into a state analogous to that existing in chorea, but manifesting itself in disordered actions of the vaso-motor more than of the musculo-motor system. Generally, there seem to be three factors concerned, or liable to be concerned, in the phenomenon: (1), a stimulus mostly of a morbid kind; (2), an altered hyperæsthetic condition of a sensory surface; (3), a more or less excited or mobile condition of one or more nervous centres. In most cases the coexistence of two of these is necessary. Billroth[2] states with regard to the rigors attending on fever of surgical affections, that their principal condition is a very rapid increase of temperature; another is a peculiar irritability of the patient, which may vary much in different cases, or in the same case at different times. He does not consider the rigors in pyæmia as necessarily dependent on blood-poisoning. There is no doubt that increased heat of the blood most frequently coincides with rigors; but inasmuch as they may occur where there is no fever (*vide supra*), and *vice versa* (as in an ague paroxysm having no cold stage), it seems to me most probable that the increased temperature is only a co-product of the original cause. The poison by paralyzing the vaso-motor nerves causes fever, and by acting on the nervous centres produces rigors. Here we have an example of the generation of spasm and paralysis by the same cause.

---

[1] Mr. Paget relates cases in which tetanic or epileptiform seizures took the place of rigors; *v.* Brit. Med. J., Aug. 16, 1862.
[2] Vid. Syd. Soc. Year-book, 1863, p. 193.

(XI.) We may now pass to the consideration of some general points in reference to neuralgia; a condition which in many respects contrasts strongly with fever, and rarely coexists with it. Schramm,[1] however, states that the remittent form of sciatic neuralgia in his experience has been generally attended with fever, and in many cases all the three stages of a paroxysm of fever (malarious) have occurred. The opposition of the two states is well manifested in some cases of malarious fever, where one febrile paroxysm in a series is, as it were, replaced by an attack of neuralgia. This, as well as the common production of some form of neuralgia by malaria, goes far to warrant the view that the morbid phenomena are determined very much by the part on which the poison fixes: pain ensuing if the cerebro-spinal nerves are specially attacked, fever if the vaso-motor, the exciting cause in both being the same. The prevalent opinion respecting the nature of neuralgia seems to be that its existence implies an excited or over-active condition of the sensory nerves. Romberg uses neuralgia and hyperæsthesia as convertible terms, and states—in hyperæsthesia we find that not only the irritation is increased, but that also the irritability of the nerves of sensation generally is exalted both during the paroxysms as well as the intervals. It is very evident that we can have no knowledge from actual observation of the state of the affected nerves during the attack. We must form our conclusions as best we may from consideration of the attendant circumstances, the "juvantia," and the relation of the disorder to others. For the moment let us put aside all cases of neuralgia which may be regarded as depending on a local irritation of any kind—either direct, as a splinter imbedded in a nervous trunk; or remote, as a worm in the bowels; or, again, on demonstrable poison generated in the system, as in gout, or received into it, as in lead intoxication. There remain, then, all those cases in which the disorder is dependent upon no ascertainable cause, except it be malaria, a draught of cold air, exposure to damp, overwork of mind or body, or some other cause of exhaustion. These form a group which may be distinguished as Nonorganic or Immaterial Neuralgia. Now, in these the existing debility and prostration is at least very often almost as marked a symptom as the pain. It is also more abiding and unvarying; and the conviction becomes wrought in the mind of the observer that it is the fundamental state upon which the pain is, as it were, engrafted—the appropriate soil, without which the morbid germ would not grow. It is proved by experience that unless this debility and prostration can be to a great extent removed, and replaced by healthy vigour, no real progress can be made in the cure of neuralgia. The task is like that assigned to Sisyphus: the patient's and the physician's hope is worn out by ever-recurring relapses. The debility seems in a special manner to affect the nervous system.

Bayer, Arztl. Intell., Bl. 34, 1859.

The brain is languid and dull, and inapt for mental labour; sometimes its function actually fails, and delirium occurs. Stimuli are beneficial—often very markedly so, though their effect is temporary. Fresh pure air, good food, sufficient repose, alternating with exhilarating employment, supplemented, if need be, by nerve-tonics, are the real remedies; and just in proportion as they increase the general tone and strength, does the patient attain complete recovery and immunity from relapses. On the other hand, just as surely do all causes of debility confirm, increase, and render inveterate the malady. Now, it may be fairly argued that where the signs of debility, and specially of nerve debility, are so apparent, and have so distinct a relation to the particular symptom, this must be itself of like essential character. It can hardly be that the morbid state of the nerve affected can be greatly different from that which prevails so generally throughout the system, especially when we consider the means which avail for the cure of both. Romberg's mataphorical expression with regard to anæmic hyperæsthesia (neuralgia), that "it seems as if pain were the prayer of the nerve for healthy blood," is in all probability exactly true. The nutrition of the nerve being ill performed, its structure undergoes some molecular alteration which conditionates pain. What is true of neuralgia from this cause, I believe is true of all cases belonging to the immaterial class. Electrical disturbances, damp cold, malaria, seem to me all to act in the like way, as far as we can judge—viz., by deranging the molecular nutritive actions of the nervous structure, and so unfitting it for fulfilling its function. There are several circumstances which seem to me strongly to support this view. One is the very frequent coexistence of numbness along with the pain, especially in highly sensitive parts, as the fingers and hands. One cannot say wherein the condition producing numbness differs from that which gives rise to pain; but it is clear that there is no opposition between them: both are often present together, and the numbness commonly remains as the more permanent condition in the intervals of the paroxysms of pain, and even after they have ceased to occur. Now, numbness is evidently a failure of functional power. Of the same import is the occurrence of various degrees of muscular paralysis, which is often associated with neuralgia, evidently as an analogous affection of the motor nerves. It yields generally to the same treatment. The phenomena of myalgia may also be referred to in illustration of the nature of neuralgia. Here the intimate relation of pain to debility is very marked: the sensory nerves of the muscles suffer because the associated motors are weak; whatever increases the debility increases the pain, and *vice versâ*. In many well-marked neuralgic affections there is evident paralysis of the vaso-motor nerves in the seat of the pain; the vessels are injected, and lachrymation or some similar phenomenon ensues. This makes it probable that the sensory nerves are in a similar state. Lastly, we may allude to the cure of neuralgia by Faradization as an illustration of its nature. The pain of a sensory nerve and the paralysis of a motor may both be removed by the stimulus of the interrupted current. This surely indicates that both states are similar. Even in organic neuralgia, it seems to me open to much question whether the affected nerve is in a state of exalted excitability, or simply of deranged and disordered nutrition. In lead-poisoning, the motor-nerves of the muscles are certainly paralyzed, the pains are diminished "by pressure and friction" (Romberg), and the whole phenomena are indicative of diminished rather than of increased vital action. In gouty neuralgia, if we take colicky and spasmodic affections for examples, the disorder is much more of an asthenic than of a hyperæsthetic character. The pain and suffering attending a characteristic outbreak of gout in the foot have much more the features of hyperæsthesia than the colicky disorder. The latter usually requires some stimulant for its relief, and can by no means be dealt with as the articular inflammation. That a nerve which receives for nutrition blood poisoned by uric acid should be disordered in its acting, and thrown into a state conditionating pain, is very intelligible; but it can hardly be regarded as having its functional powers exalted. On the other hand, the nerve lying in a focus of inflammation by reason of the active hyperæmia would seem really to be in a state of hyperæsthesia. Its condition is analogous to that of the nerves of one posterior limb in Brown-Séquard's experiment of transverse semi-division of the dorsal cord, where hyperæsthesia is produced in consequence of the hyperæmia resulting from paralysis of the vaso-motor nerves. Again, where neuralgia results from the impaction of a spiculum of bone, the development of a tumour or the like in a nervous trunk, although severe pain may be produced, it does not seem very clear that the nervous irritability is necessarily exalted—*i. e.*, that the nerve-filaments, either on the distal or proximal side of the irritant, are more sensitive than they would be naturally. In a case of neuroma of a portion of the auditory nerve recorded by Mr. Toynbee,[1] the only symptom was a diminution of the power of hearing. In a case reported in the *Dublin Medical Journal*,[2] a female, æt. 27, had a neuromatous tumour of the size of an almond developed in the course of the median nerve. If anything, even her dress, touched the tumour, severe pains shot down to the hollow of the palm, and upwards to the shoulder. She complained much of numbness and coldness of all the parts of the hand supplied by the median nerve. The nerve was cut across, and the neuroma removed. Fifteen months after the operation, she was quite free from pain, and observed nothing abnormal except a remarkable coldness of the fingers supplied by the median nerve. It is clear in this case that the neuroma, while it occasioned pain, did not increase the sensory power of the nerve. In some cases, however, it is

---

[1] Patholog. Soc. Report, 1851. [2] Dublin Med. Journ., May, 1848.

certain that the peripheral nervous filaments are truly hyperæsthetic, as in the case related by Romberg (vol. i. p. 37-44). In this, however, the hyperæsthesia may be accounted for by the increased supply of blood sent to that side of the face, the arteries pulsating strongly, and the eye being bloodshot and prominent. The same explanation applies to many other cases where the neuralgia is complicated with hyperæsthesia, but not to all. In any case where the sensitive power of a surface appeared to be actually exalted, so as to be unusually keenly alive to the contact of external bodies, there would, I think, be reason to look particularly to the state of the nervous centres. Hysteria, hydrophobia, tetanus, and certain toxic conditions, afford good examples of central hyperæsthesia. At the same time, I think it must be admitted that there is also such a condition as peripheral hyperæsthesia, of which we have examples in photophobia, gastric irritability, and cutaneous pruritus. This is certainly a very different state from neuralgia, especially in relation to remedies, but has affinities with it. It occurs under nearly the same causative conditions. Hyperæmia from vaso-motor nerve paralysis is by no means a necessary antecedent. The above view respecting the nature of neuralgia and hyperæsthesia is strongly supported by the occasional occurrence of acute pain and tenderness in limbs affected with embolism of the main artery. Motor and sensory paralysis are constant, but in some instances there is also pain and hyperæsthesia. Mr. Erichsen describes arteritis as attended with excessive sensitiveness of the surface, and with deep-seated burning and lancinating pain striking through the limb in different directions. The hyperæsthesia persists even after the limb has begun to get cold and pulseless.

From the preceding discussion we pass to the question—What is the *seat* of neuralgia—the nerves or the centres? Obviously, this is no easy question to answer. According to the law of excentric phenomena, every sensation of which we are conscious is referred to the peripheral termination of the sensitive fibres (so Romberg writes). Bowman and Todd add, that the sensation is referred to those parts, and to those only, to which the fibres irritated are distributed. According to this view, all appreciation of sensations as referred to any point in the course of the nerve is out of the question. An irritation, wherever set up, must be felt at the peripheral extremity of the fibres implicated, and never in any part of their intermediate course. But there are facts which seem strongly opposed to this exclusive dogma, and which go to prove that a sensation may be referred to various points in the course of the nerve-fibres. If we hit our funny-bone, although, no doubt, pain and tingling are felt at the peripheral distribution in the fingers, yet the chief agony is in the trunk of the ulnar nerve at the part struck, and certainly not merely in the skin covering it. The circumstance dwelt on by Valleix, that the specially painful points in nerves affected with neuralgia are always those where the nerve becomes superficial, is also a proof of a sensation being referred to other points besides the terminal. The same may be said of the pains which patients describe as shooting down along the track of a nerve, as often exemplified in sciatica. These certainly are not located merely in the skin which covers in the nervous trunk. From these considerations I am led to admit the possibility of very numerous exceptions to the law of eccentric phenomena, and to believe that pain in a nerve may really indicate by its situation the seat of the irritation, or rather morbid action. This is a conclusion of some importance to the local treatment of neuralgia. It justifies our empirical habit of applying sedative remedies as near as possible to the seat (apparent) of pain. But, of course, we cannot affirm in any case of pain involving the trunk of a nerve that the morbid action *may* not be central; the law of eccentric phenomena holds true, so far as that central disorder may certainly give rise to peripheral sensation. The only certain means of distinguishing the site of the pain causing action is division of the affected nerve. If this arrests the neuralgia, we know the disorder is seated peripherally; if it fail to do so, we know that we have to seek more centrally. In a very large number of cases, I fear, it must remain problematical where the real seat of the disorder is. If—the pain being specially referred to some intermediate spot—injection of opium subcutaneously at that part should give decidedly more relief than the same dose at a distance, it would afford ground for believing that the cause of the neuralgia was localized in that spot. In the ordinary way of rubbing sedative liniments on the cutaneous surface covering the seat of pain, we have no means whatever of proving a local action on the suffering nerve, but rather the reverse. For, take the case of the sciatic, where pain is acutely felt at the back of the thigh, and notably between the ischiatic tuberosity and the great trochanter; if this be relieved by sedative applications to the covering tegument, we are sure that the chief action of the remedy must be on cutaneous ramifications of the gluteal, lesser sciatic, and branches of the external cutaneous and other nerves on the front of the leg. These will convey impressions to the spinal centre, not far from the part where the roots of the sciatic are implanted; so that if the neuralgia were of central origin, it is very conceivable that the morbid action might in this way be beneficially modified. But, considering the depth at which the sciatic nerve lies from the surface, it seems quite impossible that the aconite, chloroform, opium, &c., should penetrate so far through skin, fat and fascia, and even large muscles. There exists some evidence to show that any strong impression made on the nervous centres (such as cauterizing the ear, galvanizing the columna nasi—*v.* Duchenne's[1] work) through incident nerves may put a stop to some neuralgias. This, if confirmed, would very much corroborate the view above expressed.

[1] Traité Thérapeut., par Trousseau et Pidoux, vol. i p. 787.

The pathological relations of neuralgia are, of course, very different according to the cause which gives rise to it. If, however, we take the commonest kind—viz., that which arises from cold, malaria, or debility—we must allow that it manifests a very close affinity with non-febrile rheumatism. Rheumatic and neuralgic pains are frequently so very similar, that they are only to be distinguished by the action of remedies. Iodide of potassium cures the rheumatic, quinine and iron the neuralgic; while often it occurs that in the same case, after having begun with the former, we have to finish with the latter. The beneficial action of muriate of ammonia in neuralgia noticed by several recent observers can scarcely be dissociated from its remarkable and positive remedial action in muscular rheumatism. The interesting but obscure phenomenon of rheumatic paralysis is closely similar to, if not identical with, the paralysis or paresis of motor-nerves, which so often forms a part of neuralgia. Catarrh is allied to neuralgia by the similarity of its causes, the diffused pains in various parts, the resemblance of its inflammatory actions to those sometimes accompanying and depending on neuralgia, and in a large number of cases by its "juvantia." If exhaustion aggravates a neuralgia, so does it also a catarrhal flux; while rest and toning means have an opposite effect. The affinity between neuralgia and ague in malarious disorder is strikingly apparent; the two disorders so evidently replace one another, that there can be little doubt that the difference is only one of situation; the sensory nerves being chiefly affected in the former, the sympathetic in the latter. The therapeutical effects of arsenic, iron, and quinine in the two disorders *rapprochent* them not a little.

(XII.) It seems a well-ascertained fact that the nervous tissue, both in the centres and in the peripheral extensions, becomes more excitable and mobile in proportion as its power becomes weaker. The motor nerve is more readily thrown into action, though the impulse it communicates is weak and cannot be long sustained. The sensory nerve is alive to the least impression, and becomes in certain cases gifted with almost preternatural acuteness. The brain is highly impressible, but incapable of any continuous effort; and headache is easily induced. Stimulants or tonics, which seem and are highly necessary, are tolerated with difficulty. The vaso-motor nerves rapidly alternate between a state of excitement, producing chills, and one of depression, giving rise to heat-flushes and perspirations. It is very probable that this difference in the vital state of the nerves depends on some molecular change in their composition, in consequence of defective nutrition; but no chemical research, that I am aware of, has yet proved such to be the case. Buhl's examinations go to show that a state of unconsciousness coincides with a watery condition of brain, such as is apt to exist in anæmia.

(XIII.) The tendency of nerve disorder to aggravation, or to make its first onset at night, is a very noteworthy point. Attacks of cholera and of choleraic diarrhœa, of epilepsy, asthma, and paresis, are very prone to ensue at night; while neuralgic, rheumatic, and other kindred disorders, are almost universally aggravated at that time. A talented but woeful hyperæsthetic female with whom I am acquainted, whose nervous disorder verges towards insanity, has for some time been always much worse towards the close of each day. In the malarioid remittent of children, the paroxysm is invariably nocturnal. The copious nocturnal sweats of phthisis and of obscure aguish disorder seem to be referable to lowering of the power of the vaso-motor and other nerves during this period; since we find tonic, astringent, and strengthening means to have a preventive effect. It is certain that malaria is most potent at night; and this is probably owing to the circumstance that the system is then less capable of resisting it. I believe a similar explanation applies to all the above cases. The morbid causes remain the same, but the nerve-power is feebler and less capable of withstanding them. It is not always easy to say how much of the increased morbid action may be owing to the state of sleep, or to the particular diurnal period. I believe that sleep does increase the liability to some affections, especially to sweating; but in most it is evident that this is not the principal cause, as sleep is entirely banished by the disorder.

Another period at which nerve disorders of all kinds are very apt to be aggravated is the catamenial. This is well called the monthly sickness, for it is certainly a season of lowered general and nervous power; and it has repeatedly occurred to me to find improvement which was previously going on smoothly interrupted by this somewhat troublesome interlude.

(XIV.) It is impossible, in a work of this kind, not to take some notice of the theory which Dr. Radcliffe has espoused, and to the illustration and establishment of which he has devoted so much labour and skill. His general position, as conveyed in his own conclusions (*vide* Lectures, Coll. of Phys., 1863, *Lancet*), is (1) that living muscle, when left to itself, is kept in a state of relaxation by the action of the natural electricity of the muscle; (2) that muscle passes out of the state of relaxation into that of contraction, when the attractive force which is inherent in the physical constitution of the muscular molecules is no longer antagonized by the action of the natural electricity of the muscle; (3) that the natural electricity which antagonizes contraction is extinguished for the moment by the instantaneous electrical currents of high tension (analogous to the discharge of the torpedo) which are developed when muscle or motor nerve passes from the state of inaction into that of action, and that, ordinarily, muscular contraction is brought about in this way; (4) that the natural electricity which antagonizes contraction is extinguished permanently at a certain time after death, and that the permanent contraction of rigor mortis is brought about in this way. Further on, he states that he believes that the same conclusions are necessary with respect to the action of a motor sentient nerve in sensation, as those which are necessary with respect to the action of a motor nerve in the production of muscular contraction. Radcliffe proposes to substitute these views for the doctrine that contractility is a special vital endowment of muscles and sensibility of sentient nerves, which on the application of stimuli are aroused into functional activity. He applies his views to explain the pathology of convulsions, spasms, tremor, and pain—and concludes that all depend on vital exhaustion, and not on vital stimulation. It is impossible for me to attempt here any critical examination of the scientific experimental evidence which Radcliffe so copiously adduces. I can only consider how for his main views are accordant with familiar and established facts, which cannot be left out of sight. The gist of his theory seems to be, that alike in health and in disease, muscular action as produced through the nervous system, and sensation, are the results, not of increased, but of diminished vital action. It appears to me, first, that he does not sufficiently distinguish between the nutritive process which maintains the structure and vital properties of the tissues, and the functional action in which these properties (as we regard them) are brought into play. The former is, of course, directly conservative, and can only tend to increase the vital powers of the part; the latter is, from one point of view, wasteful, expending those properties which are generated by nutrition. It is, therefore, very conceivable that certain electrical currents and other phenomena should be interrupted during the period of a muscle's action, which go on steadily while it is at rest. Again, the common fact that muscles well exercised by their motor nerves gain in size and strength, while the reverse is the case when they are either unused or their motor nerves are paralyzed, seems very subversive of the theory. If muscular contraction implies diminished vital action of both muscle and nerve, how can it be that the frequent repetition of such weakening acts produces development and increase of vital force? How can death cause life? Again, it seems impossible to admit that a steady, sustained effort of voluntary contraction can be at all fairly classed with a clonic spasm of convulsive disorder, however violent. True, there are muscular contractions in both cases; but in all other respects they differ widely. The kind of contraction is different; in one it is brief, violent, but unsustained; in the other, uniform, and steady. The state of the brain is very different: in one, active, conscious, with its functions of sensation and volition in full play, and its vessels traversed by full streams of arterial blood; in the other, the functions of sensation and volition in abeyance, and the vessels anæmic or filled with dark blood. The respiration and circulation in the convulsive attack are deranged from their healthy state. The fact that a very powerful emotion will sometimes animate even weak muscles to perform feats of extraordinary strength, seems capable of no other interpretation than that a higher amount of nervous energy than usual is excited in the centres, and put forth through the nerves. The force so exerted is surely far greater than any which could be developed in the rigor mortis, which is all that the muscle on Radcliffe's view can claim as its own. It seems, also, that Radcliffe makes no distinction between pain the result of some morbid action in a nerve or nervous centre, and a natural sensation: both he regards as the results of diminished vital action. This again seems quite erroneous. The *morbid* sensation is, as already shown, often associated with numbness, motor paralysis, and other signs of depressed vital power. But this is not the case with healthy sensation, which, indeed, requires for its perfection a state of active circulation in the sentient surface, as well as an active condition of the sensorium. Inflammatory pain is certainly of a different nature to neuralgia; it is intimately connected with active hyperæmia of the affected part, and is unquestionably much more likely to be relieved by depletion and cold than by any stimulation. Certainly, no man would treat it in the same way as the pain of anæmia or brow ague. In the close of his lectures Radcliffe states that the pathology of pain agrees in all essential particulars with the pathology of tremor, convulsion, and spasm; and that the process on which it depends implies vital exhaustion, and not vital stimulation. He advocates the treatment of all these disorders by supplying the weak nervous system with appropriate nutrients, such as oily articles of food and medicine, with phosphorus in various forms, by upholding and arousing the vital powers in general, and the nerve power in particular, by a stimulant plan of treatment, in which alcoholic drinks, ether, and phosphorus, in suitable doses, figure most conspicuously. The use of sedatives, as opium or belladonna, he discountenances. This quotation must, we think, convince any experienced man that Radcliffe's view is far too partial, and is by no means applicable to all the forms of sensation, healthy and morbid. The pain-relieving efficacy of opium, belladonna, and aconite, is as well established as any medical fact that we possess. That the morbid states he refers to are very often dependent on depressed vital action, there is no doubt; and we really are not aware that any one maintains the contrary. But to endeavour to prove that *all* phenomena involving motion and sensation, physiological and pathological, are of the same kind, seems to us contradictory to familiar fact, and we cannot consent to take any such principle for the basis of our practice. If prolonged experience convinces us more and more or any one thing, it is of the utter diversity and radical dissimilarity of many pathological states and symptoms called by the same name and outwardly seeming much alike. It is the fashion of the day to try to refer all disease to diminished vital action, and to assume (I think very unfairly) that previous authorities have always referred it to increased. It would be more correct to say that disease has been ascribed to deranged or perverted vital action which may be increased or diminished. Beyond this I believe we have not advanced yet.

CHAPTER III.

CEREBRAL ANÆMIA.

As one of the simplest morbid states of the brain, we may take anæmia, which properly implies a simple decrease in the amount of arterial blood passing through the organ in a given time. The observations of Kussmaul and Tenner on six male adults, backed by those which they made on rabbits, show very conclusively what are the results of this state when it is speedily induced. When both carotids were compressed in the human subject, the vertebrals of course remaining open, the principal phenomena were, pallor of the face; loss of consciousness; dilatation of the pupils; slow, deep, and as it were sighing respiration; and, in two cases of weak intellect, a choking sensation, followed by vomiting and general convulsions, which disappeared in a few seconds after the compression was removed. Ligature of the common carotids, one or both in succession may produce no symptoms, or may cause paralysis and convulsions; the convulsions affecting the same, and the paralysis the opposite side. The paralysis may precede, accompany, or follow the convulsions. The eye of the operated side sometimes becomes blind. Other symptoms which have been observed are, "dizziness, stupefaction, insensibility, loss of consciousness, of speech, and of free play of the muscles in general; difficulty in swallowing, nausea, vomiting, swooning, and coma." The authors whom we are quoting proceed to state that post-mortem examination traces the cause of the paralysis to anæmia and softening of the corresponding cerebral hemisphere, to a greater or less extent. They are satisfied that "epileptic convulsions only manifest themselves in man, when, together with the cerebrum, some or all of the parts of the encephalic mass lying behind the thalami optici are suddenly deprived of blood to a sufficient amount, but that sudden falling down, announcing the approach of an apoplectic attack (?), unconsciousness, and insensibility, originate in causes proceeding from the brain proper." The affection termed by Trousseau, "congestion cérébrale apoplectiforme," in which he believes there is no congestion at all, but that the disorder is rather allied to epilepsy or syncope, seems to be essentially of anæmic character. A man falls down suddenly, as if stricken by apoplexy; is taken up in a state of stupor, and for a quarter of an hour, or even longer, remains more or less in the same condition—his intelligence confused, and his gait uncertain. The following day he is quite well. In slighter cases, the patient is attacked, all at once, with giddiness; loses sight and speech, and staggers, sometimes falling down, but getting up again immediately. In three or four minutes he is quite recovered. In these cases, as in ordinary epilepsy, the face is pale at the commencement of the attack, and only becomes flushed afterwards. It is a curious circumstance, which was observed in the compression of the carotid experiments above quoted, that on the removal of the pressure, the face became suffused. Indeed, Kussmaul and Tenner state, as a general result of their observations, that releasing the ligature from the cervical arteries always produces temporary hyperæmia of the brain. Profuse hemorrhage after delivery, says Dr. Gooch, will cause the woman to have a distressing headache, with throbbing in the head, noises in the ears, a colourless complexion, and a quick, weak, often thrilling pulse; all which symptoms are greatly increased by any exertion. Abercrombie[1] describes how children may lie, for a day or two, in a state of stupor closely resembling coma from organic disease—insensible, with dilated pupils, eyes open and insensible, the face pale and the pulse feeble, and yet recover under the use of wine and nourishment. This state is induced by causes of gradual exhaustion, going on for a considerable time. It may occur in adults, though less frequently than in children. "It differs from mere exhaustion in the complete abolition of sense and motion, while the pulse can be felt distinctly, and is in some cases of tolerable strength." A case is related where deafness was induced by the erect posture, and hearing immediately returned in the recumbent. The patient was in a state of extreme weakness and emaciation. A weakly female, aged 22, under my care, convalescent from catarrh, stated that her head ached, and she became giddy and fell, when she threw her head upwards and backwards. Comparing syncope with apoplexy, Abercrombie says,[2] "It is preceded by giddiness, tinnitus aurium, and impaired vision; and is accompanied by blindness, dilated pupil, perfect insensibility, and not unfrequently *passes into convulsion.*" (The Italics are my own.) Kussmaul and Tenner state that convulsions from hemorrhage do not ensue—(1) when the hemorrhage is slow; (2) when the animals are very much debilitated; (3) when the nutrition of the spinal cord has suffered; (4) when large pieces of the excitable districts of the brain have been removed; (5) in animals subjected to etherization; (6) doubtless, when the excitable districts of the brain have undergone certain pathological alterations. The first and second clauses afford a reasonable explanation of the non-occurrence of convulsions in many cases of cerebral anæmia. Gooch's own personal experience, as he describes it, illustrates well the chief effects of cerebral anæmia in a chronic form. He says, any one who, from long defect in the organs of nutrition, is reduced so that he has neither flesh on his body nor blood in his veins, well knows what it is to lay down his

---

[1] On the Brain, p. 309.   [2] Ibid., p. 300.

head and doze away half the day without any congestion or inflammation of the brain. It is clear that in most cases, in all except those where cerebral anæmia is suddenly induced during a state of health, the condition will not be one of pure diminution of blood-supply, but of diminished and altered blood-supply. The system will be not only anæmic, but spanæmic. Further, this state cannot exist for any length of time without modifying injuriously the nutrition of the brain, and rendering it more excitable and weak, according to the general law which we see so constantly exemplified. This altered vital quality of the great nervous centres may exercise a considerable influence on the subsequent phenomena, as has already been shown by the above quoted statements of Kussmaul and Tenner. It is a most important fact observed by these excellent inquirers, that arrest of the blood-supply to a muscle, and the nervous apparatus with which it is connected, produces at first spasmodic contraction, followed after a time by complete paralysis. This is true in the case of the iris and the sphincter ani, and, no doubt, holds good with regard to the other muscles of the body. " Suddenly withheld nutrition" causes a sudden commotion, and molecular change in the dynamic matter, which acts in the same way as a stimulus on the nerves. The effect of slowly-impaired nutrition, as just observed, is somewhat similar: it renders the nervous apparatus much more mobile than natural. On the other hand, good and full nutrition renders the nervous tissue much more calm and steady in its actings.

We may now proceed to gather up into some general conclusions the chief results of the preceding discursive review. (1) It appears that anæmia of the previously healthy brain, when speedily induced, abolishes its functions and those of the chief organs of special sense. (2) When slowly induced, and associated with spanæmia, it produces effects similar in kind, but less in degree, except in some extreme cases. (3) Anæmia of the cerebral hemispheres, even occurring suddenly, will probably produce unconsciousness, but not convulsions. This may be regarded as the pathological condition giving rise to the minor forms of epilepsy, the "congestion apoplectiforme cérébrale," and certain forms of vertigo. (4) The true complete epileptic paroxysm probably requires for its production an at least tolerably active and excitable state of the brain-tissue, and a suddenly induced anæmia, involving not only the hemispheres, but the medulla oblongata, or at least the pons Varolii and tubercula quadrigemina. (5) Venous hyperæmia is well known to be equivalent in its influence on nutrition to anæmia. It may give rise to convulsion when it is rapidly induced in the brain, or to mere sopor when it occurs gradually. Of the first we have an example in some severe attacks of hooping-cough, and in apnœa. Of the second, the following instance came under my own observation. A male, æt. 60, was under Dr. Sibson's care in St. Mary's with an aneurism of the aorta, pressing upwards towards the right, and bearing upon the left brachio-cephalic and superior cava veins. His face, as well as the neck and upper part of the chest, was swollen, and of a deep dusky tint from venous congestion. The appearance was very much as if his skin had been darkened by nitrate of silver. The breathing was quiet, 17; pulse 96, open, soft, and equal in both wrists. The cerebral functions were much impaired. The patient remained constantly in a soporous state, very similar to that of the patients described by Abercrombie. There were no convulsions.

The following cases, though not simple instances of cerebral anæmia, are, I think, very illustrative of that state, and altogether are of considerable interest:—

No. 1.—H. B., æt. 31, female, seen in consultation with Dr. Palmer, Jan. 14th.—For about seventeen years has led a very dissolute life, drinking at intervals large quantities of brandy and port wine. After these bouts she would remain sober for a time. Had jaundice and swelled ankles in Scotland two or three years ago. No indication of syphilis. Her general condition five or six weeks before I saw her Dr. Palmer describes as sufficiently startling. There was general œdema from the forehead to the toes, a pasty wax-like complexion, complete anorexia and almost hourly tenesmus, with pain in micturition. The motions consisted almost solely of jelly-like mucus. There was marked tenderness on pressure all over the liver, but nowhere else in the abdomen. Frequent vomiting. Urine cloudy, and usually depositing red or pale lithates: it was examined again and again, but no albumen was detected. Complains of severe pains across the under parts of the roots of the toes, like those of atonic gout: has pains also in the legs and insteps. Mental faculties blunted and dull. Pulse about 100. Amenorrhœa for three months. Under treatment she improved; the œdema almost disappeared, the skin generally began to look natural, but still she was very weak in mind and body. She could eat a little meat, and slept fairly. After having gone out and taken supper one evening, the symptoms recurred, attended with smart bronchitis of right lung. This subsided under treatment; but she remained in a feeble, semi-somnolent state, with frequent sickness and anorexia—Feb. 5th. Some appearance of peritonitis, no somnolence, purged freely.—9th. Several epileptic fits occurred yesterday and to-day; is incoherent, scarcely knowing her mother, and using bad language. —14th. Up to this date, incoherent, somnolent, talking, or screaming with occasional periods of partial consciousness; sometimes clutches eagerly at food, and eats a little ravenously. Sphincters do not act. Died same evening. My impression, when I first saw this case, was very decided that it was one of renal degeneration, with uræmic poisoning. The urine, however, was unlike any that is usually passed in such states. I examined it carefully on Jan. 14th and Feb. 5th: on neither occasion could I discover in it anything manifestly morbid, except that the last specimen deposited numerous nuclear corpuscles, which appeared to be those of renal epithelium. It was full-coloured, sp. gr. 1017 to 1012, thick, with amorphous lithates, and contained no casts or albumen. As to the amount passed, it was below the normal, but was not very scanty. At the post-mortem, we found evidences of slight recent peritonitis. The spleen was large, very dark, and contained several small fibrinous masses. The liver was enlarged, and in an extreme state of fatty degeneration, but free from cirrhosis. The kidneys were very flabby and lax, but not apparently wasted; their surface was quite smooth. The matrix appeared thickened, the Malpig tufts normal; the epithelium seemed to have accumulated in the tubes in excessive quantity, but its particles were stunted and ill-formed. On the whole, it could not be said that the kidneys were at all incapable of functioning. The supra-renal capsules were carefully searched for, on both sides, but no trace of them could be found. There was much fat both within and upon the abdomen; no bronzing of the skin: head not examined. This case goes quite to corroborate Traub's view,[1] who ascribes uræmic phenomena to cerebral œdema and anæmia. Although the kidneys and their secretion were by no means perfectly normal, yet they were, I think, sufficiently so to make it pretty certain that the somnolence, delirium, and convulsions were not the result of poisoned blood. The nutrition of the cerebral centres was evidently seriously impaired for some weeks before death. The cause of the anæmia is obscure. I am scarcely inclined to attribute it to atrophy of the supra-renal capsules, since these organs may be removed from animals without any bad effects ensuing. Moreover, simple atrophy might affect the system very differently to the usual atheromatous degeneration. It seems most probable that the anæmia, the supra-renal atrophy, and the degeneration of the liver, were coincident results of some general cause—perhaps of the intemperate habits.

No. 2.—A. B., æt. 46; March 28th.—A rather strongly-made man, of medium height, not at all anæmic, rather the reverse; hair gray. Has usually led an active life, much in the open air. Ill for fifteen months, had at first an attack of painful griping diarrhœa, with some rheumatism; this was followed by loss or impairment of speech, so that he could not express what he wanted. In a few hours, with the aid of a glass of gin, he recovered. Subsequently, during the same journey in Australia, he was unable to get off his horse from stiffness and weakness in the left limbs. A week afterwards, his mouth was drawn aside a little. Two or three months later, having been quite well in the interval, he had a severe attack; for three weeks he was quite delirious, and was under medical care three months. He lost all his memory; was heavy and dull; but after a seton had been put in his neck, he became quite lively. He wears the seton still. He could not walk from giddiness at one time, nor use his right arm. Now he can walk, and has tolerably good use of the arm. He used also to have pain, and a sense of heaviness in the head, as well as a feeling of pins and needles in the legs; but these symptoms are much diminished. Pupils are now equal and natural. Speech slow, intellect does not seem vigorous, memory in particular is impaired. Right hand is unsteady; he cannot use it to write. No disease of the thoracic or abdominal viscera. Urine highly acid; deposits lithates.—April 10th. Seton removed; skin cool; head fairly cool; pulse weak and quick.—April 16th. Head seems too warm; its circulation tends to be over-active. He says, however, that he has less pain in the head than he had a week ago, and that he can now stoop and move his head better without feeling giddy.—21st. Can write since his forearm has been faradized; not, however, as freely as he used; but this seems to be from a defect in his mental actions, rather than from any want of manipulative power. He finds he misspells words, and uses wrong ones, or cannot recollect the right. In speech he seems to have the same defect; is slow in

[1] Schmidt's Jahrb., vol. cxiv. p. 308.

expressing himself, and does not recollect or comprehend as readily or quickly as he might. But he walks about well, goes long distances, and manages all his matters. Is remarkably active in the mornings.—30th. Was at the Crystal Palace the day before yesterday; was fairly well last night, but had pain in the head all night; and this morning when he got up, he felt ill and weak. His mental power was much impaired, he could not find his way, dropped his gloves and handkerchief, lighted a paint-brush instead of a match, &c. I found him with cold skin and feet, head cool, lips pale, bowels open, no appetite, pain still in head, but no tenderness; pupils natural. A dose of ammonia et spt. æth. s. co. did not rally him. He had a hot mustard bath to feet and hands, was put to bed, and took hot brandy-and-water; after which he was better. He slept all the day, ate a tolerable dinner, and by the evening was free from pain in the head, and had regained his consciousness.—May 3d. Last night as he was going to bed, he suddenly became unable to see to read, and felt giddy. This passed off by the next day. His right hand has got more steady since the faradization, he can shave himself.—June 10th. He has had two or three small attacks since last report, always directly traceable to over-exertion and subsiding with rest and a little stimulus. In these his hands are cold, his pulse weak, he staggers, and his brain evidently fails to function properly.—9th. Yesterday, he went to the Zoological Gardens, having been to the Crystal Palace the day before; he remained well until dinner-time, when he seemed stupefied, and was unable to feed himself properly. When brought home, he was cold, with a feeble pulse, and could only mutter inarticulately. In the morning he was much the same, quite speechless. After hot coffee and brandy-and-water, his pulse rallied, and became full but soft, and his head hotter than before. About two hours after, finding him still unable to speak, and with an active circulation, I bled him to 14 ounces; he bore it very well, but did not improve materially. He got out of bed himself some hours later, and walked down two flights of stairs.—13th. Yesterday he continued in nearly the same state; but to-day at 11 A. M., he had a severe epileptic paroxysm, and another at 4 P. M. After the first, he had liq. opii sed. m xv, but did not sleep. The convulsions affected both sides, the right especially; they lasted fifteen to twenty minutes. During their continuance, the face and neck were congested, and covered with sweat; the eyelids were constantly opened and shut; the respiration at one time was embarrassed. The second paroxysm ceased when I raised his head to put a seton in the neck.—16th. Since the last report, he has had very numerous epileptic paroxysms, many of them very severe, and the intervals sometimes shorter than the attacks. He is quite unconscious; urine is passed in bed; body bathed in sweat. In evening of the 14th, he began to take morphia by Dr. Sieveking's advice, who saw him with me, and I administered chloroform by inhalation. By noon of 16th he had taken about six grains; the pupils were contracted, the pulse good, 96, and the epileptic attacks had ceased for twelve hours.—18th. Remains still unconscious; no convulsions; he continued to sink all day, and died at 6 A. M. of 19th. During the last twenty-four hours, the right arm was evidently paralyzed.—P. M., twenty-eight hours after death. Scalp pale, cerebrum very pale. Arachnoid of surface white-spotted, lifted up by clear fluid which was abundant everywhere. The gray matter was everywhere very pale. The vessels appeared fairly healthy; there was no trace of emboli. All the parts, cerebellum, mesocephale, medulla oblongata, and cerebrum, were carefully examined; but to the naked eye there was no evidence of morbid change in any of them; only the roof of the ventricles was, perhaps, abnormally firm. Careful microscopic examination was made of the thalami optici, and corpora striata, as well as of the cerebrum, cerebellum, and medulla oblongata; but the only change that was detected was the deposition of orange-coloured pigment masses, along the vessels of the two cerebral ganglia, there was nothing else that could be pronounced certainly abnormal. In the fornix, however, the fibres seemed to be in great measure disintegrated. No exudation corpuscles were found anywhere. The heart was very flabby indeed, but the muscular tissue of the left ventricle was fairly healthy. Kidneys very flabby, but not diseased.

Remarks.—The primary disorder in this instance is, unfortunately, obscure, All that can be affirmed is that it left no unequivocal traces of organic change. and yet it impaired and weakened the functional power of the brain. It may have been an attack of congestion, or, what I rather incline to, an affection of the nature of sunstroke. There seems no doubt that the seton for some time was highly beneficial, but its removal was not apparently injurious. Some strychnia, which was given on two occasions, did not seem to have much effect, although it caused some spasmodic twitchings. The patient was of a very active disposition, and greatly disregarded my repeated admonitions to keep himself more quiet. The enfeebled state of his nervous power was clearly shown by the frequent recurrence of failure of cerebral function, generally in connection with over-exertion. The circulation was always depressed at these times; but this seemed to be secondary, and there was no indication of ordinary syncope. It appeared as if muscular exertion consumed the nervous force, and left the cerebral centres enfeebled. The last attack clearly was produced in this way. In this it was evident that it was not only depression of the circulation which caused the failure of cerebral power, but that the paresis of the latter, to some extent at least, was primary. This may be fairly inferred from the circulation having become vigorous without the restoration of the cerebral functions. The venesection had no immediate effect, either for good or bad; but there is too much reason for suspecting that it may have been concerned in inducing the convulsions which came on three days later, and caused death by asthenia. The results of this dissection, taken together with the history of the symptoms, incline me much to believe that the impairment of function proceeded rather from dynamic than from an organic defect, and that under more favourable circumstances, nearly complete recovery might have been attained. Admitting —which is, I think, probable—that some amount of organic lesion had occurred, it seems from the history of the disorder that this was rather general than local, and probably it effected chiefly the gray matter of the convolutions. The anæmic condition of the brain after death certainly corresponds very well with the symptoms which occurred during the last few days of life; and the supposition seems very probable that during the previous less severe attacks the condition of the brain was similar, especially as during these attacks the general circulation was evidently much depressed. How this failure of circulation was brought about is not at first sight clear; most probably it is to be ascribed to the close commissural connection existing between the cardiac centres in the cord and the superior encephalic. We know that a sudden shock to the brain will powerfully depress the heart's action; and we may conceive that the central collapse would have the same effect in this case. On the other hand the slackening of the circulation would, of course, considerably increase the primary cerebral paresis. The sub-arachnoid effusion was, I believe the result of the paresis of the brain, whose nutrition was no longer adequately carried on, and so there ensued a kind of passive exudation from the bloodvessels to fill the space of the shrinking organ. The fatal convulsions resulted, no doubt, from the increasing debility, and anæmia of the encephalon having produced, according to the general law, *v. p.*, a state of hyperæsthesia of the excitable districts, the mesocephale, &c., which displayed itself in this manner. They were too prolonged, and recurred too frequently to have depended on mere spasm of the carotids and vertebrals, though this may have occurred at intervals, and had some share in the phenomena. Kussmaul and Tenner state that the brains of rabbits could not be deprived of blood more than two minutes without death actually ensuing. On the whole, I regard the case as one in which, owing to some unknown influence, such as sunstroke, the functional power of the brain had become much impaired, and was left in a condition liable to be still further depressed from slight causes.

The morbid changes induced by cerebral anæmia, so far as they are demonstrable, are such as might have been anticipated. The insufficiently nourished tissue falls into a state of decay, termed "white softening." This occurs in the human subject in about five days, or rather sooner, according to the reports which are given of the operation of ligaturing the carotid. It is no uncommon thing to find in connection with an anæmic state of the brain after death an excessive amount of interstitial and sub-arachnoid fluid. This is secreted to take the place of the more or less shrunken cerebral mass, and is poured out all the more readily in consequence of the loss of tone in the coats of the vessels. According to Buhl's researches, this condition of a "wet brain" coincides with a tendency to stupor. In cases of softening, affecting part only of one hemisphere, resulting from embolism of an artery, it is affirmed by Panum[1] that the appearance of the softened part depends on the time at which it is examined after the deprivation of blood. Red softening commences in twenty-four or forty-eight hours, and lasts from eight to fourteen days: it is succeeded by yellow softening, and this again, after several months have elapsed, by white. The cerebral tissue in the affected part becomes gradually softened and more disintegrated, and paler in colour, as time elapses. In red softening their is always increased tension and injection of the collateral vessels. The colour is produced not only by vascular injection, but by capillary extravasations. Subsequent changes consist in fatty degeneration of the tissues and decolorization of the blood-globules.

The diagnosis of cerebral anæmia is evidently a point of the highest importance, and one which may by no means be always easy. When the face is pale, the scalp cool, the eyes uninjected, the general circulation quiet—when there is no appearance of cerebral excitement, but rather of failing power—when the recumbent position affords relief, and the distressing sensations in the head are described

---

[1] V. Meissner's Report in Schmidt's Jahrb., vol. cxvii. p. 209.

as a weight at the vertex, or a feeling of opening and shutting, and as if the top of the head were being lifted off—the nature of the case is clear. But there may be conditions of the most marked general anæmia and spanæmia, in which, of course, the cerebral circulation participates, and yet in which there may arise temporarily a state of cerebral hyperæmia. By this I mean that though the blood is evidently of very imperfect quality, deficient in solids and in red cells, yet that an excess of this blood is sent to the brain above what it ought under the circumstances to receive. Nothing is more common than to find anæmic patients complaining of headache from the administration of necessary tonics, because their nervous centres have been brought into such a state of hyperæsthesia by the impaired nutrition that they can hardly tolerate anything of a stimulant nature. A little excess, therefore, even of spanæmic blood, may cause distress to a feeble brain, which after it has regained more healthy tone, will bear and be benefited by a larger amount of much better blood. The case is similar to that of the starved man, whose very preservation depends on his being fed most sparingly for some time. The following case is of interest both as regards diagnosis and treatment:—

No. 3.—J. W., æt. 31, smith, admitted august 4, 1862.—Is in a state of the most extreme anæmia from rectal hemorrhage, which commenced nine years ago, and has recurred at intervals ever since. Latterly it has been constant; he bleeds whenever he has a motion, and even sometimes when he urinates. Has lost as much as a pint at once. His head throbs; he has pain at the precordia, palpitation and giddiness in walking. Bowels usually loose. A *bruit de diable* is heard on both sides of the neck, very loud when he turns his head to the opposite side, feebly when he holds it straight. Skin cool; pulse feeble. No piles could be discovered. On examination, the mucous membrane was pale and rather relaxed. Ordered lead and opium pills *ter die*, with castor oil and sulphur *o. n* —7th. No bleeding, or very little, since. Became unconscious to-day about noon, and is now (7 P. M.) quite so; he lies with his head low, thrust down into the pillow, turns away from me, and struggles pretty strongly if I attempt to turn him; perspires a good deal, and is rather hot; pupils dilated, pulse over 100, and rather forcible; some stomach disturbance to-day. His condition was rather one of soporose delirium than of coma. Opium was ordered, $\mathfrak{m}$ xl of tr. opii *statim*, and $\mathfrak{m}$ xx *o. h.*, until he appeared to sleep; but he would not take it, kept his mouth firmly closed, and at 12 midnight I found him very restless, thrusting his head repeatedly into the pillow, and quite unconscious. Tr. opii $\mathfrak{m}$ xl 2 *dis horis in enemate*.—8th, 10 A. M. Is in much the same state; has had two or three enemata, works much with head against the pillow, has not spoken or given any sign of consciousness. Blister to neck. —6 P. M. Is now cool. Pulse quieter, smaller, feebler. Has become more conscious, and has spoken, but is still wild and restless, throwing himself about; looks deathly pale. Has taken a good deal of milk and egg with brandy, and small doses of tr. opii.—9th, 10 A. M. Is still very restless, and perfectly pale, but quite sensible, with a cool skin and a medium-sized pupil; some little bleeding this morning.—10th. A large protrusion of inflamed piles, partly mucous and partly cutaneous, was shown me to day.

The skin was divided, and the mucous portion tied with ligatures in two separate masses. Some blood that flowed I observed coagulated perfectly. Tr. opii ♏xxx were given in brandy-and-water after the operation. He says he did not know me till to-day.—11th. Going on well; has had several hours' sleep; temp. of axilla 99°, of hand held out of bed 97° F.; is taking tannin and ol. morrh.—15th. Doing well. P. c. oleo. Tr. ferri mur. ♏xij *ter die.*—Sept. 1st. Quite convalescent, is getting stronger every day, feels better than he has done for nine years, has lost the cardiac palpitation and that in the neck. Pulse very much weaker and smaller than it was during his illness. Bowels act well, no bleeding. Feb. 10th, 1863. Has had no return of the bleeding; says he is a better man than ever he was. *Remarks.*—This man has been long under treatment, which had quite failed, because the source of the hemorrhage had never declared itself, as it happened to do while he was under my observation. There was not the least trace of piles when I first examined him, and I had no idea that any would be found. The case is instructive in this point of view, as showing how long concealed the cause of such serious hemorrhage may remain, and how closely it behooves us to search after the "causa mali." But this by the way. The bearing of the case on our present subject is to illustrate how in the extremest anæmia a state of relative hyperæmia may arise, and bring the patient into serious peril. The brain in this man during his acute disorder was evidently seriously implicated, irritated, and over-excited. His forcible struggling and resistance showed that it was no state of mere passive stupor from failure of nutrition. The open, forcible pulse, the increased cardiac action, and the dilated pupil, as well as the heat of the surface, were evidence to my mind that the cerebral arteries were dilated, and that the weak and irritable brain was oppressed by an overflow of blood. There was grave reason to fear that ventricular or subarachnoid effusion was imminent, and that as this took place and the active congestion declined, fatal coma would ensue. Opium was given, with the view of contracting the arteries, and so by lessening the blood-flow of reducing the cerebral excitement. Though not administered so regularly as I wished, it was yet given in sufficient quantity to produce an effect; and this certainly seems to have been beneficial. The blister did not rise very fully, and had not, in my judgment, much to do with the improvement. It was very remarkable how, as he became convalescent, the pulse grew small and weak, compared with what it had been during the cerebral attack. This indicates the recovery of the sympathetic system from the state of paresis into which it had been plunged —*v. p.* It is a question of material importance to determine how far the state of the skin of the head and face may be taken as an index to that of the intra-cranial organs. One would think it *à priori* probable that the external and internal carotid and their branches would be influenced similarly by the nerves which supply their coats, and, therefore, that the state of the circulation would be alike in both sets of vessels. To a great extent I believe this is actually the case, though not invariably. It must be remembered that the brain is very much more vascular than the skin, and also that it is supplied by two other arteries besides the internal carotid, which receive vaso-motor nerves from a different source. It is, therefore, quite conceivable that the brain might be receiving an excessive supply of blood, although the vessels of the external tegument were but moderately filled. Moreover, if there existed any tissue excitement of the brain, this would create an attraction of blood to the internal viscus, which would tend to leave the external tegument in a minus state. However, I can speak from personal experience to the coincidence of a cold state of the skin of the forehead, with overpowering drowsiness, *i. e.*, cerebral anæmia, and to the converse. I have met with patients who looked at first sight most blooming, but who complained that their cheeks were burning and their heads throbbing, and who wished, in fact, to be cured of their extra and intra-cranial hyperæmia. As a general rule, if the skin of the head is cool and pale, we may conclude that the intra-cranial arteries are admitting but little blood; but the converse, probably, has many exceptions. The state of the eye is, perhaps, a more sure guide than that of the skin. A red, injected, eager eye can scarcely imply anything else than an hyperæmic brain; and a pale dead, white languid eye almost certainly indicates the reverse. The state of the urine may give valuable information. Pale, copious, low specific gravity urine will surely coincide with an absence of arterial hyperæmia; while scanty, red, lateritious, dense urine will invest the cerebral symptoms with an opposite meaning. It is scarcely necessary to refer to the pulse, except to that of the carotid. If this is open and bounding, it indicates that the arteries are uncontracted, and admitting a full current of blood. Of course, the reverse would not necessarily imply cerebral anæmia, any more than in peritonitis the small, wiry pulse implies an absence of inflammation. Panting, hurried, or irregular respiration (the lungs being healthy) would point towards anæmia. The state of the pupil is so much controlled by that of the brain, as also indeed by that of the cord,[1] that its indications are not reliably definite. An excited brain or a depressed cord will produce a contracted pupil, or *vice versa;* though in medium states I think a contracted pupil generally coincides with contracted cerebral vessels, and a dilated with uncontracted.

The treatment of anæmic states of the brain is sufficiently evident if the anæmia be general; the only needful caution being "*festinare lente:*" that is to say, as fast as the weak and hyperæsthetic nervous centre will permit. Good air and good nourishment, and sufficient rest, are, of course, essential; and for medicines, steel wine, citrate of quinine and iron, carbonate of iron, and cod-liver oil, will generally do good service. In cases where the digestive power is feeble, the lactate of iron, or *fer reduit*, will probably be more easily assimilated than the more common preparations. Rennet wine may be recommended to promote the digestion of azotized food.

Where the anæmia is partial the object of treatment must be either to stimulate the languid brain moderately, or to prevent and allay arterial spasm. This subject will be considered under the head of epilepsy.

For the following case I am indebted to the kindness of Dr. H. C. Stewart, whose correct diagnosis deserves great praise:—

No. 4.—A general officer, æt. 60 years, who had been with our peninsular army and at Waterloo, and subsequently with the army of Don Pedro in Portugal, has had frequent attacks of intermittent fever, and during the last twenty years has suffered from spasmodic asthma. Dr. St. was sent for

---

[1] Dr. Fraser's paper on Physostigma Venenos., Edin. Med. Journ., July, 1863.

in a great hurry, and found on arrival that his patient had lost all power over the left side, and had very partial sensation. The muscles of the face on the affected side were all relaxed, while those on the opposite side were rigid and drawn. His tongue when protruded was also drawn to the opposite side. He had great difficulty in swallowing his saliva, and his speech was imperfect. His urine was constantly dribbling away from him. B. opened three hours before this attack. There was considerable difficulty of breathing. Consciousness was retained, and but for the difficulty of speaking he would have answered questions correctly. Left pupil contracted, right mobile. Pulse 100, weak and small. Skin hot and dry; thirst; tongue coated thickly. On inquiry St. found that he had had similar attacks before, for which he had been bled and mercurialized; that he had also had frequent attacks of intermittent fever, and spasmodic asthma. This information led him to believe that the prostration of the nervous power might be dependent upon some miasmatic poison, particularly as he had recently been staying near Woolwich. He gave therefore six grains of quinine, and some warm drink. About forty-five minutes after St. learned that he had had a very slight rigor, which was followed quickly by heat, and almost instantaneously by profuse perspirations, while as the attack passed off the symptoms of hemiplegia subsided. For a week afterwards the ague recurred every other day, and with it the hemiplegia, but in a slighter degree. The disorder yielded to quinine. Since then he has had one other attack in every respect similar, but less severe. *Remarks.*—There can be little question that the phenomena in this highly interesting case were produced by spasm of the cerebral arteries, which was so complete on one side as to prevent the nervous centres from functioning. Such spasm of the arteries is constantly present in the cold stage of ague to a greater or less extent, and may be, as in a case I shall subsequently relate, sufficient to obliterate the radial pulse. The symptoms produced by one-sided cerebral embolism are very similar, but the record of the case makes it perfectly clear that no morbid cause of this kind was in action. The paralysis of the sphincter vesicæ shows that the cord must have been affected to some extent, probably in the same way as the brain. It is worth remarking that the facial nerve was palsied on the same side as the limbs according to the usual, but unexplained, event in all hemiplegia.

The following remarkable history is quoted by M. Bailly[1] from *Wirtenson's Memoirs on Opium:*—

No. 5.—A lady of distinction was attacked at 11 P. M. with fever, attended the next day with continual nausea, and vomiting of all food. After a small dose of tartar emetic remedies were resorted to, to relieve the vomiting, and with advantage. But the second night the fever returned at 11 P.M., and scarcely had the patient complained of feeling ill, when she lost the power of speech and consciousness. Hoffman of Munster, who happened to be at hand, was summoned. He found her speechless and in a kind of sopor, her eyes open and fixed, her limbs stiff, as in catalepsy. Her pulse was small and intermitted frequently, and her breathing was difficult. In short she had a well-marked soporous intermittent fever. All who were present feared that she would die speedily. In such cases eminent authorities advise emetics, irritating enemata, or blisters, and stimulants, but Hoffman, who

---

[1] Bailly—Traité de Fièvres Intermittentes, p. 436.

had no confidence in such measures, whose inutility he had often experienced, followed a very different method. It was not the case to temporize, and in order to save the patient it was urgent to have recourse to effectual means. What remained then to be done?—try the administration of opium. But how could one venture to counteract an unnatural sleep with a remedy which causes sleep? These considerations did not weigh with this physician taught by experience. He poured into the patient's mouth ninety-five drops of liquid laudanum, and he saw that she swallowed it. After the lapse of a few minutes the pulse was developed, and the breathing more free, and in less than half an hour the lethargy was dissipated, and the danger past. The pulse was full, the limbs had regained their suppleness, the patient regained consciousness and began to speak. Febrile heat succeeded, and afterwards sweating concluded the paroxysm. The next day bark was ordered to prevent the return of the disorder, but the stomach rejected it in every form. Enemata of bark were ineffectual, for at the same hour the next night the paroxysm returned and with the same alarming symptoms as before. The laudanum was given again successfully. The next day the stomach was still intolerant of bark, and a third fit was apprehended. On the suggestion however of the husband, the laudanum was given one hour before the time of recurrence; it did not prevent the paroxysm, but it deprived it of the sopor and the alarming symptoms. After it was over the patient was able to take a vinous infusion of bark, and was soon cured. *Remarks.*—The correct reading of this most interesting case is I think similar to that of the preceding. The soporous symptoms came on at the onset of the paroxysm in the cold stage, at the time when arterial spasm is prevalent. They were removed and obviated by a powerful sedative, which we must presume to have acted on the over-excited vaso-motor nerves, and to have thus quelled the spasm. As the blood-flow returned to the encephalon its functions were restored. Trotter's experience of the good effects of opium given at the commencement of a paroxysm is quite in accordance with the above history. He found the pulse, from being weak, quick, and sometimes irregular, become less frequent, full, and equal; an agreeable warmth was diffused over the whole frame, and every unpleasant feeling vanished. This action of opium is analogous to that which it exerts in cases of renal and hepatic calculus, and spasmodic stricture of the urethra, where it seems to relax contracted muscular fibre. I am well aware that it has been thought even more efficacious in the hot stage of ague, and that it has actions apparently of a contrary kind. These points will be hereafter noticed. It need scarcely be stated that the administration of opium would not be suitable to every kind of soporous intermittent. If the coma depended upon hyperæmic congestion it would be of course contra-indicated, at least in a full dose. It may be remarked with regard to the view I maintain as to the action of opium (v. remedies), that there is nothing inconsistent with it in supposing that a stimulant may cause relaxation of existing spasm, as in Dr. Salter's cases of asthmatic paroxysm arrested by alcohol.

CHAPTER IV.

ANÆMIA OF THE SPINAL CORD.

WE are chiefly indebted to Kussmaul and Tenner for any accurate knowledge on this head. They tied both subclavian arteries close to their origins in several rabbits so that the blood was conveyed to their brains solely through the carotids. They then compressed the arch of the aorta so that all afflux of arterial blood to the trunk of the body was cut off. The results are described as follows. Respiration becomes at once slower, and gradually in the direction from back to front weaker and weaker. The hinder part of the body soon becomes completely paralyzed, while the fore-legs are only partially so. In most of the animals paralysis of the hinder part of the body came on without any convulsions. In three of them a short slight trembling preceded; whilst these trembling movements were in one case only somewhat more rapid, resembling those occurring in paralysis tremulans, and lasting for some seconds. Within a few seconds, or at most within from one to one and a half minutes the paralysis of the hind legs was complete. Peculiar movements similar to those witnessed in cholera are regularly observed in the fore-legs some time after tying the arch of the aorta. It is not at first clear whether these movements are voluntary, or are involuntary convulsions: the latter however is found to be the case. They are frequently repeated, and are produced by a reflex act when the legs are touched. They gradually cease as life becomes extinct. Respiration ceased in from eight to eighty-one minutes after the last constant compression. The heart stopped beating in from eight to twenty minutes after the last breath. Consciousness appeared but little disturbed up to the last moment. In one experiment the subclavians were tied, and the aorta compressed, which produced almost immediately complete paralysis of the hind and partial of the fore legs. The carotids were now compressed, whereupon a violent epileptic attack ensued within a few seconds, but ceased on removing the compression from the carotids. This experiment puts in a clear light the part which anæmia of the encephalon plays in producing general convulsions, and shows that anæmia of the spinal cord is marked more by paralysis than by convulsion.

Such being the results which experiment teaches us we may look for when anæmia of the cord exists, we have now to inquire how far we are likely to meet with this condition as an actual morbid change, and how far we are to recognize anæmia of the cord as a *vera causa* of disease. The mode in which the cord is supplied with arterial blood, viz., by a succession of small arteries entering the vertebral canal through the intervertebral foramina to anastomose with the anterior and posterior spinal derived from the vertebral, makes it less likely that it should be deprived of blood by constriction or obstruction of its vessels than is the case with the encephalon. It is not very likely that a large number of small arteries would become and remain constricted simultaneously, and if only a few remained open they would supply blood to the tracts of capillaries. The cases where it seems to us most probable that a paralysis may be dependent on anæmia from arterial constriction are those where the affection ensues paroxysmally apparently in connection with malarious fever. Romberg relates a case of this kind where motor paraplegia occurred according to a tertian type, disappearing spontaneously. After the due administration of quinine the paralysis ceased to return. M. Bailly describes how, during his stay at Rome, when he was evidently under the influence of malarious infection, he experienced every day about three or four P. M. an extraordinary weakness of the legs, so that he could hardly get along, and was obliged to use his arms, which were unaffected, to pull himself by the banisters up stairs. He was cured of this symptom by quinine. The following case, for which I am indebted to my friend, Mr. Moullin, was probably of the same kind:—

No. 6.—H., æt. 45, labourer, was seized July 9th, while at work, with violent pain across the loins and with numbness running down the legs. The urine was retained so that he could not pass it, and there was involuntary discharge of feces. When first seen he was lying on his back at full length, the toes pointing straight out, the skin cold, the legs paralyzed and insensible, even when pinched with the nail. He was quite unable to stir. No pain or disorder elsewhere. Quite conscious. Ordered an enema of turpentine with aloes, and calomel gr. v + pulv. jalap. co. gr. x. After the enema and purge had acted freely the limbs still remained powerless; the pain continued, but was relieved by a croton-oil liniment. July 11th. Quin. disulph. gr. x *ter die.* The next day sensation returned, and the next he could sit up in bed. In a week he walked to the dispensary, and soon after was quite well. The record sufficiently proves that no organic disease existed in this case, the suddenness of supervention and the speedy recovery are quite unlike simple or direct paralysis of the cord, the non-success of the purgatives and the good effect of quinine negative the existence of inhibitory irritation, so that *par voie d'exclusion* we are almost obliged to refer it to anæmia from arterial spasm. I have before recorded a similar case where hemiplegia ensued in a like way, and it does seem to me most probable that such cases depend on arterial constriction, principally because we have pretty certain evidence that at the commencement of an ague paroxysm the involuntary muscles as well as the voluntary are thrown into a state of abnormal contraction.

These instances are, however, very rare, and we think they afford no sufficient warrant for extending the same view of causation to all instances of so called reflex paralysis. It is worth remarking that general anæmia sufficient to produce complete loss of vision does not cause paralysis, *v.* Gooch's case of fatal flooding. The results of the habitual use of ergotized grain as food are not very favourable to the view of permanent paralysis being occasioned by anæmia. Dr. Brown-Séquard states indeed that ergot produces a contraction of the bloodvessels of the spinal cord and of its membranes, and, therefore, diminishes the amount of blood circulating in these organs. If this be so, we should certainly, on the above view, expect to have paralysis as a much more constant and early symptom than it appears to have been. It does not seem to have occurred in the earlier period of the affection, but to have succeeded to severe spasms affecting the limbs, and producing even trismus and opisthotonos. Violent convulsions and tetanus are produced by ergotism as well as paraplegia. I have given tr. ergotæ ʒss *ter die* for more than a month in a case of proptosis, &c., without observing any effect which could be ascribed to anæmia of the cord. Of course, a relative anæmia may be produced without materially impairing the functions of the spinal centres. Just as the skin of the fingers retains much of its sensibility, even when the supply of blood is much diminished, so it will be with the cord. On the whole, it appears to me, that we have no sufficient grounds for regarding spinal anæmia as a pathological state which we are likely often to meet with. It is probable that in cases of paresis which we shall presently consider more or less of anæmia may exist, but this is not the primary condition, and does not rule the treatment.

In the treatment of my case of supposed spinal anæmia from arterial spasm, the moderate inhalation of chloroform, friction with stimulating liniments to the spine, the administration of quinine with diffusive stimulants and sedatives, and a prolonged warm bath would probably be the most efficient remedies.

CHAPTER V.

HYPERÆMIA OF THE BRAIN.

By this term we understand an increased flow of arterial blood to the encephalon. This true hyperæmia should be distinguished from venous congestion, which is common enough in the closing periods of various diseases, and at post-mortem examinations, but is rarely the object of treatment, and in its action upon the brain approaches much more to anæmia than to true hyperæmia. The common varicose ulcers of the legs afford proof how unfit stagnating venous blood is to nourish the integument, and it may well be imagined how much more susceptible a tissue, of so high an order as the brain, will be of the deprivation of its proper nutrient and stimulant. With venous hyperæmia, we have here, therefore, nothing to do. Of arterial we have first to remark that it may be either physiological or pathological. The first, when it is subordinate to the functional power of the nervous tissue, and ministers to its activity; the second, when it surpasses this limit, and becomes excessive. To quote a sentence from the *Manual of Pathology*, p. 81: "In the one case it supplies a want, in the other it imposes a burden." The very same amount of blood-supply may be either beneficial or injurious, according to the vital quality and condition of the cerebral structure. A weak and irritable organ will be oppressed by that which only supplies the necessary pabulum to the more active life of the stronger. When our brains are jaded and weary with work, we find that we gain little by increasing their blood supply with vinous stimulants, and that repose is essential to enable the organ to regain its power. When, however, there is less exhaustion we are familiar with the invigorating influence of wine on the mental faculties.

Pure cerebral hyperæmia, considered apart from primary cerebral excitement, is by no means very common, at least in this country. Theoretically, it requires for its production increased action of the heart and relaxation of the contractile coats of the cerebral arteries. It is mostly in certain malarious fevers that we find these conditions existing. In a case of double quotidian paroxysm under my own care, the patient, a male, aged 46, became quite delirious in the fever, "singing and quite out of his mind." The disease soon yielded to quinine. Copland describes the symptoms of the period of reaction as consisting of flushed face, tumid features, prominent, red, and watery eyes, and pain of head attended by a feeling of distension and throbbing, often passing into delirium. Ranald Martin writes of the remittent fever of Bengal during the stage of reaction: "The blood-current/ previously oppressed, becomes now hard and quick, ranging from 110 to 120 pulsations in the minute, and the force and frequency of the circulation through the brain, superadded to the already disturbed condition of the nervous functions, give rise to confusion of ideas and loss of mental control, amounting occasionally to actual delirium." Such is the hyperæmia that he states his life was only preserved by a profuse hemorrhage from the nose during the height of the first two paroxysms in a severe attack of jungle fever he underwent. He cites from Dr. Henderson a most proving history to show how powerfully the cerebral congestion, occurring during remittent fever, tends to issue in apoplectic extravasation. So often did the one terminate in the other that it was "hard to draw the line between them."

It is highly probable that in these fevers the hyperæmia is both greater and more injurious because of the impaired state of the nervous force in the brain which is depressed by the primary action of malaria, the original cause of the disease. Convulsions do not seem to be a usual result of this cerebral congestion, neither of the authors above quoted mention them. Bailly, however, seems to have observed numerous instances at Rome of intermittent fever which he calls "convulsive." The motor disorder showed itself, however, more as tonic contraction than clonic, and there was no spasmodic closure of the glottis. The following instance affords a good example of severe cerebral hyperæmia passing into actual meningitis.

No. 7.—J. C., æt. 51, admitted July 18th.—He was furiously delirious, so that it was necessary to confine him. His pulse was strong and vibrating, but uncountable at first from the continued movements of the arms and body. Two hours later it was 124. The forearms were tensely flexed at an acute angle on the arms, and could not be extended without causing pain to the patient by the attempt. The jaws were firmly closed, the muscles of the lips in continual motion, as were also the lower limbs. Sensibility of surface not impaired. Epigastrium tender. Tongue dry and red. He continued in much the same condition till his death, July 20th. P. M. The arachnoid was thickened, and of brown red colour; the vessels were so injected that their minutest ramifications could be traced. At the posterior part was a false membrane saturated with the red colouring matter of the blood. The arachnoid of the cerebellum was in the same state. The gray substance of the brain was of a remarkably deep red. The vessels of the corpus striatum were injected. Spleen enlarged and much softened. Traces of former inflammation of the stomach, and recent of the intestines.

The distress occasioned by cerebral hyperæmia varies much according to the condition of the nervous centre. When this is highly sensitive and excitable the suffering may be great. Dr. Williams (C. J. B.) narrates the case of a gentleman subject to attacks of determination of blood to the head, which caused him so much suffering and loss of moral control, that he cut his throat to destroy his life. Whilst recovering from the wound attacks came on first with heating of the carotids, then with flushing of the face and head, suffusion of the eyes and feelings of distraction in the head. A writer in the *Journal of Psycholog. Med.* (Jan. 1863, p. 50) says: "Even in healthy persons, or persons of plethoric habit, this determination of blood may occasion transient delirium, with various signs of encephalic disturbance, such as extreme sensibility to light and sound, restlessness, pain in the head, and visual hallucinations. A flood of distorted ideas flows through the mind, and overwhelms it; bewilderment and incoherence follow, and for the time being the patient is to all intents and purposes maniacal."

CAUSES.—Hyperæmia of the encephalon will be induced by all stimulating agents which act directly on its tissue, and excite it to increased functional activity. The chief of these are alcoholic liquors; small doses of opium and camphor have a similar effect. The hyperæmia thus produced is secondary. Various conditions causing paresis of the vaso-motor nerves of the cerebral arteries will also give rise to hyperæmia, which in this case is primary and pathological. It is no uncommon thing to meet with persons who flush very much in the face after a meal. A lady under my care suffered so much in this way, her face and neck becoming of a deep red, that she was unable to dine out. She was of a highly sensitive temperament, and had occasionally some choreic symptoms. Mr. Langston Parker, in his excellent work on the stomach in its morbid states, relates (p. 258) the case of a lady, who when placed under his care had recently recovered from hemiplegia of the right side, but continued to have pain and throbbing in the head, thirst, flushing of the face, and occasional numbness of the limbs. The head was continually hot, the seat of severe pain at the vertex with occasional violent and sudden darting pains through it, which made the patient scream out; the carotids and temporal arteries throbbed violently, and the pulsations were seldom less than 100 per minute. The epigastrium was the seat of a violent beating, was full and hot, exceedingly tender on pressure, and the seat of internal pains shooting in the hypochondria, where she had also fixed uneasiness. The stomach and intestines were become so morbidly sensible to impressions, that everything she took produced pain, sickness, and very frequently vomiting; there was constantly an intensely acid taste in the mouth. The patient had previously been recommended rich diet and stimulants. She was now treated with a few leeches to the epigastrium, and a nightly mercurial aperient; which brought away at first pitchy stools. Her diet consisted of farinaceous food. In a week she was well. Several other interesting cases of the like kind are recorded. Mr. L. Parker seems to consider that the irritation of the stomach was directly conveyed to the brain, and set up there a similar condition. When, however, we consider that the only direct connection of the stomach with the brain is by means of the pneumogastric nerves, which are implanted in the medulla oblongata as their centre, and that there was no special disorder of the respiratory function, we shall, I think, be inclined to admit that the gastric irritation affected the brain in a different way. This probably consisted in a morbid impression being conveyed by the sympathetic nerves of the stomach to their ganglia, and thence to the vaso-motor nerves of the cerebral arteries which in consequence became dilated, and thus hyperæmia ensued.[1] The vaso-motor paresis, in such cases, is of the inhibitory kind explained at p. 22. The extensive diffusive character of the cerebral irritation, in these cases, and the non-production of organic disease, at least for a long time, indicate pretty clearly that the morbid action is not actually located in the cerebral tissue itself. In not a few cases determination of blood to the head is dependent on a primary state of paresis in the nerves of the cerebral arteries.

[1] The record shows that the carotid and temporal arteries were paralyzed.

It is a very curious and important fact, which is mentioned by Kussmaul and Tenner, and which would not, I think, have been anticipated *à priori*, that releasing the carotid arteries from compression causes intra-cranial hyperæmia. It almost seems as if the nervous tissue by the temporary deprivation of blood was brought into a state of excitability, which induced it subsequently to attract the blood with more force. Or where the arteries have been occluded by a spasm of their own circular fibres it may be presumed that this as it yields is succeeded by a state of paresis and dilatation. The following case exemplifies this:—

No. 8.—A merchant, æt. 65, seen in consultation with Dr. Barrett, Oct. 10th, 1861. He had in July a first epileptoid seizure preceded for some hours by hemiplegia, which passed off with the fit. A second attack occurred on the morning of the 10th; he lay in coma till the morning of the 11th, and was gradually recovering the following evening, but not yet wholly conscious. The circulation after the fit at first was depressed, but by the evening it became very active in the scalp and ears, which were red and hot, and did not give a pale spot on pressure, not even for an instant, after the compression ceased. On account of the manifest determination to the head, and the danger of effusion, ʒiv of blood were taken by C. C.; the night of the 10th, he had also calomel, and enema terebinth. The urine after the attack was free, highly albuminous, not high-coloured, sp. gr. 1022, deposited lithates on standing. 14th. The stupor has now nearly passed off, though his mental faculties seem rather torpid. Has passed two very dark scybalous motions. Tongue clean. Heart rather enlarged, otherwise apparently normal. Lungs healthy. His legs have been enfeebled for some months past; he walks like a person crippled by rheumatism. He has been generally very healthy. May 9th, 1862. He has remained pretty well till two or three days ago, when he had an attack of stupor without convulsions. He was relieved immediately by mild purging, and is now tolerably conscious. Pulse of apparently good force, large. Gets weaker in walking. Urine continues constantly albuminous. Some months after he had another attack, and died comatose. *Remarks.*—This case is one of great interest in more respects than one. It illustrates very well the occurrence of coma together with an over-active state of circulation as a sequel of epilepsy, and the danger that this hyperæmia may occasion if excessive. It also indicates the probability that hemiplegia may in some instances depend on a similar pathological condition to that which gives rise to convulsions. It seems for instance tolerably certain in this case that the hemiplegia, which disappeared so speedily, depended like the convulsions on closure of the cerebral arteries; only that during the palsy a different set of vessels was affected, perhaps those of one hemisphere and one corpus striatum only. Subsequently the arterial spasm became more general, and involved the vessels of both sides, and those of the excitable districts. In the attack of stupor without convulsions the arteries of both hemispheres were probably constricted. The renal affection, I believe, only so far contributed to the nervous disorder that it rendered the blood less fit for maintaining healthy nutrition, and so induced a state of weakness and excitability of the nervous centres. The loss of an autopsy is much to be regretted, still it seems tolerably certain from the absence of permanent morbid phenomena that there was no material organic change, except perhaps in the lower part of the spinal cord giving rise to the paresis of the lower limbs.

Malaria is of course the great cause of cerebral hyperæmia in inter- and re-mittent fevers. This complication is not so frequent among us as it is in tropical climates; it is nevertheless occasionally met with, and according to my experience most often among children in that form of disorder which I have termed malarioid remittent. Exposure of the head to the rays of a powerful sun seems certainly to cause in some cases cerebral hyperæmia. Dr. Murray, quoted by Sir R. Martin, thinks that this effect is to be distinguished from that of the same temperature in the shade where the action of the heat is more general. In this view I quite concur. The phenomena in the latter condition seem to be essentially those of extreme nervous exhaustion, which we shall subsequently examine. Dr. West mentions an instance in which exposure to the sun's rays clearly induced an inflammatory state of the brain. Burns, as in a case I shall presently relate, sometimes have a similar effect. The injury to the skin causes inhibitory paralysis of the cerebral vessels, from which hyperæmia results. The poison of the exanthemata before the eruption appears, *i. e.*, before it directs its action to the vasomotor nerves of the skin, often causes considerable cerebral congestion, apparently from direct irritation of the brain. Dental irritation in children is a frequent cause of cerebral hyperæmia, the head being hot, the anterior fontanelle prominent and pulsating strongly, the brows knit, and the skin febrile. All these symptoms subside on the tooth passing through the gum, or sometimes on effectual lancing. I have seen the flushing of face subside in a few minutes after the gums were lanced in a child who had just had an attack of convulsions succeeded by stupor. In this case it seems to me certain that the convulsions and the cerebral hyperæmia were caused by the uprising tooth (a posterior molar); the question is how. The convulsions probably depended on the increased excitability of certain parts of the brain affected by the irritation. The hyperæmia from its involving the extra- as well as the intra-cranial parts, and from its speedy subsidence on removal of the exciting cause must have been owing to inhibitory vaso-motor nerve paresis.

The morbid changes produced by cerebral hyperæmia are well exemplified in the following case.

No. 9.—J. R., m., æt. 16, ad. Nov. 11th with a burn of the third degree affecting the lower part of his abdomen, and the upper and inner part of his thigh, as well as the genital organs. The shock was severe. Pulse feeble. Respiration slow. Pain severe at night. On the 13th an erythematous eruption appeared on the chest and abdomen closely resembling that of scarlatina; the tongue also was in a very similar state to that observed in this fever. He passed two very delirious nights; on the 15th the eruption became more dusky, the hands and feet cold, and he sank at 2 P. M., having been perfectly sensible before death. At the autopsy there was found extravasation of blood under the scalp, and effusion of blood between the dura mater and the bone. All the membranes of the brain congested. Effusion of fluid beneath the arachnoid. The white substance displayed numerous puncta vasculosa. The ventricles did not contain an abnormal quantity of fluid. The lungs and all the viscera were congested. Brown-Séquard's experiments have shown that the various remote effects produced by burns are brought about through the intermedium of the spinal cord, which he regards as reflecting the irritation from the burnt part of the secondarily affected organs. In my opinion the remote action of the burn is not on the tissue of the organs themselves, but on the vaso-motor nerves of their blood-vessels, which in consequence of the morbid impression are paralyzed. It seems in this case, as not uncommonly happens in such instances, that the textural quality of the minute vessels was impaired so that extravasation of the blood ensued. Paralyses of vessels are, I think, not unfrequently associated with such loss of retentive power in the capillaries. Common epistaxis with its cure by putting a cold key down the back affords an example where a like state is remedied by the tonic effect of cold acting on vaso-motor through afferent nerves of the cord. The resemblance of the eruption to that of scarlatina in this instance was very close, the chief difference being that the face was but little affected. The mode of causation in both I believe to be the same. It seems distinctive of reflex vaso-motor paralysis that the hyperæmia it produces is *diffuse*, while that of tissue irritation is more localized and tends more to exudation and suppuration.

The *treatment* of cerebral hyperæmia must depend very much on the view taken of its causation. If it depend on direct irritation as on heat, exanthematous poison, alcohol, &c., it will be desirable if the strength of the patient permit, to deplete locally, apply cold, and promote afflux to the feet by hot mustard pediluvia. Internally we may purge, or employ Graves' tartar emetic and opium treatment, or repeated doses of colchicum. If the hyperæmia depend on paralysis of the vaso-motor cerebral nerves from malaria, or other influences, depletory and counter-irritant measures must be adopted to stave off the risk of hemorrhage or effusion if it appear imminent, and in the remissions nerve tonics, especially quinine, must be administered to remove the primary paralysis. If the vaso-motor paresis depend on a remote morbid impression, this must be mitigated or removed if possible. For this in cases of burns opium is probably the best internal remedy, and a continuous warm bath the best external. Hebra[1] relates that he kept a patient who was severely burnt continuously immersed for 21 days with the best effects. Another patient with a frightful and inveterate pemphigus was kept in the bath 100 days with the best results. The soothing influence of moist warmth takes off the depressing inhibitory influence. Mr. Windsor's experience is to the same effect (v. *Syd. Soc. Year Book*, 1863, p. 205).

The following cases of hyperæmia are of interest:—

No. 10.—E. L., f., æt. 16, ad. Aug. 20th. Ill three weeks; complains of a burning flushed state of both sides of face, extending to the head, which puts the head into much pain, makes it feel hot. She is obliged by attacks

[1] "Lond. Med. Rev.," Jan. 1860.

of this kind to go to bed every day. They occur indifferently at all times of the day. She sleeps well at night. Digestion weak. Tongue clean. Bowels open. Pulse soft. She continued under treatment till November 21st, when she was well enough to be discharged. After she had improved I noticed one day that one cheek only was hot, the other being cold. The remedies employed were strychnia and tr. ferri muriatis, and assafœtida. Tannin with gentian and henbane benefited the digestion, but the disorder was certainly not chiefly if at all of gastric origin. It was a primary paresis of the nerves of both external and internal carotids, as evidenced by the juvantia and the general character of the symptoms. It is very evident how a depleting lowering treatment would aggravate such disorder.

No. 11.—Ch., m., æt. 55, of short, broad make, very short neck. Has been suffering two or three years with an uncomfortable sensation in his head, most felt on the right side, but extending all over it, not worse on lying down, but much increased by a warm close atmosphere, and relieved by the open air, and by cold bracing weather. Seems to be of excitable temperament. If he goes to church can only stay for about an hour, after which he gets so excited and irritable about the head, that he is obliged to come out. His bald scalp flushes with blood while I speak to him. Head apt to be hot, when he is better is cold. Has rushing noises in the head. Feels sometimes weak in his legs, and is relieved by a purge of blue pill + scammony + jalap. Is not subject to rheumatism or gout, nor is the latter in his family. Urine free and natural. Heart's sounds and position normal. No indigestion. Pulse 75, of moderate force. He was ordered nitric and hydrocyanic acids with cascarilla infusion *ter*, and quinine, tannin, and henbane in a pill *bis die*. This treatment proved decidedly beneficial; he found more inclination for mental work, and less tendency to procrastinate.

In the latter case it was remarkable that the patient did not find the uneasiness in the head increased by lying down. The same was observed in another patient, whose symptoms were very similar, the carotids throbbing strongly, but who stated that his head was relieved by the recumbent posture. In one of the epileptic series the same is mentioned. It is not easy to explain this peculiarity, perhaps it may depend on the heart's action becoming less in the reclining position. Even when the cerebral hyperæmia is of traumatic origin the same is sometimes the case.

No. 12.—J. H., m., æt. 16, ad. Sept. 13th. Ill seven days, was struck by a ball on the head the day before he became ill. He has great pain in the head, throbbing in the temples, nausea and loss of appetite. Head hot, Has not more pain on lying down. With eight leeches to the temples, a blister to the neck, some Gray and Dover's powder he soon got well.

It is clear that there was direct irritation of the brain in this youth, yet he did not need to keep his head elevated. On the other hand, in the following instance the peculiar attacks seem to have been promoted by the recumbent posture. H. H., æt. 26, a sufferer from sub-acute rheumatism, but rather inclined to plethora, has seizures which he describes as follows: They begin with a sense of fluttering at the heart, and a feeling of fright, then all the blood in his body rushes to his head, which throbs violently, and seems full as if bursting. This state lasts five to ten minutes, during which he cannot move at all, tries to move but can't, is however quite conscious. The attack subsides spontaneously. It always occurs at night while he is lying down. It is worth observing that neither in this nor in five or six other cases of cerebral hyperæmia were there any convulsions. In Nos. (10) and (11) the pathological condition was essentially different from what it was in (12). There was active hyperæmia no doubt in all three, but in the two first it depended solely or chiefly on relaxation of the arteries, or vaso-motor nerve paresis; in the last it was the result of irritation of the cerebral tissue, and was produced by a *vis a fronte*. It is evidently a most practical matter to distinguish cases having one origin from those which have a different. The treatment must be determined by the diagnosis, and in some cases it is by no means easy. In the case of H. H. I think there ensued at first a spasm of the cerebral arteries, which was followed by sudden relaxation. The affection was akin to epilepsy.

CHAPTER VI.

SPINAL HYPERÆMIA.

THE spinal cord is evidently very differently circumstanced compared to the chief mass of the encephalon with regard to its supply of blood. That furnished to the latter is very abundant, and this large amount appears to be necessary for the due performance of its special functions—a failure or diminution of the supply being immediately felt, while on the other hand an overflow has equally injurious effects. In the case of the spinal cord these variations seem to be of much less moment, and we can by no means point with so much confidence to morbid results produced by them. No doubt the phenomena of meningitis, and myelitis, or apoplexy are evident enough; but these affections do not come within my plan as they involve actual organic change. With regard to spinal hyperæmia much importance has been attributed to it by various Continental writers of an older date as the cause of numerous morbid phenomena. Frank imputes certain pains of the back and lower extremities, certain sciatic neuralgias, certain species of lameness, divers tremors and convulsive movements, stupor or paralysis of those extremities as well as several epileptic and tetanic phenomena to congestion and distension of the vertebral sinuses and veins (Ollivier). Ludwig also views the very acute dorsal pains which so often exist in severe intestinal colics, and the pains in the back and limbs which occur at the onset of fevers as depending on a like condition. Portal explains convulsive and paralytic affections of the extremities occurring in various inflammatory diseases by congestion of the spinal vessels. Ollivier relates the following case. "I examined the body of an individual who had been affected with incomplete paralysis in the movements of the trunk and extremities with morbid exaltation of the cutaneous sensibility. This paralysis . . . had gradually diminished and was nearly gone, when it again appeared simultaneously with a pleuropneumonia. This latter disease made rather rapid progress, and the paralysis was observed to go on increasing till his death; so that a few days before he died the patient had relapsed into the same state of paralysis with extreme sensibility of the integuments. The upper and lower extremities performed but very feeble and general movements; respiration was extremely painful, and the movements of the chest were almost imperceptible. He preserved to the last the free use of his intellects. At the post-mortem we found rather excessive pneumonia and pleuritis of the right side; there existed at the same time considerable sanguineous congestion in all the meningo-spinal veins, which were manifestly dilated. The nervous cords were enveloped in a collection of veins very much gorged with blood, which evidently compressed each spinal nerve at its exit from the spine, a circumstance which perfectly explained the phenomena observed during life." Another case is related (from Dance), the subject of which was a female, æt. 31, who a month after a favourable confinement was attacked with formication of all the limbs, which speedily became paralyzed, while sensibility remained. The respiration became difficult and she died asphyxiated on the second day, having been bled twice. A very careful examination showed nothing abnormal in the brain or cord. All that could be detected was some red points on the cut surface of the brain, and slight infiltration of the cellular tissue of the spine external to the dura mater. The organs were all sound. O. explains the paralysis by the assumption of a congestion, which disappeared after death. This assumption seems to me quite inadmissible, for the death was of that kind which specially tends to increase and perpetuate venous congestion by reason of the impediment to the return of the blood to the right heart. There was just as much reason for finding the venous plexuses gorged in this case as in the preceding, and I must think the explanation of the paralysis in both is erroneous. The loss of motion alone cannot be explained so far as I can see by the congestion, as the distended veins would press equally on both anterior and posterior nerve-roots. Nor can I admit that the cord surrounded as it is by subarachnoid liquid is at all more likely to be compressed at its anterior than at its posterior part, because the former is nearer to the wall of the canal. These cases afford a good illustration how much more prone we are to be impressed by the visible than by the invisible, though the former may be very inadequate to account for the phenomena. A case which ended in recovery is given by the same author. The patient, æt. 38, led an active and laborious life, but was habituated to alcoholic and venereal excesses. The latter especially induced a pain in the loins and trembling of the lower extremities. For two months before his attack he had general debility of the legs and wandering pains, yet followed the same mode of life. It was not surprising that paralysis of all the limbs, and of the erector spinæ muscles should have ensued with some numbness and sense of formication. Venesection was useless, and after the application of twenty leeches to the back the paralysis became complete. After four blisters there was some improvement, but nux vomica given in gradually increasing doses was of no avail, and was discontinued, only dry frictions to the spine and to the extremities were occasionally employed. After three months' illness the paralysis entirely disappeared. The cause assigned for the paralysis by Ollivier is the recurrence of sanguineous congestion, and increased exhalation of the vertebral liquid. I cannot but think that a more natural and truer reading of the case is that the essential pathological condition was exhaustion of the nerve-power of the cord, which, with rest, was gradually restored. On reviewing the above cases, which seem to be fair specimens of the kind in question, I cannot but join with Abercrombie in feeling considerable doubt how far spinal hyperæmia (venous) is ever a cause of failure of the functional power of the cord. Arterial (true) hyperæmia we may be sure would (supposing it to exist apart from actual inflammation) lead to increased activity of the nervous tissue, such as exists in tetanus and in similar states. It is impossible, however, to separate the effect of the hyperæmia in such instances from that of the agent, as strychnia, which has induced it. Duclaux[1] has recently described as spinal congestion various phenomena, which were produced by excessive heat, and which were evidently very similar to those of heat-apoplexy. Patients were suddenly attacked with headache, muscæ volitantes, general cyanosis, and derangement of the digestive functions. Insensibly and in a short space of time there occurred a failure of strength in the limbs, substances held in the hands were permitted to fall listlessly to the ground, and the gait became uneven and irregular; there was giddiness and frequently syncope. Pain was commonly complained of at different parts of the vertebral column. Antiphlogistic and purgative treatment was usually successful, especially mercurial friction along the spine. Blood-letting was seldom required. The symptoms in these cases appear to me to have depended much more on a state of paresis, of exhaustion and enfeeblement of the nervous tissue than an active hyperæmia. The morbid influence of heat is invariably depressing. It is very possible that active hyperæmia did occur secondarily to some amount, and the results of treatment go to prove it, but I cannot view this as the primary morbid change.

[1] Lond. Med. Gaz., Aug. 1860.

I conclude this subject with expressing my entire concurrence in Kussmaul and Tenner's 22d conclusion, and in extending it to the spinal as well as the cranial cavity. The last few hours of life must almost invariably induce considerable alterations in the distribution of blood, and we know that even after death the position of the corpse has a very considerable influence.

CHAPTER VII.

CEREBRAL PARESIS.

By this term I mean a state in which without demonstrable organic change there is greater or less enfeeblement of the functional power of the brain. Perhaps the simplest instance of it is when after much exertion of mind or body we feel incapable of any sustained mental effort. By repose the functional power in case of mere fatigue is early restored, but in various morbid states repose alone is insufficient. Prolonged extreme mental exertion may induce such a degree of paresis as to constitute dementia, and the same may result from any severe mental shock. The non-dependence of this state on actual organic alteration in some cases is evidenced by the temporary restoration of the intellectual power under stimulants, as wine. Paresis may affect any or all of the cerebral functions, either the intellectual, or the voluntary motor, or the sensory. The liability to paresis will vary much according to the original vigour and endowments of the individual, and also according to the wear and tear to which he has been subjected. The phenomena of cerebral paresis are of course very varying, but all bear the stamp of debility, mingled it may be in certain cases with indications of abnormal excitability. In many instances the phenomena of primary cerebral paresis and of general anæmia will be very similar, the anæmia in fact being the cause of the failure of power. Paresis, however, is most often quite independent of anæmia. In some cases paresis of the brain seems to be the reflex of inhibitory irritation.

Instead of attempting to give an abstract description of the state in question, I propose to record briefly the leading features of various cases I have met with, which as actual occurrences seem to me more impressive than any general statement. A lady, aged 80, of strong constitution, calm mind, and energetic disposition, had a moderate attack of influenzal catarrh. In this she had the following symptoms referable to the head. She lay in a dozy torpid state, the stupor being so marked that she could hardly believe she had not taken opium. If she did not get her food when she wanted it she felt as if her understanding were leaving her. Bark and ammonia with wine benefited her, but even some days later, when convalescent, she could only lie quite still without speaking or doing anything, and felt as if she had no use of her mental faculties. The pulse was intermittent, but not specially weak. This was an instance of simple paresis of the hemispheres. F., male, of middle age, stout, is attacked suddenly one evening with faintness, giddiness, severe retching and vomiting. He could not stand, and his head felt as if it did not belong to him. He had felt unwell during the day, but the faintness, giddiness, and sickness came on all in five minutes. There was no epigastric tenderness, no headache, no pain, but drowsiness. He could not raise his head, except for a short time when he was sick. In four or five days the sickness had subsided, and he was gaining strength, but was only just able to read, and his head was still very apt to be giddy on any quick motion. His tongue was clean all the time, and his pulse not at all weak correspondingly to the peculiar debility of the head. Under a tonic treatment he recovered, but it was long before he lost the tendency to giddiness. In this case it is clear, I think, that the brain was affected by a stroke of influenza, which partially paralyzed its action, and perhaps also that of the vagi nerves. There was no indication of cerebral anæmia, the giddiness seemed to be the result of direct debility, which continued for a long time.—R. F., æt. 17, male, admitted January 28th. He complained of stupidness, nervousness all over, a great sense of weight at the vertex, and great sleepiness. Functions in fair order. With ammonia, iron, nux vomica, and valerian he was well in three weeks. The cause of the disorder is not clear in this instance, but it is evident that the cerebral functional energy was impaired.

M. W., æt. 8½, female. She has been ailing with nerve disorder ten to eleven months, has improved much on tonic treatment, but has relapsed last fourteen days. She has been at school, and has been over-exerting herself a little. She is silly, irritable, and bad tempered in mornings, and then her right arm gets affected with shaking, and her right leg aches, and the foot is everted, so that she cannot walk. At the same time her speech fails, and she stutters. At times she gets quite unconscious; the other day she was so for some hours; she then is pale, and makes a snoring noise in breathing (paralysis of the velum palati). The unconsciousness is apt to come on when she is tired. Has pain in back at times, but there is no tenderness in the spine on percussion. No anæmia. In this case the general condition was allied to chorea, but there was disorder of the intellectual centres as well as of the motor.—M. H., æt. 11, female. Ill two months, right side is partially paralyzed; her movements are also unsteady as in chorea; cannot grasp anything with the right hand. Leg dragged; tongue drawn to one side; functions in good order. With strychnia, iron, and chloric ether, she got well in less than two months. There can be little doubt, in this case, that the brain was the seat of the disorder from the unilateral character of the affection. The motor centre was weak and irritable, and as it regained tone and power under the use of the roborants, recovery ensued. This clearly was a paresis.—J. J., male, æt. 17, ill with catarrh fourteen days. Stomach disordered, memory much impaired, cannot be trusted alone; appears very nervous; speech impaired and power of holding things in his hands; is ready to fall if at all irritated or startled. Of large lax make. In three weeks he was cured by iron, quinine, and nux vomica, after three mild aperients.—F. F., male, æt. 14, ill fourteen days. Seems silly, strange, and very wandering, but answers questions. Pulse slow, weak. No other apparent disorder. Recovered in three weeks with quinine and nux vomica.—L. W., æt. 13, female. Health generally good, ill three weeks. Was attacked at first, at 10 A. M., by a kind of fit; lost the use of her legs and arms; her speech was quite altered; she looked livid; and, according to her father's account, appeared "taken for death." She did not recover consciousness by the evening of the day on which she was attacked. At the time of her admittance she had in great measure regained the use of her limbs, but still could not dress or undress herself; she often complained of pains in her arms, more in her head. She recovered with iron, quinine, cod-liver oil, and nux vomica in eight weeks. In the last three cases the symptoms indicate that the brain had been affected by some depressing influence interfering more or less seriously with the exercise of its functions. Of the nature of this influence there is no certainty, but it seems a probable conjecture that it is some miasm akin to that which produces epidemic catarrh. The length of time during which the morbid phenomena continued makes it certain that they were not of epileptic or syncopal character. Neither is there any indication of their resulting from reflex inhibitory irritation. I have chosen to record the above instances, not because I think them very unusual, but because their import scarcely seems to be appreciated by practitioners generally. It is to my mind a capital fact in neuro-pathology, that the great nervous centres are liable to have their functional power so seriously impaired by obscure (atmospheric) causes, apart from any organic lesion, or manifest cause of debility. It is clear that the nervous centres may be vexed and depressed by the same kind of agencies that harass the nerves. They may also become gradually debilitated from various causes till they give way in a sudden collapse. This should be borne in mind in dealing with all obscure cases of central affection.

Dr. Prichard applies the term leipothymia to certain fits of epileptic character, "consisting in a sudden loss of sense and consciousness, the muscular system being relaxed, and the patient lying in a state resembling sleep, at the same time without that state of the circulation which is peculiar to syncope." The affection does not appear to be a frequent one. In the only case where I remember to have witnessed it there was no indication of cerebral anæmia, but extreme weakness of the nervous system generally.

The following quotation from Mr. Austin's work on General

Paralysis affords a well-marked example of the production of cerebral paresis, of the most complete kind, by remote irritation. The paresis in these cases is of inhibitory character, and is the result of two factors, viz., on the one hand the impaired state of the vis nervosa in the encephalic centre, and on the other the intestinal irritation. That the paralysis is not the result of spasm of the cerebral bloodvessels is apparent from the gradual manner in which recovery takes place in most instances, unlike the complete cessation of the phenomena as soon as a fit of epilepsy has terminated.

"A recognized paralytic is suddenly found completely hemiplegic. The fit, which usually happens in the night, is unattended by shriek or scream, and is frequently free from convulsion. It is accompanied by semi-coma and suspended utterance, and often announces itself to the attendants or to the sufferer's fellow-patients by loud teeth-grinding, or by the seized person falling out of bed. Then the neighbours find he has fallen because an arm and a leg are powerless. Frequently the paralytic who may have been retained in bed by the well-tucked-in clothes is only discovered to be hemiplegic when the attendant comes to get him up in the morning. When he comes under medical inspection he is semi-comatose, his utterance is in abeyance, he is quite hemiplegic, but with sensation only slightly impaired. If the arm or leg be pinched, vigorous movements of the affected limbs ensue. Though sometimes apparently insensible to all going on around him there is frequently a hopeful glimmer of intelligence in the eye. The mouth is rarely distorted, and the movements of the eyeball are more perfect than might have been expected. The pupils are more unsymmetrical than usual. An attendant now administers an injection of eight tablespoonfuls of common salt dissolved in a pint of warm water. In nine cases out of ten, in at most an hour, a copious stool is the result, composed of small, hard, quite distinct rounded lumps. After an evacuation of this kind I have known a person quite hemiplegic at 2 P. M. recover a free mobility of the arm and leg by midnight. Usually, however, several similar enemata and their resulting stools are required before an approach to the ordinary movements of the limbs is obtained. Occasionally castor oil, and calomel + colocynth are employed the sooner to clear out the intestinal tube, or at least the large intestines. The object of these simple remedies is not, by serous evacuations to drive from the head, but simply to expel the hardened feces, of which the colon is full, and which I regard as the eccentric cause of the seizure. The cause removed, nature aided by a moderately generous diet, will soon restore the affected limbs to their former condition. Such measures as blistering, cupping, leeching, purging, and the like, are not only superfluous, but I believe in the highest degree prejudicial during these seizures. At any rate without their exhibition I have seen nearly weekly rapid recoveries from the completest hemiplegia. Under injections, castor oil, a pill of col. c. calom. in a day or two the patient's leg begins to move, and his utterance for monosyllables to return. Later the movements of the arm commence, and the memory becomes sufficient to enable him to recognize and name correctly those around him. Day by day the amelioration proceeds; and I have frequently seen a person, hemiplegic for the first time a week previously, again walking, and with his former gait in the infirmary. Usually, however, two or three weeks may elapse before the patient quite regains his former mobility. During this time all that is required is simply to watch, and gently to sustain the peristaltic action of the intestines."

Dr. Palmer records[1] the following interesting case, which seems to me plainly of reflex inhibitory nature:—

No. 13.—A. B., æt. 63, a temperate male, free from rheumatism, gout, or constitutional syphilis; has no teeth, but eats meat. April 4th, 1859, he was suddenly seized in the morning with left side hemiplegia, which was almost complete. 'His face was pale, he looked dull and bewildered. He was laid horizontal, cold applied to his bald head, and calomel gr. iv. given. Marked improvement ensued in two hours, and the bowels acted two or three times. He felt much better, and had regained considerable power over his leg and arm. Six leeches were applied to the temples, salines, and aperients given. In four days all paralysis was gone. He remained well for four years except an annual attack of bronchitis. He still ate meat with toothless gums. Early in 1863 he began to have irritation of the diaphragm, and unbearable restlessness and oppression in the early morning. Subsequently his mind became enfeebled, any trifling business matter threw him into a state of agitation, excitement, and sense of impending death or insanity. Then he became the subject of severe nervous dyspepsia. Marked and complete relief was afforded by narcotics, but after a few days the effect was lost, and he was worse than before. All this time his tongue was almost perfectly natural, the bowels acted regularly every day, the head was hot, and the temporal arteries pulsated rather strongly. The cerebral irritation was justly regarded by Dr. Palmer as the analogue of the past hemiplegia. It was however unrelieved by a great variety of treatment including repeated aperients, stimulants, and complete rest of mind and body, until, on Dr. Goolden's advice, a larger dose of calomel was given followed by a powerful cholagogue of manganese. This brought away a large quantity of very offensive feces, and the patient was permanently and completely relieved. His mental faculties were quite restored.

There can be no question that on the second occasion the morbid impressions conveyed from the intestines affected the brain directly, enfeebled and disordered its actings. The state of the circulation in the scalp makes it almost certain that the brain was not anæmic, rather the reverse. In the first attack it is uncertain whether the hemiplegia should be referred to arterial spasm, or to inhibitory irritation. The pallor of the face and the suddenness of the seizure point rather to the former as the more correct view. If this be so,

[1] Lancet, Dec. 19th, 1863.

we must regard the vaso-motor nerves as primarily affected in the first case, the hemispheres in the second.

In the following case the cerebral disorder appears to be plainly referable to gastric distress, which acted in the same way as the intestinal irritation in the preceding :—

No. 14.—Mr. W., m., æt. 42, seen Sept. 26th. Ill since the previous November, has been unable to sleep at night for a long time until lately, has lost flesh and got rather weak. Has very marked tenderness in the region of the stomach, particularly at the epigastrium, which has increased lately, and pain after food. The uneasy feeling in the stomach comes on in such a way at times that he is obliged to run out, or move about in some way; he feels as if he should go out of his mind. He had strong suicidal impulse while suffering from the pain. Sometimes gets relief from crying. Says he does not know whether his mind or his body is affected, but strives against it all he can. Has conceived a dislike of his best friends. Does not appear at all hypochondriacal. Is a temperate man, can't take wine or beer, but has been obliged to take several glasses of neat brandy at night to make him sleep; the brandy does not affect his head as it used, but seems to go to the stomach and relieve it. Used to have piles, but not bleeding. Bowels regular. Pulse weak, quick. No tumour in stomach. Liver and spleen not enlarged. Lips rather anæmic. Heart's sounds normal, except the second, which is not quite pure. Urine generally clear, deposits a very few small oxalate of lime crystals. Has much flatulence. He had a morphia dressed blister to the epigastrium, and took a mixture of tr. cinch. + tr. valerian. + tr. hyoscyam. + ammon. carb. + inf. valerian. *ter die*, and ferri carb. saccht. *ter die*. By Oct. 9th he was decidedly better, sleeping very well; his epigastrium was almost quite comfortable, he could take a beefsteak very well.

The *causes* of paresis of the encephalon are all such as produce nervous exhaustion. Excessive mental toil, monotony, unhealthy malarious climates, oppressive heat, venereal excess, and influenzal miasms, are the principal. The possible dependence of the prostration on some inhibitory irritation should be borne in mind. The injurious effects of overwork of the brain are well known. I should not do more than name it here, were it not that I would fain add my voice of warning to those which have already been given. Almost while I write, a youth is brought to me, whose father is intent on pushing him forward in his studies, unheedful, though a kindly parent, of his son's failing nervous power, as marked by an abdominal neuralgia, pallor, nocturnal restlessness, and a sense of unusual incapacity for mental exertion. Stern necessity may oblige those who are engaged in the thick of the battle of life to strain their powers beyond what is prudent, but in the case of those who are being trained for the strife all approach to such over-exertion should be discountenanced. It is sad when early promise of excellence is blighted by inevitable destiny, but much more sad if the collapse must be attributed to our own want of care. The ill effects of monotony are best illustrated by the languor, ill health, and sometimes mortal disease which are apt to ensue among soldiers and sailors when reduced to compulsory inactivity; while cheerful excitement has an almost magical opposite effect. The melancholy chant of the Count of Toulouse[1] expresses no futile apprehension.[2] Nature, in her insatiable love of variety, in the changing seasons, and the ever-varying weather, seems to indicate clearly enough the advantage of frequent change. All experience of malaria testifies to its specially depressing influence on the nervous system, not to mention the cretins, the inhabitants of malarious districts are spoken of as feeble in body, and spiritless in mind, phlegmatic and melancholy, stupid, languid, and apathetic. The action of heat in producing languor and general enfeeblement of nervous power is a capital fact, and one I have often thought is by no means sufficiently regarded. It is surely a very significant circumstance that an ordinary man can carry, without inconvenience, a heavy overcoat on a cold day, and walk much further and faster thus laden than he could on a hot day more lightly equipped. This surely implies a much greater amount of energy in the motor nervous apparatus in the one case than in the other. A rifleman will tell you that his aim is much more true and steady in cold bracing than in warm relaxing weather. Men endued with great nervous power are capable of enduring heat much better than others. Napoleon, it is said, when in Egypt habitually wore his coat buttoned up. The British soldiers in India, in general, bear the fatigue of forced marches under the burning sun of that climate better than the native Hindoos.[3] In fact, the stronger and better toned the nervous system is the more capable is it of resisting the enfeebling and enervating influence of heat. This is very well exemplified in the affection termed heat apoplexy, of which I propose here to take some notice. Intemperance, especially in the use of spirituous liquors, predisposes powerfully to this disorder, and so also do close crowding and bad ventilation. On the other hand, temperance, cheerfulness, and the energetic pursuit of duty, have been proved, as in the memorable siege of Delhi, to have a wonderful influence.[4] Paley, with admirable wisdom, re-

[1] "Oh dear, what will become of us?
Oh dear, what shall we do?
We shall die of the vapours if some of us.
Can't find out something that's new."
J. of Psychol. Med., July, 1863.

[2] *V.* also an instance of the appearance of scurvy among American troops, who were fairly well supplied with fresh food, but who had no active employment, and became homesick and disgusted with the service. Several died of scurvy. Several who were sick began to recover from the moment they were told they should have their discharge.—*Amer. Med. Times*, June 1st, 1861.

[3] Allison's "Hist. of Europe," vol. xvi. p. 71, note.

[4] Sir R. Martin writes, p. 410 of his work: "Officers before Delhi describe themselves as marching all day in the sun of June, July, and August, and serving in the burning trenches for weeks together; and yet they preserved their health under a temperature of 130° or more through temperance to a wonderful extent." Contra, Dr. Barclay states, as the result of his observation, that men whose nervous systems had been injured by intemperance were much more disposed than others to attacks.

commends the manful discharge of duty as the best remedy against "sinkings and oppressions of the spirits." The action of heat, whether it be direct solar, or a simply elevated temperature, is evidently the prime motor of heat-apoplexy, as the other causative conditions are chiefly predisposing, though in this respect their influence can hardly be over-estimated. The observable phenomena will vary according to the particular part of the nervous system, which especially succumbs under the morbid influence. In the worst cases where death occurs almost instantaneously the medulla oblongata is probably the focus of morbid action. Death ensues from arrest of the respiratory changes in consequence of the paresis of the vagi, and the lungs are found intensely engorged, even to the production of apoplectic extravasation, while the brain is almost free from lesion. In other cases of slower progress where the disorder commences with feverish debility in the morning, and terminates in stupor in the afternoon, the cerebral hemispheres are more especially affected, their vessels are found exceedingly congested, and those of the lungs less. Assuming the paresis to be primary, cerebral congestion ensues, according to the well-known law that impairment of function is intimately connected with impediment to the free transit of blood through the part. Thus the lungs become congested in apnœa. The circumstance that in the milder seizures the phenomena take the form of fever, either ardent or remittent, or intermittent, points to the strong probability that in these instances the vaso-motor nervous system is specially implicated.

I subjoin here the notes of two cases of this affection as it has occurred in my experience :—

No. 15.—M. G., f., æt. 14, ad. July 18th. Ill six days; was out in a field, sitting in the sun, carrying children, suddenly became faint, and got pain in the head and vomiting, and has had vomiting ever since. She is always wanting to *lie down*, and complaining of her head. Skin cool. Pulse soft, open. Bowels very costive. Epigastrium not tender. With tannin and mineral acids the sickness quite ceased in a week, and she was much better.

No. 16.—E. L., f., æt. 24, ad. Oct. 25th. Ill since the beginning of August. "She went reaping without a bonnet, and the sun affected her brains." It was about 2-3 P. M. when she was attacked, on a hot day with a bright sun. She was taken up senseless, and remained insensible for one whole month, during which her head was blistered. Legs have been much swelled, but are not so now. Has not suffered with pain in head. After the first attack she used to get slightly chilly in the afternoon, the chill was soon succeeded by much fever and cold sweats. Abdomen has been much swelled, is much distended with flatus now. At present she feels very weak and languid, is very anæmic. Has much nausea, can take no food. Very thirsty. B. regular. Urine sometimes red, sometimes pale. Head not hot, is rather better when lying down, "feels lost" when she gets up. Loses consciousness at times, finds her memory failing, spirits very low. Has dreadful cold sweats at night. The fever affects somewhat a tertian type. Skin cool.

Pulse not particularly weak. She has just returned from Kent, where she was taken ill. She was ordered quinine *ter die* with mercurial alteratives *alt. noct.;* under which she improved a little, and discontinued attendance.

REMARKS.—In both these cases the phenomena are a sudden cerebral "coup" followed by failure of functional power, and stomach disturbance. The second case is much the more severe, the prostration was very prolonged and considerable, and the tendency of the disorder to assume the character of malarious fever apparent. It seems plain that whatever amount of hyperæmia of the brain may have occurred, the history is by no means that of mere cerebral congestion, but rather reminds one of the results of concussion. If we bear in mind the primary exhausting action of heat, it will not be difficult to conceive how an excessive application of this agent may produce such phenomena as above detailed. The occurrence of anguish disorder as the result of severe nervous prostration is highly significant as to the especial implication of the nervous system in malarious disease.

The *after symptoms*, as Sir R. Martin well remarks, "are of extreme interest, and they, as well as the more chronic and subdued influence of isolation, throw much light on the pathology of the disease." The list which he gives appears to me remarkably to confirm the opinion I have expressed that heat-apoplexy essentially consists in the functional paralysis of one or more great nervous centres. It runs as follows: "(1) Severe mental depression with sense of weariness along the spine. (2) Impression of the sun being always shining on the person with tinnitus aurium. (3) Distressing formication sometimes accompanied by a peculiar and general eruption and desquamation of the skin. (4) Deafness more or less severe with impaired vision, and inability to use the eyes in reading and writing. (5) Various paralytic affections, more or less general, as hemiplegia, and local palsies, as of the eyelids, cheeks, or upper extremities, with and without loss of sensation. Heaving and difficult breathing. (6) Distressing hysterical states of the nervous system, with absence of self-control in laughing and crying—the paroxysms being followed by great prostration of nervous power. (7) Interruption to natural sleep, with incapacity for any kind of business. (8) Impression of alarm on any sudden movement of the body, and upon the occurrence of sudden noises. (9) Sudden epileptiform seizures, without loss of consciousness, followed by great nervous prostration." The foregoing have been observed in sufferers who have returned to England. In India, he proceeds, "we are familiar with the acute sequelæ to sunstroke, as ardent fever with acute delirium, remittent and intermittent fevers complicated with dysenteries, hepatic inflammations and congestions." These statements merit the most careful consideration, not only from the light they throw on the nature of heat-apoplexy, but from that which they shed on the pathology of a multitude of nervous disorders. Any man of experience in the manifold disorders of jaded and exhausted nervous systems will recognize at once how close is the resemblance between the results of tropical heat, and those produced by the ordinary causes in operation among the struggling multitudes of our large towns. It may be observed, (I.) That the most abiding results of heat-apoplexy are almost all referable to impaired functional energy of the cerebro-spinal system. (II.) That this impairment shows itself either in motor paralysis (5), sensory paralysis (4 and 5), either of common or special sensation, hyper- and dysæsthesia of the nerves of common and special sense (2 and 3), in debility and undue excitability of the emotional centres (6, 8, 9), and in similar states of the cerebral hemispheres and spinal cord (1, 7). (III.) The earlier sequelæ appear as the well-known consequences of vaso-motor nerve paralysis. The picture which Sir R. Martin gives of the manifold and varying sequelæ of sunstroke is altogether unlike that presented by actual organic disease. It is unlike in its causation, its non-progressive character, the inconstancy of the phenomena, and in the "juvantia."

The occurrence of eruption in connection with, and apparently as the result of cutaneous dysæsthesia is of much interest, and probably may be explained as the result of vaso-motor nerves becoming implicated in the morbid action. It will be remembered that one of the results of division of the sympathetic in some animals is cutaneous eruption. Romberg describes in the same way the development of prurigo from pruritus, a lichenoid eruption from a mere nerve affection. The action of summer heat in promoting the occurrence of lichen urticatus is familiar to many of us. The effects of heat-apoplexy illustrate very forcibly the development of morbid excitability and hyperæsthesia simultaneously with impairment of motor power. It is difficult to say how far malarious poison is concerned in producing the phenomena we have been considering, probably it acts chiefly as a predisposing cause. The parallel, however, between these two morbid agencies is extremely close, and it is curious and instructive to observe that their results are sometimes identical. The cause of the correspondence no doubt lies in the fact that both act principally on and through the nervous system, and that in the way of paralyzing its power. Admitting cholera poison to be a form of malaria, of which I think there is some notable evidence, we find in some recorded epidemics as sudden a death-stroke as can be occasioned by heat; malaria will produce various forms of paralysis and epileptoid attacks, cutaneous eruption, and mental depression, besides the well-known fevers. This however may be said that malaria affects more specially the vaso-motor system, and heat the cerebro-spinal.

As an imponderable influence, obscurely though unquestionably related to heat and malaria, we may notice electricity in its morbid action on the nervous centres. Dr. Radcliffe states in his lectures[1] that a continuous electrical current of low tension seems to have the power of producing temporary paralysis of a nerve or nervous centre which is traversed by it. Eckhard has shown that if the nerve of a frog's leg prepared for the purpose be included in a galvanic

---

[1] "Lancet," Feb. 28th, 1868.

current it is impossible to produce contractions in the muscle by acting upon that part of the nerve which lies between the poles. In other words the part of the nerve along which the continuous galvanic current is passing, is paralyzed by the action of the current.[1] It is also a fact that the spinal cord may be paralyzed by the same means. If for example the spinal cord of a rabbit be included in the circuit of a voltaic battery the part between the poles may be cut, pricked, torn or even electrified without giving rise either to pain or convulsion. Although the above-mentioned effects are expressly ascribed to low-tension electricity it seems indubitable that a shock of high-tension electricity produces very similar, and even more abiding. Numerous instances are on record in which individuals having been struck by lightning have suffered temporary paralysis of motion, and special or common sensation, from which they recovered either spontaneously, or with the aid of tonic remedies. In these cases there can be I think little question that the nervous tissue is directly paralyzed from some molecular change taking place in its cells or fibres. I once experienced myself a severe shock from a very large Leyden jar, and well remember the overpowering general prostration I experienced, although the shock only passed through my forearm. It is impossible, I think, to conceive that any arterial spasm can explain the effects produced in this and similar instances. Certainly in the case of the frog's nerve dissected out, and remaining attached to the muscle above mentioned, there can be no question of local anæmia as the cause of the paresis. The "juvantia" also, as in Dr. Watson's case,[2] where steel and tonic treatment effected a speedy cure of paraplegia in a girl who had been struck by lightning, decidedly indicate that the paresis from this cause is one of simple functional debility.

Venereal excess is a powerful cause of cerebral paresis, as well as of spinal, few exceed it. Good Hufeland says, "it is proved beyond all doubt that nothing renders the mind so incapable of noble and exalted sensations, destroys so much all its firmness and powers, and relaxes the whole being as this dissipation." It is not too much to affirm that a state bordering on dementia has often been produced by sexual excess, and perhaps still more frequently by solitary vice. Esquirol says that immoral habits and the use of mercury are very frequently productive of that deplorable species of paralysis which becomes complicated with dementia and monomania.[3] It is somewhat remarkable that sexual excitement should have so pernicious an effect, for the nerves of the genital organs are by no means large, their origin is remote from the brain, and the loss of excreted matter can

---

[1] On one occasion I went to sleep with the negative pole of a 40 links Pulvermacher's chain in my hand, the positive being applied to my back. In the course of the night I found my hand was quite numb, but after removing the chain the numbness soon went off.

[2] "Lectures," vol. i. p. 332.

[3] V. Ritchie on same subject, "Lancet," Feb., March, 1861.

hardly be regarded as any serious drain on the system. The only way that I can see of accounting for the remarkable collapse which attends on any abuse of the generative faculty is, that owing to the intimate commissural connections between the lumbar enlargement of the cord, where the pudic nerves are implanted, and the superior and nobler nervous centres, the intense excitation of even a small and remote centre is communicated to the others, which as this subsides fall as much below as they have previously been stimulated above par. The depression is proportional to the previous excitement.

Influenza is a common enough visitant among us, and familiar though its phenomena be, they seem to me of no little interest. That a person should be prostrated, as occasionally happens, almost instantaneously, and remain for some days in profound debility is surely very remarkable. Without speculating on the nature of the cause, let us simply consider how it seems to act. There can be I think no question that the nervous system is the one on which the stroke especially falls, and as little that the encephalic centres are prominently affected. The debility is by no means mere muscular weakness; it is described by Dr. Shapter as "an overwhelming feeling of lassitude and prostration of strength, with in many cases a loss of all muscular power, together with great anxiety of the precordia, and agonizing fears of death." The expression of the countenance is *abattu*. There are pains in every part, sensations as of being sore, beat, and bruised all over. Pain in the temples sometimes prevents rest for several nights. Many observers have noticed the occurrence of neuralgia of the face. Apoplectic and convulsive attacks have occurred in some instances, in some also delirium, in others coma. These citations of the experience of others,[1] coinciding as they do very much with my own, may be considered sufficient proof that the cerebro-spinal centres are chiefly affected by the miasma, and that in a paralyzing way. The catarrhal symptoms are for the most part such as indicate vaso-motor nerve paralysis, and atony of the capillary walls rather than actual tissue irritation. They, as Dr. Watson states, are not so essentially a part of the disorder as the peculiar prostration, since they are occasionally absent. It must appear to every reflecting mind as a very important and thought-exciting circumstance that there should exist such a subtle, undetectable poison, or agency, as this of influenza. Standing as it does quite separate from the exanthemata, it links itself on the one hand closely with some of our commonest disorders, and on the other hand manifests no obscure affinity with pestilence, and with that most widespread of all maladies, malarious fever.[2] The intensity of its operation on the nervous system, and the fact that it is now

---

[1] *V.* "Annals of Influenza," Syd. Soc., p. 320.
[2] Various good observers, Cleghorn, Petrie, and H. Greenhow, testify to the origin of re- and intermittent fevers from influenzal affection.

as it were domiciled among us, makes it important to take count of it in dealing with a variety of obscure nervous disorders. It is probable that the more we come to know of disease the more we shall find that there exist a few great distinct morbific causes, which by acting on different parts, in different combinations and degrees and with slight modifications give rise to ever-varying forms of morbid action.

The treatment of cerebral paresis must essentially consist in the avoidance or removal of all existing causes, as well as in the employment of all means that can recreate and invigorate nerve-power. The possibility of the paresis being dependent on remote irritation should be borne in mind. If, however, as is oftenest the case, it is primary and direct, we must endeavour to act on the enfeebled centre itself. Among the means at our command pure and bracing air, generous diet, and healthful mental excitement are perhaps the most powerful. The influence of the latter is often marvellous; it is really curious for any one to observe himself and note how much more exertion he is capable of when his mind is thoroughly occupied and interested, than when the occupation is distasteful. I always ask my patients who complain of failing power (not of course dependent on organic disease) what recreation they *like*, and *that* I send them to, as the best for them. Under the head of food I may allude to the popular combination of rum and milk as being one of the very best restoratives that can possibly be given. A daily morning dose of it to weakly subjects is of great value, and in cases of an acute kind it may form almost the staple of the nourishment. As to medicines, our ordinary stimulants and tonics must be employed, the drug and the dose being matters for consideration in each individual case. I shall only mention particularly one or two remedies. Strychnia I have come to regard as a truly valuable cerebral toner, its action on the encephalic being not far inferior to that which it exerts on the spinal centres. It is a perfectly safe remedy with due care, and although I have employed it for years very largely I have never seen more than slight inconvenience produced by it, when it disagreed with some patients of unusual susceptibility. It should always be given in solution, and combines very well with quinine and iron. Phosphoretted oil I have used occasionally, but it is apt to cause considerable gastric disorder, and I have had but little encouragement to persevere with it. Dr. Radcliffe has recently spoken highly of the hypophosphites as remedies for states of nervous depression. My own experience of them in phthisis would not lead me to expect much benefit from them. Cod-liver oil is, I think, a remedy of real value, whether it act according to the chemical view of ministering to the nutrition of the nervous tissue, or not. An excellent and rather elegant tonic is a combination of ammon. carb. gr. iv + ferri ammon. citrat. gr. vij-x + tr. nucis vomic. ℨx-xv + tr. calumbæ ℨxx + aq. ℥i *ter die*.

No. 17.—Mrs. P., æt. 48, broad and fat, seen July 24th, 1862. Has always been a weakly-nerved person; has had ten children. For six or seven years has suffered with bleeding piles. Her first attack of head symptoms was in October, 1861, the second in April, 1862. She did not lose consciousness in either, but had pain at the top of head and backs of eyes. She recovered from the first attack in six weeks; from the second she still suffers. Complains of burning heat at top of head, at times has pain and great heat of head, the pain is increased by the recumbent position. Feels some numbness in both hands along the back of the fingers. Has double vision from paralysis of the right external rectus muscle. Head not tender. Pulse of good force. Does not feel weak. With strychnia and citrate of iron and quinine the external rectus regained its power, and I lost sight of her after October 23d till March 17th, 1863, when she returned to me feeling very weak, languid, and incapable of exertion. A week later the paralysis of the external rectus was complete. Much hemorrhage had been going on from the piles. She had great pain at the right posterior part of head, increased on lying down. The double vision caused her much annoyance from the objects passing her in the streets confusing her. Her piles were now got rid of by operation, but the hemorrhage from the bowel continued whenever she had a motion, and the state of the right eye was unchanged. Nothing could be detected in the rectum to account for the bleeding except a loose and baggy state of the mucous membrane. This was at last arrested by tannin taken internally, aided very materially by removal to the country, where her general health and strength much improved. By the middle of June she had regained a good deal of power over the external rectus. I urged a return to the country, but this was not carried out; however, the improvement continued, so that November 10th, when I last saw her, she had almost perfect power over the formerly paralyzed muscle. Some bleeding had recurred, but not to any great extent.

REMARKS.—This case is an interesting example of a limited paresis of the nervous centres, involving the origin of one small nerve only. That the paralysis did not depend on organic disease must I think be admitted from the beneficial effect of strychnia, iron, and quinine on the first, and of country air on the second occasion. There can be little doubt that the long-continued hemorrhage was the cause of the general debility and local paresis, but it is remarkable that the latter existed before the former was felt to any notable extent. The pain in the head was probably neuralgic, yet it was aggravated on lying down. Enemata of krameria infusion, lead and opium pills, and sulphur internally failed to arrest the bleeding after the piles had been removed. The case is instructive in various respects, as showing (1) the connection between debility and paresis; (2) the necessity for close inquiry into the possible causes of paresis; (3) the superiority in some instances of a pure air to tonic medicines; (4) the dependence of hemorrhage in some cases on atony of vessels.

CHAPTER VIII.

SPINAL PARESIS.

THE nature of this state in general, and its efficient causes have been sufficiently described in the previous chapter; it only remains to illustrate its phenomena when it affects a different locality. This I shall endeavor to do by the relation of some cases, which appear to me of considerable interest.

No. 18.—C. M., æt. 39, butler, ad. Aug. 17th, having been ill five weeks. He states that his illness came on gradually, apparently from excess in drinking, not in venery. He is paralyzed to a considerable extent in both hands, so that he cannot dress himself, nor pick up anything. His feet are also weak and flap down in walking. There is a great if not complete loss of sensibility in the paralyzed limbs. The paralysis is getting worse. He feels very weak all over. Head hottish, but there is not much pain in it; he has never lost consciousness. Tongue coated at back. Bowels costive. Pulse large, soft. Urine of sp. gr. 1014, of good full colour, not albuminous. Blisters to the neck have been of no service. He was treated with quinine gr. v *ter die*, till Sept. 3d, subsequently with ferri et quin. citr. gr. x + tr. nucis vom. ♏x *ter die*. He improved gradually and was nearly quite recovered by December 20th. I have seen him lately, and find he has had no return of the paralysis during the six years and a half that have elapsed since he was under my care. In some cases it appears as if alcoholic stimuli taken in excess acted on the spinal centres much in the same way as they do on the cerebral, impairing and depressing their functional power. Last year I attended a female, who had been extremely addicted to brandy-drinking for years; as far as I heard her history she had never had delirium tremens, but she lost both motor and sensory power to a great extent in both upper and lower limbs for some months before her death. In her it is possible that the alcohol had caused sclerosis of the cord, as no remedies were of any avail.

No. 19.—N. D., æt. 20, m., ad. September 10th, 1858. Ill one month with inflamed sore-throat, which has got well; but since then he has begun to lose the use of his limbs, the legs being the weakest. He can now stand, but not walk; the legs are very numb and cold, but he is conscious when they are touched. He has no pain at all, nor tenderness of the spine. Sphincters act. Intellect clear. No reflex actions are excited on tickling the feet. Pupils large and almost motionless. Skin cool. P. natural. T. white. No cough. Heart-sounds natural. Residence damp. Never had syphilis. As I could find no clear indication of organic disease of the nervous centres, I prescribed strychniæ gr. $\frac{1}{30}$, quin. disulph. gr. ij, acid. s. dil. ♏viij, aq. ʒi *ter die*, with ordinary diet and porter. 14th. Feels much better, has more use of his hands and legs and can walk a little. 17th.

Worse last two days. Has now sore-throat and much diarrhœa, with copious perspirations, and loss of appetite. "Has no use of the hands or legs again." P. c. mist. et tr. opii ♏ viij ad. ℥i. 18th. T. very coated, yellowish. P. 120 full and weak. Some diarrhœa continues. Nausea and headache. Skin hot and moist. Cannot raise or turn himself in bed. P. c. mist. *quater die*. Vini rubri ℥vi *in die*. 20th. Bad cough. P. 96, full, occasionally intermittent. B. quiet. Adde quinæ gr. ij sing. dosis mist. 21st. No sleep from cough, sputa watery and of a rusty colour. 22d. Feels much better, appetite improving. B. quiet. T. cleaner. No use of limbs. 25th. Galvanism was applied yesterday with great benefit; he is able to move his hands and arms much better. Appetite very good. Sleeps well. October 4th. The legs are now much more weak and numb than the thighs. A much stronger current required to excite the leg muscles than those of the thigh; the calf muscles are greatly wasted. The feet used to be very cold and numb, but are not now. The hands feel weak and are rather numb, he has "pins and needles" sensation in them at times. Strychnia gr. $\frac{1}{18}$, tr. ferri muriat. ♏ xv, acid. hydrochl. ♏ ij, aq. ℥i *ter die*. 8th. Can now walk and feed himself; he cannot bear so strong a current as before. The same treatment was continued till the end of November, when he was discharged with only a slight degree of weakness remaining in the legs, which was referred to the knees. It seemed that the extensor muscles of the thighs had not regained their full power; he was able however to walk very well, and his arms had become quite strong. The dose of strychnia was gradually increased to gr. $\frac{1}{9}$ *ter die*.

A curious circumstance observed by himself was that his feet swelled during the night, so that he could not get his boots on in the morning, but after walking about the ward a little the swelling subsided. His urine was free from albumen and was otherwise healthy, except that at one time during the catarrhal affection it deposited much uric acid. I cannot but regard this as a very proving case. A man is admitted with incomplete paralysis consecutive (as he reports) to catarrh, after improvement has commenced he relapses, and becomes considerably more paralytic than at first, while simultaneously he is affected with asthenic bronchial and gastro-intestinal catarrh. Under a persistent tonic treatment he makes a good recovery. It seems impossible not to recognize in such a case as this the operation of a depressing miasm (influenza), acting with unusual potency on the whole nervous system. There is no indication of the paralysis being other than primary and direct, or that it is in any way attributable to remote irritation. The phenomena of vaso-motor paralysis were well marked in the skin and the mucous membranes, and the nocturnal swelling of the feet was owing, I believe, to the same condition. Is it conceivable that the vessels of the nervous centres were in a state of spasm, and that the paralysis depended on anæmia? What would have been the result of treating this case in the same way as the one recorded by Ollivier, v. p. 73?

No. 20.—A. W., female, æt. 9, has had paraplegia last three months, it increased rapidly after it commenced, and in fourteen days was as bad as it is now. She cannot stand or walk, but can move her legs as she sits. There is no loss of sensation in the lower limbs, they have wasted considerably. The muscles of the lower limbs are very sensitive to the interrupted current, more particularly the extensors. The spine is much curved, convex backwards and to the right side. When the legs first became weak she had more constant pain in back, but it did not seem to be increased by friction. Beginning from the two lower dorsal vertebræ there is tenderness on pressing the spinous processes all the way down to the sacrum. No sign of any tumour in front of the abdomen or thighs, no trace of any abscess. At times she has constrictive sensations in the abdomen. The legs have been painful and aching lately, they start sometimes. Urine pale, aqueous, sp. gr. 1016, not albuminous, often thick and offensive, is passed in small quantities and with discomfort. It deposits phosphatic crystals, consisting of aciculæ united in stellar groups. B. very costive, only opened by enemata, motions very dark and hard, when the b. act has much pain in the lower abdomen and all over her. After a dose of aperient medicine the legs have often appeared weaker. Appetite always poor, capricious, aversion for meat. Had constant nausea when her legs began to fail, but this is less now, is most felt in mornings. The last six weeks has complained of constant pain in the forehead, and all over the head. Sleeps badly. ℞. Strychn. gr. $\frac{1}{32}$, ferri et quin. citr. gr. v, aq. ʒss *ter die*. ℞. Ol. morrh. ʒi *ter die*. The limbs to be faradized daily. This was continued for a month, to October 30th, without any advantage, indeed she was reported altogether worse. The circulation was very feeble, the legs hypersensitive. ℞. Liq. cinch. flav. ♏ 40, pot. iod. gr. xxxv, ammon. carb. gr. xxv, tr. bellad. ♏ 80, aq. ʒvi. M. ʒss *ter die*. Vini aloes ʒss p. r. n. Empls. bellad. 3 × 6, spinæ dolenti. November 24th. The belladonna disordered her vision, and did no good, the plaster was worn for a time, but caused discomfort and was left off. The other remedies have been discontinued, the dose of bark and ammonia being increased, and infus. chirett. substituted for the water. The aloetic wine moved the bowels well for a time, but even ʒi doses fail now; it produced no depression like all other purgatives. The faradization has been continued, and the muscles of the leg as well as of the thigh are much more lively, acting briskly to the current. She cannot stand, but wriggles herself about pretty actively on her knees. The back appears much straighter than it used to be, she can at any rate sit quite upright without showing any deformity. There is still local tenderness in the lumbar spines as tested by pressure, or applying a hot sponge. She has also pain in the front of abdomen, on both sides, and all about it, but does not make her wince under steady pressure. Feels still very cold. She is much more active mentally, amuses herself one way or the other all day long. Pt. To have warm wine at night and rum and milk in the morning. December 8th. Better, can walk from chair to chair leaning on her hands. Very pale. Is so pleased to be able to get about that there is risk of her over-exerting herself. 23d. After a relapse for a few days lately of debility and languor she has again improved so much that she now walks alone quite well, goes all around the room, and even up stairs, though she halts on the right leg. She says she has nothing like so much pain in the back as she used, she bears pressure on the spine much better. Appetite very poor still. Taking tr. cinch. flavæ ʒi *ter die*, and strychniæ gr. $\frac{1}{20}$ *bis die*, with rennet wine at meals. B. are comfortably moved by syrup. rhamni cathart., one day they acted of themselves, which they have not done for months. January 6th. Can now walk about very well, but is soon tired. The mornings are her worst time, always complains then of being tired and languid. Sleeps and eats better. B. open without medicine. Feb. 13th. Has not made any distinct progress since, a fortnight ago had a relapse, which took her off her legs, and was attended with pain in her back and side, and sleeplessness. Her palpitations sometimes severe. P. good. Urine very thick and offensive last week, clear and natural now. Is extremely nervous and sensitive at night, has great difficulty in getting to sleep, is alarmed and trembles at every sound. Has had cold dashing every morning. B. in good order. F. + Q, citr. c̄. tr. nuc. vom. *ter die.* P. c. oleo. To be much in the open air in a vehicle. March 12th. Has not been much out; one day after being in the open air about twenty minutes she became almost insensible and could hardly speak. Is now better again, and pretty active on her legs in the house. The strychnia and bark have been resumed. ℞. Steel wine ʒi *ter die.* 17th. Has been moved to the country, has a better appetite last two days than she has had for a year, and sleeps beautifully. Walked yesterday three quarters of an hour without fatigue. April 15th. Is looking much better and is in all respects much improved. Still she has not the free action of her legs that she ought to have, if she trips in walking she feels it in her back. September 1st. Has been again in the country for two or three months, latterly at Margate. She runs about for hours without being fatigued, and is altogether a different being to what she was. Still a little over fatigue, especially in the *sun*, has a good effect upon her.

This case contrasts in several points with the preceding, although I believe the pathological condition was almost identical. The cause in the first case was a miasm acting upon an average system. In the second there was none to be traced, except it be admitted that some might have been generated from some broken up clayey ground near the house where building was in progress. Solitary vice was of course suspected, but I believe there was no ground for the suspicion. The "grundleiden" seems to have been a most feeble state of the nervous centres especially of the cord, which was constantly lapsing into exhaustion, and which required persevering tonic treatment not only by drugs, but by pure air, and all that could recruit the feeble power. The excessive hyperæsthesia was both a product of the debility, and reacted on it and increased it, *v.* p. 44. In the first case there was little difficulty in forming at once the diagnosis of functional paralysis; in the second I felt considerable doubt for a long time. The chief circumstance that weighed with me in regarding the disorder as functional was the presence of such marked signs of general debility and hyperæsthesia. Had these been absent, I should have been much inclined to set down the case as one of organic disease. The local tenderness of the spine, the constrictive sensations, the phosphatic urine, and the paralysis were formidable symptoms, and might well have proceeded from chronic inflammation of the cord with softening. The insusceptibility of the muscles to the interrupted current was rather a favourable circumstance than otherwise; had the reverse been the case, it would have made the existence of actual central change much more probable. The progress of the case was by no means plain sailing, the tendency to relapse from imperceptible causes was very marked, and nothing but steady perseverance carried us through. In all such cases it is wise to follow Dr. De Ricci's example[1] and refuse to undertake the responsibility unless the friends consent to give one fair play.

It appears to me a very important question in regard to such states as the above, whether what was originally functional may not by long continuance pass into actual organic disease. Obviously it must be almost impossible to ascertain this certainly; analogies might be adduced both for and against its occurrence. I think the conversion of the one state into the other by no means impossible, and I feel assured that no time should ever be lost in adopting effectual treatment for the restoration of functional power. The experience of physicians in cases of what is termed infantile paralysis is strongly to the same effect; my own observation quite confirms the truth of Dr. West's remark as to the importance of early treatment. Though it is very possible that paralytic affections occurring in children, and much resembling one another, may originate in different pathological conditions, as Dr. Heine has lately asserted, yet I think the absence of signs of inflammation of the cord or brain, or their membranes, the existence of more or less debility and disorder of health, the non-progressive character of the disease, and especially the "juvantia," will not leave us long in doubt whether we have to deal with a paresis or any organic affection.

No. 21.—J. G., æt. 3 years, male, admitted Feb. 23d, having been ill three weeks. He has lost the use of his limbs, can move his feet, but not stand, or walk. The power of the arms is somewhat impaired also. Appetite bad. The palsy came on in the night; the child was quite well on going to bed; in the morning his mother found his legs quite palsied, the arms to a less extent, and the face drawn to one side; this last symptom lasted only a few hours. Steel wine was given for fourteen days without benefit, and afterwards ferri et quin. cit. + tr. nuc. vom. Turpentine liniment was applied to the back and legs. April 4th. He is able to stand and walk round a table, holding by it. The improvement was soon after interrupted by his having got some wrong medicine, and then by an attack of dysenteric diarrhœa, so that on April 22d, when the tonic was resumed, he had lost the power of standing. After this, however, he went on steadily to recovery, and in the beginning of July he had gone to school. The disorder in this case at first was somewhat extensive, involving not only the nerves of the upper extremities, but one of the facial. It soon however subsided in the higher parts of the spinal centre, and confined itself to the lower. Under tonic treatment it disappeared, after a temporary interruption by some debilitating circumstances. Clearly this is not the history of any organic disease. The tendency of the kind of paralysis we are considering to supervene during the night is quite a feature that belongs to the family of neuroses, *v.* p. 44.

No. 22.—L. S., æt. 2¾ years, f., ad. February 11th. Ill three months. Has lost the power of walking all the time, cannot now even stand alone;

[1] Dub. Med. J., Aug. 1862.

but can move her legs, which are not wasted nor cold. The paresis came on suddenly one day, she never had a fit. No pain in spine, nor distortion. No injury to the back at any time. Sphincters act. Has nearly all her teeth. Looks healthy. Some vaginal discharge. Strychnia was given till March 3d, the dose being raised from gr. $\frac{1}{60}$ to gr. $\frac{1}{50}$ *bis die*, and ol. morrh. ʒi *ter die* given also. In a fortnight she was able to toddle round a chair holding by it, in another week she could just walk alone. Citrate of iron and quinine was then substituted for the strychnia gr. iv *ter die*, and in fourteen days she could walk across the room and pick up anything from the floor, though her gait was very straddling.

No. 23.—E. C., æt. 2, m., ad. Feb. 4th. Ill four months, became gradually worse; has lost the power of walking; bends forwards in sitting, cannot hold himself up. His legs tremble so that he cannot stand well. Arms all right. Has pain at lower abdomen, bowels loose, motions offensive, is thirsty, appetite bad, has lost flesh. Sleeps well. Has all his teeth but the last molars. Head distorted since birth, right forehead bulging, left eyelid droops. Never had fits. He was ordered ferri et quin. citrat. gr iij *ter die*, a grain of Gray and of Dover's powder *o. n.* for three nights, and subsequently a little tr. opii was added to the mixture. Ol. morrh. was given besides. March 21st. The report is that he is getting on nicely, is a great deal better, runs about. April 4th. Improvement continues.

No. 24.—W. W., æt. 2½, m., ad. Feb. 8th. Ill 1½ year, unable to move the right arm and leg properly all that time, no material wasting of arm, halts in walking on the right leg; can walk a little, but often falls. Health now good. Had a fit for 2¼ hours when 1¼ year old, when he was cutting two molars, and has had the paralysis ever since. His health was affected, at the same time he was languid and weakly. He was ordered cod oil and iodide of iron, which he continued till March 14th, when citrate of iron and quinine was given in place of the iodide. On 24th the report is that he is doing nicely, gets quite strong on his legs, can use his hand.

REMARKS.—In these four cases the palsy came on without apparent cause in three, in the last it succeeded to a fit. In all I think it may be fairly argued that no material damage had occurred in the centres. That the palsy was not of reflex origin I think certain, both from the absence of any cause of irritation as well as from the "juvantia." Had the vessels of the centres been in a state of anæmiating spasm, as Brown-Séquard assumes, would not the starved tissue have certainly degenerated and gone into white softening in cases of such long standing as Nos. 22, 23, 24?

When one limb only is affected it may not be always easy to form an opinion whether the disorder is seated in the cord, or in the nerves of the part, especially if one or two nerves only are involved. In proportion to the extent of the paralysis is the probability that the disease is central.

The following case affords an instance of some uncertainty in the diagnosis of the exact seat of morbid action:—

No. 25.—M., æt. 56, m., seen April 2, 1862, having been ill fourteen days since exposure to cold. He had a catarrhal affection when the paralysis came on. He suffers with wearying, aching, dragging pain about the right shoulder, with loss of power in its abductor muscles. The arm hangs closely by the side of the body, and cannot be raised or abducted except by a jerk of the body. The deltoid and trapezius and other muscles about the shoulder are not wasted, but are more excitable and sensitive to the interrupted current than those of the opposite side; a moderate current causes much pain in these parts, and well-marked contraction of the deltoid especially. Two years ago he had similar enfeeblement of the right shoulder, but not nearly to the same extent as at present; it lasted nine months. This morning he could not feed himself with a spoon, nor tie his cravat, nor put on his coat. His vision fails at times, and he has had other signs of disordered nerve-action, as tremblings, twitchings, &c. He is very weak and thin. Skin warm. P. good. Urine used to be very thick; last three weeks it has been clear and of good colour. ℞. Ammonio-citrate of iron, carbonate of ammonia, tinct. of nux vomica, and infusion of calumba thrice daily; the shoulder to be rubbed daily with compound camphor liniment, and to be faradized. April 8th. General state improved, that of shoulder not much. A spot about the size of a shilling near the acromion is extremely sensitive to the current. ℞. Strychniæ gr. $\frac{1}{10}$ + tr. cinchon. ʒi *ter die.* 17th. Is decidedly improved, can abduct the arm to some extent. May 13th. Is quite recovered, and has full use of the arm. At times he has felt sensations in his legs of weakness and semi-paralysis.

REMARKS.—Had there not been some indications of failing nerve-power in other parts besides that principally affected, as in the nerves of the eyes and lower limbs, I should have felt much uncertainty as to whether the circumflex nerve alone was affected in some parts of its course, or whether the disorder was central. The latter opinion, I have no doubt, is correct.

The nature of paresis, cerebral or spinal, is, I think, somewhat elucidated by reflecting on the condition of a nerve, such as the median or ulnar when affected with severe neuralgia. The function of the nerve is temporarily abolished, the skin which it supplies is utterly anæsthetic, and the muscles palsied. Under the influence of quinine and perhaps galvanism the sensory and motor power is restored. It is certain that these remedies would not amend a state of neuritis; and I can see no other view to adopt than that, owing probably to some minute molecular derangement of their tissue depending on impaired nutrition, the nerve-fibres are no longer capable of conveying centrad and peripherad the impressions they normally transmit. There is no difficulty in considering that the white fibres of the brain and cord may fall into a like state as those of the nerves, in which case the result would be the same as in peripheral neuralgia. The cells of the gray matter may probably be affected in the same way as the tubules, whose axis cylinders are continuous with their interior. This I am inclined to think is especially the case when the paralysis appears to be the result of a morbid impression (as cold and wet) made on the sensory surface of the skin. The following is an instance of this kind.

No. 26.—J. G., æt. 45, ad. Feb. 11th, ill two days. Has usually good health, does not admit drinking habits, but there is some doubt about this.

Is much exposed to wet in following sportsmen. He got very wet before the present attack, which came on suddenly; he was unconscious at first for a few minutes. He is now very giddy, and so weak on his legs that he can barely stand alone, and was brought to the hospital in a cab. Head rather hot, not painful, aching pains in neck and shoulders. Right hand is closed, he cannot extend the fingers, it feels numb. T. clean. P. soft. No strength, no appetite, no sleep at night. Bark and ammonia with valerian were given, and after ten days, two grains of opium *o. n.* March 7th. Able to walk to hospital, right hand numb and crampy. 28th. Arm galvanized three times without benefit. April 4th. Quinine and iron ordered. 18th. He improves, but states that his arm has been better every other day for the last week. May 28th. He can now carry a large basin and jug filled with water. July 4th. Getting on well.

I have recorded another case (*v.* Brit. Med. J., April 16, 1859), in which symptoms of paralysis with impairment and disorder of sensation appeared in a young man the day after he had been standing a long time in wet grass. The paralysis without being complete was remarkably extensive and diffuse, affecting not only the arms and legs, but the masticatory and ocular muscles. Death occurred in about a week from asthenia. Nothing was found in the autopsy in the brain or cord that accounted for the phenomena, nor did microscopic examination discover any exudation cells, any granular coating of the minute vessels, or any indication of structural change. In cases of this kind it seems that the nerve-cells of the cord, as the first recipients of the morbid impressions, have their nutrition in some way disordered, in consequence of which their functional power fails. Graves, in his lecture on paraplegia, records cases where the disease was induced apparently by exposure to cold and wet, and in which it came on gradually, though with very varying rapidity in different instances; some being rendered almost completely paraplegic in a few weeks, others not for months or years. He finds stimulating liniments, and blisters applied to the parts of the affected limbs most copiously supplied with nerves, the most effectual means conjoined with the administration of strychnia and sulphur internally. He records one case in which a very careful autopsy discovered no diseased condition of any organ.

The conditions above noticed embrace the most frequently occurring forms of paralysis of the cord not dependent upon organic disease. Reflex paralysis appears to me to be a much rarer affection. I have not met myself with an instance of it. As there appears some tendency to use the term rather loosely, I will repeat that it seems to me properly to belong only to cases where the paralysis is evidently dependent on a persistent irritation, increasing when this is increased, and *vice versâ*. It is characteristic of *true* reflex paralysis that removal of the irritation proves curative, while all other means fail. It is certain that no true case of reflex paralysis would be benefited by strychnia, or galvanic excitation of the nerves or muscles of the affected part, nor by stimulating applications to the cutaneous surface. These are appropriate to the paretic state, and form by their success a good test of its presence.

There is another group of instances, which are not very uncommon, but the pathology of which is very obscure, and which I allude to without by any means affirming that they truly belong to the class of paresis. The following is an example:—

No. 27.—E. S., female, æt. 7½, seen Aug. 2, 1861. A month ago became feverish; her head or rather her neck was stiff. She had been treated for rheumatic fever, but does not seem to have had inflamed joints; the urine has deposited a thick whity sediment. Her legs became weak at once; after two days she had quite lost the use of them; the left arm was affected similarly a little before the legs, and remains so. She was delirious at first and had pain at the top and back of the head, which has ceased. For fourteen days she could not sleep at night for restlessness, sleeps now. There is no loss of sensation in the legs, but rather pain, she cries out when her calves are touched. No tenderness in spine. The muscles of all the paralyzed parts are very insusceptible to the interrupted current. She is quite unable to stand. Functions in tolerable order. I prescribed strychniæ gr. $\frac{1}{40}$ + ferri et quin. citr. gr. vi, aq. ℥ss *ter die;* the dose of strychnia was afterwards increased to gr. $\frac{1}{30}$, and the limbs were occasionally faradized. Oct. 5th. Is decidedly improved, can stand. The right leg is far the worst, and its muscles are insensible to the current, but the skin is hyperæsthetic, more so than it used to be. The left arm remains very useless; she has no power or but little over the flexors. Some stiffness in the muscles of the jaws from the strychnia. March 28th, 1862. Is decidedly improved, moves about actively, but the left hand and arm are still deformed, the hand drawn back on the forearm; she can however hold things with it. Dec. 31st, 1862. Walks about well, has walked some miles in a day, but halts still on the right leg. The flexors of the left hand are deficient in power, though she can use the hand tolerably. No medicine taken the last year.

The first question here for consideration is whether the disease was essentially acute rheumatism, attacking the cord. I am quite aware that rheumatism may appear primarily in the heart, but I doubt whether it is ever confined to this or any other internal organ, without sooner or later manifesting articular symptoms. There must evidently have been some resemblance to acute rheumatism in the febrile attack to have induced the attending practitioner to make this diagnosis. It is not easy to regard the disease simply as myelitis. The delirium, the very early supervention of paralysis affecting the cord as high as the origin of the brachial nerves, the absence of spinal tenderness when I first saw her, and as far as appears from the commencement, the preservation of sensibility, and the "juvantia" seem to me to afford evidence against viewing the disorder as myelitis or meningitis.

It is a highly important point to which Dr. Gull has drawn attention that lesions of the cord are occasionally attended with an affection, which in many respects is closely similar to acute rheumatism.

The explanation of this probably is that the vaso-motor nerves of the whole system are paralyzed, and that in consequence pyrexia is set up. Case 27 recorded by this physician[1] is of very high interest. The patient, a widow working hard at a mangle, had for two years, when exerting herself much, felt pain in the back between the shoulders, and a sense of constriction and coldness round the chest. Ten days before admission she was seized with pain in the left leg, and spasmodic contraction of the muscles, with increase of the pain and constriction of the chest. She could extend the leg, but not walk. The next day there was febrile heat and diarrhœa, the hands, knees, and ankles were swollen and painful. A slough formed on the sacrum. On admission the hands were swollen, stiff, and painful with some erythema. The legs were so far paralyzed that she could only move them very feebly and slowly; the muscles very wasted, but retained their electro-contractility. Sphincters weak. Sensation nearly normal, but at times both legs felt numb, and were drawn up involuntarily. Touching the feet gave rise to formication and to very lively excito-motor movements. Eight days after admission the hands were still swollen and erythematous, the face flushed. Pulse 100, full. Perspiration had an acid smell. Pupils large. Nights sleepless. Urine ammoniacal. Opii, gr. i 6*tis horis*. Wine 6 oz. daily and a chop. Under this treatment with faradization of the limbs she completely recovered in about six months. This case seems to me to have been essentially one of paresis of the cord with implication of the vaso-motor fibrils. The history is wholly that of nervous exhaustion, the symptoms are not contradictory (no pain or tenderness on pressure of the spine), and the "juvantia" are entirely corroborative of this view. The state of the urine and the good effect of the opium afford some tolerable evidence that the disease was *au fond* different from acute rheumatism. The occurrence of a slough on the sacrum in the existing condition of the vascular system is pretty good evidence, that the local death was not dependent on arterial constriction and anæmia as Brown-Séquard supposes it to be. It is much more probable that the impairment of nervous influence left the integument so enfeebled in its vital qualities that it was unable to resist the injurious influence of pressure. On careful consideration it appears to me highly probable that the case I have above recorded was essentially similar to Dr. Gull's, the quasi-rheumatic disorder in each being produced in the same way. In my case however the cause of the affection was probably some obscure influenzal or malarious miasm acting on a weakly nervous system. The child resided in one of the outskirts of London where house-building was in progress, a kind of locality which I have often observed to be favourable to the generation of such influences. The long persistence of the paralysis suggests its dependence on some organic

[1] "Guy's Hospital Reports," 1858, p. 127.

lesion, but this is opposed by the decidedly good effect of tonic treatment, though it was by no means effectually carried out.

Diphtherial paralysis is very evidently a paresis. From its proneness to extend so widely over the nervous system, affecting not only nerves of motion, but those of common and even special sensation, it seems most probably to be a central affection. This is also inferrible from its being generally, if not invariably, bilateral. It is stated by Dr. H. Greenhow that diphtheric paralysis at its outset is peripheral, extending gradually upwards from the tips of the fingers and toes towards the trunk. This certainly is the usual description of what is termed peripheral paralysis (as distinct from a central affection), but it is obvious that it by no means implies that the extremities of the nerves are first affected, and that the morbid action gradually advances centrad to the cord. It really means that one set of nerves is affected after another, leaving it entirely an open question whether the nerve-roots are the seat of the disorder or the distal extremities. It is clear that the same phenomena would ensue if we suppose the morbid action to be located in the cord and to proceed gradually upwards from below. The view of the paretic nature of diphtherial paralysis is strengthened by the occurrence of similar paralysis after typhus, in which, as Leudet affirms,[1] there is an absence of any morbid change in the brain or spinal cord. As far as I can find it does not appear that any organic change has been discovered in the nervous centres in fatal cases of diphtheric paralysis. The only exception is a case recorded by Mr. Humphrey,[2] who found in one case a small suppurated spot with softening of the adjacent brain substance in the superficial part of the left cerebral hemisphere. Hemiplegia of the right side had been present, but had gradually disappeared. The connection of this lesion with the paralysis seems open to some question. Perhaps the strongest argument in favour of the paretic nature of the paralysis in question is the good result of a highly tonic treatment, which we shall presently notice.

The interval which most observers have found to occur between the cessation of the primary disorder and the supervention of paralysis is an important point for observation, as remarked by Dr. Greenhow, since it tends to show that the nerve affection is not attributable either to albuminuria or to anæmia. It seems also as if it could hardly be the result of the original poison or influence, as no indications of it appear while the action of the latter is in its full intensity. In this respect it resembles the renal sequelæ of scarlatina, which sometimes ensue at a period when convalescence has decidedly commenced. As numerous cases of even severe diphtheria recover without any paralysis it follows either that some special modification of the original poison must be generated in the system; or, what is

[1] "Gaz. de Paris," 19, 1861.   [2] "Brit. Med. J.," July 4, 1863.

more probable, that a certain peculiar state of the nerve-centres is requisite to allow them to be rendered paretic by the poison. This state may be gradually induced during the progress of the disease. The opinion expressed by Gull with regard to typhus fever,[1] that elimination of the poison from the system by no means coincides with convalescence, seems to be verified also in the case of diphtheric paralysis. The basis of this view is a due appreciation of the importance of the vital state of the solids with reference to their liability to be affected by poisons. It is by no means necessary that the presence of a poison in the blood should evoke phenomena of disease; the latter may not ensue or may cease because the tissues either are, or have become inapt to be affected. This is a most material point for the practitioner, who often has no power to prevent the entrance or the stay of a poison in the system, but who may do much to render the system tolerant of it. *V.* a paper on the theory of elimination in the treatment of disease, *Brit. Med. J.*, April 24th, May 1st, 1858.

The treatment of diphtheric paralysis is wholly that of a paretic affection, and may stand for that of spinal paresis. This at least expresses the general opinion of those who have had experience. Wade is the only writer who finds more advantage from pot. iodid., ferri iod., and hyd. bichlor., than from strychnia, quinine, and iron. These, and especially the first, are the remedies to which I should always have resort, together with ol. morrh., a pure air, and a generous diet. The dose of strychnia may possibly require to be increased in some cases rather largely. I should not abandon its use in any refractory case, where the diagnosis of paresis was certain, until I had carried it to the extent of producing slightly its physiological effects. Dr. Bardsley[2] gave it in some cases of paralysis to the enormous amount of a grain and a half daily. Sulphuret of potassium baths have proved useful in this kind of paralysis, as well as in various kindred affections. This affords an instructive example of the beneficial effects of suitable stimulation of the sensory nerves of the general cutaneous surface. Although the effect produced on any one part is small, yet the total impression conveyed to the nervous centres is considerable, and probably by its mildness and general diffusion acts with great advantage. Dr. Copland relates a case of general motor paralysis removed after other means had failed by frequent recourse to warm baths containing stimulant substances. In one case of paraplegia under my care lamp baths and the cold douche to the spine had been of benefit. These remedial actions are just the opposite to the morbific inhibitory, but in both the same principle is involved, viz., that of affecting nervous centres through afferent or excitor nerves; the result in the one case being to depress, in the other to arouse the functional energy. Everything depends on the *kind* of impression made, and on the vital state of

---

[1] "Med. T. and Gaz.," April 5, 1862.   [2] Hospital Facts and Observations.

the nervous centre. The virtues of pine-leaf mud baths, and those made with the contents of ruminants' stomachs, are to be accounted for in the same way. The following is a well-marked case of diphtheric paralysis.

No. 26.—H. W., m., æt. 11, ad. April 23d. Ill two months. Has had severe attack of diphtheria, followed by violent sickness, albuminuria, ascites, and lastly the symptoms of paralysis of the soft palate and extremities. Liquids are apt to return through his nose when he tries to swallow. His arms are very weak, but not quite paralyzed. The legs are very useless, he cannot stand, and has very little sensation in them. His vision is affected, he cannot see near things well. The paraplegia has come on the last three weeks. The sickness has subsided. Three children and the mother of the family were attacked and one died. Ordered strychniæ gr. $\frac{1}{30}$, ferri sulph. gr. ij, spt. æth. s. co. ♏x, aq. ʒss *ter die*, et ol. morrh. ʒi *ter die*. Lin. terebinth. dorso. The dose of strychnia was gradually raised to gr. $\frac{1}{20}$, and he was almost quite well by the end of June.

CHAPTER IX.

CEREBRAL EXCITEMENT.

THIS state is of course the opposite to paresis. The functional energy of the various encephalic centres is aroused, and shows itself by corresponding phenomena. Perhaps the stimulating influence of good wine, not of course its intoxicating, affords as good an example as we can have. The face is somewhat flushed, and the brain we may believe is too, the eye is bright, the flow of ideas is rapid, the tongue eloquent, the temper cheerful, and the spirits elated. Of the same kind, though altogether unnatural and infallibly pernicious, are the stimulating effects of opium. Cocoa, except in large doses, produces less intoxication, and its use is not followed by depression. All physical agents are however surpassed by intense mental excitement. Not to mention acute mania, the maternal instinct does unquestionably develop an extraordinary amount of energy and endurance in the weaker sex, sometimes overpassing it may be affirmed anything shown by the stronger. A mother will watch by her child's sick bed for days and nights together, till one marvels how it is that nature does not sink under the effort. In a milder degree mental stimulus shows its energizing influence in enabling us to endure fatigue to a much greater extent than we could do without it. A sportsman will keep on foot for many hours in pursuit of game who would declare himself "dead beat" with half as long a constitutional. The following story is so beautiful that I cannot forbear quoting it.[1] "After the crossing of the Green River the whole party went on foot, and the men were becoming weaker every day for want of food. The painter who had one foot badly frozen became at last through lameness constantly the last man on the trail, and once his energy almost deserted him. He was at the top of a mountain of snow with not a tree to be seen for many miles. Night was approaching, and in the direction taken by his comrades not a sign of life could be descried. He sank exhausted on the snow bank, and took out of his pocket for a farewell look the miniatures of his wife and children. *Power came to him out of their faces.* He thought how little his wife could afford to be a widow, or his children to be fatherless, beat down his despair and struggled forward. It was not till late at night that he arrived at the camp fire."

The effect of cerebral excitement varies extremely according to the previous condition of the organ. A strong well balanced brain will bear a great deal of excitation without showing any irregular or violent reaction, or subsequent debility; while a weak and excitable one will be provoked by a less amount of stimulation to manifest phenomena of morbid activity, and will fall subsequently into great collapse. It is just in the difference of capacity for enduring the wear and tear of excitement that original endowment and training show the greatest influence. One man will sleep soundly and digest well under the same anxiety which renders another wakeful and dyspeptic. It is related that the Iron Duke, on the eve of an engagement, was aroused during the night from his sleep by a message that some important point was seriously menaced. Having reflected for a moment he pronounced it erroneous, and turned off to sleep again. He was right, but few men could have composed their brain to sleep after such an awaking, even though they were persuaded that the alarm was groundless. In these days of feeble and sensitive nervous systems it seems to me to be one of the most important parts of education to develop by physical and moral training a robust and non-excitable state of brain, so that the individual may be well able to confront the strain and struggle of actual life. It is in not affording this robust vigour but generating hyperæsthesia instead that tender nurture becomes often positive cruelty.

The *morbid* states characterized by cerebral excitement are chiefly those in which delirium is a conspicuous feature. Quiet muttering delirium tending towards coma may be left out of account. Active delirium, sthenic and asthenic, and the so called delirium tremens, are the states we propose to examine. Sthenic delirium is a common result of meningitis, and of ardent, and of other high fevers. The gray matter in such cases is usually found after death of a darker colour than normal, and sometimes especially in young persons is distinctly reddened. The white substance exhibits numerous bloody

---

[1] Household Words, March, 1857, p. 264.

puncta. There can be no doubt however that fierce delirium may occur when there is no remarkable vascular injection, at least when no traces of this are found after death. In fact in this as in a multitude of similar instances the excitation of the tissue is the primary change, and the vascular repletion is secondary and varying. If the normal tissue activity be great, though the gray matter will probably be dark, yet there will be no effusion of lymph, and no material capillary engorgement. If however the functional power of the tissue fails, and an inflammatory condition commences, we shall have considerable vascular repletion, and probably more or less exudation, which however may not extend beyond mere coating of the vessels with granular deposit. There is no inconsiderable analogy between a diarrhœal or a salivary flux, and active delirium. In both extensive tracts of cell-growth are stimulated to an excessive and rapid nutrition, which interferes with the due development of the individual particles. In the former instance the cells being disposed on a free surface are shed rapidly; in the latter we are unacquainted with the precise changes which the cells undergo. Assuming the correctness of the general opinion, that the axis cylinders of the nerve fibres are continuous with the granular interior of the nerve-cells, it seems almost a necessary consequence that disordered and hurried nutrition of the latter would communicate itself to the axis cylinders, and so give rise to abnormal sensations, and disorderly motor impulses. The very varying amount of cerebral excitement in different instances of the same kind of fever must be admitted to depend in part on corresponding differences in the quality of the nervous power. The poisons are doubtless the same in all cases, but the condition of the recipients may vary greatly. Of course much will also depend on whether the poison be specially determined to the head or not.

It is not yet fully determined what changes occur in the urine in cases of sthenic delirium. In meningitis and acute mania it is probable that the phosphoric acid is much increased, but this is not yet fully established. It would be highly desirable if we had some trustworthy indication, from this or from any other source, to guide us as to the existence of really sthenic delirium in any given case, but we fear we have none such at present, and that we must rely in this as in many other instances on our discriminative tact. Of course if a patient has a flushed face, and hot head, a firm not very frequent pulse, a ferrety eye, a contracted pupil, and shows considerable muscular power and energetic action there is no room for doubt; but in such a case as that recorded by Graves (v. *Clin. Med.*, p. 175), where the patient, though violently delirious and unmanageable, "on the borders of frantic madness," had a pulse almost uncountable from quickness and exceedingly weak, with cold extremities, the most experienced would hesitate as to the proper means to be adopted. Graves says, a very few leeches would kill him, blisters would be too slow in their action, and might even aggravate the disease, cold affusion seemed inadmissible. Yet this man took in less than forty-eight hours 12 grains of tartar emetic without any prostration being produced, while the cerebral excitement was calmed, sleep induced, and the pulse rendered slower, and much softer and fuller. A right discrimination in such emergencies as this is indeed a high attainment, the more so as the remedy is quite capable of being very pernicious as well as beneficial.

Active delirium in rheumatic fever is in the great majority of cases the result of an increased excitability of the nervous tissue, and is not dependent on inflammatory movement. In the cases referred to by Dr. Fuller where actual meningitis had occurred the delirium had been rather of a low kind. Dr. Copland distinguishes two sets of cases, one where delirium or mental disorder occurs in the course of acute rheumatism, without any abatement, or but little either of the fever, or of the local disease. In these cases, he says, the head affection is chiefly nervous, and contingent upon the febrile condition, in connection with depression of nervous or vital power. In the other, the head symptoms appear at an advanced stage of acute or sub-acute rheumatism, and are generally followed by the subsidence of the disease of the joint. The patients are exhausted or cachectic, and the head symptoms are more or less indicative of inflammatory irritation of the brain or its membranes. In my own experience the form of delirium I have mostly met with in rheumatic fever has been of the first kind, and has chiefly occurred in cachectic or feeble subjects. In one instance which I shall presently relate the head symptoms, which were of a highly sthenic character, coincided with cessation of the articular affection, which reappeared again to some extent as the former gave way. There seems much reason to think that the exciting cause of acute rheumatism, whether it be an imponderable influence, or a material virus, attaches itself especially to the nervous system, and works through it. If the nervous power is strong and steady, the inflammatory phenomena will proceed in an orderly manner to the termination of the disease. But if the reverse is the case, if the nerve power is weak originally, or gets exhausted by injudicious treatment, the irritability of the brain becomes greatly increased according to the general law (*v.* p. 44), and it is affected in a much more intense measure than it would have been in a stronger state. This is an instance we think where a judicious solidism is essential to true pathology, and to successful treatment. The exciting cause of rheumatic fever must be no doubt the same in all cases. Yet in the great majority the delicate structure of the brain is unaffected by the poison, or the morbid influence whatever it be. In a few however who have less resisting power the function of the nervous tissue is disordered. Clearly the principal object of treatment should be (in such cases) to strengthen and aid the weak organ to bear up against the perturbing agency. For this opium and stimulants are requisite. Though theory might incline us to try to quell the irritation by thorough alkalization of the system so as to neutralize the presumed acid materies morbi, yet practically we find that this is insufficient, and that we must deal with this and with all the visceral complications of rheumatism as substantive disorders. The same indeed holds true of delirium in all cases; it must be treated according to its quality, without regard to its presumed cause. In such asthenic delirium as we have been considering the disorder of nutrition may be well compared to that existing in neuralgia, a non-inflammatory molecular derangement of the tissue. In sthenic delirium it approaches more to inflammatory action, and probably in extreme cases may pass into meningitis.

As regards the treatment of active delirium very much of course depends on the nature of the affection, and the presumed pathological state. If the disorder be of sthenic character, various depressant measures will be found essential. It is the fashion with some to depreciate Abercrombie, but there seems to be no question (unless we accuse him of deliberate falsehood) that he has left us most valuable records of the successful treatment of cerebral disease as it occurred in his day. I do not see if we accept his cases as truthful records that we can question the beneficial effect of general and local bleeding, and of hard purging. Abercrombie candidly states that the cases terminating favourably form but a small proportion to the whole of those he has met with, but this does not alter the fact that in certain cases this evacuant treatment was successful. I am not at all disposed to be a blind worshipper of authority; I desiderate carefully-recorded observations in proof of general views, but when I have these I shall not reject or ignore them because they do not accord with my own experience. Abercrombie's testimony is fully corroborated by that of other observers, and looking at the whole no doubt exists for a moment in my own mind as to the propriety of adopting the means he recommended when we have sthenic conditions of system to deal with. Dr. Marshall Hall places congestion of the brain at the head of the list of disorders which increase tolerance of bloodletting. It is scarcely necessary to say that if venesection be requisite it should be performed in such a manner as to make a speedy impression on the system, and induce semi-syncope. The importance of choosing the right time for venesection has often been pointed out. As a remedy it belongs to the initiatory period of inflammation, before exudation to any amount has taken place, while the heart's action is forcible, and the bloodvessels retain their tone. In tropical fevers it is of vital consequence to employ it seasonably. Ranald Martin writes, "What was a saving means at the commencement of the paroxysm is as surely destructive at the end of it." In minor degrees of sthenic delirium leeching the head may be sufficient; Graves and Corrigan speak very favourably of its effects. The application of cold to the head is also a means of prime importance. Southwood Smith adduces cases to show that where headache and delirium are present, and the lancet is inadmissible, placing the patient in a warm bath, and directing a forcible stream of very cold water on his head, soon renders him more calm, relieves his headache, and for the time dissipates the cerebral symptoms. Graves adds his testimony that the effects of this remedy are extremely remarkable, and thinks that many of the cases in which he has employed tartar emetic with such signal advantage would derive equal benefit from this mode of treatment. Von der Decken and Brand[1] have lately found baths and cold affusions of eminent service in typhus, especially in tranquillizing the brain and preventing delirium. Abercrombie prefers the cold stream to the application of pounded ice, but warns us that it is a remedy of such power that it requires to be used with discretion lest it produce excessive prostration. It is most probable that the *modus operandi* of the cold douche to the head consists in its exciting in the cutaneous nerves an impression which is propagated through the centre to the vaso-motor nerves of the cerebral arteries, and induces their contraction. On the same principle, viz., of inducing anæmia, a stream of water has long been used in some countries as a means of sending children to sleep.[2] Tartar emetic combined with opium has already been mentioned as a powerful remedy in violent cerebral excitement. Graves by no means proposed it as a specific to be given in all conditions; he does not advocate its use at the commencement of fever, when other antiphlogistic measures may be more advisable, but at a later period, when symptoms of general debility announcing the typhoid type begin to predominate; and when the condition of the patient approximates to that observed in certain varieties of delirium tremens. Graves lays down that the relative portions of tartar emetic and laudanum must be varied according to circumstances. "When congestion of the brain is known to exist or is feared, the tartar emetic must not fall short of 4 grains in the 8 ounces, while the laudanum should not exceed half a drachm; but when nervous symptoms predominate the laudanum may amount to ʒi, and the tartar emetic to gr. ij; no general rule, however, can be laid down, and the practitioner must in all cases watch the effect of this medicine from hour to hour, until he ascertains whether it agrees with the patient or not." It is clear from Graves's cases that he considers the existence of very marked debility no contra-indication to the treatment. He states that it has sometimes disappointed him, but makes no mention of any disastrous effects produced by it. We have heard from those who have employed this remedy that such are by no means impossible. It was not for mere nervous disorder that Graves used tartar emetic and opium, but for nervous disorder combined with cerebral congestion. Wine, musk, porter and opiates would control the nervous symptoms alone, but not when they were blended with the effects of cerebral hyperæmia. In some of the cases, but by no means in all, the pulse before the tartar emetic was given was

---

[1] Schmidt's "Jahrb.," vol. cxvii. p. 125.
[2] Graves's "Clin. Med.," p. 745.

small and wiry, as well as frequent. The action of the medication was always to reduce the frequency of the pulse and render it fuller, and in some cases much softer. It is unfortunate that we have no information as to the quality of the first sound of the heart in the cases which Graves relates. One cannot but entertain much apprehension that tartar emetic would be a perilous drug to exhibit when the heart's tissue was seriously softened and enfeebled. Ackermann[1] always observed after injection of tartarized antimony a diminution of the force of the blood in the aorta, which took place whether the frequency of the pulse increased or diminished, but was greatest with a slow pulse. In dogs killed by tartar emetic the irritability of the heart examined immediately after death was remarkably diminished, and sometimes altogether extinguished. On the whole the safest conclusion that one can arrive at with regard to this medication seems to be that it is chiefly appropriate to conditions characterized by high nervous excitement associated with more or less active cerebral hyperæmia. One of the best criteria for judging of the degree of cerebral activity will be the capacity displayed for muscular exertion. If this be considerable, it is clear that a good deal of vis nervosa must still exist, and we may proceed more boldly. Some important general inferences may be drawn from the remarkable facts ascertained by Graves. (1) That in certain morbidly excited conditions of vital power depressing remedies are well borne and may be essential to preserve life. (2) That this morbid excitation may be confined to one organ, as the brain. (3) That tartar emetic operates as a tissue sedative, and when it acts most favourably confines its sedative action to the morbidly excited organ. The case first alluded to illustrates forcibly the two last propositions; the brain was violently excited but the heart was far from being so or any of the other organs;—the antimony produced no depressing effect but seemed to expend itself on the brain. This is what it has been found to do, when it has acted most beneficially in pneumonia, but this is just what it is often at the present day impossible to insure.

Colchicum is a remedy which has been found of admirable effect in calming high delirium of sthenic character associated with cerebral hyperæmia. Dr. Hamilton Roe gives gr. v of the powder every two or three hours until the face is blanched, and the morbid action quieted. In some visible inflammatory affections of the eye it acts similarly. It is a remedy of the same kind as tartar emetic, and to be used with the same precautions.

Hydrocyanic acid has lately been strongly recommended by Dr. M'Leod[2] as a powerful calmative in acute maniacal conditions where no grave structural change exists, and where the morbid action has not become as it were stereotyped by frequent recurrence. He con-

---

[1] Virchow's "Archiv"—"Brit. Med. J." Aug. 29, 1868.
[2] "Med. T. and Gaz.," March 14, 21, 1863.

siders that it checks the morbid activity of the brain, "the excessive and purposeless cerebral vigour." Sound sleep sometimes follows, but is by no means a necessary result of its beneficial action. The dose is ♏v every quarter of an hour till some manifest effect is produced. If there is any difficulty in administering it by the mouth, the method of subcutaneous injection may be employed. In the latter case the ♏v of acid are to be combined with ♏xxx of water. M'Leod has no doubt from his experience that it has the power of promptly staying cases running on to chronic insanity on the one hand, or exhaustion and death on the other. As its best ascertained therapeutic effects consist in removing various neuralgic affections, it is probable that it is more appropriate to states of the brain in which simple excitement of the tissue constitutes the disorder, than to those of which hyperæmia forms an essential element. It is a less depressing remedy than the two preceding, but an over-dose produces a stuporous condition and other phenomena resembling those attending an epilepsy.

The foregoing remarks relate to the treatment of sthenic delirium, but we have seen that acute or active delirium may be asthenic. It may be no easy matter to distinguish between cases requiring depressant measures, and those for which stimulating are essential. If we read Graves's remarks on the subject of giving wine and opium in fever we cannot but remark that he felt it not uncommonly to be a difficult question to decide when they were to be given, and when withheld. He states, "that we must rely in the more advanced stages of fever on the tact acquired by previous experience and reflection, and must often depend more upon a correct estimate of the general state of the patient than upon the appearance or absence of any particular symptom."[1] Sleeplessness with restlessness and irritability, the patient constantly endeavouring to leave his bed and having delusions—these symptoms may urgently demand wine and opium. Violent and continuous delirium forbids, in Graves's opinion, a stimulating treatment, but this does not hold if though there be a good deal of raving it is nocturnal. Stokes gives a case (p. 404)[2] where there was violent delirium throughout the night (two days later it is simply reported that there was such delirium without specifying that it was nocturnal), in which 16 ounces of wine daily with camphor, musk, and opium appeared to be highly beneficial. In one of Dr. Todd's cases of erysipelas[3] the patient had such violent delirium and created so much disturbance that he was obliged to be placed in a separate ward. With ʒss of brandy every two hours and ♏xx of laudanum every four hours the delirium was unabated, but diminished considerably and soon ceased after the brandy had been given every hour, and the laudanum had been replaced by bark, chloric ether and ammonia. In another case, one of epileptic

[1] "Clinical Med.," p. 187. [2] "Dis. of the Heart and Aorta."
[3] "Clin. Lect. on Acute Diseases."

delirium, very violent and constant delirium subsided in about four days under ʒss of brandy every hour, with carbonate of ammonia and laudanum every four hours. The pulse steadily declined in frequency during the administration of the stimuli. Todd speaks very confidently also of the efficacy of alcohol in preventing delirium in patients suffering under various acute diseases. He evidently holds that it is better to err on the side of giving too much than too little stimulus. The points to which we should have most regard in endeavouring to determine the quality of the delirium we have to deal with are: (1) The general condition and constitution of the patient; (2) The state of the urinary secretion; (3) The state of the pulse; (4) The quality of the first sound and impulse of the heart; (5) The state of the pupil; (6) The state of the skin; (7) That of the bowels. If the patient be enfeebled from any cause, and has not previous to his illness enjoyed vigorous health; if his urine is in good quantity, not highly acid, red, or of high spec. grav.; if the pulse is easily compressed; if the first sound of the heart and its impulse are weak; if the pupil is dilated; the skin not very hot and dry, and the bowels relaxed, we have good grounds for expecting that stimulants will be beneficial. In proportion as the above signs are less marked, the indications become less clear, and we must resort to what is often a wise proceeding, viz., testing the condition of the system with some remedies, the result of which may lead us to take the right course. The more we can perceive the signs of excitement without power in the cerebral disturbance, the more bold we may be in our administration of stimulants and support. In cases of this kind opium is often necessary, and its dose must depend on the degree of excitement, and on various other circumstances. Too small doses may only aggravate the excitement, and too large may bring on dangerous or fatal stupor. The determination of this point is one of the most delicate in therapeutics, and cannot be solved, at least in all instances, by administering small tentative doses in succession. I am much inclined myself to give large doses of hyoscyamus, as ∋j of the extract, in cases where it might not be safe to give a full dose of opium. If we prefer the latter the amount of cerebral excitement is the chief measure we have of the quantity of the drug which will be requisite to calm it. If the pupil be contracted, belladonna may be given as an hypnotic with advantage as Dr. Murchison tells us. Hyoscyamus would probably be suitable in the same state. In cases of the kind we are now considering brandy mixed with milk will be found one of the best forms for administering stimulus and food. It should be given of course at very short intervals, say ʒij of brandy + ʒss or ʒvj of milk every hour or half-hour.

No. 27.—W. L., æt. 25, of spare frame, delicate constitution, carpenter, seen March 28th. Ill with acute rheumatism about ten or twelve days, his head began to be affected two days ago. Five years ago he was under Mr. Culpepper's care for a very severe attack of acute rheumatism, attended with endocarditis and pericarditis. Five years before that he was under my care with similar disease. On March 21st he had ten leeches to the precordia for threatening cardiac inflammation, poultices were subsequently applied, and calomel and Dover's powder given every three hours with a draught of pot. nitras, potas. bicarb. and sod. phosp. 25th. Is nearly free from the pains and swelling of the limbs except in the extensors of both feet; skin still exudes an offensive copious perspiration. 26th. Gums affected. Rheumatism has quite disappeared, just as it did five years ago suddenly while the pericardium became inflamed. Calomel omitted, Dover's powders and salines continued. 27th. In the course of the night he became quite delirious and incoherent, uttering alarming shrieks so as to disturb the neighbours, with fits of fearfulness and apprehension that the ceiling was about to fall, &c. Eyes wild and restless, can scarcely be made to comprehend any question. Head hot and skin generally. Tongue dry and covered with yellow crust. No urine passed since last evening. Hands are tremulous as in delirium tremens. Hair cut short and cold applied to head, hot mustard fomentations to the feet. Opii gr. j 3tiis horis with effervescing draughts. Curious delirium continued all the day; four persons were required to keep him in bed, he would not take the pills or mixture. At 5 P. M. Mr. Culpepper gave him gr. j of opium, and at 9 P. M. gr. ij, matters were then greatly worse. At 11 P. M. Mr. C. was sent for, the patient was said to be in a strong fit of convulsions. When he saw him, he was in a terribly excited state, eyes staring, jaws clenched, heart beating violently. Pulse 130. Great heat of surface. Tr. digitalis ℨij + tr. opii ℨj was directed to be given in two doses, at 12 and 3 A. M. At 6 A. M. he had liq. opii sed. ℨj in two doses. I saw him with Mr. Culpepper at 9.30 A. M., and learned the above history and that he had had no sleep for two nights. Pulse 117, of good force. Tongue denuded, cracked, red, covered with sordes. Is partially conscious, does what he is told, says he has no pain anywhere, is constantly talking deliriously. Rheumatism has quite disappeared in spite of counter-irritation to the limbs. Urine passed in bed. Head rather hot. Heart's sounds fairly clear, no pericardial effusion, slight questionable exocardial bruit. Right pupil dilated until lately, is now of medium size and fixed. Left eye lost. No pneumonia or bronchitis. We agreed that he should have six leeches to the temples, cold to his head, and gr. ¼ of tartar emetic every half hour.

31st. He began the treatment at 11 A. M. of 28th, and took gr. ¼ every half hour till 11 P. M., when the pulse was 95, the skin was cool, and the delirium nearly abated, in short everything going on well, which induced Mr. C. to give the mixture less frequently, every one or two hours. At 5 A. M of 29th he was not so well, so the mixture was given as before with liq. opii sed. ₥iv in each dose, and from that time to 10 P. M. of 30th he has made rapid and permanent improvement, and is now quite himself again in every respect, asking for and taking food, and knowing every body about him; delirium quite ceased. In fact but for the return of the pain and swelling of the right hand one could not say what had been the matter. The left shoulder is also painful. Complexion clear, countenance calm, pulse 86, and respiration tranquil.

April 1st. Sleeps and eats well; omit the antimony and opium. 2d. A light tonic with sodæ phosp. was given, as the urine still deposited lithates. Joints free from rheumatism. 6th. Is up and dressed and considers himself quite well. Mr. Culpepper, to whose kindness I am indebted for the report of the case, adds that during the four days he took over 30 grains of tartar emetic and ℨij of liq. opii sedat. Rheumatic pains reappeared on night of 29th and continued till April 3d; all other symptoms gradually but most distinctly abated, and not the slightest bad effect was produced by the antimony, no approach even to nausea or sickness, or purging, or depression of the heart's action. After the 30th the medicine was given less frequently.

REMARKS. There can be no question that the tartar emetic was really the efficient means of this patient's recovery. Opium had been taken previously without benefit, and was not given the first day, when nevertheless a considerable sedative effect was produced. The relapse which ensued when the antimonial was given less frequently, and the steady improvement after it was resumed at the former rate, prove that it was the chief remedial agent. Its action seems to have been remarkably limited to the brain calming the excitement of its tissue without producing any other notable effect. The case was evidently not one of ordinary rheumatic fever delirium; there seems to have been actual metastasis of the morbid action from the joints to the brain with subsequent recurrence of it in its usual site. Considering that the heart had been severely attacked before I think it is very doubtful whether there was any actual affection of it on this occasion. If there was it was slight, and had I believe no connection whatever with the cerebral symptoms. Altogether the case may stand for a Παραδειγμα of sthenic delirium.

The following case related by Dr. Posner[1] is worth comparing with the foregoing:—

No. 28.—A man, æt. 37, fell ill of acute rheumatism. Both hands were affected, the pulse was 100, and the other symptoms were as usual except that he was remarkably restless. The inflamed parts were much relieved by leeching, but the elbow-joints became engaged, and the upper arm and neck muscles were painful. On the next day after considerable delirium the joints became quite painless, the pulse was 65, the patient only complained of occipital pain. There was no indication of intercurrent delirium tremens, the cerebral disorder was viewed as a rheumatic meningitis, and treated by local detraction of blood, and ice applications, with tartar emetic opium internally, and mustard poultices to the joints which had been inflamed. The delirium continued two days and nights in spite of repeated bloodletting, the pulse fell more and more, and the joints remained painless until large doses of opium were administered, which produced on the third night sleep for seventeen hours, out of which the patient awoke rational but with severe pains in the neck and stiffness of the elbow-joints. The pulse had risen moderately and the general condition was better. After a second tranquil night the pain returned in the joints which had become affected with all its former severity, and this condition lasted some days, when it suddenly ceased, and in its place the old cerebral symptoms returned. These yielded again to the opiate treatment, and the joints became affected for the third time, and remained so until the disorder disappeared entirely in about fourteen days. The heart was never attacked.

No. 29.—Mr. L., æt. 25, a delicate man, seen in consultation with Mr. G. Brown, Dec. 13th. He had been ill about ten days suffering with

[1] "Med. Centr. Ztg.," xxviii., 27; 1859.

rheumatic pain and latterly with some pleuro-pneumonia of both lungs at the posterior bases, most marked and extensive on the right. Respiration very quick and shallow, 60 in the minute. Pulse 108, weak. Skin cool. No cough, or expectoration. Extreme thirst. Tongue thickly coated. Heart's sounds normal. Ordered mist. pot. citrat. efferv. ʒj, tr. opii ♏vj, pot. iod. gr. jss, spt. æth. chlor. ♏xij, 4*tis horis*. Opii gr. j *statim*. Dec. 14th. Slept well, respiration 30; feels better. In the course of the following night Mr. G. B. was sent for, as the patient had become "raving mad." He gave him gr. j of acet. morph. + gr. v of calomel, and repeated the same in two hours. This speedily quieted him, so that the following day he was quite rational. He was now well supported with a very generous diet, and made a good recovery.

No. 30.—W., f., æt. 30 (about), seen Sept. 10th. Has had swelling and purpuric eruption on right leg last four days, and the last two on right elbow. Leg much swelled and very tender. Is markedly weak, has not been without vegetables. In two days with iron and quinine and citric acid the purpura had disappeared, and two days later rheumatism commenced. Nitre and citrate of potash saline. 18th. Was delirious all last night, is rational this morning, but intellect not quite clear. Heart's sounds normal; ordered mist. ammon. acet. ʒj + ammon. carb. gr. iij, 4*tis horis*. Brandy ʒss 2*dis horis*. Broth diet. Beef tea. After this there was no more delirium, but the rheumatism though never more than subacute lingered about her for a long time. She did not leave the hospital till the end of October.

No. 31.—Mrs. B., a young-looking primipara, confined six days ago, seen Jan. 27th with Mr. Ferguson. She had a quick and on the whole favourable labour: the pains being sharp and strong. The milk and lochia have continued: she has had no unfavourable uterine or other symptoms, no indication of fever. She has been quite sleepless and maniacal, raving and talking continually ever since her confinement in spite of large doses of opium, as much as ʒss of liq. opii sed. in one day, and some large doses of henbane. They have quieted her a little, but not much. She answers quite rationally when spoken to by me, but as soon as she is left talks deliriously. Urine normal. Bowels have been confined, are open now, and she has been better since. Pulse of tolerable strength, 88. Circulation active in forehead, the skin reddish and is scarcely pale for a moment after the pressure is removed. We agree to give ant. pot. tart. gr. ¼ + liq. opii sedat. ♏x 2*dis horis*. This medication made her much more delirious; it was difficult to keep her in bed. Mr. F. then administered tr. hyoscy. ʒij, 3*tis horis*, with which she became quieter; had a good night Feb. 2d, and improved materially. The antimony caused vomiting after four doses and flushing of the face. She went on taking tr. hyoscy. About ʒx daily for some days and quite recovered.

REMARKS.—In this last case the treatment which succeeded so well in the first was evidently inappropriate. Yet from the appearance and condition of the patient I had great hopes that it would prove successful. Perhaps it may not have been altogether useless, by rendering the brain more amenable to the influence of the henbane than it had been previously. In this respect the utility of what are called lowering remedies is I think sometimes overlooked. They may not apparently effect much themselves, but they prepare the way for others. The conclusions to be drawn from the above cases seem to be these. (1) That the quality of the *vis nervosa* in delirious disorder varies greatly. (2) That it may be very difficult to appreciate or gauge this quality correctly. (3) That nevertheless it is most important to do so, as the treatment depends upon it. (4) That any exclusive mode of treatment by stimulation, or the reverse, or by sedatives is out of the question.

CHAPTER X.

DELIRIUM TREMENS.

WE next come to the state known as delirium tremens. This is for the most part considered to be invariably the result of alcoholic excess, but I think there can be little doubt that a state closely resembling it, if not identical, may be generated by other causes. Watson states that this may happen from prolonged anxiety, J. Johnson from over-study. In continued fever a state closely resembling delirium tremens is not unfrequent. The case is narrated[1] of a stoker of good character serving on board H. M. S. Reynard, who fell apparently in consequence of excitement at the murder of two of his shipmates by the Japanese into a state of perfect delirium tremens, not one symptom being absent. It was proved that he had not been indulging in alcoholic excess. He was put to sleep with tr. opii $m40$ + chlorof. $m xv$. Fox records[2] a case to the same effect, the disorder supervening on exposure to cold and wet. He is positive that no indulgence in intoxicating liquors had anything to do with its production. Dr. Monckton[3] relates the case of a female, æt. 28, who rather more than three months after her confinement presented an almost typical state of traumatic delirium tremens; "the breast abscess consummating the overthrow of brain equilibrium," for which previous and successive mental shocks had prepared the way. The testimony as to the production of delirium tremens by other causes than alcoholic seems to me very important, as proving that the peculiar morbid state is not necessarily one of poisoning at all. It may be sequela, or result of poisoning matter, which has passed away from the system, or may be solely a diathesis. The discussion which has lately arisen respecting the proper treatment of delirium tremens makes a careful reconsideration of its pathology necessary. Those who contend that the disease is specific and dependent upon alcoholic poisoning deny that it ever originates from deprivation of the customary stimulus, and assert that in all instances where this is apparently the case the paroxysm has only been accelerated in its arrival by the accident or disorder, which has interfered with the usual indulgence. Dr. Marston however

---

[1] "Lancet," Oct. 11th, 1862. [2] "Lancet," May 7th, 1859.
[3] "Edin. Med. J.," Oct. 1860.

adduces evidence[1] which very materially corroborates the older view, and taken together with other experience renders the above-mentioned hypothesis very questionable. He shows that delirium tremens does come on in soldiers commonly from the first to the seventh day after the privation of liquor, and this in men who had not suffered from it before. He argues, I think, convincingly, and conformably to the analogy of other similar agents, that the nervous system becomes habituated to the constant use of alcoholic stimulus, so that, although more or less injured by it, it feels seriously the deprivation. Probably most of us have some familiar experience of a similar kind. Thus men who have been accustomed to take wine or beer moderately have tried to leave them off for some reason or other, but found their efficiency for work so much impaired thereby, that they were obliged to resume their usual allowance. This is on a minor scale much the same thing as occurs in some cases of delirium tremens. On the other hand, it seems to me that if this disease was invariably the direct result of alcoholic poisoning, the good effects of abstinence ought to show themselves very speedily and decidedly, so as to put the matter out of all question.

Dr. Laycock, who has taken a principal part in advocating the abandonment of the former routine treatment by opium, considers delirium tremens as " a vague term." He thinks that various cerebral affections of melancholic character are grouped under this head, that our diagnosis is imperfect, the etiology obscure, and the pathological anatomy altogether erroneous. He does not appear to distinguish, certainly not pointedly, the acute disease termed by some D. ebrietatis from the more chronic affection attended with depression. Yet this seems to be a main point. Dr. Blake regarded them as opposite and distinct diseases, the one being the immediate consequence of intemperance, the other arising from the sudden cessation of accustomed intemperate stimulation; the one requiring the cautious use of depletion, the other the administration of stimuli; the one belonging to the phlegmasiæ, the other to the neuroses. Copland makes a similar division of the disease into species; " the one being evidently connected with inflammatory irritation of the arachnoid and associated with great irritability; the other consisting chiefly of this last state attended by exhausted nervous energy." He adds, however, immediately, and this seems very important, " yet it often presents intermediate forms or modifications, which cannot be referred to the one species more than the other." He insists that the treatment should be modified according as it approaches to the one type or to the other. Dr. Marston in his excellent paper (loc. cit.) makes the same distinction, and further groups in a separate class cases which are complicated with visceral disease, renal, hepatic, gastro-enteric, central. The first form, he says, evidently implies acute alcoholic poisoning, while the second is a delirium of drunkards in

[1] "Brit. Med. J.," Dec. 19th, 1863.

contradistinction to a delirium from drink. The subjects of the first class are soon right after an emetic purge, and two or three days' quiet. Those of the second after free purgation will probably require opium and stimulants. Graves, though not separating his cases so widely from the etiological point of view, lays down most positively the necessity for very different treatment in different cases. In the young and robust the disease may demand strictly antiphlogistic measures, including venesection, leeching, and cold to the head; while in the old debilitated and confirmed drunkard, "we are often obliged to exhibit opium from the very commencement, and that in large doses combined with stimulants." Between these extremes, he proceeds, there are many intermediate varieties, each requiring a special modification of practice. Tartar emetic boldly exhibited is often our sheet anchor in delirium tremens, especially when there is evidently active determination to the head. In some cases it may be given alone, in others combined with opium. Mr. Solly, we suppose, states only the general experience of surgeons as to the liability of habitually excessive drinkers to suffer from delirium tremens, when after the shock of an injury they are restrained from their usual indulgence. Mr. Erichsen[1] only differs in recognizing two distinct types of traumatic delirium, "the one inflammatory, the other irritative," the treatment of the first being strictly antiphlogistic, that of the other requiring full doses of opium continued until either sleep is induced, or the pupil contracted:—while if there be also much depression, stimulants are requisite. He distinctly admits that this disorder may befall persons who are not intemperate, but who have an irritable nervous system. Dr. Peddie[2] considers that the state of the brain in delirium tremens is one of alcoholic erethism, the alcohol occasioning those relative changes in the sanguiferous system of the encephalon, the tendency of which is to pass from irritation, from abnormal activity of circulation and function, to inflammatory action, according to the severity of the attack, and other circumstances. He treated eighty cases with uniform success by tartar emetic in doses of gr. $\frac{1}{4}-\frac{1}{2}$ in simple solution every two hours, or at shorter intervals, according to the degree of excitement and irritability. The action of the antimony appears to be chiefly sedative. Its direct influence is to reduce the vascular excitement of the brain, soothe the nervous system, and diminish muscular power, and its more indirect action is exerted on the functions of the skin, kidneys, and intestinal canal. The advocates of the more recent view hold that delirium tremens is a specific toxæmia from alcoholic excess, and does not consist merely in the nervous irritation and exhaustion consequent on the withdrawal of a favourite stimulus. They insist that many persons cease from alcoholic excess, and become sober without suffering in any degree from this disorder. The records of prisons are appealed to to es-

---

[1] "Science and Art of Surgery," p. 90.   [2] "Edin. Med. J.," June, 1854.

tablish this point. The occurrence of traumatic delirium in drinkers is explained by supposing the injury to induce the earlier occurrence of a paroxysm which would have ensued without it, just as an attack of influenza or some other casual disorder might have done. If a mere expectant treatment be followed, according to Dr. Ware, of Boston, a paroxysm of delirium tremens terminates by natural sleep in from sixty to seventy-two hours, dating from the time when the state of entire watchfulness and delirium commences. The mortality on this plan is stated to be extremely small, only one death having occurred in twenty-nine, and this case being complicated with acute disease; while out of fifteen cases treated with opium in small or large doses six died, two of these being complicated. On the other hand in the Edinburgh Infirmary, where for many years the disease seems to have been treated with laudanum and whiskey in a very careless manner, the mortality is stated to have been 35 per cent.; and in St. George's Hospital 14.6 per cent.; in the infantry regiments 17.6 per cent.; and in the cavalry 13.8 per cent. Dr. Gairdner's recent experience at Edinburgh is of one death among thirty cases treated in an extremely simple and natural manner, and that one being complicated with a very extensive double pneumonia. Laycock himself has treated sixty-eight cases without opium or stimulants, and has had only two deaths. These statements certainly deserve grave consideration. The one which is of main importance is the assertion that the paroxysm of delirium tremens is self-limiting, ceasing as Dr. Ware affirms in from sixty to seventy-two hours. Dr. Laycock indeed extends this period considerably, to from four to fourteen days (his cases averaged six). This is certainly a considerable discrepancy, the shortest period assigned by Dr. Laycock being a day longer than the longest given by Dr. Ware. It would indeed require a considerable faith in the spontaneous tendency of the disease to a favourable termination to allow a man to remain sleepless and raving day after day without making judicious efforts to procure sleep. Dr. Laycock indeed seems to think that sleeplessness is no such serious matter; he says that he knew one gentleman who never slept a moment for a month yet with no bad results. Drs. Watson, Latham, and Grattan think very differently as regards the state of fever patients, which the former expressly compares with that of delirium tremens. They state that two or three nights spent in restless delirium are followed by the worst consequences, and that patients who pass three nights in succession in that way almost invariably die. Now though we admit that the delirium tremens patient may, at least in some cases, have more vital resistance than the fever-stricken one, yet it can by no means be granted that continuous sleepless delirium will not tend very materially to induce exhaustion, and death by asthenia. That a routine treatment by laudanum and whiskey is not advisable is most freely conceded; we no more wonder at the high mortality under such a regime, than we do at that which results in pneumonia, when a number of patients are taken indiscriminately, and all are treated by bleeding. Our belief is that our practice in delirium tremens, as in all other diseases, should be to a very great extent governed by the vital condition of the patient. If we had a case of continued fever where the symptoms were mild, and there was no remarkable excitement or depression, we should not interfere and require the patient to swallow a dose of wine or brandy every hour as we should do if there were indications of perilous depression. We hope we have learnt the truth of Schönlein's wise saying that it often happens to good physicians to find no indication for treatment, to bad ones never. On this view we quite understand that there may be many cases of delirium tremens in which a purely expectant treatment would be the best proceeding. This will specially be the case when the disorder supervenes upon a recent debauch; and when all that is needed is to enable the patient quietly and safely to recover from its injurious effects. Dr. Laycock seems to have met with this state so often, twenty-one out of twenty-two patients alluded to by him in his first paper[1] being actually alcoholized when they were admitted into the hospital, that we cannot but think that his cases are mostly of the acute toxæmic character. The only one which he details in his second[2] paper was a case of prolonged debauch, in which, though sleep did come on in nine days without sedatives, we are by no means convinced that it might not have been advantageously induced much sooner. The points which seem to us fully established by the widest experience are the following. (I) That cases of delirium tremens differ often very widely from each other, and that their management must vary accordingly. (II) That this difference may depend, (*a*) on the original strength of the constitution; (*b*) on the degree in which the nervous and other systems have become impaired by habitual excess, by anxiety, or other causes; (*c*) on the tendency to sthenic inflammatory excitement of the brain; (*d*) on the circumstances whether the disease succeed immediately to a drinking-bout, or supervene on a condition of chronic regular tippling, which has been accidentally interrupted.

Before proceeding to illustrate the above points we would remark that it does not seem wise to set aside and ignore the experience of our predecessors because it does not agree with our own. We hold that all facts, faithfully observed and recorded, have an undying value, they may not accord with others which occur at different times and places, nay, they may seem to be contradictory, but if they be real facts, they *must* be taken into account in any attempt to construct a true theory of the disease. It is marvellous how prone the best of us are to one-sided views, how averse to look fairly at all sides of a question. We remark further that with regard to what Dr. Laycock calls the heroic treatment of delirium tremens, it is impossible to suppose that it is entirely negative.

[1] "Edin. Med. J.," Oct. 1858.   [2] Ibid., Mar. 1862.

Either it must do good, or be injurious in the great majority of cases. He himself is not sparing in his anticipations of evil, concluding that "the continued or increased use of the causes will aggravate the effects, and change that which would otherwise be acute and transient into a chronic and permanent, if not a fatal disease." It is also we think to be considered that we need in the practice of medicine not only to have general rules for the management of ordinary cases, but special directions for various exigencies. Dr. Laycock is scarcely consistent with himself in allowing the use of alcoholic stimulants (4 to 6 oz. of brandy daily in one case) where there is prostration, and in admitting that in one class of cases opium and its salts have the "most beneficial effect." This seems to me to concede nearly all that a judicious practitioner, who was not prepared to adopt expectancy, would contend for.

Now, taking up our last point first, we think that all cases where the symptoms ensue immediately on casual alcoholic excess, should be distinctly separated from others where this is not the case. In this we agree with Dr. Blake, Mr. Solly, Dr. Copland, Dr. Marston, and Dr. Morehead. These cases may require very little treatment, perhaps only an emetic and a purgative. Dr. Morehead[1] gives calomel gr. viij + gr. j of morphia at bed-time after a hot foot-bath and cold affusion to the head. In robust young men he finds cupping to the neck often useful. The nervous system in such cases being in a tolerably sound state rights itself before long as soon as the morbid influence has passed off. In other cases the attack supervenes on a debauch, but the patient is also more or less habituated to alcoholic excess previously, perhaps for many years. Here it depends very much on the condition to which the nervous system has been reduced by the previous intemperance what effect the debauch will have. If the nervous power be tolerably intact, the case will be nearly of the same kind as that first considered; if the reverse is the case, it may be much more serious. Dr. Brinton gives a good example[2] of a man who had been long addicted to hard drinking, and was admitted after ten days' nearly continuous debauch in a state of incessant struggling delirium, which continued for more than twenty hours. He was allowed 3 to 6 oz. of brandy daily, and vin. ipec. ♏xv + tr. opii ♏vij + spt. æth. chlor. ♏x was administered every three or four hours. In twelve hours he slept, and was calm and rational the next day. When admitted he was in the third or fourth day of his third attack of delirium tremens. Now it is evident that the nervous system of this man could not have been very profoundly deranged in spite of all his excesses, if he could recover so rapidly under such simple means. But now, had this patient had a tendency to inflammatory excitement of the brain, such as Dr. Morehead describes as common among Europeans in

[1] "Researches on Disease in India," vol. ii. p. 533.
[2] "Lancet," June 16th, 1860.

India, one may feel very confident that he would not have escaped so lightly. He would then have been in the condition which Mr. Solly describes as essentially one of hyperæmia, and as more relieved by a general warm bath, and cold to the head, than by any form of opium. A case recorded by Dr. Peddie[1] illustrates this state well. A man, æt. 41, on the sixth day of his third attack of delirium tremens was highly excited and delirious, attempting to get out of a window. He had had previously smaller and less frequent doses of antimony, but was now ordered gr. ½ every hour with beef-tea liberally. After each dose, he was observed to become calmer and more rational, slept soundly in the afternoon, and next day was quite convalescent. This case would surely have been rendered much worse by opium and stimulants. It is on account of the prevalence of such conditions in India, that Dr. Morehead has recourse so frequently to tartar emetic and opium, giving gr. ¾ of the former + $\mathfrak{m}$xxx of tinct. opii 2*dis horis*, and employing, if need be, at the same time stimulants and cold affusion. The importance of the original strength of the patient's system is well illustrated by the following case which occurred in the practice of Dr. Hamilton Roe. A publican, habitually intemperate, a strong thick-set man, was walking about his shop in a state of considerable excitement, incoherent and wild, flourishing a knife, and refusing to take any medicine. He was coaxed to take a pot of porter in which were dissolved 6 grains of tartar emetic. The result of this "quietner" was that in one hour he was subdued, so as to take willingly gr. iij of opium, which put him to sleep, and he awoke after six hours, perfectly well. "Il va sans dire" that there are not many cases of delirium tremens which it would be advisable to treat in the same heroic way. But it is abundantly clear that the remedies were highly appropriate, and answered their purpose admirably. We cannot think that an expectant treatment involving prolonged delirium for many days, (Dr. Laycock gives a limit of fourteen) would have been preferable to the above sharp and short cure. Such a case, or that quoted from Dr. Peddie, may stand as a type of truly sthenic delirium tremens, in the management of which stimulants are of course undesirable. Dr. Fraser[2] records two cases of delirium tremens in both of which the pulse was full and rather hard, and the symptoms had supervened on a recent debauch, the patients being robust working men. In the first, sleep came after $\mathfrak{m}$xx of tr. physostigmatis had been administered, in the second where there was also limited pneumonia after $\mathfrak{m}$xxvj. Both were quite convalescent in two days. Dr. F. limits the use of the remedy to sthenic cases, and weak pulse he regards as a contraindication. He believes the physostigma to act by depressing the action of the heart, and so lessening the supply of the blood to the brain, in consequence of which the disposition to wakefulness is conquered. The following history probably de-

---

[1] V. Loc. citat.   [2] "Edin. Med. J.," Aug. 1863.

scribes a condition in which the nervous power was less resisting, though its excitement was equal to that displayed in the first case. A strong male, of mid-age, habitually intemperate, had drunk hard up to the time of attack. He was seen by Dr. H. Roe about forty-eight hours after delirium had commenced, and had been treated previously with small doses of opium ineffectually. His pulse, when seen, was full and quick, skin rather hot, head hot, eyes and face red and flushed, delirium rather fierce. Three grains of opium were given at first, but had only the effect of causing further excitement. Two hours after, 6 grains were given, which quieted, but did not sleep him; and three hours later he took 6 more, slept almost immediately, and woke after six or eight hours quite rational and recovered. No stimulants were given. It seems to me that it would be quite unfair to object that in this case the opium was not the cause of the sleep which would have come on spontaneously without. Fifteen grains of opium in five hours is no placebo, and beyond all question had not the nervous system been in such a state of erethism as to tolerate, and in a measure resist it, the dose would have proved fatal. The administration of opium in such full doses requires a master's discrimination, and I am by no means inclined to advocate a frequent resort to such practice. That, however, in *appropriate* cases it produces excellent results, is, I think, undeniable. In many instances I am inclined to think large and repeated doses of extr. hyoscyam. afford a safer sedative. Trousseau's rule for the administration of opium is a good one; he says if the disease is 20, opium must be 21. The difficulty is to measure the disease correctly; we have no *meter* wherewith to gauge vital power. In strong contrast to both the preceding cases we place the one recorded by Mr. Jones, of Jersey.[1] A male, æt. 48, seen Sept. 9th. Has had previously fits of the horrors, and has been muddled for the last two months. Has had no sleep now for four days and nights. Has taken opium in moderate doses, but has become worse. Pulse almost imperceptible, skin covered with cold clammy perspiration, face deadly pale, lips blue, hands tremulously grasping the air, the eye expressive of great fear, the mind gone, incoherent muttering. Tr. digitalis ʒss was given, in a few minutes the pulse was felt more easily. No sleep occurred in four hours, but he was rather more sensible, less tremulous and warmer:—the same dose of digitalis was repeated. Three hours later he had had no sleep, but in other respects was improved. A further dose of ʒij was given, making ʒx in seven hours. After this he had some sleep, and slept at intervals during the night. The next morning he was sensible, his fears had disappeared, the skin was warm, pulse full and regular at 90. Heart's sounds and impulse normal. Bowels open. Urine in natural quantity. After this he took some broth, drank freely of imperial and lemonade, but took no stimulus of any kind, nor any

[1] "Med. T. and Gaz.," Sept. 29th, 1860.

other medicine. He slept some hours in the afternoon; the next night was a good one, and the next morning he was almost well, and calling out for a mutton chop. It is sufficiently clear that this case was not one for the tartar emetic treatment whether in large or small doses. Opium in moderate doses had failed, and large ones would beyond doubt have soon destroyed life. The especial indication was for a cardiac tonic, to restore the flagging circulation, and this was well fulfilled by the digitalis, which, as I have elsewhere endeavoured to show, has eminently this property. Had one to treat such a case without digitalis, camphor, ammonia, tr. cinchon. and stimulants would be the best means. In the three cases now recorded we have examples of the three principal characteristics which the disorder may assume: (1) that of inflammatory excitement; (2) that of nervous erethism; (3) that of asthenia. In the first the overwrought cerebral energy must be calmed by tartar emetic with or without opium in adequate doses, cold to the head, leeches or cupping if necessary. The iced bath has recently been recommended by two American practitioners[1] as a potent sedative. They warn however that it may produce depression verging on syncope. It is a remedy of the same kind as the cold douche in mania, and like it must be used cautiously. In the second the non inflammatory nervous erethism must be quieted by some sedative. Full doses of opium often affect this well, but small or insufficient ones are apt to aggravate the disorder. In some cases where opium has failed chloroform given by the mouth has succeeded. It is questionable whether it should be employed by inhalation. Dr. Corrigan thinks it highly dangerous in this disease, having known it prove fatal in two cases. It should certainly not be used if there is the least tendency to failure of the heart's action. Henbane may be used I think with advantage in this form of disorder; ℈j should be given at once, and subsequently gr. x 2*dis horis*, till the pupils are dilated or sleep is produced. In the third form the great danger is from the tendency to death by asthenia, which requires some form of stimulants. At the same time the brain may be so irritable that there is risk of its being injuriously affected by the very means which are necessary to maintain the circulation. Digitalis itself is perhaps as little likely to do this as any tonic, but in two cases mentioned by Dr. Mackenzie it had the effect of changing a state of timidity into the fury of acute mania, and in one I observed myself (large doses being given) it acted similarly. Where it acts favourably it must tell more on the sympathetic ganglia and nervous centres influencing the heart than on the hemispheres. I believe it to be more appropriate than opium to conditions of marked asthenia, as there is decidedly risk of the latter still further depressing the heart's action, while digitalis has the reverse effect. It is hardly necessary to say that digitalis would be altogether un-

---

[1] "Amer. Med. Times," March 8th, 1862.

suitable for a case of sthenic delirium tremens, with fierce delirium and inflammatory excitement. Hanbury[1] relates a case of delirium tremens where digitalis given to the amount of ʒvij in a few hours succeeded completely after opium had failed. The indications of asthenia were well marked. Before sleep ensued the patient became rational and laughed at his illusions, and the nervous agitation which had been excessive subsided completely. M'Rea[2] states that he has given the digitalis treatment an extensive trial, in eighty cases of mania and delirium tremens. He reports favourably of it. Of 37 cases 3 died, 2 with arachnitis and effusion. Carey reports[3] four successful cases by the same method; in all opium had been given without good effect.

From the above exposition it must appear how necessary it is to exercise a sound discrimination in treating a case of delirium tremens, and how injurious any mere routine proceeding is likely to be. Probably few things are more difficult than to judge correctly of the vital condition of that vast accumulation of delicate cell-growth which forms the cortical substance of the hemispheres. No appreciable sign that we know of indicates it certainly. The pulse is no sure guide, a weak pulse by no means always indicates a state of cerebrum that will tolerate stimulants and tonics; and on the other hand a pulse may have much apparent force when these are urgently needed. A cool or moderately hot, and clammy state of skin, a languid lustreless eye, pale and copious urine very deficient in phosphates, and a timid delirium are we think the signs most indicative of a state of nervous system which will tolerate and be benefited by a stimulant and tonic treatment.

Believing as we do that delirium tremens, except in cases of acute occasional excess, is much more than mere alcoholic poisoning, we cannot doubt the propriety of administering judiciously the ordinary so-called stimulants. If the system appeared to be in a state requiring them, we should sanction their use without any reference to the causation of the disease. If there appeared no necessity for them, we should certainly forbear them. With regard to the expectant method, we have no doubt that it will afford better results than any blind routine treatment, but we fully believe that a well-directed medication is far preferable. We cannot think it a matter of indifference whether a patient is allowed to go on raving for a week or more until sleep naturally comes, or whether he is speedily calmed and put to sleep. Nor do we think it can be other than injurious to allow a patient to continue for days with his brain in a state of semi-inflammatory excitement, when we have positive evidence of the power of tartar emetic to control it. In most diseases it is better to trust the unaided powers of the "vis medicatrix" than to interfere blindly and rudely, but this does not lead us to conclude that medi-

---

[1] "Madras Q. J. of Med. Sc.," July, 1863.
[2] "Australian Med. and Surg. Rev.," vol. i.
[3] "Med. T. and Gaz.," Aug. 24th, 1861.

cine is useless or pernicious, but rather that its exercise requires not seldom considerable skill and judgment.

The following cases were treated with full doses of henbane, and as it seems with benefit.

No. 32.—J. H., æt. 33, ad. September 16th, a robust, vigorous-looking man. He had been under Mr. H. Smith's care, who kindly gave me the following particulars respecting him. For the last year he has been in a very excited state, at intervals drinking to excess spirit, beer, and large quantities of port wine. Generally after these bouts he has been exceedingly violent, so that his wife has been obliged to fly for her life into the street. He has no sleep at night sometimes for a fortnight, has strange fancies about the inconstancy of his wife. He has always been eccentric, and has an uncle who is said to be out of his mind and subject to fits. Some time ago he had a fit of apoplexy and has been more excitable since. The cause of his last attack was its being hinted to him by a malicious woman that his suspicions of his wife were well founded. He became extremely excited and violent, broke all the furniture in the house, and threw the milk (he is a dairyman) into the street, &c. Mr. S. on being called in gave him tr. hyoscy. ʒij + spt. æth. chl. ♏xx, mist. camph. ʒij at once, and an ʒi more of tr. hyoscy. in the next twelve hours. He was calmer afterwards, but did not sleep. The next day he was very outrageous and was removed to the hospital, where he came under my care. He was not violent then. Pulse quick. Skin moist. Tongue coated. A good purge of calomel and jalap was given, and in one hour after gr. xv of extr. hyoscy., after which he slept for two hours. He had not slept before for three or four nights. The next day he had ʒss in three doses, and as much the day after, the pupil became dilated, and the throat quite dry. He was very fairly quiet immediately after the first dose of henbane, slept well on the night of 19th, and was quite recovered by the 21st. It seems to me pretty certain that this man was tranquillized to a great extent by the henbane, and that it was of great value in thus procuring the gradual subsidence of the cerebral disorder. He had on former occasions been fourteen days without sleep, and now he was convalescent in about half the time.

No. 33.—J. G., æt. 45, ad. May 31st. A strong-made broad-chested man, an habitual toper. Has recently attempted while intoxicated to cut his throat, did not lose however much blood. He had no delirium tremens when admitted, but on June 1st, in the evening, he became suddenly very violent, and has been intermittingly so since, being rational by day, but towards evening becoming violent. This has been the case the last three days; he was worse last night than at any time before; the delirium lasted from 12 to 3 A. M., was calmed by tr. opii ʒss + ant. pot. tart. gr. ⅛, 4tis horis. Is now (June 4th) quite rational and quiet, did not sleep last night, but did the one before. Pulse of moderate force, head not hot. Has porter Oij daily. Ordered extr. hyoscy. gr. xv at 4 P. M. 5th. Went to sleep soon after taking the pills and slept all night; is rational and comfortable this morning. 6th. No delirium, slept well last night. Tongue dryish and red, taking since yesterday bark + ammonia + chloric ether 4tis horis. Pills given 4tis horis till 6 P. M. yesterday, but they made him very sick after about that time. 8th. No return of delirium, takes food well, slept well last night. Takes extr. hyoscy. gr. v, o. n., and the tonic. 18th. Discharged.

CHAPTER XI.

TETANUS.

The state of excitement of the spinal cord constitutes the disease called tetanus. It seems to me impossible to regard this otherwise than as a functional disorder, although I am quite aware of Demme's researches confirmed by Flechner and others as to the presence of new growths of connective tissue in the cord in various fatal cases which they examined. It seems to me by no means improbable that this new formation was rather the result than the cause of the disease. Just as the Pacchionian granulations result from repeated excitement and hyperæmia of the brain, so we may believe that a condition of violent excitement of the cord would very probably lead to some similar effusion in its substance. Moreover the same fibroid formations have been met with in cases of ataxie locomotr., a very different disease. The unpractical character of Demme's results appear in his recommendation of pot. iod. as a remedy more likely to be useful in tetanus than any other. This will hardly meet with the assent of any experienced man. The functional nature of tetanus appears also from its being induced by the poisonous action of strychnia, which, according to the testimony of Todd and Bowman, produces no discoverable change in the nerve tubes and cells of animals killed by it. The curative action of aconite which appears to be the physiological opposite to strychnia may be cited as having the same import. The tolerance of this drug in tetanus is very remarkable, and clearly shows that the system must be in a very opposite state to that which it induces. The effects of long-continued heat as a predisposing, and of exposure to cold as an exciting cause also go to show that the disease is essentially functional. These are common causes of nerve disorders, and it is not surprising that they should be of this. Heiberg[1] concludes that tetanus is not a nerve disorder, but an affection of the blood localizing itself in the muscles. This localization expresses itself by deposits in the muscular tissue and metamorphosis of the same probably directly induced by altered or diminished innervation. The immediate result of this is shortening and stiffness of the muscles; the tetanic convulsions are consequently not spasms, but contractures. The reflex spasms which he admits do occur are only accidental, and do not belong essentially to the disease. He compares the disease to diphtheritis, and recommends the local application of argenti nitras,

[1] "Norsk Magaz.," xv., 1861.

or iodine, naphtha, or nitromuriatic acid baths. A theory which seems much more probable than Heiberg's, maintained by Richardson, Roser, Wells, Thomson, and Betoli, regards tetanus as the result of a poisonous matter formed in the blood, or absorbed into it from an unhealthy secretion of the wound. This acts like strychnia, setting up that peculiar irritable state of the cord which is the essential condition of the phenomena, and without which the various slight excitants which produce the spasms would take no effect. The supporters of this theory justly insist on the prime necessity of accounting for this condition of exalted polarity, which they think can hardly be explained on the sole view of peripheral irritation. They insist further that it gives an explanation of the idiopathic form, and of the occasional epidemic or endemic prevalence of the disease. They notice also the close resemblance between hydrophobia, a disease undoubtedly of toxic origin, and tetanus. It may also be added that division of the nerve proceeding from the seat of the injury in traumatic tetanus has by no means proved so frequently successful as one would expect on the view of peripheral irritation being the sole and essential cause. There is much in this theory to commend it, but until it is proved that any secretion of a wound can on being inoculated give rise to tetanus it must remain a mere hypothesis. We have no example of any similar morbid production setting up notable nerve disorder. In glanders and farcy, in malignant pustules, in pyæmia, in syphilitic and smallpox inoculation, and in the action of snake poison, the phenomena are much more those of disordered circulation and blood crasis than of nervous derangement. It is certainly extremely rare if it ever happens that a foul ulcer, not the result of traumatic injury, becomes the cause of tetanus.

On the other hand, the theory which assigns to local irritation the chief place in the causation of the disease has, especially if somewhat modified, much evidence in its favour. The well-known greater tendency of lacerated wounds to be followed by tetanus is very strongly shown by Mr. Poland's figures. He states that at Guy's Hospital the disease occurred only in 1 case out of 1364 when the wound was made by a clean sharp knife, but in 1 out of 55 when the nerves were injured as in accidents. Dr. Macleod[1] relates two cases of fatal tetanus in which the spasms were almost entirely limited to the side injured. It is clear that in all cases a certain predisposition of the cord must exist before the spasmodic symptoms declare themselves. As Dr. Watson says, "the real mystery lies in this predisposition." It will tend to throw some light on this dark subject if we look at some of the points of affinity between tetanus and other nervous disorders. Prolonged exposure to heat is known to have a considerable influence in promoting the occurrence of tetanus, and that it enfeebles the nervous system and

---

[1] "Notes on Surgery of Crimean War," 1858, pp. 155—161.

renders it more liable to a variety of derangements is also notorious. Exposure to wet and cold is a recognized cause of tetanus, and from a history recorded by Maisonneuve we learn that it may produce epilepsy. Eighteen sailors after escaping from the enemy by swimming to a rock were for seven days exposed to great privation and severe cold; four weeks after they had been received into a hospital they were seized with epileptic attacks, and in twenty-eight months fourteen died. The action of cold in producing cramp, sometimes pretty severe, even in healthy persons, is a familiar fact. It has caused the death of swimmers. There can hardly be any question of poison here. Yet cramp is a minor tetanus. When tetanus supervenes on exposure to cold and wet, this is perfectly analogous to the invasion of paralysis under similar circumstances. Such paralysis as we have seen is of inhibitory, and therefore of functional character. It is true there is a wide difference between the two results, between the spasmodic and the paralytic affection, but there is much to justify the view that both may be varieties of deranged action of nerve-cells. Just as numbness and pain, which are certainly very different sensory disorders, are co-products of the cause giving rise to neuralgia, so it may be with spasm and paralysis. In a case of brachial neuralgia now before me the patient suffered at night after about two hours' sleep with unbearable pain and complete stiffness of the hand. This was the case after any hard work, but when she had a quiet day she experienced only numbing and tingling pain at night. The affection yielded to quinine and iron. If prolonged action of our muscles causes fatigue, the same when one position is maintained for a long time causes cramp. These facts go to show that causes producing impairment of nerve-power may give rise to spasm. To the same effect is a case recorded in the *Brit. Med. Journ.*, Nov. 29th, 1862, where it is stated that the removal of an osseous nodule from the right thyroid of a young woman cured her both of aphonia and dysphagia (palsies), and also of a spasmodic affection of the arm. In some instances of non-organic paralysis there is rigidity of one limb and simple immobility of the other on the same side, the same cause having given rise to both conditions, and the same treatment removing them. *V.* Moodeen Sheriff, on Contraction or Rigidity of the Muscles in Paralysis; *Madras Q. J. of Med. Sc.*, April, 1863.

The following history is of much interest in many respects, and especially as showing how an influence which generally tends to enfeeble and paralyze may produce an (apparently) opposite effect:—

No. 34.[1]—Mrs. S., æt. 22, had had "dead ague" a little before April, and expected her second confinement in July. At the age of 14 she had fits brought on by excessive fright in which she had bitten her tongue. April 19th. She had a severe seizure of emprosthotonos, the limbs and trunk being in a state of rigid spasm, and the hands firmly clenched. This lasted

[1] "Lancet," Sept. 27th, 1862.

half an hour, and then changed to opisthotonos, which lasted three-quarters of an hour. Severe congestive head-pain followed the attack. She was purged with calomel, took quinine, and the next attack was much modified as well as the consequent congestive headache. One or two other attacks occurred from neglecting precautions, but by taking quinine, and attention from time to time future ones were averted. She went her full time and was delivered of a living child. Before the first attack she had previous threatenings on two or three consecutive days, and always at the same hour. The district is malarious. Rabe[1] has recorded the case of a child four months old, who had epileptic convulsions and hemiplegia of the right side with deafness of that ear, and distortion of both eyes to the left. Otorrhœa existed, but the membrana tympani and the walls of the meatus were not materially injured. All these symptoms ceased after the removal of the body of a centipede from the auditory meatus. A similar case is recorded by Fabr. Hildanus, where a piece of glass in the same situation gave rise to similar phenomena. Here we have examples of the production of spasm and paralysis by the same cause in the same system.

Chorea, which seems to stand intermediate between tetanus and paralysis, is sometimes excited by terror like the former. Epilepsy, like tetanus, requires a certain predisposition, a peculiar irritability of certain nervous centres. Without this, exciting causes known to produce the disorder fail to take effect. The case of which Pflüger quotes from Dieffenbach shows that a tetanoid state of one arm, and general epileptic paroxysms may be co-results of the same traumatic irritation, and cease with its removal. This indicates that the morbid condition in both is diathetic rather than toxic. Dr. Prichard[2] states that conversions of chorea, epilepsy, and paralysis are by no means rare occurrences. He cites a case he saw himself of a child who three years ago had pertussis, and the fits of coughing threw her into paroxysms of tetanic epilepsy. These symptoms subsided after continuing some months. She was next seized suddenly with hemiplegia of the right side from which she nearly recovered, but is now troubled with chorea of the same parts. I had recently under my care a girl, æt. 15, who suffered from a severe abdominal neuralgia, and occasionally from fits of unconsciousness. I saw her in one of these, and found both lower and the left upper limb quite rigid. Under tonics and sedatives she recovered. It deserves I think to be considered that the muscular contractions in tetanus are attended with severe pain, the pain of cramp. Now this shows of itself that they are very different from voluntary muscular contractions, which how forcible soever are never painful. The association of pain approximates the nerve disorder to neuralgia.

The case related by Swan seems to put in a clear light the influence of an injury in inducing tetanus. The patient, a female, had been operated on for popliteal aneurism by opening the sac, and applying a ligature above and below it. Everything went on satis-

---

[1] "Gaz. des Hôpit.," 123; 1861.
[2] "On Diseases of the Nervous System," p. 64.

factorily until one day the attempt was made to change the position of the limb from the flexed to the extended, when the patient uttered a terrific scream, was soon after attacked with tetanus and died. At the post-mortem it appeared that the cutaneous nerve which accompanies the lesser saphenous vein had been divided in the operation, and that the upper end which had been adherent to the surrounding parts had been abruptly separated in the attempt at extension. Romberg, who quotes the case, weakens its force by the remark that tetanus must have been already making its approach; but I think this is not a fair comment on the facts. The case seems to be an example of the effect of shock. Langenbeck[1] records three cases which go to prove that tetanus may be dependent on local irritation. In the first he removed by an incision the fragment of a needle, the symptoms immediately lessened, and next day the patient was well. In the second removal of a ligature from the spermatic cord, which had been tied *en masse* after castration, at once stopped all the symptoms. In the third case the reduction of a fracture which was attended with great displacement had the desired effect. In examining any case of tetanus we ought to bear in mind the investigations of Froriep,[2] who found in seven cases the nerves proceeding from the injured part to the spinal cord affected at intervals with a peculiar inflammatory change, consisting in nodulated tumefaction and reddening of isolated points separated from one another by healthy tracts. He thinks these are peculiar to tetanus. Lussana's statement[3] goes to confirm this, who makes one of the points of diagnosis between neuralgia and neuritis that in the latter the muscles are affected by severe and violent, continuous, tonic and clonic, tetanoid contractions. Mr. Erichsen also says that he has never failed to find the nerve running from the wound more or less inflamed, and often for a considerable distance, whenever it has been carefully looked for. The nature of the effective cause in some cases of tetanus makes it most highly probable that no poison was concerned in its production. Such injuries as the blow of a whiplash, the bite of a finger by a sparrow, the cutting of a corn (Watson), can scarcely be supposed to have any toxic action. To give this argument more weight it should be contrasted with the circumstance that the most various kinds of ulcers so far as I am aware never give rise to tetanus. Syphilitic sores primary and secondary, tuberculous cavities, the intestinal ulcerations of typhoid fever and dysentery, varicose ulcers of the legs rarely if ever have this result. Yet it is surely probable that a poison might be generated in them which would give rise to tetanus if this were the true pathology of the disease. Moreover, in various cases tetanus has commenced some time after the wound, which may have been but a slight one,

[1] "Med. Centr. Zeit.," 1862, No. 34; "Syd. Soc. Year-book," 1868, p. 220.
[2] V. Romberg, vol. ii. p. 104.
[3] Prize Essay, Milan; Schmidt's "Jahrb.," vol. cviii. p. 168.

has healed. The general bearing of all this seems to be that the influence of shock, or irritation, or of some morbid surface impression is much more potent in producing the disease than any condition which might generate a poison. The acknowledged influence of sudden variations of temperature, of mental emotions, and of certain epidemic constitutions in producing tetanus, seem to me to approximate it much more to maladies depending on imponderable agencies, than to the so-called zymotic. Trousseau describes under the name of tetanilla a disease allied to tetanus, and which in grave cases passes into it. It consists in contraction of the hands, arms, or lower limbs, one or all being affected, but the upper being usually the first to suffer. The attacks are preceded by formication, anæsthesia, and impairment of voluntary power in the limbs, and are attended with more or less pain extending along the principal nerves, and radiating sometimes into the trunk. In grave cases the whole body becomes involved, and there is some amount of pyrexia. It is characteristic of the disorder that the spasm commences in the limbs, and extends subsequently to the muscles of the trunk and neck, contrary to what occurs in tetanus. Further the muscles of the limbs and those of other parts are seldom attacked at the same time, and what is specially distinctive is that the contractions can be brought on immediately by compressing the nervous trunks or the vessels of a part. The most effective causes of the disease are lactation, diarrhœa, attacks of cholera, and of enteric fever, and exposure to cold. It is however remarkable that the application of cold to the contracted parts often immediately arrests the spasm as long as it is continued. Trousseau regards the disease as of rheumatic character. He finds bleeding from the arm or cupping along the spine, where the strength of the patient permits their employment, to have most efficacy. Quinine is the next most useful remedy, and then follow opium and belladonna in small doses. In violent paroxysms chloroform inhalation may be cautiously used. Aran has found the internal administration of chloroform beneficial combined with its local application to the contracted parts.[1]

As to the therapeutics of tetanus, it does not matter which view we adopt of the pathology of the disease. If the symptoms depend upon a poison, we have no means of eliminating it, or destroying it in the body. Our efforts are confined in this as in all other cases of the same kind to counterworking the morbid action. Certainly it will always be desirable to promote, as far as possible, a healthy state of the wound if there be one, to correct a faulty state of the secretions, and especially to provide for an ample supply of pure, cold, fresh air. The importance of this in preventing pyæmia and hospital gangrene is acknowledged, and I am sure its sedative influence on undue nervous excitability can hardly be over-estimated. I should be inclined to ascribe the recovery of the soldier whose case

---

[1] "Clinique Méd.," vol. ii. p. 107.

is related by Dr. MacGregor,[1] as much or more to free exposure to the fresh air, as to the effect of cold, which, except under proper management, is apt to be injurious. Cold affusion, however, is said to have proved useful, and Dr. Todd recommends the application of ice along the spine. Carpenter[2] affirms that he cured sixteen out of seventeen cases by this means. Probably the cold douche would be beneficial. Careful examination of the wound should be made to detect any foreign substances which might be lodged in it, and act as a cause of irritation. A highly interesting case has lately been recorded by Mr. Wood[3] where division of the internal saphenous nerve, which was irritated by a comminuted fracture of the leg, arrested permanently the tetanus which had set in two days before with severe convulsion. Dr. Fayrer, of Calcutta, divided the median nerve in a case of wound of the hand with decided advantage.[4] Should any evidence of neuritis be discovered in the course of nerves proceeding from the injured part, this state should be the object of treatment. The exhausting nature of the disease should be kept in mind from the first, and wine and nourishment should be freely administered. Among the special means which may be employed in the view of subduing the abnormal excitability of the cord there are but very few that have any real claim to notice. Recoveries have taken place under many, but the share of the drug in the recovery is open to question. With regard to the anæsthetics, chloroform and ether, Thamhayn[5] reports that they certainly afford considerable temporary relief. The pulse falls to its normal frequency, and the breathing becomes regular. The spasms and the concomitant pains vanish, as well as the distressed expression of the countenance, and tranquil sleep ensues. The external appearance of convalescence is complete, but all the while the disease is powerfully and insidiously advancing onwards towards its fatal termination. Its course is not delayed, nor its intensity diminished. As soon as the remedy is omitted the whole array of fatal symptoms reappears. Often the intensity of the disease, and of the pain is proportional to the time during which both have been suppressed by the anæsthetic. Saurel's report is in a much more favourable strain; he states that he has procured recovery in 29 cases by chloroform or ether, 11 of them being idiopathic, and 18 traumatic. He thinks the chief cause of failure lies in having recourse too late to these remedies. The possibility of restoring the power of swallowing by these means is certainly a great gain. The conclusions arrived at in a report on 43 cases in the *Medical Times and Gazette*, June 17, 1854, are nearly to the same effect as Thamhayn's. The writer states that the continuous administration of chloroform over long periods of time is

---

[1] He had violent tetanus from a slight injury, and was carried for sixteen hours exposed to severe weather. On his arrival at the halting-place he was half-frozen to death, but the tetanus had disappeared.
[2] New York J. of Med., January, 1860.   [3] Brit. Med. J., July 4, 1863.
[4] Brit. Med. J., Oct. 10, 1863.   [5] Schmidt's Jahrb., vol. cxii. p. 210.

not to be recommended, since the patient sinks as fast at least, if not faster, than when the disease is allowed to display itself. There is some ground for believing that ether gives more favourable results than chloroform. With regard to the various narcotic drugs which have been employed, it appears from a review of the cases recorded in various journals during the last four years that aconite and nicotine are the most successful. Woorara shows only two recoveries out of eight cases in which it was tried. One point which seems noteworthy is the great tolerance of aconite which is produced by the disease, a dose being well borne during its continuance, which proves poisonous when it has passed away. The aconite may be given at the rate of ℥xv of the tincture (Pharm. Brit.) 4*tis horis*, of course, watching carefully its effects. It is as well to give it with a stimulant, as in brandy and water, to obviate its depressing effects on the heart's action. Some systems are extremely susceptible of its toxic effect. I am acquainted with an instance where so small a quantity as half a drop of the Pharmacopœia tincture (1851) applied to the mucous surface of the lower lip produced distinctly poisonous symptoms, which continued nearly twenty-four hours. The dose of nicotine varies from ℥j to ℥ijss, given from four to six times a day, according to the urgency of the tetanic spasms. Its effects are stated to be lowering of the pulse, in one case from 130 to 88, in another it caused an increase of 10 beats; immediate relaxation of the spasm of the muscles of expression, respiration, deglutition, of those of the back and of the abdomen; cessation of delirium and feeling of relief from agonizing pains; profuse sweating with an intolerable odour of snuff; tendency to sleep. The hamstring and abductor muscles were more refractory to its influence than the others. Mr. Tufnell[1] records a case of severe traumatic tetanus in which 56 drops of nicotine were given in six days. Chloroform had been given by the mouth for three days without benefit. The nicotine certainly seems to have been beneficial, but had ultimately to be given *per anum* owing to the disgust it produced. The tetanus ceased in fifteen days. The reporters of the *Medical Times and Gazette*, April 6, 1861, recommend the free use of quinine in all except the most acute cases. The bowels should be effectively acted on once.

The diet should be such as to support the strength; easily-digestible food and wine should be administered at short intervals. Trial should be made in all cases of the continuous galvanic current transmitted along the spine. A Pulvermacher's chain of 120 links may be used, or a series of 15 to 20 cells of Daniell's battery. Of course it is not to be supposed that more than a very small part of this current actually reaches the cord, which lies so surrounded by moist tissue capable of transmitting electricity, and this is a reason for employing a larger battery than would be requisite if it were possi-

---

[1] Dublin Med. Press, Jan. 7, 1863.

ble to act on the cord directly. It appears that the direction in which the current is passed is of no importance. Dr. Radcliffe states that if a frog be poisoned with strychnia it is possible to prevent the development of the characteristic spasms, or to suspend them after they have actually commenced, by subjecting the spinal cord of the animal to the action of a continuous galvanic current. Moreover, Matteucci refers to the case of a man suffering from tetanus in which the patient was able to open his mouth, to breathe freely, and to move his body and limbs without much difficulty so long as a strong galvanic current was made to pass continuously along the spine from the occiput to the sacrum.

As regards prognosis, the following may be stated. The later the disease commences after the infliction of the injury the more hope there is of recovery. Prolongation of the disorder is generally hopeful, but it has been known to terminate fatally after fourteen months (Meadow's case).[1] Continued difficulty of swallowing or hindrance to respiration are perilous signs—death mostly occurring from exhaustion or asphyxia.

CHAPTER XII.

CATALEPSY.

THIS rare and curious affection doubtless belongs to the family of functional nervous disorders. It occurs chiefly in those who have weakly and excitable nervous systems, feeble health, and ill-governed minds, and who may be said to possess neither a "mens sana," nor a "corpus sanum." In fact many subjects of these disorders claim more properly the care of the alienist than of the ordinary physician. At least it may be said that after the cessation of the actual attack judicious moral treatment will almost invariably be of as much, if not more consequence than medical. One case is however recorded[2] where it seems to have resulted from an intracranial epithelioma. As regards the nature of the disorder it may be said that it is evidently allied to tetanus, but differs in the circumstance that the brain is involved as well as the cord, and that consciousness is more or less in abeyance. In a case very ably recorded by Mr. Jones[3] it is stated that all the muscles of the extremities and of other parts were so rigid that they could not be moved for two or three hours, and in three other cases which he refers to occurring under the observation of others the same symptom was well marked. "The extreme degree of rigidity," he says, "generally exists about the

[1] "Medico-Chir. Trans.," 1861.   [2] Canst. "Jahresb.," 1861, vol. iii. p. 77.
[3] "Brit. Med. J.," June 6, 1863.

commencement of the attack and passes off before the termination." Recently an account has been published[1] of an endemic cataleptic disorder prevailing at Billingshausen near Würzburg. The population consists of peasants who are well off, but who intermarry very much, and are all small and deformed. The affected individuals constitute half of the number, males as well as females. They are called there "the stiff ones" (*starren*). A chill is commonly said to be the exciting cause of the attacks. The patients are suddenly seized by a peculiar sensation in their limbs, upon which all their muscles become tense, their countenances deathly pale, they retain the posture which they first assume, their fingers are bent and quiver slightly, and the eyeballs in the same way, the visual axes converging; their intellects and senses are normal, but their speech consists only of broken sounds. The attack ceases in from one to five minutes, and the body becomes warm. The indications of a tetanoid affection are very evident here both in the arterial and in the voluntary muscles, and the same is true of the following case recorded by Mr. Austen.[2] "A male, the subject of large delusions and markedly dilated left pupil, having once apparently recovered was readmitted. He was now depressed and apprehensive. On the sixth day he became heavy, and was got to bed with difficulty. Half an hour afterwards he was completely comatose and motionless; the pulse was scarcely perceptible, and could not be counted. A salt injection having been given, he was placed on the night-stool, and then it was at once discovered that he was cataleptic. His limbs remained exactly as the attendant left them; his figure without support was as erect as a statue. The legs and arms were put in positions the least convenient and the most opposed to gravity: thus the legs were extended straight from the hips, and the arms at right angles to the thorax. In this singular state and posture he remained a quarter of an hour, when suddenly the enema operated, and the utensil was filled with an immense number of hard fecal lumps. The pulse on the instant rose, the rigid limbs fell, and the statue vanished. In twelve hours he was sensible, and understood questions. In thirty-six hours he was walking about as usual. This case illustrates excellently the effect of intestinal irritation in producing quasi-tetanic affection of the voluntary muscles, spasm of the cerebral arteries, and probably of the radial. If the latter was not the case, there must have been inhibitory depression of the heart's action. Either might result from reflected morbid stimulus. In the Billingshausen cataleptics it is pretty certain that spasm of the branches of the external carotid existed during the attacks, but none of those of the internal. In other instances, according to Dr. Copland, there is evidence of active congestion of blood in the head. In any case as in Mr. J.'s where *sudden* complete unconsciousness with tetanoid rigidity of muscles occurred I cannot think that the brain could be

---

[1] Schmidt's "Jahrb.," vol. cxx. p. 301.   [2] Austen on General Paralysis, p. 55.

otherwise than anæmic. In a case recorded by Dr. Bellingham (*Dub. Med. Press*, July 8, 1846) a female, æt. 18, amenorrhœal, had for more than six months daily fits in which the cheeks were flushed, the limbs almost tetanically rigid, the pupils mobile, the heart's action violent, pulse 120, respiration tranquil. There was complete unconsciousness and loss of voluntary motion, no recollection of what occurred during the fit. After the first ten minutes of the attack the tetanic rigidity diminished, and the limbs could then be placed and retained in any position. She was cured by leeches to the nares, purgatives, spt. ammon. fœtid., and shower-baths.

In the three cases to which Mr. Jones refers consciousness was but partially abolished, and the same is true of his own case. The degree of unconsciousness may vary with the degree of anæmia of the hemispheres which is produced. In two of these cases the temperature was not materially altered, in one the surface everywhere was of icy coldness, the countenance pallid, and the muscles were rigid as iron, while the pulse was of fair strength. The patient was a stout male, well made, but of nervous and excitable temperament. He had two attacks exactly of the same kind at an interval of about eleven months, both of which were brought on by the same conditions, viz., excitement, fatigue, and want of food. They subsided after lasting about twenty-four hours by means of rest, warmth to the feet and the epigastrium, and an opiate (in one).[1] On two subsequent occasions after a day of unusual fatigue he became very restless and troublesome, very stubborn, and partially insensible, but had no cataleptic symptoms. He was soon restored by rest and an opiate. I have cited some of the details of this case because they seem to illustrate very well how causes of exhaustion may give rise to excitement and violent muscular action instead of, as they ordinarily do, producing languor and prostration. In this young man on four several occasions the same cause was followed by the same or similar effects, the chief difference being that the brain alone appeared to be affected in the two last. In the chapter on Tetanus I have remarked on some facts analogous to the above, and will only add here that they are all probably ultimately referable to the general law that debility of nerve-tissue often coincides with increased excitability.

Catalepsy evidently is a disorder intermediate between epilepsy and tetanus, with both of which it has affinities. It resembles very much the variety of epilepsy termed tetanic. The peculiar qualities of nervous tissue in different individuals which terminate the special form and manifestation which dynamic disorder shall assume are far beyond our observation. One thing, however, we can see, viz., that much depends on which group of nervous centres most readily takes on morbid action. If it be the spinal, we have tetanus; if the medulla oblongata and adjacent superior region, we have epilepsy; if the

---

[1] Case of Catalepsy by J. Buchanan, Esq., *Glasgow Med. Journ.*, 1857, 1858.

mesocephale alone, we have so-called hysteria; if the hemispheres alone, we have "le petit mal" of epilepsy, or "congestion apoplectiforme cérébrale." Two or perhaps more of these centres may be affected simultaneously and the resulting disorder will be complex, which appears to be the case in catalepsy.

Treatment must have for its object the removal of existing exciting causes (as in Mr. Austen's case), and the calming of nerve irritation. The latter will in some instances be best effected by sedatives, in others by diffusible stimulants. In conditions of great rigidity and coldness of surface a warm bath, or still better wet packing would be I think very beneficial. In prolonged cases galvanism should be employed, and I should prefer using the continuous current first. In Mr. J.'s case the interrupted current materially diminished the rigidity of the muscles, but the cold douche was rather injurious.

CHAPTER XIII.

EPILEPSY.

THERE can be little question that epilepsy is primarily and essentially a functional malady. Graves records a case of great severity in which idiocy and paroxysmal mania had supervened for years before death, but where not the slightest deviation from the normal condition of the brain and cord could be discovered on a very careful post-mortem examination. It is true that minute microscopic research was not employed, but I more than doubt whether this can be trusted to detect changes which give no sign of their presence to the experienced eye. When it is apparent that *some* kind of change has taken place the microscope may give us most valuable aid in determining the nature of that change, but I am not inclined to trust it for much more. The various alterations which have been found in the cerebral hemispheres and their membranes, the induration of the white substance, the adherence of the gray to the investing pia mater, the dilatation of the bloodvessels, &c., are certainly rather consequences than causes of the paroxysms. One of the most recent and successful investigators of this disease, Schrœder v. der Kolk, states that we "have sufficient reason to conclude that the first cause of epilepsy consists in an exalted sensibility and excitability of the medulla oblongata, rendering the latter liable to discharge itself on the application of several irritants, which excite its involuntary reflex movements." Even when commencing dementia has shown itself, as evidenced by a high degree of silliness and dulness, complete recovery may ensue.

The causes which induce epilepsy are partly physical, partly immaterial. A great number of lesions about the head and even in remote parts are known to have given rise to the disorder. Such are injuries to the cranial bones, cicatrices of the scalp, tumours in the meninges, wandering wisdom-teeth, worms in the bowels, calculi in the ureter, or bile-duct. The disease originated in this way is termed eccentric. It should, however, be clearly understood that these physical excitants are by no means mere provocatives of the paroxysms, the convulsions being supposed to ensue as the reflex results of irritation, but that they actually *set up* in the nervous centres that state of excitability which is the essence of the disorder. They are therefore both predisposing and exciting causes. They require, however, a certain amount of predisposition in the nervous centres to become operative. In many individuals the quality of these centres is such that the morbid impression fails to take effect, they are proof against it. In others, and this is very remarkable, the same cause which might have induced epilepsy has a different result. Thus intestinal worms may cause paraplegia or amaurosis, a neuroma may cause only severe neuralgic pain, and an exostosed wisdom-tooth permanent infra-orbital neuralgia. Causes of centric epilepsy are the following: Poisoning of the blood from retention of excrementitious matter. This by deranging the nutrition of the nervous tissue generates the abnormal excitability which then manifests itself without any special irritant. Various causes of exhaustion, such as hemorhage and excessive discharges, venereal excesses, prolonged want of sleep, unremitting pain act very much in the same way. Sudden fright seems to rank rather higher as a cause. Copland indorses Esquirol's statement that fits of passion, distress of mind, and venereal excesses hold the next rank to terror in exciting the disease. This shows the relation of the malady to chorea, which is so commonly produced in the predisposed by fright. Grief, prolonged anxiety, the sight of a sufferer in the paroxysms, and in fact almost any very powerful mental emotion may give rise to epilepsy. From the above facts one conclusion of much importance may, we think, be deduced, viz., that epilepsy is for the most part a diathetic, and not a toxic affection, and that the elimination of a materies morbi is not to rule our therapy. The effective causes are mainly those which produce dynamic derangement, and which so far as we know can generate no poisonous matter.

There is one condition which has not yet been mentioned, and which according to my experience is rather infrequent, but which Copland declares to give rise to the most common form of cerebral epilepsy, especially in this country. I refer to sanguineous plethora. Prichard also in the interesting cases he relates, found repeated venesection so often of essential service that one cannot doubt that an excess of the circulating fluid may be a *vera causa* of the disease. Schrœder v. der Kolk's experience is nearly to the same effect. Copland says that he has found the disease most frequent in persons who were either very plethoric, or very much the reverse. My own observation leads me to the contrary opinion, I should certainly say that the epileptics I have had to deal with have been of a medium temperament, neither sanguine nor anæmic. With regard to individuals in the latter state, I have often remarked their freedom from epileptic disorder. In some exquisite instances of anæmia there has been nothing of the kind. With respect to local plethora, *i. e.*, determination of blood to the head, the case is different. This is often associated with very marked debility, and seems indeed to a great extent dependent upon it. The vaso-motor nerves of the cerebral arteries participating in the general weakness become unable to keep the vessels properly contracted, in consequence of which a relative excess of blood is sent to the encephalic centres, and produces a state of excitement. In some cases the local determination of blood may be due, at least in part, to the state of excitement of the nervous tissue induced by other causes, and which then attracts *à fronte* an undue amount of blood to the part. The condition here is similar to that which exists in some cases of retinal hyperæsthesia, where the morbid excitability is complicated with and aggravated by a degree of hyperæmia. The state in fact is one of semi-inflammatory nisus.

The irritating effect in certain conditions of an excess of blood coursing through a tissue has not, I think, been sufficiently considered. It was excellently illustrated by Vanzetti in his observations on inflamed limbs, where the inflammation was found to subside permanently after the main artery had been compressed for about twenty-four hours. The following remarks seem to me to set forth the pith of the matter. The circulation of arterial blood not only maintains the nutrition of the several tissues, but also acts as a sustaining stimulant to their vital powers. Of this I think we can be sure from the phenomena attendant on embolism. A patient is attacked suddenly with violent pain in the left groin, " exactly as if he had been shot." From that moment, so runs the report,[1] the limb became numb, cold, and quite powerless, and pain continued intense for some hours, at least twenty-four. Death occurred from gangrene in thirty-seven days, and an embolon three-quarters of an inch long was found in the femoral artery two inches below Poupart's ligament. Now, as the muscles and nerves of an amputated limb manifest their functional power for some short time after its removal, we are sure that the powerlessness in the above and in similar instances did not depend on any immediate abolition of contractility and of vis nervosa, but on an impairment of these vital faculties, so that the organs were unable to respond to the stimulus of the will. Kussmaul's and Tenner's conclusion, that the brain of a rabbit can remain deprived of arterial blood for two minutes without losing its capability of again performing its functions upon the renewal of the

[1] "Lancet," June 7th, 1862.

circulation, the convulsions ceasing immediately at the same time, shows also that nervous centres retain to a considerable extent their vital powers when deprived of blood. In cold-blooded animals this independence of the tissues on continuous circulation of blood is much more marked; frogs and snakes will certainly perform voluntary movements when circulation has ceased. From these facts, then, as well as from the immediate arousing and exciting effect on the brain of an increased flow of arterial blood, while its deprivation as rapidly induces an opposite state, I conclude that blood is not merely a nutrient to the parts it traverses, but also an excitant. Now in plethoric states, whether general or local, this excitation may be excessive, and the so-called excitable districts of the brain, the medulla oblongata and the parts situated just above it, may be thereby wrought into a condition of abnormal irritability, which bloodletting or checking of the blood flow may much relieve.

It is of much interest and importance to determine what is the condition of the brain and nervous system for a short time before and at the time of the paroxysms. This seems to have been pretty well settled by observation. Dr. Copland's long list of premonitory symptoms may be summed up in the statement that they all of them indicate a state of abnormal irritability or incitability, associated with a very varying condition of blood-flow, which may or may not be in excess. The due and regular nutrition of the nervous centres is evidently deranged. The aura with which the paroxysms sometimes opens is one of these nervous derangements. It is an extremely remarkable circumstance that interference with this aura should in a certain number of cases enable us to arrest the paroxysm which is on the verge of exploding. That the aura is really of central origin can scarcely be doubted, its appearing to extend along the nerves indicates only the involving of one central termination after another. There is no sort of reason for supposing that there is any peripheral disorder in the nerves which are its apparent seat, and where there is such disorder, as in neuralgia, it does not concur with epilepsy. It remains therefore a very curious and suggestive fact that we should sometimes be able to modify the vital state of a nervous centre, and that too beneficially by acting upon the nerves to which sensations of central origin are referred. Something of the same kind has been observed in sciatica, and in other states.

Almost up to the moment at which the paroxysm commences the circulation is not notably disturbed, but just at this time, according to very accordant testimony, marked pallor of the face ensues, followed by the shriek, the insensibility, and the convulsions. The sudden complete insensibility of the "grand mal," the giddiness and more or less complete though briefer unconsciousness of the "petit mal" seem to me capable of being explained only by a suddenly-induced anæmia of the hemispheres; and the convulsions are, as we know from Kussmaul's and Tenner's researches, necessary consequences of the same state of the medulla oblongata and the mesocephale. That the cerebral anæmia is not the result of mere syncope we are sure. There seems then nothing left but to assume that a sudden constriction of the cerebral arteries occurs. It is highly probable that the greater the hyperæmia and excitability was just before the attack, the more violently will the nervous centres resent the succeeding anæmia. In the majority of instances the cerebral anæmia is of short duration, and is immediately replaced by a hyperæmia which at first is of venous character, both from the retardation of the blood in the large veins, and also from the non-aëration of the blood which the left heart sends into the arteries. As the respiration is restored the hyperæmia becomes arterial just as was observed in Kussmaul's rabbits. This hyperæmia results from dilatation of the vessels, which seems to be the natural sequence to sudden constriction, as in the common reaction and glow which ensues in healthy persons after the shock of a cold douche. That the sopor depends chiefly on exhaustion is apparent from its absence in cases where the attack consists in simple unconsciousness without convulsions.

The foregoing seems to give a rational account of all the ordinary instances of epilepsy, but it may be questioned how far it applies to cases where the paroxysms are unusually prolonged. In many of these the paroxysm is made up of a series of attacks separated from one another by a longer or shorter interval of soporose exhaustion. There seems no difficulty in understanding that the anæmia may recur at the commencement of each, and that thus the same phenomena are repeated again and again. It is impossible to determine how long the anæmia (which of course is not complete as it was in Kussmaul's and Tenner's rabbits) may last, nor how long its effects may continue to be manifested by muscular agitation. If indeed the anæmia were immediately replaced by a moderate flow of arterial blood, it is probable the paroxysm would rapidly be at an end. But this is not the case in the fully-developed attack, the disorder of respiration and the remora of the venous current fill all the cerebral vessels with blood that is very imperfectly depurated, and the disorder and commotion of the vesicular neurine continue longer than they otherwise would. Much no doubt depends on the quality of the nervous centres; if they are highly irritable, and the "vis nervosa" is considerable, the disorder will be more violent and prolonged than when the reverse is the case. Thus, in the later periods of the disease, when the brain has become more or less damaged, the paroxysms are often less severe than at an earlier date.

In all instances then of true epilepsy, I conceive a temporary, more or less complete anæmia from spasm of the cerebral vessels, to be the determining cause of the paroxysm, and to give it its special features. Without this we may have various symptoms of cerebral irritation, but no epilepsy. A case recorded recently by Dr. Palmer (*v.* p. 178) is surely an instance which might well have assumed the form of enteric epilepsy, but inasmuch as there was no tendency to arterial spasm the morbid phenomena took a different direction.

It is however quite certain that long-continued convulsions may be produced by the irritation of tubercles in the brain, by acute hydrocephalus, by exanthematous miasm, and by certain poisons. In such states there will be no spasm of the cerebral arteries, and no consequent anæmia. The medulla oblongata and other parts of the encephalon are directly irritated, and convulsion ensues, as when the same parts are excited by the touch of the scalpel in a living animal. The chief distinction between epileptiform attacks depending on direct cerebral irritation, and those occasioned by arterial spasm lies in the paroxysmal and intermittent character of the one, and the more continuous character of the other. In any given case of course it will be essential to consider carefully the attendant circumstances, as the state of the urine, and of the bowels, the existence of any indications of intracranial disease, or of commencing smallpox, &c. In young adults we should not forget the possibility of an errant wisdom-tooth being at the bottom of the disorder. The case which I have given at p. 51 shows however that epilepsy, to all appearance idiopathic and centric, may at its supervention persist through so long a succession of paroxysms as to prove fatal by exhaustion.

It is a question not easily to decide how far arterial spasm without any previous abnormal state of the encephalon may *per se* give rise to epilepsy. If the disease is ever produced in this way we should expect to find instances of it among the manifold pranks of malarious miasm, and it actually appears to be so. Mr. Lowe says,[1] "within the last twelve months, many cases of jungle fever, contracted in the Upper Godavery district, have been attended with severe epileptiform convulsions." Dr. Payne[2] has observed epileptic attacks ensuing as the result of malarious infection, which may have occurred long previously, and not have shown itself in paroxysms of ague at any period. Cases of infantile convulsion are frequently seen at Calcutta which stands in very close relation to malarious epilepsy. In all these quinine affords a cure. Payne considers that a hydræmic state of blood is the most important element in the pathology of this class of disorder. Dr. Mackay[3] recognizes the occurrence of malarious epilepsy, and records a case of the kind, in which the attacks were arrested by quinine. In some of Torti's cases of lethargic pernicious fever the condition during the paroxysm was not unlike that of the epileptic attack. In one case convulsive movements occurred continually, and such a profound lethargy that no kind of painful stimulation had any effect in arousing the patient. The disease was cured by bark. Even in these cases, however, it is

[1] "Madras Q. J. of Med. Sc.," Jan. 1863, p. 67.
[2] "Indian Annals," No. xiv. p. 597.   [3] "Edin. Med. J.," Oct. 1863.

not certain that the cerebro-spinal nervous centres were not to some extent directly and primarily affected by the poison. Now that we know so much more accurately the effects which are produced on the brain by sudden arrest of the blood-flow, it seems to me that very much of the mystery which has long attended on epilepsy is removed. Indeed, so far from regarding it as a very strange and wonderful occurrence, a "morbus sacer," one is rather surprised that it and its allied disorders are not much more common.[1] It is truly a small inconvenience if from long sitting still, or from cold, our hands or feet get benumbed from contraction of the arteries; as soon as we restore the circulation all is speedily in order again, and no damage is done. But if from any cause our brain gets into a like state, it is no such light matter—the delicate and complicated organ whose function is of so high a nature cannot tolerate the suspension of its due nutrition and stimulation so easily as the skin can, and its disordered actions are manifested in the grave derangement of all the functions of the body over which it has sway. Some time ago a child was under my care for some slight ailment, and on one occasion I observed that its arms and hands were livid and cold. I was told that this occurred not unfrequently without any exposure to cold. I could not help thinking, how if the cerebral circulation was affected in a like way? would not serious symptoms declare themselves? I cannot but think that many of the peculiarities of epilepsy depend on the peculiar arrangement of the encephalic arteries. The large mass of the superior nervous centres is supplied with blood by four trunks which are amply furnished with nerves, and liable therefore to be influenced by them. It is clear that any spasm of these vessels is likely to be attended with much more considerable results than where, as in the case of the spinal cord, the vessels are small and numerous, and not likely to be affected many of them at once. The case of retinal hyperæsthesia, commonly called scrofulous ophthalmia, is worth considering with regard to the pathology of epilepsy. The disorder is essentially one of debility, a neurosis, at least I can affirm this of some exquisite cases. The debility gives rise to the hyperæsthesia according to the general law, and this determines the most intense spasmodic muscular contraction. It is true this contraction is sub-continuous, but we have instances enough to prove that a permanent irritation acting on the encephalic centres may give rise to intermittent phenomena. So in many cases of epilepsy primary exhaustion sets up a state of undue nervous excitability in the medulla oblongata and adjacent parts which then gives rise to intermittent motor disorder.

The treatment of epilepsy and of its kindred states may be designated as either empirical or rational. To the former I entertain a decided aversion, yet would thankfully accept any proofs of the

---

[1] The divine old man of Cos clearly foresaw this. Hippocrates' Works, Syd. Soc. Edit., vol. ii. p. 843.

real virtue of remedies, which must be regarded in this light. Alisma appears once to have done good in my hands, but probably it would fail in most cases as it did in the next I tried it. I have no notion of any reasonable ground on which we could expect it to be beneficial. Cotyledo umbilicus has perhaps more claim to notice, but I have had no success in its use. The list of such remedies is endless, and the encouragement to experiment with them but small. Still I think we should not wholly abandon remedies of this class, and in many refractory cases we are sure to meet with we shall do well to follow the example of Dr. J. W. Ogle, and test the virtues of the galium album, and similar herbs. Considerable allowance should be made for manifold idiosyncrasies, which are in all probability more numerous and developed in the cerebral tissue than in any other. Under this head we may allude to the desirable gift possessed by some men, so much more than by others, of inspiring confidence and hope by their mere presence and speech. It is unfortunate that experience does not tend so much as one could wish to develop this quality.

The aim of *rational* treatment is first to remove exciting causes of the disease, if any such can be detected, as worms, misplaced teeth, masturbation, &c. Next we must seek to correct any evident faulty state of the system, anæmia plethora, debility, syphilitic infection, or the like. We may then proceed to combat the especial vice, which is the "fons et erigo mali," viz., the undue excitability of the nerves or nervous centres. For this we have various sedatives of considerable efficacy. In violent, rapidly-recurring paroxysms morphia, as Dr. Sieveking has shown, will do good service. In ordinary chronic epilepsy belladonna or henbane long and steadily continued is preferable. They should be given in sufficient doses to produce some decided effect. It is common with me to give gr. j extr. bellad. *ter die* after having commenced with gr. $\frac{1}{2}$ or gr. $\frac{1}{3}$. Henbane may be given in gr. v to gr. x doses of the extract *ter die*. These sedatives may often be advantageously combined with zinc, tannin, or nitrate of silver; ol. morrh. may also be given in many cases along with the sedative. Counter-irritation by means of an issue in the arm, a seton in the neck, or remote blisters, should be used when there are signs of over-active circulation in the head. The good results obtained by v. der Kolk from the insertion of a seton in the neck, the actual cautery, issues, and cupping are certainly very striking. In some instances considerable improvement of the mental faculties which had been impaired by the disorder ensued on the use of these means. Purging may be advised in cases which are tolerant of it with the same view. On the other hand, we shall meet with many cases where the indication is to tone and invigorate. Here we have to select the least irritating tonics, as tannin, zinc, nitrate of silver, and cod-liver oil. Dr. Anstie has specially commended the latter of late in all chronic convulsive disorders, and I am much disposed to agree with him as to its beneficial action, at least wherever there is evidence of nervous exhaustion. He finds it, however, useful even where the general nutrition is excellent. In states of great nervous prostration I think strychnia is of material use, just as it is in chorea. Determination to the head may depend upon loss of tone in the vaso-motor nerves, or the arteries, and tonics may then be the most effectual means of controlling the hyperæmia. This is a case, however, in which much tact and judgment are requisite, especially at first, lest the tonics prove irritants to the over-excitable brain. Tannin, which is no mean tonic, has also the very desirable property of constringing the bloodvessels, and on this account is very appropriate in a disease where there is so much tendency to dilatation of the vessels by repeatly-recurring congestion. I have heard on good authority of bichloride of mercury having been employed with the best results. The action of this drug is a mystery to me; by some it is ranked as an excellent tonic, and certainly it is unlike any other mercurial that I am acquainted with. If it be regarded as a mercurial, it would be appropriate, I think, to conditions where, together with increased excitability of the nervous tissue, there was also local attraction of blood, a quasi-inflammatory nisus. That mercury *properly employed* has the power of annulling this morbid attraction of blood I am convinced. Bromide of potassium is highly spoken of by good observers as a remedy which is of great value in diminishing the number of fits. It will keep them off for long periods, even for a year, but they are prone to recur when the medicine is discontinued. The dose is gr. v ad xxx *ter die*.

Much importance is attached by several authorities to the arrest of any aura that can be detected, and there seems sufficient evidence to show that the repeated suppression of it may be curative. It occurs, however, only in about half the total number of cases, and when it does occur it is not by any means always in a part where any means of averting it can be employed. Further there is I think some ground for apprehension that it may but prevent the manifestation of the disorder for a time which will ultimately break out with increased severity. Schrœder v. der Kolk says this is to be feared even with our ordinary drugs, leading even to a fatal result.

One *sine quâ non* to successful treatment is that the patient should repose a cordial reliance on his physician, and that the latter should gird himself to a prolonged and difficult contest. Obstinacy on the part of the disease must be met with patient determination not to be discouraged; and I speak from experience when I say that we shall sometimes achieve good success after we have often been almost ready to despair.

The hygiene should be most carefully regulated, and everything should be avoided which can tend to diminish strength and increase excitability. The diet should be simple, but nutritious, coffee and tea had better be forborne, or sparingly indulged in. Good malt liquor may be allowed if it agrees, or instead, if need be, a little wine. Tolerably robust persons will no doubt do wisely to become as a rule, water-drinkers. Romberg recommends to erethetic subjects a milk and vegetable diet. Cold affusion in the form of a morning douche or shower-bath will be serviceable in most cases. As much open-air exercise should be taken as the intervals of the fits will allow, as there is probably nothing which tends more to diminish morbid excitability. The good effect of the exercise will be much enhanced if it can be taken in the pursuit of some interesting recreative occupation. To many patients who cannot abandon their occupations it will of course be impossible to carry out these latter regulations completely, but they must be encouraged to do what they can, and reminded of the proverb, "that half a loaf is better than no bread." To unmarried patients strict chastity of mind and body should be commended, to the married a sparing use of the conjugal bed. This is of course an extremely delicate matter to touch upon, but the effect of sexual indulgence on the nervous system is so considerable, especially in weakly persons, that a medical adviser can by no means leave it unnoticed. That which is quite innocuous to a sound man may be very pernicious to one of epileptoid tendency. In young persons of both sexes the existence of vicious habits must be considered possible, and measures must be taken for the detection of this wretched practice. It is one of the most unpleasant tasks that can befall a medical attendant to have to institute such inquiries, scouted as the very idea is likely to be at first by the parents; but too much is known of the prevalence of this vice and of its ruinous effects to allow us in doubtful cases to ignore it. There is abundant room here for tact and discretion, and perhaps the best way of proceeding is for the ordinary attendant to divide the responsibility of the inquiry with another, who appears more as a stranger, and is less likely to give offence.

The subject of puerperal convulsions has so much connection with that of epilepsy that I cannot but allude to it here. Not that we can regard the two disorders as identical, for there is evidence to show that epileptic females are by no means prone to suffer from puerperal convulsions. It is plain, however, that while they are different there is a considerable resemblance between them, and that any conclusion we arrive at respecting one must have a bearing on our views regarding the other. Of true epilepsy albuminuria forms no part, while in puerperal convulsions it is almost constant. It is probable that the toxic state of the blood materially modifies the condition of the nervous centres. In true epilepsy arterial spasm plays a prominent part, in puerperal convulsions this is not the case. The latter are in a much greater degree dependent on remote irritation than the former, whether we regard this irritation as acting indirectly through the renal disorder it produces, or directly on the nervous centres, or, as is most probable, in both ways. However, regarding the two disorders as certainly very much allied, the point to which I wish to draw attention is the following—viz., that there exists good evidence to prove that the pathological state giving rise to puerperal convulsions may vary considerably from a highly sthenic to an asthenic quality. Excellent authorities testify that copious venesection is a very valuable remedy in many instances as well as nauseating doses of tartar emetic; while in many others it is admitted that chloroform inhalation tranquillizes satisfactorily the morbid excitement. Sir C. Locock says[1] that these convulsions "appear sometimes to depend upon a loaded (congested?) state of the brain; at other times the brain appears to be influenced by distant irritation either in the uterus or digestive organs; and again in some cases puerperal convulsions are induced apparently by a peculiar irritability of the nervous system." I cannot but think that these views are very applicable to epilepsy, and that we may affirm almost the same of the one disorder as of the other. At any rate they must be admitted to add considerably to the probability that the essential morbid state in epilepsy may be very different in different instances, and may require extremely different modes of treatment.

I append here a summary of cases of epilepsy.

No. 35.—W. B., m., æt. 29, had suffered two years off and on with attacks of non-convulsive epilepsy occurring every fourteen days. Has warning by sensations in head for two or three minutes before each attack. Under increasing doses of strychnia carried up to gr. $\frac{1}{10}$ ter die, the interval was prolonged to eighty-nine days.

No. 36.—S. H., f., æt. 16, ad. with convulsive epileptic attacks; last two intervals were fourteen and seventeen days. Catam. regular. Under alisma plantago the interval was prolonged to thirty-four, and again to seventy-one days, at which date she was discharged, having had no return. Admitted again with recurrence five weeks later, same treatment pursued; —the first interval was thirty-three days, then she had three fits in ten days: —alisma was continued and she took beside tr. ferri muriat. $\mathfrak{m} x +$ tr. opii $\mathfrak{m} v$ ter die; the next interval was twenty-seven days, and then the same treatment was continued 100 days without relapse; she was then discharged, and has not, though more than a year has passed, presented herself again.

No. 37.—E. B., m., æt. 17. Ill four years with epileptoid attacks on ad.; he has four to six in the day and many at night. Digestion bad. Alisma of no benefit. Tannin, and subsequently tannin and opium, with at first acid. muriat. + acid. hydrocy. dil. and afterwards tr. arnicæ was given for eighty-four days with great advantage, so that he was free from attacks in the day, but often had a "touch" at night. For the last six weeks he was under my observation he did the work of a light place.

No. 38.—W. S., m., æt. 20. Subject to fits seven years, had three fits last week, has usually about twelve a month. His head aches much and gets hot before the attacks, and he has sparks before his eyes. Under extr. bellad. gr. $\frac{1}{2}$ ter die with mist. ferri laxans he had no fits for eighteen days, and did not attend afterwards.

No. 39.—J. N., m., æt. 22. Has had fits for eighteen months, about

---

[1] "Cyclop. of Prac. Med.," art. Puerp. Convulsions.

two a week generally, but is sometimes a month without any. He took extr. bellad. gr. ½ *bis die* for 105 days, and had no fits all the time, only threatenings, in which he stated that his hands twitch and start, and his legs get weak; medicine omitted.

No. 40.—E. E., m., æt. 48. Has epileptic attacks at intervals of about one month; has had none now for ten months. Head cut deeply several years ago by a fall from his box while driving. He was senseless for a week, and had bleeding from the right ear. He seemed to recover from this, but in about two months had a fit partly induced by the heat of the weather, ever since then has been subject to the fits, which occur without warning. There is a cicatrix on the forehead which is adherent to the bone, but not very tender. This cicatrix was blistered, and he took tr. hyoscy. $\mathfrak{m}$xx *ter die*, with ol. morrh. ʒj. Under this treatment he improved very much, became less nervous, his vision which had been misty got clearer, and no attack occurred. He described himself at the end of sixty-seven days "as a man compared to what he was." Subsequently, however, the attacks recurred.

No. 41.—F. B., f., æt. 31. A very nervous subject, has fits occurring at irregular intervals; is weak and trembling. She took strychnia in doses gradually increased from gr. $\frac{1}{20}$ to gr. ¼ *ter die*, with iron and liq. opii sed. with great advantage. Subsequently she had tannin with small doses of morphia and argenti nitras. The frequency and severity of the fits appeared to be controlled, and her general condition was improved.

No. 42.—A. R., m., æt. 11. Ill for a year with fits, recurring at first every two months, but every day for the last week. They last five minutes to an hour. In the fits he bites his tongue and struggles much. Severe pain in left hypochondrium after, and is very sleepy. Has lost his speech three months. Health pretty good. Pupil of medium size. Ordered, April 23d, tr. hyoscy. $\mathfrak{m}$xv *ter die* and ol. morrh. ʒj *ter die*. May 14th. Two fits since April 23d, the last on 26th. Is much better in himself. Does not speak above a whisper. 28th. Has regained his speech. June 11th. Feels better than he has been for years; no return of fits. Discharged. He had a relapse in September, and was treated by tr. bellad. $\mathfrak{m}$5 + ferri et quinæ citrat. gr. vj *ter die* with ol. morrh.; three fits occurred from Sept. 24th to 28th, none afterwards up to Oct. 22d, when he ceased attendance.

No. 43.—J. P., m., æt. 19, ad. Oct 2, 1862. Ill six months, is subject to fits, has had nine. Last interval three weeks. Before they come on he feels unsettled in his head for a day. In the fits he shakes, has singing in the ears and falls down, lies unconscious ten minutes, but it is thirty before he is fully recovered. They occur mostly of a morning. Health otherwise good. Is growing fast. Pulse very small and feeble. He thinks that suppressed perspiration of the feet may be the cause of his attacks, but admits that he has practised masturbation. His forehead on various occasions has appeared notably hot, and the circulation in the skin over-active, while the feet and hands are apt to be cold. At one time, while they were perspiring, he felt much better. The face and ears he describes as burning for twenty minutes at once. He has various other symptoms indicative of nerve disorder, and seems to be rather of a fanciful tendency. His condition is certainly not one of plethora, but is equally remote from anæmia; the most evident abnormality is the irregularity of the circulation, the arteries of the head being disposed to admit an undue supply of blood. Atropine and belladonna did not appear to be beneficial, his head was cooler and quieter while taking extr. hyoscy.

gr. v *ter die*. An issue in the arm was of no avail, besides much other treatment, including tannin, argenti nitras, and pot. iod.

No. 44.—F. L. æt. 11, f., ad. Nov. 16th. Had fits when three years old, and was ill a long time, lost all his faculties for a month, and was paralyzed on one side. Recovered and remained well for seven years and free from fits, but since then he has had them at intervals of about six weeks. Two fits occurred in the last week. Becomes quite unconscious in the fits, which always occur during sleep; the following morning he is dull, stupid, has headache, and is very irritable. Head rather hot, has some pain in it now. Large face, red lips, pulse regular, quiet. Some warning is afforded of an approaching fit by his being tiresome and irritable the previous day. He remained under observation till Feb. 22d, when he had had no fit for three weeks, previously they occurred about once a fortnight. Tonics and blisters to the neck did not seem of benefit, zinc gave more promise of good.

No. 45.—M. S., æt. 20, f., ad. Nov. 15; ill two days. Had a fit at first, in which she bit her tongue; since then has had nine or ten fits, but not "insensible ones," left side only affected by the convulsions. Some frontal pain, better when recumbent. Has felt giddy lately, but not weak. Has passed ascarides. Cat. regular. B. open. Nov. 18th. The shaking fits in left side continue, and she has temporary loss of power over the arm, leg not affected. The fits occur very frequently, more so at night. In four days the fits had ceased, and Dec. 20th she was discharged, well. The improvement commenced as soon as she was ordered ferri et quin. citr. + tr. nucis vom. A blister applied at first to the neck was of no benefit.

No. 46.—J. K., æt. 41, m., ad. Sept. 6th. Suffers from nervous debility, which brings on fits; has been getting worse last three months. For last ten years has not debauched. Looks ill, and his face sunken. Skin cool. Pulse weak. Takes food well. B. regular. Has much pain all over his head as if his brain was on fire. Is subject to attacks of headache, lasting three or four hours, in which he vomits much yellow bile. In evenings, he feels the blood flowing up to his head for two hours, and has dreadful sensations; at other times it seems as if his life was departing he is so chilly. Every other day he experiences nervous tremblings and low spirits, with fearful apprehensions, which come on worst in the evening. The fits occur at various intervals once a month or oftener; he affirms that he is more liable to be attacked at the changes of the moon. The fits come on, he says, with palpitation and fluttering of the heart; the blood then flows to the head, and when it has reached a certain part at the back he becomes unconscious. This man was highly hyperæsthetic, and a very unpromising subject for treatment. Full doses of tonics did not seem to benefit him, but assafœtida gr. x 3*tis horis* did considerable good; "a world of good," as he stated. He remained under treatment till Feb. 27th, and had no fits during the last two months. · I regret that I did not give him ol. morrh.

No. 47.—W. A., æt. 53, male. Ill two months. Was at first confined to bed; was quite insensible at times, and used to talk wildly; had pain in head; no paralysis; no fit; since then he has recovered a good deal, but is attacked many (fourteen or fifteen) times a day with loss of speech, weakness of limbs, some giddiness. This affection soon passes off, leaving him quite well. While in the consulting-room he had an attack during which he was unable to speak plainly as before. He compares the attacks to a sudden cloud passing over the sun. When they occur while he is walking he has to stop. Pulse weak, languid, 86. Pupils nearly equal, mobile. Syphilis denied; some stricture. No worms passed, not even after a dose of male fern. On one occasion I dilated the pupils with belladonna, and examined the fundus of the eye while an attack occurred, but I could perceive no manifest pallor of the red field. Opium in gr. ½ doses *bis die* seemed to check the attacks for a while; afterwards he benefited with strychnia and tannin. His health became better; he had not to stand still when the fits came on, and they were less severe, but as frequent. This was a well marked instance of "le petit mal."

No. 48.—M. A. S., æt. 12, f., ad. Jan. 21. Ill one year. Has something like fits in which she is unconscious, and appears as if strangulated; her eyes water. They occur about once a week. Has often violent pains in eyes and head; sight dim. When six years old passed round worms, but a dose of male fern now brought none away. With tannin she benefited materially, but ceased attendance too soon. Belladonna in small doses, and a seton in the neck, did not seem beneficial.

No. 49.—H. W., æt. 64, m., ad. June 6th. Subject to epilepsy eleven years from an injury to his head, on account of which he was discharged from the police. No attack for two years till eight days ago. Has numbness in right side of face, right arm and hand, and pain down back of right leg. Feels giddy and trembling, and shaky if excited. No pain in head. If he gets up suddenly he cannot see for a time, and everything swims before his eyes. Is a painter now; has dirty teeth, no blue line. Urine quite clear, and normal-looking, not albuminous, sp. gr. 1018. With ammonia, valerian, tr. hyoscy. and tr. nucis vom. and ʒj doses of ol. morrh. *ter die* he recovered from the above symptoms, which were probably sequelæ of the attack, and felt almost as well as ever he did in his life.

No. 50.—W. H., æt. 5, m., ad. Sept. 21st. Ill since one year old with fits which occur at intervals of one to nine months, several often occur together. In the fits he cannot get his breath, is black in the face, and unconscious; screams much. After fits, has fever for several days, and is ill for three or four weeks. Last fit three weeks ago. Pulse not weak; skin hottish. Another fit occurred Oct. 14th. He took tr. ferri mur. with much benefit, and afterwards liq. pot. arsen. and ol. morrh. when some eczema appeared, and improved still further.

No. 51.—E. F., æt. 9, f., ad. Oct. 8th. Ill three months with fainting fits, but has struggling fits last fourteen days. She struggles and screams; complains that her head is coming off; loses consciousness for three-quarters of an hour. The fits begin with drowsiness; she lies down and goes to sleep, in about ten minutes the fit comes on. Had two fits yesterday in the afternoon. Before the fits commenced she used to have pains in the abdomen, and in the side like cramp; these have ceased. Is restless at night, talking and tossing about. Head not hot; urine rather pale; no appetite for meat. Is weakly. Has scrofulous disease of one foot; not anæmic; tongue clean. Nov. 6th. Appears as if her intellect was affected; is unaccountably lively after pain in head, which comes on generally about 6 P. M. The forehead is very hot then. Before this she had materially improved. She was treated till Dec. 22d with ferri et quin. citras, and improved very much, so that she was not like the same child. The fits had ceased for some time before she quitted the hospital.

No. 52.—W. S., æt. 49, m., ad. Feb. 24th. Ill ten weeks with catarrh and fits. He was suddenly seized with unconsciousness while at his work (bootmaking), and remained so for half an hour. Did not struggle, or bite his tongue; foamed at the mouth. During the fit his mouth was drawn to one side. Has only had two fits; the first came on nine, the last three weeks ago. He had one fit previously seventeen or eighteen years ago. When he talks his mouth is drawn to one side, and his tongue to the opposite. He was ordered carbonate of iron and tr. nucis vom. with bark, and subsequently ammonia. During five weeks that he remained under observation he had no return of the fit, and became much less nervous. He had one bout of sharp abdominal pain (neuralgia).

No. 53.—M. B., æt. 19, f. Ill four or five months. After having had a sore on her finger became low and weak, and then fits came on. Last week she had fits every day but one; she is much convulsed in them; they continue as a succession three-quarters of an hour. Screams in the fits, has sopor after. Complains of a lump in throat, and is very nervous. Skin cool; pulse natural; catam. regular; bowels regular; head very hot. During the six months that she remained under my care this heat of head was a constant and remarkable symptom; it was attended with very marked activity of the circulation in the head, contrasting strongly with an opposite condition in the hands and feet. The forehead presented a uniform red flush, scarcely obliterated for an instant by pressure, while in the hands the blood after being pressed out returned again very tardily. At times she had much "swimming in the head, feeling as if she should fall when she got up," and much headache in forehead and temples. The distress of the head was relieved by leeches to the temples, blisters to the neck, ice locally applied, and dry cupping. She was better during cold frosty weather. The fits occurred at various times of the day, not at night. Her speech was lost on some occasions for two hours. Debility was marked. Except that she gained strength, and that the fits were not so frequent or so strong as they were at first, not much was accomplished. She took quinine, iron, strychnia with some advantage, large doses of assafœtida seemed also beneficial, and small doses of morphia and henbane. Hydrocyanic acid was of no avail. This case was certainly not mere hysteria; the state of the circulation in the head was distinctly abnormal, and assuming the intracranial to be similar it would account for most of the symptoms. There was no real plethora, the primary and essential defect was loss of tone in the cranial vessels and nerves, a permanent sympathetic paresis.

No. 54.—A. W., æt. 32, f., ad. July 6th. Ill five weeks, has had one fit each Friday. In each fit the two inner fingers begin pinching and shooting, and twitch; the pricking, &c., extends up the right arm to the side of the head, "the arm works," and then she loses all consciousness; she falls down, her face is drawn to one side, she is convulsed and bites her tongue (seen). The feeling in the head sometimes occurs without a fit. Is always drowsy. Does not sleep well. Suckling five months. Has had eight children, some born dead, only two living. None of them have had eruption. Not anæmic. Very nervous and excitable. Dyspepsia lately. Bowels irregular, open much at times. She only remained seventeen days under observation in which time no improvement took place. She took iron, ammonia, and henbane.

No. 55.—E. F., f., æt. 15 months, seen April 25th. Ill nine months, first had severe diarrhœa which was followed by slight convulsions, and then by bad fits, which have continued ever since, occurring generally every week. Sometimes the fits occur on Saturday morning, at 8 A. M. for several weeks together, though there may be fits also in the intervening days. The most remarkable phenomena as I see her at present are the great collapse of the ribs in inspiration, the prolonged groaning character of the inspiration, a certain amount of cough and attempt at expectoration. She swallows well. Consciousness is impaired since her illness, but not lost; there is no evident paralysis. Urine appears natural, but very scanty. Pupils of medium size. No fit now for eight days, the fits last about five minutes, but it is half an hour sometimes before she is quite restored. She has been breathing as at present for ten or eleven days. Crams very much her fingers into her mouth, no trace of teeth, is fed from a bottle. Death occurred a few days after; a careful autopsy discovered nothing morbid in the brain, nor in the organs of the chest and abdomen.

N. 56.—S. S., æt. 45, m., ad. December 22d. Ill about four weeks, since a fall from a height of about eight feet. Is of stout, rather short make and sanguineous aspect. He had been cupped at the back of the neck ad ʒviij, had a seton put in the left arm, tartar emetic ointment applied to the neck, and had been purged without benefit. He suffered from attacks of the following kind occurring five or six times a day. He begins to wink, and then both eyes become drawn quite under the lids towards the right, one inwards and the other outwards; he then loses consciousness for four or five minutes, and falls down, does not scream, but moans as if choked. I witnessed the attacks more than once; they were perfectly involuntary, not attended by much flushing of head. He feels tremulous and nervous; does not sleep well; has a trembling in the head when he lies down. Not an intemperate man. No syphilis. Bowels open. Pulse of good force, skin warm. Was similarly affected two years ago, and got well after six months. He remained under observation till Feb. 20th, when he ceased to attend, having had only slight attacks in the previous fifteen days, and having been nearly free during several former weeks. Assafœtida in gr. x doses 2*dis horis*, and iron and quinine seemed to be the efficient means in subduing the neurosis.

No. 57.—A., æt. 39, m., has had a touch of African fever formerly. Ad. April 2d. Ill three or four months, on and off. At first he lost his speech, it is now impaired. His arms and legs feel weak at various times, chiefly on exertion. Has a dull pain across the forehead, not constant, and not worse when lying down. Head rather warm; no tenderness in cranium or spine; intellect seems obscured, memory impaired; skin cool, pulse weak, pupils sluggish, left larger than right. Subsequently he had trembling of the right arm and leg. Two blisters to the neck. Pot. iod. et hydr. bichl. produced improvement; he ceased attendance, having, as he afterwards stated, got quite well. He was readmitted Feb. 23d of the following year, having then been ill a week. His condition was sufficiently obscure, he appeared to be in a state of general excitement and fussiness. His knees and right arm tremble. Sometimes he falls down, sometimes loses consciousness. He is pallid, free from fever, head rather hot, urine not albuminous. I gave him ammonia and arsenic with which he improved a good deal, his right arm became steady, his speech improved, no loss of consciousness occurred, but he had on two occasions some appearance of rheumatism in the right knee. Just after this in the night at 10 P. M. he suddenly lost his speech, and remained speechless till his admission into the ward March 31st (two days later). The day after he had a fit, consisting of convulsive movements of all the body, but chiefly of the right side, with rigidity of the flexors of the arm and extensors of the knee. April 5th. There is complete paralysis of motion and sensation in the right arm and leg, which are relaxed. Mouth is drawn to the left. Reflex movements could be excited in the paralyzed leg. The fits above mentioned recurred frequently during his stay in the hospital, the intellect remaining clear. They lasted two or three minutes, several occurring one after the other; they were not succeeded by coma; he was able to recognize his children immediately after them. No fits occurred for about twenty-four hours before death, which took place April 10; but he became very weak, unable to swallow, and gradually sank, his intellect remaining clear to the last. His evacuations were all passed under him. At the P. M. the cerebral veins and sinuses were found full of dark blood, the smaller veins were filled, but the gray matter was not dark, nor the minute vessels injected. Considerable subarachnoid effusion existed, and there were some patches of opacity over both hemispheres. The substance of the brain was firm and consistent, the white matter congested. In each lateral ventricle there were ℨvj of serous fluid, and the vessels on the walls were congested. Nothing morbid at all was found in the brain or cerebellum, though they were very carefully examined for two hours; nor was there anything morbid in the spinal cord. Microscopic examination detected nothing in the brain. The thoracic and abdominal viscera were fairly healthy.

No. 58.—E. C., f., æt. 28, mar., no children, ad. March 28th, 1861. Has been ailing since she had inflammation of lungs and liver three and a quarter years ago. Three months ago was first attacked with giddiness, and just three weeks after an epileptic fit occurred. After this (the first) they returned at the rate of four or five a day, and now occur three or four times a week. When the attack comes on she turns pale and giddy, feels as if a blow was given her on the head, falls down, loses consciousness, and becomes very sick five or ten minutes after. She has constant giddiness, is very anæmic. No tenderness about head. No worms. P. 132. Catam. regular, but excessive. Her health is better during the summer. Her mother may have had fits, but a brother and a sister are quite free. Pupils equal. In January, 1863, she stated that her head always felt hot, and was benefited by cold applications; when she becomes giddy her head is dreadfully hot. The recumbent posture relieves her head generally, it aches less; when erect it feels weary as if she needed to rest it against something. She feels weak and weary, and looks languid. March, 1864. During the last five months she has become the subject of very marked proptosis, the globes are not nearly covered by the lids, they feel tense, and (especially the right) are notably injected; the lids are also very red. The vision is pretty perfect; she can read for a short time, but afterwards the letters become confused. There is great fulness and bulging of the upper eyelids, and great pain in, and above and behind the globes. This pain is much aggravated at night, and destroys her sleep. There is also very forcible pulsation of both carotids, when one of them is compressed the pain in the eye is somewhat relieved. No thyroid enlargement. No palpitation. Ice applied to the eye and to the neck gives more relief than anything else, but it is only temporary; she goes to sleep, but is soon aroused by the pain. The radial pulse is very weak and rapid, varies (sitting) from 120 to 140. The pupils are very small. The fits have become much less frequent. In the summer of 1862 she had a period of 110 days with only one slight attack, and in 1863 she remained exempt from June 16th to December 23d (189 days). Since then she has had two or three attacks. The remedies which have done most good have been tannin gr. x + extr. belladon. gr. j in pil. ij *ter die*, and sulphate of zinc + extr. hyoscyam. gradually increased up to 18 grains of the former and 21 of the latter daily. An issue was made in the left arm in 1861, and has been kept open most of the time since. Large doses of morphia have been given to procure sleep at night lately and with good result, but quin. disulph. gr. xx h. s. was even more efficient for some days. The urine is sometimes pale and clear, sometimes deposits lithates; it is not albuminous, deposits no casts.[1]

No. 59.—H. H., m., æt. 38, ad. Oct. 5th. Had a fit yesterday evening at 11 P. M., had none since his first, five years before. He went into the fit with a loud cry, fell down, and bit his tongue. Does not know how long he was in the fit, but was told by his friends that he had another at 4 A. M. this morning. The attacks occur during sleep, without any previous intimation. Not at all anæmic. Is a teetotaller. No worms. Syphilis denied. Does not suffer from pain in head. Pulse steady. No epilepsy in his family. Is out for many hours cab-driving. He took. pot. iod. + ammon. carb. with benefit, but attended only about a month.

Among the above 25 cases there are 16 males and 9 females, and among sixteen other cases I have notes of, there are 7 males and 9 females. In the total number, therefore, the males are to the females in the proportion of 23 to 18. The oldest patient was a male, æt. 64, the youngest a female æt. 15 months. There are 10 under the age of 20 years, and only five above that of 40. The attacks were non-convulsive in three instances; No. 47 was a marked example of "le petit mal." Injuries to the head were the assigned cause of the fits in Nos. 40 and 49. In almost all the remaining cases the cause was quite obscure. General hyperæsthesia and nervousness was marked in Nos. 41, 43, 46, 53, and 54, but in quite as many or more instances there was no trace of it. The fits were few and far between in Nos. 49, 52, and 59. There were other indications of nervous disorder in Nos. 39, 40, 42, 43, 46, 51, 52, 57, 58. Hyperæmia of the head was a notable symptom in Nos. 38, 43, 53, 58. Debility was evident in Nos. 41, 43, 46, 51, 53, 54, 55, 58. There were premonitory symptoms in Nos. 35, 38, 43, 44, 51, 54. In 54 there was a regular aura commencing in the hand, in the other cases there were various sensations in the head. Pain in the head was complained of to a notable extent in Nos. 46, 51. Giddiness was a marked symptom in Nos. 45, 49, 53, 58. In 52 there was some amount of facial paralysis after the fit. In Nos. 35 and 41 strychnia appeared to have a good effect. In 53 and 56 large doses of assafœtida appeared useful. In No. 36 alisma plantago was perhaps curative, but in 37 it quite failed. In Nos. 38, 39, 40, 42, 58 belladonna or henbane seemed decidedly beneficial, though as they were mostly given with other drugs it is difficult to tell how much of the result was due to their action alone. The remedies with which they were usually associated were zinc, tannin, and ol. morrh. In Nos. 45, 51, 52, 56 tonic treatment, ammonia, iron, and quinine seemed to be really curative. The nocturnal restlessness and *quasi*

---

[1] The sequel of this case has been very sad, but instructive. After the proptosis and congestion of the orbital tissues and lids had existed nearly six months the pain became greatly exaggerated, the conjunctiva in both eyes greatly chemosed with fibrinous exudation, and effusion of lymph took place into both anterior chambers. Prolonged hyperæmia has thus issued in destructive inflammation.

delirium, and the previous neuralgia incline me to think that No. 51 was *au fond* a case of malarioid remittent. No. 59 is a case of great interest. The patient is a calm, sensible, uncomplaining sufferer, tractable and reliable, and regular in her attendance. The improvement in her state has been so marked that I am hopeful she will ultimately be quite restored. The recent development of proptosis with great vascular congestion in and around the globes and strongly-marked pulsation of the carotids is highly suggestive, especially when the absence of thyroid enlargement is taken into account. It is difficult not to regard the proptosis, &c. as a part of the original nerve disorder, a variation probably of its seat. The head had previously been very hot, when giddiness came on, indicating that an increased flow of blood to some part of the encephalon ensued at such times. Latterly the branches of the ophthalmic artery seem to have been unduly relaxed and to have given rise to the orbital hyperæmia. The carotids are in the same state. The fact that there is no thyroid enlargement seems to prove that the smaller arterial ramifications are the main controllers of blood-supply. As long as they retain their due tone and consequent calibre no excessive flow of blood to a part will ensue, though the main trunks may be throbbing violently for lack of tonicity in their coats, or from paresis of their regulating nerves. When, however, the small arteries, and ultimate ramifications of the sympathetic are thus affected the tissues which they supply have their vital actions increased, and we then get various phenomena according to the normal function, original excitability, and tendency of the organs concerned. It is very curious thus to find an excess of vital manifestations essentially depending upon a failure of vital power (vis nervosa). It is most probable I think that in the earlier period of this case increased blood-flow took place towards the medulla oblongata and mesocephale. It is very evident how important it must be to distinguish cases where the cerebral excitability is primary, and where the hyperæmia if any occur is consequent on this excitability, and those where as in the above instance the pathological order is reversed.

In those instances where long intervals of apparently perfect health intervene between the fits there does not seem to be any indication for the administration of drugs. The diet and mode of life should be however duly regulated, the object kept in view being to increase power and diminish excitability.

In the two fatal cases which occurred the autopsy manifested no cause for the disorder. The general conclusion which I am led to adopt from the above review of my cases is that epilepsy in its nature is a disorder of the nervous centres quite analogous to neuralgia and hyperæsthesia of the nerves. Some cases approximate to the former, but the majority to the latter condition, and in some the morbid action is maintained and aggravated by hyperæmia, either depending on arterial relaxation, or on local attraction of blood. The disease which it most resembles is, I think, scrofulous ophthalmia.

CHAPTER XIV.

HEADACHE.

HEADACHE is a symptom present in so many and different conditions that it has no claim to be considered a distinct disease. The article upon the subject in Dr. Copland's Dictionary treats of the various kinds in a very exhaustive manner. I shall only enumerate the various kinds of inorganic headache that are met with, and give some illustrations of them. One of the commonest kinds is that which coexists with prostration of nervous power, in which I conceive the state of the brain much resembles that of a nerve suffering from neuralgia of debility. A second is hyperæsthetic headache, where, along with more or less debility, there is considerable excitement and hyperacute sensibility to all impressions. The two forms are certainly distinct, though transitional instances are more frequent than typical. The means which relieve the former are apt to aggravate marked cases of the latter. A third form of headache is the result of active hyperæmia, and is characterized by fulness of the vessels, heat of head, by being aggravated (this is not invariable) by the recumbent posture, and by the relief afforded by cold applications, purgation, and depletion. A fourth form is sympathetic, depending on disorder of the stomach or of some other organ. Dr. Sieveking describes a hæmorrhoidal form of headache, sudden, violent, and vertiginous, attended with impaired vision and irritability of temper, and probably dependent on rectal irritation. (V. Med. Times and Gaz., Aug. 12, 26, 1854.) In all these I consider the encephalon itself to be directly affected. In hemicrania and other forms of neuralgic headache the nerves of the scalp suffer. In rheumatic headache the same occurs in some instances, in others the nerves of the dura mater are implicated in the morbid action. Gouty headache may present various grades of irritative or inflammatory phenomena correspondiug closely with the neuralgic or inflammatory results of the action of the materies morbi in other parts. In many cases there will be indications of the existence of the gouty diathesis, but it is very important to be aware that, as Dr. Copland states, it may be the first manifestation of the disorder. Trousseau relates an interesting example of hemicrania replaced by gout, and states that the articular and the neuralgic affection often alternate in the same individual, and that the latter may be the sole manifestation of the diathesis in the offspring of gouty parents. Rheumatic and neuralgic headaches are often very difficult to distinguish except by testing them with remedies. Pot. iodidum or guaiacum is usually curative of the one as tonics are of the other. The urine is more often lateritious in the rheumatic than the neuralgic disorder, and there is less debility. In gouty affections we shall generally find a deficiency of uric acid in the urine if the total amount passed in twenty-four hours be estimated. Syphilis not unfrequently occasions headache, or rather pain in the head, of varying degrees of severity, often much resembling the results of rheumatism. It is generally amenable to full doses of iodide, but may require mercury.

No. 60.—Mrs. F. S., æt. 38 (?), seen July 27th, 1861. Has been much in India, but never had fever or ague. Has no mental distress. Looks thin, wan, and poorly; forehead large, peculiar expression of countenance giving one the idea of impending insanity. Has suffered for three or four years with headache paroxysmal, but very severe indeed while it lasts, which is from twelve to forty-eight hours. It returns once or twice a week, is relieved by nothing but chloroform (inhaled) and morphia; the latter acts slowly, she takes 2 grains without any soper ensuing; chloroform relieves immediately. At the time when the headache is present is almost distracted by violent throbbing at the vertex, which is somewhat relieved by firm pressure. Head then seems hot to her, it is cool now. She can lay her head down without increasing the pain. Superficial veins of neck very large. Does not sleep well always, has sometimes restless nights preceding the attacks of headache. Some decayed teeth, but they cause no notable uneasiness. No worms. Urine palish, free, acid, sp. gr. 1011. P. soft, weak. Skin cool. She was ordered strychnia with citrate of iron and quinine *ter die*, and to take supper with malt liquor at night. In about six or seven weeks she had benefited very much, slept better, but still had to take a cup of cocoa in the course of the night. At this time she had hemicrania of the right side, which she said was quite different from the head-attacks she had had previously. The veins of the neck did not appear full now. A month later she suffered pain extending down the right leg from the hip to the toes, apparently in the centre of the limb, quieted by cold, and induced by heat. Nov. 8th. Pain has shifted from leg to arm, the right shoulder and arm are stiff and painful each morning, the pain runs down the arm. "It is a misery to turn or move in bed." During the day the pain subsides. Headaches less and less. This arm-pain was soon cured by chloroform liniment and the Turkish bath. Jan. 6th, 1862. The headache has recurred the last three weeks with hysterical symptoms and depression. It is most probable that the neuralgia in this case was of malarious origin, although there was no history of fever. The tonic treatment plainly averted to a great extent its recurrence. The disorder exhibited the usual shifting tendency of neuroses, its hemicranial manifestation, and the quasi-rheumatic affection of the limbs was less distressing than the original in which the brain itself seemed to suffer.

No. 61.—Mrs. W., æt. 24, has been much in India during her early life, and has been under my care previously for neuralgia of the side, and for erythematous flushing of the face. Has had brow-ague three or four times. Pregnant about seven weeks. She has been suffering severely for three or four days with pain in the head chiefly on the left side, and such great irritability that mere rustling of paper distresses her. Her face looks somewhat flushed and oppressed. P. rather excited. Appetite tolerable. T. clean.

Urine pale. B. open. The headache remits during the day, but comes on severely about 5 or 6 P. M. During the night she is markedly feverish, and wakes often from short dozing sleep. With quinine at first, and quinine and iron afterwards, the headache was reduced to a minimum in about a week.

No. 62.—A. P., æt. 20, f., ad. April 29th. Ill five or six months. Suffers with head; "comes over with such sensations that she quite goes out of her mind." Head cool; it feels giddy and confused. Left hand and arm get numb at times and her speech fails. Cat. regular. Much palpitation. Functions in order. Ammonia, iron and calumba were highly beneficial.

No. 63.—A. H., æt. 50, f., ad. Nov. 16th. Ill three months, head feels light, and sore and weak, occasionally has sharp darting pains in it, which make her stagger. Can't sleep at night for tenderness of head. Some deafness. With iron, calumba, and cod-liver oil, and henbane at night, all her symptoms very much improved.

No. 64.—H. P., æt. 10, m., ad. Feb. 6th. Never well from birth. Has frontal headache almost every day, eyes feel as if on fire. Suffers with violent attacks of sickness, retches much. "Eyes work continually." Has occasionally swelling of the dorsum of the left foot. Ague has occurred in the village where he lives. Is languid. With citrate of iron and quinine + tr. nucis vom. he got a great deal better; after an accidental relapse (perhaps from some wrong medicine being given) pot. iod. was added to the tonic and ol. morrh. given, which he continued till June 10th, when he was fairly well except being still rather weak. In the first of these four cases there was extreme neuralgic suffering, in the second there was much of this and also of hyperæsthesia, in the third the brain seems to have been in a condition resembling that of "anæsthesia dolorosa" in a nerve; the last affords an example of cerebral debility and neuralgia, with associated stomach disturbance. That mere exhaustion of the brain will cause gastric disorder I am satisfied. A lady, æt. 70, of very feeble power told me that she had always been very liable to sick headache, she remembered perfectly that going about sight seeing used constantly to induce an attack of sick headache attended with nausea and retching.

No. 65.—M. A. B., f., æt. 39, ad. Nov. 3d. Ill a week, has been suckling eight months. Has a peculiar pain in the head which she cannot describe; is very irritable, and at times says she is quite violent. Is afraid to be trusted by herself. Does not sleep at night. Memory very failing, can't remember from one day to the next. Can't endure the slightest noise. Pulse 100, small. Pupils of medium size. She benefited very much with ammon. carb. gr. v + æth. chlor. ℞ x + liq. opii sed. ℞ xx *ter die*. In a week she slept better, appetite was better, the pulse had fallen to 72, and was of good volume. In this case there was a marked blending of the symptoms of cerebral exhaustion with those of hyperæsthesia and excitement; pretty full doses of sedatives were certainly beneficial combined with stimulants, but did not act so well alone, as they were given for the first three days.

No. 66.—C. W., æt. 44, ad. Jan. 12th. Has suffered from headaches almost constantly for the last two years. Is of stoutish make, not anæmic. States that she suffers from pain in the chest, and in the arms and legs, which is much worse at night; can't lie down in bed, feels suffocated and is obliged immediately to get out. Has frequently frightful dreams. At times feels almost induced to commit suicide. Bowels very confined unless she takes medicine. Pulse 108. Has much pain at mid-sternum extending up into throat with sensation of choking. March 12th. Is in a state of the most extreme hyperæsthesia, crying and agitated, can't sleep, walks about the room all night long. No appetite. Urine scanty and thick. Says her illness commenced with rheumatic pains in left arm extending up to shoulder, these have been gradually leaving her, and the arm, which was very weak so that she could not hold a teacup, has become much stronger. Her head and nerves became affected three or four days after the rheumatism came on. June 4th. She was discharged very much improved, had been mending steadily since March 16th. She was treated at first with aperients and antispasmodics and with material benefit, but after the relapse March 12 she took calomel and colchicum at night, daily *ad vices iv.*, then *alt. noct.* for a week, then twice a week for more than a month. Black draught was given almost daily for nearly the same time. The hyperæsthesia and nervous distress in this case were very great, quite verging on insanity, and proving that the cerebrum was essentially involved in the morbid action. There was no indication of gout. I doubt whether mere purging was the efficient remedy as she had taken aperients pretty freely before her relapse, including at last nightly doses of ol. Crotonis ♏ ½.

No. 67.—T. A., æt. 26, m., ad. May 2d. Ill four years, always weakly. Is very nervous, and has pains in his head. Complains that strange almost uncontrollable thoughts come into his mind. Anything that excites him in the day makes him wake up and call out at night. Feels very weak. Bowels costive. Quinine, iron, strychnia, and opium were of very great service to him. He remained under treatment over three months.

No. 68.—J. D., æt. 7, m., ad. Dec. 4th. Ill twelve months. Is very violent and excited at times, tries to get out of the window, throws things about, is restless at night and has delusions. Takes food ravenously, is never satisfied. Complains at times of pain in the head and chest. Is much worse last three months, much worse at the change of the moon. Skin cool. Pulse feeble. Tongue clean. Bowels open. He took at first ferri et quin. citrat. gr. vj + pot. iod. gr. iij *ter die*, and a small opiate at night for three weeks, subsequently tr. nucis vomicæ was substituted for the pot. iod. He ceased attendance March 2d, but I heard of him on April 18th that he continued much better, more submissive and controllable, and attended school both Sunday and weekday, which he had not been able to do previously. In all these three cases there was very marked cerebral hyperæsthesia and excitement with more or less pain in the head. In the first the condition was of asthenic character, purgatives were of marked benefit and stimulants unavailing. In the two latter tonics and sedatives were of marked remedial efficacy. It is most probable in the first case that the disorder was induced by some morbid condition of the " primæ viæ," while in the others it seems to have been based chiefly on debility. It may depend very much whether the morbid action affect the nerve-cells or the white fibres which result is produced, viz., mental excitement or pain. Pain we know is caused by an enfeebled condition of nerves, and delirium we also know results from cerebral exhaustion. The phenomena vary with the tissue affected.

No. 69.—E. A., f., æt. 32, ad. Aug. 30th. Ill fourteen days, ailing a long while. Suffers with dreadful headache and sickness; the headache extends from the front to the back, is constant, and is not affected by position. Left side of face, and tongue, and arm, and hand are numb; the numbness begins in the tips of the fingers, and extends upwards to the face, lips, and tongue. At these times her speech becomes thick, and continues so for an hour at times. The attacks of numbness occurred two or three times a week or oftener. Has no appetite, food causes pain, and is vomited directly. Has a sensation of tremor at stomach. Bowels open. Tongue whity. Skin cool. Pulse good. Feels very weak. Head a little hot. For the first three days she had strychnia gr. $\frac{1}{20}$ ter die, but without any benefit. A blister was then applied to the epigastrium, and she took acid. hydrocy. dil. $\mathfrak{m}$ v + mist. pot. citrat. ʒj (efferv.) ter die. This soon stopped the sickness, and then tannin pills were given bis die in addition. By Oct. 16th she was very much better, the stomach was right; she had had two returns of the numbness but much less than it used to be. In this case the gastric disorder was primary and the head-pain and cerebral paresis were produced as I believe by an inhibitory action exerted through the sensory nerves of the stomach on the higher nervous centres. Various morbid conditions of the primæ viæ will give rise in predisposed persons to headache. Dr. Prout[1] describes excessive acidity of the cæcum as producing in certain persons severe frontal headache, attended with complete intolerance of light and sounds and a state of mind bordering on delirium. After a longer or shorter duration the pain ceases, sometimes quite suddenly; and this sudden termination Prout connects with a relaxation of a spasm of the bile-duct, and a flow of bile into the intestines, partly from a description of the sensations which others have invariably experienced, and partly from his personal experience of the disorder.

CHAPTER XV.

VERTIGO.

This symptom, for it scarcely attains the rank of an independent disorder, is of sufficient interest and importance to require a brief notice. Its relation to epilepsy is recognized in the term epileptic vertigo, which is applied to the lesser form of the malady. It is eminently a dynamical disorder, as though often occasioned by toxic agents its most exquisite forms are certainly generated by influences of a totally different kind. It occurs as Dr. Copland justly observes in predisposed persons both from excess and from deficiency of blood supply to the brain. It is also produced by various causes of cerebral debility without any notable variation of the circulation. Any sudden diminution of the pressure exerted upon the encephalon by the blood circulating through it and by the subarachnoid liquid seems to induce giddiness. As regards the blood the effect of impending syncope is familiar. As regards the subarachnoid fluid we may cite Cruveilhier's experiment. He states that if the sheath of the dura mater in a dog is punctured between the atlas and the occipital bone, and the spinal fluid allowed to escape, the animal reels about like a drunken man, and lies down for hours in a state

[1] "Stomach and Renal Dis.," p. 81.

of stupor. The day following he is quite recovered. Probably the giddiness which we experience on rising quickly, after having been stooping down for some time, depends in great measure on the reflux of the subarachnoid fluid towards the spinal cavity, which while the head was depressed gravitated towards the cranial. It is worth observing that the giddiness does not occur while the pressure is increasing, but when it ceases. The vertigo which is felt after rapidly turning round, or in states of nervous debility from any quick movement of the head, cannot I think be owing to any change in the circulation or in the external pressure, but to a dynamic derangement of the cerebral structure. It is induced the more readily in proportion to the weakness of the nerve-power. Its nature is somewhat elucidated by the fact that the same feeling is experienced on looking down from a great height, when we have not a distinct perception of the objects below, or when we look at a rapidly-flowing stream when wading across it. Mayo says, "we lean upon our eyesight as upon crutches," and if we cannot lean securely, we become giddy.

I shall cite a few cases in which giddiness was the prominent symptom, partly for the sake of illustration of the subject, partly for their bearing on other affections.

No. 70.—T. C., æt. 55, admitted Feb. 5th. Of large make, face red. Ill four or five months with constant giddiness, which is better when he lies down, and after meals, except breakfast. Has had some rheumatism, but no gout. Otherwise quite healthy. P. excited and soft. Marked pulsation of the abdominal aorta. Sleeps very well. He remained under my care six months, and during almost all that time there was marked hyperæmia and heat of head, his hands and feet being cold. He was not at all hyperæsthetic. I exhausted all my skill to relieve his giddiness, but in vain. Pot. iod., antimony, colchicum, mercury to mild salivation, purging, alkalies, strychnia, and other tonics failed to effect any material improvement. Belladonna (gr. ½ of the extract *ter die*) made his throat dry, but availed nothing to lessen the hyperæmia and giddiness. A seton in the neck was the only measure that accomplished this for a time, but soon it also failed to benefit. The noteworthy points in the case are the connection of giddiness with hyperæmia of the head, the absence of any epileptoid affection, and the relief to the giddiness notwithstanding the hyperæmia in the recumbent position. The latter circumstance is to be explained by assuming that the effect of gravitation is more than counteracted by the slower action of the heart, and the greater steadiness of the head. The absence of morbid excitability in the encephalic centres was probably the element wanting to give this case the epileptoid character. This the hyperæmia did not generate.

No. 71.—E. M., æt. 63, admitted Feb. 9th, ill three months. Had smart epistaxis at first. P. now of fair force. Complains of great weakness, has not strength at times to speak. Her eyesight fails now and then, she turns giddy and falls. Much sense of pressure at vertex. Is obliged to lie with her head high. With strychnia and ol. morrh. continued for some length of time she got well. This case was clearly one of cerebral debility, yet the recumbent position was not beneficial.

No. 72.—W. C., m., æt. 54, admitted June 22d. Ill three weeks. A short, strong, thick-set man. Was attacked with giddiness suddenly, when walking about is giddy, feels as if he should pitch down; forehead hot, eyes dull, is better on lying down. Skin cool. P. Soft. B. open. Urine very clear, pale. T. clean. He had strychnia increased from gr. $\frac{1}{16}$ to gr. $\frac{1}{12}$ *ter die*, blisters to the neck and aperients, and quite recovered in two months. The tonic was certainly the efficient remedy, the others were employed rather to guard it, on account of the peculiar robust appearance of the patient. In both the latter instances I think the marked effect of the strychnia shows that the pathological state was one of cerebral debility, more than of anæmia general or local. In the latter case there was none certainly, and it was not marked in the former.

No. 73.—C. C., æt. 12, admitted Dec. 11. Ill since about June, when he was struck on the back of the head with a cricket-bat, and since then has suffered from dizziness and violent headache, not constantly, but at various times, and especially if he exerts himself. When he is ill in this way he has repeated vomiting. The attacks last one or two days. No tenderness of head. Pupils large, active. P. weak. Skin cool. Sleeps well. He took citrate of iron and quinine with tr. of nux vomica with great benefit. This case is certainly interesting as showing how the dynamical disorder remaining after a concussion may be aggravated by expenditure of the nerve-force, and removed by invigorating treatment.

Among the debilitating causes which produce giddiness none is more efficient than influenza. It is very remarkable how suddenly and severely the cerebral affection supervenes, and how long it continues. In the case recorded at p. 75, it was weeks before the patient could move his head as usual without feeling dizzy. In the following case the cause is not so clear, but I think it very likely that the total abstinence may have predisposed to the attack.

No. 74.—E. W., æt. 48, conductor, admitted Sept. 15th. Ill four days with giddiness and headache, could hardly stand this morting. Has not the least pain in head, but it feels light, he can scarcely see anything. Is not anæmic. Says he is a strong man, never ailed with his head till a month ago. Left off taking alcoholic liquor three months ago. Never drank to excess. With strychnia he improved very much.

In a case of nearly complete paralysis of both legs and the right arm from exposure to cold and wet, giddiness was at first a very marked symptom, and continued for more than a month. Tonics effected a cure. Venereal excess is often a cause of vertigo, as it is of epilepsy. A case was recently under my care in which irritable dyspepsia, general hyperæsthesia, and giddiness were very marked, and had evidently originated from this cause. He was greatly benefited by nitrate of silver, creasote and opium, and subsequently by quinine and arnica. The tendency to relapse on leaving off the quinine was evident. Even when his digestion was fairly good, he experienced some days giddiness and confusion in the head with a sense of dulness and temporary double vision. Moving his head quickly would bring on these symptoms. There is a form of giddiness which occurs in old persons, the nature of which is very obscure.

It appears as a single symptom unassociated with any special state that can account for it. It occurs paroxysmally, and is sometimes quite absent. I will not affirm that it is peculiar to the aged, but I have not met with it in others. The practical point to be aware of is that such giddiness is often curable by hydr. bichlorid., given alone or with tr. cinch. Rheumatism and syphilis affecting the brain or its membranes may cause giddiness, but, according to my experience, pain is a much more marked symptom in such states. In numerous instances of renal degeneration that I have met with giddiness has been but rarely complained of. Organic disease of the head is of course often attended with giddiness, but it is seldom, I think, a very prominent symptom, and the nature of the case is evidenced by other and graver phenomena.

CHAPTER XVI.

CHOREA.

CHOREA is a disorder of great interest to the student of nervous affections, inasmuch as its very various and curious phenomena are not only capable of being explained to a considerable extent by established principles, but also when duly considered afford valuable aid to the inquirer into the nature of analogous forms of morbid action. It is unnecessary for me to give any detailed account of this well-known disorder. I shall only allude to the facts of its being sometimes confined to the muscles of one side; of the irregular muscular action being sometimes replaced in a great degree by paralysis, the affection then bearing a notable resemblance to imperfect hemiplegia; of the frequent impairment and enfeebling of the memory, temper, and intellect; and of the occasional dependence of the phenomena on some peripheral irritation, such as is occasioned by pregnancy, dentition, constipation, &c. Some comments on these facts may be of value. Taking the one-sided form of the disorder we remark that it seems to afford a proof that the encephalon is the part essentially involved. Unless this were so it would be very difficult to conceive how the affection should be limited to one-half the body, which if this be admitted is quite intelligible. The same inference is supported also by the frequent impairment of the mental faculties, the cessation of the movements during sleep, and by the circumstance mentioned by Dr. Watson, that he has known it in several instances to be attended by pain of the head on that side only which was opposite to the agitated limbs; the disease also being speedily cured by local detraction of blood from the painful part. The enfeebling of the mental faculties, the hemiplegic form of the disorder, the promoting causes, and the usual "juvantia" clearly indicate that the disease is essentially one of debility. This debility is evidently not mere common general weakness, which is met with every day without any choreic features, but especially befalls the nervous system. Chorea is thus most correctly regarded as a paretic affection of the brain and cord; but, owing to the great tendency of weak nervous tissue to irritability, the phenomena partake as much or more of undue mobility or convulsion, as of paralysis. We have here one of the most complete exemplifications of the oftenmentioned law, that irritability and mobility rise as power fails. The production of the disorder by peripheral irritation appears to me to afford an interesting instance of inhibitory action, the morbid impression impairing the functional power of the nervous centres, and thus inducing a secondary paresis. This is certainly the case when chorea is produced by intestinal accumulations, dentition, &c., but in some instances, among which perhaps those where pregnancy is concerned should be included, the morbid impression made upon the encephalon is of a more directly irritating character. Romberg describes the chorea of pregnant females as almost always bilateral, the muscles of the face and tongue being invariably affected. "The intensity of the movements is very marked, and they are often complicated with convulsions of an epileptic character. Many complain of a sense of numbness in the affected parts. The brain is almost invariably affected, and this is shown by headache, vertigo, a wild expression of the features, rolling eyes, unconnected speech, loss of memory, and great irritability." The signs of paresis and of excitement are here evidently blended together. In connection with the production of chorea by peripheral irritation may be mentioned its repression and cure by sulphuret of potassium baths, which must act by stimulation of the cutaneous nerves, and rousing of the nervous centres to a more healthy action. Beneke believes that it is in this way that all baths produce their general effects (*v.* Schmidt's *Jahrb.*, vol. cxv. p. 101).

The result of a well-devised tonic treatment in ordinary chorea is so satisfactory that no question can exist as to the functional nature of the disorder, and that it depends upon a failure of vital power, and not at least in the great majority of cases on any morbid matter circulating in the blood. It may stand as the type of a great class of diseases, in which a primary alteration of the vital endowment, a failure or perversion of functional power is the essential circumstance. As, however, most diseases may arise from different causes, so it may fully be admitted is the case with chorea. This, as we shall presently see, the test of remedies proves. When the malady appears to be a simple paresis, a steady use of tonic treatment is clearly the course to pursue. In most cases I find citrate of iron and quinine with liq. pot. arsenitis to act very effectually. Cod-liver oil I almost always administer at the same time in small doses. In some instances strychnia is preferable; it has been highly praised by Trousseau, and I have had some experience myself of its utility. He recommended it to be given in doses sufficient to produce its physiological effects. This I have not found necessary, but it might be so perhaps in cases of great severity. The use of the interrupted galvanic current is of great service in many cases of chorea, and probably might generally be used with benefit. The two latter therapeutic results increase still further the *rapprochement* between chorea and functional paralysis. Cold bathing judiciously managed is probably second to no remedy in its calming and invigorating action on the nervous system. This means should be employed whenever it is practicable. With regard to cases where the disease is of such severity as seriously to threaten life by exhaustion, sedatives must be had recourse to. In a very bad case, detailed by Dr. Graves, morphia with arsenic proved less serviceable than stramonium with quinine, but recovery seems to be chiefly attributable to the persevering use of tepid salt water shower or douche baths three times a day.

Purgation is sometimes of marked advantage. Dr. Prichard states that he saw a boy who had nearly the aspect of an idiot after a long-continued and severe chorea restored by a course of purgative medicines. Dr. Hamilton's cases prove that purgation may be curative even when the general state seems to contra-indicate it. A boy under his care, æt. 8, was emaciated and exceedingly puny, and his abdomen lank; but he recovered after having had during ten days a "most wonderful" discharge of feces nearly equalling in weight (as H. estimates it) that of his whole body. It is very mark-worthy that the appearance of the feces is sometimes healthy at first, then becomes unnatural, "black and fetid," and subsequently healthy again. So that in a case proving refractory to other means it would be desirable to continue steadily the administration of purgatives for some time. The best drugs would probably be podophyllin and aloes, combined with extract bellad. Or aloes with a little blue pill might be given with extr. nucis vomicæ. The beneficial action of purgatives may be explained either in accordance with the inhibitory theory of the disease, or on the supposition that they remove a materies morbi from the blood. Both views may be true in different instances. The great majority of my choreic patients have had no indications of any liability to rheumatism. Of fifteen cases, I find only one in which there was any valvular cardiac affection, and this patient is reported never to have had rheumatism or anything like it. On the other hand, rheumatic affections, though abundantly common, rarely show any tendency to choreic complication. It is quite possible that, in some cases, the rheumatic diathesis, whether that mean a poison (lactic acid) in the blood or no, may be an efficient cause of chorea, just as in certain cases benefited by continued purgation we may assume the presence of some "materies morbi" in the circulation, but there is certainly no necessary or intimate connection between the two disorders. Dr. Kirke's view is that the association is not between chorea and rheumatism, but between chorea and valvular disease of the heart, excited by rheumatism. (*V. Med. Times and Gaz.*, June 20th, 27th, 1863.) He thinks the valvular disease produces the chorea. Believing as we do that one important factor of rheumatism is a paretic condition of the vaso-motor nerves, and that chorea is especially characterized by a similar state of the musculo-motor, there is certainly so far a degree of affinity between them. Just as in epilepsy, a certain predisposition being given, a fright or a worm in the bowels will set up the morbid process, so it may be that, the tendency to chorea existing, the exciting cause of rheumatism will evoke the malady. Other causes will act similarly. Thus M. Zambaco quotes two cases of chorea depending apparently upon constitutional syphilis, and ceasing under the employment of specific remedies. Increasing experience leads us to attribute a very main part in the causation, location, and shaping of disease to the previous conditions which dispose the general system, and the particular part to suffer from the subsequent morbific influence. The former are the more essential, the latter may vary greatly, both in kind, and in degree. When the former are very potent any even a slight exciting cause will, as it were, explode the mine. When the reverse is the case, the exciting causes must be much stronger, and may often fail to take effect. Though I am rather digressing I cannot help observing how these views of the supreme efficacy of the predisposing causes go to establish the retributive character of very many disorders which are often imagined to be accidental. We go on a long time infringing some law of our being, unknowing the while that every act of disobedience has added to the cumulating force of those deranged vital qualities, which one day some slight cause will call into terrible activity. The transgression is straightway followed by the dark shadow of its punishment. Chorea is quite an instance in point; the permitted indulgence in enervating habits, the neglect to insure a robust vigorous frame slowly generate the feebleness and mobility of the nervous system, which is the essence of the disease. Even though the transgression be rather the result of necessity than of indulgence, as too often occurs among the poor, or has been the act of a progenitor, the organic law is inexorable. Inflammatory affections, softenings[1] of the brain or cord, or hemorrhages[2] can very rarely be regarded in any other light than as sequelæ, or complications of chorea, and not as causative. Still Dr. Watson's important observation above quoted should be borne in mind, and the possibility of the disease being dependent on cranial or spinal meningitis is perhaps not to be denied. The analogy of epilepsy would afford some support to this view as we have already seen that exceptional cases of this disease do occur, in which free depletion is of marked advantage. In one instance under my care, chorea

---

[1] *V.* Stoffella, Schmidt's "Jahrb.," vol. cxiii. p. 160.
[2] *V.* Fuller's case, "Lancet," May 17th, 1863.

appeared as a complication of psoriasis of long standing in a girl, æt. 12. Both chorea and eruption yielded to arsenic with the aid of an issue.

Certain cases of chorea are beneficially treated by tartar emetic. My friend, Mr. Gay, has mentioned to me an instance which had been treated ineffectually with many remedies, but which recovered under small doses of this. Gillette[1] advises it to be given for successive periods of three days with intermissions of the same length. He administers it in increasing doses, so that on the sixth day of its use, the patient takes 9 grains. Vomiting, and we may presume prostration, is not desirable. It is probable that the cases where this medication succeeds are of a sthenic character, and are analogous to those of delirium in which the same remedy proves sometimes so successful.

Regulated gymnastic exercise is often very useful in this disease, even where it is very severe. For the first three or four days passive exercise alone is employed, the trunk and limbs being rubbed and moved. For the next eight or ten the limbs are made to perform regular movements, and after this the patients are able to go to the gymnasium, and pursue systematic exercise. Great improvement occurs during the first ten or twelve days of the gymnasium, then there is a check, and after this improvement proceeds steadily. Choreic grimaces and contortions may be treated on the same plan by making the patient perform regulated movements. The beneficial effect results no doubt from the improvement produced by the exercise in the functional power of the motor nervous apparatus.

With regard to the curious nerve disorders occasionally met with, which have more or less resemblance to chorea, epilepsy, and hysteria, as I know nothing of them from personal experience I shall only remark that they seem either to be connected with irregular menstruation, or to be produced by imitative sympathy, or by some morbid emotional excitement. Probably in most of these cases the liberal employment of cold affusion, both actually and metaphorically, would powerfully tend to arrest the morbid manifestations. Nothing we know promotes such proceedings more than sympathy and attention, and nothing is more decidedly repressive than "throwing cold water" upon the exhibition. Bricheteau[2] gives an account of an epidemie of chorea in one of Monneret's wards. Eight females contracted the disorder from the spectacle of one who was severely affected in the course of five days, and more would probably have been attacked had not the contagious influence been arrested by isolating the patients. Constans[3] records the occurrence of an epidemic of hysterical demonomania. The inhabitants of Morzines in Haute Savoie, amounting to about 2,000, live in a state of great poverty and bad hygiene. The epidemic lasted four

---

[1] "Ann. de Thèrap.," 1859, p. 102.
[2] "Gaz. des Hôp.," No. xlvi., 1863.
[3] Med. Critic and Psycholog. J.," Jan. 1863.

years and affected as many as 110 persons. They were termed possessed, were mostly celibates, chloro-anæmic, or scrofulous, and suffered from gastralgia or dysmenorrhœa. Everything gave occasion for a paroxysm, especially the expression of a doubt that they were possessed. The phenomena were partly hysterical, partly maniacal. The affected retained sufficient consciousness not to injure or expose themselves in the most disordered actions. The epidemic was arrested by removing the priest, and intimidating the people by the presence of soldiers. The influence of diseased morale is sufficiently apparent here.

CHAPTER XVII.

PARALYSIS AGITANS.

It appears to me a question whether two distinct affections are not often comprehended under this name. For on the one hand it appears pretty certain that there is one form which is met with in old persons, is quite incurable, and is associated with if not dependent on organic wasting changes in the nervous centres; while another form occurs in younger persons, is more curable, and therefore is presumably not dependent on organic change. Stoffella[1] relates the case of a man, æt. 79, who had the affection five years before his death. At the autopsy he found traces of atrophy of the brain with secondary dropsy of the ventricles and of the cerebral membranes, and an apoplectic cyst as large as a pea in the right optic thalamus; the pons Varolii and medulla oblongata were remarkably stiff, the arteries at the base calcareous, and the lateral columns of the cord, especially in the lumbar region, traversed by grayish opaque streaks, which as well as the indurations in the pons and medulla resulted from embryonal connective tissue. Cohn,[2] who has recently published a paper founded on an experience of six cases, gives two autopsies,[2] in one of which there was marked cerebral atrophy, and in the other wasting of the cord opposite the second cervical vertebra. The ages of the patients, both males, were 49 and 74 years. The first had been employed in using mercury. Skoda[3] details the autopsy of a female, æt. 34, who had been affected about 2½ years, and died of variola. The brain was tough, the pia mater œdematous, the walls of the ventricles, the fornix, pons Varolii, medulla oblongata, and cord were remarkably stiff, both optic nerves were flattened and stiff. In some opaque reddish spots in the brain the nerve-tissue was destroyed by embry-

[1] Schmidt's "Jahrb." vol. cxiii. p. 39. [2] Ibid., vol. cviii. p. 303.
[3] Ibid., vol. cxix. p. 294.

onal connective tissue, which occasioned also the induration of the pons and medulla. The muscles were very fatty, the neurilemma of the nerves of the upper limbs was thickened.

The following histories may serve as an example of the more curable forms of the disease. A male,[1] æt. 57, came under Dr. R. Reynold's care suffering with vertigo and general disturbance with paralytic tremor of the whole right upper limb, which in the situation of the biceps was 4° F. hotter than the other. The sensibility was unaffected. After five applications of an 120-link Pulvermacher's chain each lasting an hour the spontaneous jactitation completely ceased. By continuing the same treatment every other day the power of the arm was almost quite restored in a month. The disease was recent, having commenced only fifteen days before he was submitted to treatment. Graves[2] gives the case of a female, æt. 25, who after a severe fright became vertiginous and hemiplegic and was laid up in bed three months. The hemiplegia gradually declined, but the muscular power remained weak, and very imperfectly under voluntary control, most of the muscles being in a state of perpetual motion. Amaurosis also affected both eyes during the disease, but one recovered completely, the other very imperfectly. She could not walk slowly, and when she had commenced walking she could not stop without considerable difficulty. The following cases have come under my observation at St. Mary's, the two latter being under my own care.

No. 75.—S. M., f., æt. 12, ad. April 3d. Of healthy aspect. Ill three months with catarrh and cough, last three weeks has had vomiting which has got worse. She rejects everything which she takes shortly after swallowing it, but has no pain in the stomach. Slight epigastric tenderness. B. costive. T. whitish. Much thirst. P. 70. Appetite good. Her right arm is in continual vibration ever since her illness commenced. Lung and heart sounds healthy. 4th. I found her asleep to-day and her arm quiet. She had two purges of calomel and haust. sennæ. On 6th she was electro-magnetized for about ten minutes, and in about one hour after the arm became quiet, and has remained so ever since, and the vomiting also has ceased. 13th. Discharged.

No. 76.—J. K., labourer, æt. 60, ad. March 16th. A broad-made strong-looking man, not anæmic. Had rheumatic fever seven years ago, not so well since. Thirty years ago he was frightened by a bull who tossed him into a hedge, and he has shook ever since. His hands and arms tremble, his hands shake so that I cannot feel his pulse. He has pretty good muscular power in his arms. He does not seem to have been intemperate. He only attended a short time on account of some lumbar rheumatism.

No. 77.—J. H., æt. 47, labourer, ad. Sept. 24th. Is a large man. Complains of tremor of the right upper extremity; the muscles of this limb have full power, but quiver and twitch constantly except while he is quiet as in bed; the pectoral muscles of that side are involved. There is some

---

[1] Schmidt's "Jahrb.," vol. cxix. p. 294.   [2] "Lancet," Dec. 3d, 1859.

tremor of the legs, but nothing like that of the arms. Both however are decidedly weak; the knees are sometimes very stiff. No numbness of the right arm, but has pins-and-needles sensations in hand sometimes. When the shaking stops he has aching in the right scapula, and along the biceps. No pain or tenderness in the spine. When first attacked his eyes were always "winking," not lately. Sight and hearing are quite good now, but his speech, memory and vision are occasionally impaired. The least excitement makes him worse. He sleeps, eats, and drinks well. Sweats very easily, much at night. Was affected in the same way two years ago, was under my care and soon got well, remained quite well for one year, then the disorder came on again at intervals; some days he would have it and others not. I gave him at first strychnia, iron and other, and faradized his arm. This treatment, especially the electricity, was rather injurious than otherwise. I changed it after eight days for tr. hyoscyami ʒss *ter die*, under which he rapidly improved and ceased attendance in a fortnight.

Petræus[1] relates two severe cases, observed in the Copenhagen Hospital, one of which proved fatal. Nothing was found at the autopsy but fatty degeneration of the heart, and pneumonic consolidation of the right lung. He remarks on the tremor not being constant in many cases, ceasing for some days and then recurring with fresh force; or changing its seat from one part to another. The tendency to steady increase is, he thinks, specially characteristic of the disease. All weakening influences whether of mind or body are apt to produce the disorder. Cohn distinguishes tremor from paralysis agitans. He considers the first as paretic debility and not as a spasm; and derives it from failure of the tone of the voluntary muscles which they receive from the nervous system. The causes of spasm and of tremor are the same. Paralysis agitans he considers as tremor complicated with palsy, the latter involving even the muscles concerned in swallowing and the sphincters, and being attended with anæsthesia. The paralysis generally supervenes at an advanced period of the disease and is usually less extensive than the tremor. Both Cohn and Copland consider mercurial tremor as an example of the paralysis agitans. Frank[2] relates the case of a widow, æt. 40, who after exposure to cold on coming out of a vapour-bath was attacked with this disorder. The movements seem, however, to have been more active than usual, and as she recovered in no long time after cupping the spine it may be doubted how far the case is comparable to the chronic affection.

It appears to me that the cases I have cited warrant the view that there exists a functional nervous affection which at least bears a very close resemblance to paralysis agitans. Between this state and chorea there is certainly no very material difference. From the success of the continuous galvanic current in Reynolds' case, and of henbane in my own especially after faradization and strychnine had failed, it seems probable that the disorder depends in some instances

---

[1] Schmidt's "Jahrb.," vol. cxvii. p. 163.
[2] Copland's Dict., art. Paralysis, p. 25.

at least on increased excitability of the nervous centres of such a quality that it will not tolerate tonics, and requires rather calmants. This varying quality of nervous matter is just one principal thing that makes the treatment of epilepsy and its allied disorders so uncertain and difficult. Whether the slighter forms of the affection may pass by long continuance into the graver and more incurable, attended with organic change, is difficult to determine, but I think it quite possible. The analogy of chorea, which, as we have seen, is complicated sometimes with decided morbid changes, is very confirmative of this view. Prolonged restless excitement of the nervous tissue in the centres is very likely, as in epilepsy, to induce a local determination of blood which gives rise to slow exudation and induration. It is somewhat remarkable that these changes affect the same localities in paralysis agitans, as they do in epilepsy. The wide difference between the irregular purposeless tremors of paralysis agitans, and the strong, steady contraction of a muscle in voluntary effort needs no exposition. It is clear that no theory can be correct which would class them together, because in both there is muscular action. The one circumstance common to both is that *some* disturbance of the molecular state which the nerve-cells assume during quiescence occurs in each. In the one this disturbance is perpetual except during sleep, owing probably to deranged nutrition of the nerve-cells. In the other the disturbance is regulated by the will, and is compensated by sufficient repose. The tendency of a habit of action, as well insisted on by my friend Dr. Sieveking, to perpetuate itself and become inveterate is not to be left out of account. The tremor, which at first, excited by some casual cause, might by appropriate means have been stilled permanently, when allowed to become habitual exceeds our power to control. The treatment of paralysis agitans in its earlier stages must I think be substantially the same as that of chorea. In its later, though there can be small hope of benefiting the patient materially, I should use hydr. bichlorid. in tr. cinchon. with ol. morrh., and sulphuret of potassium baths.

As mercurial tremor has been alluded to above as a species of paralysis agitans, a view in which I quite coincide, I will observe here that mercury may be regarded with good reason as a very poison to feeble nervous systems. The disorder of the motor nerves which it produces is essentially a chronic affection, as evidenced by the similarity of the symptoms, the existing debility, the "lædentia," and the "juvantia." Dr. Watson writes that it is aggravated by all kinds of mental emotion, and relieved temporarily by anything that tends to stimulate and fortify the nervous power. Steel is one of the best remedies for this disorder as it is for chorea and other neuroses. The inflammation of the buccal mucous membrane induced by mercury is evidently not of phlegmonous character, but of diffuse, and quasi-erysipelatous. It may be referred, I think, very reasonably to a paralysis of the vaso-motor nerves of the part.

Eczema mercuriale is a similar affection of the skin; it is apt to be attended with adynamic fever, and sometimes with delirium and convulsions. The practice of taking or giving frequent blue-pill aperients is worthy of all reprobation.

CHAPTER XVIII.

SPASMODIC AFFECTIONS.

HYPERCINESES, as Romberg terms them, seem to be of rarer occurrence than the corresponding hyperæsthesia. The same may be said of the kindred paralyses as compared to anæsthesia and neuralgia. This is somewhat remarkable inasmuch as in organic disease the relation is reversed, motor power is much more frequently impaired than sensory. In many cases spasms depend on some organic alteration, but in quite as many they are independent of it. They present two principal forms, viz., clonic and tonic; the latter are more often the result of asthenic excitement than the former. In all spasms there is a defect of volitional power, the cerebral centres no longer rule the actions in an orderly manner, and some of the lower centres seem to have usurped their authority. In some instances, the emotional are the seat of morbid excitability, in others the spinal. Often the excitability is intimately connected with debility, but this is by no means necessarily the case. Remote irritation, in the intestines or elsewhere, is a frequent determining cause of spasm. Romberg in his first volume has given one of the best accounts we possess of the different manifestations of spasm. I shall notice briefly in this place the less commonly recognized forms, having described the classical elsewhere.

Trismus is a clonic or tonic spasm of the muscles concerned in the movements of the lower jaw, and sometimes of the adjacent. It may be produced in predisposed persons by cold. One of Romberg's patients, a male, æt. 43, is subject to a *dying away* in a marked degree of the upper and lower extremities accompanied by numbness of the muscles. At the same time the masseters and the tongue become rigid, and there is dysphagia. These symptoms are brought on immediately by exposure to cold. Evidently spasmodic contraction of the arteries of the limbs coincides, in this instance, with a like state of the masticatory and lingual muscles. Various other causes may produce trismus, as dental and intestinal irritation, epilepsy, the gouty diathesis, abscess in the abdominal parietes, and hyper-excitability of the nervous centres. Dr. Fraser relates a case of severe trismus resulting from exposure to wet and cold, which was treated beneficially with Cannabis Indica given in gradually increased doses up to gr. iij. *o. h.* He improved gradually, and made a good recovery. (V. *Med. T. and Gaz.*, Feb. 7, 1864.)

Facial spasm may show itself in one or several of the muscles supplied by the seventh nerve. It may affect the orbicularis palpebrarum alone, or the buccinator. A patient under my care, suffering with periodic frontal neuralgia attended with giddiness, had also twitching of the left eyelids. The pain and giddiness were cured by iron + quinine, but not the twitching, nor was the endermic application of morphia more effectual. A lady, who had had chorea when a girl, and whose nervous power was weak and overtasked, suffered with twitchings of the face, her mouth being frequently drawn awry so that she had to hold it with her hand to steady it. She was wonderfully better in frosty weather. Immediately on eating, her face and neck became quite flushed and crimson. Here we have a paresis of arteries associated with a clonic spasm of adjacent muscles, the vaso-motor and musculo-motor nerves being no doubt in a like state. Mitchell[1] records the case of a female, æt. 50, in whom the muscles of the face, and tongue, and neck on the left side were affected at intervals of ten minutes, with rigid spasm lasting for three minutes at a time. The left side of the nose and chin was numb, the teeth were closely compressed, the nose was drawn over to the left side, and the forehead and eyebrows corrugated. The muscles of the neck rotated the head to the left shoulder, the left arm became extended, and a sense of numbness ran down in a straight line from the neck to the thumb and forefinger. The disorder ceased after the extraction of all the carious teeth. Romberg had under his care a robust man, æt. 36, who after a powerful mental emotion was attacked with slight paralysis of the left side. This disappeared after bloodletting and purging, but violent spasm set in, affecting exclusively the left half of the mouth and the platysma myoides; it persisted for four days and nights, and gradually yielded to cupping and tartar emetic, and the endermic application of morphia. Oppolzer[2] relates a case in which along with pain of the right side of the head and face, and right shoulder twitchings occurred in the facial muscles, the sterno-cleido-mastoid, the muscles of the external ear, and those of the shoulder. The muscles of both external ears were affected, the right most. The twitchings were attended with severe pain which preceded and outlasted them. Pressure on any part of the face, or head, or shoulder, arrested the twitchings, but not the pains. Volition also controlled the spasms. In the preceding cases we have examples of the causation of facial spasm by simple nervous hyperæsthesia, by remote irritation, or by sthenic excitement of the brain (probably). It is evident that much discrimination is requisite to judge correctly of the pathological state.

Strabismus is sometimes a spasmodic affection, and is produced

---

[1] "Med.-Chir. Trans.," vol. iv. p. 25.   [2] "Wien Wochenbl.," 6—8; 1861.

by dental or intestinal irritation, by inflammatory disorder at the base of the brain, and by any emotions which temporarily derange mental equanimity. Böhm states that idiots whose eyes were in a normal state at other times squinted egregiously while engaged at their lessons. As the cerebral power increases the squint lessens and disappears. This seems to indicate a diversion of *vis nervosa* from the centres of the ocular nerves to the weak and struggling hemispheres. The same author relates an interesting instance of the replacement of ague paroxysms by spasmodic strabismus. The type was at first quartan, then tertian, and lastly quotidian.

The muscles of the neck are not unfrequently affected with spasm, which is often produced by rheumatoid influences, but in other cases, as in that related by Brodie, where a wry-neck alternated with melancholia, seems to depend on dynamic nervous derangement. In one of Romberg's cases dentition was evidently the cause of the spasm. In a weakly girl, æt. 7, under my care, there was very marked tonic contraction of the left sterno-cleido-mastoid. The head was drawn to the left, much more so at some times than at others. Under the use of iron, ether, and valerian with veratria ointment locally the spasm ceased, recurred again with earache, and ceased again under the administration of pot. iod. + ammon. carb. There was a rheumatic element in the case as evidenced by some affection of the feet.

The two following cases are instances of spasms probably originating in the upper cervical region of the cord, of very obscure causation, and but little modified by treatment.

No. 78.—E. B., æt. 43, seen Oct. 3d, 1862. Has been affected for about twelve months as at present, his health, however, remaining good. Is a broad-made man with rather short neck, works at china-riveting, and thinks his work may have something to do with the disorder, as he sits with the right side of his head facing a window, and has to turn frequently to the left. He is subject to almost continual clonic spasm, especially of the left sterno-cleido-mastoid and trapezius muscles, by which the head is bowed to the left side and the shoulder is raised. Any mental excitement increases the spasm greatly. He is much worse sometimes than at others. He has a sensation of cramp in the left neck which extends down the outer side of the same arm, and is relieved by stretching it out. The muscles of the right side of the neck do not appear to be paralyzed; he can straighten his neck occasionally by a voluntary effort. In June, 1863, he had an attack of rheumatism of the right leg. April 5th, 1864. Is much better since he went down to Brighton last autumn and had sea-bathing; while in the water he was quite free from spasm, and so he is now in the morning and when he is warm, but on cold, wet and foggy days he is worse. The spasm is very much less than it used to be. Much treatment was employed in this case with but little advantage, he took ferri carb., zinci valerian., tr. aconiti, pot. iod., and citrate of quinine and iron, but with very little advantage. Subcutaneous injections of atropine and opium were fairly tried, but they disappointed my expectations. Galvanizing was apparently of benefit, the antagonist muscles being faradized, and the affected ones subjected to a continuous current. This was done under Mr. Lobb's supervision. On the whole I think the "vis medicatrix" had as much share in the improvement as the remedies. The affection seems to be specially referable to excitement of the left spinal accessory nerve, but there is nothing to show how this originated. May not such states of excitement arise in nervous centres apparently *suâ sponte*, just as they seem to do in centric epilepsy?

No. 79.—St. W., æt. 33, f., seen Nov. 14th. Aspect "spiritual." Has suffered a long time with indigestion, does not often vomit. Feels sinking in fifteen minutes after food as if she had not taken any; this is relieved by spt. ammon. fetid. Is not anæmic. B. very costive. P. above 100. Urine clear. Catam. regular. She suffers with attacks of vibratory movements of head, sometimes with arms, which are made worse by the showerbath. At times has paroxysms of violent spasmodic contractions of the diaphragm resembling hiccup attended with constant expectoration of white frothy mucus. I witnessed one of these, which lasted some minutes and appeared very distressing. They continued sometimes a quarter of an hour and were succeeded by sensations of sinking. The vibratory movements of the head from side to side were much more continuous than the spasms of the diaphragm, they occurred sometimes while she was lying down. There were sometimes intervals of four to eight days between the paroxysms. During one fortnight they occurred very frequently, she could not take anything even water without bringing them on. Her nights were restless. She had sometimes pain and throbbing in head. She could not walk without some slight assistance, as a finger held out to her. Her disorder did not seem to be at all simulated, in fact both the cervical and the diaphragmatic spasms were clearly involuntary. She remained under observation till towards the end of the succeeding March and was then dismissed materially improved; she could walk a good deal better. The chief remedies employed were aperients, citrate of iron and quinine, and iron electuary. The pulse varied from 108 to 132. It seems most probable that this was a dynamic disorder, and also that it was not dependent on remote irritation. Had it been otherwise the progress would rather have been to worse than better. I think we must assume the existence of a state of erethysm of the cord in the vicinity of the origin of the phrenic and upper cervical nerves. Counter-irritation in both these cases would probably have been advantageous, in fact in the latter the head was much quieter some time after a blister to the loins.

The following case was, I think, closely related to neuralgia, or at any rate to neuralgic disorder, judging from the anæsthesia and the "juvantia." It was probably a peripheral neurosis, but is of interest specially as showing the affinity between · spasm and paralysis (sensory).

No. 80.—A. N., f., æt. 17, got suddenly spasmodic contraction of the flexor muscles of the left hand and forearm a week before she came under Mr. Bryant's care. The health was good, catamenia regular, sensation of the parts perfect. Iron was given and in three weeks the natural movements of the part were restored; the nerves of sensation, however, now became involved, complete anæsthesia of the whole hand and forearm making its appearance. This condition also disappeared in two months under the same treatment, sensation and motion being at last perfect. (V. *Med. Times and Gaz.*, 1862, June 14th.)

The affection termed *writer's cramp* seems to depend on undue excitability of the muscles and nerves concerned in writing, such that they are unable to execute the necessary delicate movements, but start off into larger ones. When much engaged in writing during cold weather I have experienced a tendency to it, which makes it needful to write more slowly and steadily in order to keep the muscles under control. There is at such times a sense of fatigue in the hand and wrist, and for some way up the arm. Zuradelli considers that there is primary paralysis of some muscles, and secondary spasm of others, and that various forms of the disorder may occur according to the particular muscles affected. Thielmann relates a case of similar disorder occurring in a sempstress. When she attempted to sew, the thumb flew away from the needle, and a burning pain extended up along the outer side of the wrist to the elbow, and if the effort was continued a red streak formed in the same situation. She was cured in twelve days by quinine and opium. Haupt states that other neuroses are not infrequent as complications of writer's cramp. He mentions squinting, stuttering, choreic disorder, laryngeal or pharyngeal spasm, strangury, palpitation of the heart, solar plexus, neuralgia, headache, &c. Rheumatism appears to be one of the inducing causes, over-exertion of the muscles concerned, and general impairment of nervous power inducing undue excitability are also powerfully influential. it is evident that resting the enfeebled part is necessary, and in many cases if not indeed in all, I should strongly advise the patient to discontinue entirely writing with the affected hand, and to accustom himself to use the other. This would not cause much inconvenience after a few weeks' practice. Pitha relates a case cured by electricity. Chorea, which is so analogous a disorder, is sometimes so much benefited by faradization, that I should expect much good from the same means in writer's cramp. Dr. Althaus employs the interrupted current when the disorder appears to be paralytic, but the continuous if it is spasmodic. I have no doubt that the latter remedy is especially indicated in spasms due to sthenic excitement, but where the condition is rather one of hyperæsthesia and debility the stimulus of the interrupted would be I think more beneficial. It is certain that some spasms are cured by stimuli. Tonic or sedative treatment internally would also be very advisable. In cases where there was any indication of a rheumatic element potass. iod. usually with ammon. carb. should be administered. Cold douching would probably be beneficial, and local bathing with sulphuret of potassium lotion.

Spasms of the muscles of the lower limbs, especially of the gastrocnemii, are not uncommon, and give rise to various distortions. Remote causes of irritation are probably the most frequent, but in some instances there is centric disorder. It is remarkable that in some cases the weight of the body pressing on the feet against the ground seems to have induced the spasm which was absent in the recumbent posture. This illustrates the reflex production of certain distortions. Bamberger relates the case of a youth, æt. 19, convalescent from pneumonia. As soon as he touched the ground with his feet all the muscles of the lower extremities fell into a state of tetanic rigidity, interrupted by the most violent sudden contractions, which threw the patient upwards, and during their rapid recurrence increased in intensity so that the patient had to be supported. At the same time the face was flushed and distorted, the pulse accelerated and extremely forcible. The moment that the patient sat or lay down all the movements ceased. If while lying in bed the soles of his feet were pressed, the same phenomena appeared but with much less intensity. He was cured by sedatives and cold affusion (*v.* Schmidt's *Jahrb.*, vol. cii. pp. 23, 24). The congenital development of *pes equinus*, &c., which is not unfrequent, stands probably in connection with the greater tendency to reflex action during fœtal life in consequence of the imperfect control exercised by the brain.

The most practical facts to bear in mind with reference to spasms are, (1) their frequent dependence on some removable cause of irritation; and (2) that when there exists no such exciting cause the *quality* of the nervous derangement producing them may be very various, either sthenic requiring depletion and counter-irritation, or hyperæsthetic calling for sedatives, or connected with exhaustion and needing stimulants and tonics. It may be no easy matter to estimate correctly the existing pathological state.

Mr. Smith, of Leeds, finds that permanent involuntary contraction of muscles may be successfully treated by the following simple proceeding. Place their origin and insertion as far apart as possible; maintain them in that state for some time, their opponents will then be gaining strength, and the balance of power will be restored. He states that he has cured cases of spasm of the masseter, sterno-cleido-mastoid, and various other muscles by this means. (*Lancet*, Sept. 20th, 1851.)

CHAPTER XIX.

SLEEPLESSNESS.

THE requirements of different individuals with regard to sleep differ considerably. Some are able to do with comparatively little, others need much more. It is generally those of great mental and nervous energy who at any rate for a certain time can bear the privation of their ordinary repose. Alison says of Napoleon, that like Wellington and all great generals he had an extraordinary power of commanding sleep when it suited him to take rest, and of doing without it when circumstances required such a privation. Boerhaave, according to Forbes, Winslow, is recorded not to have closed his eyes in sleep for a period of six weeks in consequence of intense study. We may perhaps take this account *cum grano salis*, as we read in a note of the same page that a Chinese criminal lived but nineteen days when condemned to be put to death by being kept constantly awake. There is, however, no doubt that in the state of mania patients will pass an extraordinary length of time with little or no sleep, and that all very strongly exciting passions and emotions will have a similar effect. The above remarks may seem to show the propriety of distinguishing a sthenic variety or form of sleeplessness depending on cerebral excitement, or on a state of semi-inflammatory irritation. It has much in common with the sthenic form of delirium tremens, and occurs in various fevers, in inflammation of the cerebral membranes, and in commencing insanity. Mr. Solly reports a case where repeated copious leeching with purgation followed by gentle mercurials and aconite produced sleep in about five days, of which otherwise there was but little prospect. Dr. Graves also mentions a case of delirium tremens in which watchfulness was a prominent symptom, but disappeared rapidly under the use of tartar emetic with opium. Such cases are, however, comparatively rare with regard to those of the opposite type where the sleeplessness is dependent upon a state of debility and irritability induced by bodily or mental causes. Dr. Russell has published an excellent paper[1] in which he illustrates forcibly the powerful influence of mental excitement and trouble in causing sleeplessness. The effects of such inflictions are only too familiar, and too often are the secret cause why the best therapy proves inefficient. When, however, the depression is not yielded to and encouraged, or is not too overwhelming in proportion to the strength of the system, judicious medication may often do much to make the burden less felt, the edge of the sorrow less keen. It is most true, and Dr. Russell illustrates it well, that the feeble hyperæsthetic brain collapses under the pressure which an organ of better quality and power can sustain. Now we have means whereby we can often improve this quality and power to a greater or less extent. Further, the mere procuring a regularly recurring oblivion of distressing impressions is no slight boon, and makes the sufferer more capable to bear his waking burden. Our nature is so compounded of the material and immaterial that what benefits the former is almost certain to do the same to the latter. A girl recently under my care with very various and marked signs of prostration of nerve power suffered for many months with exceedingly restless nights, the cause of which appeared to be chiefly great hyperæsthesia. Although she improved materially in other respects she did not sleep well until she was removed from

[1] "Brit. Med. J.," 1861; May 25th, Nov. 9th, 16th.

London to a healthy part of the country. I have had several patients, two especially, both temperate males, who for a length of time were quite dependent for good rest at night on wine taken either on going to bed, or in the course of the night. Graves mentions that in persons of irritable and nervous disposition he has found musk or assafœtida given more or less frequently during the day effectual in procuring sleep at night. In some cases of this kind it answers well to divert the patient's attention from the idea of remaining sleepless by giving it a new direction, as the importance of being awake to take his medicine at fixed times. In others a placebo, such as a bread-pill, proves a powerful sedative if only the patient can be inspired with faith in its efficacy. Dr. Laycock mentions a case where so long a sleep followed such a medication that it excited alarm. It is not easy to form a precise idea of the state of the nervous centres in which "a night-cap," as above mentioned, is so effectual in procuring sleep. Debility is certainly one marked feature of it, but there must be surely another, even more important, as the most profound debility does not by any means always interfere with sound sleep, nay, rather seems to conditionate it. This other element we are much disposed to think is hyperæsthesia, or irritability, which as already noted so commonly increases *pari passu* with weakness. The condition may be compared with that of neuralgia when it is beginning to give way under treatment, and is so easily reproduced by anything that causes exhaustion. Now as the stimulant recruits the exhausted nerve-force the hyperæsthesia ceases, and the brain-tissue subsides into a state of calm repose. It may be added here that it is often well to give not only a stimulant, but also some digestible nourishment, about the time of going to rest, or even in the course of the night where debility to a serious extent exists. It is quite certain that a craving empty stomach is by no means favourable to quiet slumber, and in this point of view moderate suppers are far from being unsuitable to many invalids. I well remember the case of a lady, who the night after a natural confinement woke up with severe gastric disorder and flatulence, which resisted various medication, but subsided immediately after a plate of cold meat, and some brandy-and-water.[1] Among the various soporifics I doubt if there be any more potent, especially for the weakly and hyperæsthetic, than prolonged exposure to the cold open air. This should be so managed as not to cause great fatigue, and if well timed, and followed by a sufficient meal, it will be found an admirable preparative for sound nightly slumber. Where this is impossible, as in cases of severe disease, and especially where, as often happens, narcotics disagree, it is well to try the effect of a monotonous voice. There is no question as to the soporific influence of such tones particularly when the speaker or reader is detailing

---

[1] A medical friend informs me that he finds a mustard poultice to the epigastrium an excellent hypnotic in some cases. This probably depends on its stimulating a languid solar plexus.

some matter which is not without a considerable tinge of dulness. The old monk's prescription for sleeplessness, viz., to tell your beads, was sound advice. The removal of any existing cause of irritation is of course often essential to procure sleep. Surgical cases exemplify this well. A gentleman about whom I was consulted lately told me that while suffering with torpid liver in India he had no sleep for five months until he commenced the nitro-muriatic acid bath and sponging. He thinks that he never slept an hour, and besides had lost taste and smell. He had no jaundice all this time, but objects appeared yellow to him. In less than a fortnight the function of the liver was restored, and with it the senses of taste and smell. Then followed sleep, at first for thirty hours on end, and in six months he was in perfect health.

The conditions necessary for the sleep-repose of the brain seem to be essentially these two, (1) a non-excited or active state of the cerebral tissue; (2) in most cases a diminished afflux of blood to the organ. We have already sufficiently noticed the importance of the first; the following observation illustrates well the need of the second. A gentleman, æt. 24, after considerable mental strain, experienced the following symptoms. He was thoroughly weary and drowsy at the close of the day, and felt, as well he might, the need of nature's restorer; scarcely, however, had he laid down his head, when the cerebral arteries began to throb forcibly, and soon all inclination for sleep was banished, and for hours he lay wide awake but deadly weary. The *causa mali* here was evidently deficient tonicity in the cerebral arteries, or more exactly paresis of their vaso-motor nerves. As the arteries relaxed they admitted an undue flow of blood to the brain which goaded its weary tissue into abnormal activity. The effect of altered blood-flow on the brain is also apparent in the following account which Graves quotes from Vigne's work. He states that in Kashmir it is a common practice for mothers to put their children to sleep by exposing the head for two or three hours to a small stream of water. This, as in Brown-Séquard's and Tholozan's experiment of lowering the temperature of one hand by chilling the other, must certainly have the effect of causing cerebral anæmia by contraction of its arteries. In children, attacks of malaroid remittent, a disease I shall subsequently describe, are invariably productive of very marked sleeplessness. The nocturnal febrile paroxysm seems to generate a state of excitability of the brain, and at the same time to stimulate it to morbid action by accelerating the circulation. Quinine in these cases is a most efficient hypnotic. Adults also occasionally suffer much with restlessness at night in connection with obscure aguish phenomena, as chills, cold sweats, prostration, and feelings of alarm, or strange terror. In some instances of this kind there is that very peculiar sensation of dread which makes the person afraid to sleep lest it should be a sleep without waking. I have met with this in both sexes. Closely allied to the insomnia of fever is that which occurs from over-fatigue, where the sufferer, though sorely in need of repose, lies vainly expecting it, and finds himself instead wakeful, feverous, and exhausted. Tea-drinking, though in moderation, will sometimes seriously interfere with sleep. I believe the following is an instance of its poisonous action when taken in excess.

No. 81.—J. R., æt. 47, m., a large stout man, works at a kiln in a brickfield, ad. April 27th. Ill one month. Complains of a tormenting feeling which goes all over his chest and head, and prevents sleep; when he does, he has terrific dreams. Does not suffer more after eating. T. clean. P. quiet. B. not regular. Sounds of heart normal. Sanguine aspect. Slight rheumatic pains in the knees. His symptoms did not vary much; he constantly complained of a tormenting feeling "like evil spirits," referred to the præcordia, and attended with palpitation. He was besides weak, and had some tenderness of the scalp and some lichenous eruption once. I was quite unaware of the nature of the case, and gave him various medicines with little or no benefit till June 22d, when as he complained of being restless at night, I ordered him half a grain of morph. mur. o. n. and a mixture of tr. valerian. ammon. + tr. arnicæ + tr. opii *ter die*. He improved by this, and was quite well by Aug 3d. His wife told me then that she had thought he was out of his mind; he used to lie awake at night without sleep; fancied he was going to be taken away to an asylum. He wanted to tell the hospital chaplain that he was going to be stoned. His illness began with nocturnal restlessness and sleeplessness. He was never a drinking man, but used to drink last summer three or four quarts of tea a day while at work. After his recovery he was conscious of his former delusions. From the præcordial dysæsthesia, and the sleeplessness, and the good effect of morphia I am strongly inclined to regard the preceding as a tea-neurosis. The history is unfortunately deficient as to whether he had continued his copious libations of tea up to the time of his being taken ill, and as to whether he subsequently discontinued them, but the probability is that he made no change. In all obscure neuroses we ought to consider whether tea may be not the culprit.

With regard to soporific drugs I think that henbane, in spite of the doubts which have lately been thrown upon its efficacy, approves itself frequently as a really valuable remedy. It seems to act as a direct cerebral calmant, affecting evidently the vaso-motor system in a much less degree. It is rare that it has any injurious effects, but I have met with some very susceptible systems, who could not take it nor any other form of narcotic. The action of opium on the other hand, though more potent, is more uncertain, and more apt to be injurious. It exerts unquestionably in many persons a stimulating power, at least when given in moderate doses, and in the early period of its action. Thus it comes to pass that if the cerebral tissue be highly hyperæsthetic, opium, unless given in large doses, is apt to produce an effect the very reverse of sedative. It seems appropriate to cases where there is some but not profound debility, where the cause of the insomnia consists in some peripheral nerve irritation, where the brain is not highly hyperæsthetic, where the secretions are tolerably free, and generally where there exists any grave and severely distressing affection. When given to obviate sleeplessness of cerebral origin it should be administered in a sufficient dose some time before the period when it is desired, that its soporific action should be manifested. I quite agree with Dr. Graves as to the advantage of using it in the form of enema in many instances, and, as Dupuytren held, the dose need not exceed that which is given by the mouth. The administration of high doses of opium is one of the most delicate points of practice, and though in skilful hands it gives often excellent results, had better be avoided if possible. The previous use of antimony, of a cold douche to the head while the body is immersed in a warm bath, of the latter alone may render a smaller and safer dose of opium equally efficacious with a larger. The symptom which would most warrant the exhibition of large doses of opium is severe pain provided at the same time there were no indications of failure of pulse. Large doses of henbane, as gr. xx of the extract, may in many cases advantageously replace opium. I have recently given for several nights gr. xxv to a man on the verge of delirium tremens and sleepless previously even with morph. mur. gr. $\frac{1}{2}$. When sleeplessness depends on some frequently-recurring irritation, as cough, much smaller doses of opium may be sufficient, and they may be repeated according to need. In maniacal excitement, as Dr. M'Leod[1] has recently pointed out, hydrocyanic acid in m_v doses, frequently repeated if necessary, is often effectual in inducing sleep.

Forbes Winslow says "a warm bath a short period before retiring to rest, bathing the head at the same time with cold water, particularly if the scalp be unnaturally hot, will often insure a quiet and composed night, when no description of sedative, however potent its character and dose, would influence the system." (*Lect. on Insanity*, p. 73.)

In the foregoing remarks the nature and causes of drowsiness, which we meet with occasionally as an independent affection, have been incidentally noticed. In a great majority of cases it depends on cerebral debility or exhaustion, but in some I am pretty certain it is one of the results of anæmia of the hemispheres. In these cases I believe it may be materially lessened, if not cured, by the administration of belladonna with the view of procuring relaxation of the arteries. In one instance, where drowsiness came on so much about 5 P.M. every day that the man was unable to go on with his work, I gave atropia gr. $\frac{1}{100}$ in infusion of valerian *ter die* with a curative result. In another instance, however, the drug failed. On the other hand I do not deny that drowsiness may be associated with cerebral hyperæmia, but this is almost invariably of a more or less venous character. I doubt how far an active cerebral circulation ever coincides with drowsiness, except of course in cases of actual organic mischief. When drowsiness depends on

[1] "Med. T. and Gaz.," March 14th, 21st, 1863.

cerebral exhaustion strychnia may be resorted to in aid, and *only in aid*, of the natural restoratives. It is never wise to goad a feeble organ beyond its strength.

No. 82.—F. W., æt. 22, clerk, ad. March 22d, ill nearly one year. Of strong make. His face, the cheeks especially, are flushed and of a deep red, and hot. He finds benefit from dipping his head into cold water. Complains that he has shocks in his system as he walks about, drops on his knees, at home is continually falling asleep, even in the streets he has fallen asleep while walking and tumbled against the railings. Is comfortable after 6 P.M., is as strong as ever, but till then from 11 A.M., has great debility and drowsiness. Gets worse if he walks much or is startled. Has a great appetite. Had fits when a child. Never passed worms. Bowels open. Never had ague. Flushes more in face after meals. When the drowsiness comes on he begins to wander and talk at random. He remained under treatment till the end of May and improved very decidedly. The state of the face did not alter much. He took strychnia gradually increased up to gr. $\frac{1}{12}$ *ter die*, besides quinine and iron. These remedies were certainly beneficial, which puts it, I think, out of the question that the drowsiness depended on cerebral hyperæmia. Tonics would surely have aggravated the results of such disorder. On the other hand there were marked indications of cerebral debility, and the state of the circulation in the face may be ascribed to paresis of the nerves of the arteries. I have notes of a quite similar case (externally) where there were no cerebral symptoms, only debility; tonics were beneficial. These cases give us the practical hint not to conclude too hastily from the outside to the state of the inside.

Soporose affections are stated by Schramm[1] to be of very frequent occurrence in the malarious district where he practises, especially in children. In them they are usually not serious, but in persons advanced in life they sometimes prove fatal. The sopor depends in some instances on cerebral anæmia, in others probably on a direct action of the poison on the brain. The following case has lately occurred to me.

No. 83.—E. L., æt. 7, f., ad. March 21, ill four weeks. Her mother states that she is sick three or four times a day, brings up a little froth; after the retching she sleeps for four or five hours, and then is very deaf for two or three more. She sleeps well, but wakes up with dry throat in the morning. No tenderness of the epigastrium. Has lost much flesh last fourteen days. I gave her ferr. et quin. citrat. gr. vi *ter die* and ol. morrh. ʒi *ter die*. In about three weeks all the symptoms had disappeared. In two of Schramm's cases a paroxysmal gastric neuralgia was replaced by a profound sopor. In a gentleman lately under my care, suffering with great exhaustion of nervous power and occasional neuralgia, extreme drowsiness was a marked symptom. In all cases of this kind where we have no reason to suspect narcotic poisoning, intracranial extravasation, or the like, we should look to the state of the urine, as latent renal degeneration might be a very possible cause of sopor.

[1] Bayer, Arztl. Intell. Bl. 38, 39, 40; 1861.

CHAPTER XX.

FACIAL NEURALGIA.

THERE are several varieties of this form of affection, which it is practically important to distinguish. One is the sympathetic, or reflected, where the pain depends on some cause of irritation seated in a more or less remote part; it may be a decayed tooth, and over-acid stomach, a gravid uterus, intestinal accumulations. Another is where the pain is produced by some organic central disease, as in Romberg's well recorded case. A third is where the pain is associated with marked tenderness; and where, judging from the "juvantia," we must consider the nervous disorder to be of a different kind to that which exists in other cases. It is clear that the conditions cannot be identical in cases which are cured by aconitine ointment, and those which yield to tonics. Fourthly, there are the instances which often are evidently produced by the special miasm which gives rise to ague, and which when their causation is not so evident are still attended with similar states of nerve debility, and are cured by the same means. These cases are sometimes markedly paroxysmal, sometimes show no periodicity. They are of very frequent occurrence in malarious districts; Schramm observed 195 in the course of four years at Bodenwöhr in the Palatinate. A transition between the two last varieties is exhibited in those cases referred to, by Watson and Brodie, in which after the pain has existed a long while the affected skin becomes swollen, red, and exquisitely tender. In these it is reasonable to suppose that the paretic state of the cerebro-spinal nerves has extended to the adjacent vaso-motor, in consequence of which the skin becomes highly injected with blood, and its sensory function is consequently exalted. Romberg terms the condition where the painful part is quite tolerant of pressure "anæsthesia dolorosa," which he regards as quite distinct from tic douloureux. Even in the fourth variety, however, there are many instances in which there is great tenderness of the skin without any vascular injection.

With regard to the first form of facial neuralgia, I have chiefly to mention that while we should always have an eye to its possible existence, and be on the lookout for any indication of remote irritation on which it may depend, we should not be in the case of suspected teeth over-hasty to have them removed. It has occurred to me more than once to relieve effectually by medicine neuralgic pain on account of which several teeth had been fruitlessly extracted; and on the other hand, the presence of numerous decayed stumps in the jaws has not prevented my curing a distracting neuralgia of the face and head. Dr. Brinton well remarks,[1] "There are plenty of facts which suggest that lesions of nerves not necessarily painful may become so from causes originally by no means local. Thus I believe there are hundreds of people walking about London this minute, the diseased nerves of whose carious teeth would be speedily roused into severe neuralgia by two or three nights of sleepless watching, and anxiety, or by two or three days of insufficient nourishment, or of violent and exhausting exertion of mind or body. And conversely I am sure that a generous diet will often relieve the agony arising from sheer involvement of nerves in a cancerous deposit." The case related by Sir B. Brodie where a pain in one foot was immediately relieved by dilatation of a stricture of the urethra, which the patient had not even mentioned at first, affords a good example how latent and remote the real *causa mali* may be in all cases of neuralgia, and how carefully we should search for indications of it. Friedberg records[2] four cases of severe pain of the face, involving in three all the divisions of the fifth nerve, and refractory to all internal treatment, which at length yielded to the extraction of one carious tooth. The remarkable circumstance was that other carious teeth had previously been extracted without relief, though they were painful and aching, while the tooth which appeared to be the cause of the neuralgia was painless. I would say generally that in all cases where the general health and strength did not appear much impaired, I should think it very necessary to make particular inquiry after possible determining causes of the neuralgia.

Oppenheimer[3] relates two cases of neuralgia of the fifth pair which obstinately resisted all treatment until the condition of the nasal cavities was investigated. In the first case a male, æt. 20, had regular paroxysms affecting all the divisions of the right nerve, which were cured by removing a nasal polypus that was accidentally discovered. In the second case there were very frequent and irregular attacks of ill-defined pains, which were materially relieved by zinc injections into the nasal cavities. These were not, however, adequate to curing completely the catarrh, which persisted along with the pains to some extent.

With regard to facial neuralgia depending on central alterations of structure, I do not know how it is to be diagnosed unless there are existing symptoms of such disease, as paralysis of some limb or group of muscles. Inefficiency of all remedies would of course make it highly probable that some organic alteration was at the bottom of the mischief. It is, however, worth remarking that even in such cases remedies may produce a certain amount of benefit. Thus in Romberg's case, sesquioxide of iron and assafœtida at first proved

---

[1] "Lancet," April 11th, 1863.
[2] Canstatt's "Jahresb.," 1860, p. 25, vol. iii.
[3] Schmidt's "Jahrb.," vol. cviii. p. 178.

very serviceable. In the case of a female[1] who had long suffered from intense pain in the balls of the toes, depending, as the result proved, on a bony tumour in the internal popliteal nerve, relief was always derived from arsenic, though it was transient.

The third form must, I think, be rare; I have scarcely met with a marked example of it, though analogous hyperæsthesias in other situations are not uncommon. A typical case of this affection would, I think, occur in a person of tolerably good health and strength in whom tonics did not appear indicated. Such a one Mr. Skey's patient seems to have been whom he treated in St. Bartholomew's with aconitine ointment. He describes him as a fisherman, æt. 40, of dark, swarthy complexion, apparently of healthy constitution, and not intemperate. (V. *Med. Gazette*, vol. xix. p. 158.) It is probably in cases of this class that two remedies which have been highly recommended for their occasional success may be expected to prove beneficial. I allude to muriate of ammonia, and croton oil. Mr. Skey found the former of more benefit in Mr. Spey's case than any other internal medicine, though the good effect soon failed. Barralier recommends it to be given *during* the paroxysm at half-hour intervals. Besides the temporary relief it was observed that in cases of headache returning in periodical paroxysms several times a month the intervals gradually became longer, the attacks diminished in intensity, and ended by disappearing completely after having been several times arrested by the remedy. It has proved effectual in idiopathic hemicrania, in headache consequent on recurring ague, in those occurring in the decline of low fevers, and in the period of irritation in typhus. (V. *Edin. Med. Journal*, Aug. 1859.) It is a remedy which would certainly not avail in cases suitable for quinine and iron. My chief acquaintance with it is as a remedy for muscular rheumatism. I have found it useful in one case of abdominal neuralgia, but my experience of it as an antineuralgic is very limited. With regard to croton oil our knowledge is purely empirical; we know that it has achieved great results in a few cases, but we have scarce any indications to guide us as to the state of system to which it is appropriate. *A priori* we may suppose that constipation, and an absence of prostration would be prominent features of cases where it was to benefit.

The following case belongs rather to the transitional instances above alluded to, than to this form.

No. 84.—J. R., ad. July 25th. Ill two months, worse last three weeks. Has pain from his chin to the top of his head, mostly towards right side. Is obliged to get up at night, sometimes thrice, and bathe his head with cold water to relieve the pain. Sweats very much at night. Feels very low, so as to be unable to work at times at his trade (shoemaking). Pulse large, very compressible. B. open. T. clean and red. Never had ague, or lived in the way of it. The pain is sometimes relieved by pressure, at

---

[1] *V.* Lancet, Aug. 11, 1860.

others increased. He was almost free from pain in a week after treatment was commenced, but he was still weak when he ceased attendance Sept. 4th. In about eighteen months he came under my care again with the same disorder. He mentioned now that his head felt hot; he could hardly bear to lay it on the pillow, it was so sore. After a fit of pain he trembled all over. He had six decayed teeth, but felt no inconvenience from them, except perhaps that he could not drink hot liquids. He ceased attendance much relieved in five weeks. In about two years he was again under my hands with the same symptoms, great soreness of the head, and inability to take hot ingesta into his mouth. He was quite cured in five weeks, and I have not seen him since (three years ago). His treatment consisted of quinine and iron, arsenic and belladonna. The latter seemed perhaps even more efficacious than the former. This man had very much of the stamp of aguish disorder upon him, as marked by great general debility, nocturnal sweating, and "cold shivers" which at one time succeeded each fit of pain. The cutaneous hyperæsthesia was well marked, but it yielded to the same remedies which subdued the pain. The presence of the decayed teeth did not prevent the final cure. The relapsing tendency of the disorder was very marked.

The last form is certainly far the most frequent, and corresponds with the most frequent forms of neuralgia in other localities. Schramm[1] finds the disorder to prevail much more in the female than in the male sex in the proportion of 136 to 59. In the former the disease increased in frequency up to the 30th year, in the latter up to the 40th. More cases occurred in the first than in the last six months of the year, 72 from January to April out of 195. The kind of pain varied very much; it was often attended with indications of vaso-motor paresis, injection of the eyes, redness and swelling of the skin, lachrymation and salivation. Most cases were apyretic, but in several there was shivering and fever, or shivering and sweating. Sometimes the neuralgia suddenly replaced a pneumonia, or a gastro-enteritis, or other inflammation. Supra-orbital neuralgia was always very obstinate. Arsenic was found an invaluable remedy in such cases, and where there was a tendency to relapse. It also appeared to be a specific in chronic inflammation of the eyes and of the lids. The treatment of this kind of facial neuralgia and of similar in any part, may be thus formulated. Either quinine is to be given in full rapidly repeated doses until deafness is produced, and afterwards in smaller doses: or, arsenic in doses of gr. $\frac{1}{30}$ dissolved in distilled water by heat is to be taken *ter die*, and extr. belladon. in doses of gr. $\frac{1}{2}$-gr. 1 *2dis horis* until either the pain yields, or disorder of vision and dryness of throat ensue. Both of these modes of treatment are thoroughly efficacious, but it is of little use in severe cases to adopt half measures.

Rheumatic neuralgia of the face rarely, I think, corresponds to the course and distribution of the divisions of the fifth, but is more purely a peripheral affection. The following case seems to illustrate this.

[1] Schmidt's "Jahrb." vol. ciii. p. 177.

No. 85.—A returned Indian officer, æt. 65, came under my care on account of some diffused swelling and redness of the nose and left eye. The nose had a bulbous appearance. He has never had gout, nor had any of his family. The affection was of three or four days' duration. He took pot. iod. + pot. bicarb. + ammon. carb., and in six days the disorder had ceased, but the previous night he had a good deal of pain in the left jaw and teeth. This was doubtless a rheumatic neuralgia, as the original affection had been a rheumatic inflammation. .

The following case is a good illustration of the fourth kind. I am indebted for the report of it to my friend Mr. Smith, of John-street, under whose able care the patient was.

No. 86.—Mrs. S., æt. 39, mother of seven children, the last born nine years ago; she has never been pregnant since till last autumn (1856), when she miscarried at the second month. Is very stout and leucophlegmatic, circulation languid; left eye often somewhat everted, especially when she is weak and tired. Is hardly ever free from pain in the head. Comes of a nervous family; one sister, æt. 42, has never menstruated, and has now mental delusions; another has been epileptic for sixteen years, and is hysterical in the highest degree; a third is subject to neuralgia, and has a cast in one eye; a brother is also neuralgic. Mrs. S. suffered at Hampstead, where she had been living several years, about fifteen years ago, a fearful attack of "tic douloureux" for weeks, and was only cured by Dr. Elliotson giving gr. xx doses of quinine till she was quite deaf; she was then quite cured. She has had slight attacks since, one rather severe at Marlow eight years ago. After miscarrying last autumn went to Scarborough for two months and got pretty well. Nov. 10th, 1856. Has neuralgia of left side of face, principally in the situation of the mental nerve, of moderate severity. Quinine was given at first in rather small, subsequently as the paroxysms became more severe and of longer duration, in larger doses until 48 grains were given in the twenty-four hours, when she became quite deaf, and the pain quite ceased (15th). The day before she was delirious and suffering fearful pain. This evening at the usual hour of paroxysm she had shivering, but no pain. For two hours there ensued an attack of hysteria with partial syncope, only relieved by stimulants in large doses. 18th. For the last three nights has had similar attacks coming on at precisely the same hour with shivering, but gradually decreasing in severity. The amount of quinine has been diminished; she takes 10 or 12 grains in twenty-four hours with as many drops of liquor arsenicalis. 22d. Hysterical attacks quite gone, slight pain in the face. She slowly gained strength, went to Brighton, and improved, but had still in spite of quinine slight returns of the disorder. Towards the end of the succeeding January she had neuralgia again in the same part, not paroxysmal, and not attended with shivering, but with some numbness extending down the right arm. The attack yielded to 24 grains of quinine in the day. Various external applications were tried, as opium, chloroform, belladonna, Fleming's tincture of aconite, Morson's aconitine ointment, but none of them afforded so much relief as poppy fomentation applied almost boiling hot. *Remarks.*—There are several points well worthy of notice in this highly interesting case. (1) The liability of the patient by original constitution to derangement of the nervous system, and the affinity clearly indicated between neuralgia, epilepsy, insanity, and hysteria, all varieties of dynamic disorder. (2) The resemblance of the affection in many respects to disease of malarious origin; this resemblance depending, I believe, on the circumstance that the same structures are the seat of morbid action in both cases. Nerve debility, *however* produced, easily generates neuralgia. (3) The hysterical attacks which ensued as the neuralgia ceased were evidently a part of the same disorder, and were subdued by a continuance of the same treatment. They were surely as much a physical disorder as the neuralgia itself. (4) The involvement of the hemispheres in the morbid action when it was at its height, and the cessation of both pain and delirium under the same remedy. The nerve and the nervous centre suffered alike, but expressed that suffering differently. (5) The evidence the case affords, by the subsequent recurrences at intervals after the first attack, that the remedy which proved so serviceable did not remove or destroy the cause of the disease, but simply rendered the system more capable of withstanding it. The long periods during which she was free from disease prove, I think, that it was not dependent on any structural lesion.

I have lately treated in a similar way a female, æt. 33, who had been suffering with facial neuralgia six months, and had taken quinine under medical advice without benefit. The pain occurred about twice a day in paroxysms of such severity that she became quite beside herself. She found that stooping forward, so as to promote the flow of blood into the head, relieved the pain. The pain was speedily arrested by quinine gr. v *2dis horis* till her ears were buzzing. Other tonics were given afterwards and the improvement has been maintained. She attributed the attack to sleeping in a damp bedstead, but she had also suffered much mentally, which was probably the more efficient cause.

The following case illustrates the efficacy of the other mode of treatment alluded to.

No. 87.—H. W., æt. 45, m., ad. under Dr. Markham's care Feb. 9th. He was suffering severely, and was very much relieved by iron and quinine, and a liniment of chloroform + aconite. His symptoms relapsed after resuming work at shoemaking. Dr. Markham kindly transferred him to my care Feb. 29th. His history was that he had been ill quite five months, with pain in face and head; he had some decayed teeth removed from left upper jaw, after which an abscess formed, but this is now quite well. The pain before the teeth were removed was toothache, not like the present, which he says is frightful, and worse than it has yet been. The pain is paroxysmal, it comes on the last three days about noon, and gets to its acme about 1 P. M., subsides about 5 or 6 P. M. It used to be very severe at night, but is not now. The pain affects both temples and all the top of head, is attended with a sense of opening and shutting, and with great soreness. The skin of the forehead is not more than just warm, not flushed or injected, but feels very tender. No pain now in eating. He feels very weak. Is not gouty, nor were either of his parents. Never in the way of ague. T. quite clean. P. feeble. B. open. Urine has been very thick. Pupils of medium size or rather small. No blue line on gums. Quindisulph. gr. v *3tiis horis*. Ferri carb. sacch. gr. xx *ter die*. March 3d. Head not at all relieved; pain seems to shoot through the brain. P. extremely feeble. Has not been made deaf. Acidi arseniosi gr. $\frac{1}{20}$. Aquæ distil. ℨss *ter die.* Extr. bellad. gr. i *2dis horis,* olei morrh. ℨij *ter die.* 7th. Was almost quite free from pain yesterday, not quite so well to-day; has taken about twenty of the belladonna pills, three yesterday; pupils not at all large, eyes very photophobic. March 21st. Is much better, has scarcely any pain at all in head now, has gained flesh, but still feels weak on exertion; has worked three or four hours a day. Is a great deal stronger and better than he has yet been; has not taken any belladonna for some time. 28th. Head quite free from pain; can't sleep at night for pain in *arms* if he works, but has no pain if he does not.

Division of the suffering nerve is a remedy which seems to have succeeded in a few instances, but has failed in many more. It can of course be useful only in peripheral neuralgia, and I should think in states of system when the general nervous power was not materially depressed. The nearer to the point of exit of the nerves from the cranium the section is made the more likely the operation will be to prove beneficial, but it will be also much more severe. It is not to be thought of until all other means have failed. J. Kühn[1] records an instance in which the inferior dental nerve was divided with apparent success, no relapse having ensued during six months at least. Ch. Frank[2] records five cases, in four of which the operation was successful. In the first, the second and third divisions of the fifth were the seat of disease. The infra-orbital neuralgia was cured by division of the nerve at its exit from the foramen, and the mental by section of the inferior dental nerve before its entrance into the canal. In two other cases the infra-orbital nerve was successfully divided. In a fourth the supra-orbital and frontal nerves were divided with good results. In the fifth case the inferior dental nerve was twice divided, at an interval of above four months between the operations, but the result seems not to have been satisfactory. Bratsch[3] gives the histories of nine patients, all of whom, except one, at the time of the report were freed from their sufferings. In several, however, the operation had been so recently performed that it was by no means certain that a relapse would not ensue, which indeed seems not impossible, seeing that the nine patients had shared no less than twenty-five operations among them, nearly three a-piece. Eisenmann remarks that these cases support the view that idiopathic neuralgias are of central origin, and agrees in the opinion attributed to Sir C. Bell that it is not the division of the nerve, but the operation, and its influence on the nervous centres, which removes the pain temporarily or permanently.

Trousseau distinguishes epileptiform neuralgia, as he terms it, from ordinary facial neuralgia. The former is characterized by sudden violent darts of pain, attended in some instances with rapid convulsive movements of the facial muscles, lasting about a minute, but returning ten to a hundred times a day, with longer or shorter periods

[1] "Archiv. Phys. Heilk.," iii. 1859, p. 226.
[2] Schmidt's "Jahrb.," vol. ci. p. 293.
[3] Canst. "Jahresb." 1860, p. 25.

of exemption, varying in duration from days to months. The attacks are induced sometimes by any movement of the face, as in speaking, drinking or eating. The suffering is terrible. No treatment cures effectually, but very large and repeated doses of opium procure, as long as they are continued, great mitigation of suffering, or even complete exemption. When the drug, however, is omitted, the disorder soon returns. Section of the trunk of the nerve also affords great temporary relief, lasting for days or even months, but the disorder recurs obstinately. Quinine is of no avail.

CHAPTER XXI.

FACIAL PARALYSIS.

THE plan of my work excludes from notice under this head all cases depending on organic lesion. Inorganic paralysis in this situation has long been known, and designated as rheumatic. Trousseau[1] says that the action of cold is one of its most frequent causes; it surprises those whom it affects in the midst of most perfect health, and produces no derangement of the economy. A mere current of air, remaining in a damp place, as in a house whose walls are not well dried, is enough to give rise to it. Other causes are violent emotions, as terror, of which he gives an instance, anger, grief. Sometimes it comes on without apparent cause. Sudden supervention is a pretty constant character of this paralysis. J. Frank states that seven of his patients were suddenly attacked with this paralytic affection on putting their heads out of the window in the morning when it was very cold, though only for a moment. Romberg says, "It is very common for pain and tumefaction, accompanied by febricitations, to occur in the affected side of the face after the patient has caught cold; these symptoms disappear after a few days, and the paralysis remains." The facts above cited illustrate and confirm, as it seems to me, the views already advanced as to the causation of paralysis. When the facial nerve is suddenly palsied by a "coup de vent," it is impossible to suppose that the cold has acted directly on the nervous filaments lying well covered with fat and skin. On the other hand it is certain that the sensory nerves of the skin *must* be affected, and they produce the paralysis by a reflex inhibitory influence. When the affection results from excessive emotions, such as terror whose enfeebling effect is notorious, there must be a direct paresis of the nerve-cells at the origin of the facial, unless we assume with Brown-Séquard that a spasm of the minute vessels takes place

---

[1] "Clin. Med.," vol. ii. p. 286.

in this situation. The occurrence of quasi-inflammatory swelling in the affected side of the face I should refer to a paralysis of vasomotor nerves inducing hyperæmia of the part. The paralysis in rare instances affects both sides of the face. (I am still confining myself tó non-organic affection.) Dr. Gairdner relates[1] and comments very instructively upon a case, which was entirely of eccentric origin. All facial expression is completely lost, and labial articulation also. According to M. Davaine, if the branches of the nerve given off before its exit from the stylo-mastoid foramen are paralyzed, there is also dysphagia, a nasal twang of voice, and impairment of lingual articulation. In the double paralysis the mouth is not drawn to one side, as it often is in the single. The diagnosis of inorganic from organic facial paralysis is a point of much importance. Romberg asserts that they are often confounded. Trousseau admits it possible that a facial paralysis, having all the characters of the disorder we are considering, may result from a very limited hemorhage in the mesocephale; though he adds that in all his practice he has never met with such a case. He grounds his admission on Vulpian's experiments, who produced facial paralysis in a dog by a small wound of the fourth ventricle. The distinguishing signs which Trousseau confides in are the possibility of closing the lids in all cases of facial paralysis from cerebral disease, and the retention of the electric excitability of the muscles, which is lost in the functional disorder. In most cases of cerebral disease the facial paralysis will be associated with hemiplegia or other symptoms. If the facial nerve be involved in disease of the petrous bone, or have received traumatic lesion, the nature of the case is generally sufficiently clear.

If there be any indication of inflammatory action in the vicinity of the parotid gland, we may apply a few leeches and purge. If, as usually happens, there are none, the interrupted current should be passed for fifteen minutes daily along the track of the paralyzed nerve, and stimulating embrocations should be rubbed on the skin of the face. Strychnia may be administered internally, or, as Trousseau recommends, endermically. In exceptional cases the paralysis gets well in twelve or twenty-four hours of itself. Some cases, however, resist all treatment, though there is apparently no organic lesion. In some cases refractory to other remedies we may employ the continuous current. Schultz[2] has succeeded in curing six cases of grave facial paralysis by this means. When the paralysis has been considerable and of long duration, it is apt to be followed, as in analogous instances, by permanent contracture to a greater or less extent of one or more of the facial muscles. Here we observe again the affinity between paralysis and spasm.

I subjoin an illustrative case.

[1] V. "Lancet," May 18, 1861.
[2] "Wiener. Med. Wochenschr." No. xxvii.

No. 88.—J. E. L., æt. 22, m., ad. May 11th, ill one week. Has paralysis of the right facial nerve, the eye cannot be closed, and the cheek is puffed out in expiration. He can close the mouth, but not so perfectly as normally. No numbness of skin of face. Hearing of right ear good. The affection came on quite gradually, after exposure of the right side of the face to a draught two days before. No pain in head. Some bad teeth, but none ache. He was faradized once, used linim. terebinth. to the face, and took strychnia, and was all but quite well in a month. He improved materially with the liniment and one galvanization in the first three days.

CHAPTER XXII.

RETINAL HYPERÆSTHESIA.

THIS common affection befalling one of the nerves of special sense corresponds closely in its essential features with the neuralgiæ. It is true that in most of the latter the disorder tends rather to the production of anæsthesia than of hyperæsthesia, and that we are not warranted in regarding the pain as a manifestation of the latter state. Still it is evident that the retinal affection occurs just in those states of system which are favourable to the production of neuralgiæ, that the general tenor of the concomitant symptoms is indicative of nervous prostration, and the "juvantia" are precisely those which avail to cure neuralgia. The term "scrofulous ophthalmia" commonly applied to the disease is, I cannot but think, a bad one, as it is not uncommonly met with in children who have no clearly marked strumous peculiarities, but who are weakly and cachectic. Very possibly it may be more frequent in strumous than in non-strumous children, but it certainly is not limited to the former. It is remarkable that it should prevail so much among children; it seems in them to take the place of the manifold sensory neuralgias which are such a plague to adults. The treatment which I have found most satisfactory is to apply an aconite lotion to the eye, and to administer ferri carb., or ferro-citrate of quinine with ol. morrh. A healthy state of the alimentary canal must of course be secured by gray powder, &c., if requisite.

The following cases are instructive:—

No. 89.—J. S., æt. 10, m., ad. April 7th, with strumous ophthalmia, and treated with F. + Q. citr., ol. morrh., collyr. bellad. and blisters till 22d, when he was transferred to my care. He had then extreme photophobia, such that he had not opened the left eye for four months; the right eye was almost as bad. He kept his hand constantly pressed over the eyes. He had suffered with the disorder for six years more or less since he had had hooping-cough. Pulse weak, jerky. T. clean. B. costive. Quinine, + iron, + tr. aconite (the latter in ℨvj doses) *quater die*, strychnia +

iron + hydrocyanic acid, ol. morrh., lead lotion, blisters, occasional leeching, small doses of morphia, gr. ⅛ *ter die*, the same with ferri carb., tannin + opium, emetics, and tr. ferri mur. ℞ x *2dis horis* were given till March of the following year, when he was nearly well, and remained so, or rather improved still further till May 6th, taking ferri ammon. citr. + ammon. carb., + inf. calumb. He then ceased attendance. Of all the above remedies, which were pretty fairly tried, there were two which produced signal benefit, so much as to make it worth while to notice them particularly. The first was tannin given in doses increased to gr. x *ter die*, with liq. opii sedat. ℞ v; under this the eyes almost perfectly recovered, and remained well for a month; he was able to face the light well, and was in the open air all day long. After getting a wetting he relapsed, and the tannin failed to restore him. For a month he then took ferri pot. tart. and ol. morrh., but with no gain. I then gave the tr. fer. mur. ℞ x, *2dis horis*, determined to see what a "coup sur coup" treatment would accomplish. In fourteen days he was able to bear the light quite well, and during the remainder of the time he was under observation (three months) no relapse occurred. I have no wish to exaggerate the efficacy of these remedies, and have no expectation that liberal tanning and ironing of the system will always or often be requisite. I should generally expect more good effect from a pure bracing air. Still I think the above example may be worth remembering in dealing with obstinate cases. The amount and frequency of the dose of a remedy are most important items for consideration, and are often by no means sufficiently regarded. Treatment may entirely fail from this cause alone.

No. 90.—A. A., f., æt. 10, ad. July 26th, 1860. Had measles in April; has been ailing ever since. Skin cold. P. weak. Extreme photophobia of both eyes, the lids red externally, much lachrymation. T. clean. Appetite indifferent. B. open. Tr. ferri mur. with acid. hydrocy. dil., the same with morph. muriat. gr. ⅛ *ter die*, powdered bark and soda, tannin + opium, tannin, colchicum + henbane, belladonna alone, and with iron, ol. morrh., tr. ferri mur., *2dis horis*, continued till Feb. 18th, 1861, failed to do any good; the photophobia was as extreme as possible, and there was very extensive redness and excoriation around both eyes from the constant irritation of the discharge. She now began to take ferri ammonio-citrat. gr. v + ammon. carb. gr. ij + tr. nucis vom. ℞ v + inf. calumb. ʒi *quater die*, which she continued till July 8th, when the eyes were quite well except a slight film of opacity on the cornea. She improved steadily from the time of commencing this medicine. She was seen again Nov. 21st, the eyes continued well, she had been in the country. These two cases were as nearly as possible exactly alike, save the difference of sex, yet the remedies which had availed most in the first were useless in the second. It seems to me that such experience as I have just recorded, which of course is frequently paralleled, affords us some valuable guidance in dealing with other disorders whose nature is more obscure, as epileptic affections, or other neuroses. It seems as if, though the *kind* of remedy is clearly indicated, it is a matter of exceeding difficulty to find that which shall be exactly appropriate to the particular instance. Not only so, but the amount of dose is a matter of material moment. I have seen a sixteenth of a grain of strychnia *ter die* cause considerable stomach disturbance, while one-twentieth was well borne and cured. Where nervous tissue acquires an extreme susceptibility it is no easy matter to adjust a remedy so as to tone and calm without injuriously exciting—and this is what is wanted. If these points were well considered, we should have fewer sceptics with regard to the virtue of remedies. In a third case the patient, a female æt. 23, of marked strumous diathesis, all whose family were consumptive, was treated for more than eighteen months with a great variety of remedies, iron + quinine, strychuia, bark + soda, tannin, colchicum in full doses, aconite, tr. ferri mur. ℞ x, 3*tis horis*, with occasional blisters, leeches, and various sedative collyria, but without permanent relief;—even two or three months of country air failed. She was then admitted into the Charing Cross Hospital, where she took bark and iron, and had the eyes repeatedly vaporized with bisulphide of carbon. This appeared to cure; I saw her some good while after she had left the hospital without any trace of the photophobia, which had been very great, but with a very opaque right cornea. As her circumstances were tolerably good, and she had had the fullest trial of internal remedies, it seems fair to ascribe the cure rather to the bisulphide than to the rest and nursing of the hospital.

The following case, though not identical with the foregoing, has much in common, and is of practical interest.

No. 91.—W. O., æt. 38, m., ad. June 18th. Suffering with his eyes for seven months; for the first three or four he was at Moorfields, during the rest of the time he has been under the care of an eminent ophthalmic surgeon. He had been treated since April 26th with an issue in the temple, liquor cinchon., bark + soda, + colchicum, pot. iod., opii gr. ¼ *ter die*, ungt. hydr. c. opio, hydr. c. cretâ gr. iij *ter die*, besides leeches on three occasions. He was still, however, in a very suffering state when he came under my care, had been unable to work at his business, that of a carpenter, for seven weeks. The right eye could not bear the light, but appeared healthy. The left eye was in a state of marked conjunctivitis and sclerotitis, with great lachrymation, the cornea was cloudy and the iris muddy. There was great intolerance of light, so that he was obliged to hold a kerchief to the eye, though vision was lost. The globe of this eye was very tender. He had pain at the forehead and back of head. When lying down he was easier. Urine natural. B. costive. P. exceedingly weak and soft. T. quite natural. Appetite good now, has not been so till last three weeks. Has been a teetotaller last twelve months, used to drink hard before; I had the great advantage in treating this case of knowing that the best means which could be employed had been fully tried, and that by the most skilful hands. It was therefore clear that it was useless for me to attempt to deal with it purely as a tissue inflammation. Whatever hope there might be of success must lie in endeavouring to improve the general condition of the nervous system, which was evidently depressed, and in calming the local hyperæsthesia. If this could be accomplished the inflammatory phenomena might be expected to yield also. I ordered him quiniæ disulphat. gr. v *ter die*, and extr. bellad. gr. ¼ *ter die*. In five days he could see a great deal better; the pupil was less contracted, the iris clearer, the inflammation much reduced, the pain around the eye much less. He felt very nervous. June 27th. He was ordered quiniue gr. iij + tr. ferri muriat. ℥ss + spt. æth. chlor. ℞ x *ter die*, and ten days later ol. morrh. was added. By July 21st he could see with the left eye every letter of his card, the cornea and iris had become clear, the photophobia had ceased, he had gained much flesh, and had been working for several days exposed to a hot sun. By August 21st he was well enough to be discharged, though he had passed through an attack of diarrhœal disorder. This case was treated on the principle of having regard to the pathological condition rather than to the local phenomena, and it may fairly be said that the result was satisfactory. The case proves, if proof be needed, that *some* inflammations are dependent upon nerve debility.

Retinal Anæsthesia.

This is a much rarer affection than its converse. It seems, however, to constitute the disorder termed nyctalopia, which appears to be chiefly produced by debilitating agencies, and the neurotic character of which is further affirmed by its nocturnal occurrence. Romberg mentions cold, scurvy, malaria, self-abuse, and the exclusive use of coarse vegetable food as ascertained causes. It occurs, according to Ruete, in Russia, extensively among the poor in Lent. In an epidemic referred to by Mackenzie, fatigue and inhabiting small dark rooms seemed to give rise to the disorder. A residence on board ship is thought by Dr. Mackenzie to conduce to the disease. A succession of blisters to the temples is recommended by Bampfield except in cases depending on scurvy. Cold bathing of the eyes, and quinine, with good food, will probably be advantageous in most cases.

CHAPTER XXIII.

THROAT DYSÆSTHESIA.

This affection is a neuralgia differing in no respect essentially from the same disorder in other parts. It is certainly, at least in its well-marked forms, of rarer occurrence. From the peculiar susceptibility of the throat a dysæsthesia of this part produces considerable distress. Patients complain of feeling as if they should be choked, and the sense of impending suffocation is sometimes very urgent, of dysphagia, of a sense of heat, dryness and burning. The throat on inspection is found either normal, or but slightly inflamed, and the nervous distress is out of all proportion to the visible alteration, if there is any. The patients are mostly females, but the affection is quite unconnected with hysteria, in so far as that term is intended to imply a tendency to simulate or exaggerate disease. Where a rheumatic element can be discerned, pot. iod. or ammon. muriat. should be given, generally with bark or ammonia on account of the existing debility. If the neuralgia appear to be simple, quinine and iron, with ol. morrh., and sometimes arsenic steadily administered, will effect a cure. For some illustrative cases, I refer to the

Med. Times and Gaz., May 2, 1863. The following is of the same character.

No. 92.—E. G., f., æt. 36, married, ad. Nov. 5th, ailing three years, ill one month. Complains of pain in neck and head, of a sensation of swelling in throat and tongue; wakes up at night with palpitation of heart, and a sense of being very ill, attended with choking. From 8 to 12 P. M. a feeling comes over her as if she could hardly keep life in her; it seems to proceed from the left hypochondrium, causes palpitation, and takes away her speech. Throat is not at all sore. Has no dyspepsia. Is weakly. Heart's action a little excited. When first attacked she was purple all over, and seemed to be dying; had then been up three nights nursing. Brandy relieves her. Ordered F. + Q. citrat. gr. x + tr. nucis vom. ♏xij + aq. ℥j *ter die*, and subsequently ol. morrh. On this treatment she has improved in a very marked manner. Dec. 3d, she was better a great deal. Jan. 11th, has been up at night nursing a sick child; disorder relapsing. A lady recently under my care suffered most severely with this disorder; her distress was so great she felt as if she should lose her reason. At night she was much worse; could get no sleep in spite of several doses of chlorodyne. She had had the affection on and off for a long time; when it ceased, which it did at intervals, she got well immediately. Bromide of ammonium and pot. iodid. were beneficial.

Dr. L. Türck[1] seems to have noticed this affection, which he designates as neuralgia and hyperæsthesia of the throat. He states that the pain is increased by continued talking or singing, which I should think very probable. The treatment he employs consists in resection of the gustatory nerve and cauterization with solid nitrate of silver.

CHAPTER XXIV.

LINGUAL NEURALGIA.

This is a very severe and intractable variety of nerve disorder, at least in bad cases, far more so than the preceding. I have termed it a neuralgia, and believe that it is such essentially. There is, however, in well-marked instances more or less of morbid alteration of the mucous membrane. The surface appears over-red, insufficiently covered with epithelium, as it were denuded in patches, between which are others of whity coating. The edges are often indented, and there may be some appearance of ulceration, but this is only exceptionally present, and is certainly not of the essence of the disorder. The distress from the sore or burning sensation is very great, and the patients are apt to have a morose, unhappy look. The disorder is remarkably persistent; in one of my cases it had continued twelve, and in another six years. Of five cases, three were

---

[1] "Wien. Allg. Med. Zeit.," vii. ix. 1862.

females. In the way of treatment iron and quinine, arsenic, ol. morrhuæ, tr. aconite have proved beneficial as internal remedies, and among these I think arsenic holds the highest place. Locally borax with glycerine affords some relief. I must acknowledge, however, that I feel far from confident, when entering on the treatment of a case of this kind, of achieving any decided success. Milder cases certainly are cured, but old standing ones are very obstinate. The cause of this is, I think, partly the high degree in which the organ is endowed with nervous susceptibility, and partly is almost continual exposure to causes of irritation. *Il va sans dire* that the state of which I am speaking is not merely the result of bad and decayed teeth pressing against the organ. The following cases are worth recording:—

No. 93.—M. C., f., æt. 52, ad. May 26th. Ill one year as at present, worse the last six weeks. The disorder commenced first six years ago. The tongue at its anterior third looks red, denuded, eroded somewhat, with thin white patches on its surface. A sensation of burning rather than soreness is complained of. P. of good force. Never had any cutaneous eruption. Lotion of borax and glycerine. Liq. pot. arsenit. ♏ iv *ter die*. June 16th. Is getting better. T. much easier. 30th. Mouth very painful, burning sensations in throat, slight indications of an eruption on the tongue. July 10th. P. full and rather excited, has burning pain in tongue and throat. T. has the same appearance as at first. Can't take any food. Quinine gr. vij *ter die*. Ol. morrh. ʒi *ter die*. 24th. Is a great deal easier, has none of the burning heat now. T. more comfortable, but feels parched at night. Takes food better. Aug 4th. Doing well. T. looks healthier, more covered with epithelium. 18th. T. a great deal better, only a little place at left side which is sore. Pt. Ferri carb. saccht. gr. 20 *ter die*. 28th. T. very painful last four days. Pt. She did not attend again; probably the relapse was not of long duration, but it marks well the obstinate character of the disorder.

No 94.—M. S., f., æt. 30, ad. Decr. 16th, 1861. A large, fine-looking woman, unnaturally flushed in cheeks, at present they are hot. Skin of hands cool, damp. P. quick, weak. Is weakly, suckling nine months. Has headache and loses her sight at times. Has five healthy children, two dead with measles, and one with teething convulsions. She has been ill for twelve years, suffering with her tongue; it feels sore along the edges, which are indented, but not ulcerated. Some weeks later, when she was suffering much, it was noted that there were small streaks or spots of red elevated papillæ, where the mucous membrane appeared denuded; in the intervals the surface was pale and depressed. The tip was the tenderest part. Teeth pretty sound. Digestion often imperfect. Manner morose. Urine very clear and pale, sp. gr. 1010, deposits only scaly epithelium. T. is much better some days than others. The affection has been regarded as syphilitic; she has taken hyd. bichl. and pot. iod. and pot. chloras, without benefit. She never had any cutaneous eruption. Treatment was continued, though not regularly, up to July 28th, 1862. She benefited more by liq. potas. arsen. ♏ vij—x *ter die*, but at the time of her taking this she became pregnant, which induced, as it had on several previous occasions, stomach derangement, and aggravated the lingual disease. I saw her again Feb.

6th, 1863, when she had been confined fourteen days. She stated that she had suffered much with her T. all through her pregnancy, but was relieved soon after. This is the only pregnancy where this has been the case; usually the neuralgia continues a long time after. She is now again under treatment.

No. 95.—J. G., m., æt. 33, ad. March 19th. Ill two years with tongue affection. Some spots form on one or other margin and under surface, which appear slightly depressed, and partially covered with a whity layer, detached epithelium. These were seen on several occasions during the time he remained under observation (about five months); they never appeared to be more than excoriations. He had had a chancre once, but there was no cicatrix to be seen on the penis. No trace of syphilis. Arsenic with tr. aconite and ferri + quin. citras was of much benefit, so that on one occasion he thought himself quite well. He soon, however, relapsed. At the time when he appeared recovered there were still traces of the whity patches remaining. In this case more than in any other there were indications of some quasi-eruptive affection like a vesicular skin disease; but I doubt whether this was more than secondary. I think there was more sensory disorder than the small amount of visible local alteration could account for.

No. 96.—W. W., m., æt. 50, ad. July 27th. Ill six months. His tongue looks at anterior part of dorsum denuded, and semi-raw, with whity coating here and there, and some tendency to fissure, especially at the tip, the edges indented. He can scarcely eat anything for the soreness, which is relieved by hot water, but cold causes smarting. Never had eruption or sore throat. Had a chancre twelve years ago, and suppurating buboes thirty years ago; no cicatrices in groins or on penis. Pain is always worse at night. About October 1st, when the tongue was feeling quite well, I observed a characteristic arcuate group of syphilitic tubercles encompassing the left commissure of the lips. Subsequently this group spread peripherally. Arsenic with cod-liver oil has been of material service to the tongue, so that it is kept pretty easy as long (Jan. 7th, 1864) as he continues the remedy, but on two occasions, when pot. iod. and nitric acid have been substituted, he has immediately relapsed. Painting the eruption on the lips with iodine has lessened it a good deal. Jan. 25th. The state of the tongue is aggravated; there are in the middle of the dorsum two or three fissure-like depressions with intervening induration; the surface of the cheek is red and sore; he feels very low and languid. The tongue is in more pain at night. Quinine gr. v + liq. pot. arsenit. m_x ter die. Pt. c. oleo. He continued this with decided benefit up to Feb. 15th, when I gave him besides Plummer's pill gr. v, o. n. March 3d. The eruption of the face had improved very much, his tongue looked much better and healthier, and felt to him nearly well; he could eat anything. The mixture was omitted, and the oil and pill continued. 10th. Still doing well. It is doubtful in my mind whether this was a case of actual syphilitic neuralgia, i. e., depending principally on the poison of syphilis, or whether it was ordinary neuralgia occurring in a syphilitic subject. I rather incline to the latter, inasmuch as pot. iod. was injurious while arsenic was beneficial. The mercurial, however, has certainly done much good.

No. 97.—E. R., f, æt. 55, had suffered since the spring of 1858, with more or less of a choking sensation, which at times came on "so fearfully" that she thought she must be choked. She described her state from this sensation as not feeling "ill exactly, but out of spirits, and fearful, as I suppose one would feel if a halter were about one's neck." Her tongue was so very·sore that it was painful to eat difficult to talk. She thought that the principal seat of the disorder lay in the tongue, which caused constant efforts to swallow, and that produced the dryness in the throat. Occasionally she was quite free from the distressing dysæsthesia. She took quinine with decided benefit, as well as a generous diet. In the autumn of 1859 she came under my care again in a state of great depression, with a cold, pallid skin, very weak pulse, anorexia, nausea, and very distresing sense of dryness of the mouth, her tongue feeling like a piece of leather. The night was the only time when she was quite free from the distressing sensation. Tongue appeared indented, but not ulcerated. Bark + ammonia was given, and acidi arseniosi gr. $\frac{1}{30}$ *ter die*, and she removed to the seaside. In three weeks she was almost if not quite well. In this case there appears to have been a combination of lingual and pharygeal dysresthesia. I have considered several times how far the condition of the tongue described above could be regarded as the result of lichenoid eruption, but I have never seen any such state of the tongue in ordinary lichen or prurigo, nor have I seen in lingual neuralgia any such eruption of the cutaneous surface, nor has the appearance of the tongue itself sufficiently warranted the supposition. In severe cases of this disorder Dr. L. Türck's practice of dividing the gustatory nerve might, I think, be adopted.

CHAPTER XXV.

BRACHIAL NEURALGIA.

ROMBERG gives but a short notice of this form of neuralgia; he considers it less frequent than crural, and less isolated than sciatic and facial neuralgia. Lussana and Bergson have entered fully into the subject in their prize essays published at Milan 1859, 1860, and reported fully in *Schmidt's Jahrb.*, vol. 108, p. 168, and vol. 113, p. 296. Lussana describes at length the various symptoms produced by neuralgia in the several nerves proceeding from the plexus, noticing particularly the terminal painful points, the superficial and the intermediate painful track (via dolorosa). The superficial painful points are where a nerve is given off from its trunk, where it perforates a muscle, or runs round a cylindrical bone, and where it becomes subcutaneous. In its direction the pain may be centripetal or centrifugal; in the latter case it is continuous, and without any elevation of temperature. The pain is as a rule increased by pressure, and, except in the case of the internal cutaneous nerve, by motion. With regard to the temperature of the affected parts Lussana finds it objectively or subjectively increased in neuralgias of cutaneous and sensitive nerves; objectively or subjectively lowered in neuralgias of nerves that are chiefly motor. Whenever the affected nerve is compound, *i.e.*, motor as well as sensory, muscular symptoms are observed which vary much in degree, but may amount to complete paralysis. If the short and long thoracic nerves are affected, the respiration may be short, laborious, and painful. Pyrexia rarely occurs except in plethoric habits; nausea and gastric disorder may be present, or even delirium. The type is generally inter- or sub-intermittent. The diagnosis between Br. Neuralgia and Neuritis is made to turn on the greater rarity of neuritis, on the more apparent causation of the latter, on the absence of pyrexia in neuralgia, on the more continuous character of the pain in neuritis, on the absence of signs of local inflammation, and of local tenderness on pressure of the affected nerve, on the greater amount of pain in the terminal points in neuralgia, and in the trunk in neuritis, on the greater constancy and earlier appearance of paralysis in neuritis, on the greatest severity of the muscular cramps and spasms, and on the different state of the terminal points in chronic cases, they being painful in neuralgia and anæsthetic in neuritis. In neuroma the pain extends more in a centripetal direction than it does in neuralgia. Lussana notices the existence of neuralgic pains in disease of the heart and great vessels, in disease of the lower part of the cervical region of the spinal cord, and of the vertebral column, in hepatic disease, in constitutional syphilis, and in lead poisoning which might be mistaken for essential brachial neuralgia.

Bergson arranges branchial neuralgias more according to their causes, as traumatic, rheumatic, sympathetic, hysteric or chlorotic, saturnine, such as depend on spinal irritation, and finally the idiopathic or essential. He rests the diagnosis of neuritis on the almost invariable previous occurrence of an injury, and on the increased size of the painful nerve, which can be detected through the skin. True chronic idiopathic neuralgia he considers to be very rare, and very refractory to treatment, while acute is much more tractable.

I have records of seventeen cases in which the nerves of the hand and arm, especially the median and unlar, were the seat of more or less severe neuralgia. As the affection has not been described so particularly in our own country, it may be worth while to record them shortly. Fifteen of them were females. The oldest patient was sixty-six, the youngest twenty.

CASE 1.—M. C., æt. 25, f.; ill three months with pain of right hand affecting all the parts supplied by the median nerve. It is worse at night, destroys sleep. After other treatment continued for a month had failed, I gave quinine gr. v *ter die*, and subsequently gr. x *ter die*. Under this she was well in three weeks.

CASE 2.—H. O., f., æt. 54.; ill for a long time with a numb and sleepy feeling in her hands at times, aggravated to violent pain at night. Cured in about ten days by small doses of quinine and iron.

CASE 3.—C. B., f., of mid-age; is awoke during night by a numbness or pain in the fingers of both hands, those supplied by the ulnar nerve being first affected. The morbid condition extends to the forearm. During the day the neuralgia ceases. Cured in five or six weeks by moderate doses of quinine + iron. Slight rigors occurred at night as the neuralgia yielded.

CASE 4.—M. J., f., æt. 29, four months pregnant. Ill one month with pain in hand and forearm not extending above elbow, severe at night, but felt only as a numb sensation during the day. There was marked debility. Quinine gr. xv and ʒss in the day failed, and so did arsenic and ferri carb.; quinæ gr. ij + ferri sulph. gr. iv *ter die*, was now given with morphia and henbane at night, and cured in three weeks.

CASE 5.—E. E., f., æt. 56, complains of pain in right forearm extending from fingers up to elbow, commencing in mid-finger. It is of more burning character at night, does not disturb her rest, but is very severe in morning, when she cannot move her hand to open or close it. The fingers often feel burning when she touches or holds anything, at other times are numb. Foot somewhat similarly affected. Small doses of quinine + iron, larger doses of quinine, carbonate of iron, muriate of ammonia and cod-liver oil failed to do more than to give some temporary relief. Under strychniæ gr. $\frac{1}{12}$ *ter die* and extr. col. co. gr. v, o. n., with the continued use of ferri carb. she improved considerably, so that she was able to do needlework, whereas she had at first been unable to hold a needle. She continued this treatment five or six weeks, having had for the last fourteen days pot. iod gr. ij *ter die* in addition, and was then well enough to be discharged. One galvanization appeared to be beneficial, a second rather injurious.

CASE 6.—J. M., f., æt. 48, suffers with bleeding hæmorrhoids. Ill three months with pain in centre of right palm extending up the arm over the shoulder to the spine; it is constant and gets worse, is increased at night. Hand is numb except the fingers and thumb; there is much burning sensation in it. No sleep at night. Cured in a month by small doses of quinine + iron, and morphia at night. It was remarkable in this instance how the pain extended itself upwards like an aura, not in the track of a nerve, and how the fingers were exempted from the disorder. The affection was evidently peripheral.

CASE 7.—E. M., f., æt. 47; ill three weeks with pain, chiefly of right mid-finger, in day-time it is numb. Left hand slightly affected. Urine very thick. Pot. iod. liq. pot. arsen. and liq. pot. for a week were of no avail, quinine in gr. xv and xx dose daily was more beneficial, but recovery took place under quinine + iron + liq. opii sed. in small doses with henbane at night. Some pruritus pudendi occurred during the last few weeks of treatment, and was much benefited by a borax and opium lotion.

CASE 8.—J. T., f., æt. 66. Ill more than six months. Is quite well except in her arms, which get stiff and numb, and ache, and are very cold. She suffers thus most at night. She took ferro-citrate of quinine gr. x + tr. nucis vomicæ m̨x + aq. ʒj *ter die*, and used locally lin. camph. co. In six weeks she was nearly well.

CASE 9.—S. K., f., æt. 47. Ill more than a year. Has pains in hands, extending up arms to shoulders, giddiness and general weakness. Most pain in right arm. Pain shifts from hands occasionally to the left side. With pot. iod. + citrate of iron and quinine, she recovered in about three months.

CASE 10.—E. L., f., æt. 46. Ill fourteen days. Cat. ceased three years. Some rheumatic symptoms lately. She took at first pot. iod. with alkali and colchicum with benefit for a week, her head being relieved; but she complained of her hands being attacked with numbness and cramp in the morning about 5 A. M., which continued in fits of ten minutes duration off and on till noon. A week later the pain came on earlier in the middle of the night, and was severe. With quinine and iron in moderate doses she improved, but did not recover. Probably rest and good food were essential as affording a basis for medical treatment. In this respect the disadvantages of external hospital patients can hardly be exaggerated. Success with them is a real test of the efficacy of drugs.

CASE 11.—R. B., m., æt. 65. Ill three or four days. Stout, healthy looking. Has lost the use of right hand, can hardly grasp at all with it or use a knife or pen. The parts supplied by the median nerve are numb, but never in pain. Feels some stiffness up to the elbow. The affection came on suddenly. No pain in head, no giddiness. Not subject to rheumatism. Skin warm. Glands in axilla not enlarged. He took for a week hydr. bichl. gr. $\frac{1}{8}$ + pot. nitrat. gr. x + inf. gent. co. ʒj ter die with slight benefit. Afterwards he had citrate of iron and quinine gr. 8 ter die, and was well in a month.

CASE 12.—C. G., m., æt. 20. Ill one week with pain in left arm, from elbow to tips of fingers; worse at night, relieved by heat. With gr. xij of quinine daily he was quickly well.

CASE 13.—C. R., f., æt. 40. Ill three weeks with pains in arms and hands; after much exertion her fingers get quite straightened so that she cannot bend them at all, she then feels "awful" pains in fingers extending up to shoulders. The pain is a great deal worse at night, is a sort of tingling and numbing pain. Can hardly dress herself in the morning. Left arm but little affected. Skin warm. Urine pale. Pulse not weak. Small doses of quinine + iron and pot. iod. were of no avail; she complained eleven days after admission, that if she had any hard work during the day her hand at night got quite stiff, and was in unbearable pain after she had slept about two hours; while if she had a quiet day she suffered only numbing and tingling sensations at night. The fingers got numb if she tried to write or sew. She suffered in exactly the same way eleven or twelve years ago. She was considerably improved by full doses of quinine gr. 20—30 in the day. An interlude of dyspepsia then occurred, after the relief of which she took ferri carb. gr. 20 ter die, and was nearly well at her last visit. The effect of exertion in aggravating the disorder was very apparent in this case.

CASE 14.—A. R., f., æt. 43. Ill seven days, was attacked in sleep all of a sudden, pain came on in the left shoulder, ran down the arm, and settled in the hand, which feels very powerless; the two inner fingers are much more numb than the others, but all are much affected. The pain in the hand keeps her awake at night, being worse then; it shoots down from the elbow. Hand sometimes very cold, at others hot, when hot the pain is increased. Urine clear. Aspect pallid. P. weak. The pain quite ceased under full doses of quinine, gr. xl—l a day with ol. morrh., and the numbness also diminished, but the hand remained almost completely paralyzed with scarcely the least movement of flexion or extension. The quinine alone seemed only to weaken her memory and sight a little; when ferri sulph was added, she became nearly blind and deaf. After this she was ordered strychnine gr. $\frac{1}{30}$—$\frac{1}{8}$ with tr. cinch., under which she regained some motor power, but in spite of galvanizing both with the interrupted and continuous current (she wore Pulvermacher's chain for some time) and a month in the country there was still very little power over the hand, when I last saw her after three months' treatment.

CASE 15.—A. L., f., æt. 47; ill at first for six weeks with sore throat and debility, got much better. At end of three months began to complain of agonizing pain extending from shoulder to wrist, and to the finger ends, continuing day and night, destroying all rest, and extending up the side of neck. No difference in appearance or temperature of affected parts. P. of good force, rather frequent. Of large make. Feels very weak, but otherwise well. Quinine in daily dose of gr. 20 to 28 failed to benefit, as well as extr. belladon. gr. ½ 2*dis horis*, and liq. pot. arsen. ♏ v *ter die*. Pot. iod. gr. v—vij *ter die*, with two opiate subcutaneous injections was of some service, but most benefit was obtained by the local application of tr. aconite undiluted with arsenic internally, under the use of which the arm became quite well. Just after this, the aconite having been continued about one month, and the arsenic five weeks, an eruption appeared on the upper arm attended with fearful itching and much heat and redness. The aconite was replaced by a strong lead lotion, and the arsenic continued. Three days later erysipelas had markedly developed itself over most of the arm and shoulder, attended with swelling and papular eruption, and pinching and burning pain in the part. She felt shivery. P. excited and feeble. Bark and ammonia were ordered, and the arsenic omitted. In four days all the redness had subsided, the swelling continued with much pain about the arm of scalding character. Much thirst. In ten to fourteen days she was well. In this case aconite and arsenic appeared to be the most effectual remedies. I can scarcely think the aconite had anything to do with producing the erysipelatoid inflammation, as it had been used fully three weeks without any such result. I have however, known aconite to cause cutaneous irritation. If this cause be put aside, I see no other view to take than that as the cerebro-spinal nerve disorder yielded the vaso-motor nerves became implicated, and this in the way of paralysis. There does not seem in this case to have been any musculo-motor nerve paralysis, which was so marked in No. 14. In a case I saw only once the patient, a female, æt. 45, suffered with nocturnal burning, throbbing, and painful sensation in hands and arms extending up to the shoulders with numbness of the fingers. The urine was clear, she had no indigestion.

Case 16.—E. G., f., æt. 26; ill two months ago with scarlet fever, on making any exertion experiences a pain in chest, and loses sensation and power in left arm. P. 96, weak. She took strychnia and iron, and was nearly well in fourteen days.

Case 17.—S. H., f., æt. 34, ad. May 19th, ill five weeks. Her right hand "goes dead" three or four times a day; it is constantly weak so that she cannot hold things with it, and she has constant pain and tenderness at the styloid process of the radius; no swelling of the wrist. T. whity and indented. B. costive. Urine rather dark. Has lumbar pain. Is weak and languid. She was not benefited by small doses of quinine and pot. iod., became worse with exceeding pain about the wrist and up the arm; a blister had caused much irritation. The hand was so cold one night (May 28th), that she was obliged to put it for relief into hot water. There was some diarrhœa and nausea, and she felt extremely depressed and languid. The quinine was increased to Ɔi in the day and the bowels quieted with opium and chloric ether. June 2d. A great deal better; the other fingers are comfortable, but she has much pain in the index and thumb. While the blister was open she was free from pain in the styloid process, now it has returned to that part, and to the adjacent articulation of the thumb. The quinine was increased to gr. viij *ter die*, and by the end of June she was convalescent and went into the country.

The above histories are sufficient to prove that branchial neuralgia is not, at least in this country, a very rare affection; it is rather curious that unintentionally I have recorded just as many cases of this disorder as of sciatica. The two seem to be essentially similar in their nature, relation to rheumatism, causes, and treatment. A rheumatic element appears, however, to be much less frequent in brachial than in sciatic neuralgia, and in correspondence with this pot. iod. and arsenic are found to be less efficacious. The influence of debility in predisposing to and maintaining the disorder is very decided. Besides this, however, we must assume some special agent to be affecting the nervous system injuriously. What that is cannot be precisely stated, but it seems to me that we shall not err greatly if we suppose some general miasmatous influence, widely dispersed and varying much in its potency at different periods, to be the efficient motor of the phenomena. There seems to be some sound reason for believing that neuralgic and epidemic catarrhal (influenzal) disorders are rather closely correlated in their origin, the cause of the latter giving rise also to the former. Mr. Norris, of Petherton, and Mr. Ewens, of Blandford, have recently stated[1] their experience as to the occurrence of sequelæ of hemicrania, and intermittent cephalalgia in connection with influenza. Hjaltelin[2] says that influenza in Iceland was followed by various neuralgic pains, especially lumbago, otalgia, odontalgia, facial and intercostal neuralgia and hemicrania. Similar observations have been made long ago as already stated by others. Several points of the above histories illustrate the neuralgic habitudes of the disorder. The nocturnal aggravation of the pain; its remission or absence by day; the intimate relation between it and numbness so that the latter seems to be a less degree of the same condition; the coexistence in some instances of motor disorder; the prevalence of general debility; the absence of self-limitation are family features of neuralgia. The results of the treatment above detailed seem to me to show pretty conclusively that the malady was not depending on any remote cause of irritation, as decayed teeth, worms, intestinal accumulations, &c.; nor on gouty poison or dyspepsia. These, however, are very possible causes, and we should be prepared to meet with them. The influence of heart-disease in producing a certain form of brachial neuralgia should also be remembered. The cases illustrate sufficiently the treatment which should be pursued. One main point is to improve the general tone and strength. If this be effectually accomplished, there will not generally be much more required. Good air and food, and the usual tonics with occasionally a nightly sedative are the most reliable means. In some instances ammonia, valerian, and arnica, with nitrate of silver prove more beneficial than quinine. In local applications I have not much faith, but they may sometimes, as in No. 15, afford much benefit. The interrupted current will I think chiefly be found useful where there is motor paralysis; I am

---

[1] "Med. Times and Gaz.," April 11,,1853.
[2] "Edin. Med. Journ.," Feb. 1863.

sure that it should be used cautiously to weak and hyperæsthetic nerves lest it aggravate rather than relieve the pain. Becquerel,[1] however, maintains that an induced current passed through a nerve in its long axis will always cure neuralgia if the stream is sufficiently strong, and the intermissions are very rapid. I confess I should not like to be the patient so treated. With regard to the continuous current it might, I think, be serviceable as a means of procuring temporary relief, but it is a very troublesome means to use (I speak of Pulvermacher's chain), and would be of little real avail unless the morbid tendency of the general system were amended by tonic treatment. Dr. Radcliffe has recently praised the use of the hypophosphites in neuralgia, together with cod liver oil and fatty food, viewing the disease from a chemical stand-point. I have not found any special advantage from the hypophosphite of iron and quinine in a few instances of various disorders in which I have tried it, and I certainly should not be disposed to rely on the acid alone to the exclusion of the two bases whose efficacy is so well proved. As an occasional sedative I am as much disposed to rely on chlorodyne as on anything else. A patient of mine told me she had cured herself with this of a sciatica which had proved refractory to orthodox medical measures. I must say, I should never use willingly any preparation whose composition was kept secret. The following history seems properly to find its place here as it refers certainly to a peripheral neurosis, and not to a central affection. The disorder was probably of the same nature as neuralgia, but, inasmuch as it was located in a mainly muscular nerve, it produced rather paralysis than pain. There was, however, very marked loss of sensation, which is often as much a part of neuralgic disorder as pain.

CASE 18.—G. W., æt. 40, ad. Nov. 11th; ill fourteen days. Has lost the use of his right arm, so that he cannot raise it from the shoulder-joint and abduct it by the action of the deltoid; he can move the forearm, but not so well as the other; has had great pain about the insertion of the deltoid, which came on in the course of the night, and has been replaced by numbness. The anæsthesia does not extend quite to the elbow. Is not subject to rheumatism. Functions generally in good order. Does not feel weak. Works in a damp place in a brewery. Dec. 20th. Right deltoid much wasted, unexcitable by galvanic current, skin covering it also very numb; the adjacent muscles and integuments are quite lively and sensitive. Whichever pole is applied to the highest part of the arm while the current (interrupted) is passing he feels the shocks there, not in the lower. But if I place the poles opposite each other on either side of the deltoid, he feels the shocks in both. He finds the arm stiffest in cold weather, and he suffers more pain then in it. The chief pain is a little below the seat of numbness. Jan. 7th. Deltoid much wasted, remains insensible to the strongest current, which has been used almost daily. On one occasion the current was sent directly through the muscle by needles passed through the skin. No good effect ensued, but he was unable to bear nearly so strong a current as before. It

[1] L'Union Med., Nos. i. and iv., 1861.

is very observable that the cold air produces "gooseflesh" all over both upper arms and shoulders when he is stripped, except over the paralyzed deltoid. Some weeks later the interrupted current had precisely the same effect, the anæsthetic skin remaining quite smooth, while the sensitive contracted. Feb. 4th. I have passed a continuous current from a 6-cell battery through needles stuck into the muscle, no muscular motion nor any sensation was produced while the current was passing, but on interrupting it the muscle contracted. The deltoid has shrunk and wasted much since I last saw him. He was now directed to wear a small Pulvermacher's chain on the affected part. In three weeks there was no improvement; the deltoid and infra-spinatus muscles were quite irresponsive to faradization, the skin over them still numb. March 12. Slight improvement. April 16th. Is recovering more use of arm, and the numbness diminishes. By about the middle of September, up to within a month of which he wore the chain, he had quite recovered save a little numbness in the skin over the insertion of the deltoid. Medicine had a fair trial in this case, and appeared ineffectual. Pot. iod. in gr. v doses *ter die*, pil. hydr. c. opio to salivation, sulphuret of potassium baths, strychnia carried up to gr. $\frac{1}{4}$ *ter die*, and ammon. murias failed to produce decided amelioration.

The strychnia was certainly continued at the rate of gr. $\frac{1}{12}$ *ter die*, during a good part of the time during which he was wearing the chain, but as it had been fairly tried before without benefit I think it cannot lay claim to the improvement, which was due either to the continuous current or to the *vis med. naturæ*. The chain is no favourite with me; it is a troublesome and rather painful remedy, but I think there is much ground for regarding it as the really effectual agent in this case. Paralyses such as the one above described are much more apt to remain as chronic and incurable affections than to disappear of themselves. The pathology of the above case is obscure, the most probable view is that the disorder was essentially similar to neuralgia of sensory nerves, but it remains unexplained why it was so refractory to treatment. It yields, however, in this respect to Case 14, which was not benefited by the chain, but which in most respects quite corresponds to the picture of neuralgia. It is quite possible and probable that in certain cases the molecular change which conditionates neuralgia may pass on to larger and more complete alteration, even to organic lesion.

CHAPTER XXVI.

SCIATICA.

CASES.—(1.) G. N., æt. 56, m, ill nine months with severe sciatica; cured by cinchonine and iron with ungt. veratriæ. As the sciatica yielded he had attacks of frontal pain, and gastrodynia. He was weakly, and his affected leg was specially weak. Treatment till convalescent=thirty-five days, total=three months.

(2.) Mrs. Ab., æt. 30, f. Ill two days with severe sciatica, not extending below ham, attended with great tenderness. Cured by pot. iod. + alkali at first, + bark afterwards, and aconite lotion in a week.

(3.) F. B , f., æt. 48. Ill three weeks with severe sciatica, unrelieved by quinine gr. v *ter die*, or by the same + iron, cured by pot. iod. with arsenic subsequently. Morphia injection failed. Treatment=forty-five days.

(4.) J. H., m., æt. 36. Ill six to seven months with sciatica, health otherwise good. Very much benefited, if not cured by arsenic internally, and tinct. aconite with belladonna to the limb. Treatment=thirteen days.

(5.) Mrs. H., f., æt. 30. Has had several previous attacks of left sciatica much relieved by hypodermic opiate injection. The present came on with marked signs of failing nerve power, syncopic attacks, delirium especially nocturnal, restlessness and exhaustion. Recovered well with ammon. carb., tr. valerian., tr. arnicæ, liq. opii sed., inf. valerian. 4*tis horis*, and arsenic with change to country.

(6.) W. W., m., æt. 43. Ill five weeks with left sciatica, most pain over exit-point of nerve from pelvis, with numbness and crampy pain extending down limb. But little benefit from iron + quinine, and veratria ointment, but was cured by two morphia dressed blisters to hip, and pot. iod. + tr. cinchon. + inf. cascarill. Debility was marked. Whole treatment=two months.

(7.) J. L., m., æt. 44. Ill three weeks with right sciatica; no benefit from arsenic and veratria, or arsenic + pot. iod. Cured by cinchonine, and cinchon. + iron, alterative aperients and emetics.

(8.) W. F., m., æt. 65. Ill one year with severe sciatica not extending beyond knee; great pain over exit of sciatic nerve. Much benefited by blister to hip, and veratria ointment subsequently with arsenic internally. Treatment=seventeen days.

(9.) T. H., m., æt. 38, right sciatica relieved by ol. tereb. m_x *ter die*, and linim. tereb. c. opio.

(10.) E. D., m., æt. 46. Ill fourteen days with left sciatica, nervous debility very marked. Hypodermic morphia injection gave no relief, nor did pot. iod., nor colchicum, nor ferri carb., nor croton oil aperient at night, but under the steady use of arsenic gr. $\frac{1}{20}$ *ter die* he recovered. The least exertion caused extreme perspiration

(11.) L. C., f., æt. 52. Ill fourteen days with left sciatica, marked debility, and vaso-motor nerve disorder. Has flushes of heat succeeded by perspiration three or four times a day; "fingers die now and then, turn numb and cold as marble, and the nails become black." Under F. + Q. citr. and aconite lotion she benefited very much. The motor power of the limb was impaired somewhat. The neuralgia affected also the right side of the face. Treatment=thirty-nine days.

(12.) T. D., m., æt. 45. Ill four months with right sciatica, making him walk lame. Is getting worse, very weak and emaciating. Most pain over exit of sciatic nerve. Much affected by change of weather from fine to wet. Cured in fourteen days by arsenic, and linim. terebinth. c. opio. He had had ague, been in India, lived at Woolwich.

(13.) J. N., m., æt. 42. Ill three weeks with left sciatica, very much benefited by quinine + iron, and ol. morrh., and one hypodermic opiate injection.

(14.) H. A., m., æt. 49. Ill two months with sciatica of the right thigh, great debility and starvation. Unrelieved by pot. iod. and tr. colch., or arsenic and tr. cinch., or opiate hypodermic injections, but very much by hospital care and good diet, aided by valerian, ammonia, chloric ether, and ferri carb. internally, with a morphia blister.

(15.) E. W., f., æt. 49. Ill two or three months with left sciatica, affected limb colder than the other. Not benefited by pot. iod. + bark, with morphia blister, but materially by quinine + iron. The neuralgia showed a tendency to affect the head.

(16.) C. P., æt. 38, f. Ill six months with left sciatica. A morphia blister, pot. iod. + vin. colch., iron + quinine, and ferri carb. were of no avail. Quinine gr. 20 in the day was of material use, but arsenious acid appeared to be the most effectual remedy. Liq. opii sedat. was injected several times with temporary relief. Treatment=six months.

(17.) M. M., m., æt. 63. On ad. had had sciatica four to five months since a wetting while perspiring; health generally perfect; pain increased by changes of weather. Left leg *feels* very cold, but the actual temperature of both is about the same, 90° F. Pain extended quite down to ankle, was replaced to some extent by numbness in the course of the treatment. He remained in the hospital seven weeks, had quinine, arsenic, iron, pot. iod., croton oil, subcutaneous opiate injections, and morphia blisters, but did not make very satisfactory progress.

The above cases show pretty clearly that sciatica is for the most part essentially a neuralgic affection quite similar to neuralgia in any other situation. The proportion of males to females in my cases is considerable, 11 : 6, a circumstance which, if not accidental may be explained by the greater exposure of the male sex to chills, &c. The impairment of motor power which often occurs has been well noticed by Romberg, and is certainly almost as noteworthy a feature as the pain. It shows that the morbid action is not confined to the sensory nerves, but affects the motor in juxtaposition with them. Of the nature of this morbid action we can say little more than that it appears to be identical with that which produces neuralgia in other situations, that except perhaps in recent rheumatic cases it is not inflammatory, and especially that it has usually a positive relation to debility, and will not yield permanently until at least some degree of strength and vigour is restored. Dr. Radcliffe's suggestion that owing to impaired nutrition some breach occurs in the oleaginous investment (white substance of Schwann) of the axis cylinder as I think probable, and at any rate may serve provisionally as a representation to our minds of the state of the parts concerned.

Romberg admits the occurrence of a spontaneous cure in connection with critical symptoms, as diarrhœa, menstrual, lochial, or hæmorrhoidal discharges. I do not wish to question the possibility of this; but according to my own experience the continuance of any discharges of this kind is much more likely to perpetuate than to cure a sciatica. Neuralgic disorder is occasionally met with which affects more the superficial nerves of the lower limb than the deep-seated sciatic trunk. It is essentially similar to the more common affection. The *diagnosis* of sciatica does not generally present any material difficulty. Pain extending down the posterior aspect of the limb in the course of the nerve, especially felt, and increased by pressure between the ischiatic tuberosity and the great trochanter, but not aggravated materially by the movements of the joint, or by pressure of the articular surfaces together, can scarcely be due to other causes than sciatica. The most important point in refractory cases especially occurring in the female sex is to determine whether or not the pain is dependent on any intra-pelvic, or other organic disease. Churchill mentions a case (*Diseases of Women*, p. 253) where an ulcerated uterine cancer produced no pain except in the whole course of the sciatic nerve. In such cases there will however almost always be other symptoms, such as discharge, or hemorrhage, which will indicate the true nature of the disease. It is most probable that the pain from cancer uteri is of reflex character, and not occasioned by direct irritation of the nerve. This I conclude partly because the uterus is too remote from the sciatic nerve, and partly because fibrous and ovarian growths which are more likely to press on the nerve do not have the same effect. Trousseau[1] declares that sciatica is often dependent on disease of the vertebral column, kidneys, testes, uterus, and rectum, and states that Chomel went so far as to disbelieve in the existence of essential sciatica. He mentions a case where it occurred in a young female after delivery in consequence of a slow inflammation of the sacro-iliac symphysis ending in abscess. The condition here was probably one of neuritis. Though I have the highest respect for Trousseau's opinion I must say that my experience does not confirm his and Chomel's view as to the frequency of the remote origin of sciatica.

The disease in some cases has a rheumatic character, the urine being lateritious and acid, a certain amount of pyrexia being present, and the strength not much impaired. Here potass. iod. and vin. colch. with alkali are curative, but the iodide should be given in pretty large doses, gr. vij—x, *ter die*. In the majority of instances, however, there is more or less marked debility, the urine is free and pale, the tongue clean, and tonics are evidently indicated. Among these I am inclined to rate arsenic rather highly, as it has served me well in cases which would scarcely I think have recovered without. I am rather partial to the simple solution in distilled water, which easily dissolves gr. $\frac{1}{10}$ per ℥j. As a means of improving the general nutrition, as well as that of the affected nerve, it will be well to administer ol. morrh. in all cases bearing the stamp of debility. I am aware that some physicians have found repeated small doses of croton oil of great efficacy, but it has not occurred to me to meet with such. The remedy should however be borne in mind in dealing with refractory disease of this kind. I say of this kind, for it is by no means useful only in sciatica, but also in other neuralgias. This goes far to disprove the view of the mechanical cau-

---

[1] "Clinique Européenne," No. iii., 1859.

sation of sciatica, viz., that it is produced by the pressure of scybalous masses in the lower bowel. This may occasionally be the case, but certainly it is not common, and on the other hand constipation very often produces no sciatica. I remember an old man in whom by reason of a large epithelial cancer of the lower rectum the feces concreted above into masses about as large, and almost as hard as a walnut, which enemata would bring away; yet he had no sciatica. I am rather inclined to look upon croton oil as acting in certain cases as a specific stimulant to the nervous system. Cases no doubt occur where local bloodletting is necessary, but I can scarcely believe that venesection can be requisite as Romberg states. If this is ever the case, it must be when there exists considerable pyrexial disturbance of a sthenic character, and this might be always allayed I should think by other means. Ol. terebinth. has maintained for some considerable time its reputation as a remedy for sciatica. I have used it but little, chiefly because the state of the general system has seemed to require more decided tonics. I consider it most appropriate to those conditions where there is no marked debility, or indication of recent rheumatism, or of organic disease. Hypodermic opiate injection gives considerable temporary relief in some cases; it is apt, however, to cause much distressing nausea and sickness. It is scarcely desirable to use it except where the suffering is severe. As a local application if the pain be severe, and the limb intolerant of pressure, I think aconite lotion is the best. If the pain be more gnawing and wearying and tenderness be not marked, chloroform and opium liniment is preferable. Veratria ointment and belladonna are appropriate to cases where the tenderness is less than in those requiring aconite. Some physicians have much confidence in "firing," I do not mean using the actual cautery, but iron heated by being dipped in boiling water. Dr. Graves indeed states that in very obstinate cases the actual cautery applied to five or six spots along the course of the painful nerve is the means most to be relied on. I should consider this, however, quite a "dernier ressort," and certainly not to be employed unless I was well satisfied of the absence of organic disease as well as of general debility. It cannot be too clearly kept in mind that as long as the latter continues no real improvement can be effected. Dr. Fuller speaks highly of acupuncturation, and there is no doubt of its frequent efficacy in this and other neuralgic affections, although I am not convinced that its virtue depends on the evacuation of effused fluid. Dr. Althaus has found faradization of the affected nerve effectual in sciatica. I can quite believe that this is the case, but it is requisite in using the interrupted current to take care, (1) that the condition is not one of inflammation, and (2) that the strength of the current is not too considerable. I am satisfied that the pain may be aggravated if this caution is disregarded. Torri[1] relates ten cases of sciatica cured by weak con-

---

[1] "Gazz. Med. Ital. Toscan." 1857, Nos. xlii., xliii.

tinuous currents kept up uninterruptedly for two days. The positive pole was applied to the leg, the negative to the thigh, the epidermis having been previously removed at each spot, and a sponge moistened with saline solution placed in contact with the cutis. The pain of this proceeding we can aver must have been severe, and we are not surprised to read that the skin in contact with the zinc always became gangrenous and required some time to heal. The pain may have been lessened by the half grain of morphia which was placed upon the denuded cutis. A case is recorded by Hooker[1] in which division of the popliteal nerve was successfully resorted to for severe neuralgia of the leg. Jobert de Lamballe[2] had also divided the sciatic (and crural) nerves in a case of great severity, but though much relief was afforded the patient died from sloughing of the skin over the sacrum and pyæmia. He renounces this operation in favour of the actual cautery. Finco[3] reports that he has treated 48 cases of sciatica by cauterizing the *ear*. In 30 the operation was quite successful, in 10 partially so, in 8 it failed. The failure is ascribed by F. to the presence of various complications. In almost all his cases vigorous antiphlogistic treatment was employed before the cauterization, and in some its effect was aided by mercurial or belladonna ointment. The operation had to be repeated only in 3 cases. Duchenne[4] rejects the use of the cautery, but thinks that the interrupted current may be employed in its stead. He prefers, however, to act *loco dolenti*, using dry conductors.

Crural Neuralgia.

My experience accords with Romberg's that this is a much rarer affection than sciatica, but that in essential points it closely resembles it. Direct irritation of the nerve from a loaded intestine or some similar cause may give rise to it, but less frequently I think than the obscure influences which so commonly produce nerve disorder. The possibility of neuralgia and impaired motor power of the thigh being dependent on the existence of obturator hernia should be borne in mind, and if any symptoms of intestinal obstruction are observed, an operation should be at once performed. The following case is an example of non-organic crural neuralgia.

CASE 18.—Mrs. F., æt. 65, seen June 14th. A frequent sufferer from neuralgia affecting various parts. Was attacked yesterday in afternoon with intense pain affecting both lower limbs from the hips to the ankles and heels. The pain was diffused over the front and exterior of the limbs, and was attended with a sense of powerlessness. She kept rubbing the parts constantly in hope of relief. Functions in order. The pain continued severely from 5 P. M. to 1 A. M., remitted then somewhat, but returned

[1] "Lancet," Oct. 1, 1859.   [2] "L'Union Méd.," No. lxxvii., 1859.
[3] "Gaz. Lombard." xxxviii., xxxix., xli., 1860.
[4] "Tr. de Therapeut." par Trousseau et Pidoux, vol. i. p. 787, 788.

again at 6 A. M. severely for a short time. Up to noon of 14th she had no sleep in spite of ♏ 120 of liq. morph. bimecon. given since the previous evening. A liniment of chloroform, belladonna, and opium gave no relief. Quinine given to moderate cinchonism subdued the pain; on 15th she was quite free. Some slight nocturnal fever occurred as the neuralgia yielded. For some weeks before her attack her nervous system had been much deranged in consequence as she thought of a thunderstorm.

In another case a delicate boy, æt. 9, had agonizing pain in his feet occurring in paroxysms succeeded by copious perspirations. Pot. iod. + pot. bicarb. was of no benefit, but with citrate of iron and quinine he soon got well.

CHAPTER XXVII.

ANGINA PECTORIS.

My noticing this disorder among the functional diseases of the nervous system will show that I consider it to be *au fond* a neuralgia. Dr. Watson objects to this view:[1] (1) because the paroxysm is excited by such causes as are especially calculated to disturb the natural action of the heart, bodily exertion, and menal emotion: and (2) because the disease is so very frequently and suddenly fatal, which is not the character of mere neuralgic diseases in general. To this it may be replied that exertion and mental emotion are causes which do very much increase and even induce various neuralgiæ. A gentleman about whom I was lately consulted suffered with an obstinate neuralgia of the side of the chest, which subsided on his remaining perfectly still, but was immediately reproduced by moving about. Neuralgia in other parts is not fatal just because the function of the organ is not essential to life. No one can be surprised that "tic douloureux," or sciatica, or the like should not endanger life. Dr. Stokes,[2] from his examination of the subject, concludes that the special group of symptoms described as angina pectoris is but the occurrence in a defined manner of some of the symptoms connected with a weakened heart. Obstruction of the coronary arteries he considers as no necessary condition. According to this view a weakened state of the heart is essential. I cannot agree with this, as I have certainly had patients under my care with considerably weakened hearts who presented none of the symptoms of angina pectoris. And again I can adduce one if not two cases where after death from this affection the heart was found in a toler-

---

[1] "Lectures," vol. ii. p. 259.
[2] "Dis. of Heart and Aorta," p. 487.

ably healthy state. Something there must be I think beyond simple weakening of the organ to account for the peculiar phenomena of the disease. It is however quite reasonable to believe that a variety of morbid changes may predispose to it, and indeed this seems to be the fair inference from the observations which have been collected by Dr. Forbes. This opinion seems to be that entertained by Dr. Copland. Dr. Latham regards the disease as spasm of the heart, insisting on its analogy to cramp in the voluntary and involuntary muscles, and on the efficacy of opium in relieving the distress. Lussana adopts the same view, citing an observation of Morgagni's who found at an autopsy the heart "durum valde et robustum," and another one of Carron d'Annecy where the heart was very much contracted. He thinks it demonstrated that the heart's muscular tissue during the attack is in a state of cramp-like contraction, and remarks that the character of the pulse as generally observed is in conformity with this view, being brief, small, hard, and often accelerated. V. *Schmidt's Jahrb.*, vol. 108, p. 312. Dr. Walshe[1] says that "angina pectoris seems to be constituted by spasm of the heart, and neuralgic pain," and doubts whether it ever occurs without some kind of structural change in the organ. It may be remarked that a cramp-like condition of the heart's tissue would quite as much interfere with its functional action as a paralytic state. It is quite as essential for the heart to relax duly to admit blood into its cavities, as it is that it should contract and expel it. The pallid face, sunken features, and feeling of impending dissolution may quite be accounted for on the view held by Latham. Lussana states, what seems scarcely in accordance with general experience, that after the attack the continued contraction of the muscular fibres is succeeded by languor, exhaustion of irritability, and finally paralysis, to which even the pain itself contributes. Therefore the heart of anginose patients falls after the attacks into a condition of collapse, and the circulation is languid and feeble, so much so in some cases that the pulse and the heart's impulse become imperceptible, and the patient at last becomes faint and dies quietly. Dr. Stokes, on the contrary, speaks of the pulse during the attack as being almost imperceptible, and says nothing of any subsequent syncopal state. Morgagni and Carron found in two patients who died during the attack the right cavities completely empty, and the left ventricle nearly so, the pulmonary artery and the vena cava on the contrary distended with blood, which was black and quite fluid. In patients who had died in the intervals of the attacks coagulated or fluid blood was found in larger or smaller quantity in the cavities. Lussana regards the latter as indicating paralysis, the former tetanus of the heart. He thinks generally that the blood of anginose patients is but slightly coagulable; in one of my own cases the fluidity of the blood was

---

[1] "Dis. of Lungs and Heart," p. 434.

remarkable. His final conclusions are that the disease may be dynamic or organic; but that for the most part it is the latter, being in fact produced by mechanical irritation of the cardiac plexus resulting from calcareous degeneration of the coronary arteries of the heart, or some similar cause. It is thus invariably a neuralgia, whose sole and constant seat is the cardiac plexus.

The three following fatal cases in which autopsies were made came under my own observation.

No. 98.—J. O., æt. 39, m. Seen Dec. 15th. Always had a rosy colour. Never had rheumatic fever, but had pain in left temple, stopped by local applications. Has been ailing several months. About nine weeks ago had the first attack of pain in his chest, "it turned his face white." Up to Nov. 16th, when he was admitted as in-patient, he had the attack once in two or three days. While in hospital he had a short hacking cough, pain in epigastrium extending up to the throat increased by walking, which also brought on palpitation. Heart's action regular, loud diastolic bruit at base and apex, cardiac dulness not increased, impulse at times heaving and strong. Weak breathing all through both lungs. Urine healthy. Temper irritable. Left hospital Dec. 8th in same state. When he came under my care he complained of a constrictive sensation at the epigastrium, "like a rope round him." The same sensation was brought on by walking to some extent. At times he had a dreadful amount of flatulence. Appetite very good, but is afraid to eat. Looks well. Pulse 54, weak, intermitting every now and then. Heart's action trembling, the contractions appear to be not steadily sustained. Ordered argenti nitrat. gr. $\frac{3}{4}$ + extr. hyoscy. gr. ij *ter die*, with ammonia, spt. æth. s. co., and tr. hyoscy. On 21st and 22d he suffered much from pain in front of his chest during the night up to 4 A. M. On 24th he had pains in his chest as usual till 7 A. M. when he screamed out violently, turned over, and died immediately. I was informed that he had latterly had an attack twice or thrice daily, each attack lasting one hour, during this time the epigastrium was hard and swollen. In the intervals he was quite free from pain. Taking even very light food, or riding, or walking brought on the paroxysms. In one of the latter, if not the last, the pain extended to the left arm, affecting it severely. He used to open his dress and rub his chest when suffering. His wife thought he had a tendency to insanity. *Post-mortem.*—Lungs quite healthy. Some fluid in pericardium. Heart about normal size, very decidedly flabby, muscular tissue appeared healthy, large loose clots in auricles. Aortic valves did not hold water; they were thickened, but quite flexible. Just above one of them, in the sinus of Valsalva, there was a large patch of calcareous deposit, about $\frac{1}{4}$ by $\frac{1}{4}$ inch; it lay close to the orifices of a coronary artery. The coats around were healthy. Mitral valve a little thickened, but quite efficient. Right valves healthy. Muscular tissue of the heart was markedly affected with fatty degeneration, the fibres full of minute oil molecules, and their nuclei broken up into masses or streaks of oily molecules. Liver and stomach quite healthy. Body in good condition, muscles of a good dark colour, and in a decided state of rigor mortis, which was not the case with the heart.

No. 99.—Mr. H., æt. 57, a stout, large-made man, had been to the races on 27th, and rather deranged his digestion as he thought with melons and champagne. He complained on 30th of a very distressing pain across the upper part of his chest "as if an iron network was there instead of flesh," but there was no disorder of the sounds or rhythm of the heart. He was very fidgety and nervous, and anxious for relief, and of his own accord applied hot water to his chest, so as to raise a small blister. The pain in his chest came on while he was walking up a hill on 27th and continued till his death. He had always a presentiment of sudden death, often spoke of it; his father died of disease of the heart. On 30th he had a dose of calomel + opium, some brandy, and olei ricini, and one dose of soda + acid. hydrocy. dil. ℞ iij. Shortly after this he died suddenly, just after leaving the nightstool. *Post-mortem.*—Lungs much congested, but crepitant throughout and healthy. Heart of normal size, cavities open, containing as well as the large vessels much fluid blood, and scarce a trace of clot. The heart's tissue was rather flabby, of good colour, the muscular fibres of both ventricles showed only fatty degeneration of their nuclei, the bulk of each fibre was quite healthy. The subpericardial fat encroached to some extent on the muscular tissue in some parts, but the walls of the cavities were not thinned. The left coronary artery was extensively affected by atheromato calcareous deposit, which narrowed at some parts of its canal decidedly. The right coronary appeared healthy, the mitral and aortic valves were healthy, the others were not specially examined. No coagula in the large pulmonary vessels. Tracheal and bronchial mucous membrane was very highly congested and dark. The abdominal viscera all appeared healthy. The stomach contained a little fluid; its mucous surface was pale and normal.

No. 100.—X. Y., a robust man, æt. 54, was under treatment a short time with inflammation of the left testis of moderate severity. It was getting better, and he was not otherwise ill at all. He had been under treatment on previous occasions, but had never had any serious illness. About the middle of the day he was suddenly attacked with severe pain in the region of the heart. His medical attendant had seen him the same morning, and found him apparently well. In fifteen or twenty minutes the man was dead. Six leeches had been applied on three separate occasions to the testis; the patient had suffered some mental anxiety, but was in tolerably good circumstances. At the *post-mortem* the rigor mortis was well marked, the body muscular, and in good condition. Heart flabby, its walls were perhaps rather thinner than normal, and its tissue of a less decided red. On microscopic examination some degree of fatty degeneration of the fibres was found, but not by any means enough to account for the fatal event. There was slight atheroma of the coronary arteries. Brain not examined. Thoracic and abdominal viscera healthy.

Remarks.—The morbid changes in these three cases were materially different, and yet the disease was in all I believe the same. In the first it is probable that the patch of calcareous deposit pressed on and irritated some nerve, which then exerted on the cardiac ganglia a depressing inhibitory influence. The degenerated muscular tissue would be all the more readily paralyzed from its enfeebled state. In the second case there seems no adequate explanation to be given of the sudden supervention of the symptoms, as it must be supposed that the disease of the coronary artery had existed for a long time, and the heart so to speak must have become habituated to it. In the third case there appeared absolutely no cause for the fatal event. The occurrence of such cases as the last, the absence of any constant morbid condition in instances where organic disease is found, and the frequent existence of all kinds of organic lesions without any trace of angina incline me very much to believe that the essential circumstances in the disorder under consideration is an attack of neuralgia, quite similar to that which would be unimportant elsewhere. This seems to be nearly the opinion entertained by Trousseau, and is further supported by the complete cures of the disease which have occasionally been accomplished.

Bernard tells us,[1] and the observation is highly important, that irritation of a posterior spinal root causes temporary arrest of the heart's action continuing for fifteen or twenty seconds; he even intimates that in a weakened animal fatal syncope might be produced in this way. It is however noteworthy that cerebro-spinal neuralgia however violent does not (in the human subject) seem to have much tendency to induce syncope, whereas this is apt to ensue on irritation of the sympathetic plexus. If we conceive such a pain as a severe gastralgia befalling the cardiac plexus we may well imagine that it would occasion arrest of the heart's action. I am much inclined to coincide with Laennec's statement, quoted by Romberg,[2] to the effect that "in a slight or moderate degree angina pectoris is an extremely common affection, and exists very often in individuals who are free from any organic affection, of the heart or of the large vessels. I have seen many persons who have experienced only some smart attacks, but of short duration, and who have afterwards been freed from them. I even believe that the influence of the medical constitution contributes to its development, for I have observed it frequently in the course of certain years, and I have hardly met with it in others." Romberg's statement that arthritis and hysteria are the chief predisposing causes of this disease appears to me by no means well founded, certainly at least as regards the latter. Neither can I remember to have met with angina in any of my gouty patients; I can scarcely think that the podagrous are notably more liable to the disorder than others. Rheumatism appears to me to have much more relation to angina pectoris than gout has, and this may be the reason that certain states of cardiac disorder of anginose character are remarkably relieved by pot. iod. I am speaking here of the apyretic form of rheumatism, such for example as produces a stiff neck. Believing as I do that angina pectoris is essentially a neuralgia, there is nothing surprising to me in the occurrence of minor degrees of it, or to speak more exactly, of various forms of dysæsthesia or neurosis of the heart. True, these are not likely often to pass into the graver disease, but they indicate nevertheless

[1] "Leçons," vol. i. p. 269.
[2] "Dis. of Nervous System," vol. i. p. 126.

the tendency of the nervous structures of the heart to be morbidly affected. This is a material point, as any tendency to implication of vital organs is always to be regarded with suspicion. Thus of two persons who on exposure to malaria should contract, the one a severe tic of the face, the other a moderate cardiac neurosis, I should have no question in estimating the former as the more lightly visited. It is perhaps impossible to offer any satisfactory arrangement of cardiac neuroses, the most useful way will be I think to cite some interesting examples I have met with, and to make some comments upon them.

Before doing this I would remark shortly on the great influence of gastric disorder on the heart. This is a matter of the commonest experience, but it seems to me to be by no means sufficiently explained. In the first place I think it must be allowed that mere flatulent distension of the stomach disturbs materially the action of the heart, the relief procured on dispersing the flatus being immediate. I should be much inclined to ascribe this disorder of the heart solely to inhibitory action of the gastric nerves, were it not that it is certainly aggravated by lying on the left side, which by bringing the weight of the liver and other viscera to press on the stomach pushes it upwards against the diaphragm and the heart. The cardiac uneasiness from this cause sometimes takes the form of a sharp precordial pang, which forces the person to turn immediately from the left side position from the sensation that if he did not the heart's action would be arrested. The distress in this case seems to be of mechanical origin. There is certainly I think some peculiar relation between flatulency and cardiac disorder. A gentleman whose heart is apparently free from organic disease, and who has no gouty tendency, but some rheumato-neuralgic, finds that when he has been debilitated by various causes, over-exertion in walking produces a tendency to syncope and flatulence. It appears as if both resulted from the same cause. He has no dyspepsia, but has found that sudden mental excitement or emotion will suddenly bring on flatulency when he was previously quite free from it. The extraordinary rapid development of flatus (rectal), which occurs not uncommonly in malarious dysentery, ceasing as suddenly as it commenced, and taking the place of diarrhœal discharge is almost sufficient to prove that flatulent disorder may be dependent upon nerve affection. No one can I think have had to deal with these cases without being impressed both with the neurotic character of the disorder and the utter insufficiency of any mere decomposition of intestinal contents theory to account for the phenomena. From my own observation of both gastric and rectal flatulence I am much disposed to lay down as a proposition, that mucous membranes under the influence of enfeebled innervation may secrete large quantities of gas. Trousseau[1] affirms that flatulent distension often occurs

---

[1] "Cliniq. Méd.," vol. ii. p. 354.

quite independent of fermentation. Cardiac distress and debility may be co-results of the same nerve disorder. The best remedies for cardiac uneasiness depending on flatulence are creasote in pills with quinine and a little ginger, or creasote in solution with muriatic acid and tr. calumbæ. The following case is a well-marked example of the association of cardiac and gastric disorder.

No. 101.—M. L., f., æt. 53, ad. January 23d, ill three months. Complains of dreadful palpitation of the heart mostly felt at night, preventing her from lying down or getting sleep for hours; sometimes she can hardly breathe. The palpitation causes a hammering noise in head. Has much flatulence and spasm at the stomach (severe pain darting from between the scapulæ to the sternum, and up into the neck). If she can disperse flatus is easier. Food does not digest, turns to wind. The heart does not appear enlarged, there is a loud rough systolic bruit at the base extending some way along the aorta, second sound distinct lower down, rhythm normal. She says the heart seems to stand still at times. Is very weak, always thirsty. Epigastrium very tender. Takes no tea. Has prolapsus ani. Nitrate of silver with henbane was given with good effect in calming the excited action of the heart, but muriatic acid with prussic and inf. calumbæ was rather prejudicial, a combination of strychnia, ferri sulph. and tr. zingib. proved however most useful. As long as she took it she had tolerable appetite, and was able to digest and to lie down and sleep at night. The heart's action became much quieter, and the pulse notably *weaker* than it had been at first. Stout she found beneficial, but had to omit it occasionally. Mutton, cocoa, and bread she was able to digest very tolerably.

In this case it is quite certain that the gastric disorder as well as the cardiac was a neurosis. Had it been otherwise the strychnia and iron would surely have proved the reverse of beneficial. Flatulent distension of the stomach no doubt aggravated the cardiac disorder, but did not originate it. Both were I believe co-results of the same neurotic condition, and both were benefited by the same treatment. The calming of the excited heart's action under nervine tonics is a curious and interesting phenomenon, and almost necessarily suggests to us the opposite results of dividing and galvanizing the pneumogastric nerves. In one very marked instance which occurred to me many years ago the patient had had diarrhœa, vomiting, loss of appetite, and sleepless nights for two or three days; she was very weak, inclined to faint, and felt as if she would sink through the bed on which she lay; yet the pulse was regular, large, rather forcible, 100. Under quinine 9 grains a day, she gained much strength, and the pulse became weaker, from the heart acting more quietly. The effect of large doses of quinine in slowing the pulse is very similar to that of galvanizing the pneumogastrics, and the result is probably attained through the same channel. It is in instances of the kind above related, well known to practical men, that we have good examples of the truth of the distinction made by Barthez[1] between *radical* and *acting* forces. The former may be

---

[1] "Traité de Thérapeut.," par Trousseau et Pidoux, vol. i. p. 43.

nearly exhausted while the latter are in full play; and *vice versâ* the latter may be but slightly manifested while the former are powerful. The amount of the radical forces represents a person's capacity of vital resistance to disease and to fatigue. Two persons may have the same apparent strength and capacity for action, but one, to use an expressive term, has much more "last" in him than the other, withstands fatigue much longer, and resists hardship and morbific causes much better. The acting forces according to Barthez have their origin in the radical, and these are especially increased and sustained by quinine and other tonics, though of course they are dependent essentially on the due maintenance of the various vital processes by food, pure air, repose, &c. It is very noteworthy that there is often a distinct consciousness in the system that these radical forces are failing. The pulse and respiration may be good, there may be no evident signs of impending collapse, and yet the patient may feel that he is gravely stricken, and have a presentiment of dissolution which is not unfrequently verified. I well remember myself during the cholera epidemic of 1854, a full hour before I was attacked with a form of the disease, laying down the pen as I was writing at night surprised at the sudden strong presentiment of death which came over me. My mind was quite calm and clear, my bodily functions were unaffected, and I looked upon the feeling for some time as a curious psychical phenomenon. This however by way of digression. The depressing influence of certain matters taken into the stomach upon the heart is well known, as for instance that of large draughts of cold water, or of lumps of undigested food. Mr. Higginbottom has recorded[1] some well-marked examples of "syncope senilis" resulting from the latter cause, and relieved speedily by the administration of an ipecacuan emetic. Such cases seem to me best explained on the view of inhibitory action, the *morbid* stimulus being reflected from the nervous centres on the cardiac nerves. Tea is so notorious a disturber of the heart's tranquillity that it needs little more than a bare mention. I am satisfied that it is not solely an idiosyncrasy which renders it a very poison to some individuals, but that acquired nervous debility may have the same effect. The gentleman whose case I have alluded to above used to take tea freely and enjoy it until the last five or six years without experiencing any ill effects. Now it renders him sleepless, hyperæsthetic, weak, and produces a sensation of precordial uneasiness and of failing action of the heart. Coffee if continued a few days has the same effect, but cocoa has not. The remedy in such instances is not only omission of the injurious article of diet, but the employment of all means capable of increasing nervous energy. It may be mentioned as illustrative of the change wrought in the nervous system by the toils and cares of life, that the same man to whom tea is now a poison drank it instinctively as the most reviving

"Lancet," April 20, 1856.

beverage twenty-four years ago towards the close of an eighty miles' rowing match. Many Alpine tourists find cold tea an excellent refresher in their mountain clamberings. It is plain enough that to a tolerably firm nervous system tea is a grateful and useful stimulant. Its poisonous and depressing action on the weak and shaky system may be explained I conceive on the principle before referred to, viz., the production of hyperæsthesia by debility. When the nervous power has become enfeebled the plexuses of the coronary arteries partake of the morbid sensibility, and are excited by tea to produce contraction of the vessels. The heart is thus imperfectly supplied with blood, and its action is consequently feeble and flagging. In other instances where palpitation is produced it is probable that the stimulus tells more upon the muscular tissue of the heart than upon the coats of its vessels. M. Beau[1] has lately remarked on the production of angina pectoris by the use of tobacco, and records eight cases in evidence, two of which proved fatal. Judging from the action of nicotine in tetanus, and from the effect of tobacco enemata it would seem probable that tobacco exerts a directly paralyzing influence on the heart. Rouget[2] however shows by experiment that its action is the reverse, that when applied directly to the heart it causes a permanent tonic contraction; and that if it be applied to the motionless and dilated ventricles of birds and mammals killed by the inhalation of chloroform, it restores for a time the contractions, and at last induces tetanus of the tissue. This statement goes to support the theory of spasm.

The cases I propose to relate may be distinguished as rheumatic, malarious, saturnine, and connected with "goitre exophthalmique."

No. 102.—C. R., æt. 35, (?) of sanguine habit, but rather weak nerve power, had been exposed to cold more than once, and suffered from stiff neck and a most unaccountable malaise. His digestion was usually good. Four days later, having had a fresh chill in the interval, he took a hurried meal, and on returning had a nap as usual. He awoke with a very curious sensation of spasmodic choking all along the œsophagus. He went to bed and felt somewhat relieved by the warmth, so that he slept for about one hour. He then awoke in the most excruciating pain, could only lie in one position, viz., on the back slightly inclined to the right side with the left leg drawn up. He could not breathe without great pain. "I dared not," he says, "close my eyes from experiencing that most awful sensation as if my heart would cease pulsating, the agony I went through that night baffles all description. For two hours he was involuntarily kicking; though well aware that he was doing so he seemed to have no control over his limbs; and if he chanced to kick himself the feeling was a most curious one, "as if one leg did not belong to the same body." A mustard and turpentine poultice to the chest afforded some relief. When I saw him early the next morning the pulse was excited, the tongue pretty clean, urine scanty and high-coloured, sounds of heart and lungs healthy. He took calomel and opium of each gr. ij immediately, and had his chest rubbed with a liniment of aco-

[1] "J. de Méd. et de Chirurg. Pratiq.," July, 1862.
[2] "J. de la Physiol.," 1860, p. 569.

nite and opium. After sleeping two or three hours he awoke and began to take muriate of ammonia and bicarbonate of potash *quater die*. The next day the urine deposited a lateritious sediment; he was much better, and in forty-eight hours from the time I saw him he was convalescent, and had no relapse. Both before and after this attack he has suffered from rheumatism, muscular and periosteal.

In this instance it is quite certain that the disorder was a rheumatic neurosis, and that there was nothing whatever imaginary in it. The nervous and muscular apparatuses of the heart and œsophagus were especially involved, as well as the intercostal nerves. According to Bezold[1] the nervous centre of the cardiac movements furnishing three-fourths of the entire propulsive force of the heart occupies the cervical region of the cord including the medulla oblongata, and extends as low as the fourth dorsal vertebra. Its fibres run through the cervical spinal cord, and pass out between the seventh cervical, and fifth dorsal vertebra, probably passing through the lower cervical and upper dorsal sympathetic ganglia, and proceeding to the heart. If we suppose that in ordinary circumstances the rheumatic disorder in the above case would have assumed the form of intercostal neuralgia it is not difficult to understand how by extending backwards and involving the origins of the upper dorsal nerves it induced the very peculiar cardiac distress. The involuntary kicking seems to have depended on an excited state of the lower dorsal and lumbar cord, the action being of a somewhat reflex character. The altered sensation was probably also due to central disorder. The case seems to me of interest from the evidence it affords that neurotic as well as febrile rheumatism has a tendency to affect the heart.

No. 103.—M. A. W., f., æt. 44, ad. March 12th. Resides near Uxbridge; no ague in vicinity. Had rheumatic fever two years ago, since which time her heart has never been quite right. Ill now one month. States that at 10 A. M. and 7 P. M. daily she experiences a sense of fulness in præcordia, and of faintness, with pricking and shooting in the same situation, and "deathly feelings." She can't lie down well at night. The heart's action is now quite normal and regular, and the P. also. She is a stout person, rather full coloured. Appetite is bad; she has thirst, but her food digests fairly. B. open. Urine sometimes thick. Tea twice a day. Tea was forbidden, and she was ordered creasote and rhubarb in pills *bis die*, with ferri pot. tart. + pot. iod. + pot. bicarb. + inf. calumb. *ter die*. 26th. A great deal better, pain at heart nothing like it was, nerves much better, urine clear. She continued in an improved state, but with some relapse from exertion in nursing, and on April 20th the mixture was changed for pot. bicarb. + spt. ammon. co. + inf. gent. co. On this she kept very well as long as she persevered in taking it, but if she omitted it and the pills for two days the symptoms recurred. June 11th. She described the attacks which came on when the medicines are omitted as follows : " The heart feels so cold as if it lay in cold water ; she could feel a stifling sensation which obliges her to get up and go into the open air; her sight gets dim, her head feels lost, and all her senses

"Wien. Med. Wochenschr.," Dec. 20th, 1862. "Brit. Med. J.," Feb. 7th, 1863.

leave her." The attacks last half an hour and occur at irregular times now. After this she took F. + Q. citr. + pot. iod. gr. ij *ter die*, with which she benefited very much, and by July 2d was fairly recovered.

I regard the disorder above described as of rheumatic nature from the previous attack of rheumatic fever, which probably inflicted some damage on the nervous apparatus of the heart, from the good effect of pot. iod. and alkalies, and from the occasional lateritious state of the urine. I believe, though I cannot put my hand upon the notes of the case, that she had a son who died soon after of rheumatic heart disease. In her case the affection was evidently a neurosis, and though quite controlled for the time I think it is highly probable that it will return, and may be aggravated by gastric disorder or the like so as even to end fatally.

The next group are instances of malarious infection.

No. 104.—M. S., æt. 41, of active but nervous temperament, latterly residing in London, but having lived for many years in Australia, was subject to winter bronchitis. Jan. 9th. Having had on the previous day marked symptoms of commencing catarrh she was attacked about 8 A. M. with distress referred to the heart, a sensation as if she were dying, breathlessness and anxiety. I saw her about 10 A. M., when I found the P at the wrist almost utterly gone, the hands cold, the same distress continuing. The action of the heart on auscultation was very rapid, the sounds normal and loud, the face pale, and the eyes sunken. Her voluntary muscular power was not materially impaired; she sat up readily, and stretched her limbs vigorously. More than once she expressed a dread of going to sleep lest she should never wake again. She seemed too restless and anxious to sleep or lie down. Stimulants were given freely, mustard poultices applied to the precordia, and the interrupted current passed from the nape of the neck to the same part. Very little improvement was produced for some time; the P. continued fluttering and most indistinct, but at last warmth began to return in the hands, and the P. improved. She took gr. iij of quinine at 11 A. M. and 1.30 P. M. For a good while before and after the latter hour the cerebral functions were much disordered. There was evident delirium. About 4 P. M. she became much quieter, but complained of extreme weakness. The P. was 108, of tolerable force; the T. remained clear, but appeared to her to be dry, though it was fairly moist. She vomited once about the middle of the day, and coughed up a few times a little phlegm; but almost all the catarrhal symptoms had disappeared; 10 P. M. complains of extreme debility and perspiration breaking out. Quinine gr. iij at 5 and 9 P. M. In the course of the next day gr. iij of quinine were taken, and at the same rate for another half day. She then had a little calomel and rhubarb, after which she slept well. No medicine was now given till 15th, when she began citrate of quin. and iron, gr. v *ter die*, which she took for nearly fourteen days, and was quite well by 30th. The cardiac symptoms never recurred severely, but she had more than once uneasy sensations about the chest, which made her fear a relapse, such as fluttering action of the heart and great weakness. One of her daughters about the same time had an attack of bronchitis attended with a decided aguish disorder recurring every morning, consisting of shivering and depression, and ceasing under the administration of quinine together with the bronchitis.

Feb. 3d. M. S. was attacked again about 11 P. M. with decided rigors, and violent beating of the heart in repeated paroxysms, with great depression and mental disturbance manifested as before by constant loquacity, and a tendency to repeat the same question over and over again. The P. at 2.30 A. M. when I saw her (4th) was soft and quick; the skin fully warm; the T. parched and dried up and coated. She complained of breathlessness, threw the clothes off her, her legs felt as if they did not belong to her, and her hands tingled. I gave her liq. opii sed. + spt. æth. chlor. and the symptoms gradually subsided. At 7.30 A. M. she began to take quin. dis. gr. ij 3 *tiis horis*. 5th. Was better all yesterday until 11 P. M. when the same symptoms recurred, but less severely. She got some tolerable sleep, but experienced in the morning some disorder of the heart's action with a feeling as if she were dying. This subsided after some time, and she remained till the afternoon weak and depressed. She was cinchonized. 7th. After a tolerable day on 6th, the appetite however being very bad, she began to have about 9 P. M. "internal tremors," and exceeding restlessness, which passed into high fever and was succeeded by profuse sweating when she at last got to sleep. This morning is very weak and prostrate with utter aversion to food and much nausea. Ice to swallow and mustard poultices to epigastrium. On 8th resumed quin. dis. gr. ij *ter die*, and on the 10th began ferri and quin. citr., this she took with benefit for four days, and then went to the country. She returned in about a month much improved, but having still in the evenings slight but distinct paroxysms of aguish character. Nov. 7th. Up to about this date she continued well and active; she woke up about 2.30 A. M. with palpitation and distressing uneasiness at the heart and pain in the back. I saw her at 4.30 A. M. and found the heart beating rapidly, its sounds very clear and sharp, the P. thready and indistinct, and the hands coldish. She was wakeful and afraid to sleep; her legs felt as if they did not belong to her. After two doses of chloric ether + liq. opii sedat. the P. became more distinct, the pain in the back less, the hands warm, and she went off to sleep. With quinine and iron she was well in about ten days. It is now nearly six years ago since these attacks occurred, and there have been no signs since of any serious heart affection.

I have the most perfect assurance that in the above case there was an entire absence of all hysterical fancy. The patient had passed much of her life amid the stirring scenes of a colony, and was one of the last persons in the world to plague herself and others with imaginary disorders. She had once been accidentally poisoned with sulphate of zinc, and had never had the same health since. She had also once suffered with a head affection from excessive heat, which subsided after an eczematous eruption had appeared on the scalp. The first attack, which was the severest, had a very serious aspect; her own apprehensions of impending death were very strong. I was puzzled by it at first, as I could not see why the pulse should be absent while the heart was acting violently. In the subsequent attacks when I had a clearer notion of the causation of the phenomena the course to be pursued was apparent. The attack was in fact essentially the cold stage of an ague, in which, owing to a peculiar irritability of the vaso-motor nerves, the arteries were unusually constricted. The circulation was thus seriously interfered with, and the heart had to struggle against the obstruction. As soon as the arterial spasm yielded the difficulty and danger were over. The cerebral disorder shows how specially the nervous system was affected by the poison. In the subsequent attacks there seems to have been less spasm of the remote arteries than in the first, and perhaps the cardiac plexus was more directly affected. The feeling of impending dissolution assimilates the state a good deal to angina. It is worth remarking that in this instance, as well as in No. 102, there occurred the peculiar symptom of not daring to sleep, and of the lower limbs feeling as if they did not belong to the body. The apparent relation of the disorder to influenza, its distinctly aguish character and the occurrence of aguish bronchitis at the same time in another member of the family are points of much significance.

The remarkable case related by Dr. Stokes[1] seems to me to have resembled the one just recorded. In the former, a rather mild case of maculated typhus, the heart's impulse was strong and the sounds remarkably distinct on the 8th day, and continued so until the 15th, though no pulse could be perceived at the wrist. The surface was icy cold, and of a violet hue, the countenance sunken, and the skin and breath cold. Stimulants were of no avail. On dissection no organic lesion of any kind could be discovered in any part of the body; the heart was firm and its muscular structure natural; no obstruction existed in any artery, but the whole quantity of blood seemed much diminished; its consistence was somewhat pitchy and its colour very dark. The wound made in the arm (for injecting blood) was still gaping, and presented not the slightest appearance of adhesion or inflammation. Knowing as we do how weak a contraction is sufficient to send a pulse-wave through *open* arteries I cannot conceive that in this case the vessels were free from obstruction, and as no embolon, &c. was found at the autopsy it seems pretty certain that they were occluded by spasm of their circular coats, which naturally disappeared after death. This view is strongly supported by the icy coldness of the surface, and of the breath, phenomena which are rarely if ever observed except under such conditions of the nervous system as exist during the algide stage of fever. Had the failure of pulse been owing to cardiac debility, the organ would not have been found firm after death, nor would stimulants have been so ineffectual. The warm bath would probably have been the best remedy, as it proved in a case to be presently mentioned. The observation is one of great importance as showing that algide symptoms, the result of vaso-motor nerve irritation, may occur in typhus fever. On talking this case over with Sir R. Martin he made the sagacious remark that the patient must have had malarious disease previously. Nothing is said about it, but it is highly probable.

[1] "Dublin Q. J. of Med. Sc.," 1839, p. 7; and "Dis. of Heart and Aorta," p. 384.

No. 105.—X. Z., m., æt. 37, had previously suffered from ague and from recurring neuralgia, and had just returned from a malarious district. About the middle of the day he was attacked suddenly with faintness, and after taking some ether vomited. The syncope increased and became alarming, requiring the frequent administration of restoratives and friction to the surface. In the evening he had a dose of calomel and a rhubarb draught. The night was sleepless, and the next day he was very prostrate, remained in bed, unable to eat or to exert himself. In the evening another attack of syncope came on from which he was rallied as before. Ten grains of quinine were now given, and early the next morning, ten more. He was feverish in the night, but with an opiate had some sleep. The next day he was better, had no faintness. From this time he gradually recovered, but was unfit to work for some time. Several years have elapsed since the above illness, but there has been I believe no recurrence, nor any indication of disease of the heart.

Recamier cites two very instructive instances of the same character as the foregoing. In the first, a man, æt. 35, of good constitution, felt some lipothymic symptoms which soon ceased, and recurred the next day at the same hour. No preventive means were used, and in the third attack the man died. No adequate cause for the fatal event could be found at the post-mortem. In the second a young lady, æt. 19, was affected in the same way, but after the second attack bark was administered rapidly in full doses, and she was speedily cured. Torti relates (*Therapeut. Spec.*, p. 435) a case of syncopal tertian which appeared almost utterly desperate, but yet after the last rites of the Romish Church had been administered the patient was snatched as from the jaws of the grave by the use of bark. Hamilton mentions[1] a case of "terciana syncopal" occurring in Peru. The subject was a negro, æt. 40, with a finely developed head who managed an estate for his master. He was as usual in the field in the morning when he fell on the ground and was conveyed on a mule to his master's house in town. When first seen after his arrival, he was more like a corpse than a living man; the pulse at the wrist was scarcely to be felt; skin cold and dry; little or no shivering; speech lost; but his vision and hearing appeared intact. The first thing done was to put the patient into a warm bath, which seemed to operate as a charm, for the breathing became freer, the pulse rose, and speech returned. After leaving the bath the hot and sweating stages of the disorder appeared. It was ascertained that the bowels had been confined several days. He was freely purged with calomel and rhubarb, took quinine and was well in ten days. It is stated that such cases there are generally fatal, and that those who are taken ill are given up for lost. Trousseau (*Clinique Médicale*, vol. ii. p. 763) mentions two cases in which death seemed actually to have taken place, but which were nevertheless restored by bark. Cardiac paralysis was no doubt the

---

[1] Hamilton's "Practical Obs. on the Intermittent Fever of Peru." Highley, 1842, p. 27.

cause of death in some of the cases at Walcheran, of whom Sir G. Blane says, " Under the influence of the endemial air recoveries were slow and imperfect, and relapses very frequent, so that some of the convalescents when apparently doing well would unaccountably drop down dead. Slighter degrees of the same affection are I believe by no means uncommon as sequelæ of malarious fevers. In a case of remittent fever under my own care the patient was attacked one night by an alarming sensation referred to the heart attended with faintness and a failing pulse. He thought himself dying, and said it seemed as if life was ebbing from him. After he had become convalescent this cardiac disorder continued to recur about every second day, and was especially induced by any painful emotion or agitation. As the testimony of an independent observer is of great value, I subjoin an abbreviated account of an attack in which this same patient came under the observation of Dr. Symonds, of Clifton. He was called one afternoon to see him in haste, and found him, he says, in a rather puzzling condition. "There were indications of some very distressing sensations about the precordia; he pressed my hand against his side as if suffering some spasmodic pain." He had complained the day before of pain in the heart. "He was, however, so very delirious that one could not be quite sure that the local feeling was not some delirious dysæsthesia. His pulse was weak, small, not quick, hands and feet cool, head hot, eyes suffused. He talked delirious of matters in which he had been engaged some months before. Dr. Symonds doubted whether some decisive remedies should not be applied to the head, but guided by the state of the circulation and the character of the neurotic symptoms, he ordered for him brandy, a full dose of calomel + opium, Hoffmann's ether and ammonia. Five hours later he was much better, quite conscious, had passed an enormous quantity of pale limpid urine, but still had pain in the region of the heart. "The case was now clear—feeble heart, pseudo-angina pectoris, and a neurotic diathesis heightened and disordered by the malarious influences to which he had been subjected. With quinine, valerianate of zinc, creasote, and opium, and occasional alterative doses of calomel, he was soon convalescent. I was consulted in the case of a young officer, a model of physical conformation, and apparently in good health, who had been the cock of Eton, but after his return from India suffered with such a distressing dysæsthesia referred to the heart that he could not walk a mile without feeling that death was imminent. There was nothing apparently wrong about the action of the heart, nothing to be detected on the most careful examination. Yet I do not think he was malingering, both from his serious alarm about his malady, and from his not applying for any certificate to prolong his leave of absence. Sir R. Martin informs me that cardiac debility, as marked by an intermitting pulse is an extremely common result of residence in India, and my own observation of returned Indians has generally shown a markedly weak state of the circulation.

Whether this debility affect the nervous apparatus of the heart solely, or its muscular tissue, or, as is most probable, both, I do not undertake to decide. There can, however, be no question that the nervous system is principally implicated; no one can have had much to do with malarious disorder without observing how large a part the nervous system plays in the multiform phenomena that present themselves. The treatment of these cases is in one respect plain enough, viz., that they require invigorating tonic remedies, among which we must always rate highly pure air and generous diet. But in another respect, and that one which may be of momentous importance in perilous cases, our course is not so clear. Supposing in an attack of cardiac angina of presumed malarious origin we find the heart's action very depressed and we dread death from its failure. This condition may arise on the one hand from irritation of the sympathetic plexuses causing constriction of the coronary arteries and so depriving the heart of an adequate supply of blood; or it may depend on a paralysis of the cardiac nervous centres and nerves. In the first case sedatives would be needful, in the second stimulants. The diagnosis must, I think, chiefly rest upon our being able to ascertain whether or not the affection can be regarded as coinciding with the algide stage of an intermittent, as marked by the usual signs. If so, it is probable that the coronary arteries are in a state of constriction, and we may either give opium with chloric ether, and a warm bath; or, if the distress is less urgent, wait till the spasm spontaneously subsides. In the other case a large dose of digitalis would probably be advisable together with free stimulation. In doubtful instances it will be safest to give stimulants and to apply an effectual mustard poultice to the precordia. This may by its powerful excitation of the cutaneous nerves both arouse the cardiac centres, and remove the irritation of the sympathetic plexuses. It sounds rather contradictory to talk of removing a state of irritation in one set of nerves by setting up irritation in another. Yet as a matter of experience it seems true that such may be the case. The common practice with the laity of applying a mustard poultice for the relief of all sorts of pain, including neuralgia, is not so bad as at first sight it would appear. Duchenne, quoted by Trousseau (*Tr. de Thérap.*, vol. i. p. 787), says, " It is a capital fact that a sharp and sudden pain excited at any point of the cutaneous surface possesses the property of modifying profoundly certain sciatic neuralgias." The matter may be put in this way. When we feel a pain, or have an irritation in any part, all that we can say is that the nerve or nervous centre belonging to that part is in a morbid state, which is generally functional and removable. Now if we transmit through some other nerve a strong excitement of a different kind to that centre we may succeed in abolishing the original morbid action, supposing it to depend on no actual organic change. We all know how any matter that interests us much makes us unconscious for the time of any minor disorder, and cases are on record where a strong mental emotion has dissipated actual articular gout. The virtue of emetics in certain inflammations depends on their action on the nervous centre of the inflamed part. In giving opium in any case of cardiac affection we should be guided very much by the degree of pain. Should this be severe, we may give a moderate or full dose, ℳ xxv—l, but if the syncopal tendency predominate, we should be very cautious in giving opium lest we increase the depression. The good effect of the warm bath in Hamilton's case was very striking. It acted no doubt as a relaxant, opening up the arteries and allowing the circulation to run freely. Of course it should not be so prolonged nor the temperature so elevated as to cause faintness. In the case of X. Z., No. 105, on the contrary, I am much in doubt as to the exact state of the heart, the general tenor of the phenomena was much more that of direct depression and semi-paralysis of the organ than of arterial constriction and anæmia. I have been the more inclined to notice the point I have just referred to, as it has occurred to me in some painful instances to observe the utter inefficiency of stimulants when sinking had set in. Brandy poured down as long as the patient could swallow had no effect. Of course I do not doubt the value of stimulants in states of depression, but I cannot avoid posing the question, whether failure of cardiac action may not arise in different ways, in one from direct paralysis of the cardiac nervous centres and nerves, in another from irritation of the vagi or of the medulla oblongata, and in a third from general arterial constriction combined or not with a similar state of the coronary vessels.

The following instance of cardiac disorder was confidently referred by the patient to the use of lead under his anvil, and he has had no relapse since the lead was removed. I do not, however, feel absolutely convinced that the case was one of saturnine intoxication, as the gums presented no blue line, but I think this is the most probable view. Lead was found I believe in a quantity of powder removed from under the anvil.

No. 106.—J. R , æt. 28, a hearty man, ad. Dec. 27th, ill fourteen days. Was attacked between twelve and one at night while asleep with great palpitation and giddiness, great weakness and sense of illness; has had palpitation more or less ever since. No bruit about the heart, nor enlargement, its action is excited. Lungs healthy. No dyspepsia. T. coated, clammy; bad taste in mouth; some thirst. No epigastric tenderness. Was quite exhausted by walking about two miles to the hospital. States that he works as a smith at an anvil beneath which is a piece of lead to deaden the sound, which lead gets cut up into dust and gets into his throat. His employer affirms that men have been destroyed by this kind of dust. He has been exposed to the action of the lead four months. He was ordered strychnia, iron, spt. æth. S. Co. and henbane, and improved, but on returning to work found that "it almost killed him." There was then slight paralysis of two fingers of the right and of one of the left hand. Is pallid, nervous, weak and tremulous. He was now (Jan. 6th) ordered ammon. carb. + tr. nuc. vom. + tr. opii ℳ v ex. inf. gent. co. *ter die*, with ferri carb. sacch , under which he nearly recovered in a month and was at work (without the lead) the last week.

Mr. Pye Chavasse records[1] a remarkable case of great nervous prostration with right side anæsthesia, anxiety, and palpitation of the heart (which was sound) on the slightest exertion, which seems certainly to have been occasioned by the use of water impregnated with lead. "The blue line on the gums if not altogether absent was at all events very faint." In my own case, as in Mr Chavasse's, it is a strong point in favour of the lead poisoning view that the patient recovered so completely after removal of the presumed cause. Had it been otherwise, had he suffered from foul air, general debility, influenzal miasm or any other depressing cause, he would have been much longer in recovering, and would in all probability have relapsed. He is now strong and hearty. In such cases the cardiac nervous centres seem to be directly affected, to be semi-paralyzed.

No. 107.—A. R., f., æt. 26, ad. Jan. 22, 1858. Complexion florid, has lived in London last twelve years. Subject to rheumatism last nine years, suffers from it every winter. Had rheumatic fever nine years ago, has had palpitation more or less ever since, but not to such an extent as to cause her alarm till three months ago. Action of heart very tremulous, complains of constant pain in the region of heart of dull wearing character, increased when palpitation comes on, which it does several times a day, especially on the slightest exertion. Has pain in knees increased at night, a little dry cough in the morning. Thyroid gland enlarged equably; it first enlarged six years ago, is now less than it has been. Evident proptosis. P. very small. Breathing natural. B. costive. Feb. 11th. Heart beating with considerable violence, extended dulness over precordial region more especially at right side. Complains still of pain, gets but little sleep. A blowing sound is heard all over the heart, but a distinct rough systolic bruit is heard in the second intercostal space immediately to the left of the sternum; a thrill is also felt here. Same bruit is heard over right carotid. To the right of sternum both aortic sounds are heard clear. Health greatly improved. 22d. Pain very severe last night and palpitation increased, no sleep. March 4th. Pain not nearly so severe, and referred entirely to one spot near the apex of the heart. P. 112. T. clean. Less proptosis, goitre decreasing. March 12th. A severe attack of pain and palpitation last night relieved by empl. bellad. c. opio. March 18th. Much improved. 19th. About middle of day became worse with increase of pain, and severe vomiting; the latter was allayed by hydrocyanic acid and digitalis in effervescing salines, but the pain continued very severe till 8 P. M., when eight leeches were applied to the precordia; she expressed herself as much relieved, but died the following morning at 7.30. She was leeched over the heart on Jan. 25th with relief, and blistered about the same part on Feb. 9th, 22d, and March 1st, with some advantage. She took small doses of tr. digitalis, spt. ammon. fœtid., sal volatile, and tr. ferri ammon. Her P. was generally about 120. *Post-mortem.*—Bronchial and cervical lymphatic glands enlarged, supra-renal capsules, liver, spleen, kidneys healthy. No pericarditis. Heart of normal size, its valves effective, some vegetations on the mitral, its

[1] "Brit. Med. J.," April 23, 1859.

muscular tissue of good colour. Both lungs in a state of pneumonic engorgement, the left at posterior part grayly hepatized. Thymus gland very large, weighed 1,200 grains; it overlapped the pericardium, lay upon the aorta and pulmonary artery, and reached down to root of left lung. Thyriod gland much enlarged. Brain healthy.

The symptoms in this case indicate the existence of a primary neurosis of the vagi nerves of a paralytic kind. The phenomena bear considerable resemblance to those produced by division of these nerves. The excited quick action of the heart is a constant result of this operation, and, after death the lungs are often found more or less engorged and condensed. The attack of pneumonia which so suddenly supervened and so rapidly proved fatal was probably the result of some casual catarrhal (influenzal) agency affecting a system highly predisposed to pulmonary congestion and consequent effusion. Budd[1] and Gull[2] have both noticed the occurrence of low or gangrenous pneumonia from the compression of the pulmonary nerves by tumours of various kinds. The slight anatomical change found in the mitral valve is quite insufficient to explain the pain and palpitation which so frequently recurred. It seems impossible to regard them as other than functional disorders, especially as they varied so much. How far they were dependent on injurious pressure exercised on the vagi nerves by the enlarged glands must remain uncertain, though my belief is that no such pressure existed. I have certainly seen cases with very much greater glandular enlargement where no such symptoms were present. The thyroid enlargement and the proptosis are difficult to account for satisfactorily; but the common occurrence of goitre as the result of malaria indicates its dependence on the vaso-motor nerve paralysis and consequent hyperæmia, and the same conditions were probably concerned in inducing the proptosis. Thus if we suppose hyperæmia of the tissues contained in the orbital cavity to issue in serious effusion, which is no very unlikely event, the globes would be protruded. I have at the present time two cases under my care which exemplify the influence of hyperæmia and serious effusion in causing this condition. In one where the proptosis has supervened quite recently, there is strong pulsation of the carotids, pain in and behind the globes, tension of the lids and great congestion of the conjunctiva. The patient is epileptic. In the other the proptosis is of old standing, there is no tension or redness of the lids, but there is a quasi-œdematous swelling all round the orbit, an evident pushing out of the integument. Pressure on the eyeball does not cause it to retire much into the orbit, but it certainly makes the bulging integument more tense. In this case there is serious effusion, in the former congestion. It is possible also in some cases that an enfeebled state of the recti muscles contributes to the proptosis. For further remarks on this

[1] "Med.-Chir. Trans.," 1859, vol. xlii. p. 215.
[2] "Guy's Hosp. Reports," 1859, p. 307.

subject I may refer to a highly interesting case published by me in the *Med. T. and Gaz.*, Jan. 2d and 9th, 1864. In this though cardiac symptoms were not so prominent there was extreme debility, cough, and gastric disturbance, which brought life into very considerable peril. Under sedative and tonic means she was quite restored excepting the goitre. It is abundantly clear from the preceding cases that an affection of nerves supplying vital organs may be a very serious thing, and that the prognosis should in such cases be guarded.

A common form of cardiac neurosis is that where the action of the heart is much accelerated, ranging from 110 to 140 in the minute in the standing position, and not falling much below the former figure in the sitting. The contractions are abnormally sharp and vivid, the organ seems to spring up with a quick forcible leap against the ribs. The apparent excess of action misleads the practitioner sometimes to suppose that there is hypertrophy. Percussion however shows that no enlargement exists, and auscultation detects no vascular bruits, nor derangement of the rhythm. The feeble stroke of the radial pulse often contrasts markedly with the vivid action of the heart. The general condition of the patient exhibits more or less evident indications of debility. Dyspepsia is often present to some extent, but it is by no means always the essential cause. Tea on the other hand seems in some cases really to be the "fons et origo mali," the symptoms subsiding materially on its omission. I think the pathological condition in such cases is essentially hyperæsthesia either of the nervous centres or of the sensory nerves of the heart, perhaps especially of those fibres distributed to the endocardium of the ventricles. The hyperæsthesia is as in other instances the result and associate of debility. The feebleness of the pulse shows how ineffectual the apparently forcible contractions of the heart are. In fact the ventricles do but grasp the blood for a moment, and relax again immediately before they have fully emptied themselves. A case at present under my care illustrates well how much more efficient a slower and more sustained action may be. An elderly man complains only of lassitude, has no dyspnœa, no indication of defective circulation. He is anæmic, but has no nerve disorder whatever. His pulse when first seen was only 20; there was scarce any impulse to be felt, the sounds were indistinct, and similar to each other. With iron and ol. morrh. the pulse has risen to 32, and he has become stronger. In this man it is evident that the heart contracts steadily and quietly on the blood in its cavities and expels it fully. There is no spasmodic jerk in the contraction, and consequently no notable impulse.

Dr. Lyons[1] has recorded a remarkable case which is as follows. A male, between 30 and 40 years of age, began to suffer at first with debility and unpleasant sensation in the chest; after a time

[1] "Dublin Q. J. of Med. Sc.," May, 1862.

could not leave his room, and scarcely could stir without increasing the heart's action. During the periods of excitement of the heart's action the debility was extreme, the patient's sufferings most intense, and the cardiac action almost more violent and tumultuous than Lyons had ever before witnessed. The face was flushed vividly, the pulse was 120, regular, and not remarkable for force or volume. The impulse was very violent, and a loud, diffuse, systolic bellows murmur was audible with great and equal intensity over the whole precordial region. Iron and tonics failed to give any relief, but vesication continued for ten months was of some service. After about five to seven years he completely recovered, and the most careful examination was unable to detect anything in the least degree morbid about the heart or any other part. Lyons considers this case to have been one of pure uncomplicated myocarditis. To me it appears more probable that it was an intense neurosis of the above kind, for these reasons: I cannot think that a myocarditis could exist for years without destroying life, or at the least seriously damaging the tissue of the heart, or of its valves by extending to them. Moreover an inflammation would so weaken the muscular fibres as to prevent the action of the organ from being excessive.[1] On the other hand the extreme debility, the intense suffering, and especially the long continuance of the disorder are much in favour of its neurotic character.

The treatment of cardiac hyperæsthesia is too often unsatisfactory, probably because it is impossible to obtain rest for the organ. An irritable brain or stomach may be soothed by giving them timely repose, but we can do this but very partially with the heart. Avoidance of all emotion and excitement is very desirable, and the diet must be scrutinized to see whether some of its component articles may not produce or increase the hyperæsthesia. In severe cases occasional small leechings may be recommended. Belladonna plasters are generally useful, and I should expect benefit from hypodermic injection of opium into the precordia. Internally I have seen most benefit from tr. digitalis, ♏xv *ter die*, but I am not altogether satisfied how far it is quite safe to give this drug in states of cardiac excitement. In conditions of cardiac languor I have no fear of it, but in the opposite I think we need to be cautious. In some cases aconite and hydrocyanic acid may be useful, but they have not served me well. Opium and nitrate of silver might be suitable remedies, especially where there was irritable dyspepsia. The very possible dependence of the disorder on some remote, perhaps little heeded, irritation should not be forgotten.

---

[1] Demme states that the most constant and manifest symptoms of myocarditis are decrease of the heart's energy, loss of rhythm in its movements, increasing frequency of the pulse, steady diminution of its size, and its continuous undulatory character.— *v.* "Schweiz. Ztschr. f. Heilk.," i. pp. 79, 461; 1862.

CHAPTER XXVIII.

RESPIRATORY NEUROSES.

The pulmonary enjoy no exemption from the disorders which are apt to befall other nerves. Some of their neuroses have long been accepted as classic diseases. I purpose to notice some of the more practical points relating to different typical forms, founding my remarks on cases of actual occurrence.

No. 108.—M. T., f., æt. 27, ad Oct. 13th. Ill six days. Complains that she can't get her breath, can't sleep at all soundly for dyspnœa at night. Her chest is not tight, she has no cough, air enters freely into lungs; sounds of heart normal. P. good. Has cold perspirations frequently. Menorrhagia exists to some extent, the catamenial flow lasts seven to fourteen days. Feels faint and giddy. Takes food fairly well. With ferri carb. saccharata, ammon. carb. and tr. arnicæ and liq. pot. arsen. she improved materially during the six weeks she attended; the last time I saw her "her breath was nothing near so bad."

No. 109.—Master H., æt. 9, seen December 9. A fair-haired, intellectual-looking, lively boy. Ill for more than a year. Is decidedly feverish and is thirsty at night, not by day. Is frequently sighing deeply, about once a minute or oftener; this "besoin," he says, keeps him awake at night. The lungs and heart are quite healthy. He has pain also in the abdomen about the upper and mid-part, not increased by pressure Appetite bad. Tongue clean. Skin cool. Pulse weak. With quinine + iron he recovered completely.

Remarks.—In both these cases the phenomena seem to be referable to a semi-paralysis of the pulmonary branches of the vagi, a sort of anæsthesia in consequence of which the reflex inspiratory actions could not be performed with their normal facility, but required the assistance of volition. Debilitating disorder was present in both instances, viz., menorrhagia in the female, and obscure nocturnal remittent in the boy. The good effect of nerve tonics was very marked. As under these the general power was improved, the anæsthesia yielded. In contrast with these I may cite some instances of an opposite kind.

No. 110.—E. C., f., æt. 52, ad. January 29th. Ill eight months with severe catarrh and cough, pains between shoulders, dyspnœa, anorexia. The cough is very violent but dry. No râles heard on ausculting the chest. Is very weak. Atropiæ gr. $\frac{1}{120}$ + tr. ferri mur. $\mathfrak{m}$ xv + oxym. scill. $\mathfrak{m}$ xv + aq. ʒj *ter die*. February 12th. Cough very much better. Strychnia with tr. ferri mur. was now given, and the atropia omitted. 19th. Wonderful appetite from this medicine, but it does not quiet cough like the other. Pt. addendo atropiæ gr $\frac{1}{130}$ ad. sing. dos. The cough was soon relieved and she was discharged March 12th.

No. 111.—W. M., m., æt. 59, ad. April 12th. Ill all the winter with cough, but not enough to lay him up; worse last six days. Gets weaker and weaker; can't work now. His breath fails on exertion. Much thick expectoration. No râles in backs, breathing obstructed in right front, fairly good in left. No sleep at night from cough. When he has an attack of cough it affects his head so that he falls off the chair and becomes insensible for a minute; this often occurs at the instant the cough comes on. Appetite very bad. Vomits up his food at times. P. large, soft. Skin cool. B. open. Lungs rather emphysematous. During the treatment he experienced for a time a sensation in his head as if he was half stunned, making him feel stupid; this was relieved by putting his feet in hot water. His treatment consisted of strychnia, nitric acid, and opium with morphia and stramonium at night, subsequently of quinine and arsenic. He benefited very decidedly, and was cured in less than a month.

No. 112.—D. P., f., æt. 42, ad. December 17th. Of short broad make. Ill two to three weeks with a dreadful screaming cough, which causes much trembling and exhaustion, and lasts for four or five hours at once. The cough strains her chest so that she fears that some extensive cicatrices on the chest from erysipelas, which she had last year, will give way. No insensibility ever induced by cough. Pulse of good force. T. clean. Urine copious, thick. No appetite. Always very weak since her illness. She was ordered acid. nitrici ♏iij + atropiæ gr. $\frac{1}{120}$ + aq. ℥j *quater die.* This was taken up to January 18th, the doses being increased in number up to seven or eight a day. It produced very considerable improvement both in the cough and expectoration, and was then changed for quinine + iron + liq. opii sed. ♏vij *quater die*, with which she improved still further, and the cough completely ceased.

No. 113.—G. F., m, æt. 28, seen November 15th. Ill one month, never suffered in the same way before. Of very stout plethoric habit. Pulse 100, soft, large, not notably weak. Heart's sounds normal. Urine lateritious. Suffers from severe cough, paroxysmal and suffocatory, attended with substernal pain; it occurs in a succession of expiratory acts like the cough of pertussis. Cannot lie down at night. Is easy sitting in a warm room, suffers much more on exposure to cold. No râles in chest. His mother states that he never had hooping-cough, and it is prevalent in the vicinity. There is a good deal of blood in the mucous expectoration. With nitric acid, strychnia, quinine and opium *ter die*, and stramonium and morphia at night he improved rapidly, and in a week was convalescent.

Remarks.—These cases are examples of a not uncommon pulmonary neurosis, in which together with marked general debility, and more or less local vascular congestion there exists predominating hyperæsthesia of the nerves of the air-passages. When the hyperæsthesia is considerable, and there is but little catarrhal affection, atropine has approved itself a very valuable remedy. If there were much vascular congestion I should prefer opium. Where the debility is great strychnia and iron, aided usually by the sedatives, should be employed; they seem by imparting tone to lessen the undue excitability of the nervous structure. The peculiar attacks of insensibility which occurred in No. 111 were not, I believe, at all dependent on congestion of the brain, but rather on a spasmodic contraction of its arteries, such as we suppose to occur in the "petit mal" of epilepsy. They ceased under the tonic treatment together with the cough.[1] I look upon

---

[1] In a patient under my care with pretty severe bronchitis attacks of insensibility sometimes occur when he has coughed less than half a minute, so complete that he has fallen down and hurt his face, while at other times he coughs for a long while without losing consciousness.

them as analogous to the cerebral disorder which a gastralgic patient recently under my care complained of. He stated that the pain made him light-headed at times; he felt as if his senses were going away. He was cured by strychnia, iron, and opium. In this case there could be no question of any cerebral congestion.

Pertussis is of course the capital example of a specific bronchial hyperæsthesia. The excitement of the vagi nerves, however induced, is clearly peculiar and not identical with that just noticed. It is consequently much less under the control of remedies. I do however by no means agree with Romberg that treatment is so ineffectual as he seems to consider it, and I believe that most physicians still retain faith in the utility of various measures. Dr. Whitehead has adduced[1] evidence showing how much the duration of the disease can be diminished by treatment. Thirty-five cases not treated till the disease had lasted three months were cured on an average in less than twenty-five days; and eighty-seven whose treatment was commenced within fourteen days after the onset were cured in the same time. Opium, usually as Dover's powder, and belladonna were the principal remedies. Trousseau, referring to Bretonneau's treatment of the disease by belladonna, says,[2] "Nous avons pu nous-mêmes constater l'extrême efficacité de ce moyen," and Vollant[3] affirms the same in the strongest terms. The latter uses only the powder of the root which he gives in doses of gr. $\frac{1}{4}$, increasing the number from one to four or five a day till the paroxysms begin to subside, when it is given less frequently.

Dr. West confirms to a great extent Dr. Hamilton Roe's testimony of the efficacy of prussic acid, and has only in one instance out of many hundred known any actually poisonous effects to be produced by it.

The evidence for the real remedial power of this drug is worth considering, and our conclusion in this case may be applicable to others. Its sedative effect in some gastric hyperæsthesias cannot we suppose be questioned. It may therefore be admitted that it acts as a calmative to the filaments of the vagi distributed to the stomach, and consequently it is very probable that it will affect in the same way those which proceed to the lungs. An unbiased and thoroughly reliable observer as Dr. West, tells us that in some cases it "exerts an almost magical influence on the cough," while in other cases it seems perfectly inert and sometimes injurious. Does not this warrant our regarding hydrocyanic acid as a remedy which may serve us well, but may also fail us, and forbid our rejecting it altogether? Moreover there is some ground at least for believing that it is not a matter of indifference what preparation we use. Much of the variability in the results obtained from this as well as from

---

[1] "Third Report of Clinical Hospital for Children at Manchester, 1859."
[2] "Traité de Thérap.," vol. ii. p. 71.
[3] "J. de Méd. et de Chirurg. Pratiq.," vol. xxxiii. p. 361.

other remedies depends no doubt on the dissimilarity of the preparations employed in different instances. We have just seen that Vollant lays stress on the use of belladonna root, deeming the leaves to have little efficacy. Hepp insists on the importance of carefully following Withering's directions in collecting and preparing digitalis. Not more than a year's supply he says should ever be kept. Is it not pretty nearly certain that nearly worthless drugs are too often employed? Bearing in mind the above, I am not at all shaken in my belief of the utility of treatment by finding that a great variety of remedies have been found or considered capable of arresting or diminishing the disorder in some instances while they have entirely failed in others. This, even admitting the purity and equal virtue of the preparations, as I have already observed, is a feature common to many disorders and especially to neuroses. The idiosyncrasy of the individual patient, and the existence of numberless shades of difference in the nature and quality of the morbid processes are quite sufficient to prevent our remedies from having that certainty of action which many look for, and not finding become sceptical of all therapeutic agency. Even with regard to non-specific bronchial hyperæsthesia after considerable experience I have no certain foreknowledge as to whether atropia, opium, or cannabis indica will be successful in a given case. I am quite ready to charge some of this uncertainty to my own want of discernment, but I am certain that cases are not uncommon where the symptoms are to all appearance quite the same and yet the same remedies will have very different effects. One of the chief mistakes current at the present day is to regard all diseased states to which the same name can be applied as exactly and essentially similar, whereas the truth is that the same name covers a multitude of morbid conditions which vary *ad infinitum* in their component elements. The gross, outward resemblance leads us to overlook and neglect the concealed but more important differences. This is the more to be regretted as the latter rule the treatment.

With regard to pertussis I am much inclined to regard hydrocyanic acid as suited to an earlier period of the disease than atropine is; I give it during the catarrhal stage with vin. ipecac. and a saline. Combined with nitric acid it is very suitable also to a later period when the catarrhal affection is less acute, the dry have given place to moist râles, and the febrile movement has subsided. When the cough is very violent and the catarrhal affection is slight I expect great benefit from atropine. I have however seen it in combination with nitric acid act exceedingly well in an infant suffering with severe bronchial catarrh complicated probably with miliary tubercle. As to the objections raised by some against employing such potent agents especially in young subjects I think it may be fairly replied that medicine cannot be practised at all without care and attention, and a very moderate amount of these is quite sufficient to prevent the possibility of any injurious consequences from the administration of any of the alkaloids. It may be affirmed that atropia is actually safer to use than opium. The latter, if an overdose is accidentally taken, is more likely to be lethal than atropia, unless indeed the dose is very large. In the convulsions occurring in severe hooping-cough I have found atropia of some benefit, but not of so much as I had expected. I am doubtful at present whether opium is not preferable. The following case is a good example of a combined treatment which will be suitable in many instances.

No. 114.—A. S., f., æt. 7, ad. Nov. 12th, ill two months with hooping-cough; in mornings has hard strangling fits of coughing after which she brings up about ʒij of blood. Some slight large-tube râles in back. Takes food fairly. Has about twelve fits of violent cough in twenty-four hours. P. weak and soft. T. dark mahogany coloured in morning. Atropiæ gr. $\frac{1}{120}$ + acid. nitric. ♏ij + aq. ʒss ter die. 26th. Is quite a different child, cough a great deal better, does not spit any blood now, or complain of her head. Pt. c. mist. subinde. Dec. 30th. Ol. morrh. ʒj ter die; vini ferri ʒj ter die. 14th. Recurrence of cough. Reptr. mistr. atropiæ. 31st. Better, does not cough so often, but has violent attacks now and then. Pt. Jan. 11th. Does not whoop now at all, but has very bad cough at night for one hour. Ferri et quin. citrat. gr. v ter die. Pt. c. oleo. 25th. Cough nearly gone.

Bromide of potassium has lately been given by several physicians with very good results. From two to five grains is the dose for a child from two to five years old. Bromide of ammonium may be used in the same way.

The affection termed laryngismus stridulus, or spasm of the glottis, is one of peculiar interest, not only as a well-marked instance of nerve disorder capable of receiving a satisfactory explanation from established principles, but also on account of the great peril to life attending it. The child which but a minute before appeared tolerably well may the next be laid lifeless in its parent's arms. The suddenness of the stroke which we know may fall at any moment adds much to the painful interest with which we must regard these little patients. The two following cases will serve as a text for some comments.

No. 115.—A. R., m., æt. 2, ad. April 6th, ill two months. Has had from the first attacks of convulsive character, apparently consisting of laryngeal spasm. A baby belonging to the same mother was attacked last week suddenly and died immediately. This child had the disease when 8 months old, got better during the summer, but has been worse the last winter. Has some cough, varies much, some days the attacks occur every hour. B. open. T. much coated. Lives in a kitchen. Is a very weakly child, does not walk. Two upper incisors are just making their way through the gum (lanced). The condition of the alimentary mucous membrane was corrected by small doses of gray powder and olei ricini, and ferro-citrate of quinine was steadily administered for nearly eight weeks, during which he was taken out into the open air. Under this treatment he improved so much that he ceased attendance by the end of May. No relapse occurred or none of importance till the beginning of the following November, and then the repetition of the same treatment together with ol. morrh. proved curative.

The relation of the disorder to dentition in this case was not at all well marked, nor was there any other apparent exciting cause. I believe the nervous centres were more at fault than the peripheral structures. The tonic probably arrested the disorder by lessening the excitability of the medulla oblongata. The weakly condition of the little patient was presumably the cause of the morbid state of this centre. The nervous erethism was neurolytic.

No. 116.—G. H., m., æt. 10 months, seen Jan. 17th, 1861. Is suffering severely with attacks of spasm of the glottis which occur about every twenty minutes. The affection commenced gradually with very slight attacks six weeks ago; it has been much worse during the severe frost. About sixteen days ago he had a well-marked convulsive seizure which had not recurred since. In the attacks he first turns pale, throws his head back, the commissures of the lips are drawn backwards in a kind of grin, the face becomes sub-livid, there is a period of silence, and then comes the peculiar stridulous inspiration, which recurs several times, and is followed by a natural cry. He is greatly depressed, his face looks sunken, he seems ill and rather emaciated. B. rather costive. No fever. Is teething and has had the gums lanced twice or thrice, but the last time it appeared to be of no benefit. Until lately has been a remarkably placid and healthy infant without any tendency to diarrhœa. He has been brought up by hand. Three or four times a day he takes small doses of ol. ricini + ol. terebinth., besides ferri carb. sacch., and a small opiate at night. 19th. This afternoon he had a sharp attack of convulsions, and during the whole evening and early part of the night had frequently glottic spasms, and was crying with pain. Chloroform was repeatedly administered and with good effect in tranquillizing him, but its influence soon passed off. After taking ♏ij of liq. morph. bimec. he was quieter and slept. 21st. Yesterday began to take extr. belladon. gr. $\frac{1}{12}$ + ol. tereb. ♏iij *ter die*, had morphia in the night; is on the whole quieter; a second dose of liq. morph. bimec. ♏iij was given to-day. B. open. 24th. Last two days is decidedly bettter, taking little but the morphia, the attacks of glottic spasm are much less frequent and severe, but diarrhœa has begun, the bowels which before were costive being loose and gripy and the stools green. 28th. Worse last three days, has severe and frequent attacks; great restlessness especially at night and suffering evidently referred to the mouth; the gums look natural. He takes tr. bellad. ♏iv-v 2*dis* vel 4*tis horis*. 29th. The belladonna entirely failed to give relief, although it evidently deranged his vision; he has to day been taking liq. morph. bimec. in ♏ four doses *bis* vel *ter die*, and is now quieter. Takes very little food. 31st. Is better and has less attacks, takes morphia. Feb. 4th. Is very much better, the attacks of laryngismus have ceased. 7th. Going on well, no medicine. 18th. Has had a little return of the laryngismus, but not material; is otherwise fairly well. March 9th. Has still the laryngismus occasionally, but is doing well, gaining strength; takes morphia daily. 18th. Had yesterday some very severe attacks. April 19th. Numerous and severe attacks of laryngismus lately, and this morning a fit of convulsions, in which his face was markedly pale. The upper lateral incisors are now advancing, but the gums do not appear tense or red (lanced). After this the attacks gradually ceased. Nov. 21st. At the beginning of

June he went into the country where he remained about three months, and returned quite restored. He is now cutting his first molars, and though he has had some catarrh there has not been the least return of the laryngismus. Jan. 1864. No return of the disorder, the child has thriven well.

The relation of the disease in this case to dentition is by no means clearly established. It certainly supervened about the commencement of the process, but it subsided long before it was over, and the aggravations of the disease did not evidently correspond to the period of eruption of a tooth. Whether there was some deep-seated irritation connected with the development of the teeth can only be conjectured; if so, it only existed during the formation of the earlier teeth. The three points which the history seems to set forth prominently are, (1) the connection between the disease and general convulsions; (2) the good effect of morphia and the inutility of belladonna; (3) the importance of change of air. The occurrence of general convulsions in connection with laryngismus indicated that the morbid action extends to and involves some larger group of nerve cells than in the local spasm, probably either the whole of the medulla oblongata, or the corpora quadrigemina also. The convulsions as well as the glottic spasms appeared to depend much more on a state of erethism of the nervous centres than on any peripheral irritation. I mean that the former was much the more important causative element, the removal of which would have arrested the morbid phenomena. This is evidenced also by the "juvantia," sedatives affording relief, while lancing the gums had no decided good effect. I am much inclined to refer the supervention of the disorder to the severe cold of the winter which depressed and deranged the "vis nervosa." The first attack of general convulsions occurred during a hard frost. In this instance as in some others it has certainly appeared to me that the prevalence of severe cold has materially promoted the occurrence of general convulsions. The cold seems to depress the nervous power of the little patients, and make exciting causes of disorder more operative. The inference from this is that the child should be kept during cold weather in a well-warmed room, at a uniform temperature say of 64 deg. F., and that this should be maintained night and day. The sudden death which is by no means uncommon in this disease depends I conceive on the transmission of irritation along the cardiac fibres of the vagi to the heart, which is then arrested in its action just as when the pneumogastrics are strongly galvanized. Life truly hangs by a thread while we know not whether in any one of the attacks the nerve disorder may not take this fatal direction, instead of invading the recurrent laryngeals only. The superiority of morphia to belladonna was unequivocal, a result which was not anticipated, on account of the greater tendency of opium to cause tetanic phenomena. It is very possible that in another instance the result might be different, but it is as well to remark that in the fatal case of epileptic disorder recorded at p. 51 the attacks subsided under the administration of morphia. The doses given were certainly large, the strength of the bimeconate being about equal to that of tr. opii; they produced however no trace of narcotism. This shows that the erethism of the centres must have been considerable. The carbonate of iron which was tried was certainly of no benefit, if not injurious. This result contrasts strongly with the good effect of tonics in the other case. It may be accounted for I think by observing that the subject of the first case was a very weakly child, while that of the second was the reverse. The condition of the latter was more sthenic than that of the former. All this corroborates what has been before said as to the difficulty of determining exactly the remedy suitable to an individual morbid state, and shows how the self-same symptoms may result from different pathological conditions. The attacks had indeed ceased before he was removed into the country, but the great improvement which ensued in his health makes it eminently probable that his subsequent immunity depended on the calming and toning influence of the purer air. Considerable intermissions had previously occurred, but had been followed by relapses. Romberg writes respecting the free intervals, "the first thing to attend to is the atmosphere and the diet." This is quite my own feeling, and indeed in all neuroses attended with a high degree of sensitiveness and excitability, and not depending on an eccentric cause, I look to the influence of a pure rather bracing air as the most sovereign remedy. Tonics are apt to prove too irritating and sedatives to lose their efficacy.

In an able paper on this disorder (v. *Brit. Med. J.*, March 7th, 1857) Mr. T. Paget lays down the following directions for treatment with which to a great extent I concur. After removing all peripheral causes of irritation, whether dental, intestinal, or elsewhere seated, he contemplates the subjection of nerve excitement by means of narcotics as the most important object. "Upon the narcotic to be used, and the mode of giving it, or the dose required, I need lay but little stress, especially since it is well known how varied is the susceptibility of individuals in reference to this class of medicines. Suffice it to say that the drug I have most used is opium; that beginning with small doses and cautiously regulating them according to their effect, I do not stop short of producing a constant drowsiness and some slight pallor, that when this state is obtained, the paroxysms decrease in force and frequency, the infant is calmly sleeping its day away, no longer devil-torn, nor are its friends racked with anxiety; and that when the paroxysms have failed to occur for some forty-eight hours, which will usually happen in from three to six days, the drug is gradually withdrawn, the quantity taken off each dose being immediately restored if the attacks show the slightest disposition to encroach again. I may say also that to attain to the required effect I have usually been obliged to give to children 4 or 5 months old (the age at which the disease most commonly perhaps invades) from 1 to 5 minims of tr. opii in a dose with 4 or 6 of sal volatile two or three times a day; or if in enemata 5 to 7 minims."

Asthma is by general consent acknowledged to be essentially a neurosis, though it is rare to meet with it in a pure form. Usually it is attended with more or less of bronchitis just in the same way as retinal hyperæsthesia is with conjunctivitis, while spasm of associated muscles is a prominent feature in both cases. The view usually taken of the special seat of the neurosis is that it affects those branches of the vagi which are distributed to the bronchial muscles, and that the latter being spasmodically contracted seriously obstruct the access of air to the cells of the lungs. It would be expected according to this view that the chest would be rather diminished than expanded in size, and such appears to be actually the case. That excellent observer, Dr. Walshe, states that there is sinking of the epigastrium, and elevation of the diaphragm (evidently from the diminished mass of air in the lungs). Dr. Flint[1] says that "if emphysema be not present, the volume of the lungs may be so reduced by the expiratory efforts as to diminish appreciably the clearness of percussion." It appears, however, that this is not a constant and invariable condition, but that it may be replaced by the opposite. Wunderlich[2] describes one form of asthma as consisting in a gradual augmentation of the dyspnœa which reaches its maximum at the end of two or three days. At this stage the chest is almost motionless in spite of the most violent muscular efforts, the percussion resonance is everywhere preserved, and after many hours the limbs of the chest are extended downwards. The liver also descends, the heart is thrust into the epigastrium, and the thorax is excessively distended." Théry[3] also describes the thorax during the paroxysm as being in a state of the greatest distension, as in forced inspiration. The diaphragm, however, contracts sometimes so forcibly as to depress the lower end of the sternum backwards. Kidd[4] and Sanderson[5] describe this state of great distension as that which is characteristic of asthma, though they differ as to the mode of its production. The former refers it to a tonic spasm of the muscles of inspiration; the latter to a relaxation of the dilator muscles of the glottis, as well as of the contractile fibres of the lung tissue, in consequence of which expiration cannot be properly performed. There can be I think little doubt that the view held by the two last observers is too exclusive, and that except in cases complicated with extensive emphysema there is no notable if any dilatation of the chest in the earlier part of an attack of pure nervous asthma. That in the course of a prolonged fit the chest should become distended is quite intelligible if we consider that the inspiratory power is much superior to the expiratory, and

[1] "On Respirat. Organs," p. 397. [2] "Pathologie," III. 316.
[3] Merkel's "Report on Asthma," Schmidt's "Jahrb.," vol. cix. p. 229.
[4] "Dublin Q. J. of Med. Sc.," May, 1861.
[5] "Med. T. and Gaz.," May 16, 1868.

that the air gradually accumulates in the lungs being locked up as it were by the bronchial constriction. Salter, who has most ably studied the whole subject of asthma, adopts the theory of bronchial spasm of nervous origin, and states that the chest distension is dependent on the demand for air, and is observed in all states of insufficient aëration of the blood. The circumstance that during the worst of an attack the expectoration is scanty or nil is tolerably good proof that the small arteries of the bronchial mucous membrane are constricted during this time, and adds to the probability that the bronchial tubes themselves are in the same state. It must be admitted I think as pretty certain that hyperæsthesia of the sensory filaments of the vagi cannot be the essential pathological state, for this as we have lately seen induces, not spasm of the minute bronchi and exaggerated action of the *inspiratory* muscles, but violent action of the *expiratory* in cough, with more or less copious expectoration. The shifting of the dry râles heard during the paroxysm from one part of the chest to another affords some evidence that the smaller tubes are at intervals narrowed so as to produce such sounds and again relaxed. The depression, the chilliness of the skin, the smallness of the pulse, the aqueous quality of the urine, remind one somewhat of the cold stage of ague[1] in which, by the way, along with various spasmodic phenomena there is "distressed and anxious breathing." If the inspiratory muscles were primarily affected so as to keep the chest in a state of almost permanent inspiration, there is little doubt that the will would be able to interrupt occasionally this morbid action, and to procure every now and then a forced expiration, so that the used-up air might be expelled from the lungs. This, however, there seems no power to do. From these and other considerations, I am led to regard true asthma as a tetanoid disorder of the motor nerves of the bronchi, and as in great measure dependent like epilepsy on morbid excitability of certain nervous centres, which are probably located in the spinal rather than in the encephalic districts; this I conclude from the absence of any tendency to general convulsions in the asthmatic paroxysm. No doubt there are many cases where the peculiar excitability would remain inoperative except for some peripheral irritation, just as in epilepsy; and there may be great varieties in respect of the relative importance of the central and peripheral causes; the former, however, I hold to be the more essential and constant element of the malady. The necessity of a peculiar predisposition is fully as apparent in asthma as in epilepsy. The nature of this predisposition may vary very much, it may consist in a tendency to skin eruption, to gout, or rheumatism, or hæmorrhoids, or periodic hemicrania, or uric acid deposits. All these as Trousseau states are affections which asthma may re-

---

[1] Théry says "Agues run parallel with, or alternate with, asthma . . . . . the primary cause may determine both disorders."—Schmidt's "Jahrb.," vol. cix. p. 237.

place, and which in turn may replace asthma. This diathetic tendency which so often leads to asthma is frequently derived from hereditary descent. The extraordinary capriciousness of asthma is notorious, and is certainly a matter of high interest and significance. It proves how wonderfully slight and subtle may be the influences which act with great effect on certain states of the nervous system. Were it not well ascertained how very slight a change in locality will make all the difference to an asthmatic, we should feel much disposed to consider the notion as the result of a morbid imagination. This should be remembered by us in dealing with other and still more obscure neuroses. The influence of the withdrawal of light on asthmatics is remarkable. One of my hospital patients, a male, æt. 35, declared that "when it gets dark he is done altogether," and another, a female, æt. 75, found her paroxysms come on at nightfall, whether this occurred early, as in the winter, or late, as in the summer. Trousseau[1] mentions the case of an asthmatic who when his attacks came on had five or six moderator lamps lit in his room, and was immediately relieved. Though the neurotic character of asthma is, as these and many other facts show, extremely marked, yet it is clear that it differs from many of the more common, and especially the sensory neuroses, in that it is not associated at least frequently or intimately with marked signs of nerve debility. On the contrary, as Mr. Pridham observes, asthmatics are for the most part gifted with extraordinary energy and talents. The admirable Trousseau, who acknowledges his infirmity in this respect, is an instance in point.

The treatment of asthma is eminently that of neurosis. It consists first in the removal of all causes of irritation, such as catarrhal inflammation of the bronchi, dyspeptic disorder, unwholesome diet, and unsuitable climate, &c., and secondly in the use of various appropriate tonics and sedatives. The prophylactic management of asthma involves as one of its most important parts the selection of a suitable locality for the invalid's residence. This can scarcely be determined except by trial. It should be borne in mind that the air of large towns is in not a few cases more beneficial to an asthmatic than that of the country, and that where there is a tendency to asthenic bronchitis a relaxing climate is unsuitable. Though the averting of pulmonary catarrh is highly desirable, we must remind our patients that no amount of guarding against cold will protect them against the stroke of influenza, which by the way seems to me to be far the most frequent cause of catarrh; and also that the best way of effectually resisting the morbific action of cold is to tone and fortify the system so that it may be well able to endure it. It is truly a remarkable thing how the same temperature that withers and destroys the feeble vitality of the two extremes of age, invigorates and increases the life of the strong and healthy. An old lady, however,

---

[1] "Clinique Méd.," vol. i. p. 539.

under my care told me once that she was "quite well and wound up" as long as a sharp frost continued in December; as soon as the thaw set in she got a cold, tracheal cough and expectoration. On the frost setting in again sharply she rallied and became more vigorous. It was remarkable this year, 1864, how very general catarrhs became as soon as the frost ceased. Cold bathing or sponging, regular outdoor exercise, a sufficient but not excessive amount of clothing, avoidance of damp, chilling draughts when sitting still, are the main points to be observed by the invalid who is fearful of taking cold. Of course, in every case judicious adaptation of general rules to the individual condition is essential. The importance of a duly regulated diet is well known, and has lately been especially illustrated by Mr. Pridham.[1] He restricts his patients at first to two ounces of fresh meat with as much dry bread for dinner at one P. M., and the same for supper at seven, allows a cup of tea with cream and dry bread in the morning and for drink weak brandy or whiskey and water, which is not to be taken till three hours after animal food. Rest is also enjoined for the same period, though air and exercise are recommended. Three grains of extr. conii are given four times a day, just one hour before each meal. As the symptoms improve the diet is increased, though it is still very spare and simple. The rationale of this proceeding is very evident; it is manifestly well adapted for patients who betray any symptoms of disordered digestion or assimilation. As there seems no doubt that the materies morbi of gout may give rise to asthma, so it is very possible that unhealthy products of digestion may act in a like manner. In most of Pridham's cases the urine was habitually loaded with lithates, indicating an excess of acid passing off by the kidneys. The more our pathological knowledge increases, the more do we find that many different causes are capable of producing the same effects. Pridham professes to treat in the above way only what he terms dyspeptic asthma, though he seems inclined to extend the significance of the term rather widely, as he says that he is convinced that an asthmatic person can never with impunity eat and drink as other people do. An inveterate asthmatic who was once under my care told me, however, that though he was obliged to be careful in his diet, yet he could go out to a dinner party and eat and drink like any one else and not be the worse for it. He also found, as indeed occurred while I had him in view, that when he got bronchitis the asthmatic attack ceased. Trousseau gives an exactly similar case. Such instances show clearly the essential difference between inflammatory catarrh and asthma. Gymnastic exercises, riding, sawing, bowling, have been praised for their good effects; and as tending to diminish excitability and increase tone and strength, they are likely to be useful. Compressed air has recently been introduced as an

[1] "Brit. Med. J.," June 9th, July 28th, Sept. 1st, 29th, Nov. 17th, Dec. 29th, 1860.

agent in the treatment of various pulmonary affections, including asthma. Sandahl in his paper[1] states that of fourteen cases of asthma and pure simple pulmonary emphysema all were improved, and twelve as far as could be made out had experienced no relapse. Of seventy-seven who suffered with asthma, emphysema, and chronic bronchitis, fifty-seven were improved and twenty either doubtfully or not at all. From Vivenot's observations[2] it appears that the effects on the system are slowing of the pulse and the respiration, diminution of the pulmonary and cutaneous exhalation, increase of the urinary secretion, and prevention of congestion in the parts on which the air acts. It may reasonably be expected that benefit would result from these baths in all cases of catarrhal affection of the air-passages, but in pure spasmodic asthma it is not very apparent how they could act beneficially, nor does there seem sufficient evidence to prove that they have done so. M. Beau[3] finds sulphuret of potassium baths not only to relieve the attacks of asthma, but to prevent their recurrence. Each bath should last twenty minutes, and thirty should be taken, one every other day. The temperature should be 86° F. Certain tonics seem to be of real use in not a few cases. I have found arsenic sometimes of much advantage, administered in doses of m_iv—v of Fowler's solution *ter die*. It may be given with ammonia and tr. camph. co., or alone, or with an ordinary cough mixture, according to circumstances. We should assure ourselves before giving it that it is likely to be tolerated by the stomach. When there are indications of gastric as well as of bronchial catarrh, nitric or muriatic acid is preferable in combination with acid. hydrocy. dil. and tr. calumb. When there is bronchial catarrh alone, atropia with or without nitric acid is a valuable remedy. I have had a case recently under my care which has terminated very satisfactorily under atropia gr. $\frac{1}{20}$ *ter die*, and tannin with Canada balsam in pills. Atropia is a remedy on which I feel much inclined to rely both from experience of its power as a sedative, and from the observations of Dr. Williams as to its abolishing the contractility of the bronchi, which is just what is desirable in asthma. Cannabis indica has occasionally proved very useful, gr. $\frac{1}{2}$ doses of the extract immediately checking the spasm. In one case where asthma supervened upon phthisis great relief was afforded by the subcutaneous injection of liq. opii sed. m_x into the left front of the chest. M. Courty[4] has also obtained very good results from subcutaneous injection of atropine (gr. $\frac{1}{35}$ thrice repeated) in the vicinity of the left vagus nerve. Dry cupping should be persistently employed as long as there are signs of congestion of the bronchial mucous membrane. In some cases pot. iod. proves very beneficial. With regard to the shorter and severe paroxysms I can do little more than

---

[1] Schmidt's "Jahrb." vol. cxx. p. 178.
[2] Ibid., vol. ci. x. p. 335.
[3] "J. de Méd. et de Chir. Pratiq.," vol. xxxiii. p. 440.
[4] "Gaz. Méd," Nov. 1859.

enumerate the various remedies which have been found efficient. Ice pills according to Romberg often afforded instant relief, and inhalation of sulphuric ether or chloroform may be very serviceable. Smoking tobacco, or stramonium, or a compound of the latter with belladonna, will sometimes quell the spasm. Ipecacuan emetics may be given for the same purpose. Opium combined with spt. æth. s. co. has in some cases a good effect. Nitre paper should not be forgotten, made according to Dr. H. Salter's formula by soaking red blotting paper in a solution of ʒiv of pot. nitras in aq. Oss. In some instances Ducros' medication or a modification of it is beneficial. He brushes the posterior wall of the pharynx with a strong solution of ammonia, liq. ammon. + aq. āā ʒj. The first time that Trousseau tried it he thought the patient would have died suffocated. He states, however, that "employé dans une juste mesure il a rendu de réels services." Probably M. Faure's plan is preferable. He puts ʒss of liquid ammonia in a bowl, and desires the patient to inhale the vapour, taking care, however, to close the nostrils. The inhalation is to be continued for fifteen minutes, and to be repeated four times a day. Trousseau relates that the captain of a ship was always exempt from the paroxysms while his vessel was loaded with guano, or he was staying at the gathering grounds. Various stimulants are occasionally beneficial, strong coffee, tea, ammonia, and alcohol. Dr. Salter[1] has recently published some remarkable evidence of the power of very large quantities of the latter to subdue paroxysms of the disease which had proved refractory to all other measures. Intoxication was not necessarily produced. The efficacy of alcoholic and other stimulants I believe to depend on the circumstance that their action on the nerves or nervous centres replaces advantageously the morbid action which previously affected them. We have here another instance of the affinity between spasm and paralysis, both being advantageously treated by the same means.

To prevent recurrences, Trousseau advises a compound medication consisting of ten days of small doses of belladonna, as many of turpentine, and the remaining ten of the month of arsenical cigarettes, besides a sixty grain dose of powdered calisaya bark in coffee every ten days. This plan must be followed out a long time and very exactly.

Sneezing and *hiccup* are two minimum disorders as they usually occur, but they occasionally develop themselves to the dignity of a disease. Romberg cites several instances of the former occurring either in his own experience or in that of others. It is met with occasionally as an accompaniment of hooping-cough, and of verminous disorder, as well as in the so-called hysterical state. Mosler relates a case[2] in which a scrofulous female was computed to have sneezed 50,000 times in eighty hours, and the neighbourhood was alarmed! She was amenorrhœal, and the disorder returned a month

---

[1] "Lancet," Nov. 14, 1863. [2] "Med. T. and Gaz.," June 25, 1859.

after its first attack. The only instance I have met with was in the person of a mid-aged gentleman, who had suffered from dysentery in India, and had quite recovered, but no doubt still retained something of the malarious influence, which gave rise to the nasal flux. Romberg describes ordinary sneezing as a reflex act excited by irritation of the nasal filaments of the fifth pair, as well as by other filaments of the same nerve, and of other and remote nerves, such as the intestinal and uterine. This is no doubt true in many instances, but it seems to me also pretty certain that the morbid action is very often central rather than peripheral in its seat. In fact where no cause of peripheral irritation can be discovered it seems most reasonable to suppose that the seat of disease is in the part where most vital action and change is going on. At any rate the possibility of this cannot be denied. The circumstance which I have often observed that a hot room will cause sneezing which subsides when the air is cooled is in favour of this view. The heat relaxes the general tone, but could not irritate peripheral nerves. One circumstance which appears very noteworthy in sneezing is the muco-watery secretion, which is sometimes very considerable. In one of Brodie's cases the watery fluid dropping from the nostrils was sufficient to wet a handkerchief completely through. Now it is certain that the exudation is not the mere result of the air-blast passing through the nasal cavities; it seems to be, as well as the morbid sensation which determines the expiratory act, the result of deranged innervation. We can scarcely err in regarding the vaso-motor nerves as implicated in this occurrence, and that necessarily in the way of paralysis. How this comes to pass is not so clear by any means. Of course, when an irritant, as snuff, is directly applied to the mucous surface we may consider that the tissue and the nerves are both directly affected, but this will not serve for the cases where no local irritant is applied, or where the local irritation is remote. I see no way of rendering a rationale of this common occurrence, except by referring it to the theory of inhibitory action. The muco-watery profluvium is the result of reflex inhibitory irritation, congesting the vessels and promoting exudation. If indeed the profluvium were derived from any large gland the reflected irritation might be supposed to affect this in the ordinary way, but as in all probability it is poured out from the general mucous surface this explanation will hardly apply. Another mode in which we can conceive the phenomena to be linked together is that some central change gives rise at one and the same time to the pain and the paralysis, each being expressive of disorder of a similar kind in a particular kind of nerve. Romberg's case of facial neuralgia gives support to this view (*v.* p. 37, "Syd. Soc. Transl.")

When there is no discoverable cause for the paroxysms the usual anti-neuralgic treatment is generally indicated. One of Romberg's cases was cured by carbonate of iron, and my own was very much benefited by iron and quinine with Fowler's solution.

Hiccup is described by Copland as consisting of a sudden and rapid contraction of the respiratory muscles, of the diaphragm especially. Romberg thinks this erroneous, and does not allow that irritation of the phrenic nerve is concerned in producing it. He bases this opinion on two cases recorded by Bright in which organic disease affecting the right phrenic nerve produced other nervous disorder, but no hiccup. He ascribes its occurrence to reflex irritation having its starting-point in the alimentary canal, the liver, or the uterus, but admits also that its cause not unfrequently resides in the central nervous organs. Copland states that it is often produced by locomotive biliary and renal calculi, as well as by strangulation of internal parts, and external injuries and fractures of the ribs. It is not an uncommon and distressing symptom towards the fatal close of acute diseases and fevers, especially in advanced life. The form of hiccup which most concerns us here is that which constitutes *per se* the whole or chief disorder and is not merely symptomatic. This seems for the most part referable either to obscure nervous disorder such as is loosely called hysterical, or to malarious infection. Of the latter a good instance is recorded by Widal (*Gaz. Méd. de l'Algérie*). The patient was admitted at first suffering under the consequences of cerebral congestion. Five or six days after having committed excess in drinking he was seized with violent hiccough, the incessant spasms of which compelled him to remain in bed, and resisted all treatment by anti-spasmodics. The hiccough was so intense and noisy that it was heard outside the hospital. The number of diaphragmatic contractions reached 55 in the minute, and their energy was so great that all the muscles of the trunk participated in them. There was considerable dyspnœa, short inspirations, red face, white tongue, loathing of all kinds of food, pulse small, 80. Opii gr. $\frac{1}{8}$ was given every two hours, and a blister to the epigastrium was dressed with morphia, but no improvement ensued. The patient had no sleep, and his strength was failing. At last quinine in pretty full doses was given, which speedily put an end to the disorder, after it had lasted nineteen days. In all cases where the patient has ever been exposed to malaria we should consider whether this may not be the cause of the disorder. It is rather remarkable in the foregoing case that the neurosis was continuous, not periodic. Romberg mentions a case occasioned by violent fright, in which the hiccup was complicated with, and alternated with attacks of spasm of the glottis The patient was a female, æt. 21, with regular catamenia. I see no reason for denominating such a case hysterical any more than one of chorea, produced as it often is in the same way. The seat of the disorder in both the above instances, and indeed in most, I believe to be central, though it is difficult to say precisely what nervous centre is affected. Probably, however, it is the upper part of the cord about the origin of the fourth cervical nerve. The causes which give rise to hiccup are most often of a debilitating kind, and there can be no question that the condition of the nervous centre is rather one of exhaustion than of increased energy. The affection may be viewed as a kind of local chorea, and like it is the result of abnormal excitability and weakness in the nervous tissue.

Very various treatment has succeeded in cases of non-malarious hiccough. In individuals exhausted by profuse discharges a full dose of opium is praised by Sydenham. In an opposite condition, viz., suppressed menstruation, Berends obtained a cure by taking three ounces of blood from the foot. Blisters to the neck are sometimes useful. Mental influences occasionally are potent remedies. Cruveilhier seems to have cured two bad cases by half drowning them with water poured down their throats. Swallowing lumps of ice I think would prove often an effectual remedy. Laennec was successful with milder measures in the form of magnetic(?) plates applied to the epigastrium and opposite region of the spine. Electricity, as it has proved beneficial in chorea, might be so also in this allied disorder. In some cases the interrupted, in others the continuous current might be suitable. The former should be used in cases where there was evident asthenia, the latter in those where there were indications of sthenic excitement. Various stimulant and tonic medicines might be administered internally according to the condition of the patient. One of the best is assafœtidæ gr. x in pil. ij, 2*dis horis sd*. The practitioner will do wisely in cases where the neurosis is idiopathic and obstinate to mingle with his treatment as much of the "medicina mentis" as possible. Nothing is more certain than that even actual bodily disorder is very materially influenced by mental affections, and this is eminently true of the neurosis.

Yawning is a small neurosis, which however has some points of interest for the thoughtful practitioner. Thus, though clearly a muscular *action*, it must be ascribed to diminution of nervous energy, and is thus a similar pathological instance to chorea and hiccough. Then it is unquestionably a communicative neurosis, and though of course we must take into account the circumstance that a number of individuals who are together are likely to be in the same state of fatigue, &c., yet it is certainly remarkable that witnessing this small spasm in a companion should cause others to imitate it involuntarily. One's thoughts of course recur to the communication of epilepsy in the same way, and one cannot but observe how in smaller as well as in greater matters our organism is swayed by the same rules. As these are communicated other neuroses may be so too, a circumstance which should make us not indifferent to the protection of the young and impressionable from sights which might affect them injuriously. Mothers firmly believe that squints are catching, and I am not sure that they are not right. At any rate it is best to err on the side of safety. Romberg assigns to the uterus a large share in the production of yawning, and affirms consistently that it is much more frequent in the female than in the male sex. This I take leave to doubt, and am much more inclined to acquiesce in his admission that it may be of central origin, as is seen in apopletic attacks. To my mind it is commonly of centric origin, at least when it results from fatigue, and betokens a state of temporary nervous exhaustion. It is worth observing that it is a common occurrence at the commencement of the cold stage of an ague.

CHAPTER XXIX.

MYALGIA.

In this disorder it appears to me that the sensory nerves of the muscles must be essentially implicated, as if they were not it is impossible to conceive how the pain which gives its name to the affection should be experienced. The muscles, it is plain, are weak and readily exhausted, their functional power is low. But if this were all, the phenomena would be simply those of paresis or imperfect paralysis, and there would be no pain. The pain is like that of ordinary neuralgia in being calmed by repose, reproduced by exertion, and removed by nerve tonics. I therefore regard myalgia as a muscular neuralgia, and believe that it is to be treated exactly on the same principles as neuralgia in any other situation. The weak and aching muscles are to be rested sufficiently, but not left on the other hand without adequate exercise. The general strength and vigour must be promoted as much as possible by diet, air, and medicines. The following case is a well-marked instance.

No. 117.—S. B., m., æt. 25. Ill three months. Pallid, of small make, ordinary temperament. Functions in fairly good order. Complains of pain at top and back of right shoulder which ceases if he leaves off work for a few days, but returns again on resuming it. The seat of the pain is in the supra-spinal fossa. When passing his stitches in boot-making he feels as if the shoulder were pulled out of its place. Has been ordered warm baths without benefit. Under steady perseverance in the administration of quinine with iron, or strychnia, and ol. morrh., he recovered completely in about three months. During the last six weeks he was able to follow his employment. It is very easy to confound this disorder with chronic rheumatism; from which it is chiefly to be distinguished by its complete subsidence during repose and aggravation by exertion. The profession is much indebted to Dr. Inman, of Liverpool, for having first accurately described and distinguished it.

CHAPTER XXX.

ABDOMINAL NEURALGIA.

UNDER this head I propose to consider various more or less painful affections, which appear to have their seat either in the viscera, or in the parietes of this cavity. They are often difficult of management, and their existence is as yet far from being generally known to the profession. What I know respecting them I have learned almost entirely from experience, and I believe I shall do best by relating various cases which have occurred to me, and subjoining some comments upon them. In the first group of instances I shall give, pain is the chief or only symptom, the sensory nerves seem to be alone affected.

No. 118.—J. B., m., æt. 14, pupil-teacher, intellectual-looking and delicate, worked rather hard in a school. Ad. January 28th. Ill three days. Has pain in abdomen causing him to bend double at times, some cough and pain in chest; food causes no pain. Much headache at times. Forehead cool. Abdomen somewhat tender to pressure; the pain in it ceases when he is recumbent. I urged his being removed from school, as the confinement was evidently injurious, but this was not done. Citrate of quinine and iron with a little pot. iod. and chloric æther was given for fourteen days without advantage. Subsequently he took a combination of ammon. carb., ferri ammon. citr., tr. nucis vom. and infus. calumb., with which he benefited immediately, and was discharged well by the end of April.

No. 119.—J. N., m., æt. 13, ad. June 4th, ill two days. Was attacked while at work with pain in abdomen and violent sickness and purging. These have ceased, but the pain continues, and there is considerable tenderness on pressure over the umbilical region, but not elsewhere. P. small, 100. T. slightly furred. Pupils of medium size. Has had a dose of ol. ricini. Although I have had an eye to detect abdominal neuralgia for some length of time, I doubted seriously in this case what was the exact state of matters. The boy had walked to the hospital, and his aspect was scarcely that of a person affected with peritonitis. Yet the tenderness was so marked, and there was such an absence of hysterical exaggeration, that I was fearful of treating the disorder as mere neuralgia. So I gave him then and there tr. opii m̨xxx in an enema, and after he had lain still awhile and seemed freer from pain I ordered him pil. saponis co. gr. v, 3$tiis$ vel 4$tis horis$. 8th. Apyretic, has still much abdominal pain, but some appetite. The course was now clear; I gave him ferri et quinæ citratis gr. vij $ter die$, and in fourteen days he was almost well, ailing only with great debility.

No. 120.—G. E., æt. 13, m., ad. Nov 21st, ill three months. Has frequently violent pain in his bowels, "and is all drawed into a lump." Flinches very much from pressure on abdomen. When lying down the recti muscles are very tense, but when his attention is distracted he lets me manipulate his abdomen without much complaint. Has "cold shivers" when the pains are present. B. open, has pain when they act. Has taken his food pretty well till last two days. Very languid and drowsy. Has been under medical care and been salivated for supposed inflammation of bowels. I gave him at first citrate of iron and quinine, *ter die*, and lin. opii; from this in a week he was little if at all better; it was then changed for muriate of ammonia, gr. x *ter die*, but without any advantage; the paroxysms of pain lasted from ten to sixty minutes. He then had ferri carb. saccharati gr. xv vel xx *ter die*. This was of material service, but still the enemy was not quelled, the pain reappearing two or three times a day. A bismuth mixture with hydrocyanic acid given along with the iron only caused sickness, and I was beginning to get disheartened, and to suspect malingering, when at last I prescribed pot. iodid. gr. jss *ter die*, continuing the iron, and in a fortnight he was quite well.

No. 121. H. H., m., æt. 13, ad. March 19th. Has been laid up two months. Looks very healthy. T. clean. B. open. Has pain in abdomen commencing in the region of the cæcum and following pretty regularly the course of the transverse and descending colon. He describes the pain as "wretched agony," lasting five to fifteen minutes. His father thought he would have died some days ago. Exertion brings on the pain; is not attacked nearly so much at night when lying still. Has been blistered without benefit. Skin cool. P. weak. Citrate of iron and quinine and spt. æth. s. co. did good, but was not nearly so efficient as muriate of ammonia with bark, on which he improved so much that he was nearly well when he ceased attendance a month later.

No. 122.—J. G., f., æt. 23, ad. March 26th. Ill three days with severe pain all over lower part of abdomen and extending to back, not relieved in bed. Pain increased when bowels act. Abdomen not swollen. Catamenia just ceased, lasted only two days. Not anæmic. T. clean, moist. The pain was very much like that of limited peritonitis, but not so much influenced by pressure. I injected liq. opii sed. ♏x into the hypogastrium subcutaneously, ordered an opiate liniment, and pil. saponis co. gr. v, *ter die*. 30th. Was very much relieved by the injection, "it seemed to expand her stomach and remove the pain." Catamenia returned and continued three days. B. confined. Urine much paler. P. very feeble. With ferri and quin. citr. + chloric æther she improved materially and soon ceased attendance.

In the case of a young female æt. 15, whose catamenia were regular, and who showed no traits of hysterical character, there was a history of numerous fits of epileptic nature, which continued to recur at longer intervals. In one, which I witnessed, both the legs and the left arm were rigid, the right was mobile, and there appeared to be complete unconsciousness. She had very severe abdominal neuralgia, which was temporarily quieted by opium and decidedly checked by full doses of quinine. She went on very well for some time afterwards with citrate of iron and quinine and ol. morrh., but afterwards had some relapse. Country air had been of great advantage to her health previously, but she drooped as soon as she returned to London.

REMARKS.—It may be observed that the subjects of most of the above cases were boys, who probably have less tendency to hypochondriacal exaggeration than most persons. Nevertheless I must confess that on one or two occasions I was much inclined to suspect the patient's honesty until the speedy success of a particular remedy proved that it was my skill that was defective, and not his "morale." In none of the cases related did the neuralgia appear to be referable to lead; the gums showed no trace of blue line (my notes mention this specially in three). One very practical point which the above histories illustrate is the different quality of the morbid action in different cases which appear very much alike, and the great difficulty there may be in selecting the right remedy in any given instance. Where pot. iod. succeeds, we may regard the aponeuroses as most affected; where muriate of ammonia avails, the muscular fibres; and where iron and quinine carry the day, we may consider that the neuralgia is more of a simple than rheumatic character. This knowledge after the event does not avail us however before it, and I believe it will often be necessary to have recourse to trial, which however need not generally be prolonged. It would be easy to indicate points, as the state of the urine, the previous history, the effect of moving about, which might serve as aids in diagnosis, but I believe they are unreliable. Increase of pain, for instance, on moving, which would be a sign of muscular rheumatism, might easily be present in fibrous. Pale and low sp. gr. urine would certainly indicate most probably simple neuralgia, but lateritious urine would be no certain sign of rheumatic disorder. As to the exact locality of this neuralgia, it seems to me that we may agree with Romberg in referring it to the superior mesenteric plexus and its ramifications. From the neuroses which are so definitely referred to the epigastrium, and which probably have their seat in the solar plexus, it is certainly distinct. In the case where subcutaneous injection acted so efficiently it may be thought that the disorder was seated in the anterior parietes of the abdomen, but I doubt whether this is sufficient ground for the opinion, as in another instance a severe and well-marked gastralgia was relieved equally well by the same means. The relation of this disorder to common neuralgia in other situations is marked by its being associated almost invariably with general debility, by its being cured by the same remedies, and by its occuring occasionally as a result of malarioid fever in children.

That the affection now described is not well known in the profession seems pretty clear from the history of a case recorded in the *Brit. Med. Journ.* by Dr. Martin, of Rochester, July 16th, 1859. A boy, æt. 10, tall and active, suffered with attacks of pain in the bowels, which had become gradually longer and more severe. The abdomen felt soft and bore pressure well when pain was absent, but the least touch was intolerable, and all the surface of the body was preternaturally sensitive, when the pain was present. When the attack began to come on he appeared frightened, and threw himself on the ground writhing to and fro in great agony; the pulse became very rapid, and the face covered with profuse perspiration. The pain seemed to begin in the cœliac plexus of nerves, and to shoot into all the abdominal viscera, and to the region of the heart. A London physician who was consulted thought that the disorder might depend upon lead poisoning, and prescribed alum and change of air. These and much other treatment failed, until at last ferri carb. was given, which cured the disease.

The neuroses which occupy the upper abdominal region, and commonly involve the stomach, may be reasonably supposed to affect, at least in many instances, the solar plexus. Romberg describes a cœliac neuralgia or hyperæsthesia of the solar plexus, the pathognomonic feature of which is a peculiar sense of fainting and annihilation accompanying the pain. The treatment of this he says does not differ in any essential point from that of gastrodynia. I find great difficulty in making any arrangement of the very various and interesting cases of nerve disorder which affects this region. Some rough discrimination may be made of instances in which some hyper- or dysæsthesia predominates, of those in which motor disorder (vomiting) is the prominent feature, and of those in which the rejection of various morbid products is a chief phenomenon. In some cases it appears that the terminal ramifications are more affected, in others the disorder appears to be more central.

No. 123.—R. T., f., æt. 9, ad. Feb. 15th. Ill five weeks, pale. Complains that she has pain after eating, and at other times. It is severe at night. No marked epigastric tenderness. No appetite. All her food lies heavy at her chest, but she never vomits. Has constant thirst. P. feeble. T. clean. Skin cool. With citrate of iron and quinine and ol. morrh. she recovered speedily.

No. 124.—M. A. T., f., æt. 60, ad. Oct. 29th. Short and stout, of rather sanguine aspect. Ill two or three years. Suffers with pain commencing under right ribs which passes to middle of abdomen and epigastrium, and backwards to the interscapular space; "a dreadful burning pain it is," and attended with much flatulence and nausea. It lasts five or six hours, and goes off leaving much soreness and depression, "so that she does not know what to do." Food does not affect it at all. The pain used to come on for six weeks every day while she was at Swindon; after coming up to London she was free for fourteen days. She has been dosed with emetics, which made her bring up much blood (Oss at once) mingled with phlegm, and has taken opiates which made her sick. T. white. Urine generally pale and copious. Appetite good, except when pain is on her. B. regular. P. good. No fever. Never had ague. With quinine, iron, pot. iod., ammon. carb. and bark she improved very much, so that on Dec. 5th she reported that she was getting quite well except some pain about the head. It seemed, she said, like new life to be relieved from the stomach pain. This patient had had rheumatism severely two years before, and her gastralgia probably contained a rheumatic element.

No. 125.—J. S., æt. 2, m., ad. Aug. 27th. Since he had measles seven or eight months ago has suffered much with pain at lower sternal region, "is always beating it day and night." Has had pertussis recently. Lips swelled, cracked and ulcerating. With citrate of iron and quinine and ol. morrh. he benefited greatly.

REMARKS.—In the three preceding cases it is clear that the pain was not a mere gastric disorder, as it was independent of taking food; it was essentially a similar affection to the mesenteric neuralgiæ which we have just noticed. In the first case there was constant thirst, a very misleading symptom, and which one may certainly affirm would not have been quieted by salines. It is a less common dysæsthesia than pain, but was present (periodic) in the case recorded by Brodie.[1] In the second case the burning pain and the sanguineous vomiting might have raised suspicions of ulcer. Gastralgia is rare in such young subjects as that of the third case.

No. 126.—S. H., f., æt. 39, ad. Jan. 7th. Ill fourteen days. Suffers with pain in stomach, chest, and back, which is as bad in the intervals of her meals as directly after. No pain on pressure. One article of food has the same effect as another. Is quite free from pain when lying down. Drinking warm water gives great relief to pain. Has been worked hard. Appetite tolerably good. T. clean. B. costive. With ferri sulph. gr. iij. + pulv. cinnamomi co. gr. v + aloes gr. j in pil. ij *ter die* she quite recovered in about seven weeks. Citrate of iron and quinine was tried for a short time, but was less efficient than the first combination.

No. 127.—A. F., æt. 43, f., ad. June 30th. Ill two years with pain in abdomen, at lower chest, and between shoulders, much worse after eating; one kind of food causes as much pain as another. Wine or beer disagrees, and even gruel brings on the pain. Never vomits, but has nausea, and watery fluid rises up into her mouth. No appetite. Not thirsty. Urine very high coloured, clear, scanty. Argenti nitras with extra. hyoscy., bismuth with tr. opii were of little avail, and strychnia was injurious, but ferri carb. ʒj *ter die*, with lactic acid at meals continued for about eight weeks effected a cure.

REMARKS.—The two last cases form a kind of transition to those where the disorder has more the character of hyperæsthesia than pain. The combination used in the first is nearly the same as that employed by Abnercrombie (*v. Dis. of Stomach*, p. 51) with success in a very intractable case of gastralgia. The lactic acid was very beneficial in the second case. I have used it now for several years, and am quite satisfied of its value as a peptic when the functional power of the stomach is low, and its nerves are weak and irritable. In certain cases it is I think decidedly preferable to muriatic acid. That which I have used has been prepared for me by Mr. Blades, 52 Edgeware-road, a most careful pharmaceutist.

The following history is worth recording from the distinct connection which it exhibits between a respiratory and an abdominal neurosis.

No. 128.—Mrs. ——, æt. 43, seen April 9th. Has been suffering for some weeks with bronchial catarrh, and latterly also with pain of a wearying aching kind of the epigastrium, and along the margin of the ribs. She has been getting weakly and nervous for some months. I prescribed citrate of iron and quinine + chloric ether + tr. nucis vomic., and the pain soon disappeared, but one night a violent attack of asthma came on, so severe that she seemed to be in danger of actual suffocation, and at the same time

[1] Local Nervous Affections, p. 30.

bronchitis was set up; she had cough, expectoration, and wheezing, with dry large tube râles in both lungs. Under the use of ipecacuan, morphia, &c., this subisded, but she became extremely weak, and had again pain in the former situation, and also in both loins. She again took iron and quinine, and the pain diminished much, but on account of some nocturnal febricitation I changed this for quinine gr. ij *ter die*. In a day or two after she had a most severe attack of the pain in the abdomen attended with retching. It occurred at night, entirely prevented sleep, and was relieved at last by a glass of brandy about 4 A. M. The next day she was free from severe pain, but exceedingly sore and tender all about the epigastrium, right hypochondrium and loins. There was decided tenderness, and the discomfort and dysæsthesia were much aggravated by turning to the left side. The urine was clear, acid, not red. The next night she slept well with a "nightcap" of hot brandy-and-water. She subsequently took carbonate of iron and tr. cinchonæ, and I ceased to attend her. The bronchitis had been attended with more or less of asthma every morning, for which she had been smoking stramonium with benefit, but after the severe attack of gastralgia the cough and chest affection almost disappeared.

No. 129.—J. N., æt. 36, m., ad. April 9th. Has been ill since last August except for about six weeks altogether, and those not occurring continuously. Is a painter, but has no blue line on gums; has colic six years ago. Always was a nervous man. Eyes prominent, expression of countenance hypochondriacal. Lips red. T. coated, dryish. Skin cool. P. feeble, quiet. Appetite very bad, is thirsty. B. costive. Urine thick, pretty free. Has continual nausea. Suffers from violent pain at epigastrium passing right through to shoulder, attended with sickness which comes on after eating and at other times. The epigastrium is tender, most so towards the left side. Vomited matters are greenish, mucousy, strongly acid. Food causes pain as soon as swallowed. Pain relieved by lying on the back. On 15th the urine had an iridescent pellicle on the surface, was neutral, effervesced strongly with acid, and deposited a large amount of white phosphates. This tendency of the urine to deposit phosphates continued up to May 12th, soon after which time he was made an extern patient and came under my care. He had previously been treated with lime-water, bismuth, prussic acid, hyposulphite of soda, repeated blisters, leeches, and pepsine. May 17th. His symptoms were less severe, he had no sickness for six days, but felt much oppression at the stomach. Argenti nitratis gr. $\frac{1}{4}$ + extr. hyoscy. gr. iv in pil. *ter die* was ordered. At the end of ten days he was a great deal better, could take food "quite nicely," felt his chest more free, and was getting more strength. He then went to the country. Urine was then pale and clear.

No. 130.—J. W. æt. 22, seen Sept. 6th. Ill seven to eight years. Suffers with pain and tenderness in left side passing round and extending to both scapulæ, worse after food and exertion. She is often sick and vomits in a few minutes after food. The vomited matters are very acid. Only streaks of blood ever brought up. Light food agrees best, but milk is rejected. Arrowroot or sago suit. Is easier in morning when stomach is empty. T. too clean, over-red. Cat. regular. B. open. P. weak. No fever. Not much flatus. Much emaciated lately. Urine very pale sp. gr. 1010, not albuminous. She has been treated six years before for gastric ulcer. She took argenti nitrat. gr. $\frac{1}{4}$ and opii gr $\frac{1}{4}$ in pil. *ter die* for three and a half months; in fourteen days she was able to take meat; she gained two stone in weight and quite recovered. Not a trace of cutaneous discoloration was produced.

No. 131.—Mr. Tw, æt. 25, seen in consultation with Mr. Cooper. Has been ill about four years since a bilious fever in America; in three months after this his stomach symptoms set in, and have continued wherever he has been. He suffers uneasiness at the epigastrium immediately after taking food, and is not relieved until he has got rid of it, which appears to be effected partly by vomiting, partly by digestion. The matter vomited is very acid (tested) and tastes hot and bitter. He vomited about Oj in the day, by small quantities at a time. It does not appear that he finds much difference between meat and lighter food; he suffers even more after beef-tea than pie-crust. No tumour to be detected in the epigastrium; the whole abdomen is collapsed and soft, the bowels appear empty. Liver descends low in epigastrium, probably from the loss of any support from below. No notable tenderness at epigastrium, but some soreness. At times has much flatus with his sickness. T. smooth, rather too red. He is very emaciated, his eyes of a clear white, and his aspect much like that of a phthisical person. His lungs and heart appear sound. Urine full-coloured, feebly acid. He is very thirsty, but dares not drink for fear of causing irritation of the stomach. Has taken bismuth, pepsine, hydrocyanic acid, and strychnine, but with very little good effect. It was agreed that he should take iced milk in dessert-spoonfuls every twenty minutes, and nothing else for some days, except argenti nitrat. gr. $\frac{1}{4}$ + opii gr. $\frac{1}{8}$ in pil. *ter die*. In six weeks he came to see me at my house, and reported that he was much better, had gained flesh and strength, had no sickness, and was able to take meat and other solids pretty freely. The nitrate of silver had been omitted the last week; he had had some nausea the last two days. I have not heard of him since.

REMARKS.—The last three cases are good examples of gastric hyperæsthesia, though I do not assert that this was the sole disease. The question will occur to most readers whether the symptoms were not due to ulcer of the stomach. I think it is quite possible that ulcers may have existed, but I doubt very much whether they were the cause of the symptoms. In the first case the irritability of the mucous membrane was such that it led to an excessive pouring out of acid, in consequence of which the urine was left in a minus condition, and deposited phosphates. I have seen this kind of draining off of acid in a few other instances. In the two other cases the amount of acid secretion was not so great, but the functional power of the organ was extremely impaired, and there was great hyperæsthesia (local). To diagnose the condition of simple gastric hyperæsthesia from that which is associated with ulcer is, except where perforation of a bloodvessel has occurred, a matter of exceeding uncertainty. It is notorious that ulcers may go on to perforation of the whole wall of the stomach without having given rise to any symptoms at all, and it is quite common to meet with instances where the symptoms preceding an attack of hæmatemesis have been only those of very moderate dyspepsia. Quite recently I have had a good proof how distinct the ulcer and the dyspeptic symptoms may be in relation to treatment. A cook, æt. 42, had been under my care several times with disorderd digestion, but of quite an ordinary character. She had always been pretty speedily relieved by appropriate treatment, and was so on this occasion. She had been free from pain at the stomach for some time, was discharged on a Thursday feeling quite well, and continued so until the following Sunday, when towards night a copius gush of blood, about Oiij, took place from the stomach, declaring too plainly that her previous malady had not consisted solely of the symptoms of which she was conscious. After long attention to this subject I incline more and more to the opinion that, except in some particular instances, ulceration *per se* produces no distinctive signs until perforation ensues, and that the pain and functional disorder with which it is often attended are no necessary results of the lesion.[1] Their existence depends much more on the state of the general mucous surface than on the presence of ulceration. Of the value of nitrate of silver in conditions of gastric hyperæsthesia I have myself not the least doubt, though I feel how difficult it is to account for its action. I do not rely at all on the above cases to prove its virtue, because it was given (except in the first) along with opium. This is usually a useful adjunct, but I have certainly seen the nitrate beneficial when given alone, and I am satisfied that its action is more and other than that of the sedative. Its influence on nervous tissue is attested by the good effects it produces in "ataxie locomotr. progressive." The difference between gastrodynia and gastric hyperæsthesia is well illustrated by these cases.

No. 132.—G. C., m., æt. 49, ad. April 15th, getting gradually ill two months. States that whatever he eats or drinks all returns again, either in a few minutes, or in one or two hours. Food does not cause pain immediately. Epigastrium not notably tender. The vomiting begins with a pain about the umbilicus, which "works upward" and produces the sickness. No sign of any tumour. Of placid quiet demeanour. Rather pale. T. natural. B. regular. Urine copious, has not full control over it. With strychnia and liq. opii sed. *ter die*, he was quite well in a month.

REMARKS.—In this case, and such are not infrequent, motor disorder was a much more prominent symptom than pain. The affection might almost be called a chorea of the stomach. The chief action of strychnine is on the nervous motor apparatus, and thus it proves a suitable remedy in conditions like the above by its toning and steadying influence.

No. 133.—E. H., æt. 30, labourer, ad. Jan. 16th. He had been suffering eight or nine months with violent pain in head and chest, aggravated after taking food. He was treated at first with bismuth and hydrocyanic acid or opium, and a blister, but with only temporary amendment. February 5th. He has still great pain after eating, and vomits all his food in one hour after taking it. Much tenderness in epigastrium and pain all about præcordia. Great thirst. Pulse small and feeble. Skin cold. Urine very clear and pale. A blister was ordered to the epigastrium, and muriatic +

---

[1] Dr. Wilkes informs me that Dr. Habershon concludes from his dissections that the presence or absence of pain depends on whether the ulcer does or does not involve nervous filaments. I doubt whether this expresses the whole truth.

hydrocyanic acid *ter die.* 9th. Symptoms unchanged. Is shaking with ague tremor, and states that he does so several times a day. States that last year he was under my care with distinct ague of tertian type, the paroxysms being however rather obscurely developed. He was not thoroughly cured, having discontinued treatment too soon, and has suffered in the same way off and on ever since. He comes from Pinner near Harrow, where ague is prevalent. The case was now clear. He took quinine + iron with benefit, but ceased attending before he was thoroughly well. After he had had the tonics for three days, as he was still suffering, though less, I injected liq. opii sedat. ♏x subcutaneously into his epigastrium. Four days later he reported that he had felt very giddy in walking home (ten miles), but that in about six hours he was relieved of the stomach pain, which had quite ceased until his dinner yesterday reproduced it to some extent.

REMARKS.—The resemblance of this case to ordinary gastric catarrh was at first considerable, subsequently its true character was quite apparent. The good effect of the subcutaneous injection was very evident. I have used it in a similar case, in one of palpitation and præcordial uneasiness, and in one of asthmatic dyspnœa with decided advantage. In all these the remedy was applied as near as possible to the apparent seat of the distress, and I think this is not a matter of indifference. The patient in the above case had taken tr. opii ♏vj *ter die* for three days without relief previously, which shows that it cannot be merely the absorption of a certain amount of the drug into the circulation which produces the beneficial effect. The influence of a remedy introduced into the parietes of a serous cavity upon the subjacent viscera is I confess very difficult to explain, but not more so than that of leeches and blisters similarly applied, which I think cannot be contested. There seems some reason to think that the nerves distributed to the parietes of a serous cavity are co-ordinated in a considerable degree with those of the contained viscera, so that an impression made on the external affects through the centres the internal. I cannot omit a remark as to the cruelty of the Poor-law medical arrangements, which oblige a poor ague-stricken peasant to walk twenty miles a day to get a supply of a remedy which is needful to cure him. Why do not the unions keep their own dispensaries and exempt their medical officers from all the mere mechanical work of dispensing medicines ? If the system is not a sham, the *deserving* poor ought to have what is needful, and it ought not to be a matter of question to the medical attendant whether he can afford to give an expensive remedy or not. His remuneration should be for his skill, and with the providing of drugs he should have nothing to do.

No. 134.—B. J., m., æt. 52, ad. July 27th. Ill seven days. Is suffering from pain under the right ribs, which comes on unless he eats very sparingly. It is very severe, extends towards the back, is sharp and pricking. Liver not at all enlarged. Epigastrium and all the adjacent region covered with marks of leech-bites. While in India he was bled from the arm thrice, had seventeen dozen leeches applied, and took two hundred and five grains of calomel, presumably for hepatitis. P. weak. T. clean. No fever. Urine of good color. Eyes clear. Liver not at all enlarged. A blister to the painful part; pot. iod. and prussic acid were of no benefit, but liq. opii sed. ♏x injected subcutaneously into the painful part took all the pain away, and when I saw him three months later he had had no recurrence of it. It caused, however, very great sickness. He was liable to gout. I do not know whether this was a gouty neuralgia, but it is clear that it was effectually quelled by the injection. Possibly there are some cases of supposed liver disorder which might be well treated by the same means. I have placed this case next to the preceding as illustrating the efficacy of the same mode of treatment. It is I think a valuable means, but certainly should not be used except in cases of rather severe pain on account of the troublesome sickness it is apt to produce.

The following are instances where the vomited matters were peculiar.

No. 135.—E. S., æt. 36, f., of rather sanguine habit, ad. May 11th. Affected with pityriasis all her life. At the catamenial periods, which occur regularly, and the intervening fortnights she has copious vomiting of stuff like brown water, which lasts for twelve hours, and is preceded by violent headache. In the intervals she is tolerably well. Digestion pretty good. Very apt to take cold. No râles in lungs posteriorly. Is worse after any exertion. Functions in good order. Lives at Chiswick near the river, in an open meadow. A week later the urine was found exceedingly pale, aqueous, and non-albuminous. Bi-weekly doses of calomel with nitro-muriatic acid and taraxacum were given for five weeks without avail. She described herself as suffering with a sense of dreadful weight round the chest for several days before the vomiting came on. On June 7th she brought up much thick stuff like brown phlegm. B. relaxed, as they always are in warm weather. Strychnia, quinine, opium, arsenic were now given; at a later period iron was substituted for the latter. She improved steadily under this treatment, and was discharged apparently quite well Aug. 27th.

REMARKS.—I read this case as one of periodic congestion of the stomach issuing in exudation of bloody fluid, which became darkened by the gastric acid. The result of the treatment proved that the pathological condition was one of nerve-disorder, and not of hepatic congestion and obstruction. The cause of the nerve-disorder is obscure, but the locality of her residence affords some ground for suspecting the operation of malaria. The concurrence of severe head-pain and paralysis of the vaso-motor nerves of the stomach deserves to be noted.

No. 136.—E. T., æt. 35, f., married, five children. Of rather sanguine aspect. Ad. Feb. 9th. Ill one month. Has some cough and spits much blood (a teacupful in one day), and some phlegm. The blood comes up with nausea, but no vomiting, and is of a very bright color. This hemorrhage has been going on the whole month that she has been ill. The first of her illness was that she felt extreme debility, and fainted several times a day. About eight days later blood came up. She has copious cold sweats at night, and feels very shivery in the morning. P. soft. B. costive. Catamenia were delayed a week when the blood first was brought up. Chest deformed, right front flattened; there is right lateral curvature. No dulness anywhere, but weak breathing all throughout both lungs. Some epigastric tenderness. She always experiences extreme exhaustion a quarter of an hour after taking food; it lies heavy, but does not cause much pain. She continued under observation till April 20th, having lived part of the time in Paddington instead of Walworth, where her home was. The former locality agreed much better with her than the latter. The treatment consisted of quinine, opium, iron, and strychnia variously combined, and had a markedly beneficial effect. Gastric hemorrhage recurred several times, but she had none for the last three weeks of her attendance.

Extreme weakness was a prominent symptom, attended frequently with what she termed faintings. These I believe from what I witnessed of them were rather leipothymic than syncopal. There was apparent unconsciousness, but not the same loss of muscular power which occurs in syncope, nor the same pallor of face. The presence of gastric ulcer must be considered a probable cause of the hemorrhage. My own opinion, however, is that ulceration did not exist, or if it did, that it was not the cause of the symptoms. The bleeding I look upon as analogous to epistaxis, and as proceeding from active congestion of the capillaries of the mucous surface. For (1) it is proved by Dr. Brittan's case, v. *Brit. Med. Journ.*, April 2, 1859, that copious bleeding may take place from the stomach without any ulcer, and without obstruction to the venous current: (2) The peculiar and extreme debility was not consecutive to and produced by the loss of blood, but may be considered rather as its cause. By affecting the vaso-motor nerves of the stomach it produced the active congestion. The cause of the debility itself was probably some malarious miasm generated at Walworth, no unlikely place for such an occurrence. (3) The treatment was not such as was likely to benefit ulcer, at least while it was extending.

I will refer here to a similar case which I have recorded at length in the *Assoc. Journ.*, 1856, June 7th and 14th, in which a weakly female, whose heart and lungs appeared sound, had various symptoms of aguish disorder, with frequently-recurring hæmatemesis and extreme debility. With quinine, iron, country air, and rest she improved much, and recovered at last after a voyage to Ireland. I saw her recently in good case. A severe relapse was induced on one occasion by her resuming work while too weak for the exertion. The hæmatemesis in this case was more a kind of frequent oozing of blood than an actual gush. Once or twice, however, pretty free bleeding occurred. I quote from my remarks the following. Rejecting the hypothesis of organic disease as wholly inadequate to account for the symptoms, I observe that the view of aguish disorder being the "grundleiden" is the only one which can explain the phenomena, and it does so fully. The system was under the influence of a depressing poison operating primarily on the nervous organs. This caused the neuralgia, the toothache, the cerebral disorder resembling intoxication, the bewildered feelings, the forgetfulness and loss of sight by its action on the cerebro-spinal system; while its action on the sympathetic and vaso-motor nerves was attested by the hæmatemesis, the syncopic attacks, the aguish paroxysms, and the epigastric sinking. The periodicity of the hæmatemesis and its being checked by quinine testify to its peculiar character. The immediate relapse on recommencing work is exactly what is observed in neuralgia and other nerve disorders ;—the symptoms, which remain in abeyance during rest when the nerve-power is not expended, are speedily reproduced when exertion consumes the yet too scanty stock of strength. In inveterate cases such as this the influence of a pure and bracing air is absolutely essential to cure. Drugs seem to fail partly from actual deficiency of the vital (radical) forces of the system. Another case came under my observation in which hæmatemesis in small quantities went on for about six months, recurring at short but irregular intervals, and continuing for several days at a time. It was associated with severe pain of one knee and great nervous depression. After the ineffectual application of several blisters and much medication amputation of the limb was advised by a hospital surgeon, but the patient declined. No astringents had any effect in arresting the hemorrhage, which at last ceased under the use of carbonate of iron, and the pain in the knee at the same time became easier, so that she was able to move about with a crutch after having been for months confined to bed. The knee was never swelled, nor did it present to my eye much appearance of organic disease.

No. 137.—J. W., m., æt. 38, ad. July 2d, 1857. Ill since last Christmas, worse last three months. Suffers with pain after food, most after vegetables. Formerly the pain lasted about four hours until vomiting set in and then was relieved. Now for the last fourteen days he has had vomiting daily in the morning from 3 to 4 A. M., and about 9 P. M. The vomited matters are grayish and frothy, and have contained sarcinæ. Is sometimes quite free from pain when his stomach is empty. No tumour or anything morbid to be discovered in abdomen; no epigastric tenderness. Heart and lungs tolerably sound. Urine thick and passed with straining, and pain felt about the crest of the ilium. Is losing flesh and getting weak. B. open; when they were confined some time ago he was better, and had less sickness. Has had hyposulphite of soda without benefit, besides various other remedies. I examined the vomited matter at this date and again September 24th, and on both occasions found sarcinæ in abundance. He remained under my care till October 1st, the symptoms recurring at intervals. Generally towards night flatulence would come on to a considerable extent, and be followed sooner or later by vomiting. Occasionally the flatus passed away *per rectum*, and once was attended with sudden purging. The gastro-intestinal disorder was evidently no ordinary indigestion, it seemed to be to a great extent independent of taking food. None would occur for several days, and then an outburst would take place. It was in this respect somewhat like the group of symptoms produced by obstruction of the pylorus, but the sequel negatives the idea that there was any such organic lesion. When he came under my hands he had already been treated most judiciously by Dr. Vernon, who sent him to me, and I saw only one way of proceeding left open to me, which was to deal with the malady as rather the result of failure of power, than as a substantive disease. It seemed possible that if the innervation of the general system and of the stomach in particular could be improved the production of sarcinæ and the vomiting might be materially checked, if not arrested. Whatever part the sarcinæ play in modifying or aggravating the disease with which their occurrence is associated, they are in all probability rather accidental than essential. They are found in a variety of conditions, in ulcer, in pyloric obstruction, and simple disorder of secretion, and in fact are probably developed like other fungi where the higher organic life is waxing faint and feeble. On this view then I treated his malady as a paralytic neurosis with quinine, iron, opium, and strychnia, the quinine being increased up to gr. x *ter die*, and the strychnia to gr $\frac{1}{30}$. The result was satisfactory; the attacks of flatulent disorder, of pain, and of vomiting became much less frequent, and he gained flesh and strength.

He was still however subject to recurrences when he ceased attendance (*ut mos est* of hospital externs). I hunted him up however in April 1859, and learned from his wife that he was quite well and had been so a long time; "had been nicely" all the last year (1858). After he ceased attending at the hospital he had no further medical treatment.

I have pretty well anticipated any remarks I might have to make. The moral of the case is that it may be well worth while to treat a general condition rather than a particular prominent symptom. It may also be added that there seems some ground from this as from other cases to think that the good influence of a course of treatment may show itself long after its discontinuance, perhaps even more markedly than at the time of its being in force. Persons who have gone on a tour, or visit to some distant place, not unfrequently continue to improve in health after their return home.

CHAPTER XXXI.

NEUROSES OF THE URINARY ORGANS.

THE urinary organs seem to be much less liable to neuralgic affections than the digestive. They are, however, by no means exempt, and some of the neurotic disorders affecting them are extremely severe and intractable. They have their location mostly in the viscera, or rather in the nerves distributed to them. Romberg, however, justly describes the lumbar region of the cord as being often implicated, and states that venereal excesses (which exhaust this nervous centre) often are the cause. He gives no cases. In those I have met with the neurosis has been as elsewhere generally either of a rheumatic or simple kind. The following instance was evidently the former:—

No. 138.—G. W., m., æt. 38, ad. October 29th, ill nine days. Complains of pain in micturition of an aching kind, and felt mostly at the end of the act. Has pain also in hypogastrium varying in severity at different times. Micturates often, has to rise once or twice at night. Urine clear, no discharge at all. Pot. iodid. gr. vj with a little henbane daily for a week cured him.

No. 139.—G., æt. 80, f., seen February 19th, suffering with some irregular action of bowels, but chiefly with irritation of bladder and frequent micturition, and feeling nervous and weak. With citrate of iron and quinine + tr. nucis vom. + liq. opii sed. she improved materially in the course of a month, though some dysuria still continued. May 19th. She came under my care again for very severe dental neuralgia, which came on just after a double tooth was drawn six weeks previously. The pain was incessant, but worse at night, and had deprived her of rest many nights. She had, however, felt "bodily well" since the pain had been so severe.

With quinine + iron she improved speedily, and no complaint was made of the dysuria.

In this case the severe dentalgia, which evidently was not dependent on diseased teeth, serves as an exponent of the nature of the dysuria. Both in fact were simple neuralgias, and the latter seems to have been absorbed by the former. Bourguignon[1] has specially described neuralgia of the bladder, and states that it is produced by exactly the same causes as give rise to other neuralgias. Rheumatism is the most frequent of all, especially when induced by chilled feet. The neck of the bladder is the especial seat of the neuralgia, and the symptoms are pain, frequent calls to urinate, and tenesmus (spasm) of the sphincter. If the disorder is of rheumatic origin, the urine generally deposits lithates; if it is not, the urine is copious and clear. Long continuance of the neuralgia may lead to paralysis of the muscular coat of the bladder. In aggravated cases cerebral and spinal symptoms ensue. In the matter of treatment he recommends sedatives locally and internally, alkalies if the urine is over-acid, tonics, and electricity. Hamon recommends superficial cauterization of the skin of the hypogastrium with nitric acid.

Dr. Behrend reports the following interesting case :[2]—

No. 140.—A lady, æt. 30, without family, suffered from May, 1857, with great irritability of the bladder, compelling her to rise from three to eight or even more times in the night. The urine then was pale, insipid, but otherwise normal, except that it was two or three times as copious as in health. She had lost flesh, and suffered much from thirst, headache, and nausea, especially on rising in the morning. Her spirits were much depressed. During the day there was no little irritability, and the quantity of urine was nearly normal. Tr. ferri muriatis, valerian, mineral acids, liquor potassæ, sea-bathing, change of air were of no avail, but belladonna given ultimately in a dose of gr. ¼ of the extract in the morning, and gr. j at nine P. M. effected speedily an almost perfect cure, which remained permanent, although the remedy was at once discontinued after it had produced its physiological effects. The disease had existed sixteen months before the belladonna was given. The vesical hyperæsthesia in this instance seems to have extended to the renal nerves and to have given rise to the increased flow of watery urine. Hysterical hyperæsthesia has the same effect we know. The nocturnal character of the neurosis should be noted.

In the following instance the neurosis was probably of toxic origin:—

No. 141.—J. F., æt. 57, m., gardener, ad. September 4th, 1855. Rather short, emaciated lately. Has had gout seven or eight times, not every year, but nevertheless declares that he has always had "the greatest of health." During the last three weeks his urine has been constantly running away both by night and day. Appetite and digestion good. No thirst. Urine quite clear, light-coloured, rather highly acid, not albuminous, nor saccharine. He drinks a great deal of tea; takes tea at dinner. Bladder not

---

[1] "L'Union Méd.," 1861, Nos. xxxiii., xxxv.
[2] "Lancet," June 25th, 1859.

distended. He remained under treatment till April 2d without any real amelioration of his urinary incontinence. I gave him ammonia, bark, quinine, iron, strychnia, ol. morrh., tr. lyttæ at night, arsenic, zinc, opium suppositories, belladonna + quinine, and cubebs. The belladonna did more good than anything else. About April 5th his right hand was attacked smartly with rheumatic gout, and immediately his vesical disorder entirely ceased, and had not reappeared when I last saw him June 11th. Gout is well known as a tormentor of the nerves, and Cullen and Prout both allude to gouty irritation of the urinary organs. Strangury or spasm of the neck of the bladder, or irritability of the detrusor, seems however to occur more frequently than paralysis. In my case the condition was certainly chiefly paralysis of the sphincter. He was galvanized twice, but without advantage.

No. 142.—Mrs. A., æt. 40, seen July 11th, complaining of increased frequency of micturition with a sense of burning afterwards about umbilicus; this chiefly troubles her in the early part of the day, not at night. Health pretty good. Urine in fair quantity, full-coloured, sp. gr. 1027, deposits much octohedral oxalate, and gives some spontaneous crystallization with NO_5. I prescribed nitric acid + liq. opii sed. + tr. and infus. lupuli. In five days she was much improved, and the condition of the urine had changed remarkably; it was pale, aqueous, sp. gr. 1008, alkaline, and free from oxalates or any other deposit; its quantity was not observedly increased. The dysuria did not reappear.

In this case the vesical dysæsthesia was probably associated with exaggerated renal destructive assimilation, both conditions being dependent on nerve paresis, and both being amended by the same tonico-sedative remedy. Oppler's experiments[1] are tolerably conclusive as to the active part taken by the kidneys in forming the solid urinary excreta. If we consider with Brown-Séquard that by paralysis of the vaso-motor nerves the vital actions of a part are increased, in consequence of the unusual supply of arterial blood it receives, we can understand that the urinary solids might be notably augmented in a condition of paresis of the renal plexus. The increased excretion of urea which occurs in low fevers may be ascribed in part to the same cause, the renal being involved with the other nervous districts in the general paresis. That there was a material difference in the urinary solids on the two occasions noted in the preceding history can hardly be doubted, and almost as little that the change effected was the result of the medication. In a paper in the *Brit. Med. J.*, Oct. 12th, 1861, I have given an instance where the amount of urea and phosphoric acid during twenty-four hours was ascertained in the condition of baruria, in the normal, and while the patient was under the influence of nitric acid and opium. In the first the amount of excreta was more than four times as much as the lowest observed in the latter condition. The coincidence is worth observing, and can scarcely be without significance that the same remedy is very efficient in certain asthenic bronchial and intestinal catarrhal fluxes. In choleraic disorder it has been much

[1] Virchow's "Archiv.," vol. xxi. p. 3; "Syd. Soc. Year-book," 1861, p. 219.

relied on by some practitioners. Its action as an astringent tonic arresting destructive metamorphosis must surely be the same in all cases. There is nothing specific about this remedy, as in the following case strychnia answered the end much better.

No. 143.—H., m., æt. 35, seen July 15th. He complained of aching uneasiness in the loins, which he had had since the previous winter, with great general debility and nervousness. The hyperæsthesia was still very considerable. Appetite poor. He was chiefly troubled by a nervous feeling referred to the bladder leading him to imagine that he wanted to urinate though he had no real call to do so. If he was at all hurried, he could not urinate at all. The vesical dysæsthesia he had had for years. The urine was highly acid, sp. gr. 1036, contained an excess of urea, and deposited lithates and some oxalates. Nitro-muriatic acid + liq. opii failed to benefit, but strychnia effected a cure. The urine on Aug. 6th, after he had taken the strychnia five days, was of sp. gr 1021, of normal colour, and deposited no uric acid nor oxalate in twenty-four hours. The next year he had a return of the same symptoms, and strychnia with citrate of iron and quinine was effectual. An occasional opium suppository was also useful in calming the vesical uneasiness.

In this case there was a condition of general hyperæsthesia which did not exist in the former, but which is evidently only "un degré de plus" of the same disorder. The same remarks apply to both.

No. 144 —Mr. A., æt. 27, seen Aug. 25th. Has lived until last three years a gay life, and committed venereal excesses, but is now steady. Has had syphilis. Is pallid, thin, weakly, and nervous. Has had indigestion, but this has ceased. B. are irregular, either loose or confined. Urine full-coloured, sp. gr. 1028, crystallizes with NO_5, deposits a little mucus, no oxalates, not albuminous. There is a slight urethral discharge. Some long-standing eczema of the scrotum. He was ordered at first (before the urine had been examined) arsenic + tr. cinchon. with ol. morrh., and ungt. zinci + hydr. nitr. oxyd. to the eruption. In a week the eczema was better, but he thought his general state worse. I gave him then pills of argenti nitrat. gr. ¼ + opii gr. ¼ + extr. coloc. co. gr. j *ter die*. On Sept. 10th he was decidedly better, his countenance clearer and brighter, his urine of lower sp. gr. and giving a less crystallization of nitrate of urea. Sept. 15th. His urine is pale, sp. gr. 1013, does not crystallize with NO_5. The quantity is about Oij, the same as it was on Sept. 10th; at first it was about Ojss. He feels and looks much better, has more spirit and is more cheerful, his digestion however is weakish. He tells me that when he first came to me he had such depression that he used to feel inclined to cut his throat.

Dr. Sieveking related once to me the case of a clergyman in a state of hyperæsthesia and complete loss of tone, passing 30 to 40 oz. of urine daily, which contained so much urea as to solidify with nitric acid. Quinine given to the amount of 30 grains a day reduced the sp. gr. from 1030 to 1010, and greatly improved his state and his sensations. I am aware that the existence of such a disease as baruria (Prout's azoturia) is denied by some excellent authorities (Parkes has never seen such a state), and that it requires to be carefully distinguished from mere relative excess of urea. Also, except in the one case quoted above, I have not proved by actual figures that there was excessive excretion of urinary solids.[1] Still I am quite satisfied from repeated observation that if, in connection with general or vesical hyperæsthesia and debility, we find the urine of high sp. gr., non-saccharine, crystallizing with NO_3, or depositing lithates or oxalates copiously, we may confidently expect that an alteration in the state of the urine without much increase of quantity will coincide with remarkable improvement, and that this change will generally be effected by opium with. some of the milder tonics rather than by the stronger. Of the value of this clinical fact I have no doubt, but I am not so sure of the correct interpretation of it. That the renal disorder is not a necessary result of general nervous prostration is perfectly certain, as the urine in such states is often very pale and light. Still my experience points very much to some debilitating cause as the prime motor of baruria. Dr. Prout considered abuse of the sexual powers as principally, and generally such causes as enfeeble the vital powers and more especially the spinal nerves as producing baruria. In two females where the urine was in this state there was extreme hyperæsthesia and debility, and besides such casual conditions as would give rise to general prostration. On the other hand the great benefit to the general health which coincides with an alteration in the urine indicates the cessation of some debilitating morbid action, and this can scarcely be anything else than the excessive renal excretion. If it be objected that the amount of loss to the system in this way can scarcely be material, and would be easily compensated by a little increase of diet, it may be replied that there are several similar instances, in which a chronic discharge of no great amount produces very considerable debility. I am disposed to think that the debility is both cause and consequence; that by producing paresis of the renal nerves it sets up the morbid excretion, and is subsequently itself increased by the drain to the system occasioned thereby. There is a decided tendency in the urine passed by patients suffering under baruria to deposit oxalate of lime, and in some instances the crystals are very large and numerous. Lithates are often present with the oxalate or may replace it, and the view taken by Prout and B. Jones that the two deposits are of the same general nature seems to me well founded. It may be remarked " en passant " that there is perhaps no instance where cell-tissue and vessel are more distinctly ruled by nervous influence than this of the kidney. The common result of

[1] The following case, which I have lately met with, seems but little open to question. A gentleman, æt. 45 about, very anæmic, but strong and capable of much exertion, a small meat-eater, weighing 9 stone, passed in 24 hours 33 oz. of urine which crystallized into a solid mass with half its volume of nitric acid. The total amount of urea was 673.88 grains, of uric acid 7.68 grains. The urine contained a very little albumen; it had recently been more considerable. There was no sign of renal congestion, no febrile movement. The eyelids had been a little puffed. His parents had been very gouty, but he never had any attack. He is intolerant of tonics and of even very minute doses of opium.

an hysteric attack shows clearly that the capillary membranes of the Malpighian tufts must be remarkably altered for the time so as to allow of a greatly increased transudation of aqueous liquid, while at the same time the secreting action of the epithelium of the cortical tubes is much diminished. It is worth mention that a small dose of opium has in some persons very much the same effect, while quinine in full doses has an opposite.

The nocturnal incontinence of urine so common in children I believe to depend upon an hyper-excitability of the vesical nerves, in consequence of which the stimulus of even a small quantity of urine causes contraction of the muscular coat. Belladonna acts here as a sedative, just as it does in the case of the pulmonary nerves. Some tonic with ol. morrh. will also generally be found advisable. Trousseau takes just the same view; he gives belladonna in increasing doses if the disorder does not yield, up to even gr. iv of the extract, at night; and continues it for three, four, or five months, then gradually diminishes the dose for two, four, six, or even ten months, until the morbid habit is fairly broken. If the incontinence is diurnal as well as nocturnal, he considers that the sphincter vesicæ is paretic, and administers strychnia.

No. 145.—A., æt. 45, m., has suffered for years with symptoms of neurolysis and obscure remittent fever. Strychnia has been of great service to him. He was in all respects as well as usual when late one night he was much alarmed by finding his urine very bloody; he came immediately to me, and passed in my room a little which was very full of blood, the red globules being diffused through the liquid, and not forming casts. No epithelium was present. After a dose of tannin + opium that night the next day's urine was smoky, but much less bloody, it deposited a brownish-red sediment, consisting of red globules and numerous large octohedra of oxalate of lime. The supernatant fluid was red, clear, sp. gr. 1029, and notably albuminous. The same day at 1 P. M. at my house he passed urine which was pale and perfectly clear, and free from any deposit or albumen, sp. gr. 1013. The microscope detected nothing. The region of the bladder was quite soft and painless; he had no pain anywhere except a very slight uneasiness at the root of the penis. No relapse has occurred, though he has since married and travelled about.

From the absence of any indications of calculus in the kidneys or bladder, from the speedy cessation of the hemorrhage, and the eminently neurolytic diathesis of the patient, I conclude that most probably the hemorrhage was not dependent on any organic lesion, but was essentially analogous to epistaxis, and depended on an accidental congestion of the vesical capillaries from a freak of vasomotor nerve paresis. Watson alludes to cases of hæmaturia occurring in connection with ague. Prout notices the much more frequent occurrence of hæmaturia in certain years than in others, especially in those succeeding the epidemic cholera. It is probable that a modification of the choleraic miasm may produce this hemorrhage by paralyzing the renal nerves. I have seen a pretty copious hemorrhage from the bronchi of one lung occur in a similar way at night in a man who never had before nor has had since (though five or six years have elapsed) any symptoms of phthisis, heart disease, or aneurism.

The following case of sunstroke narrated by M. Beaupré[1] seems to me very proving as to the effect of sudden nervous prostration on the vesical and other capillaries, and even on the tissues. Towards the end of July a soldier, æt. 26, who had previously enjoyed perfect health, was brought into hospital, having by his comrades' account suddenly fallen senseless on the rampart where he had been two hours on guard exposed to the whole power of the sun; in that condition he was found when they came to relieve him. His extremities were warm, his face pale and leaden; there was total loss of motion and feeling; black dissolved scorbutic-like blood flowed from the nasal fossæ. The cavity of the mouth was filled with blood, and all the lining membrane was checkered with livid, scorbutic-like spots. A litre and half of black blood mixed with urine was drawn off by the catheter. The pulse was small and very feeble. Death occurred in six hours. On dissection the bladder was found filled with putrid fetid blood; the whole extent of the mucous membrane of the nose, pharynx, œsophagus, stomach, intestines, and bladder; presented the same livid spots as the inside of the mouth; the putridity of the corpse rendered quick burial necessary. This record shows that powerful insolation acting on the brain may destroy the tone of the capillaries in numerous parts of the body, and so impair the consistence of their walls that they can no longer retain their contents. This effect must be produced through the vaso-motor nerves which are involved in the general paresis. There is a good deal of resemblance between this case and the one of burn recorded at p. 68 as well as those of intestinal hemorrhage pp. 268, 269. In all prostration of nervous power led to effusion of blood. It is not improbable that the extreme congestions found in some cases of heat apoplexy depend, as in the above, on complete loss of capillary tone, and that therefore the term apoplexy is correct, though not in the sense that the congestion or effusion is the cause of the seizure. In all cases of vaso-motor paresis there is probably more or less impairment of the tone of the capillaries as well as relaxation of the arteries, so that we can easily understand when the heart's action is excited, as in the hot stage of remittent fever, how great is the risk of extravasation. The capillary alteration is however "un dégré de plus" beyond that which relaxes arteries.

"Treatise on Cold," p. 11.

CHAPTER XXXII.

NEUROSES OF THE LOWER INTESTINE.

THE rectum is by no means a common seat of neuroses, in this country at least. The only forms I have myself met with, and these perhaps rather belonged to a higher part of the bowel, consisted in serous, flatulent, or bloody discharges occurring under circumstances which made their dependence on nerve disorder highly probable. The following case is a good example.

No. 146.—C. R., æt. 23 (?), seen July 3d. Has been invalided and sent home from India on account of dysenteric diarrhœa; has now been at home about a year. The diarrhœa has almost ceased under Sir R. Martin's treatment, but the bowels are very easily disordered; a glass of bitter beer will act as a purge. The motions are apt to become lumpy and pale. The chief trouble he has now is great flatulence passing *per rectum*; it will come on quite suddenly and be very troublesome for some time; it mostly occurs some time after dinner. He is pallid and has lost much flesh. During a recurrence of dysenteric diarrhœa while under my care the flatulence quite ceased. Some months later the neurosis came earlier in the day, after luncheon, and not after dinner. He would then have uneasiness in the bowels, some tendency to relaxation, and pass a lot of wind. Still later, when the flatulency had almost left him, he found that it always returned whenever he became weak and prostrate, which was the case now and then. The last note I have is that the flatulent disorder came on every night exactly at 10 P. M. and lasted fifteen minutes. He could take beer and even champagne well, and had materially gained in strength. The most efficient remedies were pills of quinine + opium + creasote + pip. nigr. *ter die*, tannin + opium in pills, pepsine wine, and abundant out-door exercise.

I believe it is considered by some of our best authorities as highly heretical to hold that mucous membranes can secrete gas. I must confess that I cannot explain such a case as the above without admitting that such secretion may actually take place. In a very similar instance, but of much shorter duration, towards the termination of the disorder, the diarrhœa, which had been markedly paroxysmal, gave place to quite similar bursts of gastric or intestinal flatulence. It seems as if one might almost speak of a gaseous diarrhœa.

No. 147.—Tr., æt. 40 (?), a fine-looking, well-conducted but not very strong soldier, acting recently as drill-sergeant to a volunteer corps. Was in the Crimea, had good health all the time. Never had any kind of fever. Latterly has lost much flesh and got very weak. Lungs rather emphysematous, otherwise sound. Heart sound. He suffered first with sudden attacks of palpitation and great debility; subsequently he had symptoms of gastric catarrh and paroxysms of severe gastralgia. While improving he began to pass blood *per anum*; the first day he passed Oij, he thinks, and continued to do so in varying quantities for some days. The abdomen was full, soft, resonant all over, but less so in the left hypochondrium than elsewhere; the hepatic dulness was diminished in extent. A feeling of weight and pain which he had had in the lower part of the abdomen ceased after the bleeding. He had no piles. Under the use of lead + opium the bleeding ceased, and with quinine and change of air he recovered. His health has since been fairly good, and he has only once had a very slight recurrence of bleeding.

REMARKS.—The cause of the hemorrhage in this instance is doubtful, but I think one may exclude piles, dysenteric and tuberculous ulceration, and malignant disease. Had any of these existed there would almost certainly have been prior symptoms, and the hemorrhage would have recurred. On the other hand, the existence of marked neurolytic disorder and the previous exposure to malaria make it not improbable that congestion of the lower part of the colon or rectum may have given rise to the bleeding.

No. 148.—S. Sp., f., æt. 27, ad. Sept. 14th. During the last week has been suffering more or less pain in stomach (abdomen probably) accompanied by diarrhœa of which she took no notice, was purged yesterday several times, and early this morning was seized suddenly with severe pain in stomach with somewhat violent retching. On her admission she was cold, surface clammy; she complained of intense pain in the abdomen. P. weak and frequent. Ate some plums and apples last night.

Calomelanos, camphoræ, opii, capsici, āā gr. ½, ft. pil. post *sing. sedes liquid*. Mist. pot. citrat. efferv. ʒj. Acidi hydrocy. dil. ♏v 2*dis horis*.

The sickness was arrested, the next day she passed a motion containing large coagula of blood. 16th. Passed more blood in motions last night, much pain in abdomen, increased on coughing. Twelve leeches were applied to the belly and relieved the pain very much. She took also the above pill *ter die*. 19. No blood last two days in stools, only some feeling of soreness now in abdomen; has begun quinine. She went out well.

REMARKS.—This case occurred during the prevalence of epidemic cholera, and was clearly the result of the miasm. It is impossible to say what were the causes which determined the occurrence of hemorrhage rather than of serous discharge, but it is evident that there must have existed great congestion of the mucous membrane, probably of the large intestines. Extreme capillary congestion and extravasation of blood were observed by Reinhard and Leubuscher in some fatal cases especially in the ileum. One part at least of this congestion must have consisted in dilatation of the arteries of the mucous membrane, and another in loss of tone of the capillaries, both probably the results of nervous paralysis. That the choleraic poison acts especially on and through the nervous system is, I think, unquestionable. The remarkable and peculiar depression, the algide symptoms, the cramps, the sudden prostration and death occurring sometimes without any diarrhœa, all testify to this fact.

The following case from Torti is well worth perusal in reference to this subject.

No. 149.—A garrison soldier of our city in the third paroxysm of a tertian fever passed a dejection extremely blackish, as it were made up of blood partly coagulated and partly dissolved. It resembled somewhat a copious flow of hæmorrhoidal blood; but the black colour, and its being thoroughly mixed with excrements of softer consistence, showed that it came from higher up. The excretion was also (at times) clear and unmixed with feces, quite like the black blood called by the ancients atrabile. Very copious was this discharge, frequent and violently ejected, the countenance at the same time became Hippocratic, the extreme parts cold and livid, the whole body corpse-like, the pulse almost abolished, while the patient lay buried rather than swimming in a pool of this foul fluid from which he endeavoured to free himself with vain efforts and restless tossing to and fro. As quickly as possible all the sacraments of the Church were directed to be administered, and then the Peruvian bark in strong doses, though almost without hope. The next morning the patient was still alive but utterly prostrated, still rather cold, and with a most feeble pulse. The use of the remedy is continued according to my practice in a smaller dose, and this alone and food is prescribed. On the following day an exceedingly mild attack occurs, and in it the pulse begins to rise (in force) and the body gets somewhat heated, while there is no return of the black dejections. The patient advanced towards health every day after, had no further relapses, and completely recovered, the bark being continued by way of prophylaxis for some days.

There can be no question in a case of this kind that the hemorrhage was not the result of ulceration.

No. 150.—Mrs. A., æt. 50, f., a finely-made florid person of highly nervous temperament, but little strength. Her catam. have occurred every fourteen days since girlhood. If she gets the least cough expectorates blood. Ten years ago had copious hæmatemesis; brought up a basinful. When young has been bled many times without benefit. She had constantly-recurring slight eczema, which did not yield to the usual treatment, and as she appeared full-blooded I took on one occasion ℥vj of blood from the arm. It weakened her considerably for some time and did no good. She has several times had copious bleeding *per anum*, which, as far as I could judge from an examination I made during one of these attacks, did not proceed from piles. There was diarrhœa at the same time and tenderness over the descending colon. Tannin + opium with lead enemata arrested the hemorrhage, but it recurred at intervals a long time afterwards, and probably does so still.

The circumstances which dispose me to regard the above case as an instance of intestinal vaso-motor nerve paralysis are (1) the occurrence of hemorrhages from four different surfaces at various times; (2) the marked want of tone and nerve power; (3) the marked plethoric aspect of the patient in spite of all the frequent losses of blood; (4) the good effect of strychnia, which she has repeatedly taken with great advantage. It appears as if the quantity of blood frequently became disproportioned to the retentive power of the vessels, in consequence of which rupture and extravasation occurred. The state of the system resembles that of the so-called "hæmophilic" or bleeders. Besides the tendency to hemorrhage the only other marked peculiarity is the hyperæsthesia and nerve debility. It may be an error to regard the vascular and nervous weakness as causatively connected, but there are certainly some grounds for the opinion. Thus I have had evidence again and again that cutaneous purpura is essentially the result of debility and not of privation of vegetables, and I have more than once seen extravasation of blood take place under the conjunctiva solely as the result of neurolytic prostration. Scurvy is said to have appeared among some American troops, and to have proved fatal in some cases, which appeared to be induced chiefly by *ennui* and home sickness. *V. Amer. Med. T.*, 1861, June 1st.

Mr. Ashton, in his work on Diseases of the Rectum, thus describes neuralgia in this situation. "The disease is most frequently met with in anæmic individuals in whom the nervous sensibility is generally excessive and often deranged. Females whose systems have been depressed by menorrhagia, or frequent child-bearing, particularly if the labours have been attended with violent floodings, are liable to become the subjects of this disease, as well as of other forms of neuralgia." The quality of the pain varies in different persons and at different times; it is sometimes constant, more often remittent. As to its origin Ashton describes it as either reflex from some cause of irritation in other parts of the alimentary canal, or as induced by exposure to cold and damp, as in sitting on cold wet stones, or by the influence of malaria. He relates an interesting case in which the patient had been engaged harvesting in Essex, and had been exposed to the night air. He complained of great pain at the fundament occurring daily and continuing for some hours, not induced or aggravated by defecation. No lesion of any kind was discoverable. The local application of belladonna failed, but with quinine he soon recovered.

CHAPTER XXXIII.

UTERINE NEUROSES.

THE uterus seems to come in for a fair share of neurotic disorder. This indeed might be expected not only from its functional importance, and its extensive sympathetic connections, but from the marked depression of nervous power with which its monthly evacuation seems to be almost constantly associated. The commonest form of dysmenorrhœa is recognized by Churchill and Tyler Smith as neuralgia. Besides these periodic affections there occur more continuous ones, which seem to be, however, of much the same character. The usual causes of neuralgia affect the uterus as they do other parts. Rheumatism, miasmata, and remote irritation play the same part here as they do elsewhere. The affection described under the name of "irritable uterus" appears to be a true hyperæsthesia quite distinct from neuralgia as we have seen it to be in the case of the stomach. Dr. Marion Sims' vaginismus appears to be essentially a similar hyperæsthesia of the vulva. Common menorrhagia, not of organic origin, is evidently intimately connected with vaso-motor nerve paresis, and is restrained effectually by treatment corresponding to this view. Sir R. Martin mentions the frequency of uterine hemorrhage in females who have been long in India, and refers it to weakening of the nervous and muscular power of the organ by long exposure to heat and malaria.[1]

No. 151.—M. W., æt. 25, f., ad. July 26th. Ill since her confinement nine weeks ago. Suffers with pain round the lower part of abdomen and dreadful bearing-down. The pain causes her to bend double when it comes on; it is worse at night. Sometimes there are intervals of freedom from pain for about two hours. No discharge. Uterus appears quite normal. Appetite tolerable, but food lies heavy. Head giddy. Pulse not weak. Urine very high-coloured and copious. She took for three weeks pot. iod. gr. j + sod. carb. gr. xv. + inf. gent. co ʒj *ter die*, and used an opium and belladonna liniment. Under this treatment she improved very much, and was then ordered ammonia, soda, tr. hyoscy., and dec. cinchon., which she took until September 3d, and was then discharged well. The state of the urine, the absence of marked prostration, and the efficient remedies point out the rheumatic character of this hysteralgia.

No. 152.—E. N., f., æt. 32, no children. Ad. October 28th, ill six months. Suffers with bearing-down pains, but has no discharge. The pains are aggravated at times, and she then passes a large quantity of aqueous urine. At the catamenial periods the pains are much worse. Uterus healthy. No pain in connection. No tenderness on either side of abdomen. A cruel hernia on right. In the course of her attendance she had throat dysæsthesia for a time. She took citrate of iron and quinine + tr. nuc. vom. + spt. œth. chl. *ter die* for about two months and improved steadily and satisfactorily. This case seems to have been one of simple uterine neuralgia.

No. 153.—A. S., f., æt. 18, ad. April 12th, ill three weeks. Has violent pain at lower part of abdomen and bearing-down. Catamenial discharge

---

[1] There is an important passage in Virchow's "Handbuch der Pathol.," vol. i. p. 231, in which he states that on microscopic examination small solutions of continuity are actually seen to occur in the capillaries and small arteries and veins, through which single blood-globules escape one after another, while the current goes on uninterrupted within the vessels. If the gap in the vessel is larger the circulation may be stopped in the vessel, and the current may set from all sides towards the orifice. He states further that after the escape of a certain amount of blood the wall of the vessel may be repaired, and the leak disappear. He does not state in what tissue he has seen the phenomena. I have never witnessed anything of the kind in the frog's web, but I think nevertheless that it is extremely probable that the wall of the smaller vessels does undergo modifications which make it permeable by solid corpuscles without its losing its consistence entirely, reducing it in fact to something like a film of gelatine. Such alterations take place under various conditions in which the vital power of the tissues is impaired, and among them I think prostration of nervous power must be noted as one of the principal. The same influences which cause arterial relaxation will often cause also leakage of the capillaries, and the same means which prove remedial in the one condition avail also in the other. I believe that some change of this kind in the smaller vessels occurs in normal menstruation, and the relation of this process to lowering of nervous power seems to be unmistakable.

has continued for last three weeks, is brought on by any exertion. Abdomen soft, bears pressure very fairly. She feels very weak. B. regular. She was ordered ammon. carb. gr. iv + liq. potass. arsenit. ℥ iv + inf. gent. co. ʒj *ter die.* 19th. Pain so severe two days ago that she fainted. Catamenia ceased. 22d. Is stronger, pain continues. May 6th. Is a great deal better; the pain is felt only now and then. Pt. c. mist. ol. morrh. ʒj + vini ferri ʒss *bis die.* She did not return. In this case the affection of the sensory nerves was complicated with paresis of the vaso-motor, and as both disorders were amended by the same remedy it may be inferred, as we have done previously, that they were "au fond" of the same nature. I have recorded a case (v. *Lancet,* July 21st, 1855) in which paroxysm of severe neuralgia of the face issued in actual extravasation of blood in the eye and cheek. The pain would continue very severely for forty-eight hours, then begin to remit, and at the same time a blush would appear in the part which increased until there was actual effusion of blood.

Dr. Cahen has recorded (*Arch. Génér.*, Oct. 1863) two cases showing the influence of ileo-lumbar neuralgia on the occurrence of uterine hemorrhage, and remarks that the occurrence of congestions and hemorrhages in neuralgias is certainly to be attributed to the concernment of the vaso-motor nerves.

No. 154.—E. M., f., æt. 42, married, ad. July 16th, ill two years. Has pain at nates on sitting down, and in hips when walking. She cannot pass urine or feces without pain, and has frequent calls to both evacuations. Is never free from red discharge. On vaginal examination the os and cervix are found excessively tender, so much so that it is impossible to ascertain their condition accurately. Is very weak. Aspect very pallid and sunken. Vaginal suppositories were ordered, consisting of opii gr. ij + extr. bellad. gr. ¼, and pot. bromidi gr. x *ter die.* She continued under my observation only fourteen days, but appeared to benefit by the remedies. This was in all probability a case of hyperæsthesia. Dr. Tilt records a similar instance where a married female, æt. 30, had been confined to bed for several months by an excruciating pain in the back and in the lower part of the abdomen. The pain was constant, but was much aggravated at the menstrual periods. The womb was exquisitely sensitive, its neck swollen and slightly ulcerated. After the inflammatory condition had been relieved by leeches, &c. the pain persisted until vaginal suppositories of morphia gr. j—iij on cotton wool were used, which cured the neuralgia. M. Aran adopts a similar proceeding.

In his excellent paper on Irritable Uterus (*Lond. J. of Med.,* May, 1851) Dr. Mackenzie lays down that the disorder is rather of sympathetic than of idiopathic character, the immediate cause being reflected irritation having its origin in various organs with which the uterus has intimate relations, but the predisposing being a defective state of the blood inducing hyperæsthesia of the nervous system generally, and of the uterine nerves in particular. Spinal irritation, gastro-intestinal disorder, gout and rheumatism, he seems to consider as the principal causes of hysteralgia. From an analysis of thirty-seven recorded cases he shows that the principal complications are leucorrhœa and disorders of menstruation; the most frequent antecedents are dyspepsia, mental anxiety, and weakening discharges; the concomitant affections are anæmia, spinal irritation and disorder of digestion. My own experience would lead me to take rather a different view as regards the influence of reflected irritation in causing hysteralgia. Causes of the former in the alimentary canal and elsewhere are abundantly common in my field of experience, but the special symptoms of the latter affection are extremely rare. Leucorrhœa, menorrhagia, dysmenorrhœa are frequent enough, but it is very rare to meet with uterine hyperæsthesia, at least in a marked form. The affection seems to me strictly comparable to hyperæsthesia in other situations, and it is very difficult to say whether its essential seat is in the peripheral nerves, or in the centres. Dr. Tyler Smith has mentioned to me a case in which frontal neuralgia and ague continued until puberty, and were then replaced by "irritable uterus." In this case the nerve disorder was not of reflex origin.

The treatment of menorrhagia not depending on plethora, or organic disease, is generally very satisfactory. The patient is directed after the flow returning at the proper time has continued for three or four days to make tannin with acid. muriat. + liq. opii sed. + spt. æth. chlor. in doses proportioned in frequency to the amount of the hemorrhage. When the flow is arrested by these means I give citrate of iron and quinine + liq. pot. arsenit. *ter die* during the intervals, and I usually find that their length becomes gradually increased, while the duration of the discharge diminishes. I am sure of the virtue of arsenic in such disorders, and I am rather surprised not to see it mentioned among the remedies advised in some works specially devoted to the diseases of women. There is nothing specific or peculiar in this action of arsenic; it is a powerful nerve tonic, and as such induces a better contraction of the uterine arteries. In his excellent paper on arsenic Dr. Begbie has specially noticed its action upon the uterus, v. *Edin. Med. J.*, 1858, May. In some cases I have found strychnia + tr. ferri muriat. to answer well. In menorrhagia as in other instances a primary deficiency of tone or power produces results which react on and intensify the original defect.

CHAPTER XXXIV.

CUTANEOUS NEUROSES.

As the principal sensory surface the skin may be expected to come in for its full share of nerve disorder, and this is to a great extent actually the case. I do not intend to refer here to neuralgic pain which has been noticed elsewhere, nor to painful affections of tramautic origin, of which Romberg cites several interesting cases. The conditions I propose to illustrate are (*a*) that of increased, (*b*) that of diminished sensibility, (*c*) that of vaso-motor nerve paresis, (*d*) that of vaso-motor spasm. One or more of these may coexist.

Cutaneous hyperæsthesia is far from being uncommon as a primary affection; it is often associated with more or less of popular eruption, but certainly may be quite independent. The following cases prove this:—

No. 155.—J. A., æt. 35, m., ad. Sept. 29th. Ill six weeks, complains of continual itching all the whole day affecting every part except the hands and feet—"can't bear himself when in bed." There is no eruption whatever. His health is good. B. open. P. weak. Feels weak. Has very frequent calls to urinate, but passes very little. He was treated with aconite lotion and carbonate of iron, and quite lost his itching in about three weeks.

No. 156.—G., æt. 47, complains of having suffered during three weeks great irritation of the skin; she felt as if she could tear her back to pieces at night. At that time after scratching she says pimples come out attended with great sense of burning and scalding. There was no eruption whatever to be seen on the parts. With the aid of aconite lotion and acid. sulph. dil. m xxx *ter die* she recovered from her troublesome disorder.

In other cases there is some scanty and limited lichenous eruption, but it is evidently insufficient to account for the wide-spread and severe itching. I believe further that Romberg's view is correct, that even in marked cases of lichen and prurigo the hyper- or dysæsthesia is the cause and not the consequence of the eruption, and this for the following reasons:—

(1) Decided inflammation of the skin produced by irritants, or as occurring in erysipelas, is not attended with anything like the severe itching of lichen or prurigo, yet in such cases the papillary structure must be involved. (2) The very marked influence of warmth and of the night in aggravating these eruptions is quite accordant with the genius of nerve disorder, and, on the contrary, unlike that of true inflammation. (3) One form—lichentropicus—is produced by conditions eminently exciting, and yet exhaustive of, nervous power. (4) The relation of these eruptions to urticaria, which is evidently a neurosis. (5) The very small amount of inflammation in many severely itching eruptions. The causes of cutaneous hyperæsthesia are generally very obscure; it is rare that we are liable to influence the disorder by our knowledge of them. In the allied affection urticaria it is notorious that all sorts of things will give rise to the eruption in predisposed persons, each being especially sensitive to some particular substance. Here the predisposition is evidently the "grandleiden," and in hyperæsthesia it is much more so, as we are much less able to detect any exciting causes. The warmth of bed, or of any source of heat is the chief excitor. This renders the disorder often a grievous infliction by destroying the patient's rest. In the case of lichen tropicus, the "prickly heat," the elevated temper-

ature is no doubt the chief or sole cause, acting on nervous tissue as it so commonly does in the way of enfeebling power and increasing excitability. I have several times observed the reproduction of lichen urticatus in my own patients by summer heat. This influence of heat seems to me a very significant fact with regard to the essential nature of the disorder. Heat is an imponderable, and cannot act as a "materies morbi," nor is it likely to cause the retention in the system of "excernenda," but rather the reverse. It does however affect the nervous power very speedily and decidedly, and thus we can hardly avoid recognizing the disorders which it produces as purely dynamic, and not dependent on any morbid state of the blood. This view is supported by the fact that in two toxic disorders, gout and syphilis, itching is by no means a marked or frequent symptom. I do not remember to have observed it in any of the cases of chronic gout I have had under my care; and in syphilis the less itching quality of the eruption is notorious. Jaundice is certainly sometimes attended with much itching, but much more often is not, at least in my own experience. I am therefore inclined to regard the affection we are considering as an essential neurosis, but as one which, like many others, may differ much in quality in various instances. In some it may be of a more sthenic, in others of a more asthenic character. In lichenous and pruriginous disorder if at all severe the administration of hyd. bichlorid. or some mild mercurial is requisite. In the other cases saline aperients with a little vin. colch. may be sufficient. Soda baths and the sulphur-fume bath are often very serviceable; the latter, however, should not be used in cases of a sthenic character, at least until after due depletion has been employed. In asthenic cases tannin may be of efficacy, or arsenic. Where the hyperæsthesia exists alone, or with but a little eruption, acid. sulph. dil. in ℨss doses *ter die*, or citric acid in gr. x—xv doses with spt. æth. chlor. are beneficial. Bismuth ointment and aconite lotion are useful local applications. Henbane should be given in sufficiently large doses (gr. x—xv of the extract) to soothe the irritability of the system, and to procure sleep at night.

Urticaria by its fugitive character, by its manifold and various causation, by its nocturnal invasion, by the dysæsthesia attending it, and by the nature of its phenomena fully asserts its title to be regarded as a neurosis. Its characteristic pale wheal-like elevations are the result of a cutaneous spasm, contracting the tissue into knots or "bumps." In persons with highly irritable skins pressure with a hard point on the surface will produce the same effect. Patients complain sometimes that the bumps are produced when they scratch themselves to relieve the previously existing irritation. It is, I think, probable that the dysæsthesia and the cutaneous contraction are co-results of the same nerve disorder, and that the latter is not merely a reflex of the former. The spasm is certainly not dependent upon hyperæmia, as in urt. evanida it occurs without any. The diffuse inflammatory redness of the skin, which is so marked in some instances, and attended even with swelling, must be considered as an indication of vaso-motor nerve paresis, and we thus get in this curious malady three different pathological changes resulting from the operation of the same cause, viz., spasm of contractile tissue in certain parts, paralysis in others, and a state of hyper- and dysæsthesia of sensory nerves. It is very instructive to note these various phenomena developed under our eyes, intimating to us what may occur on internal and concealed surfaces. Like most neuroses, urticaria may be produced by remote irritation, which is in many cases seated in the intestines, but may be elsewhere, as in the female sexual organs. Scanzoni has recorded[1] some highly interesting cases where urticaria was produced by the application of leeches to the uterus. In one of these, a woman, æt. 28, had five leeches applied to the cervix. Scarcely had they taken hold when she complained of most violent labour-like pains in the abdomen, and although these soon moderated in force, they were accompanied with such intense febrile action that the entire body glowed with heat, the pulse rose to 140, the carotids pulsated visibly, and the face, neck, and chest exhibited an intensely red colour, to which were added in a very short time a large eruption of urticaria elevations of a palish colour. The eruption was accompanied by great headache, inclination to vomit, and excessive lassitude, symptoms which continued to the following day, although the exanthem with the accompanying fever disappeared entirely after three hours' continuance. Scanzoni refers the phenomena to irritation of the uterine nerves, and states that they could not depend on the absorption of any poison from the leeches, as no such symptoms are ever occasioned by the application of leeches to other regions of the body. In a third case it is stated that the leeches, had been applied eight times, and it was only on the ninth occasion that the urticarious phenomena occurred. It is clear how strongly the above history corroborates the theory of inhibitory action. Paralysis of vaso-motor nerves gave rise to the carotid pulsation, to the cutaneous hyperæmia, and through the vagi and the coronary plexuses, as well as the fevered blood, to increased action of the heart. The urticarious elevations show how a spasm may be produced together with a paralysis, as we have before observed. Imponderable miasms, as that of ague, may cause urticaria. Probably there are several which may produce the same effect. In some persons even of good health urticaria persists in a chronic recurring form for years, just as many other neuroses do. Its rational treatment consists in the removal of any ascertainable cause of irritation, and in the administration of such means as may seem appropriate to calm the nervous disorder existing in the particular instance. In " urticaria ab ingestis" an emetic should be given, and followed if necessary by an aperient with or without a dose of calomel. In the more acute febrile conditions salines with

[1] *V.* "Edin. Med. Journ.," Oct. 1860.

hydrocyanic acid may be employed and subsequently mineral acids. Cazenave recommends alkaline baths. During the presence of acute disorder lead lotion may be freely applied to allay the itching. Henbane and camphor taken at night in full doses will be often serviceable in procuring sleep. In chronic cases without evident cause cold douching in the morning, and carbonate of iron *ter die*, or arsenic, or some nervine tonic should be steadily administered. When the disorder is produced by malaria it yields to quinine.

Anæsthesia of the skin not dependent on organic disease of nervous structure is by no means rare in connection with neuralgia and diphtheria, but I am little acquainted with it from my own experience in other morbid states. Tactile sensation which judges of temperature and locality must be distinguished according to Jaksch from common sensation, of which pain is a modification.[1] The faculty of touch may remain quite unimpaired while the consciousness of pain is lost. Carpenter states, however,[2] that the ordinary sense of tact may remain while yet there is no power to judge of temperature, and *vice versa*. Romberg[3] says "that insensibility to pain with a continuance of the sense of touch occurs in various diseases, but most frequently in lead poisoning, and not rarely in hysteria, but never in cases where the sense of touch is destroyed." It seems difficult to reconcile the statements of Jaksch and Carpenter. For my own part, I think it very doubtful that there are different fibres for the conveyancing of the different sensations to the sensorium, as if this was the case the total number of cutaneous nerves would have to be extremely great. It seems quite possible that a nerve may be insusceptible of a particular impression just as the retina in certain persons is to particular colours. Romberg mentions the occurrence of cutaneous anæsthesia in washerwomen, and has no doubt that the immersion of the hands in the soapy water was the cause. The symptoms were much like those of neuralgia. Voisin[4] describes hysterical anæsthesia as by no means a constant occurrence in all cases, as Gendrin states it to be. On the contrary, it very rarely occurs except after severe convulsive attacks attended with unconsciousness. Briquet however controverts this, and states that of 221 anæsthetic females only 160 had had convulsive attacks. It is often of short duration, lasting only some minutes or hours after the paroxysm; but in inveterate cases it may persist for years. Voisin believes the anæsthesia to be dependent on the unconsciousness. The left side as a rule is the one which is anæsthetic, but sometimes the disorder affects the outer side of all the limbs, or even extends over the whole surface. While the skin is anæsthetic the muscles are usually in the opposite state.

Beau and Foisin agree that *analgesia* (loss of the feeling of pain)

[1] Schmidt's "Jahrb.," vol. cxx. p. 48.
[2] "Physiology." p. 225, 2d edit.
[3] "Syd. Soc. Translat.," vol. i. p. 200.
[4] "Gaz. Hebdom," xlviii., 1858; Canst. "Jahresb.," 1860, vol. iii. p. 98.

is always the first phenomenon in hysterical anæsthesia, that it always precedes the loss of the sense of touch. The analgesia is at first incomplete and gradually increases. It is rarely limited to small spots, usually it occupies a whole side, and that the left. When the analgesia is complete faradization with the wire-brush reddens the skin, but causes no pain. The mucous membranes of the nose, the mouth, and the vagina are sometimes affected and usually on the left side. Loss of the sense of touch Voisin regards as a higher grade of anæsthesia; it is mostly left-sided, and in rare instances extends over the whole surface. Nearly the same may be said of the loss of the faculty of distingushing temperature.

Diminution or loss of the sense of resistance depends on a deficiency of the muscular sensibility, and of the cutaneous tactile faculty; it is therefore a complex morbid state, and of rare occurrence, inasmuch as the muscular sense is only impaired in the worst cases of hysteria. When this complex paralysis is complete, patients have no perception of the size, form, weight, and temperature of bodies placed in their hands as long as their eyes are averted.

Jaksch (*v. loc. cit.*) has specially studied the subject of cutaneous anodynia. He observed it in six or eight among 120 to 130 patients at Prague. It coexisted with other nerve disorders, especially those belonging to the hysterical class. When extensive it may involve *all* the mucous surfaces continuous with the skin. Occasionally it happens that the tongue alone is affected, the cutaneous sensibility remaining normal. The conjunctivæ and the nasal mucous membrane may be insensible to the strongest stimulants, as liq. ammoniæ and mustard oil, no lachrymation or sneezing being produced. Smell is usually lost in anodynia of the nose, and taste in that of the tongue. Sir Chas. Bell relates a case of plethoric hysteria communicated by Mr. Crampton, of Dublin, in which the right eye, the lids, and the skin of the cheek and forehead about an inch around were quite anæsthetic. The sight of this eye also had been quite lost for four or five months, and had been dim for four years or more since a blow on the eye. Under depletory treatment she quite regained the sight of the eye. The anæsthesia ceased some time previously when pain and deafness recurred in the right ear, where they had existed before the anæsthesia. The anodynia may be general, or one-sided, observing accurately the median line, or it may affect separate tracts of various size. It never corresponds to the distribution of a single cutaneous nerve. The subjacent muscles are often similarly affected, at other times not, or they may be anodynic (to the electric current) while the skin covering them is normal. It is very worthy of observation that the most severe neuralgia may coexist in the same part along with cutaneous anodynia. Four-fifths of the patients were females, the disorder prevailed most from the 16th to the 30th year of life, in uneducated persons, and more among Jews than among other persuasions. A mental perturbation was the most frequent cause, and healthful mental stimuli were among the most efficient restorative means. Other useful remedies were such as are usually employed in other neuroses, zinc, musk, quinine, morphia, electricity, warm baths, as those of Teplitz. Cold affusions and counter-irritation were most effectual in recent cases.

Hysterical hyperæsthesia is so much more commonly observed with us than anæsthesia, the latter perhaps being overlooked, and the tendency in many patients of this kind to "embroider" is so great that I confess I have for a long time received the accounts I have read of the above condition *cum grano salis*, as it is not easy to be well assured that some of the symptoms might not be feigned. But with regard to anodynia there can be no doubt that it must be the result of a real alteration in the state of the nerves, and no pretence. No normal conjunctiva or Schneiderian membrane would stand the test of liq. ammoniæ or mustard without giving unmistakable evidence of sensibility. The experiment is precise enough, and unless we question the veracity of the author we must admit the occurrence of this remarkable sensory paralysis; and if of this then I think of other forms of so-called hysterical disorder, as real nerve—and not merely nervous affections. There has hitherto been far too much confusion between the bodily and the mental derangement, and because in many cases the latter has been present it has been too much taken for granted that it existed in all, and that the bodily was mythical. We shall always have much need to be on our guard against deception in the case of our meeting with a genuine hysteric, but on the other hand we have evidence enough I think that causes of exhaustion of nerve power may generate all kinds of morbid phenomena from the greatest hyperæsthesia, muscular agitation, and convulsion to anæsthesia, analgesia, and paralysis. Let us only think what must be the depressing effects of constant monotonous toil, scanty pay, poor food, bad air, and failing strength, especially where there is no bright ray of future happiness in a better state to light the gloom, and where in the absence of healthful recreation gin and prostitution are the devil's substitutes, and then say if we can be surprised at any amount of physical nervous derangement. Dr. G. Bird, speaking of paraplegia the result of enervation occurring in sempstresses says: "They are unable to procure proper food, and are often driven to intemperance to forget their miseries, or to prostitution to add to their wretched income." In awe and sadness we ask ourselves at times, "How can these things be?"

There are a good many instances, some I have alluded to already, of paresis affecting the vaso-motor nerves of the skin and its glands. The profuse sweating which affects persons whose nervous power is low depends evidently on this condition. A friend who has hemiplegia too probable of organic origin tells me that when he has a lamp-bath he perspires very much more on the palsied side than on the other. *Per contra*, I have been informed that a dose of arsenic taken before a Turkish bath will prevent perspiration being induced.

Sir R. Martin has related to me the case of a lady who had suffered from frontal neuralgia and malarious fever, in whom there appeared now and then a largish patch of redness on the forearm near the wrist from which such an abundant perspiration flowed that several handkerchiefs were saturated in about half an hour. If arsenic be allowed to be a nerve-tonic, which can hardly be denied, its remarkable efficacy in asthenic eczema, impetigo, and pemphigus must be considered tolerably good proof that one chief constituent of these eruptions is a state of vaso-motor nerve paresis. Not only is the discharge arrested, but the abnormal temperature and vascularity are reduced. This is surely very like what occurs on galvanizing a divided sympathetic. Occasionally subcutaneous effusion occurs in place of surface discharge, and yields to the same toning treatment. I have recorded the case of a child, æt. 14 months, who suffered with diffuse erythematous redness appearing in various parts, on which at first a few bullæ were developed. A few days later both hands were intensely œdematous, the swelling had been preceded by redness. Quinine + iron + arsenic cured, although there was much feverishness. Certain roseolæ, and erythemata, and cases of recurring erysipelas seem to depend chiefly on want of tone in the cutaneous vaso-motor nerves. Pemphigus hæmorrhagicus in which the bullæ contain bloody serum, of which I observed some years ago an instance in a thin, fœeble-looking man, æt. 60, forms a transition to purpura. In the case alluded to the eruption quite ceased under the administration at first of bark and ammonia and subsequently of arsenic. The weakness and fragility of the capillaries, which is the essential condition in purpura and the allied disorder scurvy, seems to be sometimes to a great extent of neurotic origin, and at any rate is often considerably amended by the administration of iron and quinine. One of the severest cases of purpura I ever saw was cured by infusion of matico, *i. e.*, by tannin. It is often, however, necessary to premise cholagogue purgatives.

M. Parrot[1] relates the case of a female, a hystero-epileptic, in whom bloody sweating occurred during many years on the knees, thighs, chest, lower eyelids, hands, and face. The tears were once also tinged with blood, and there was frequently some hæmatemesis. On one occasion together with the hæmatemesis there was severe epigastric pain, and the skin of this part was covered with a bloody dew. These hemorrhages were never an isolated phenomenon; they always succeeded to a mental emotion, and complicated a nervous attack attended with absolute loss of motor and sensory power. At one time neuralgic paroxysms were attended with sanguineous exudation at the painful parts. There was no deception; Parrot himself witnessed the phenomenon. There was never any reddening of the skin in the parts where the hemorrhage occurred. The catamenia seem to have been pretty regular, and their appearance always re-

[1] "Gaz. Hebdom.," 1859, 40—47.

lieved the cutaneous hemorrhage. Parrot cites various other recorded cases of a similar character, and observes, in conclusion, that this cutaneous hemorrhage may coexist with others of a similar character in persons of a delicate, irritable constitution, especially in females; that all these hemorrhages not only are associated with general nervous perturbation, but are further frequently connected with localized phenomena of pain and spasm; that they closely resemble these phenomena with regard to their efficient causes, the parts which they affect, the suddenness of their invasion and cessation, and their harmlessness. These hemorrhages, which he terms neuropathic, proceed he believes from the glands of the external and internal tegument. They consist of true blood, and not merely of red-stained serum.

Under the head of spasm of the vaso-motor nerves of the skin I might allude to the common "dying," as it is called, of the hands; when under exposure to cold the fingers turn white and numb, so as to be often for the time almost useless. Sir B. Brodie, in his work on Local Nervous Affections, p. 42, observes that in some of those who are subject to so-called hysterical disease of the joints the whole limb is affected with a remarkable alternation of heat and cold. Thus in the morning the limb may be cold and of a *pale* or *purple* colour, as if there were scarcely any circulation of blood in it, while towards the afternoon it becomes warm, and the evening is actually hot to the touch with the vessels turgid and the skin shining. Graves mentions a remarkable case of somewhat the same kind, the patient being a young female. One leg and foot at a time became very hot, swollen, smooth, shining, and as dark in colour as a ripe black cherry. When the hot fit ceased, the slight swelling and the discoloration subsided, and the affected parts remained during the next stage pale, deadly cold, and comparatively free from pain. Only about three hours of complete intermission ensued in the twenty-four, one leg becoming affected as the other recovered. It is remarkable that perspiration does not seem to have occurred in consequence of the hyperæmia. In these cases we have examples of alternating spasm and paresis of the cutaneous vessels; in the following I think the phenomena are mainly due to spasm.

No. 157.—A girl, æt. 17, without known cause felt violent pain in the hands; four fingers of the right and two of the left became slate-coloured, cold, insensible—in short, exhibited all the symptoms of incipient gangrene. Movement was almost entirely abolished in these fingers. The induced current was applied, giving rise at first to increased pain, but soon arresting the sufferings of the patient. After ten or twelve sittings at about the end of a week the sensibility, the normal temperature, and colour, as well as motion, were restored. The epidermis came off to the extent of the first appearance of the gangrene. During electrization a fetid sweat was noticed over the electrified parts.—(v. *Brit. and For. Med.-Chir. Rev.*, April, 1859.)

No. 158.—W. P., æt. 32, indoor servant, seen May 6th, 1856, ad. into hospital fourteen days ago. Has had no particular disease during his life;

health good when his fingers became affected and for some time after. States that from two to three weeks before he was admitted his finger-tips were quite black and cold, but not numb; every one thought they were going to mortify. Before they turned black they used to be cold and numb. This state lasted about six weeks, the numbness then went away, and they became exceedingly tender and burning. During this second period, if he had his fingers in bed they were burning, if he left them out they got very cold. Between the two dysæsthesiæ he was prevented from sleeping. During the first period when the fingers were cold and numb they used to swell much at night. Some of the fingers now are perceptibly colder than the others, and of a semi-livid tint, and the cuticle yields under pressure with a sense of crackling, the pressure causing much pain though the part is numb. In other fingers that are recovering the cuticle is detached, and the skin is rather swollen and of a brightish red; and nearly normal warmth and sensibility. The left ring-finger has quite escaped, and the right little finger. June 3d. Is exceedingly weak, pulse very weak. Right middle finger turns quite white when exposed to cold, while the other fingers of the same hand at the same time turn black and blue. All the fingers are now red and warm, the weather being so. Right index and mid-fingers are very thinly covered with epidermis and are very tender. Left fingers are all quite well. Says his fingers have not gone on nearly so well since he left off the pot. iod.+ quinine which he took for the first nineteen days. Since then he has had calomel + opium *bis die* for an attack of epidydimitis. By July 5th he was pretty well recovered, and left the hospital.

Mr. Myrtle records[1] the following case, which he terms one of anæmic sphacelus.

No. 159.—A military man, strongly built, and of sanguine temperament, æt. 46, healthy-looking, and having enjoyed uniform good health in spite of seven years' active service in the tropics and in the Crimea, complained of the following disorder. The fingers of both hands, especially those of the right, were pale and cold; the right little finger from its point to its middle felt cold as ice, and its ungual phalanx was blue—looked as if dead; under the top of each nail, and extending across, there was a purple line about one-tenth of an inch in breadth. The thumbs and the rest of both hands were natural. The last phalanx only of the right little finger was devoid of sensation. The ears were much colder than natural, had a mottled appearance, and exhibited on the outer and posterior part of each helix a number of ecchymosed patches. Heart's action normal but weak. Five days later he passed a sleepless night, having been kept awake by severe and constant burning pain in the feet and toes; the feet were pale, cold, and clammy, the extremities of the toes being bluish and tender to the touch; the fingers except the little one were well, and the ears nearly so. The extremity of the right little finger became gangrenous and was removed by Mr. Walter Coulson, who was satisfied by careful examination that there was no disease in the arteries. Myrtle is of the same opinion, and refers the symptoms to feeble action of the heart, and lowered vitality from deficiency of nerve-force. Citrate of iron and quinine seem to have been most beneficial as a remedy.

REMARKS.—In these three instances the malady seems to me to have consisted essentially in disordered innervation. The coldness and numbness

[1] "Lancet," May 30th, 1863.

were no doubt the result of spasmodic contraction of the arteries, which produced in the two first cases the death and detachment of the cuticle from arrest of nutrition in the lowermost layer of cells; and in the second actual gangrene of a part of one finger. The lividity of the parts whose supply of blood was arrested depended on the stagnation of venous blood in the capillaries; it may be easily produced by application of ice to the surface, and removed again by warmth, v. p. 30. Why the cessation of *vis a tergo* should cause this remarkable venous congestion is not quite clear, especially as it is not an invariable result. The constringent influence of cold sometimes makes a part quite pale and white, as it did the right middle finger in the second case, while the adjacent ones were livid. When this occurs we must suppose the capillaries and veins to have become emptied, perhaps by contracting like the arteries. I say perhaps, for I have seen whole tracts of capillaries in the frog's web appear *empty* and void of blood-corpuscles when their arteries were contracted, while they themselves were perfectly patent. It is probable that an alteration of the normal attraction and repulsion between the corpuscles and the tissues is concerned in the phenomenon. The exemption of one finger of each hand in the second case is a curious circumstance, and may be cited as a proof that the disorder could not depend on any external influence. The dependence of the disorder in the third case on some general "motor" must be admitted from the ears and the feet becoming affected in a like way. That "motor" may have been latent malarious infection in the one instance, but in the others there was no history of any exposure to such morbific agency. It is very remarkable that in the cases of branchial neuralgia I have seen there has never been any modification of nutrition of the suffering parts. I know not how to account for this except by supposing that the vaso-motor nerves were unaffected. If this be the true explanation, it is curious that the morbific cause should be so limited in its operation as to act on one set of nerves forming far the larger part of the nervous supply and to leave others close by intact. The peripheral character of the disorder was very evident in all the instances. Embolism may I think be quite excluded as a cause. These cases are suggestive as to the possible occurrence of gangrene or wasting in internal parts, from similar anæmiating arterial spasm. The treatment of such cases should consist I think in the administration of iron and quinine, ol. morrh., and belladonna, in full doses, in the application of warmth and mild local stimulation, and the continuous electric current, though the induced proved beneficial in the first. This result was produced I think by the stimulus exhausting the undue excitability of the nerves.

It may admit of some question how far the alterations which ensued in the two preceding cases resulted directly from deficient nervous influence. It seems quite certain that mere loss of sensation in a part from division of its nerve causes of necessity no derangement of nutrition in it. The various branches of the fifth have been divided repeatedly without any such result both in man for the relief of neuralgia, and in experiments upon animals. The glossopharyngeal has also been divided and the gustatory without the nutrition of the tongue being notably affected. Romberg (vol. i. p. 20, 22) cites two cases in which it is mentioned that the digital nerve on one side of a finger was divided, but nothing is said of any other result than the relief of pain. Büttner, after dividing the fifth nerve, protected the eye by a watch-glass, and found that so long as it was thus kept from external irritation not the least alteration occurred. Jobert de Lamballe divided the sciatic nerve for the relief of severe neuralgia and spasm of the muscles, and about three weeks after the crural nerve on account of the persistence of pain in the thigh. The patient was delivered from his pain, but got an eschar on the sacrum and subsequent pyæmia, of which he died. No ulceration seems to have occurred in the limb itself, and the sloughing of the sacrum of course could not be the result of the operation. (V. *Union Méd.*, No. 77, 1859.) Malagodi seems to have performed the same operation with a successful issue. Mr. Paget gives two cases from his own experience proving that nutritive repair may take place perfectly in paralyzed parts. On the other hand, there are cases which show that when nerves have been injured by disease or violence the circulation and nutrition of the parts supplied by them may be much impaired. Mr. Simon mentions (*Lect. on Pathology*, p. 74) the case of a man who some months previously had torn his ulnar nerve at the inner condyle; his two inner fingers had become swollen and livid with vascular injection. A female (*v. loc. eund.*) had disease of a large portion of the sciatic and lumbar plexus of nerves on one side, causing palsy and anæsthesia of the limb; neuralgia was referred especially to the vicinity of the knee, and at this spot ulceration had occurred. Sir B. Brodie records two cases of division of the ulnar nerve by accident in which three months, or some years after the occurrence, the little finger was numb, cold, of a purplish colour, and in one presented vesications followed by superficial sores wl. ch healed, but recurred again. Mr. Paget cites cases from Messrs. Travers and De Morgan, showing that the reparative process in the same person after injuries to the cord goes on well in the sound, but scarcely at all in the paralyzed parts (*Lect. on Pathol.*, vol. i. p. 43). Mr. Hutchinson and Mr. Lyle have recorded cases of paralysis of the ulnar and median nerves from wounds in which the hands were livid and from 4° to 6° F. colder than the corresponding healthy. (V. *Med. Times and Gaz.*, 1863, Feb. 14th, March 21st.)

The notorious liability of palsied parts to be injuriously affected by degrees of cold or heat which a sound part could well endure, and the great tendency of the eye to suffer from destructive inflammation when the fifth nerve is divided, make it nearly certain that loss of nervous influence does in some way impair, though it does not abolish, the nutritive power of the tissues. The paralyzed parts are more liable to disease than sound parts, but do not necessarily suffer. Further it appears that irritation of nerves may be a more potent cause of disease than even paralysis. Mr. Hilton's case proves that irritating pressure on a nerve may determine ulceration in the parts supplied by it (v. *Paget's Lect. on Path.*, vol. i. p. 43). In a case recorded by Mr. Hooker (v. *Lancet*, Oct. 1st, 1859) where the popliteal nerve was successfully divided on account of obstinate neuralgia of the leg attended with ulceration the ulcers healed soon after the operation.

It is very conceivable that where a nerve is injured by violence the cicatrix may keep up irritating pressure on accompanying vaso-motor nerves, and so the bloodvessels of the parts supplied may be persistently contracted, and the nutrition of the tissue suffer in consequence. This will be all the more likely to happen if the vital power of the part is either originally weak, or is impaired by loss of its normal *vis nervosa*.

Osteal Neuralgia.

Authors scarcely seem to recognize the occurrence of neuralgia in bone; I find no mention of it in Romberg, Erichsen, or Copland. The following is I believe an instance.

No. 160.—W. S., m., æt. 52, Dec. 7th, ill fourteen days. Is a strong-looking man, but has led a dissipated life; denies having had syphilis, but allows gonorrhœa. Never had gout, nor had his parents. He complained of a lichenoid eruption all over him, itching much when he was warm, and of great tenderness of the external condyle of the right humerus; this part feels just as if it was bruised, but there is no sign of any injury and no thickening to be felt. The disorder came on gradually. The pain caused considerable impairment of the power of the elevator muscles of the right arm; he could not raise any weight, nor take down his coat from a peg, nor put it on. Health perfect. A blister over the condyle, pot. iod. gr. x *ter die*, quinine and strychnia with ol. morrh. were of no benefit, but three subcutaneous injections of liq. opii sedat., and the inunction of veratria over the painful condyle almost removed the neuralgia by April 7th. It was remarkable that the accidental application of veratria ointment to his legs caused extreme tingling, while the skin of the condyle was affected very much less. As the neuralgia declined, the arm regained strength. The itching was out of all proportion to the amount of eruption visible by day; it was greatly amended by citric acid gr. xv + spt. æth. chlor. m x *ter die*.

A young lady is at present under my care with an evidently similar affection of the lower dorsal and lumbar spines; the tenderness, however, extends also some little distance on either side. In this situation neuralgia is by no means uncommon, and I quite agree with Romberg in believing that the phenomena ascribed to spinal irritation are nothing more than ordinary hysterical and neuralgic disorder. Certainly I can see no ground for supposing that congestion of the spinal cord or its membranes forms any part of the morbid process.

CHAPTER XXXV.

MALARIOID DISORDER.

PERVERTED and distorted as the truth respecting malarious disease has been by certain writers, so that a sober-minded man feels almost necessarily fearful of being thought to sanction in any degree their extravagances, it yet remains unquestionably true that there is no group of morbid affections of more weighty and practical interest, and which more claim our attention, than those which belong to this class. I will refer briefly to some of the points which justify this statement. (1) The almost universal prevalence of these diseases in all parts of the world is a striking fact. One can scarce open a book of travels without lighting on some reference to the endemic fever. Most intense and wide spread in the tropics, where the malarious influence sets its stamp on almost all morbid action, it prevails as far north as 62°. (2) The apparent absence of anything special or peculiar in the conditions which give rise to it. Moisture and warmth seem to be the efficient causes of this strange malignant influence. A soil, or even a rock needs but to have been wet and to undergo drying to become a source of disease. Even drying wood is adequate to produce the miasm. I am aware that evidence has been collected to show that ferruginous soils are eminently prone to generate malaria, but it cannot, I think, be contended that this fatal quality is peculiar to this kind, or to any. Rather it seems like the fulfilment of the original curse pronounced on the ground for man's sake. Excess of moisture and complete dryness arrest the development of malaria, indicating plainly that the formation of the poison is somehow connected with the act of drying. (3) The obscure (but undoubted) relation between malarious disease, influenza, and cholera, and the much greater prevalence of these disorders in some years than in others. (4) The very various diseases which malaria commonly produces, as fever, neuralgia, and dysentery. These may stand as representatives of the chief kinds of morbid action, showing how multiform may be the phenomena which spring from this origin. (5) The especial predilection of malaria for the nervous system, and the vast, almost endless variety of disorders it is capable of generating through the intermedium of this system. This circumstance, and the consequent tendency of ague to be associated with peculiar, anomalous, and alarming symptoms, as in the so-called pernicious fevers, give a deep interest to the study of malarious affections. (6) Though in our own land we see comparatively little of malarious disease in its more severe forms, yet owing to the wide extent of our colonial empire there are but few families who have not some member more or less exposed to suffer from them, and the number of those who return home invalided from such disease is large and increasing. It is quite clear, therefore, that a practitioner should be well acquainted with the manifold manifestations of malarious intoxication if he desire to meet the requirements of his day. It is by no means sufficient to know how to manage a tractable, well-behaved ague; we should be prepared for a variety of strange, anomalous, and puzzling forms of disorder which will be sure to perplex us if we have no clue to guide us to comprehend them. This clue will be found (1) in a knowledge of the laws of neuropathology as developed by Bernard and others; (2) in an acquaintance with the action of malarious influence on nervous tissue. The former topic has been sufficiently noticed. With regard to the second, it may be remarked that the phenomena from which we have to judge do not all present the same character. The contracted vessels, and skin, and the rigors of the cold stage of ague appear to evidence a stimulation of vaso- and musculo-motor nerves; while the increased temperature, the full pulse, the flushed surface, and the dilated vessels of the hot stage all show the existence of a state of paralysis of nervous and muscular tissues. The diarrhœa, dysentery, splenic, hepatic, or thyroidal enlargement which are so frequently produced by malaria, can only be interpreted as results of dilated and paralyzed arteries, and consequent excessive flow of blood to an enfeebled tissue. In some cases paralysis of some of the voluntary muscles has resulted from exposure to malaria. The state of a nerve in neuralgia, as I have endeavoured to show, is much more akin to paralysis than to excitement, and is commonly attended with more or less paralysis of the motor fibres contained in a compound trunk. The general conclusion from these facts clearly is that the action of malaria is mainly paralyzing, though its earlier operation may sometimes *appear* to be stimulating. I say appear, for I am very much disposed to think that the stimulation is only apparent, and this for two reasons. First, the voluntary power is certainly weakened, and the quasi-spasmodic contractions may proceed much like those of chorea from a state of undue mobility and excitability of the nervous centres. Secondly, there is certainly, as I can testify from personal experience, a remarkable hyperæsthesia of the cutaneous nerves, which are far more sensitive to cold than in the healthy state. This hyperæsthesia as well as the motor disorder may result from paresis of the centres according to the general law that power and excitability vary inversely. It is by no means improbable that the whole train of disorders may result from a primary vaso-motor nerve paresis giving rise to increased heat of the blood, which then might produce at first an unhealthy irritation of the nervous centres issuing sooner or later according to the quality of the nervous power in exhaustion and paralysis. It is well known that increased heat of the blood is one of the earliest occurrences in fevers. However this be whether the spasmodic phenomena result from fevered blood, or from the direct action of the poison, there is no question that the stimulation is of an unhealthy and injurious kind, and that we have in the coexistence of the apparently differing phenomena above mentioned another proof of the connection existing between spasm and paralysis. The result of the action of malaria may probably vary a good deal according to the idiosyncrasy of the individual, and according to the virulence of the poison itself. Just as to some persons a moderate dose of opium proves a powerful stimulant, while in others it causes more or less powerlessness, so it may be with malaria. Beyond any doubt the prolonged operation of malaria has a remarkably enfeebling and lowering effect on nerve power both in the cerebrospinal and sympathetic systems. In any actual paroxysms of malarious disorder we must of course be guided in our therapy by the existing circumstances. If the symptoms are such as indicate constricted arteries and anæmic organs, we must act very differently to the way in which we should if peril arose from active congestion of an important organ produced by the opposite state of nerves and vessels. Two main points to remember will be (1) that loss of functional power may result from constriction of the arteries supplying a part; (2) that over-excitement, and even inflammatory phenomena may depend upon an opposite condition. I have already given various instances of the pernicious and irregular forms of malarious fever, v. Cases 4, 5, 34, 104, 105.

I would refer for other examples to M. Bailly's work on intermittent fevers, and to Torti's Thérap. Spécial.

I shall now proceed to notice some of the obscurer forms in which malarious disease appears in this country, (1) in children, (2) in adults. I do not intend to advert to common ague, or its hemicranial equivalent, but to some maladies which are scarcely recognized in ordinary text-books, though they have not escaped the observation of Dr. Copland and Dr. Macculloch before him. As my field of experience has been a district of London, it may justly be expected that I should adduce some proof of the possible production of malaria in this place.

CASE 1.—A hard-worked medical man, resident in Paddington for eleven years, informs me that so far as he knows he has never been in districts where ague is prevalent. About 1853 he had distinct quotidian, and during three years was often subject to recurrences of similar disorder.

CASE 2.—G. S., æt. 30, ad. June 5, 1857, works in sewers. He was in Kent ten months ago; no one had ague in the place to which he went; he remained there fourteen days. After this he returned to Paddington, and has been working there ever since, not near the canal. Tertian ague began nine weeks ago; it ceased after treatment in six weeks, but ever since he has had neuralgia of both sides of the chest at the lower parts, with sinking sensation, and occasional burning heat flushes.

CASE 3.—L., æt. 19, residing not far from the Paddington canal, has a decided attack of ague, never having suffered from it before, nor having resided in any known malarious district.

CASE 4.—S. A., f., æt. 15, ad. May 13, 1857. About fourteen days ago had tertian ague for the first time. It came on without any known cause. She came from Norfolk to London; there was no ague in the part of Norfolk from which she came.

CASE 5.—May 5, 1857. A policeman, æt. 25, living at Walbrook in the city, employed on night duty, has tertian ague, the rigors occurring every other night. He was previously a carman at Maidstone, of most abstemious habits, had no ague before he came to London, where he had been about eleven weeks before the disorder came on.

CASE 6.—J. S., æt. 33, m., ad. April 8th, ill about a month, never had a day's illness before, never was in Kent or Lincolnshire, has been in London eight years. Ascribes his illness to a cold. His illness began with rheumatoid swelling and pain of hands; in about fourteen days this subsided, and marked quotidian ague appeared, which continued a few days, was arrested by quinine, and after a week relapsed again.

CASE 7.—C. M., æt. 32, m., ad. May 16, ill three weeks with tertian ague, which he thinks he got while working in wet in Russell Square. Never had ague before, never was where there was ague, has not left London for thirteen years. Always a healthy man. Has had five paroxysms. Is sick and vomits in the cold stage. The ague was arrested by quinine temporarily, but he did not attend long enough for a cure to be effected.

CASE 8.—J. S., f., æt. 40, April 27, 1863. Ill fourteen days with tertian ague. Was born and lived in a Lincolnshire fen; people around her often had ague, but she never had it; left her home at æt. 14, and resided in Cambridgeshire and Lincolnshire. Has been in London twelve years; never had ague till now, nor any particular illness.

My friend Dr. Brinton related to me the following case which occurred in his hospital experience. An omnibus driver who had always been in London suffered with severe inflammation of one eye, which had resisted all sorts of remedies for a long time, during which he had been under another physician's care. Taking the hint that there occurred a slight remission in the course of the day, Dr. Brinton gave him full doses of quinine, which acted magically, and he was soon well. I could easily add other examples to the foregoing, but they seem to me sufficient to prove that London, during the last twelve or fifteen years at any rate, has been capable of generating an influence giving rise to well-marked ague. Case 8 proves either that London may produce ague, or that it may call into activity a latent predisposition contracted in a malarious district, and which that locality did not render active. In either case the occurrence is sufficiently significant. The chief value of the facts above adduced is, in my opinion, the proof they afford that in obscure cases of disease of the nervous system occurring among ourselves it is right and necessary to take into account, in forming a diagnosis, the *possible* presence and operation of a malarious taint as the cause of the symptoms. This is no mere hypothesis, I am convinced from experience of the soundness of the view. It ought to be remembered that malarious disorder is very multiform, and that, especially in London, for one case of actual ague we may have fifty of variously modified disorder. The following is an instance: A medical friend, who had twice had ague, and had resided in a malarious district, but had been for some time in London, experienced for three consecutive mornings chills occurring at 11 A. M.; on the fourth morning he had instead acute neuralgia of the neck and shoulder at the same hour; on the fifth he had neither chills nor neuralgia, but epistaxis at the same time; he had not provoked it in any way. A very strong reason for acquainting ourselves thoroughly with the obscurer forms of these affections is, that they are not self-limiting, like our ordinary continued fevers, but are evermore, unless arrested by remedies, prolonging their weary course by perpetual relapses and recrudescences. I doubt if any diseases are more wearying and distressing than those I am now alluding to.

The first I shall more particularly notice is a disorder which is by no means uncommon in young children between the ages of 2 and 10 years, and to which I have given the name of Malarioid Remittent. It has quite the character of a re- or intermittent fever, the paroxysms occurring at night, while the day is more or less free. The illness commences gradually, and has often lasted several weeks before the little patient is brought for medical treatment. It is usually regarded at first as some casual derangement of the stomach or bowels even by medical men. In well-marked cases there is drooping, languor, fretfulness, and loss of appetite by day, while at night the sleep is restless and disturbed, and not unfrequently there is considerable delirium. This delirium may be the prominent, indeed almost the only symptom, of which the following is an instance.

No. 161.—W. H. B., m., æt. 5, seen April 1st, 1859. He had been under my care nearly two years before with considerable nightly delirium and screaming, and with lameness of the right leg and neuralgic tenderness of both. I was then suspicious of scrofulous hip disease, but neither I nor one of my surgical colleagues could discover sufficient evidence that such existed. He was then treated with quinine in 2 doses at 7 and 9 P. M., and recovered so far that he slept well, and only halted in walking without having any actual pain in the legs. He had now come into the hospital with manifest hip disease; an ulcer was discharging near the left. While awake in the day he was pretty well, but if he slept, or at night during sleep, he talked wildly and screamed so much as to disturb the other patients considerably. When asked if he was in pain he answered no, and promised not to scream again. My advice was asked respecting him, as it was found that he had been an out-patient of mine some time before. I gave him at first gr. iij of quinine in 2 doses at 6 and 8 P. M., but after three days of this treatment the screaming was even worse. The quinine, however, did not otherwise disagree, so I doubled the dose. From that time he ceased to scream and slept quietly during the three weeks he remained in the hospital. The discharge from the hip also lessened materially, and his general state improved. The persistent character of the disorder was very evident in this instance, as well as the action of the remedy, which fully justified the diagnosis. The history shows also the necessity for duly adjusting the dose of a remedy, and not rejecting it too hastily as inefficient or even injurious, which might have been supposed to be the case here. In very many cases some of the organs are more prominently affected than others. Thus we may have cerebral, or thoracic, or abdominal symptoms, which will simulate, and sometimes very perplexingly, substantive disease of the various viscera. I shall adduce instances of each.

No. 162.—T. M. A., æt. 2, m., ad. Jan. 10, ill 14 days. Had two fits first, and one last night; during the fits and at other times beats his head as if he had pain in it, and works his occiput against the pillow. Always screams when pain takes him in the head. From 5 P. M. to 5 A. M., is very restless and delirious. Is dreadfully irritable even in the daytime. Has only vomited once, and that was yesterday. No typhoid spots. Pupils of medium size. Knits his brows. Head rather hot and skin generally. Bowels costive. No appetite. Tongue clean. Pulse feeble and quick. Hirud. ij, temporibus. Hyd. c. cretâ gr. ij *h. s.* Quin. disulph. gr. j *ter die.* 13th. Had a double dose of quinine last night, and passed a very good night; did not disturb his mother once. Healthy motions. Quin. disulph. gr. ij o. n. Pt. c. gr. j *bis die*. 17th. No fever now, head cool, has fair nights. 31st. Sleeps much better, looks very well, but has no appetite. Omitted mist., hyd. c. cretâ gr. j *alt. noct.* Feb. 7th. Much better. Discharged. It is not too much to say that there was grave reason in this case to fear the existence of meningitis, probably tubercular. No doubt there was considerable hyperæmia of the brain, but this was more from arterial dilatation in consequence of vaso-motor nerve paralysis, than from actual inflammation of the cerebral tissue. As the nerves were toned and the vessels contracted the hyperæmia subsided. Had a different plan been pursued, as repeated doses of calomel, it is highly probable that the case would have terminated unfavourably. It is desirable to digress slightly here to call attention to certain rheumatic affections of the head in children which resemble the cerebral form of malarioid remittent a good deal, but require a different remedy. I allude to pot. iod., which I have found on several occasions very serviceable when the symptoms had a rather threatening resemblance to acute hydrocephalus. The following is an example :—

No. 163.—C. A., m., æt. 7, ad. Feb. 7th, ill five days. Complains dreadfully of pains at back part of head. Is restless and convulsed at night, "working with his eyes." Appears "lost in thought" at times, stupefied I suppose. Pulse feeble. Skin cool. Bowels costive. Very weak and languid. Quin. disulph. gr. ij *ter die.* 21st. Same pain, sleeps very little better. Pot. iodid. gr. iss. Dec. cinch. ℥ss *ter die.* Hydr. c. cretâ c. pulv. rhei *alt. noct.* 28th. Sleeps quite well, and does not complain of pain in head. Pt. mist. c. tr. cinch. ℥ss ad ℥ss; ol. morrh. ℨj *ter die.* No recurrence of symptoms by March 17th, when he ceased attendance. An important element of diagnosis between these and more serious diseases is the non-progressive character of the disorder in the former; the symptoms do not become materially worse, though two or three weeks have elapsed since their first appearance. In tubercular meningitis there is not the same degree of fever at night, but more tendency to irritability of the stomach and retinæ. Trousseau indicates depression of the abdominal walls, the tache cérébrale, paralysis most marked on one side, dilated pupils, strabismus, constipation, extreme rapidity of the pulse, stupor interrupted occasionally by a single loud cry, and great irregularity of breathing as the characteristic symptoms of this almost hopeless malady. In doubtful cases it will generally be well to act on the more favourable view, and to give either pot. iod. alone, or pot. iod. with quinine. A few doses will usually give us results which will materially aid to determine our diagnosis. Dr. Coldstream[1] speaks very favourably of pot. iod. in substhenic inflammatory disease of the brain in children.

The next variety I shall notice is where chest symptoms predominate.

No. 164.—E. L., f., æt. 6, ad. Feb. 2d, ill a week. A fair, pretty child. Has violent cough, no appetite, some days has much fever. Is very restless and coughs badly at night. T. red and coated. P. quick and weak. Good breathing all through both lungs. Is worse at night and very thirsty. Subject to these attacks every five or six weeks since her infancy. Ferri et quin. citrat. gr. v *ter die*, gray powder and rhubarb twice a week. In a week she was sleeping much better, in fourteen days the cough was almost gone, and the appetite was very much better. By March 12th she was well.

No. 165.—W. D., æt. 8, m., ad. Sept. 6th, having been ill on and off since he had an attack of the same kind fifteen months ago. Blue eyes, light hair, intelligent face, rather prominent forehead. Is very fond of reading. Has lost much flesh. At times has a "nasty dry cough." Complains of uneasiness at the lower part of the sternum. Good breathing in the backs, some crepitation is heard below the right clavicle. Abdomen normal. Skin hottish with perspiration on face. Does not sleep well at night, rambles and talks. He varies much; one week he is all life and spirits, the next much depressed. Hydrocyanic acid and salines *ter die*. 9th. Lies sleeping very much by day, is pretty quiet at night, takes food fairly. Râles are heard over both fronts and backs. Quin. disulph. gr. j *ter die*. 16th. Seems quite well, is up and running about. Cod-liver oil was now given with iron an quinine, and in another week he was discharged well.

In the first of these two cases there was nothing remarkable except the cessation of the cough without the use of any sedative. In the second the resemblance to phthisis was so considerable that I paused a few days before I gave tonics. The physical and mental constitution of the child, the emaciation, the cough, the sub-clavicular râle with the febricitation, pointed very much in the direction of tuberculosis. The extension of the râle all over the chest a few days later warranted the hope that the chest affection was only catarrh, and the result of tonic treatment soon made the case quite clear.

No. 166.—A. E. D., f., æt. 2¼, ad. March 10th, ill two months. Looks seriously ill, has emaciated rapidly the last week. Has a bad cough, wheezy perspiration, no appetite, bowels costive, skin hottish, tongue coated at back, tip red, thirsty, likes cold drinks, lips pallid, legs cold. Very fretful, very restless at night, but not delirious. No dulness, but moist crepitant râles all through posterior parts of both lungs, harsh breathing in fronts. Father died consumptive. This child, as she lay in her mother's arms, looked so ill, and the symptoms, together with the history, pointed so much in the direction of tuberculosis (diffused miliary), that I feel very desponding as to the result. But there was just a hope that the disease might be malarioid

---

[1] "Edin. Med. J.," Dec. 1859.

fever with chest complication, and, as this was far the more hopeful view, I resolved to act upon it. It was quite clear to me that it was not a case of mere ordinary bronchitis; the peculiar and deep prostration evidently betokened either fever or some grave organic disease. Turpentine stupes were ordered to the backs, pulv. Doveri gr. iij *o. n.* and quinæ disulph. gr. j *quater die*, dissolved by citric acid in citrate of potash saline. 17th. More cough, but appetite much better; has slept pretty well; much less râle in backs; air enters freely. Quin. disulph. gr. xx, acid. sulph. dil. q. s., liq. opii sedat. ℳxxx, aquæ ʒvj. M. ʒss *ter die.* Pt. pulv. 24th. Much better, much better night's rest; cough still troublesome; clear breathing without râles in both backs. Pt. Ol. morrh. ʒj *ter die.* April 18th. Quite well.

Abdominal complications are more rare than I should have expected; they occur both as neuralgia, diarrhœal, or dysenteric purging.

No. 167.—E. B., f., æt. 6, ad. April 7th. She had been ill one week with a bad cough and much expectoration; could not rest at night, and moaned in her sleep. During the first week a cough mixture containing chloric ether was given, gray powder and rhubarb. 14th. She complained of very severe abdominal pain, which, however, did not seem like that of peritonitis, and lay in bed constantly whining and crying. She was very weak, and perspired very profusely. No thirst. B. open. Urine red and thick. Coughs much, but there are no râles in the chest. Heart's sounds normal. Cat. lini abdomini. Ferri et quin. citrat. gr. v, acidi hydrocy. dil. ℳij, liq. opii sed. ℳij, aq. ʒss *ter die.* 17th. She had ceased to complain of pain in the abdomen, but was feverish, thirsty, and perspiring dreadfully, and had pain in her legs. T. moist and clean. Pt. 21st. Much better, but fearfully weak, and seemed to have lost the use of one of her knees. 28th. Much better, but still very weak; can move her knees better. She continued iron and quinine with ol. morrh. for another month, and made a good recovery. About a year later she came under treatment again with similar disorder, only that there was now chest affection instead of intestinal. With iron and quinine and oil she again recovered well.

No. 168.—H. J., m., æt. 5, ad. April 19th, ill four weeks. Skin hot. P. rapid. Breathing harshish in both backs, without much râle. Abdomen not very tense. B. relaxed much, motions very offensive. Emaciated greatly, used to be very stout. Slight cough. I gave him at first gray and Dover's powder *ter die* and ol. morrh. After three days the powder was given at night only. 26th. Looks very ill, lies in his mother's arms utterly prostrate. B. have been quieter, but are more relaxed again. No appetite. Pt. olio. Bismuth and opium *post sing. sedes liquid.* May 3d. Much more appetite. B. quiet; motions very dark and offensive. Pt. c. mist. et oleo. 24th. B. are in much better state, but still apt to get loose; has had marked pyrexia, but there is less now. Sweats most copiously at night, and by day if he sleeps. Gaining flesh. Quin. disulph. gr. xviij, acid. s. dil. q. s., liq. opii sed. ℳxxv, aq. ʒjss—ʒj *bis die.* After this he improved decidedly, the sweating diminished, and he was well in three weeks.

In both these cases there was exceeding prostration, which, in the absence of sufficient organic disease to account for it, should always direct our attention to the nervous system. In both also there was very copious sweating, which is often, with due regard to the circumstances under which it occurs, a valuable indication of a neurolytic state, and of the need of nervine tonics. The neuralgia in the first case was as evidently dependent on debility of sensory, as the sweating was on a like state of vaso-motor nerves. In the second case, both the intestinal and cutaneous fluxes evidently resulted from the same nerve disorder. At the time the latter case occurred I was less familiar with malarioid remittent, or I should have given the quinine much earlier. In place of sweating a roseolous rash sometimes occurs, which is evidently a phenomenon of the same kind produced by flushing the capillaries of certain districts of the skin with blood through relaxed arteries. The circumstance whether the hyperæmia affects the superficial strata of the skin or the deeper is probably one of the causes which determine whether there shall be a roseola or a diaphoresis. I think that no one can observe such cases as those I have related, and which it is difficult to describe fully, without being struck by the confirmation they afford to the doctrines stated at p. 25 *et seq*. The phenomena in some instances are as instructive as any experiment.

There is one symptom I have not mentioned which is extremely well marked in many cases of this fever. It is met with certainly in other morbid conditions, but yet it is a valuable sign, and may aid materially in establishing the diagnosis. Wherever it occurs I believe it may be taken as an indication that there is considerable nerve debility. The symptom I refer to consists in a peculiar dark rather broad rim beneath the lower eyelid, deepest in tint near the inner canthus, and gradually lessening in shade as it curves outwards. It is most evident in the early part of the day, and would not I think be observed when fever was present. As to the cause of this appearance I am uncertain; it may be owing to actual discoloration of the skin in this part with morbid pigment, which becomes more evident when there is pallor of the surface. The disappearance of the dark rim as recovery ensues would, however, be against this view.

This fever is evidently not identical with the classical remittent fever of children, which is usually regarded as typhoid. The latter is, in my experience, far from being a common affection, while the one we have been considering is decidedly frequent. The influence of remedies is besides so marked in the malarioid fever that it cannot for a moment be ranked with typhoid. I have made no post-mortem examinations, but I cannot conceive that they would strengthen essentially the evidence already adduced. The term malarioid is, I think, quite justified both by the character of the phenomena and the marked success of quinine. The occurrence of such fever is a further evidence of the existence of aguish miasm of actual London origin. As to season of the year, there has not appeared to be a very marked prevalence in one period rather than in another. In the last three months of the year it seems to be more frequent than in April, May, or June, and about as frequent as in July, August, and September.

The following history is, I think, one of much interest, though it will seem to many at first sight that it has little claim to be placed in this volume.

No. 169 —St. C., æt. 3½ years, m., ad. May 9th, ill three weeks. The abdomen has gradually enlarged without pain or tenderness; no other morbid condition preceded except some failure of health. The feet and legs are natural. The abdomen is dull and fluctuating, is considerably distended; when he is turned to one side the upper does not become resonant, there is resonance only in the epigastrium. The liver does not descend below the ribs. All the time he has been ill his appetite has been lost, and he has emaciated much. Heart's sound normal. Natural breathing in both backs. T. clean. Urine not free, not red. B. much relaxed five or six times daily. Another child died lately with large abdomen in two days. The urine examined three days later was scanty and lateritious, but free from albumen. On May 23d the urine was very alkaline, scanty, and thick, deposited phosphates, and contained a vast deal of carbonate of ammonia. The quantity of peritoneal effusion was undiminished. He slept very sound and perspired very much at night. May 30th. Urine still alkaline, and effervescing strongly with nitric acid. Appetite now very great, is always asking for food. June 9th. The urine was more free, acid, and not albuminous; his health was much improved, and the quantity of fluid in the abdomen had very much diminished. July 7th. Discharged, perfectly well, better than he was before his illness. The treatment consisted at first of gray and Dover's powder, āā gr. ij *ter die*, with iod. pot. and nitre mixture; after three days this was changed for a diuretic mixture containing digitalis and ungt. hydrag. to the abdomen, as the bowels were very relaxed and the stools green. Four days later iodine was painted over the abdomen in place of the mercurial ointment, and diuretics continued. Two days after this things were getting worse; he had passed no urine for twenty-four hours; the skin was blistered by the iodine. I thought the kidneys must be congested, and ordered a blister to each loin, and ant. pot. tart. gr. ¼ *ter die*. Three days later I had to omit this medicine, and I prescribed gr. j of quinine *o. n.* In two days there was some improvement; the urine was then as stated above on May 23d: I gave then in addition tr. ferri muriat. ♏v *ter die*, which he took up to the time of his discharge.

REMARKS.—At the time when I treated this case I knew much less about nerve disorder than I do now, otherwise I should have given iron and quinine much sooner and more boldly than I did. I suppose I need not say that I should not often advocate such remedies alone in dropsy. But this was a peculiar case in which the ascites had come on without apparent cause, where the kidneys and heart appeared to be sound, where, as the event proved, there was no peritoneal tubercle, but where there was, as the alkaline ammonical condition of the urine showed, great depression of vital power. Moreover, there was diarrhœa, which, in the absence of inflammatory disorder or organic disease, may be fairly referred to paresis of the vaso-motor intestinal nerves. From some peculiarity in the child's system the peritoneal vessels became similarly affected to those on the mucous surface, and serous effusion ensued. It is quite clear that perseverance with diuretics would most likely have destroyed life, and would not have removed the dropsy. Tonics, on the other hand, by raising the general power and contracting the relaxed vessels, had the desired effect. The case was, I believe, one of obscurely-developed malarioid remittent. It is well known that dropsy is not an uncommon sequel of intermittent fever. Flint[1] mentions that in ten cases out of twenty-two of ascites the dropsy had supervened on more or less numerous attacks of this disorder. He thinks with regard to ascites generally that more success will be attained by resorting early to tapping, and relying more on tonic medicines, iron and quinine, than by confining treatment to the use of diuretics and hydragogue cathartics. The spontaneous decomposition of the excretions has been well pointed out by Dr. Inman as a sign of failing vital power. It was present very markedly in this case, and was no doubt the cause of the highly ammoniacal condition of the urine. There was no mucus in the fluid to act as a ferment; the decomposition can only be referred to an alteration of the normal properties of the secretion itself. Lastly, I would observe how strongly the case testifies against prescribing according to the mere name of a disease, and how it sets forth the necessity of studying the pathological condition existing in each case, as well as the "lædentia" and "juvantia."

The next subject I propose to notice refers to a disorder essentially similar to that we have just considered, but presenting usually much less distinct symptoms, and affecting adults. This is the "obscure remittent" of Dr. Macculloch, which is often a very anomalous and difficult disorder to deal with. Persuaded as I am that such a disease exists, and is not very rare, I feel strongly the need for sobriety of judgment and careful investigation before concluding that in any given instance the disorder is really of this nature. As the nervous system is prominently affected, as the febrile manifestations may occur at night and seldom perhaps be well marked, as the disorder is chronic and often obstinate, and apt to be attended with anomalous symptoms, it is no wonder if the perplexed practitioner is much disposed to vote it all hysteria or hypochondriasis. I must refer here to the section on hysteria for the grounds on which our diagnosis from that state should be based, and will only remark that we should be cautious in using an ill-understood term to designate that which we feel ourselves to be obscure. Of course due pains should be taken to discover any existing organic disease, or any pernicious habit, or consuming mental distress, which may account for the bodily suffering. Supposing, however, that none of these can be detected, or appear adequate to explain the morbid phenomena, it is well worth considering whether the patient be not labouring under this form of malarioid disease. Besides the possibility of the disorder having originated in London, which has been proved by the evidence I have adduced, it should be considered how very practicable it may be for an individual on a journey of business or pleasure to "pick up" an aguish taint at some place where the causes of it are rife; and those who have most experience of such matters I believe will agree with me that, like syphilis, such a taint once

---

[1] "Amer. J. of Med. Sc.," April, 1863.

contracted is with difficulty ever shaken off, at least as long as the subject of it is exposed to the wear and tear of an ordinary active business life. The existence of the obscure remittent among us is fully recognized by Dr. Copland, whose world-wide experience of the morbific action of malaria makes his testimony peculiarly important. Writing about 1850, he states that he believes malaria to be far oftener present than has been imagined, more especially of late years, and around the metropolis. He adds that "by mistaking this fever for other diseases the sufferings of the patient are often materially aggravated, whilst having recognized its nature and cause not only the means of cure, but those of prevention become obvious." Between cases of a milder and more obscure character there intervene all grades up to those where the symptoms of bodily disease are evident and striking, although the nature of the efficient cause may be matter of great question. I proceed to relate sundry cases in illustration of this subject, taking first those of the more positive stamp just alluded to.

No. 170.—G. R., æt. 32, a carpenter, ad. July 19th. Generally has good health, has been ill three weeks. He was first attacked at Dover with shivering occurring every night followed by violent sweating; he had pains in the knees and soles of feet. He still shivers every night more or less, but has no sweating. He complains of debility, pain at the back of the head, and exhaustion on the least exertion; has bad nights, no appetite. The pulse is very feeble, the tongue covered with white-capped papillæ, skin cool. B. costive, urine dark coloured. Has pain across loins and in the left shoulder. The stomach and intestines are shrunken; there is no enlargement of spleen or liver. The thoracic organs are healthy. Pot. iod. with ammon. carb. and tr. cinchon. was given at first for three days, besides two doses of calomel and colocynth, but without any advantage. 22d. The stomach can retain only milk and beef-tea; there is no epigastric tenderness. He is so feeble that he can hardly stand. Quin. disulph. gr iij *ter die*. 25th. Somewhat better. P. very weak. Urine exceedingly dark coloured. Pt. c. quin. *quater die*. Chop and porter. From this time he went on steadily improving, and was discharged well Aug. 12th. As he improved, the urine became of a much lighter colour.

This man undoubtedly had quotidian fever, though while under my care the febrile symptoms were but slightly developed. It would be more exact to say that he was under the toxic influence of malaria, which caused the remarkable prostration. It did not appear that there was any other cause for this extreme debility, and the speedy way in which he rallied under treatment founded on this view confirms the opinion. The source of the poisonous miasm was by no means clear; if produced at Dover, as seems most probable, it certainly suggests the possibility that other towns may have the same undesirable privilege. The very dark colour of the urine, while the spec. gr. was moderate, shows that considerable waste was taking place in the blood-globules, whose decay furnished the abundant pigment. The arrest of this decay by quinine is a fact I have often observed; it seems to indicate that this wonderful nervine acts in part through the nerves on the blood in the vessels, diminishing over-active vital changes. The beneficial action of alcohol in acute disease is probably of the same kind.

No. 171.—W. C., m., æt. 32, excavator, ad. Sep. 16th. Ill four months; his illness came on gradually. I have no note as to his having been in any known malarious locality; my impression is that he had not. He seems to get worse every week. Aspect anæmic. Has the appearance of a man affected by some serious disease; his speech is slow and hesitating, and his whole manner of the same kind. Has headaches at night. Is very ill in the morning, can hardly draw his breath, and has cramps in the legs. Takes food fairly. Not much cough or expectoration. Skin cool. Feels very weak. P. feeble. Heart and lungs sound. Quin. disulph. gr. v *ter die*. In three days he was much better; at the end of seven he was still improving, and some neuralgia had appeared in the left frontal nerve. Soon after this he ceased attendance. This man had never had ague, and there was really nothing distinctive on which to found a diagnosis. The absence, however, of any organic disease which could account for the great prostration was strong ground for regarding the system as labouring under some serious toxic influence, and, as the symptoms did not appear to be those of the ordinary continued fevers, it was reasonable to attribute them to malaria.

No. 172.—Mr. S., æt. 40, seen Aug. 24th. Was born and lived at Wisbeach twenty-two years ago; never had ague. He has suffered from catarrh five weeks; bowels have been loose until the last few days; has a hollow cough, almost dry. Is emaciating much and losing strength. Has drenching sweats at night. Skin damp. P. weakish. Lungs emphysematous, heart displaced and liver lowered. Last four days has had pain across upper abdomen, not increased by food. With quinine + iron in pretty full doses he recovered, but his improvement was slow. It is not uncommon to meet with cases in which by day there are only symptoms of general debility, while at night some special phenomena of nerve disorder ensue. In one instance a female, æt. 32, stated that she woke up with a shivering fit at night about 1 A. M., the rigor lasted ten to fifteen minutes, was attended with palpitation, and succeeded by faintness and a sense of dread. With quinine gr. iv at 6 and 9 P. M., the attacks ceased. Another, æt. 31, after an asthenic bronchial catarrh complained of having much palpitation, which came on very often at midnight; she awoke up in trembling and perspiration. Another, æt. 40, who had been ill about four months, and had sickness and violent retching of a morning with some bowel disorder, described herself as waking up in bed at night in a state of semi-syncope. She benefited very much by quinine and change of residence from the vicinity of a canal.

No. 173.—X. Y., a strong-made medical man, æt. 40, until lately resident in the country, where he had for a long time been overworked, especially with midwifery at night. He suffered from irritability of the urethra at intervals, especially after great fatigue. His great distress now (June 13th, 1859) is from shifting rheumatoid pains, which remain scarcely more than two days in one part, but during this time make the affected part very tender and sore; they haunt the loins, hips, and shoulders. Muriate of ammonia has been taken, but without benefit. He takes food tolerably well. Urine=40 oz. in twenty-four hours, sp. gr. =1020, contains no uric acid. He complains of exceeding exhaustion; is even unable to read, which he is usually very fond of. His nights are wretched; he gets out of bed more than twenty times to change his position, as he is unable to turn in bed. Much perspiration at night. T. flabby. P. soft. Skin cool. A fortnight later, after he had improved in the interval, he had two very bad nights; the last was particularly bad. He had not ten minutes' sleep from distressing muscular spasm almost like tetanus, such that while lying on his back he could not breathe, and was compelled (though no chicken) to shed tears. When I saw him his pulse was open and very soft, and his skin damp. He told me that at night the part of the bed where he lay was so drenched with sweat that it might literally have been wrung out. I advised him to take gr. x of quinine at bedtime and two hours previously. He took this, went to bed, and lay quiet without spasm, but did not sleep for two or three hours; then he took a full glass of port wine and slept well for three hours, after which he awoke, took more wine, and slept again, so that he had a fairly good night. July 11th. Has been taking about gr. 20 of quinine every night and wine; has decidedly improved, but feels sore and stiff in various parts, and perspires copiously still. Urine deposits uric acid now pretty freely, the twenty-four hours amount = 5.53 grains. Relishes his port wine greatly and longs for it. 12th. Was quite delirious last night, and is exceedingly shaky to-day; walks tottering, and feels as if he should fall. 21st. For some days has had ferri et quin. citratis gr. x + tr. arnicæ m xv *ter die*, and is greatly better, sleeps better. 26th. Last few nights not so good. Quin. disulph. gr. v, *bis die*, and gr. x *o. n.* 28th. Is quite jolly and strong; two excellent nights; some rheumatism with swelling about ankles. Aug. 27th. Has been going on very well, taking gr. x to xx of quinine daily until this morning when severe purging and vomiting set in; he passed a gallon or more of pale liquid; had cramps in abdomen, and felt chilly and depressed. Purging stopped by sulphuric acid, spt. æth. s. co., and tr. opii. Thinks he is better than he has been for between two to three years, but still has the severe pain at night in the muscles of the back, which prevents him from turning in bed, and forces him to get out at the one side and in at the other. Sept. 17th. Is in greatly better health than for a long time, in excellent spirits, gaining flesh; has better nights, but still requires wine, and has to get out four or five times to change his position. He can walk but little. His bladder is much less irritable than it used to be; it will hold now 9 ounces, whereas last year it would only hold 3 ounces at a time. Oct. 5th. His chief complaint is now of his feet, which get very swelled and painful at night, more so than they used to be. They are easier after a night's rest, but very stiff, and do not subside to their normal size. Occasionally when he has had sharp sciatic pain the feet have been much better. Dec. 13th. Feet exceedingly tender and painful, so that he can barely walk; no quinine taken for a long time. Much depression. Pot. iod. gr. iv + ammon. carb. gr. v + tr. cinchon. ʒjss + dec. cinchon. ʒj *ter die* Sulphur-fume bath. 17th. Can walk now very much better. March 20th, 1860. Is now so far recovered that he can walk six miles without much inconvenience. He sleeps sound for five and a half hours at night, but is obliged to be lightly covered and to have the window open to avoid sweating. I have often seen him since, and know that he is in fair health.

REMARKS.—The exceeding causeless exhaustion, the great depression, the sleeplessness, the muscular spasm, the drenching nocturnal sweats, the delirium on one occasion, the beneficial effects of quinine and wine, and the asthenic rheumatic affections are very noteworthy points in this case. Mere asthenic rheumatism it certainly was not. Some toxic influence must surely have been at work so to prostrate a robust system which had long successfully battled with difficulties. This could hardly have been the less healthy atmosphere of London, because the effect of this would have been less acute and would rather have increased than diminished as time passed on. That the nervous system was especially affected was clear both from the symptoms and from the good effect of persistent tonic treatment. The under-current of rheumatism, which became so prominent as the symptoms of debility and prostration gave way, seemed to me to have a common cause with the rest of the disorder; reminding me very much of the case of a relative of my own who was invalided and sent home from India for subacute rheumatism, but recovered completely by the change to a colder climate. In this and many like instances nerve-debility, however occasioned, goes for very much more, I am persuaded, in the treatment of disease than any *materies morbi*. It is very worthy of notice that while the uric aid was absent from the urine at the time of the greatest depression, it increased and attained to a tolerably good figure as the general condition amended. This I have observed in other similar instances. It is by no means only in gout that the uric acid is deficient in the urine; this is also the case in various conditions where nutrition is much impaired. The patient was a man of more than average fortitude, endurance, and intelligence, and a better instance could scarcely be adduced of the severe and long suffering inflicted by this obscure malady. With a feebler system, or a less courageous spirit, I think it far from improbable that mental derangement might have ensued.

No. 174.—G. G., æt. 20, m., ad. Dec. 30th. Has a cough always in winter, father and mother died of phthisis. Ill one week, suffers with cough, great weakness, anorexia, night sweats. Does not sleep well at night, but is always drowsy. No dulness or morbid breath sounds under clavicles, some large bronchial râle in left lower back, none elsewhere. Never spit blood. Has now a good deal of expectoration. P. feeble, but distinct. T. rather coated. B. open. Urine rather high coloured. Is now bathed with perspiration, but is cold. Till to-day did not appear ill as at present, about noon became affected with faintness and perspiration. He appeared so seriously ill that he was made an in-patient under one of my colleagues. Dover's powder was given at night, and on Jan. 1st mist. spt. vini gall. was ordered. His further history is as follows. On the night of Dec. 31st or next morning he had three convulsive attacks, two slight fits and a severe one, was convulsed and became black in the face. He remained insensible all Jan. 1st, and did not speak; after an enema he appeared better. On Jan. 2d he appeared much better, was quite conscious, had appétite, and was well up to 11 P. M., when the sister left the ward, got in and out of bed to the night-chair by himself. Soon after this he changed, became delirious, was noisy and moaning, sank and died quietly about 9 A. M., of 3d—P. M., on Jan. 6th. Brain, heart, kidneys, liver, spleen, and stomach normal. Lungs engorged at back part, crepitant, no tubercles anywhere, but a soft cretaceo-fatty mass lay in the root of right lung. Thymus gland large. Supra-renal capsules enlarged, very firm, converted into firm scrofulous matter of marked yellow colour internally with spots of cretaceous deposit. Externally there was found a peripheral layer of grayish more translucent stuff consisting of fibroid stroma loaded with nuclei mostly round, and containing some groups of small masses of translucent homogeneous fibrin. ('speckig,' or bacony matter). The more yellow or opaque part is far advanced in fatty degeneration. The hair was curly, of demi-woolly appearance. The body had much of the dark tint of a mulatto; the penis and scrotum were large and very dark.

REMARKS.—The above was no doubt a case of Addison's disease, but yet it seems pretty certain that the patient did not die of that disease. The peculiar intermitting and ultimately fatal nervous affection must, I think, have been the result of some toxic influence acting *ab externo* on a system predisposed by existing organic disease to be dangerously depressed. The day I saw him, Dec. 30th, he was seriously ill and prostrate, the next day he seems to have been better, the day after he has severe head symptoms, the fourth day he is much better, and on the fifth he dies. This is much more like the doing of a pernicious fever than of uncomplicated supra-renal capsule degeneration. The latter alteration must have been of long standing, while the disorder which destroyed life seems to have commenced about twelve days before death as a bronchial catarrh. The same conversion seems to have occurred in this case as in No. 104, p. 220, where a similar affection transformed itself into a remittent fever with arterial spasm. Here again we have glimpses of the connection subsisting between influenza and malarious disease.

No. 175.—Mr. H., æt. 48, seen in consultation with Dr. Palmer Jan. 29th. He is a weakly man with feeble heart and emphysematous lungs. No valvular disease or hypertrophy. Insanity is hereditary in his family; his father died insane. Is a coach painter, no blue line on his gums. Has had neuralgic attacks the last fourteen days, had erysipelas before. The neuralgia began, while there were still remains of the erysipelas; it affects now both calves, and extends sometimes downwards to the feet. It comes on regularly every twelve hours at 1 A. M. and 1 P. M., and also is brought on by exertion, as in standing upright. Some similar pain has occurred in the situation of the biceps brachii muscle, and in the forearms, on both sides. The painful parts are not tender on pressure. Urine full coloured, clear, not albuminous. Agreed to give quin. disulph. gr. v *quater die*, and ferri carb. sacoht. ℈j *ter die*. Feb. 5th. His legs have been well now for three days, but he continues to suffer much in the arms and forearms, and also has shown distinct symptoms of insanity ever since the legs got well. For the last four days has had tr. opii ♏ 20 with each dose of quinine. 9th. Intellect more normal; pains shifting about, and less severe; both hands swollen, showing indications of rheumatism. Urine turbid and lateritious, deposits uric acid when treated with nitric. Gets very weak, can hardly move in his bed. Appetite very bad. Becomes very faint at night. Pot. iod. gr. viij, pot. acetat. gr. 20, spt. æth. nitr. ʒss, mist. camph. ʒj *ter die*. Pulv. Doveri, gr. x *h. s. o. n.* Wine and nourishment to be given freely. 12th. Pains much relieved, and has less faintness, is calmer. There is, however, marked anæsthesia of the feet, and complete paralysis of the right forearm muscles, so that the hand hangs powerless; the left hand being also paralyzed, but less completely. 14th. Is very much worse, rheumatic swelling gone, complete anæsthesia of the feet, and some way up the leg; same condition of hands and arms some way above elbows. Numerous petechial or purpuric spots on knees, feet, trochanters, and hands. Radial pulses barely to be felt, crural quite distinct and of fair apparent force. Sounds of heart very feeble. Is perfectly conscious. Tongue moist at edges, dry and black in middle. Bowels relaxed very much each night, not by day. Abdomen rather distended, right illiac fossa tender, distinctly more so than left. No unequivocal rose spots, one doubtful one. Both hands and feet quite powerless. Has taken a bottle of port wine daily the last two days besides Oss of brandy. In the evening vomiting began, everything was rejected; during the night he had no diarrhœa, but the vomiting continued in spite of ice. The asthenia gradually increased, and he died on 16th.

REMARKS.—It was certainly desirable to have had an autopsy in this case, and yet I doubt whether it would have thrown light on its obscurity. The patient, always a feeble individual, and having an hereditary tendency to nerve disorder, died in the uttermost state of adynamia after having presented a series of completely ataxic phenomena mainly referable to the nervous system. Erysipelas, periodic neuralgia, cerebral derangement, rheumatism, and paralysis of the extremities as to motion and sensation preceded the final collapse, during which, however, at least up to two days before death, the functional power of the brain had returned and was active. This picture is certainly not that of any of the recognized continued fevers of this country, nor do I think it is at all proved that the symptoms were the result of a malarious poison. Still the phenomena appear to me to point more in this direction than in any other. The tenderness in the right iliac fossa might certainly be the result of such intestinal ulceration as occurs in typhoid fever, but it might also occur from disease independent of this fever, as from inflammation and ulceration of the follicles of the cæcum and colon similar to that which is apt to ensue in dysentery. The agminate glands of the small intestine, according to Dr. Morehead, are affected in some cases of remittent fever. He gives two cases in his work (vol. i. p. 146, 157), in which Peyer's patches were enlarged and ulcerated. The nocturnal occurrence of the diarrhœa, the paralysis, the rheumatism, and the clear state of intellect two days before death are phenomena quite unlike those of typhoid fever. There is nothing to show that he was under the influence of gouty or lead poison. The periodic character of the neuralgia, and its replacement by rheumatism, while this again was succeeded by peripheral paralysis, are circumstances which are often paralleled in instances of malarioid disease. The previous erysipelas had no doubt further lowered the power of his originally weak system, and to this debility the severity and fatal tendency of the disorder was probably due rather than to any especial malignity in the efficient cause. Without asserting it as my settled opinion, I have long suspected, and I think there are some grounds for the view, that a form of fever exists which is neither typhus, typhoid, relapsing, nor febricula, which is more or less continued, and is allied to influenza, rheumatism, and malarious diseases. Of this I am disposed to think the following was an instance.

No. 176.—Mrs. T., seen August 15th, 1863. A married lady, resident in South Belgravia a short distance from the river, the smell of which she is persuaded affects her during the months of July and August. She has had four children in quick succession, and suckled the last seven months. She exposed herself to a chill during very hot weather, and was attacked with febrile symptoms, which increased for a week, and then obliged her to take to bed. When I saw her she had been ill fourteen days, and confined to bed the last seven. She was perfectly rational, and her countenance did not present the aspect of stupor. Her symptoms had been a very coated tongue, prostration, very high-coloured urine, loss of appetite, thirst, and frequent great flushing of the face and head in paroxysms, with succeeding perspirations. She had no splenic enlargement, nor hepatic, no decided tenderness in the ilio-cæcal region, very little diarrhœa (one day). There was a pretty copious papular eruption on her chest, the papules lowering down to spots on the abdomen, some of them resembling rose spots, but being rather larger; on the 16th this eruption had faded a good deal. She complained then of tenderness about the right upper part of the neck, and just behind the right ear, there was very little of any swelling. On 15th about 8 P. M., her pulse was 117; tongue red, denuded, moist, coated towards the base. On 16th at mid-day, the pulse was 96, skin cool and soft. The bowels, which had been confined four or five days, had been opened by a water enema; the stool was lumpy. 20th. Is gradually improving, but has considerable pain and swelling of the right parotid gland. This swelling did not suppurate, but she had a long and tedious convalescence, extending over fully three months. Towards the end of her disease evening accessions of fever and most violent evening accessions of neuralgia were marked features of her state. The neuralgia was centered in the enlarged parotid gland. Both symptoms were benefited by quinine, but ultimately change of air became necessary.

REMARKS.—It must be admitted as a not impossible occurrence that this case was *au fond* one of typhoid fever modified to some extent by malarious influence. As there was no autopsy, this cannot be disproved. The condition of the patient was altogether unlike that of ordinary typhoid fever in the aspect of face, the absence of stupor, the kind of eruption, the paroxysms of flushing of the head, the state of the bowels, the subsequent evening neuralgia, and the presumed cause. Parotitis may occur in remittent as well as in typhoid fever. I wish to avoid the typhoid controversy, but I cannot help stating that it is not demonstrated to my mind that enlargement, or even enlargement with ulceration of Peyer's patches, is a pathognomonic evidence of typhoid fever. I think it possible that enlargement, or even enlargement with ulceration, may be produced by other causes, and that of such a kind as might occur from typhoid fever. Where the symptoms during life differed considerably from those ordinarily observed in this disease, I should not regard the state of the intestines supposing them to be affected with typhoid alterations as diagnostic *per se*. Further, with the evidence I have at present, I cannot but think that a patient may have a copious eruption of rose spots, nearly disappearing in five days, considerable diarrhœa, tenderness in the ileo-cæcal region, and other symptoms of low fever, and die at the end of fifteen days without any morbid alteration being found in the intestines, or any other organ, except some congestion of the lungs. The intestines were carefully examined. My creed at present is that the great majority of continued fevers are easily distinguishable, but that the groups are not so exactly defined as to make it always possible to say whether a given instance belongs to one or to another. The case I think is similar to that of cancer and various other disorders. The types are well marked, and distinct, but in proportion as the special characters are more feebly developed we get transition instances, the exact nosological place of which it is very difficult to fix. The case I have related seems to me to have much more marked affinities with remittent malarious than with typhoid fever.

In concluding this subject I would ask attention to the bearing of a few facts, viz: (1) It has been shown that a cause capable of producing ordinary ague may be generated in London, *how*, I do not say. (2) Children in London not unfrequently suffer with disorder which has the character of a remittant, or quotidian intermittent, and is cured by quinine, or quinine + iron. (3) Neuralgia affecting various situations is not uncommon which yields to the same treatment. (4) The cause which produces influenza occasionally gives rise to inter or remittent fever and neuralgia. Now as London is not a place well calculated for generating malaria in the ordinary way, and as another cause appears to be capable of producing similar phenomena, it seems to me a question that may fairly be raised whether there may not be several causes or miasms, which, acting on the nervous system, produce the same or similar effects. When a person free from all ague taint gets a violent facial neuralgia which is cured by quinine in full doses, we can hardly avoid asking ourselves the question, what is the difference between such disorder and that of malarious origin? If the results are so like, must not the causes be like too? I think it may also be argued that it is certain that some such miasmata are very commonly and widely diffused, and that it is but reasonable to attribute to them a large share in the generation of our ordinary maladies. The results of their action are of very various character according to the state of the recipient. Generally, however, it may be stated that their main action consists in the depression of nervous power. According to the part specially affected the symptoms will vary; thus there may be cerebral depression, neuralgia, palsy, fever, or hyperæmia and exudation phenomena.

I may mention here that I have met in the course of the last year with two cases of quartan ague, occurring in labourers. One had contracted his ague at Deal, and had suffered with it at "spring and fall" for ten years. The other had received his taint at Tilbury in Essex five years previously. In the first the attack commenced about 1 P. M., in the second at 6 P. M. In the latter, as the fever gave way, a sharp paroxysm of neuralgia of all the divisions of the left fifth nerve occurred, and lasted all night from 4 P. M. This man attended six weeks, and had no attacks after the first seven days; he took quin. dis. gr. ij 2*dis horis* at first, and afterwards less frequently. The other took tr. cinchon. flav. ʒij 4 *tis horis;* he only attended eight days, but had no return after the second. These are, as far as I know, the only cases of quartan I have seen in the course of thirteen years. A mid-aged female at present under my care has a disorder which is apparently ague of octavan type. It has been arrested by quinine.

CHAPTER XXXVI.

SECRETION FLUXES.

No. 177.—J. M., æt. 28, m., ad. Jan. 14th. Ill three weeks, jaundiced, stools of a light, urine of a dark colour. Liver rather enlarged, projecting two fingers' breadth below the ribs. Some nausea. Sense of weight over eyes. Has pain referred to lower sternal region, worse after food. Tongue coated. No thirst. Skin cool. Pulse feeble. Has ear-ache. Feels very weak. Abdomen fallen. Hyd. chloridi gr. x statim, acidi nitro-muriat. ɱ v + liq. taraxaci ʒj + aq. ʒj *ter die*. 18th. Stools of a different colour altogether after the powder; mouth sore, tongue coated. Urine clear, but of a deep red. Podophyllin gr. ½ + extr. colch. acet. gr. ij *o. n. s.* Pt. c. mist. 21st. Not half so yellow as he was, but still markedly so. Stools of a good colour. Urine very red. Pulse very weak, soft. Pt. c. pil. et mist. 25th. Urine of a deep reddish colour, evidently from bile; stools dark coloured; pills have acted strongly, had seven motions on 23d, all darkish. Is still jaundiced. Perspires very much in a warm room. Pulse very weak. Appetite poor. Tongue coated. Seeing that though there was free bile flow into the intestine the jaundice continued to manifest itself in the skin, eyes, and urine, and that there was evidence of considerable debility, I thought it probable that the condition was one rather of bilious flux than of biliary retention or suppression, and I prescribed accordingly. Twelve grains of quinine were given daily. In three days there was improvement; in twelve days there was scarce any trace of jaundice; the urine was clear and of a natural colour, the stools rather light coloured. Nitric acid still detected a little play of colour when added to the urine. He was treated subsequently for another month on account of ear-ache (neuralgia) and cough, and was discharged on March 10th feeling as well and strong as ever he did. He had no cholagogue, or aperient medicine after he began the quinine.

REMARKS.—My first acquaintance with the above kind of disorder was in the case of an officer serving in the Crimea, who was highly jaundiced, but passed at the same time a large amount of bile in his stools. "Lots of blue pill and calomel" were given, as well as some emetics, to get rid of the bile, but it appeared to him "that he made more as fast as it was carried away." During his voyage to England the jaundice disappeared, but remittent fever came on and increased so much that he was much more seriously ill when he reached his destination than when he embarked. When he came under my care at home he was greatly prostrated, quite unnerved, and had nocturnal paroxysms of fever accompanied with determination of blood to the head. Quinine with change of air restored him. In cases of jaundice of this kind the probability is that the nerves of the hepatic plexus are paralyzed, and that in consequence hyperæmia ensues and increased functional activity. Salivation to some extent may be produced in the same way. Cutaneous fluxes are quite common in connection with malarioid disorder. The nocturnal sweating of phthisis has been rightly interpreted by Dr. Inman as the result of exhaustion, and, as I believe, dependent upon vasomotor paresis. Anything which causes great nervous prostration is apt to give rise to sweating. It is worth remarking that in the case above recorded there was debility and a neuralgia (ear-ache) from the first, and that he was very readily affected by the single mercurial dose. These are all indications that the nervous power was below par. The patient was a rather strongly made man. Dr. Copeland notices jaundice from exuberance of bile as one of the forms of the disorder, and refers to other authors who have described it. I have recorded in the *Med. Times and Gaz.*, Feb. 7th, 1863, a case in which this condition succeeded to one of inflammatory congestion. The practical value of correct pathological views is very apparent in such instances.

CHAPTER XXXVII.

HYSTERIA.

It seems to me quite necessary in a work professing to deal with disorders of the nervous system to take some notice of the above-named state. The term is confessedly not a very definite one, and it will be, I think, worth while to consider what meaning is generally attached to it as used by the profession. Dr. Prout states that "in hysteric cases the utmost duplicity and cunning may be displayed, where from mere appearances we should expect nothing but the most rigid truth—in short, the whole energies of the patient's mind are bent on deception." Her innate desire being to become an object of attention, if she fail to accomplish this by inspiring love, she falls back on the endeavour to excite commiseration. Dr. Watson writes: "The deceptive appearances displayed in the bodily functions and feelings find their counterpart in the mental. The patients are deceitful, perverse, and obstinate, practising or attempting to practice the most aimless and unnatural impositions." I believe that the majority of the profession agree with these statements, and that the term "hysterical" is commonly used to designate a patient whose complaints are considered to be more or less exaggerated, and who is not *bona fide* anxious to get well, and cease from being the object of nursing and sympathy. Dr. Copland considers increased reflex excitability of the nerves of the female generative organs as one principal causative condition of hysterical affections, and Romberg's opinion is nearly the same. The latter says: "From the time when hysteria has taken root, the reflex action preponderates throughout the organism and renders the individual more dependent upon external stimuli." He says, however, naïvely, when speaking of spinal irritation, "The patients generally being females, much deception is practised upon the medical men!" It seems to me that this view fitly applies to the bodily condition which is present in many hysterics, though not, I think, in all, but that it by no means sufficiently regards the psychical. An erethysm proceeding from the generative apparatus might, I can well conceive, give rise to erotomania; or to various spasmodic quasi-choreic affections, but hardly to the peculiar mental state which Prout and Watson recognize so fully, and which my own experience certainly leads me to look upon as the fundamental malady of the truly hysteric. There seems to me to be very little evidence in favour of the view that hysteria is the result of ovarian or uterine hyperæsthesia; in fact I should say the evidence of cases where such hyperæsthesia is present is opposed to it. It does not appear that females suffering with irritable uterus are more hysterical, often not so much so, than those who have no such disorder. Neuralgia of the ovaries is certainly a rare affection, very far more so than hysteria. All experience proves that much, I had said almost any, local treatment is injurious in real hysteria, but this would surely not be the case if Copland's and Romberg's theory were true. The point in question is one of most practical interest. If the essence of hysteria is a disorder of reflex excitability, it is as much a bodily disease as tetanus or chorea, and ought to have its cure attempted by remedies addressed to the deranged nerves or centres. But if the disorder *au fond* is what Prout represents it, then it must be apparent how futile such procedures must be. In arguing thus I take, as I think I have a right, typical forms of disease for instances, while I am quite ready to admit that there may be many intermediate morbid states compounded of various measures of bodily and mental disease. Having stated thus what seems to be the prevalent and to a great extent the correct opinion on this subject, I proceed to lay down and illustrate a limitation of it, viz., that the most marked and characteristic hysterical phenomena (according to ordinary parlance) may occur as the result of severe strain or exhaustion of the general nervous system in persons who are thoroughly honest, and have no morbid craving for sympathy. I will briefly relate a case of what I consider to be genuine hysteria, and then three cases of what I think would be falsely termed so.

No. 178.—M. K., æt. 27, f., ad. Sept. 12th. Has aphonia, can only speak in a whisper. Lies in bed with both legs crooked up with the heels against the buttocks, complains very much of pain when any attempt is made to straighten them. The limbs are rather but not very much wasted. Says that ten years ago she fell down and hurt one leg, which then became drawn up; two years ago she took cold and the other leg followed, and both have remained as at present ever since. Cannot pass her urine freely, she says, but on being examined is found to have passed a quantity under her. Chloroform was administered, and as soon as she became insensible the legs were brought straight down with perfect facility, and being thus disposed they were tied to the bedposts. 16th. Has scalded her face and mouth pretty smartly with boiling water on purpose; she was found with it. Sent out soon after. This girl was determined to be ill in one way or other, and as she was not allowed to persevere in her first plan she adopted another. Clearly it would have been futile to have given her physic, unless perhaps it had been the "*infusum benedictum*," which was once found effectual in curing a number of malingering soldiers, and which was compounded of a weak infusion of tobacco and Epsom salts!!

The following cases are of a very different stamp :—

No. 179.—F. U., f., æt. 30, single, ad. April 20th. Ill three years. Has no strength, legs are weak, feels suffocated at times, more so at night. Her throat is not sore, but her voice is weak. When the suffocative attacks come on her legs give way and she drops. At times she becomes quite unconscious for a few minutes. Gets worse at the end of the week, is better for the Sunday's rest. Works from 7 A. M. to 12 at night in a laundry. P. weak. T. clean. Ordered strychnia + tr. ferri muriat. + chloric ether *ter die.* May 4th. Has been better, but had a bad attack of choking and suffocation on 30th, when catamenia were present; "is always worse at those times." She continued the same mixture, or a very similar one, up to July 6th, and improved very considerably, so that the attacks occurred much more rarely than they had done; she had been without any when last seen for fourteen days.

REMARKS.—These attacks must have had much of the outward appearance of hysteria, since she herself described them to me as such. Yet surely there was cause enough in the unhealthy and excessive toil she had to endure for almost any amount of nervo disorder. Which of us, I should like to know, would not have collapsed under a long continuation of it? In spite, however, of her unfavourable circumstances, she rallied bravely, and gladly acknowledged the improvement in her health, the last thing which an hysteric is inclined to do.

The next case is similar.

No. 180.—E. S., æt. 17, f., single, ad. Sept. 22d. Ill twelve months, had improved, but has relapsed last three. Is hysterical, the attacks come on at the monthly periods; she becomes giddy, very nervous and weak at the chest, and goes off into convulsions at those times. The heat of the laundry-work seems to bring on the attacks. She takes food fairly, does not seem hyperæsthetic. T. coated. B. costive. With iron and quinine she improved steadily and satisfactorily during a period of more than two months.

No. 181.—Mrs. A——, æt. 35, seen June 28th, a very sensible calm person of well-regulated mind. Has not been feeling well for some days; her power of attention and her memory is impaired; cannot read as usual. Over-fatigued herself yesterday. Is now suffering severely with headache referred to the vertex compared to a heavy pressure, and darting through the head at times. Head not hot. Has much difficulty to restrain herself from "hysterical crying," finds a lump rising in her throat. Headache not increased by lying low. Had scarce any sleep last night. No appetite at all. With tonics and country air she soon got quite well.

Now it needs no argument to prove that these last three cases were totally different from the first, and different in the most important respect, viz., that their "*morale*" was healthy and sound, and that they were really desirous to get well. With the first mental perversion was almost the sole disorder, and I verily believe that the old treatment of lunatics, viz., a sound whipping, would have done her more good than all the drugs in the British Pharmacopœia. But the latter cases had much more of the commonly-recognized hysterical symptoms, viz., globus, crying, choking, and paroxysms of unconsciousness, than the first. Any practitioner would have called them hysterical, as indeed they called themselves. But it is plain they were not hysterical in the sense in which the first case was. Such, however, is the force of terms that I suspect very few would have acquitted them of some degree of the same mental perversion which characterized the first. Now this I hold to be an injustice against which I protest. According to the received use of the term hysterical among us, no one should, I think, be so designated whose mind is free from all exaggerating tendency, and who would scorn to practise malingering. Call them, if you please, weak-nerved, enfeebled, hyperæsthetic, or neurolytic, or anything which implies that solely their physical mechanism is failing and out of gear, but cast no suspicion on their immaterial part, perhaps braver and stronger than your own, which may never have been tried as theirs has. No doubt there are many cases of a mixed kind, where, together with real nerve debility and distress, there is more or less of mental infirmity, disposing the sufferer to exaggerate, or to make the most of their maladies. If, however, no proof of imposition can be discovered, and if the history of the patient shows that she has had much wear and tear of the nervous system, we should be slow to set her down as an hysteric because she has the classical symptoms more or less markedly. I speak from self-condemning recollections of patients whose complaints I had got weary of hearing, and whom I had come to set down as inveterate complainers not to be benefited by anything, who yet after a time have rallied, and shown that it was mere physical disorder which depressed them, and that there was no want of honesty. This, after all, is the main point; let a patient be but really anxious to get well, and there is fair hope of dealing successfully with her nervous disorders, however complicated they may be. But when the medical attendant once finds that disorder is simulated, or greatly exaggerated for selfish purposes, he had better conclude that moral treatment is needed and not medical.

CHAPTER XXXVIII.

SYPHILITIC AND RHEUMATIC NERVE AFFECTIONS.

IT is a question of considerable importance, but which I have no means of answering from my own experience, whether the syphilitic poison is capable of giving rise to nerve disorder independently of the production of organic disease. The analogy of gouty and rheumatic disease would lead us to an affirmative opinion. Dr. Williams, of Swansea, in a most noteworthy paper,[1] has brought forward evidence, showing that "one invasion of constitutional syphilis establishes a diathesis.... which may manifest itself in the system of the affected person for at least very many years afterwards. Under an apparent

[1] "Brit. Med. J.," April 12, 1862.

absence of all disease the subtle taint exists, though veiled and concealed by the deceptive garb of health, and may be communicated by the parent to the child." A diathesis he defines to be "a latent vital power which is capable of imparting a special direction to all morbid processes which may occur in the body during the period of its prevalence." He relates a case of severe bronchitis, one of pneumonia, one of apparent softening of the brain, and one of epilepsy, which were rapidly cured by remedies solely anti-syphilitic. I am strongly inclined to accept the above view, confirmed as it is by the analogies of malarious and rheumatic disease, which seem to modify other supervening disorders much in the same way as syphilis does. I am more and more disposed to think that the conception of a *diathesis* is a most important one, and that it must replace to some extent that of a poison, or "materies morbi," which has been carried much too far. Diday[1] holds that while secondary syphilis belongs to the class of virulent, *i. e.*, toxic, affections, tertiary belongs to that of diathesis, like some skin diseases and rheumatism. Individuals of feeble constitution are most liable to this unfavourable change of an intoxication into a diathesis, which renders the morbid phenomena much more inveterate. According to Williams's and Diday's views, it seems quite possible that neuralgia in any of its manifold haunts, or any other nerve disorder, might be *au fond* of syphilitic character, and most successfully treated with anti-syphilitic remedies. The following quotations from the work of a recent French writer go to confirm the above anticipation.

M. Zambaco relates three cases, which prove, he says, in the most incontestable manner that the syphilitic diathesis may attack the nervous centres, and produce profound dynamic disorders, without our being able to refer these disorders to a modification of structure; and this too even when there exists complete paralysis of motion and sensation. He quotes Gibert, Robert Melchoir, and Follin as holding the same opinion. In the first case a male, æt. 28, who had shortly before been cured of a double syphilitic sarcocele, died after having suffered about a month with almost complete paraplegia and impaired sensation of the lower limbs with paralysis of the sphincters. At the post-mortem the cord was found healthy, the lungs contained incipient metastatic abscesses. In the second case there was also almost complete paraplegia, but no loss of sensation. The patient, a male, æt. 58, presented a cicatrix on the penis and a well-marked syphilitic lichen within a month of his death. All the organs were quite sound. In the third case a chancre had existed six months before the patient came under observation suffering from an impetigo and an obstinate continual vague pain without precise seat, but felt deeply in the brain. This pain increased, and at the end of a month he was affected with incomplete right-side hemiplegia. Some days later the paralysis became complete and speech was lost, but not

[1] "Edin. Med. J.," April, 1862.

consciousness. The next day the feces and urine were passed involuntarily, the right arm was contracted, the left leg affected with subsultus, the tongue bitten by the teeth closed in trismus. Still no loss of consciousness or sensation. Violent contraction of the limbs ensued followed by coma and death. The brain and the cord were carefully examined and found healthy. A case is related of quotidian fever recurring daily at 5 P. M., which resisted quinine, but was cured by mercurials speedily. The patient, a female, had a papular eruption, but no very marked syphilitic symptoms. Two other cases were recorded of a similar kind, but in which the presence of syphilis was clearly evidenced. M. Zambaco believes that the disorders above described result from a perturbation of the nervous system under the influence of the syphilitic infection. Hysterical attacks of a well-marked kind not only coincide with the development of constitutional syphilis, but are cured by a specific treatment. Three cases of this kind are related in which the patient had been free from any hysteric affection before syphilitic disease appeared. It is worthy of remark that the attacks of nervous disorder were in all of them nocturnal, conforming in this respect to the ordinary pains of syphilis. In one instance obscure nervous symptoms continued for more than a year, until the discovery of syphilitic ecthyma declared the nature of the disease, and led to its speedy cure. Zambaco relates various cases of syphilitic neuralgia, many of them cured by specific treatment, but he does not decide positively whether these always depend on some actual lesion or not. Gjor[1] relates the case of a male, æt. 40, who three years before his death had marked symptoms of syphilis, and for the last four months paraplegia, which was at one time complete, but improved to some extent before his disease from phthisis. The cord was found perfectly healthy with the exception of some congestion of the veins of the pia mater at its lower part. There was nothing else except the usual changes in phthisis. In a second case, a female æt. 31, had had syphilis for at least five years, and died five months later completely paralyzed in all her limbs. The palsy commenced about $1\frac{1}{4}$ year before death, affected first the right side, and three months afterwards the left. It was attended with violent pains and spasmodic contractions of the limbs. Sensibility was diminished in the lower half of the body. The brain and spinal cord were perfectly normal. The lungs were congested posteriorly. Nothing else morbid. A third case is referred to in a Danish journal of the same kind.

In connection with the influence of syphilis on the nervous system I wish to make some reference to that of obscurely-developed rheumatism of a chronic kind. In the cases I have observed it seems to me rather doubtful what was the exact nature of the morbid action, but it was almost certainly either syphilitic or rheumatic, and as

---

[1] Schmidt's "Jahrb.," vol. ci. p. 299.

there were no traces of the former I am diposed to assume that the latter disease was operative.

No. 182.—R. G. P., æt. 40, m., ad. May 21st. Ill eighteen months; had a fit at first in which he seemed strangled, but did not struggle; for seven months after was very dull and silent, then went to work and continued at it till the last three months, but was not the same as before. The last three weeks he has been troublesome, has various delusions, has no power over the sphincters. On being asked, he says that he has pain all over the head. Sleeps very badly. Head hottish. Urine clear, non-albuminous. P. steady, natural. B. open. Pupils equal. No paralysis. No eruption. Denies syphilis: no traces of buboes or chancres. Used to suffer from rheumatism all about him. His treatment consisted of pot. iod. given for the first ten days at the rate of gr. vij *ter die*, and for the rest of the time at the rate of gr. x *ter die*, combined during the last month with tr. cinchon. Henbane was also given as a nightly sedative, gr. x of the extract *o. n.* This was replaced afterwards by extr. belladon. gr. ⅓. By June 8th he was, according to his wife's report, wonderfully altered for the better; he had more control over the sphincters. In fourteen days more he had become quite sensible and had gone to work. While awake he had tolerable control over the bladder, but at night there was much incontinence. My last report of him was on Aug. 3d, when he was at work and improving. Two or three weeks before he had a suppurating gland in the left axilla, but no cause of irritation existed in the range of the lymphatics.

No. 183.—W. D., æt. 43, carpenter, ad. July 3d, 1853. Subject to rheumatism about seven years, has had none for nearly twelve months. Is suffering as at present two months. His illness commenced with pain about umbilicus, followed by vomiting, which has continued about fourteen days; he keeps no food on his stomach. The pain extends over his chest and through to the back; it is increased by food, and is relieved by vomiting. Is seldom thirsty. Has little appetite. No epigastric tenderness. Pulse natural. Skin cool. Sleeps well. Bowels costive. Urine clear and free. Some slight thickening of skin, and desquamation over knuckles. Ordered pot. iod. gr. iij + ammon. muriat. gr. xv + vini colch. ♏v + tr. opii ♏iv + inf. gent. co. ℥j *ter die*. He improved at once; at the end of 14 days his appetite was very good indeed. He had no sickness, and his food digested well. July 31st. He is apparently well, but if he omits the medicine his appetite is not so good. I did not see him again until Jan. 19th, 1856, when he stated that he had been suffering two months with great pain in the left arm and between the shoulders. His stomach was all right. The pain was felt much about the insertion of the deltoid. It was very bad at night, compelling him to quit his bed and bathe his arm with warm water. He was treated with pot. iod. gr. iij — iv + dec. cinch. ℥j *t. d.* and linim. tereb. c. opio to the arm. By Feb. 2d he was very much better, had resumed work, slept till 7 A. M., and had only then a little pain. The medicide was continued with tr. cinch. When I saw him again June 13th, 1856, he was an in-patient. He stated that he had been taken ill in March with stiff neck, and the disorder proceeded over his head to the forehead, where it caused pain and aching of the eyes. He had double vision when he used both eyes except for a short time in the morning. The vision of the right was better than that of the left eye. If he shut one eye he could see objects close to him pretty well, but with both eyes they appeared misty.

This had been the case fourteen days. Had sharp pain in frontal region. No distortion of face or of tongue. During the last month he had not been able to use his left arm and leg, could move them now pretty well, but had a numbed sensation all down left side. In the fingers of right hand he had the same sensation, but had perfect use of that side. He had had no fit nor loss of consciousness. He had been at work for fourteen days after I last saw him, had been exposed to cold winds which brought on a relapse. By July 11th he had lost the sense of stiffness in the left side, the leg was well, but the hand was still lame and the vision double. He was treated with pot. iod. gr. iij. Aug. 16th, he became again an out-patient under my care. During the last week marked ptosis had ensued of the right eyelid, the pupil had become dilated and the sight of the eye was now worse than that of the left, which had previously been the weaker, but now was seeing fairly well. Both eyes appeared normal. There was throbbing pain in the right temple and across the forehead. Still has pain in left deltoid. Mouth rather drawn to right. No tenderness of scalp. Not much strength in left hand or arm. He took pot. iod. + tr. cinch. + sod. carb. + tr. nucis vomic. *ter die* till Sept. 17th, the left hand became a good deal stronger so that he could grasp fairly well, but the right pupil remained dilated, there was paralysis of the internal rectus, and the ptosis continued; the sight, however, was not much affected. I have not seen him since.

REMARKS.—It is I think certain that there were none of the ordinary signs of syphilis in this man, though I have no statement in my notes to that effect. Had any existed, they would certainly have been noticed during some of the many opportunities I had of seeing him. The affection was more like a shifting rheumatism than any other. Its location was first in the stomach, then in the left shoulder, then at the base of the brain, involving probably also the basal cerebral ganglia. Perhaps the disorder of the eyes was to some extent peripheral, the misty vision may have been produced by deranged accommodation. Iodide of potassium was of most marked benefit, but did not prevent relapses. It is tolerably certain that the head affection did not depend on any organic disease, and I think it very questionable whether there was any inflammatory action at all. In the first case the cerebral hemispheres and the mesocephale seem to have been most affected; the paralysis of the sphincters depended I conceive on a morbid inhibitory influence transmitted from the brain to the lumbar swelling of the cord. There is one reason which weighs with me to some extent to regard those cases as of rheumatic rather than of syphilitic origin, seeing that there were no clear indications of the latter, which is, that ordinarily nerve disorder seems to be much more a component element of rheumatism than of syphilis. The great tendency of the latter is to cause the deposition of a low form of exudation matter in nearly every tissue of the body, as Dr. Wilks well observes. Its affinities are decidedly with structural lesions, those of rheumatism with neuroses.

No. 184.—C. S., æt. 28, policeman, ad. April 7th. Ill two years. Has pain at lower part of back extending round left abdomen, sacral region of spine rather tender. Has seizures of tottering and weakness at times. Has much nervousness and excitement of left side, which passes away with flatus, after which he is much relieved. Has a large patch at the outer side of thigh which is numb, but that has been so for years, ever since he laid on damp ground. No sexual abuse. Has much walking which brings on the pain. Had rheumatic fever four years ago badly, and has never been quite well since. He improved to some extent with pot. iod. + tr. cinchon., but much more decidedly with citrate of quinine and iron + tr. nucis vom. The numbness of the thigh diminished materially. He was under treatment five months. It appeared to me in this instance.that there was certainly some affection of the cord itself of a rheumatoid or paretic character, and which I should compare to a rheumatic neuralgia. The disorder was certainly not mere lumbago.

CHAPTER XXXIX.

REMEDIES.

Some remarks on the action of the chief remedies employed in the diseases we have considered may be of advantage.

Quinine asserts its especial influence as a nervine by its power of controlling and curing neuralgia, not only malarious, but also when produced by influenza or mere debility. This proves that it has a special relation to the nervous system. Its power over malarious fever is explicable on the same view, it checks and arrests the paroxysms by virtue of its toning influence on the cerebro-spinal and sympathetic systems. That it is no antidote in the sense of chemically neutralizing the malarious poison, is quite certain, as it may be given to any amount in cases of visceral disease from this cause without the least curative effect; and as it often quite fails to eradicate the morbid influence from the system, as shown by the return of the disorder at spring and autumn or after exposure to trivial exciting causes, although the individual has long removed from a malarious locality. The peculiar effects which quinine produces when given in full doses, as buzzing in the ears, deafness, blindness, weakening of the pulse, can all be accounted for on the view that it tones and excites vaso-motor nerves to such a degree that the arteries of the ears, eyes, and heart become contracted, and the parts they supply anæmic. Its over-action in this way may be decidedly injurious. In one case it caused a distressing constriction of the throat, and in another a sense of fear about the heart. That the remedy is not merely an anti-periodic, as some call it, seems to me abundantly proved. There can be no question that it does actually increase and invigorate the general nerve power when given judiciously, both restoring it when depressed by debilitating disease, and enabling it as a prophylactic to resist morbid influences. The protecting power of quinine in preserving men in health who are exposed to malaria has been sufficiently demonstrated. The inference from all this is that quinine is likely to prove useful in all cases where nerve power is much debilitated, more especially when the vaso-motor system is especially at fault, and where in consequence fevers, congestions, or asthenic effusions take place. Thus in pneumonia of a low type where the lungs are gorged with blood, in asthenic rheumatic fever, in some cases of typhoid and typhus fever, in chronic relaxation of the uterus attended with menorrhagia and leucorrhœa, in bronchorrhœa, and in a multitude of analogous conditions where vascular atony is marked quinine may be given with the distinct view of toning and contracting the minute arteries and so arresting hyperæmia and exudation, while at the same time it elevates the power of the crebro-spinal system. Its use in various states of debility is in a measure limited by its tendency already mentioned to cause contraction of arteries to an undue extent so that the functional energy of the heart and other important organs may be notably impaired from defective supply of blood. This, however, is most to be feared when there exists considerable hyperæsthesia. Like all remedies of this class, quinine has the disadvantage of being liable to act as an irritant to the various tissues, so that in inflammatory disorders it is often a matter of great doubt whether it can be employed without risk of doing harm. Much, however, may be done in many instances to obtain toleration of the remedy either by giving it in small doses, or by exhibiting it in combination with some modifying agent. Thus Dr. Morehead[1] finds the administration of quinine together with small doses of antimony to produce excellent results in pneumonia both primary and attendant upon malarious fever. It also acts very well in certain cases when given along with a small quantity of calomel or blue pill. It is by no means necessary that the tongue should be clean before quinine is exhibited, but it is always desirable, often essential, that there should be no visceral congestion. Great mischief may be done by pushing quinine without giving heed to this precaution.

Arsenic is in many respects a similar remedy to quinine, and has besides some peculiar actions of its own, which are significant of its general *modus operandi*. It stands next to quinine in its power of controlling malarious fever and neuralgia. It has a very marked efficacy in preventing the recurrence of menorrhagia, more so indeed than any other remedy with which I am acquainted. It arrests the exudation of eczema, impetigo, and pemphigus when these eruptions are not of an acute and sthenic character, *i. e.*, where the tissues are not very easily irritated.' If the reverse is the case, arsenic will surely aggravate the disorder. It has a considerable effect in stilling the jactitations of chorea, and acts in a somewhat similar way in diminishing the tendency to recurrence of asthmatic bronchial spasm. Mr. Hunt mentions that small doses of arsenic are of eminent utility in checking chronic diarrhœa, or gastric irritation, although the opposite effect is apt to ensue when the medicine is given under different conditions. Mr. Spender mentions a very confirmative instance. V. *Brit. Med. J.*, Jan. 16th, 1864. The

---

[1] "Dis. of India," vol. ii. p. 370.

following is to the same effect. A healthy female, æt. 25, while suckling took by mistake two ♏ xxx doses of Fowler's solution, in consequence of which her breasts became perfectly dry. After the medicine was omitted the milk returned abundantly. The same seems to hold good of its action in conjunctivitis. Here we cannot but observe a remarkable agreement between its action on the internal and external tegument. The reading of these various facts seems tolerable easy; it seems clear enough that arsenic given either in too large doses, or in irritable conditions of the system, acts as a *tissue irritant*, inflaming the skin and mucous membranes, and perhaps other parts. On the other hand, it is evidently a nervine tonic, acting on both departments of the nervous system; increasing their vital power, and enabling them to resist the morbific influences. Its action on the vaso-motor nerves, especially those of the cutaneous and uterine vessels, is very marked, effecting the contraction of the arteries supplying these parts, so that hyperæmia is diminished, and serous and sanguineous discharges are arrested. The French commission report that arsenic is a most powerful febrifuge, and has unquestionably the property of reducing engorgements of the spleen. This latter action (like the former) must surely be ascribed to its tonic influence on the nerves of the splenic artery in consequence of which the undue supply of blood to that organ will be reduced to more nearly its normal amount. The curative action of arsenic in chorea and asthma may be explained in a like way by regarding it as a tonic of nerves or nervous centres which are weak, unduly excitable and mobile. In chorea the cerebro-spinal, in asthma the vagi nerves feel its beneficial influence. Schmidt and Stürzwage[1] have determined that small doses of arsenious acid produce a considerable diminution of metamorphosis (20 to 40 per cent). Both the urea and the pulmonary CO_2 were lessened, and corresponding quantities of fat and albumen were retained in the body. I think it will be admitted that the above exposition of the *modus operandi* of arsenic is at least consistent with itself, and that the original assumption explains naturally all the therapeutical facts with which we have become acquainted empirically. It has the advantage of doing away, as in the case of quinine, with any notion as to the *specific* action of the remedy, and of reducing the various phenomena under an intelligible and rational principle. The chief difference between quinine and arsenic seems to lie in this, that the latter is much more of a tissue irritant than the former, and has more special localities for its operation. Dr. Hughlings Jackson has suggested to me that the therapeutic virtue of arsenic may depend on its replacing phosphorus, or some other isomorphous constituent of nervous tissue which has come to be deficient. This is not at all improbable, and at any rate there can be no doubt that arsenic improves the nutrition of the nervous system. In the administration of arsenic much

---

[1] "Parkes on the Urine," p. xxiii.

may be done to adapt the remedy to the special state of the system. Thus it may be given with a saline when there is a tendency to inflammatory excitement, or with tr. cinchonæ when depression and weakness of circulation are prominent features. The addition of a little opium is a useful guard to obviate intestinal irritation, and should generally be made, when it is requisite to give rather large doses, as is the case in ecz. figuratum, in malarious fever[1] and some instances of sciatica.

Iron requires merely a brief mention as a nervine tonic. The saccharated carbonate, and citrate of quinine and iron are the most useful forms. I have tried the corresponding hypophosphite, but it does not seem to have any advantage. In cases where the urine is acid and lateritious with accompanying fever and prostration, and where it is doubtful whether quinine alone will be borne well, it often answers to give citrate of quinine and iron with citric acid and bicarbonate of potash, so as to combine the tonic with an effervescing saline to which also a few drops of hydrocyanic acid may be added. The recent investigations of Pokrowsky[2] show distinctly the chief effect of iron to be manifested in improved nutrition, the animal temperature being raised, the urea secretion augmented, and the weight of the body increased. He states that all preparations of iron act alike. I should qualify this by adding *if they are equally well digested by the stomach*. M. Cordier[3] has recently adduced evidence to show that lactate of iron interferes less with digestion than any other chalybeate, even than " fer réduit." This might be important to remember in dealing with great anæmia associated with irritability of the stomach, where the ordinary preparations of iron cannot be tolerated.

Strychnia is a nervine tonic which addresses itself specially to the motor-nervous apparatus of the cerebro-spinal system. It finds its opportunity in all cases where the nerve cells of the centres are weak, and cannot furnish the requisite stimulus to the motor nerves, whereas, it is injurious in all conditions of an opposite kind. It is not usually considered to have any action on the brain, but some very positive evidence has convinced me that it affects the superior as well as the spinal centres, arousing and increasing their nervous energy when it is defective. On the sympathetic system it acts much less evidently. Dr. Hannotte Vernon[4] has, however, shown that it powerfully stimulates the developed uterus to contraction in states of inertia, and its power of arresting vomiting in certain cases of irritability of the stomach is certainly very striking. It is occasionally serviceable in torpor of the bowels as an addition to purgatives, and I have seen it remove very formidable symptoms of in-

---

[1] *V.* Chapple, " Med. T. and Gaz.," March 2d, 1861. Almés, "Gaz. de Paris," xxii., 1860.
[2] Virchow's "Archiv." xxii. 5, 6; 1861.
[3] "Edin. Med. J.," 1863.
[4] "Brit. Med. J.," Dec. 1857.

testinal obstruction. Thalwitzer[1] has found it an effectual remedy in both tertian and quartan ague, preventing relapses much more certainly than quinine. It should invariably be administered in solution and not in the form of pill. Given in this way it is most perfectly safe, and there is not the least risk of its producing the so-called cumulative effects. I have given it very largely for many years, and have never observed anything of the kind. Dr. Fleming's explanation of apparent cumulative action is, I have no doubt, correct.[2] He considers that a number of pills remain for a time undissolved in the alimentary canal, till some change suddenly occurs, when they all liquefy and are absorbed at once. The view adopted by Dr. Radcliffe that the action of strychnia depends on its lessening the capacity of blood for the absorption of oxygen I must consider erroneous, as I cannot think that the tonic and energizing influence of the drug can be explained by the mere diminution of the arterial character of the blood. That strychnia so affects the blood may be very true, but I hold it to be a mere "neben-werk" of its action, and in no way essential to its therapeutic efficacy. Semi-cyanosis of the blood by other means does not increase nervous energy.

Digitalis has long been employed and ranked as a depressant agent, and that it may be used as such very effectively there is no doubt. Latterly, however, various observers have satisfied themselves that it may under certain circumstances produce diametrically opposite effects, acting in fact as a powerful cardiac toner or stimulator. I stated my belief of this in 1859, *v. Brit. Med. J.*, Dec. 17th, and since then evidence has accumulated considerably proving that such is the case. Winogradoff and Traube show by exact experiment that digitalis if not given in excess does not diminish, but actually increases the pressure in the arteries. The former states that digitalis acts both on the regulating and motor nerves of the heart (the vagi and sympathetic cardiac nerves), and that the degree of pressure in the aortic system is the conjoint result of these two factors. The first action of digitalis on each is to excite, and the second to paralyze. If then the motor are more stimulated than the regulating nerves, the arterial pressure will be increased, and so it will be if the regulating are enfeebled while the motor are excited. On the contrary, the arterial pressure diminishes when the regulating nerves are more strongly excited than the motor. In a dog after division of the vagi the pressure rose after injection of digitalis from 124 to 260, declining in ten minutes to 176 millim. Repetition of the injection speedily arrested the heart's action. There seems to be a remarkable correspondence between these observations and those of Hufschmidt and Moleschott as to the effect of irritation of the medulla oblongata and spinal cord on the frequency of the pulse,

---

[1] "Preuss. Militar. Arztl. Ztg.," 1862.
[2] "Edin. Med. J.," Dec. 1862.

v. p. 22. In addition to the results quoted there, it may be mentioned, that they found that irritation of the *medulla oblongata* was conducted to the heart through the pneumogastric, and not through the sympathetic nerves, while irritation of the spinal cord was transmitted to the heart through both sets of nerves. From the above evidence there seems good ground to conclude (1) that digitalis in the milder degrees of its action has a stimulating influence upon the heart, acting through the medulla oblongata and spinal cord or the cardiac nerves proceeding from them; (2) that its stronger action has the reverse effect, like galvanism or mechanical irritation, arresting the heart's movements. How this arrest is produced is not clear. On the one hand, it may be supposed that the over stimulus tetanizes the heart, producing such strong contraction that the ventricles no longer relax to admit blood, which of course would bring the circulation to a standstill. This view is supported by the fact that according to Dr. Fuller's observations and my own the heart after death from digitalis is found with its cavities firmly contracted, contrasting remarkably with the condition produced by aconite and chloroform. On the other hand, the arrest may be regarded as the result of inhibitory action, the excessive stimulus producing a morbid and depressing effect. This view is on the whole I think the most probable, as we are frequently meeting with analogous instances where it appears that an unnatural or unsuitable stimulation tends to paralyze nervous power. Besides the amount of stimulus the degree of excitability of the cardiac nervous and motor apparatus is a highly important factor of the ultimate result. This is demonstrated by the following quotation from Mr. Lister's most valuable paper: "In a healthy state of the nervous system very gentle irritation of the vagus increases the heart's action, while a slightly stronger application diminishes the frequency and force of its contractions . . . . . When partial exhaustion has occurred a much stronger galvanic stimulus is required to produce the same effect upon the heart than at the commencement of an experiment; and thus an action of the battery which when first applied causes marked diminution in the number of beats, may after a while come to have the opposite effect, and increase the heart's action as decidedly as it had previously lowered it; while at an intermediate period it may seem to have no influence at all." Just in the same way, I conceive, digitalis tones and strengthens the action of a feeble heart, but lowers that of a vigorous one.

Clinical observation in various particulars confirms the above views. Thus there is some evidence that digitalis acts in a like way upon the vessels as upon the heart. It is said to check epistaxis, and Dr. Brinton affirms it to be the best remedy for hemorrhage from pulmonary cavities in doses of ♏30 to 90 6*tis vel* 4*tis horis*. In the case of menorrhagia it is considered to act on the uterine tissue rather than on the vessels, but this seems to me problematical, seeing that the muscular fibres in the unimpregnated state are undeveloped. However this be, it is certain that it produces contraction of contractile tissue. Digitalis is spoken of highly by some observers for its efficacy in neuralgia. Mr. Harewicke[1] has always used it in "tic doulourex," with the happiest results, giving gr. ½ of the powder every three hours even in cases where he much feared its depressing effects on account of the great debility. M. Serre[2] reports the cure of several long-standing cases of hemicrania including his own of fifteen years' duration by means of Debout's pills; consisting of quin. gr. iss + pulv. digitalis gr. ⅔ in each, one taken every night for three months. The quantity of quinine is too small to produce any material effect. Boison[3] says that a pill of musk gr. j + extr. digitalis gr. iss + opii gr. ½ has a magical effect upon neuralgia. There can be no doubt that the drug acts in such instances in the way of a tonic, probably much like the quinine with which it is associated, and which has in large doses a like power of slowing the heart's action. The advantage of giving large doses of digitalis in cases of delirium tremens seems to me sufficiently proved, and I think it nearly as certain that it is only the asthenic variety of the disease which is capable of being thus benefited. If further observation establish this point it will be an additional evidence in favour of the primary tonic action of the remedy, and will accord with what we have just seen of its curative influence in neuralgia. Dr. Wilks[4] has performed a most interesting crucial experiment which absolutely proves that digitalis may revive and restore the failing action of the heart, and therefore cannot possibly be a mere depressant. The patient was a woman, who having long suffered from disease of the heart had a severe flooding after labour. She was apparently *in articulo mortis*, her limbs were cold, face livid, no pulse at the wrist, and a mere fluttering to be heard when the ear was applied to the region of the heart. The body was covered with a deathly clammy sweat. Brandy and ether had failed, but ʒss doses of tr. digitalis, *o. hora*, restored her after seven had been given, and she recovered. I had for some time intended to use the same means if a fitting opportunity occurred, and had spoken of the same to several of my friends as a possible succour *in extremis*. Two cases which I recorded, v. *Med. T. and Gaz.*, Dec. 13th, 1862, of the tonic and restorative action of digitalis in debilitating disease of the heart are worth referring to by any one who has doubts on the matter. The diuretic power of digitalis is not unfrequently very evident, but it partakes of the family infirmity belonging to all its congeners, that it is very uncertain. Dr. Christison[5] is inclined to believe that its two actions, the diuretic and sedative, are incompatible. I think this is very likely, and further that in any case where it acted princi-

[1] "Assoc. Med. J.," June 1, 1855.
[2] "Bull. de Thérap.," April 15th, 1861.
[3] "Bullet. de la Soc. de Méd. de Gent.," May and June, 1861.
[4] "Med. T. and Gaz.," Jan. 16th, 1864.
[5] "Edin. Monthly J. of Med.," Jan. 1855.

pally on the heart as a toner or sedative its renal action would be less developed. Dr. Christison speaks very decidedly as to the non-increase of renal irritation in the cases where he has administered it for the relief of the dropsy of Bright's disease.

Tannin may be taken as representative of the class of astringents. It seems to me certainly doubtful whether it has any direct action on nervous tissue, while that it exerts such on the smaller vessels is tolerably certain. It probably renders their membrane more firm and resistant, and therefore less distensible by the blood and permeable by exudation. It finds its opportunity in asthenic forms of inflammation and congestion, where it reduces the hyperæmia by contracting the vessels, shrinking up and obliterating those which have been morbidly developed. In a case of inveterately relapsing corneitis of both eyes producing very great impairment of sight, I ultimately obtained complete recovery by giving gr. xxx of tannin *ter die*. I think it is quite possible that the nervous tissue may be affected by the astringent in an analogous way to the vascular, rendered less mobile and excitable. The beneficial effect of alum in lead colic, which can hardly depend on removal of the lead from the system, points to some influence of this kind. In any condition where nervous disorder might be increased or maintained by hyperæmia tannin would probably be useful. On this ground its utility may be explained in some cases of epilepsy. Its chief advantage in such and in similar disorders depends on its having less tendency to cause irritation than most other tonics.

Sulphuric and Nitric Acids have certainly some claim to be regarded as toners of vaso-motor nerves. They cannot be supposed of course to act in their original form on the parts they influence, as their acid quality must be lost the moment they enter the circulation. They cannot be mere astringents like tannin. When sulphuric acid restrains a choleraic purging, or a colliquative sweating, these effects must surely be produced through the nerves that regulate the arteries of the internal and the external teguments. Its special nervine action is attested by the following quotation from Dr. Pereira:[1] "No remedy is so successful in relieving the distressing itching, formication, and tingling of the skin as diluted sulphuric acid taken internally." Nitric acid is certainly a remedy of considerable efficacy in catarrhal affections both of the bronchi and intestines, and it has further this special indication of its nervine operation that it is often very serviceable in the spasmodic period of pertussis. To those who are impressed like myself with the great concernment of the nervous system in all cases of malarial fever, it will not be without significance that nitric acid has been found a valuable remedy, in these disorders, in some cases surpassing quinine.[2] It is very useful also in enlarged spleen.

---

[1] "Mat. Med.," vol. i. p. 472.
[2] "Amer. J. of Med. Sc.," April, 1861—Jan. 1860

Opium is a drug the empirical use of which very far outruns our scientific knowledge of its action. Molière's quiz at physicians on this score is almost as appropriate now as at the time he wrote. There can, I think, be scarcely a more glaring instance of the necessity which exists for careful research into the *modus operandi* of remedies. Taking our common experience of the effects of opium, we know that it acts as a soporific, as a calmer of pain, and as an arrester of intestinal and other secretions and morbid profluvia, even of some hemorrhages. Graves gives a case in which obstinate bleeding from the gums was arrested by opium, v. *Clin. Med.*, p. 272. Stewart relates some cases in which opium was given in very large doses to females who were syncopic, and almost dying from uterine hemorrhage with very great advantage, v. *Med.-Chir. Trans.*, vol. iv. p. 366. Further we know that in certain constitutions it has a stimulating influence on the brain, manifested both in greater activity of the intellectual functions, and in a greater capacity of enduring fatigue. This stimulating effect when excessive may be succeeded by depression and sopor. In some inflammatory diseases, as in sclerotitis and peritonitis, opium decidedly checks and subdues the hyperæmia and tendency to exudation. The action of the drug on the cutaneous nerves seems to be rather uncertain, it does not seem by any means to cause diaphoresis frequently. Nay, even Dover's powder I have found in accordance with Deschamps'[1] recommendation materially to check the night-sweats of phthisis. The reading of these various facts is sufficiently obscure; it is not easy to refer them to any one general principle. Perhaps it is premature to make the attempt in default of accurate observations upon animals, yet as they are not by any means affected by the drug in the same degree in which human beings are, we cannot avail ourselves to any great extent of this mode of inquiry. Muller indeed has shown[2] that opium exerts a local influence on the nerves, destroying their excitability, and that this influence is not propagated either towards the periphery or centre. This is true both of the cerebro-spinal and sympathetic nerves. It may be questioned how far such a proceeding as immersing a nerve dissected out from the tissues in a solution of opium fairly represents the action of the drug when it is diffused through the whole mass of the circulating blood. However, if we accept the above experiments of Muller, it seems reasonable to refer the soporific and pain-allaying property of opium to a sedative action exerted on the nerves or nervous centres. On this view we should expect that the nerves generally would be similarly affected, that the face would be flushed in opium poisoning, that hemorrhages and inflammations would be aggravated, and diarrhœal and other fluxes increased in consequence of paralysis of the vaso-motor nerves of the facial, intestinal, and other arteries. As the reverse is the case we

---

[1] "Gaz. Méd. de Lyons," Jan. 1861.
[2] Muller's "Physiol.," vol. i. p. 679.

meet with a difficulty, which we must try to remove. It can scarcely be supposed that opium acts in a contrary way on the sympathetic to that in which it does on the brain and cord. It stills pain alike in parts supplied by either set of nerves. It might be imagined that opium acted on other tissues in an analogous way to that in which it affects the nervous, rendering them as it were torpid, and disinclined, or inapt to function. This would explain the arrest of secretions, and perhaps of exudations, and of inflammations, but leaves quite unaccounted for, or rather is contradicted by, the stimulant action of opium on the brain, its power of preventing fatigue, and of arresting hemorrhages. Two things are most necessary to be regarded in speculating on the *modus operandi* of opium, viz., the amount of the dose, and the individual indiosyncrasy, or the state of nervous power. According as these vary its effects vary extremely. It appears that the larger the dose, *cæteris paribus*, the more speedily and decidedly sopor ensues, while small doses are more apt to cause excitement. Small doses also are quite adequate to control diarrhœal exudations and to "lock-up" secretions. It may be supposed, it appears to me, with much probability that the apparently different actions of opium depend very much on the circumstances whether it acts chiefly on the cerebro-spinal or sympathetic systems, a difference which may reasonably be ascribed to original diversities of constitution. The chief action of opium in moderate doses is that of a stimulant or toner to nervous tissues, but in the majority of individuals it acts more on the sympathetic than on the cerebro-spinal system. By stimulating the vaso-motor nerves it produces contraction of arteries, and thus lessens the flow of blood to various parts. Hence the skin of the face and head in opium narcosis becomes pale and cool, while the brain more or less deprived of blood lapses into sopor. Hence also hyperæmias, hemorrhages, and morbid exudations are arrested, and even natural secretions restrained. These instances seem to be almost conclusive; if opium did not contract arteries how could it arrest a uterine hemorrhage? The calming of pain by the local application of opium, as in subcutaneous injection, may be explained according to the view I adopt if we bear in mind what has been advanced as to the essential character of neuralgic pain for the relief of which opium is most efficacious. The suffering nerves being in a state of vital debility are restored to a healthier state by the action of a stimulant. I have seen the subcutaneous injection of morphia produce immediately a good-sized patch of redness with two or three red elevations like longish wheals. Mr. Simon says, "Opium is not an anæsthetic except by the production of stupor." The mental excitement and the prevention of fatigue may be accounted for by its exerting a stimulant action on the brain and spinal cord. The chief objection to the above view is that opium if it acts specially on vaso-motor sympathetic nerves ought to dilate rather than contract the pupil. The radiating fibres of the iris, which are made to contract by galvanizing the cervical sympathetic, ought to be similarly affected when opium is administered. It is very possible that this would be the case did not the motor nerves of the circular fibres pass through, and probably receive additional fibres in the lenticular ganglion. This nervous centre must be regarded as belonging to the sympathetic, and consequently the nerves proceeding from it will be affected by opium in the same way as other sympathetic nerves are. The pupil is therefore contracted. Unless it be admitted that the gray matter of the ciliary ganglion influences the nerves which proceed from it, it is not easy to imagine what can be its purpose. If the action of opium could be limited like galvanism to the sympathetic filament proceeding to the nasal, or to the lenticular ganglion, it might produce dilatation. As it is, however, the far more powerful muscular and nervous apparatus which effects the closure of the pupil overrules the other. A case recorded by Dr. Baly in his translation of Muller's *Physiology*, vol. i. p. 828, may be noticed here. The third nerve of one eye was paralyzed, the pupil was slightly dilated and perfectly fixed, the strongest light causing no contraction, although the vision was perfect. The adjusting power of the eye was lost or much impaired. Now in this case the pupil was not much dilated because the gray matter of the lenticular ganglion still kept up an influence on the motor nerves, but the iris could not be influenced through the retina, because the communication of the ganglion with the third nerve was interrupted. Belladonna, on the other hand, dilated the pupil further by paralyzing the ciliary ganglion. There is no doubt that the optic and the third nerve constitute the nervous apparatus essential to the main movements of the iris, and the dilatation can be accounted for under ordinary circumstances simply by the unopposed action of the straight fibres, most of which may be merely elastic tissue. The sympathetic fibres are probably as in other situations chiefly distributed to vessels, and take no important part in the movements of this muscular curtain. Clearly full dilatation of the pupil occurs under circumstances which seem to exclude all stimulation of any nerve, as in chloroform, narcosis, and fatal syncope.

A second objection which may be made is that copious sweating occasionally occurs in opium poisoning, and even from moderate doses of the drug. This looks more like relaxation of vessels than contraction. To this it may be replied, that copious sweating is a common result of any cause which powerfully depresses the nervous system; it occurs in apoplexy, in profound debility of malarious origin, and in sudden embolism of the pulmonary artery. It may therefore well occur in fatal opium narcosis, where the brain is paralyzed for lack of arterial blood. As to the diaphoretic action of ordinary doses it may be explained on the following grounds. All glands, as Bernard shows, have their motor nerves, stimulation of which excites them to active function. Now retaining the view that the primary action of opium is stimulant, it is quite conceivable that in some parts it may stimulate the gland-motor more than the vaso-motor nerves, and thus promote instead of suppressing secretion. Individual peculiarity is probably largely concerned here; thus cats are, I believe, invariably profusely salivated by a dose of opium, while I scarcely have ever heard of such an occurrence in man except the case mentioned by Pereira.[1] A third objection may be raised from the circumstances that opium produces in some persons an increased flow of urine, as especially observed by Dr. Woodward.[2] I have several times observed this, but have always seen that the secretion was pale and aqueous just like hysterical urine. It is very difficult to say what condition of vessels coexists with this kind of renal secretion, but I doubt very much whether it is one of arterial dilatation. Most probably some peculiar change is produced in the homogeneous membrane of the Malpighian capillaries, affecting their filtering action. The slower and diminished breathing observed in opium narcosis depends probably on a state of torpor of the respiratory centre, itself the result of a diminished flow of arterial blood. The same condition of the hemispheres accounts for the coma, the brain being, as lately shown by Durham[3] and Bedford Brown,[4] more or less anæmic during sleep. The occasional occurrence of convulsions may with our present knowledge be reasonably ascribed to the cerebral anæmia. That these various phenomena depend principally on arterial contraction seems to me still more probable from the remarkable restorative effect of belladonna, which has now been observed in several cases.[5] If the vital power of the tissues themselves were deeply injured by the one drug, they could hardly so soon resume their action under the influence of the other. In one recorded case, v. *Brit. and For. Med.-Chir. Rev.*, April, 1858, the pulse was scarcely perceptible, though the heart's beat was strong. In another mentioned by Dr. J. W. Ogle, *Med. T. and G.*, Oct. 3, 1863, the surface was icy cold. Both these phenomena are mostly results of over excitement of vaso-motor nerves. While I cannot but attribute the chief part of the operation of opium to its influence on the vaso-motor nerves, I think also that it may in large doses (like alcohol) act paralyzingly by over-stimulus on the encephalic nervous centres. Indeed both agents have in many respects the same effects. Thus both in small or moderate doses stimulate the brain, in larger produce sopor but leave the respiratory centre efficient, and in still larger doses cause fatal coma and collapse. In all cases a very great deal depends on the degree of impressionability of the nervous force, and on its condition in different parts. If the vaso-motor nervous apparatus be very sensitive, as in young children, the arteries are very readily occluded, and coma ensues, while in older persons the gray matter of the hemispheres will be first affected in a way of

---

[1] "Mat. Med.," vol. i. p. 708.
[2] "Boston Med. J.," vol. lxv. p. 108.
[3] "Guy's Hosp. Reports," vol vi. p. 149.
[4] "Amer. J. of Med. Sc.," Oct. 1860.
[5] Ibid , Jan. 1852.

excitement, and it will require a large dose to produce a soporous state. In states of cerebral excitement it may require an almost poisonous dose of the narcotic to produce sleep. The action of the heart is commonly increased by moderate doses of opium, or at least in nowise depressed, but after poisonous doses it becomes very feeble and failing. This results partly from the contraction of the coronary arteries admitting an insufficient supply of blood to the muscular tissue, and partly from the same state of the bloodvessels of the cardiac centres, in consequence of which they cease to supply the heart with nervous influence.

Belladonna may be ranked as the physiological opposite to opium. In full doses it causes extreme flushing of the face and head with great distension of the veins, numbness of the face, dimness of sight or even blindness, confusion of head, delirium sometimes attended with great excitement, dryness of the mouth and throat, extreme dilatation of the pupils, and often an erythematous eruption. The chief points of contrast in its action as compared with that of opium are the state of the pupils, the deep flushing of the face, the delirious excitement, the acceleration and sometimes increased strength of the pulse, and the hurried breathing. Sopor is generally consecutive to delirium, and is often replaced by wakefulness. There can be to my mind but little question that the deep congestion of the skin of the face and head, the delirium, and the cutaneous erythema depend on arterial dilatation and increased afflux of blood in those parts. In one case the skin of the face had been as red as blood, but had quite returned to its natural state twenty-two hours later when I saw the patient; delirium had existed along with the congestion, and had disappeared with it. It is impossible to consider such temporary congestion as the result of tissue irritation, the effect of a mustard poultice would not have ceased so speedily. The acceleration of the pulse may reasonably be ascribed to paresis of the cardiac branches of the vagi, or of the vaso-motor nerves of the coronary arteries, the first being the more constant occurrence, and the second probably being added, when the pulse is not only rapid, but strong. The accelerated breathing is the result partly of free blood-flow through the medulla oblongata, partly of the increased cardiac action. The increased heat of the skin, the erythematous eruption, or the perspiration, all which have been observed, are easily explicable on the view of vaso-motor nerve paralysis. The evidence in favour of the pain-calming action of belladonna is very decided. Trousseau does not hesitate to affirm as the result of very numerous experiments that of all the remedies employed against the symptom pain there is none which seems more constantly efficacious than belladonna. He admits, however, the superiority of opium in internal pains. The blindness is probably in part dependent on paralysis of the ciliary muscle which is affected just in the same way as the iris, and through the medium of the same nerves. The numbness of the face and the weakening of muscular power are also indications of diminished vis-

nervosa. Botkin[1] and Michéa[2] both agree that belladonna destroys the excitability of the nerves, affecting the motor before the sensory, and lastly the cerebral hemispheres. The peripheral extremities of the nerves are first affected. The heart's action was rendered weaker and more frequent, and the pressure in the arteries diminished. Thus most of the phenomena produced by belladonna seem to be satisfactorily explicable on the view of its occasioning paresis of nervous tissue generally and especially of the vaso-motor nerves. There are, however, two very constant results of its action which seem to be of a different kind. These are the dryness of the mouth and the throat and the dilatation of the pupil. The first seems to imply a contraction of the vessels supplying the mucous membrane and the salivary glands effected doubtless through stimulation of their nerves. I have examined the throats of various persons under the influence of atropine, but have not been able to satisfy myself that there was any marked dryness. I am therefore much inclined to regard the phenomenon in question more as a dysæsthesia than as a real arrest of secretion. If, however, it actually occurs, it may be explained on the view of its paralyzing the gland motor nerves, while opium sometimes does the contrary. The dysphagia and aphonia which sometimes occur are certainly paralytic phenomena, and so in accordance with the general mode of action. The question as to the action of atropine on the pupil has been admirably studied by Dr. Harley,[3] who considers it proved, (1) that atropine does not dilate the pupil by stimulating the sympathetic as galvanism does, and (2) that it does not do so either merely by paralyzing the third nerve, supplying the circular fibres of the iris. He is most inclined to adopt Ludwig's view that the drug acts directly on the radiating fibres, and relates an experiment showing that a recently removed eye immersed in solution of atropine comes to have the pupil fully dilated in some hours, while the companion eye placed in water shows no such change. It is a very difficult question to decide completely, but after a careful perusal of the facts recorded I think there is little doubt that atropine does not stimulate the cervical sympathetic and thus produce contraction of the radiating fibres of the iris. The chief evidence is as follows:—

(1) Atropine applied for twenty-five minutes to the upper end of the divided sympathetic does not cause the contracted pupil to dilate as galvanism does. (2) When the third nerve is divided the pupil dilates immediately and permanently, and the dilatation is not increased by atropine; the cervical sympathetic being now divided, the pupil contracted to one half, both sets of fibres being paralyzed. (3) The pupil being fully dilated by atropine the sympathetic on that side was divided, the ear became warm, but the pupil remained fully

[1] Virchow's "Archiv.," vol. xxiv. p. 83; 1862.
[2] "Ann. de Thérap.," 1864, p. 8.
[3] "Edin. Med. J.," 1856, 1857, p. 431, and p. 705.

dilated for three days, afterwards gradually contracted, and was completely so by the ninth day. (4) Sympathetic divided on one side, the contracted pupil made to dilate at first to half its extent with atropine, subsequently by long-continued application made to dilate completely. The general bearing of these facts seems to me to be that atropine does not stimulate the sympathetic, but that it acts on it as it does on other nerves, paralyzing therefore the ciliary ganglion and nerves, as well as the third. The effect of atropine on the ciliary muscle should be taken into account. This, as having but one set of fibres, is a simpler structure, and its action can more easily be determined. Atropine certainly paralyzes it, and so also does disease of the third nerve. It therefore seems probable that atropine acts in a like manner upon the iris with which it is associated. As to the direct action of atropine on the iris it seems difficult to understand how it can affect one set of fibres without the other, the two being supplied absolutely by the same capillaries. It is very possible that the contraction of the pupil produced by division of the sympathetic depends on an increased flow of blood to the iris, and on an exaltation of the vital properties of its circular fibres, which then contract with greater energy, v. p. 27. When the divided sympathetic is galvanized dilatation ensues because the vital power of the constrictor is now diminished, and so it is less capable of action. The radiating fibres meanwhile, though similarly affected, meeting with less resistance shorten by mere passive contractility. Paralysis of the sympathetic makes it more difficult for atropine to dilate the pupil because of the increased energy of the constrictor, so that a greater amount of the drug is required to overcome its action. When belladonna applied to the skin of the forehead dilates the pupil of that side only it is difficult to suppose that it is absorbed, or that it directly affects the ciliary nerves. What is certain is that it must act on the sensory filaments of the ophthalmic division of the fifth, and through these it is probable that a reflex action of an inhibitory paralyzing character is communicated to the third nerve.[1] Botkin's experiments seem sufficient to prove that it cannot act as a stimulant as Wharton Jones and others think. I have examined the web of the frog under the influence of atropine, both when applied locally and injected subcutaneously, but I did not observe that the arteries were notably affected. The circulation is very apt to be affected by

[1] The above had been written a long time before I met with the following passage in Simon's *Lect. on Pathology*, p. 219. "An anæsthetic agent operating on the peripheral expansion of the fifth nerve produces the *negation of excitement* in its centre; this condition diffuses itself to the motional centre of the iris, and as excitement would have shown itself in contraction of the pupil, so the opposite nervous condition evinces itself in expansion of that aperture. Where the reactivity of the spinal cord is very highly excited a peripheral surface may by the influence of belladonna be rendered incapable of provoking reflex movements. Thus, for instance, if a frog be rendered tetanic by opium or strychnine, any contact of its cutaneous surface will produce universal spasm; if either before this poisoning, or subsequent to its manifestations, one limb of the animal be plunged into a solution of belladonna, no mechanical irritation of that portion of the body will cause the tetanic convulsion."

movements of the animal which possibly may have been a cause of error. The state of the brain in which belladonna is occasionally useful as a soporific is where there is violent excitement and wakefulness, with a contracted pupil.

Hyoscyamus appears to be chiefly a simple and direct cerebral sedative. Of its calmative and hypnotic action I have no doubt, but it produces no other distinct effect when given in ordinary doses. In poisonous quantities it acts somewhat like belladonna. The narcotic effect of both drugs is, I believe, due to direct action on the nervous centres.

Aconite is certainly of great value as an external application in cutaneous hyperæsthesia, and in some neuralgias, but I am shy of administering it internally. It may be used, however, in various conditions characterized by sthenic nervous excitement, certain pyrexiæ, neuralgias, and headache, but its effect should be carefully watched lest it induce perilous depression of the heart's action. The dose at first should not exceed m_x of the tincture (*Ph. Brit.*) *ter die.*

Cannabis Indica has certainly an influence on the brain, producing not unfrequently a kind of intoxication or delirium. There seem to be great individual differences in respect to the tendency to be thus affected. In most persons an ordinary dose produces no notable effect, but in some the cerebral disturbance, and the delusions usually of a pleasing kind are very considerable. The primary stimulant action is succeeded after a time by a sedative, but no actual narcosis appears to be produced. There is evidence that cannabis has a tranquillizing influence on the spinal cord in tetanus, but it is not to be relied on for producing this effect, and does not seem comparable in this respect to aconite. My own experience is quite corroborative of Dr. Clendinning's that it has a decidedly sedative effect in the cough of bronchitis and phthisis. Dr. Tilt says it is a wonderfully useful drug to quell neuralgia or mental excitement. In hysterical derangement, Dr. Forbes Winslow finds that the tincture will occasionally allay the excitement and produce sleep more rapidly than any other form of sedative. Fronmuller finds that it produces a more natural sleep than any other narcotic, and that its action is not attended with any unfavourable after-effects. Sir R. Martin finds it very effectually to arrest the vomiting of hysterical females, and my own observation leads me to the same conclusion. Dr. Reynolds' experience of it is peculiar; he says[1] it is useless in mere functional, psychical, sensory, or motor disorders, without demonstrable organic change; on the other hand, it is essentially beneficial in cases of congestion, softening, meningitis, or hemorrhage. The drug appears to diminish the over-activity of the nerve centres without disturbing the animal or vegetable functions. On the vaso-motor nerves I have not observed it to have any action, but Dr. Churchill speaks of it as

[1] "Arch. of Med.," Jan. 1861.

a valuable remedy in menorrhagia, classing it along with ergot of rye. The general result seems to be that it is principally a cerebral sedative, which is not appropriate to conditions of sthenic excitement, but rather to such as manifest debility and depression with hyperæsthesia. Dr. Forbes Winslow gives a hint which is worth remembering with regard to the employment of sedatives generally. This is that cases which are intractable to separate remedies, will yield to a judicious combination of several. This is probably the secret of the success of the nostrum, chlorodyne.

Hydrocyanic acid is familiar to us all as a useful sedative in gastric and bronchial irritation. It is evidently a nervine, but its *modus operandi* is not at all clear. In poisonous doses it produces tetanic convulsions and insensibility preceded by faintness and giddiness; the pupils are dilated, the pulse is small or imperceptible. In a good-sized young dog whom I injected with two ♏xxx doses of acid. hydroc. dil. subcutaneously at about ten minutes' interval the effects were as follows. He was prostrated in a few minutes, lay quiet with deep but infrequent breathing, and quick but feeble pulsation of the heart, whose sounds were just audible. After the second injection the breathing became slower, and the heart's action feebler, and so he died very gradually in about twenty minutes from the first introduction of the poison. A stimulus to the cornea caused contraction of the orbicularis palpebrarum from seven to ten minutes before death, but not about four minutes later. At the autopsy made two hours after death the limbs were not rigid, the lungs were moderately congested, the heart was well and firmly contracted, its tissue remarkably firm, the cavity of the left ventricle almost quite obliterated, that of right small, but little blood in either, coagula in both auricles. Brain decidedly pale. From this it almost appears as if the heart's action had been arrested by over-stimulus of its nerves, tetanizing it. Perhaps convulsions and insensibility are produced by similar tetanizing of the cerebral arteries. Such, however, are the effects of over-doses, and they do not throw any light on the results of ordinary ones. I believe we must for the present be content to think of the drug as a direct sedative to nervous tissue. As such it has been used lately with great success by Dr. K. McLeod in cases of insanity attended with excitement.

There is some evidence that the inhalation of *Oxygen gas* diluted, in the proportion of from 2 to 12 per cent. for small doses, and to a very much less degree for large doses, has a beneficial effect in various disorders, among which some neuroses may be reckoned. One of my own patients declares that he was restored by this means from a state of extreme depression in a marvellous way. Dr. Birch,[1] who has had the principal share in bringing this remedy forward, does not recommended it in nervous hyperæsthesia, or chronic cases of extreme debility and spanæmia. He has found its good effects most

---

[1] "Brit. Med. J.," Dec. 24, 31, 1859.

decided "in persons of a gouty or strumous habit, or otherwise in a state of general *malaise*, with sluggish circulation, either constitutional or superinduced by an atonic and oppressed condition through over-feeding and other luxurious habits." In some cases improvement coincides with critical discharges of retained excrementitious matters. Mr. Hooper[1] records an intractable case of neuralgia of the sole of the right foot which was cured after much other medication had failed by the inhalation of oxygen. The patient was a labourer, æt. 40, the whole foot was exceedingly hot, the agony beyond description. No mention is made of gouty tendency. During the inhalation the urine became increased in quantity, and loaded with urates and phosphates. It seems probable that the remedy may be useful in cases rather of indirect than of direct depression.

The operation of *Cold* on an ordinarily vigorous system is, as we have seen, tonic and invigorating, *v.* p. 31 *et seq*. It increases nervous power and specially excites the smooth muscular fibres of arteries and of the skin, as well as the nerves influencing them. Catarrhal affections are much more prone to ensue on the supervention of a thaw than during a sharp frost. In its greater degrees, and in feeble states of system it is often depressing, partly we may believe by obstructing the free flow of blood through the arteries. The suppression of the catamenial discharge by the application of cold to the feet, of hæmoptysis by ice to the chest, and the beneficial effect in cases of cerebral hyperæmia of cold to the scalp indicate I think plainly that cold acts through the incident nerves in a reflex manner upon the vaso-motor, and causes arterial contraction. We shall see presently that heat has just the opposite effect. It seems to me very probable that the extreme drowsiness which is produced by intense cold depends on a want of due supply of arterial blood to the brain, the congestion which is so often observed is probably chiefly venous, and dependent on the mode of death, viz., by coma. The paralyzing action of cold in certain states of nervous power has been already alluded to, *v.* p. 188, and forms a good example of inhibitory action. It may affect musculo-motor or vaso-motor nerves, and in the latter case may if the vital power is weak originate actual inflammation by the hyperæmia produced. The toning anti-neuralgic influence of dry cold is well shown in the following case.

No. 185.—W. L., æt. 32, a healthy man. Rather more than 2½ years ago was struck by some small shot on the head, and has suffered ever since with pains continually flying about the part, not felt anywhere else. The head felt stiff, and tender, and heavy, and dull; he could not find a comfortable position to lay it in. During the cold frosty weather the head was a great deal better, and it was much relieved by pumping cold water upon it. Health quite good all the time. The shots were removed by operation, were flattened and imbedded a little in the bone. After their removal the pain ceased. It is very noteworthy that a neuralgia of organic origin was thus

---

[1] "Brit. Med. J.," March 15, 1862.

relieved by cold. Trousseau states that tetanoid spasms are temporarily stilled in the same way.

The action of *moist warmth*, whether applied by warm baths or in any other way, is worth considering. It may be stated (1) that it is generally soothing and comforting to sensory nerves in a state of neuralgic suffering, as for instance in the headache of influenza, and in the case of tic douloureux recorded at page 185, but not so constantly in the pain of inflammatory congestion, which, as in the case of a burn, is often arrested by cold. However, there is good evidence that in these same affections, even when very severe, moist warmth may be one of the best means that can be employed. Mr. Windsor[1] says, " Many years since we convinced ourselves by a series of comparative experiments that there was no treatment for the collapse which generally accompanies severe burns so efficacious as the warm bath. In our cases the pain at once disappeared, and sometimes did not return, the pulse improved, and the countenance lost its anxious and sunken case ; the bath, however, was never continued for more than an hour." He thinks this treatment would often save life. Hebra relates a case of severe burn, the subject of which nine days after its occurrence was suffering intense pain, and could neither stand, sit, nor lie down straight. She was placed in a bath at 99.5° F., and an hour later she could stretch her legs, and the pain had disappeared. In forty-eight hours the pulse fell from 120 to 80, the thirst became less and the appetite increased. She remained altogether 504 hours in the water, the temperature of which was gradually lowered to 88° F., and recovered well. The beneficial action of cold in inflammation depends on its keeping the arteries contracted, and the part anæmic, if it does not effect this it is rather irritating. (2) Moist warmth seems to abate the tissue irritation, the attractive *nisus*, which constitutes the essence of sthenic inflammation, causing afflux to and arrest of blood in the part independent of arterial dilatation. In a case of very aggravated psoriasis under my care the skin was paler after an hour's packing in a wet sheet than at any other time. The beneficial effect of poultices and fomentations on inflamed parts, including the viscera of serous cavities, depends chiefly on this sedative action on the tissue, which extends even to the deeper parts. (3) I think we may be pretty sure that moist warmth applied to the cutaneous surface through its action on the afferent nerves and nervous centres relaxes the nerves and vessels of internal parts. A female, whose catamenia returned too frequently, informed me that soaking her feet in hot water would bring on the discharge at any time. The common prescription of a warm hip-bath in amenorrhœa probably acts on the same principle, as otherwise it would be more likely to determine a flow of blood to the cutaneous surface than to the uterus. The benefit of a warm bath in children's convulsions probably depends on its inducing re-

---

[1] " Syd. Soc. Y.-b.," 1863, p. 205.

laxation of the contracted cerebral arteries, and allowing free blood-flow to take place through the brain. It should, therefore, not be administered indiscriminately, not if the head was flushed and hot, and the eyes injected.

Beneke[1] and Clemens[2] agree that the general effects of baths depend upon their action on the nerves of the skin. The latter finds that simple or medicated baths always produce their greatest diuretic effect in the first fifteen or twenty minutes; he could detect none of the substances dissolved in the bath water in the urine. The diuretic effect was marked, especially in increasing the flow of water, and the excretion of phosphates and other fixed salts. The chloride of sodium and urea were not much increased. Beneke lays stress on the importance of the stimulus of the bath being appropriate to the state of the system; if it is, it causes a general sensation of well-being, a bodily and mental exhilaration, some increased frequency of pulse, and generally and as an ultimate result an increase of nutrition, and of the weight of the body. If, however, the stimulus is not suitable to the individual, these beneficial effects are replaced by shivering, lassitude, febricitation, restlessness, and loss of weight.

The special advantage of the warm bath consists in the circumstance that a very large sensory surface is mildly and equably stimulated, so that all the cerebral and spinal centres are moderately excited. It is on this principle that such baths as those of Gastein and Wildbad, scarcely more than hot water, act efficiently in cases of paralysis of exhaustion. This is the primary and beneficial effect, but if the temperature be too high, or the bathing too prolonged, we then have debility and nerve exhaustion produced, which may even cause a degree of syncope, such as is not uncommon to novices at a Turkish bath. The same influence which relaxes the internal arteries, and thus promotes more free circulation through the brain and cord, if carried too far, or used in too weakly a system, depresses the action of the heart, sometimes even seriously.

Similar views seem to me very applicable to various medicated baths of ascertained efficacy in different neuroses. Thus sulphuret of potassium baths are certainly useful in chorea, in lead paralysis, in some cases of asthma, and in some of eczema. It is difficult to believe that the remedy can act by removing the causes of these disorders, while it is certain that it must exert an influence on the cutaneous nerves, which, communicated to the centres, may there effect changes which materially modify the morbid phenomena. In the following instance mentioned to me by Dr. Tyler Smith the nitro-muriatic acid lotion appears to act in a way which can only be explained by the view that certain nerves of the parietes exert an influence on those of the contained viscera. A lady whose liver is habitually torpid always gets a well-coloured bilious motion from the

---

[1] Schmidt's "Jahrb.," vol. cxv. p. 101.
[2] "Med. Centr. Ztg.," xxx. 58, 59; 1861.

application of spongio-piline, saturated with nitro-muriatic acid lotion, to the right hypochondrium, but a foot-bath of the same has no effect.

In appropriate cases, such as are not suffering under active disease, there is no calmative which is more effectual than an atmosphere and climate suited to the state of the system. In asthma, in chronic sleeplessness, and in a variety of obscure nervous disorders change to a pure and suitable air may be of far more value to the sufferer than any drug, or mode of treatment. This is eminently the case in removal from London to the country. The cessation of the unending hum and clatter of London traffic, the perceptible stillness, affects the brain with a pleasant sense of rest, and contributes materially to the beneficial effect of the air. A judicious selection of locality is, however, most important. The atmosphere which tones, braces, and calms one system will injuriously affect another, and the moist relaxing air of our southern and western coasts which may calm a highly excitable, tensely nerved system will seriously depress one of an opposite quality. For many invalids convalescent, or semi-convalescent from tropical disease the Scottish moors and mountains is, I believe, preferable to any in our island. Were I similarly affected I should wish to betake myself to the Swiss Alps, avoiding, however, absolutely the close valleys, which are often most pernicious. I would say to every traveller in search for health, consider well where you make even a brief stay, for a night or two in a locality where the aspect of the population tells of malaria may infect you with a taint which it may be hard to shake off, even if no worse occur. I shall not as long as I live forget the scene that I witnessed at Martigny during the day I halted there. A week of illness spent there, commencing apparently in a mere diarrhœa, bereft a young affectionate wife of her husband, and left her to finish in grief the journey which had begun so joyously. In some cases frequent change is more efficacious than a continued residence in any one locality. This applies very much to the slight teasing febrile affections which hang about some who have previously suffered with malarious fevers. For those who are tolerable sailors sea voyaging under favourable circumstances is one of the best restoratives. To many Indian invalids the long sea voyage would I am satisfied be safer and more health-promoting than the over-land route.

APPENDIX.

The subject of inhibitory paralysis appears to me to be one of so much importance that I am desirous of entering into it somewhat further than I have done in the text. The following are, I think, interesting examples of this morbid state. Mr. Tyrrell relates the following history.[1] "I was requested to see a young gentleman, æt. 13, who had been suffering for many days from headache of severe kind, giddiness, flushed state of countenance, and great restlessness and irritability; he was also intolerant of light, and his vision was very imperfect, being obscured by a gauze or web. I found the pulse rapid, small, but very compressible; the skin dry and hot; and the tongue loaded on the median part by a thick light brown deposit, the edges being unusually red; the appearance of this organ induced me to direct my inquiries into the state of the secretions from the alimentary canal, and to examine the abdomen; I then learnt that the patient had been freely purged, principally by saline medicines; but that the remedies had been directed to the head, under the supposition that it was the seat of the morbid action; my examination of the abdomen discovered an irregular, indurated swelling in the right iliac region, which I considered to result from a collection of hardened fæces in the caput coli. A full dose of scammony and calomel was administered and produced a very copious discharge of hard scybala; the relief was immediate; all urgent symptoms subsided, and after a second dose he became convalescent—proving that all disturbance, cerebral, ocular, or other emanated from the accumulation of scybala in the colon." Tyrrell adds that such cases are rare in adults, but frequent in children or young persons. Mackenzie[2] relates the case of a girl, æt. 7, whose vision became dim after an attack of inflammation of the eyes attended with headache, when suddenly her pupils became widely dilated and immovable. The abdomen was much swollen. About a month previously to this she had passed a lumbricus. After repeated doses of castor oil and turpentine she passed at different times nine lumbrici, and vomited two; after which the belly became soft, the pupils contracted when the eyes were exposed to the light, and in the course of a few months' treatment vision was restored. Dr. Burgess[3] gives the history of a coloured man, æt. 39, who suddenly began to suffer severe pain through the right eye, and over the right side of the face and head, and about this time discovered that he had paralysis of the right side of the face. The pain continuing most severe through the globe of the right eye he soon began to experience a cloudiness of vision. For the first few days all objects viewed with the right eye alone seemed of a bright yellow colour; at the end of five or six weeks the power of vision was entirely obscured. Now began a similar set of symptoms in the left eye, resulting finally in total loss of sight in this eye also. This condition was

[1] Vol. ii. p. 280.
[2] "On Dis. of the Eyes," p. 1061.
[3] "Brit. Med. J.," June 14th, 1862.

reached in about four months after the first attack. Two months later the eyes had a staring vacant aspect, the globes being prominent, as if pushed forwards, the pupils largely dilated, and but little sensitive to light. No evidences of disease in the external coats of the eye; the deeper portions presented a greenish colour. Paralysis of the muscles of the right side of the face with partial paralysis of the tongue still existed; and pain similar in character, though much less severe than that which had ushered in the disease, still continued. He also described a sensation as of something crawling about on the top of his brain. He had chancre four years before, but had never suffered from any consecutive symptoms. Shortly after this he was delivered from a tænia nineteen feet long by means of pumpkin-seeds and castor oil and turpentine. Two or three days after this he began to distinguish shadowy outlines of objects around him, and from this time the haze cleared away so rapidly that in a week more he was able to recognize his acquaintances. At this time the power of vision was returning only to the right eye, but soon after the left improved also. At the end of thirty days the patient could read newspapers, the pain had nearly disappeared, and both eyes had a perfectly normal appearance, save the glaucomatous hue of the inner chambers, which still existed. Paralysis continued, but was less evident. Two years and a half later the patient's sight still remained unimpaired, or nearly so, and the paralytic effects had all disappeared.

REMARKS.—In the first of these cases there were signs of cerebral congestion, of retinitis, and general pyrexia; in the second, there was headache, paralysis of the ciliary nerves, and ophthalmia; in the third, pain in the head and face, paralysis of the facial and hypoglossal nerves, and retinitis leading to amaurosis. In all the phenomena were evidently dependent on remote irritation. The natural reading of the phenomena seems to me to be—in the first, paralysis of the vaso-motor nerves of the retinal, facial, and cerebral arteries; in the second, cerebral neuralgia, and inhibitory palsy of the ciliary branches furnished by the third pair and of the vaso-motor nerves of the eyes; in the third, similar but more extensive neuralgia and palsy, the latter involving also both retinal vaso-motor nerves. If any one should contend that the condition in the first case was not one of vaso-motor nerve paralysis, but of direct cerebral and retinal irritation, which I can hardly think is possible, this will not apply to the second case where there was paralysis of ciliary nerves along with the ophthalmia, and still less to the third where there was palsy of the right facial and hypoglossal together with retinitis. If the retinæ were directly irritated the origins of these nerves should have been so too, and there should have occurred contraction rather than paralysis. In the cases quoted from Scanzoni, at p. 462, it seems impossible to believe that the cutaneous hyperæmia was the result of *attraction* of blood to the skin excited by reflex irritation. It would be as reasonable to regard blushing as the result of cutaneous irritation. Tissue irritation, as when produced by a mustard poultice, is always attended with more permanent phenomena than those resulting from arterial dilatation. The diffuse character of the inhibitory vaso-motor paralysis is very apparent in the first case, and it is worth observing that both eyes were affected in all the three. If spasm of the vessels in the centres had been the cause of the palsy in the third case, should not the retinal vessels have been in a similar condition, and would not, moreover, the long period during which the nutrition of the centres was arrested have produced softening and irreparable damage? Dr. Brown-Séquard asserts that an inflammation cannot be explained by a hyperæmia from vaso-motor nerve paralysis, but, as I have before stated, my own experience quite coincides with Bernard's, that in weakly or sickly animals actual inflammation may be produced by division of the sympathetic. This conclusion seems to me quite borne out by the evidence of the above cases. No. 55 may also be cited as a proof that long-continued hyperæmia from relaxed arteries may pass into destructive pus-generating inflammation.

While, however, I think that inhibitory paralysis of musculo-motor, and of vaso-motor nerves is not an infrequent form of disorder, and that the latter often gives rise to inflammation of a more or less diffuse kind, I also think there is evidence that nerve pain or nerve palsy may cause nutritional changes of inflammatory character. Herpes Zoster is an oft-quoted instance. Graves relates a case (*Dublin Med. J.*, vol. iii. p. 342) where a gentleman, æt. 68, had an attack of hemicrania affecting the right side. Each hair felt like a minute poniard implanted in the skin, causing intense agony; at last a minute pustule that soon desiccated appeared around each hair, and in a few days his scalp got well. During the height of the disease the engaged half of the scalp was red, but not erysipelatous. The hair did not fall off. Samuel's experiments, if confirmed, prove that severe irritation of sensory and compound nerves may cause violent inflammation. He states[1] that irritation of the tissue in the vicinity of the sciatic nerve produced healthy suppuration along the course of the nerve and its divisions, but did not extend to the lower part of the leg and foot. The skin and the muscles were not inflamed. Prolonged irritation of the sciatic nerve on the contrary caused prodigious swelling and inflammation of the whole limb, with offensive sanious exudation and discoloration of the muscles. Irritation of the posterior spinal nerve roots and their ganglia in the lumbar region caused great swelling and hyperæmia of the leg and thigh. It does not appear to me quite certain whether in these experiments the irritation was not so great as to paralyze the vaso-motor nerves, at the same time that by its action on the sensory it impaired the nutrition of the tissues. Hutchinson's cases show that small whitlows may form on the fingers in consequence of their being deprived of sensation. As counter evidence to Samuel's experiments we ought to consider the numerous instances in which severe pain is produced either by direct or reflected irritation of sensory nerves, yet without any inflammation ensuing in the part to which the pain is referred. Such instances are so numerous that it is needless to cite any at length, and I will only allude to two cases mentioned by Sir B. Brodie (*Local Nervous Disorders*, pp. 4, 5), to three cases mentioned by Romberg (vol. i. p. 72, 73), and to an interesting case given by Dr. Churchill (*Dis. of Women*, p. 253) in which uterine cancer gave rise to no other pain except excruciating sciatica. In none of these was the nerve irritation attended with any inflammation. Neither was it in Denmark's[2] case where a fragment of lead impacted in the radial nerve caused such suffering in the hand that amputation was had recourse to, nor in a case given by Sir Charles Bell,[3] where a "man died of agonizing burning pain in the sole of his foot, and the poisonous drugs that were administered in hope of relieving him. Only two days before his death I found a hard tumour like a piece of bone in the ham, and that the pain in the foot proceeded from this." After death the popliteal

[1] Canst. "Jahresb.," vol. ii. pp. 53–57.
[2] *Med.-Chir. Trans.*, vol. iv. p. 48. It is true that there was an excoriation in the palm, but the skin here is supplied by the median nerve.
[3] "Nervous System," 1836, p. 370.

nerve was found involved in a soft cancerous mass. In most cases where neuralgic pain is attended with some degree of inflammation this evidently depends on vaso-motor paralysis and not on tissue irritation. This appears from the diffuse hyperæmia, the throbbing, the paroxysmal aggravation, and especially from the cure of the whole disorder by tonics. Brodie especially mentions that inflammation produced by nerve irritation is not very active, is not such as will end in suppuration, or abscess. In Mr. Paget's case where urethral irritation caused abscess in one testis we need more exact information respecting the state of things during the time that the abscess was forming. It does not seem to me fully proved that the morbid action was not communicated by continuity of tissue. This is the explanation which Dr. Mackenzie is most inclined to adopt with regard to sympathetic ophthalmitis. He says: "It is extremely probable that the retina of the injured eye is in a state of inflammation, which is propagated along the corresponding optic nerve to the chiasma, and that thence the irritation which gives rise to inflammation is reflected to the retina of the opposite eye along its optic nerve." If the view be taken that the inflammation depends on inhibitory irritation of the nerves of the secondarily-affected eye, it should be observed that, as Dr. M. states, the subjects of sympathetic ophthalmitis are debilitated and in ill-health, and that the inflammation is unhealthy. The occurrence of purulent otorrhœa together with auriculo-temporal neuralgia is clearly an instance of vaso-motor nerve paralysis, the vasal nerves being paralytically affected like the sensory.

On the whole, after comparing the teachings of science with our experiences in practice, I find that the theories of vaso-motor paralysis, of inhibitory action, and of the paralytic character of neuralgia are of great value as affording a rational basis for treatment, and as combining together in an intelligible view numerous facts which would otherwise be of little significance;—but the doctrine of special trophic nerves seems to me at present to be but sparingly applicable to the phenomena of disease. One of its principal supporters (Samuel) regards fever and inflammation as states of excitement of the trophic nerves, and atrophies as the reverse. Now certainly the view which Bernard's observations lead to as regards fever and many cases of inflammation is much more consonant with experience.

The essential idea of the inhibitory theory is that a peculiar kind of impression made on a centre may disorder or paralyze its action, may prove directly depressing. There seems to be ground for believing that such impressions may be generated within the cranial cavity as well as at the periphery. The crossed paralysis resulting from hemorrhage into one hemisphere of the cerebellum seems only explicable on the view originally propounded by Mayo that the fibres of the transverse commissure coming from the diseased side communicate "a depressing" or "withering influence" to the descending fibres conducting voluntary motor impulses. Perhaps it may be more correct to regard all the fibres uniting together nervous centres as wholly commissural, and to consider the morbid influence in this case therefore as affecting the gray matter of the pons Varolii rather than the fibres, but this is only a slight modification of the original view. One circumstance which seems to support it is that the crossed paralysis only occurs, according to Hillairet,[1] in about one-third of all the cases;—the reason being, that in the other two-thirds the morbid impression is either insufficient

---

[1] "Ann. de Méd. et de Chir. pratiq. par. Jamain," 1859, p. 89.

to overcome the volitional impulse, or takes another direction, as to the corpora quadrigemina, causing blindness or convulsions, or to the medulla oblongata impairing respiration or speech, or even to the lower part of the cord producing predominating paraplegia. The non-occurrence of paralysis in some cases of disease of the cerebrum itself is probably to be explained in the same way. It is not the lesion of the hemisphere *per se* that causes the paralysis, but the depressing influence of this lesion on the deeper-seated cerebral ganglia. Paralysis therefore may or may not exist according to the quality of the nervous power, or the peculiar kind of lesion. In certain instances, as Dr. Ogle[1] has pointed out, the morbid influence may take another route and act on the cerebral ganglia of the opposite side so that the paralysis affects the limbs on the same side as the lesion. This view may afford some rational ground for treatment in cases which would otherwise be hopeless. It is true that we may be unable to amend materially the state of the damaged part, but we may be able so to improve the functional power of a connected centre that it shall not be depressed by the "withering influence" conveyed to it from the seat of the lesion.

[1] "Med.-Chir. Trans.," vol. 42.

VINDEMIATIO.

(1.) In all cases we should be guided as to treatment by the pathological condition existing much more than by the name of a disease. Morbid conditions called by the same name may be utterly different essentially, and require most different management. We should always endeavour to estimate the quality and amount of the nervous power.

(2.) The same cause may give rise to very various and even apparently opposite effects, according to the state of the nerve or nervous centre on which it acts; thus an irritation may either paralyze a muscle, or throw it into convulsion or into rigid spasm; may cause pain or numbness or local tenderness; may produce cerebral excitement or depression. Much depends on the degree of irritation, a moderate may excite, while a powerful may depress. The same may be said of the kind or quality of the irritation, an appropriate kind stimulates, while one which disagrees has an opposite effect.

(3.) The result of a stimulant or of a sedative may be different according as it affects the cerebro-spinal or vaso-motor nerves. The constriction of the arteries produced by the action of a stimulant on the latter may diminish or temporarily arrest functional power, and *vice versâ* dilatation of arteries produced by a sedative may give rise to excessive action. The operation of these agents on the cerebro-spinal nerves or centres is just the reverse.

(4.) Hyperæmia from paralysis of vaso-motor nerves is very common, and may under conditions of general exhaustion or local irritation pass on into actual and complete inflammation. This hyperæmia or inflammation is always diffuse.

(5.) We should bear in mind the frequent occurrence of reflex inhibitory action, implying the paralysis of cerebro-spinal or sympathetic nerves, as the result of a stimulus morbid in kind or degree in relation to the centre on which it acts. Such morbid impressions may originate within the cranium from lesion of the membranes or of a nervous centre.

(6.) Debility and excitability of nervous centres and nerves very often increase *pari passu*, but the former may exist alone. When very great it constitutes what may be termed simple paralysis, a simple loss of functional power. This is specially distinguished from reflex paralysis by being amenable to repose, generous diet and tonics, while reflex requires the removal of the exciting cause. Simple paralysis of a nervous centre much more often affects motion than sensation. It occurs both in the spinal and encephalic districts.

(7.) Paresis of nervous centres constitutes the primary and essential part of the affection termed sunstroke or heat-apoplexy; the vascular congestions being induced secondarily and depending in great measure on loss of tone in the capillaries and small arteries. According to this view the intimate relation between such disorders and various forms of fever is easily intelligible, as vaso-motor paresis seems to constitute an essential part of all febrile movement.

(8.) Active cerebral excitement may be either of a sthenic, an asthenic, or a medium quality, and will require corresponding modifications of treatment, and this independently of the nature of its exciting cause. This entirely applies to delirium tremens.

(9.) Spinal excitement (tetanus) is to be regarded more as a dynamic than a toxic affection. Its affinity to paralysis, and its relation to prostrating influences, as prolonged heat and cold and wet, should be borne in mind. Catalepsy, a variety of tetanus, is sometimes produced by exhaustion.

(10.) The epileptic paroxysm is immediately dependent on spasm of all the encephalic arteries in the greater, and those of the hemispheres only in the minor form. Sudden temporary anæmia is thus the necessary condition of the occasional paroxysm, but in prolonged convulsions, as puerperal, exanthematic, of tubercular or of uræmic origin, it is probable there is direct irritation of the tubercular quadrigemina and adjacent parts with more or less secondary hyperæmia. The latter when primary may no doubt be a predisposing, but if it stop short of actual inflammation, is scarcely ever an exciting cause of convulsions. Hyperæsthesia of the excitable districts, quite analogous to that affecting peripheral nerves, is, however it may be excited, the fundamental cause of convulsions. According to the *quality* of this hyperæsthesia counter-irritants, sedatives, or tonics, or a combination of them may be requisite.

(11.) Chorea is in most cases a dynamic disorder of debility, involving a greater or less extent of the cerebro-spinal centres, sometimes only the motor apparatus, sometimes the hemispheres also. Paralysis agitans, when not of organic origin, is a similar but more limited affection involving some part of the spinal centres.

(12.) Muscular spasms and contractions are attributable to disorder of motor nerves similar to the neuralgia of sensory, and like them are sometimes of central sometimes of peripheral origin. They may also be of sthenic or asthenic quality. A series of gradations may be traced from tonic spasms, through clonic tremors, and choreic agitation to actual paralysis.

(13.) Wherever nerves exist neuralgic affections may and do occur. As to their quality they may present either that of hyperæsthesia where tenderness and excitement predominate and sedatives relieve, or that of neuralgia characterized by pain and depression, and relieved by stimulants. These are the typical forms, but of course intermediate and mixed ones are most common. As to their origin they are in most cases intimately connected with depressing agencies, or with malaria, but may be dependent on remote irritation, or gouty or syphilitic poison.

(14.) Headache may be produced either by neuralgic affection of the brain itself, or of the nerves of the parietes, and may be characterized by hyperæsthesia, or by prostration. Like other nerve disorders it may be produced by direct or remote irritation.

(15.) Vertigo may be produced by any sudden alteration in the state of the cerebral circulation, or by enfeeblement of its power, or by direct or remote irritation interfering with the due action of its tissue.

(16.) Angina pectoris is essentially a cardiac neuralgia, consisting as so often observed in other situations of sensory and motor disorder, pain and spasm. It may be produced by very different causes as well as other cardiac neuroses.

(17.) The fatal termination of laryngismus stridulus probably depends on cardiac spasm associated with the glottic.

(18.) The convulsions attending on pertussis and other severe coughs do not depend on hyperæmia of the brain, but on propagation of the motor disorder to the nerves of the cerebral vessels.

(19.) Hemorrhages to a greater or less amount may result from causes of prostration acting through the vaso-motor nerves on the small arteries and capillaries. The nerve paresis causing dilatation of the arteries flushes the parts which they supply with blood, while the same condition impairing the quality of the capillary wall allows actual blood to escape into the tissue or on a free surface.

(20.) Miasmata giving rise to ague are generated occasionally in and around London. Young children are prone to suffer from a remittent fever of this kind attended with various complications. In adults it sometimes shows itself in a very obscure form attended with great nervous prostration and depression.

(21.) In well-marked cases of hysterical disorder (so called) the mind and morale may be perfectly sound and healthy.

(22.) Remember the distinction between the radical and the acting forces, *v.* p. 216.

(23.) In treatment large allowance must be made for idiosyncrasy; the *kind* of remedy may be clearly enough indicated, but it may not be easy to determine the particular one required. It is also essential to ascertain the proper dose; a remedy may fail because given in too large or too small an amount, or because it has not been given for a sufficient length of time.

INDEX.

Abdominal neuralgia, cases of, 429
Acids, sulphuric and nitric, action of, 322
Aconite, uses of, 330
Ague, greater prevalence of, 18
Anæmia, cerebral, 48
    spinal, 61
Anæsthesia, cutaneous, 278
    retinal, 193
Angina pectoris, 210
Anodynia, cutaneous, 279
Arsenic, action of, 316
Arteritis, results of, 42
Asthma, 239
    Pridham's treatment of, 242
    Ducros' medication in, 244
Atropine in cough, 234
Aura epileptic, 137, 142
Azoturia, 263

Baruria, 263
Bath, shower, 33, 34
    warm, action of, 334
    in syncopal ague, 226
    continuous in burns, 69
    in sleeplessness, 179
Belladonna, action of, 327
Bladder, neuralgia of, 262
Bronchial hyperæsthesia, cases of, 231, 232
Burns, results of, 69

Cannabis indica, action of, 330
Capillaries, atony of, from sunstroke, 267
Cardiac neuroses, rheumatic, 218
    malarious, 220
    saturnine, 226
    connected with Goitre Exophthalmia, 227
Cardiac hyperæsthesia, 229
Catalepsy, 131
Chloroform in tetanus, 129
Chorea, 160
Colchicum, in delirium, 106
Cold, effect of, 31, 32, 332
Compressed air baths in asthma, 243
Convulsions, puerperal, 143
Cramp, Writer's, 178
Cutaneous hyperæsthesia, 275
    anæsthesia, 278

Cutaneous—
    analgesia, 278
    hemorrhage neuropathic, 282
Cutaneous arteries, spasms of, 282

Delirium, sthenic, 101
    asthenic, acute, 107
    tremens, 112
    in rheumatic fever, 103
Digitalis, action of, 319
Drowsiness, 179

Ear, cauterization of in sciatica, 209
Epilepsy, 134
    cases of, 144
    treatment of, 140
Excitement, cerebral, 100
    spinal, 123
Exercise, effect of, 30

Fever, neuropathology of, 34
    malarioid, 291
    remittent obscure, 297
Flatulence, gastric, 215

Habit of action, 168
Hemorrhage, intestinal from nervous paresis, 269, 270
    gastric from nerve paresis, 258, 259
Hæmatemesis, from nervous paresis, 259
Hæmaturia, from nervous paresis, 266, 267
Headache, 153
Heat-apoplexy, 81
    after symptoms of, 82
Hiccup, 246
Hydrocyanic acid, action of, 106, 331
Hyperæmia, cerebral, 63
    spinal, 71
Hyperæsthesia
    gastric, 255
    uterine, 273
    retinal, 190
Hysteria, 307

Incontinuence of urine, diurnal, 266
    nocturnal, 266
    gouty, 262
Influenza, effects of, 85

Inhibitory theory, 22, 24, and appendix
Iris, action of opium on, 324
    belladonna on, 328
Iron, action of, 318
Irritation unfelt, 21

Lactic acid, 253
Laryngismus stridulus, 235
    T. Paget's remarks on, 238

Malaria, action of, 288
Malarioid disorder, 287
Malarious epilepsy, 139
Menorrhagia, treatment of, 274
Menstruation, state of vessels and nerves in, 272
Monotony, ill effects of, 79
Myalgia, 248

Nerves, division of, in neuralgia, 187
Nervous influence, results of loss of, 284, 286
Neuralgia, relations of, 44
    nature of, 39
    seat of, 42
    facial, 181
    abdominal, 249
    brachial, 197
    sciatic, 204
    lingual, 194
    vesical, 262
    rectal, 271
    uterine, 272
    epileptiform, 187
    osteal, 286
    crural, 209
Neuroses, cardiac, 217
Nicotine in tetanus, 130
Nocturnal aggravation of nerve disorder, 44

Opium, 323
    action of, on iris, 324
Oppler on the function of the kidney, 263

Paralysis, facial, 188
    agitans, 165
    infantile, 92
    diphtherial, 98

Paresis, cerebral, 74
    spinal, 88
Pertussis, 233
Pflüger's laws, 21
Pyrexia, 215

Quinine, action of, 315

Radcliffe's views, 45
Radical forces, 216
Reaction, 33
Rectum, neuralgia of, 271
Respiratory neuroses, 231
Rheumatic nerve affection, 312
Rigors in fever, 37

Sciatica, 204
Secretion fluxes, 306
Shower bath, effect of, 33, 34
Sleeplessness, 174
Sneezing, 244
Soporose affections, 180
Spasmodic affections, 169
Strychnia, action of, 318
Sulphuret of potassium baths in chorea, 161
    in asthma, 243
Syphilitic nerve affections, 310

Tannin, action of, 322
Tartar emetic, action of, 106, 114
Tea, action of, on heart, 217
Tetanilla, 128
Tetanus, 123
Throat dysæsthesia, 193
Tobacco, action of, on heart, 218
Trismus, 169

Urinary organs, neurosis of, 261
Urticaria, 276
Uterus, irritable, McKenzie on, 273
Uterine neuroses, 271

Vaso-motor nerve, functions of, 25 et seq.
Vertigo, 157

Warmth, moist, action of, 333

Yawning, 247

(LATE LEA & BLANCHARD'S)

CLASSIFIED CATALOGUE

OF

MEDICAL AND SURGICAL PUBLICATIONS.

In asking the attention of the profession to the works contained in the following pages, the publisher would state that no pains are spared to secure a continuance of the confidence earned for the publications of the house by their careful selection and accuracy and finish of execution.

The printed prices are those at which books can generally be supplied by booksellers throughout the United States, who can readily procure for their customers any works not kept in stock. Where access to bookstores is not convenient, books will be sent by mail post-paid on receipt of the price, but no risks are assumed either on the money or the books, and no publications but my own are supplied. Gentlemen will therefore in most cases find it more convenient to deal with the nearest bookseller.

An ILLUSTRATED CATALOGUE, of 64 octavo pages, handsomely printed, will be forwarded by mail, postpaid, on receipt of ten cents.

HENRY C. LEA.

Nos. 706 and 708 SANSOM ST., PHILADELPHIA, April, 1870.

ADDITIONAL INDUCEMENT FOR SUBSCRIBERS TO

THE AMERICAN JOURNAL OF THE MEDICAL SCIENCES.

THREE MEDICAL JOURNALS, containing over 2000 LARGE PAGES,

Free of Postage, for SIX DOLLARS Per Annum.

TERMS FOR 1870:

THE AMERICAN JOURNAL OF THE MEDICAL SCIENCES, and THE MEDICAL NEWS AND LIBRARY, both free of postage, } Five Dollars per annum, in advance.

OR,

THE AMERICAN JOURNAL OF THE MEDICAL SCIENCES, published quarterly (1150 pages per annum), with
THE MEDICAL NEWS AND LIBRARY, monthly (384 pp. per annum), and
THE HALF-YEARLY ABSTRACT OF THE MEDICAL SCIENCES, published Feb. and August (600 pages per annum), all free of postage. } Six Dollars per annum in advance.

SEPARATE SUBSCRIPTIONS TO

THE AMERICAN JOURNAL OF THE MEDICAL SCIENCES, subject to postage when not paid for in advance, Five Dollars.

THE MEDICAL NEWS AND LIBRARY, free of postage, in advance, One Dollar.

THE HALF-YEARLY ABSTRACT, Two Dollars and a Half per annum in advance. Single numbers One Dollar and a Half.

It is manifest that only a very wide circulation can enable so vast an amount of valuable practical matter to be supplied at a price so unprecedentedly low. The publisher, therefore, has much gratification in stating that the rapid and steady increase in the subscription list promises to render the enterprise a permanent one, and it is with especial pleasure that he acknowledges the valuable assistance spontaneously rendered by so many of the old subscribers to the "JOURNAL," who have kindly made known among their friends the advantages thus offered and have induced them to subscribe. Relying upon a continuance of these friendly exertions, he hopes to be able to maintain the unexampled rates at which these works are now supplied, and to succeed in his endeavor to place upon the table of every reading practitioner in the United States a monthly, a quarterly, and a half-yearly periodical at the comparatively trifling cost of, SIX DOLLARS *per annum.*

These periodicals are universally known for their high professional standing in their several spheres.

I.

THE AMERICAN JOURNAL OF THE MEDICAL SCIENCES,
EDITED BY ISAAC HAYS, M. D.,

is published Quarterly, on the first of January, April, July, and October. Each number contains nearly three hundred large octavo pages, appropriately illustrated, wherever necessary. It has now been issued regularly for over FORTY years, during nearly the whole of which time it has been under the control of the present editor. Throughout this long period, it has maintained its position in the highest rank of medical periodicals both at home and abroad, and has received the cordial support of the entire profession in this country. Among its Collaborators will be found a large number of the most distinguished names of the profession in every section of the United States, rendering the department devoted to

ORIGINAL COMMUNICATIONS

full of varied and important matter, of great interest to all practitioners. Thus, during 1869, articles have appeared in its pages from one hundred and fifteen gentlemen of the highest standing in the profession throughout the United States.*

Following this is the "REVIEW DEPARTMENT," containing extended and impartial reviews of all important new works, together with numerous elaborate "ANALYTICAL AND BIBLIOGRAPHICAL NOTICES" of nearly all the medical publications of the day.

This is followed by the "QUARTERLY SUMMARY OF IMPROVEMENTS AND DISCOVERIES IN THE MEDICAL SCIENCES," classified and arranged under different heads, presenting a very complete digest of all that is new and interesting to the physician, abroad as well as at home.

Thus, during the year 1869, the "JOURNAL" furnished to its subscribers One Hundred and Forty-seven Original Communications, Eighty-eight Reviews and Bibliographical Notices, and Two Hundred and Eighty-seven articles in the Quarterly Summaries, making a total of over FIVE HUNDRED articles emanating from the best professional minds in America and Europe.

To old subscribers, many of whom have been on the list for twenty or thirty years, the publisher feels that no promises for the future are necessary; but gentlemen who may now propose for the first time to subscribe may rest assured that no exertion will be spared to maintain the "JOURNAL" in the high position which it has so long occupied as a national exponent of scientific medicine, and as a medium of intercommunication between the profession of Europe and America—in the words of the "London Medical Times" (Sept. 5th, 1868) "almost the only one that circulates everywhere, all over the Union and in Europe"—to render it, in fact, necessary to every practitioner who desires to keep on a level with the progress of his science.

The subscription price of the "AMERICAN JOURNAL OF THE MEDICAL SCIENCES" has never been raised, during its long career. It is still FIVE DOLLARS per annum; and when paid in advance, the subscriber receives in addition the "MEDICAL NEWS AND LIBRARY," making in all about 1500 large octavo pages per annum, free of postage.

II.

THE MEDICAL NEWS AND LIBRARY

is a monthly periodical of Thirty-two large octavo pages, making 384 pages per annum. Its "NEWS DEPARTMENT" presents the current information of the day, with Clinical Lectures and Hospital Gleanings; while the "LIBRARY DEPARTMENT" is devoted to publishing standard works on the various branches of medical science, paged

---

* Communications are invited from gentlemen in all parts of the country. Elaborate articles inserted by the Editor are paid for by the Publisher.

separately, so that they can be removed and bound on completion. In this manner subscribers have received, without expense, such works as "WATSON'S PRACTICE," "TODD AND BOWMAN'S PHYSIOLOGY," "WEST ON CHILDREN," "MALGAIGNE'S SURGERY," &c. &c. And with January, 1870, another work of similar practical value will be commenced, rendering this a very eligible period for the commencement of new subscriptions.

As stated above, the subscription price of the "MEDICAL NEWS AND LIBRARY" is ONE DOLLAR per annum in advance; and it is furnished without charge to all advance paying subscribers to the "AMERICAN JOURNAL OF THE MEDICAL SCIENCES."

III.
THE HALF-YEARLY ABSTRACT OF THE MEDICAL SCIENCES

is issued in half-yearly volumes, which will be delivered to subscribers about the first of February, and first of August. Each volume contains about 300 closely printed octavo pages, making about six hundred pages per annum.

"RANKING'S ABSTRACT" has now been published in England regularly for more than twenty years, and has acquired the highest reputation for the ability and industry with which the essence of medical literature is condensed into its pages. It purports to be "*A Digest of British and Continental Medicine, and of the Progress of Medicine and the Collateral Sciences*," and it is even more than this, for America is largely represented in its pages. It draws its material not only from all the leading American, British, and Continental journals, but also from the medical works and treatises issued during the preceding six months, thus giving a complete digest of medical progress. Each article is carefully condensed, so as to present its substance in the smallest possible compass, thus affording space for the very large amount of information laid before its readers. The volumes of 1869, for instance, have thus contained

THIRTY-FOUR ARTICLES ON GENERAL QUESTIONS IN MEDICINE.
ONE HUNDRED AND ELEVEN ARTICLES ON SPECIAL QUESTIONS IN MEDICINE.
NINETEEN ARTICLES ON FORENSIC MEDICINE.
NINETY-NINE ARTICLES ON THERAPEUTICS.
THIRTY-SEVEN ARTICLES ON GENERAL QUESTIONS IN SURGERY.
ONE HUNDRED AND SIXTY-SEVEN ARTICLES ON SPECIAL QUESTIONS IN SURGERY.
NINETY-FIVE ARTICLES ON MIDWIFERY AND DISEASES OF WOMEN AND CHILDREN

Making in all over five hundred and fifty articles in a single year. Each volume, moreover, is systematically arranged, with an elaborate Table of Contents and a very full Index, thus facilitating the researches of the reader in pursuit of particular subjects, and enabling him to refer without loss of time to the vast amount of information contained in its pages.

The subscription price of the "ABSTRACT," mailed free of postage, is TWO DOLLARS AND A HALF per annum, payable in advance. Single volumes, $1 50 each.

As stated above, however, it will be supplied in conjunction with the "AMERICAN JOURNAL OF THE MEDICAL SCIENCES" and the "MEDICAL NEWS AND LIBRARY," the whole *free of postage*, for SIX DOLLARS PER ANNUM IN ADVANCE.

For this small sum the subscriber will therefore receive three periodicals costing separately Eight Dollars and a Half, each of them enjoying the highest reputation in its class, containing in all over TWO THOUSAND PAGES of the choicest reading, and presenting a complete view of medical progress throughout both hemispheres.

In this effort to bring so large an amount of practical information within the reach of every member of the profession, the publisher confidently anticipates the friendly aid of all who are interested in the dissemination of sound medical literature. He trusts, especially, that the subscribers to the "AMERICAN MEDICAL JOURNAL" will call the attention of their acquaintances to the advantages thus offered, and that he will be sustained in the endeavor to permanently establish medical periodical literature on a footing of cheapness never heretofore attempted.

*** Gentlemen desiring to avail themselves of the advantages thus offered will do well to forward their subscriptions at an early day, in order to insure the receipt of complete sets for the year 1870, as the constant increase in the subscription list almost always exhausts the quantity printed shortly after publication.

☞ The safest mode of remittance is by postal money order, drawn to the order of the undersigned. Where money order post-offices are not accessible, remittances for the "JOURNAL" may be made at the risk of the publisher, by forwarding in REGISTERED letters. Address,

HENRY C. LEA,
Nos. 706 and 708 SANSOM ST., PHILADELPHIA, PA.

DUNGLISON (ROBLEY), M. D.,
Professor of Institutes of Medicine in Jefferson Medical College, Philadelphia.

MEDICAL LEXICON; A DICTIONARY OF MEDICAL SCIENCE: Containing a concise explanation of the various Subjects and Terms of Anatomy, Physiology, Pathology, Hygiene, Therapeutics, Pharmacology, Pharmacy, Surgery, Obstetrics, Medical Jurisprudence, and Dentistry. Notices of Climate and of Mineral Waters; Formulæ for Officinal, Empirical, and Dietetic Preparations; with the Accentuation and Etymology of the Terms, and the French and other Synonymes; so as to constitute a French as well as English Medical Lexicon. Thoroughly Revised, and very greatly Modified and Augmented. In one very large and handsome royal octavo volume of 1048 double-columned pages, in small type; strongly done up in extra cloth, $6 00; leather, raised bands, $6 75.

The object of the author from the outset has not been to make the work a mere lexicon or dictionary of terms, but to afford, under each, a condensed view of its various medical relations, and thus to render the work an epitome of the existing condition of medical science. Starting with this view, the immense demand which has existed for the work has enabled him, in repeated revisions, to augment its completeness and usefulness, until at length it has attained the position of a recognized and standard authority wherever the language is spoken. The mechanical execution of this edition will be found greatly superior to that of previous impressions. By enlarging the size of the volume to a royal octavo, and by the employment of a small but clear type, on extra fine paper, the additions have been incorporated without materially increasing the bulk of the volume, and the matter of two or three ordinary octavos has been compressed into the space of one not unhandy for consultation and reference.

It would be a work of supererogation to bestow a word of praise upon this Lexicon. We can only wonder at the labor expended, for whenever we refer to its pages for information we are seldom disappointed in finding all we desire, whether it be in accentuation, etymology, or definition of terms.—*New York Medical Journal*, November, 1865.

It would be mere waste of words in us to express our admiration of a work which is so universally and deservedly appreciated. The most admirable work of its kind in the English language. As a book of reference it is invaluable to the medical practitioner; and in every instance that we have turned over its pages for information we have been charmed by the clearness of language and the accuracy of detail with which each abounds. We can most cordially and confidently commend it to our readers.—*Glasgow Medical Journal*, January, 1866.

A work to which there is no equal in the English language.—*Edinburgh Medical Journal*.

It is something more than a dictionary, and something less than an encyclopædia. This edition of the well-known work is a great improvement on its predecessors. The book is one of the very few of which it may be said with truth that every medical man should possess it.—*London Medical Times*, Aug. 26, 1865.

Few works of the class exhibit a grander monument of patient research and of scientific lore. The extent of the sale of this lexicon is sufficient to testify to its usefulness, and to the great service conferred by Dr. Robley Dunglison on the profession, and indeed on others, by its issue.—*London Lancet*, May 13, 1865.

The old edition, which is now superseded by the new, has been universally looked upon by the medical profession as a work of immense research and great value. The new has increased usefulness; for medicine, in all its branches, has been making such progress that many new terms and subjects have recently been introduced; all of which may be found fully defined in the present edition. We know of no other dictionary in the English language that can bear a comparison with it in point of completeness of subjects and accuracy of statement.—*N. Y. Druggists' Circular*, 1865.

For many years Dunglison's Dictionary has been the standard book of reference with most practitioners in this country, and we can certainly commend this work to the renewed confidence and regard of our readers.—*Cincinnati Lancet*, April, 1865.

It is undoubtedly the most complete and useful medical dictionary hitherto published in this country.—*Chicago Med. Examiner*, February, 1865.

What we take to be decidedly the best medical dictionary in the English language. The present edition is brought fully up to the advanced state of science. For many a long year "Dunglison" has been at our elbow, a constant companion and friend, and we greet him in his replenished and improved form with especial satisfaction.—*Pacific Med. and Surg. Journal*, June 27, 1865.

This is, perhaps, the book of all others which the physician or surgeon should have on his shelves. It is more needed at the present day than a few years back.—*Canada Med. Journal*, July, 1865.

It deservedly stands at the head, and cannot be surpassed in excellence.—*Buffalo Med. and Surg. Journal*, April, 1865.

We can sincerely commend Dr. Dunglison's work as most thorough, scientific, and accurate. We have tested it by searching its pages for new terms, which have abounded so much of late in medical nomenclature, and our search has been successful in every instance. We have been particularly struck with the fulness of the synonymy and the accuracy of the derivation of words. It is as necessary a work to every enlightened physician as Worcester's English Dictionary is to every one who would keep up his knowledge of the English tongue to the standard of the present day. It is, to our mind, the most complete work of the kind with which we are acquainted.—*Boston Med. and Surg. Journal*, June 22, 1865.

We are free to confess that we know of no medical dictionary more complete; no one better, if so well adapted for the use of the student; no one that may be consulted with more satisfaction by the medical practitioner.—*Am. Jour. Med. Sciences*, April, 1865.

The value of the present edition has been greatly enhanced by the introduction of new subjects and terms, and a more complete etymology and accentuation, which renders the work not only satisfactory and desirable, but indispensable to the physician.—*Chicago Med. Journal*, April, 1865.

No intelligent member of the profession can or will be without it.—*St. Louis Med. and Surg. Journal*, April, 1865.

It has the rare merit that it certainly has no rival in the English language for accuracy and extent of references.—*London Medical Gazette*.

HOBLYN (RICHARD D.), M. D.

A DICTIONARY OF THE TERMS USED IN MEDICINE AND THE COLLATERAL SCIENCES. A new American edition, revised, with numerous additions, by ISAAC HAYS, M. D., Editor of the "American Journal of the Medical Sciences." In one large royal 12mo. volume of over 500 double-columned pages; extra cloth, $1 50; leather, $2 00.

It is the best book of definitions we have, and ought always to be upon the student's table.—*Southern Med. and Surg. Journal*.

NEILL (JOHN), M.D., and *SMITH (FRANCIS G.), M.D.,*
Prof. of the Institutes of Medicine in the Univ. of Penna.

AN ANALYTICAL COMPENDIUM OF THE VARIOUS BRANCHES OF MEDICAL SCIENCE; for the Use and Examination of Students. A new edition, revised and improved. In one very large and handsomely printed royal 12mo. volume, of about one thousand pages, with 374 wood cuts, extra cloth, $4; strongly bound in leather, with raised bands, $4 75.

The Compend of Drs. Neill and Smith is incomparably the most valuable work of its class ever published in this country. Attempts have been made in various quarters to squeeze Anatomy, Physiology, Surgery, the Practice of Medicine, Obstetrics, Materia Medica, and Chemistry into a single volume; but the operation has signally failed in the hands of all up to the advent of "Neill and Smith's" volume, which is quite a miracle of success. The outlines of the whole are admirably drawn and illustrated, and the authors are eminently entitled to the grateful consideration of the student of every class.—*N. O. Med. and Surg. Journal.*

There are but few students or practitioners of medicine unacquainted with the former editions of this unassuming though highly instructive work. The whole science of medicine appears to have been sifted, as the gold-bearing sands of El Dorado, and the precious facts treasured up in this little volume. A complete portable library so condensed that the student may make it his constant pocket companion.—*Western Lancet.*

In the rapid course of lectures, where work for the students is heavy, and review necessary for an examination, a compend is not only valuable, but it is almost a *sine qua non.* The one before us is, in most of the divisions, the most unexceptionable of all books of the kind that we know of. Of course it is useless for us to recommend it to all last course students, but there is a class to whom we very sincerely commend this cheap book as worth its weight in silver—that class is the graduates in medicine of more than ten years' standing, who have not studied medicine since. They will perhaps find out from it that the science is not exactly now what it was when they left it off.—*The Stethoscope.*

HARTSHORNE (HENRY), M.D.,
Professor of Hygiene in the University of Pennsylvania.

A CONSPECTUS OF THE MEDICAL SCIENCES; containing Handbooks on Anatomy, Physiology, Chemistry, Materia Medica, Practical Medicine, Surgery, and Obstetrics. In one large royal 12mo. volume of 1000 closely printed pages, with over 300 illustrations on wood, extra cloth, $4 50; leather, raised bands, $5 25. (*Now Ready.*)

The ability of the author, and his practical skill in condensation, give assurance that this work will prove valuable not only to the student preparing for examination, but also to the practitioner desirous of obtaining within a moderate compass, a view of the existing condition of the various departments of science connected with medicine.

This work is a remarkably complete one in its way, and comes nearer to our idea of what a Conspectus should be than any we have yet seen. Prof. Hartshorne, with a commendable forethought, intrusted the preparation of many of the chapters on special subjects to experts, reserving only anatomy, physiology, and practice of medicine to himself. As a result we have every department worked up to the latest date and in a refreshingly concise and lucid manner. There are an immense amount of illustrations scattered throughout the work, and although they have often been seen before in the various works upon general and special subjects, yet they will be none the less valuable to the beginner. Every medical student who desires a reliable refresher to his memory when the pressure of lectures and other college work crowds to prevent him from having an opportunity to drink deeper in the larger works, will find this one of the greatest utility. It is thoroughly trustworthy from beginning to end; and as we have before intimated, a remarkably truthful outline sketch of the present state of medical science. We could hardly expect it should be otherwise, however, under the charge of such a thorough medical scholar as the author has already proved himself to be.—*N. York Med. Record,* March 15, 1869.

LUDLOW (J. L.), M.D.,

A MANUAL OF EXAMINATIONS upon Anatomy, Physiology, Surgery, Practice of Medicine, Obstetrics, Materia Medica, Chemistry, Pharmacy, and Therapeutics. To which is added a Medical Formulary. Third edition, thoroughly revised and greatly extended and enlarged. With 370 illustrations. In one handsome royal 12mo. volume of 816 large pages, extra cloth, $3 25; leather, $3 75.

The arrangement of this volume in the form of question and answer renders it especially suitable for the office examination of students, and for those preparing for graduation.

TANNER (THOMAS HAWKES), M.D., &c.

A MANUAL OF CLINICAL MEDICINE AND PHYSICAL DIAGNOSIS. Third American from the Second London Edition. Revised and Enlarged by TILBURY FOX, M.D., Physician to the Skin Department in University College Hospital, &c. In one neat volume small 12mo., of about 375 pages, extra cloth. $1 50. (*Now Ready.*)

This favorite little work has remained out of print for some years in consequence of the pressing engagements which have prevented the author from giving it the thorough revision which it required. The great advance which has taken place of late in the means and appliances for observation and diagnosis has necessitated a very considerable enlargement of the work, so that it now contains about one-half more matter than the last edition. The Laryngoscope, Ophthalmoscope, Sphygmograph, and Thermometer have received special attention. The chapter on the diagnostic indications afforded by the Urine has been much enlarged, and a section has been inserted on the administration of Chloroform. Special attention has been given to the medical anatomy of regions and organs, and much has been introduced relative to pericardial, endocardial, abdominal, and cerebro-spinal diseases. On every subject coming within its scope such additions have been made as seemed essential to bring the book on a level with the most advanced condition of medical knowledge; and it is hoped that it will continue to merit the very great favor with which it has hitherto been received.

GRAY (HENRY), F. R. S.,
Lecturer on Anatomy at St. George's Hospital, London.

ANATOMY, DESCRIPTIVE AND SURGICAL. The Drawings by H. V. CARTER, M. D., late Demonstrator on Anatomy at St. George's Hospital; the Dissections jointly by the AUTHOR and DR. CARTER. A new American, from the fifth enlarged and improved London edition. In one magnificent imperial octavo volume, of nearly 900 pages, with 465 large and elaborate engravings on wood. Price in extra cloth, $6 00; leather, raised bands, $7 00. (*Just Ready.*)

The author has endeavored in this work to cover a more extended range of subjects than is customary in the ordinary text-books, by giving not only the details necessary for the student, but also the application of those details in the practice of medicine and surgery, thus rendering it both a guide for the learner, and an admirable work of reference for the active practitioner. The engravings form a special feature in the work, many of them being the size of nature, nearly all original, and having the names of the various parts printed on the body of the cut, in place of figures of reference, with descriptions at the foot. They thus form a complete and splendid series, which will greatly assist the student in obtaining a clear idea of Anatomy, and will also serve to refresh the memory of those who may find in the exigencies of practice the necessity of recalling the details of the dissecting room; while combining, as it does, a complete Atlas of Anatomy, with a thorough treatise on systematic, descriptive, and applied Anatomy, the work will be found of essential use to all physicians who receive students in their offices, relieving both preceptor and pupil of much labor in laying the groundwork of a thorough medical education.

Notwithstanding its exceedingly low price, the work will be found, in every detail of mechanical execution, one of the handsomest that has yet been offered to the American profession; while the careful scrutiny of a competent anatomist has relieved it of whatever typographical errors existed in the English edition. A few notices of previous editions are subjoined.

Thus it is that book after book makes the labor of the student easier than before, and since we have seen Blanchard & Lea's new edition of Gray's Anatomy, certainly the finest work of the kind now extant, we would fain hope that the bugbear of medical students will lose half its horrors, and this, necessary foundation of physiological science will be much facilitated and advanced.—*N. O. Med. News.*

The various points illustrated are marked directly on the structure; that is, whether it be muscle, process, artery, nerve, valve, etc. etc.—we say each point is distinctly marked by lettered engravings, so that the student perceives at once each point described as readily as if pointed out on the subject by the demonstrator. Most of the illustrations are thus rendered exceedingly satisfactory, and to the physician they serve to refresh the memory with great readiness

and with scarce a reference to the printed text. The surgical application of the various regions is also presented with force and clearness, impressing upon the student at each step of his research all the important relations of the structure demonstrated.—*Cincinnati Lancet.*

This is, we believe, the handsomest book on Anatomy as yet published in our language, and bids fair to become in a short time THE standard text-book of our colleges and studies. Students and practitioners will alike appreciate this book. We predict for it a bright career, and are fully prepared to endorse the statement of the *London Lancet*, that "We are not acquainted with any work in any language which can take equal rank with the one before us." Paper, printing, binding, all are excellent, and we feel that a grateful profession will not allow the publishers to go unrewarded.—*Nashville Med. and Surg. Journal.*

SMITH (HENRY H.), M.D., and HORNER (WILLIAM E.), M.D.,
Prof. of Surgery in the Univ. of Penna., &c. *Late Prof. of Anatomy in the Univ. of Penna., &c.*

AN ANATOMICAL ATLAS, illustrative of the Structure of the Human Body. In one volume, large imperial octavo, extra cloth, with about six hundred and fifty beautiful figures. $4 50.

The plan of this Atlas, which renders it so peculiarly convenient for the student, and its superb artistical execution, have been already pointed out. We must congratulate the student upon the completion of this Atlas, as it is the most convenient work of

the kind that has yet appeared; and we must add, the very beautiful manner in which it is "got up" is so creditable to the country as to be flattering to our national pride.—*American Medical Journal.*

HARTSHORNE (HENRY), M. D.,
Professor of Hygiene, etc., in the University of Pennsylvania.

A HAND-BOOK OF HUMAN ANATOMY AND PHYSIOLOGY, for the use of Students, with 176 illustrations. In one volume, royal 12mo. of 312 pages; extra cloth, $1 75. (*Now Ready.*)

SHARPEY (WILLIAM), M.D., and QUAIN (JONES & RICHARD).

HUMAN ANATOMY. Revised, with Notes and Additions, by JOSEPH LEIDY, M. D., Professor of Anatomy in the University of Pennsylvania. Complete in two large octavo volumes, of about 1300 pages, with 511 illustrations; extra cloth, $6 00.

The very low price of this standard work, and its completeness in all departments of the subject, should command for it a place in the library of all anatomical students.

ALLEN (J. M.), M. D.

THE PRACTICAL ANATOMIST; OR, THE STUDENT'S GUIDE IN THE DISSECTING ROOM. With 266 illustrations. In one very handsome royal 12mo. volume, of over 600 pages; extra cloth, $2 00.

One of the most useful works upon the subject ever written.—*Medical Examiner.*

WILSON (ERASMUS), F.R.S.

A SYSTEM OF HUMAN ANATOMY, General and Special. A new and revised American, from the last and enlarged English edition. Edited by W. H. GOBRECHT, M. D., Professor of General and Surgical Anatomy in the Medical College of Ohio. Illustrated with three hundred and ninety-seven engravings on wood. In one large and handsome octavo volume, of over 600 large pages; extra cloth, $4 00; leather, $5 00.

The publisher trusts that the well-earned reputation of this long-established favorite will be more than maintained by the present edition. Besides a very thorough revision by the author, it has been most carefully examined by the editor, and the efforts of both have been directed to introducing everything which increased experience in its use has suggested as desirable to render it a complete text-book for those seeking to obtain or to renew an acquaintance with Human Anatomy. The amount of additions which it has thus received may be estimated from the fact that the present edition contains over one-fourth more matter than the last, rendering a smaller type and an enlarged page requisite to keep the volume within a convenient size. The author has not only thus added largely to the work, but he has also made alterations throughout, wherever there appeared the opportunity of improving the arrangement or style, so as to present every fact in its most appropriate manner, and to render the whole as clear and intelligible as possible. The editor has exercised the utmost caution to obtain entire accuracy in the text, and has largely increased the number of illustrations, of which there are about one hundred and fifty more in this edition than in the last, thus bringing distinctly before the eye of the student everything of interest or importance.

BY THE SAME AUTHOR.

THE DISSECTOR'S MANUAL; OR, PRACTICAL AND SURGICAL ANATOMY. Third American, from the last revised and enlarged English edition. Modified and rearranged by WILLIAM HUNT, M.D., late Demonstrator of Anatomy in the University of Pennsylvania. In one large and handsome royal 12mo. volume, of 582 pages, with 154 illustrations; extra cloth, $2 00.

HEATH (CHRISTOPHER), F.R.C.S.,
Teacher of Operative Surgery in University College, London.

PRACTICAL ANATOMY: A Manual of Dissections. From the Second revised and improved London edition. Edited, with additions, by W. W. KEEN, M. D., Lecturer on Pathological Anatomy in the Jefferson Medical College, Philadelphia. In one handsome volume, with over 200 illustrations. (*In Press.*)

HODGES, (RICHARD M.), M.D.,
Late Demonstrator of Anatomy in the Medical Department of Harvard University.

PRACTICAL DISSECTIONS. Second Edition, thoroughly revised. In one neat royal 12mo. volume, half-bound, $2 00. (*Just Issued.*)

The object of this work is to present to the anatomical student a clear and concise description of that which he is expected to observe in an ordinary course of dissections. The author has endeavored to omit unnecessary details, and to present the subject in the form which many years' experience has shown him to be the most convenient and intelligible to the student. In the revision of the present edition, he has sedulously labored to render the volume more worthy of the favor with which it has heretofore been received.

MACLISE (JOSEPH).

SURGICAL ANATOMY. By JOSEPH MACLISE, Surgeon. In one volume, very large imperial quarto; with 68 large and splendid plates, drawn in the best style and beautifully colored, containing 190 figures, many of them the size of life; together with copious explanatory letter-press. Strongly and handsomely bound in extra cloth. Price $14 00.

As no complete work of the kind has heretofore been published in the English language, the present volume will supply a want long felt in this country of an accurate and comprehensive Atlas of Surgical Anatomy, to which the student and practitioner can at all times refer to ascertain the exact relative positions of the various portions of the human frame towards each other and to the surface, as well as their abnormal deviations. Notwithstanding the large size, beauty and finish of the very numerous illustrations, it will be observed that the price is so low as to place it within the reach of all members of the profession.

We know of no work on surgical anatomy which can compete with it.—*Lancet.*

The work of Maclise on surgical anatomy is of the highest value. In some respects it is the best publication of its kind we have seen, and is worthy of a place in the library of any medical man, while the student could scarcely make a better investment than this.—*The Western Journal of Medicine and Surgery.*

No such lithographic illustrations of surgical regions have hitherto, we think, been given. While the operator is shown every vessel and nerve where an operation is contemplated, the exact anatomist is refreshed by those clear and distinct dissections, which every one must appreciate who has a particle of enthusiasm. The English medical press has quite exhausted the words of praise, in recommending this admirable treatise. Those who have any curiosity to gratify, in reference to the perfectibility of the lithographic art in delineating the complex mechanism of the human body, are invited to examine our specimen copy. If anything will induce surgeons and students to patronize a book of such rare value and everyday importance to them, it will be a survey of the artistical skill exhibited in these fac-similes of nature.—*Boston Med. and Surg. Journal.*

HORNER'S SPECIAL ANATOMY AND HISTOLOGY. Eighth edition, extensively revised and modified. In 2 vols. 8vo., of over 1000 pages, with more than 300 wood-cuts; extra cloth, $6 00.

MARSHALL (JOHN), F. R. S.,
Professor of Surgery in University College, London, &c.

OUTLINES OF PHYSIOLOGY, HUMAN AND COMPARATIVE.
With Additions by FRANCIS GURNEY SMITH, M. D., Professor of the Institutes of Medicine in the University of Pennsylvania, &c. With numerous illustrations. In one large and handsome octavo volume, of 1026 pages, extra cloth, $6 50; leather, raised bands, $7 50. (*Just Issued.*)

In fact, in every respect, Mr. Marshall has presented us with a most complete, reliable, and scientific work, and we feel that it is worthy our warmest commendation.—*St. Louis Med. Reporter*, Jan. 1869.

This is an elaborate and carefully prepared digest of human and comparative physiology, designed for the use of general readers, but more especially serviceable to the student of medicine. Its style is concise, clear, and scholarly; its order perspicuous and exact, and its range of topics extended. The author and his American editor have been careful to bring to the illustration of the subject the important discoveries of modern science in the various cognate departments of investigation. This is especially visible in the variety of interesting information derived from the departments of chemistry and physics. The great amount and variety of matter contained in the work is strikingly illustrated by turning over the copious index, covering twenty-four closely printed pages in double columns.—*Silliman's Journal*, Jan. 1869.

We doubt if there is in the English language any compend of physiology more useful to the student than this work.—*St. Louis Med. and Surg. Journal*, Jan. 1869.

It quite fulfils, in our opinion, the author's design of making it truly *educational* in its character—which is, perhaps, the highest commendation that can be asked.—*Am. Journ. Med. Sciences*, Jan. 1869.

We may now congratulate him on having completed the latest as well as the best summary of modern physiological science, both human and comparative, with which we are acquainted. To speak of this work in the terms ordinarily used on such occasions would not be agreeable to ourselves, and would fail to do justice to its author. To write such a book requires a varied and wide range of knowledge, considerable power of analysis, correct judgment, skill in arrangement, and conscientious spirit. It must have entailed great labor, but now that the task has been fulfilled, the book will prove not only invaluable to the student of medicine and surgery, but serviceable to all candidates in natural science examinations, to teachers in schools, and to the lover of nature generally. In conclusion, we can only express the conviction that the merits of the work will commend for it that success which the ability and vast labor displayed in its production so well deserve.—*London Lancet*, Feb. 22, 1868.

If the possession of knowledge, and peculiar aptitude and skill in expounding it, qualify a man to write an educational work, Mr. Marshall's treatise might be reviewed favorably without even opening the covers. There are few, if any, more accomplished anatomists and physiologists than the distinguished professor of surgery at University College; and he has long enjoyed the highest reputation as a teacher of physiology, possessing remarkable powers of clear exposition and graphic illustration. We have rarely the pleasure of being able to recommend a text-book so unreservedly as this.—*British Med. Journal*, Jan. 25, 1868.

CARPENTER (WILLIAM B.), M. D., F. R. S.,
Examiner in Physiology and Comparative Anatomy in the University of London.

PRINCIPLES OF HUMAN PHYSIOLOGY; with their chief applications to Psychology, Pathology, Therapeutics, Hygiene and Forensic Medicine. A new American from the last and revised London edition. With nearly three hundred illustrations. Edited, with additions, by FRANCIS GURNEY SMITH, M. D., Professor of the Institutes of Medicine in the University of Pennsylvania, &c. In one very large and beautiful octavo volume, of about 900 large pages, handsomely printed; extra cloth, $5 50; leather, raised bands, $6 50.

With Dr. Smith, we confidently believe "that the present will more than sustain the enviable reputation already attained by former editions, of being one of the fullest and most complete treatises on the subject in the English language." We know of none from the pages of which a satisfactory knowledge of the physiology of the human organism can be as well obtained, none better adapted for the use of such a-take up the study of physiology in its reference tof the institutes and practice of medicine.—*Am. Jour. Med. Sciences.*

We doubt not it is destined to retain a strong hold on public favor, and remain the favorite text-book in our colleges.—*Virginia Medical Journal.*

The same is the title of what is emphatically *the* great work on physiology; and we are conscious that it would be a useless effort to attempt to add anything to the reputation of this invaluable work, and can only say to all with whom our opinion has any influence, that it is our *authority*.—*Atlanta Med. Journal.*

BY THE SAME AUTHOR.

PRINCIPLES OF COMPARATIVE PHYSIOLOGY. New American, from the Fourth and Revised London Edition. In one large and handsome octavo volume, with over three hundred beautiful illustrations Pp. 752. Extra cloth, $5 00.

As a complete and condensed treatise on its extended and important subject, this work becomes a necessity to students of natural science, while the very low price at which it is offered places it within the reach of all.

BY THE SAME AUTHOR.

THE MICROSCOPE AND ITS REVELATIONS. Illustrated by four hundred and thirty-four beautiful engravings on wood. In one large and very handsome octavo volume, of 724 pages, extra cloth, $5 25.

KIRKES (WILLIAM SENHOUSE), M. D.,

A MANUAL OF PHYSIOLOGY. A new American from the third and improved London edition. With two hundred illustrations. In one large and handsome royal 12mo. volume. Pp. 586. Extra cloth, $2 25; leather, $2 75.

It is at once convenient in size, comprehensive in design, and concise in statement, and altogether well adapted for the purpose designed.—*St. Louis Med. and Surg. Journal.*

The physiological reader will find it a most excellent guide in the study of physiology in its most advanced and perfect form. The author has shown himself capable of giving details sufficiently ample in a condensed and concentrated shape, on a science in which it is necessary at once to be correct and not lengthened.—*Edinburgh Med. and Surg. Journal.*

DALTON (J. C.), M. D.,
Professor of Physiology in the College of Physicians and Surgeons, New York, &c.

A TREATISE ON HUMAN PHYSIOLOGY. Designed for the use of Students and Practitioners of Medicine. Fourth edition, revised, with nearly three hundred illustrations on wood. In one very beautiful octavo volume, of about 700 pages, extra cloth, $5 25; leather, $6 25. (*Just Issued.*)

From the Preface to the New Edition.

"The progress made by Physiology and the kindred Sciences during the last few years has required, for the present edition of this work, a thorough and extensive revision. This progress has not consisted in any very striking single discoveries, nor in a decided revolution in any of the departments of Physiology; but it has been marked by great activity of investigation in a multitude of different directions, the combined results of which have not failed to impress a new character on many of the features of physiological knowledge. . . . In the revision and correction of the present edition, the author has endeavored to incorporate all such improvements in physiological knowledge with the mass of the text in such a manner as not essentially to alter the structure and plan of the work, so far as they have been found adapted to the wants and convenience of the reader. . . . Several new illustrations are introduced, some of them as additions, others as improvements or corrections of the old. Although all parts of the book have received more or less complete revision, the greatest number of additions and changes were required in the Second Section, on the Physiology of the Nervous System."

The advent of the first edition of Prof. Dalton's Physiology, about eight years ago, marked a new era in the study of physiology to the American student. Under Dalton's skilful management, physiological science threw off the long, loose, ungainly garments of probability and surmise, in which it had been arrayed by most artists, and came among us smiling and attractive, in the beautifully tinted and closely fitting dress of a demonstrated science. It was a stroke of genius, as well as a result of erudition and talent, that led Prof. Dalton to present to the world a work on physiology at once brief, pointed, and comprehensive, and which exhibited plainly in letter and drawings the basis upon which the conclusions arrived at rested. It is no disparagement of the many excellent works on physiology, published prior to that of Dalton, to say that none of them, either in plan of arrangement or clearness of execution, could be compared with his for the use of students or general practitioners of medicine. For this purpose his book has no equal in the English language.—*Western Journal of Medicine*, Nov. 1867.

A capital text-book in every way. We are, therefore, glad to see it in its fourth edition. It has already been examined at full length in these columns, so that we need not now further advert to it beyond remarking that both revision and enlargement have been most judicious.—*London Med. Times and Gazette*, Oct. 19, 1867.

No better proof of the value of this admirable work could be produced than the fact that it has already reached a fourth edition in the short space of eight years. Possessing in an eminent degree the merits of clearness and condensation, and being fully brought up to the present level of Physiology, it is undoubtedly one of the most reliable text-books upon this science that could be placed in the hands of the medical student.—*Am. Journal Med. Sciences*, Oct. 1867.

Prof. Dalton's work has such a well-established reputation that it does not stand in need of any recommendation. Ever since its first appearance it has become the highest authority in the English language; and that it is able to maintain the enviable position which it has taken, the rapid exhaustion of the different successive editions is sufficient evidence. The present edition, which is the fourth, has been thoroughly revised, and enlarged by the incorporation of all the many important advances which have lately been made in this rapidly progressing science. —*N. Y. Med. Record*, Oct. 15, 1867.

As it stands, we esteem it the very best of the physiological text-books for the student, and the most concise reference and guide-book for the practitioner. —*N. Y. Med. Journal*, Oct. 1867.

The present edition of this now standard work fully sustains the high reputation of its accomplished author. It is not merely a reprint, but has been faithfully revised, and enriched by such additions as the progress of physiology has rendered desirable. Taken as a whole, it is unquestionably the most reliable and useful treatise on the subject that has been issued from the American press.—*Chicago Med. Journal*, Sept. 1867.

DUNGLISON (ROBLEY), M. D.,
Professor of Institutes of Medicine in Jefferson Medical College, Philadelphia.

HUMAN PHYSIOLOGY. Eighth edition. Thoroughly revised and extensively modified and enlarged, with five hundred and thirty-two illustrations. In two large and handsomely printed octavo volumes of about 1500 pages, extra cloth. $7 00.

LEHMANN (C. G.)
PHYSIOLOGICAL CHEMISTRY. Translated from the second edition by GEORGE E DAY, M. D., F. R. S., &c., edited by R. E. ROGERS, M. D., Professor of Chemistry in the Medical Department of the University of Pennsylvania, with illustrations selected from Funke's Atlas of Physiological Chemistry, and an Appendix of plates. Complete in two large and handsome octavo volumes, containing 1200 pages, with nearly two hundred illustrations, extra cloth. $6 00.

BY THE SAME AUTHOR.
MANUAL OF CHEMICAL PHYSIOLOGY. Translated from the German, with Notes and Additions, by J CHESTON MORRIS, M. D., with an Introductory Essay on Vital Force, by Professor SAMUEL JACKSON, M. D., of the University of Pennsylvania. With illustrations on wood. In one very handsome octavo volume of 336 pages, extra cloth. $2 25.

TODD (ROBERT B.), M. D. F. R. S., and BOWMAN (W.), F. R. S.

THE PHYSIOLOGICAL ANATOMY AND PHYSIOLOGY OF MAN. With about three hundred large and beautiful illustrations on wood. Complete in one large octavo volume of 950 pages, extra cloth. Price $4 75.

BRANDE (WM. T.), D.C.L., and **T**AYLOR (ALFRED S.), M.D., F.R.S.

CHEMISTRY. Second American edition, thoroughly revised by Dr. TAYLOR. In one handsome 8vo. volume of 764 pages, extra cloth, $5 00; leather, $6 00. (*Just Issued.*)

FROM DR. TAYLOR'S PREFACE.

"The revision of the second edition, in consequence of the death of my lamented colleague, has devolved entirely upon myself. Every chapter, and indeed every page, has been revised, and numerous additions made in all parts of the volume. These additions have been restricted chiefly to subjects having some practical interest, and they have been made as concise as possible, in order to keep the book within those limits which may retain for it the character of a Student's Manual"—*London*, June 29, 1867.

A book that has already so established a reputation, as has Brande and Taylor's Chemistry, can hardly need a notice, save to mention the additions and improvements of the edition. Doubtless the work will long remain a favorite text-book in the schools, as well as a convenient book of reference for all.—*N. Y. Medical Gazette*, Oct. 12, 1867.

For this reason we hail with delight the republication, in a form which will meet with general approval and command public attention, of this really valuable standard work on chemistry—more particularly as it has been adapted with such care to the wants of the general public. The well known scholarship of its authors, and their extensive researches for many years in experimental chemistry, have been long appreciated in the scientific world, but in this work they have been careful to give the largest possible amount of information with the most sparing use of technical terms and phraseology, so as to furnish the reader, "whether a student of medicine, or a man of the world, with a plain introduction to the science and practice of chemistry."—*Journal of Applied Chemistry*, Oct. 1867.

This second American edition of an excellent treatise on chemical science is not a mere republication from the English press, but is a revision and enlargement of the original, under the supervision of the surviving author, Dr. Taylor. The favorable opinion expressed on the publication of the former edition of this work is fully sustained by the present revision, in which Dr. T. has increased the size of the volume, by an addition of sixty-eight pages.—*Am. Journ. Med. Sciences*, Oct. 1867.

THE HANDBOOK IN CHEMISTRY OF THE STUDENT.—For clearness of language, accuracy of description, extent of information, and freedom from pedantry and mysticism, no other text-book comes into competition with it.—*The Lancet.*

The authors set out with the definite purpose of writing a book which shall be intelligible to any educated man. Thus conceived, and worked out in the most sturdy, common-sense method, this book gives in the clearest and most summary method possible all the facts and doctrines of chemistry.—*Medical Times.*

ODLING (WILLIAM).
Lecturer on Chemistry, at St. Bartholomew's Hospital, &c.

A COURSE OF PRACTICAL CHEMISTRY, arranged for the Use of Medical Students. With Illustrations. From the Fourth and Revised London Edition. In one neat royal 12mo. volume, extra cloth. $2. (*Just Ready.*)

BOWMAN (JOHN E.), M. D.

PRACTICAL HANDBOOK OF MEDICAL CHEMISTRY. Edited by C. L. BLOXAM, Professor of Practical Chemistry in King's College, London. Fifth American, from the fourth and revised English Edition. In one neat volume, royal 12mo., pp. 351, with numerous illustrations, extra cloth. $2 25.

The fourth edition of this invaluable text-book of Medical Chemistry was published in England in October of the last year. The Editor has brought down the Handbook to that date, introducing, as far as was compatible with the necessary conciseness of such a work, all the valuable discoveries in the science which have come to light since the previous edition was printed. The work is indispensable to every student of medicine or enlightened practitioner. It is printed in clear type, and the illustrations are numerous and intelligible.—*Boston Med. and Surg. Journal.*

BY THE SAME AUTHOR.

INTRODUCTION TO PRACTICAL CHEMISTRY, INCLUDING ANALYSIS. Fifth American, from the fifth and revised London edition. With numerous illustrations. In one neat vol., royal 12mo., extra cloth. $2 25. (*Just Issued.*)

One of the most complete manuals that has for a long time been given to the medical student.—*Athenæum.*

We regard it as realizing almost everything to be desired in an introduction to Practical Chemistry.

It is by far the best adapted for the Chemical student of any that has yet fallen in our way.—*British and Foreign Medico-Chirurgical Review.*

The best introductory work on the subject with which we are acquainted.—*Edinburgh Monthly Jour.*

GRAHAM (THOMAS), F.R.S.

THE ELEMENTS OF INORGANIC CHEMISTRY, including the Applications of the Science in the Arts. New and much enlarged edition, by HENRY WATTS and ROBERT BRIDGES, M. D. Complete in one large and handsome octavo volume, of over 800 very large pages, with two hundred and thirty-two wood-cuts, extra cloth. $5 50.

KNAPP'S TECHNOLOGY; or Chemistry Applied to the Arts, and to Manufactures. With American additions, by Prof. WALTER R. JOHNSON. In two very handsome octavo volumes, with 500 wood engravings, extra cloth, $6 00.

DUNGLISON (ROBLEY), M.D.,

NEW REMEDIES, WITH FORMULÆ FOR THEIR PREPARATION AND ADMINISTRATION. Seventh edition, with extensive additions. In one very large octavo volume of 770 pages, extra cloth. $4 00.

HENRY C. LEA'S PUBLICATIONS—(*Chemistry, Pharmacy, &c.*). 11

*F*OWNES (GEORGE), Ph. D.
A MANUAL OF ELEMENTARY CHEMISTRY; Theoretical and Practical. With one hundred and ninety-seven illustrations. A new American, from the tenth and revised London edition. Edited by ROBERT BRIDGES, M. D. In one large royal 12mo. volume, of about 850 pp., extra cloth, $2 75; leather, $3 25. (*Just Ready.*)

Some years having elapsed since the appearance of the last American edition, and several revisions having been made of the work in England during the interval, it will be found very greatly altered, and enlarged by about two hundred and fifty pages, containing nearly one half more matter than before. The editors, Mr. Watts and Dr. Bence Jones, have labored sedulously to render it worthy in all respects of the very remarkable favor which it has thus far enjoyed, by incorporating in it all the most recent investigations and discoveries, in so far as is compatible with its design as an elementary text-book. While its distinguishing characteristics have been preserved, various portions have been rewritten, and especial pains have been taken with the department of Organic Chemistry in which late researches have accumulated so many new facts and have enabled the subject to be systematized and rendered intelligible in a manner formerly impossible. As only a few months have elapsed since the work thus passed through the hands of Mr. Watts and Dr. Bence Jones, but little has remained to be done by the American editor. Such additions as seemed advisable have however been made, and especial care has been taken to secure, by the closest scrutiny, the accuracy so essential in a work of this nature.

Thus fully brought up to a level with the latest advances of science, and presented at a price within the reach of all, it is hoped that the work will maintain its position as the favorite text book of the medical student.

This work is so well known that it seems almost superfluous for us to speak about it. It has been a favorite text-book with medical students for years, and its popularity has in no respect diminished. Whenever we have been consulted by medical students, as has frequently occurred, what treatise on chemistry they should procure, we have always recommended Fownes', for we regarded it as the best. There is no work that combines so many excellences. It is of convenient size, not prolix, of plain perspicuous diction, contains all the most recent discoveries, and is of moderate price.—*Cincinnati Med. Repertory*, Aug. 1869.

Large additions have been made, especially in the department of organic chemistry, and we know of no other work that has greater claims on the physician, pharmaceutist, or student, than this. We cheerfully recommend it as the best text-book on elementary chemistry, and bespeak for it the careful attention of students of pharmacy.—*Chicago Pharmacist*, Aug. 1869.

The American reprint of the tenth revised and corrected English edition is now issued, and represents the present condition of the science. No comments are necessary to insure it a favorable reception at the hands of practitioners and students.—*Boston Med. and Surg. Journal*, Aug. 12, 1869.

It will continue, as heretofore, to hold the first rank as a text-book for students of medicine.—*Chicago Med. Examiner*, Aug. 1869.

This work, long the recognized Manual of Chemistry, appears as a tenth edition, under the able editorship of Bence Jones and Henry Watts. The chapter on the General Principles of Chemical Philosophy, and the greater part of the organic chemistry, have been rewritten, and the whole work revised in accordance with the recent advances in chemical knowledge. It remains the standard text-book of chemistry.—*Dublin Quarterly Journal*, Feb. 1869.

There is probably not a student of chemistry in this country to whom the admirable manual of the late Professor Fownes is unknown. It has achieved a success which we believe is entirely without a parallel among scientific text-books in our language. This success has arisen from the fact that there is no English work on chemistry which combines so many excellences. Of convenient size, of attractive form, clear and concise in diction, well illustrated, and of moderate price, it would seem that every requisite for a student's hand-book has been attained. The ninth edition was published under the joint editorship of Dr. Bence Jones and Dr. Hofmann; the new one has been superintended through the press by Dr. Bence Jones and Mr. Henry Watts. It is not too much to say that it could not possibly have been in better hands. There is no one in England who can compare with Mr. Watts in experience as a compiler in chemical literature, and we have much pleasure in recording the fact that his reputation is well sustained by this, his last undertaking.—*The Chemical News*, Feb. 1869.

Here is a new edition which has been long watched for by eager teachers of chemistry. In its new garb, and under the editorship of Mr. Watts, it has resumed its old place as the most successful of text-books.—*Indian Medical Gazette*, Jan. 1, 1869.

*P*ARRISH (EDWARD),
Professor of Materia Medica in the Philadelphia College of Pharmacy.
A TREATISE ON PHARMACY. Designed as a Text-Book for the Student, and as a Guide for the Physician and Pharmaceutist. With many Formulæ and Prescriptions. Third Edition, greatly improved. In one handsome octavo volume, of 850 pages, with several hundred illustrations, extra cloth. $5 00.

The immense amount of practical information condensed in this volume may be estimated from the fact that the Index contains about 4700 items. Under the head of Acids there are 312 references; under Emplastrum, 36; Extracts, 159; Lozenges, 25; Mixtures, 55; Pills, 56; Syrups, 131; Tinctures, 138; Unguentum, 57, &c.

We have examined this large volume with a good deal of care, and find that the author has completely exhausted the subject upon which he treats; a more complete work, we think, it would be impossible to find. To the student of pharmacy the work is indispensable; indeed, so far as we know, it is the only one of its kind in existence, and even to the physician or medical student who can spare five dollars to purchase it, we feel sure the practical information he will obtain will more than compensate him for the outlay.—*Canada Med. Journal*, Nov. 1864.

The medical student and the practising physician will find the volume of inestimable worth for study and reference.—*San Francisco Med. Press*, July, 1864.

When we say that this book is in some respects the best which has been published on the subject in the English language for a great many years, we do not wish it to be understood as very extravagant praise. In truth, it is not so much the best as the only book.—*The London Chemical News*.

An attempt to furnish anything like an analysis of Parrish's very valuable and elaborate *Treatise on Practical Pharmacy* would require more space than we have at our disposal. This, however, is not so much a matter of regret, inasmuch as it would be difficult to think of any point, however minute and apparently trivial, connected with the manipulation of pharmaceutic substances or appliances which has not been clearly and carefully discussed in this volume. Want of space prevents our enlarging further on this valuable work, and we must conclude by a simple expression of our hearty appreciation of its merits.—*Dublin Quarterly Jour. of Medical Science*, August, 1864.

STILLÉ (ALFRED), M. D.,
Professor of Theory and Practice of Medicine in the University of Penna.

THERAPEUTICS AND MATERIA MEDICA; a Systematic Treatise

on the Action and Uses of Medicinal Agents; including their Description and History. Third edition, revised and enlarged. In two large and handsome octavo volumes of about 1700 pages, extra cloth, $10; leather, $12. *(Just Issued.)*

That two large editions of a work of such magnitude should be exhausted in a few years, is sufficient evidence that it has supplied a want generally felt by the profession, and the unanimous commendation bestowed upon it by the medical press, abroad as well as at home, shows that the author has successfully accomplished his object in presenting to the profession a systematic treatise suited to the wants of the practising physician, and unincumbered with details interesting only to the naturalist or the dealer. Notwithstanding its enlargement, the present edition has been kept at the former very moderate price.

Dr. Stillé's splendid work on therapeutics and materia medica.—*London Med. Times*, April 8, 1865.

Dr. Stillé stands to-day one of the best and most honored representatives at home and abroad, of American medicine; and these volumes, a library in themselves, a treasure-house for every studious physician, assure his fame even had he done nothing more.—*The Western Journal of Medicine*, Dec. 1868.

We regard this work as the best one on Materia Medica in the English language, and as such it deserves the favor it has received.—*Am. Journ. Medical Sciences*, July 1868.

We need not dwell on the merits of the third edition of this magnificently conceived work. It is the work on Materia Medica, in which Therapeutics are primarily considered—the mere natural history of drugs being briefly disposed of. To medical practitioners this is a very valuable conception. It is wonderful how much of the riches of the literature of Materia Medica has been condensed into this book. The references alone would make it worth possessing. But it is not a mere compilation. The writer exercises a good judgment of his own on the great doctrines and points of Therapeutics. For purposes of practice, Stillé's book is almost unique as a repertory of information, empirical and scientific, on the actions and uses of medicines.—*London Lancet*, Oct. 31, 1868.

Through the former editions, the professional world is well acquainted with this work. At home and abroad its reputation as a standard treatise on Materia Medica is securely established. It is second to no work on the subject in the English tongue, and, indeed, is decidedly superior, in some respects, to any other.—*Pacific Med. and Surg. Journal*, July, 1868.

Stillé's Therapeutics is incomparably the best work on the subject.—*N. Y. Med. Gazette*, Sept. 26, 1868.

Dr. Stillé's work is becoming the best known of any of our treatises on Materia Medica.... One of the most valuable works in the language on the subjects of which it treats.—*N. Y. Med. Journal*, Oct. 1868.

The rapid exhaustion of two editions of Prof. Stillé's scholarly work, and the consequent necessity for a third edition, is sufficient evidence of the high estimate placed upon it by the profession. It is no exaggeration to say that there is no superior work upon the subject in the English language. The present edition is fully up to the most recent advance in the science and art of therapeutics.—*Leavenworth Medical Herald*, Aug. 1868.

The work of Prof. Stillé has rapidly taken a high place in professional esteem, and to say that a third edition is demanded and now appears before us, sufficiently attests the firm position this treatise has made for itself. As a work of great research, and scholarship, it is safe to say we have nothing superior. It is exceedingly full, and the busy practitioner will find ample suggestions upon almost every important point of therapeutics.—*Cincinnati Lancet*, Aug. 1868.

It is just eight years since the first edition of Professor Stillé's work was presented to the profession, and we have now to chronicle the receipt of the third. This, we are certain, is a sure indication of the value in which it is held; it speaks more loudly in its favor than could possibly any words we could write. We consider it is of especial value to students, combining as it does therapeutics with a very excellent description of the articles of the materia medica.—*Canada Med. Journal*, July, 1868.

GRIFFITH (ROBERT E.), M.D.

A UNIVERSAL FORMULARY, Containing the Methods of Pre-

paring and Administering Officinal and other Medicines. The whole adapted to Physicians and Pharmaceutists. Second edition, thoroughly revised, with numerous additions, by ROBERT P. THOMAS, M.D., Professor of Materia Medica in the Philadelphia College of Pharmacy. In one large and handsome octavo volume of 650 pages, double-columns. Extra cloth, $4 00; leather, $5 00.

In this volume, the Formulary proper occupies over 400 double-column pages, and contains about 5000 formulas, among which, besides those strictly medical, will be found numerous valuable receipts for the preparation of essences, perfumes, inks, soaps, varnishes, &c. &c. In addition to this, the work contains a vast amount of information indispensable for daily reference by the practising physician and apothecary, embracing Tables of Weights and Measures, Specific Gravity, Temperature for Pharmaceutical Operations, Hydrometrical Equivalents, Specific Gravities of some of the Preparations of the Pharmacopœias, Relation between different Thermometrical Scales, Explanation of Abbreviations used in Formulæ, Vocabulary of Words used in Prescriptions, Observations on the Management of the Sick Room, Doses of Medicines, Rules for the Administration of Medicines, Management of Convalescence and Relapses, Dietetic Preparations not included in the Formulary, List of Incompatibles, Posological Table, Table of Pharmaceutical Names which differ in the Pharmacopœias, Officinal Preparations and Directions, and Poisons.

Three complete and extended Indexes render the work especially adapted for immediate consultation. One, of DISEASES AND THEIR REMEDIES, presents under the head of each disease the remedial agents which have been usefully exhibited in it, with reference to the formulæ containing them—while another of PHARMACEUTICAL and BOTANICAL NAMES, and a very thorough GENERAL INDEX afford the means of obtaining at once any information desired. The Formulary itself is arranged alphabetically, under the heads of the leading constituents of the prescriptions.

This is one of the most useful books for the practising physician which has been issued from the press of late years, containing a vast variety of formulas for the safe and convenient administration of medicines, all arranged upon scientific and rational principles, with the quantities stated in full, without signs or abbreviations.—*Memphis Med. Recorder*.

We know of none in our language, or any other, so comprehensive in its details.—*London Lancet*.

One of the most complete works of the kind in any language.—*Edinburgh Med. Journal*.

We are not cognizant of the existence of a parallel work.—*London Med. Gazette*.

PEREIRA (JONATHAN), M.D., F.R.S. and L.S.

MATERIA MEDICA AND THERAPEUTICS; being an Abridgment of the late Dr. Pereira's Elements of Materia Medica, arranged in conformity with the British Pharmacopœia, and adapted to the use of Medical Practitioners, Chemists and Druggists, Medical and Pharmaceutical Students, &c. By F. J. FARRE, M.D., Senior Physician to St. Bartholomew's Hospital, and London Editor of the British Pharmacopœia; assisted by ROBERT BENTLEY, M.R.C.S., Professor of Materia Medica and Botany to the Pharmaceutical Society of Great Britain; and by ROBERT WARINGTON, F.R.S., Chemical Operator to the Society of Apothecaries. With numerous additions and references to the United States Pharmacopœia, by HORATIO C. WOOD, M.D., Professor of Botany in the University of Pennsylvania. In one large and handsome octavo volume of 1040 closely printed pages, with 236 illustrations, extra cloth, $7 00; leather, raised bands, $8 00. (*Lately Published.*)

The task of the American editor has evidently been no sinecure, for not only has he given to us all that is contained in the abridgment useful for our purposes, but by a careful and judicious embodiment of over a hundred new remedies has increased the size of the former work fully one-third, besides adding many new illustrations, some of which are original. We unhesitatingly say that by so doing he has proportionately increased the value, not only of the condensed edition, but has extended the applicability of the great original, and has placed his medical countrymen under lasting obligations to him. The American physician now has all that is needed in the shape of a complete treatise on materia medica, and the medical student has a text-book which, for practical utility and intrinsic worth, stands unparalleled. Although of considerable size, it is none too large for the purposes for which it has been intended, and every medical man should, in justice to himself, spare a place for it upon his book-shelf, resting assured that the more he consults it the better he will be satisfied of its excellence.—*N. Y. Med. Record*, Nov. 15, 1866.

It will fill a place which no other work can occupy in the library of the physician, student, and apothecary.—*Boston Med. and Surg. Journal*, Nov. 8, 1866.

Of the many works on Materia Medica which have appeared since the issuing of the British Pharmaco-

pœia, none will be more acceptable to the student and practitioner than the present. Pereira's Materia Medica had long ago asserted for itself the position of being the most complete work on the subject in the English language. But its very completeness stood in the way of its success. Except in the way of reference, or to those who made a special study of Materia Medica, Dr. Pereira's work was too full, and its perusal required an amount of time which few had at their disposal. Dr. Farre has very judiciously availed himself of the opportunity of the publication of the new Pharmacopœia, by bringing out an abridged edition of the great work. This edition of Pereira is by no means a mere abridged re-issue, but contains many improvements, both in the descriptive and therapeutical departments. We can recommend it as a very excellent and reliable text-book.—*Edinburgh Med Journal*, February, 1866.

The reader cannot fail to be impressed, at a glance, with the exceeding value of this work as a compend of nearly all useful knowledge on the materia medica. We are greatly indebted to Professor Wood for his adaptation of it to our meridian. Without his emendations and additions it would lose much of its value to the American student. With them it is an American book.—*Pacific Medical and Surgical Journal*, December, 1866.

ELLIS (BENJAMIN), M.D.

THE MEDICAL FORMULARY: being a Collection of Prescriptions derived from the writings and practice of many of the most eminent physicians of America and Europe. Together with the usual Dietetic Preparations and Antidotes for Poisons. The whole accompanied with a few brief Pharmaceutic and Medical Observations. Twelfth edition, carefully revised and much improved by ALBERT H. SMITH, M.D. In one volume 8vo. of 376 pages, extra cloth, $3 00. (*Now Ready.*)

This work has remained for some time out of print, owing to the anxious care with which the Editor has sought to render the present edition worthy a continuance of the very remarkable favor which has carried the volume to the unusual honor of a TWELFTH EDITION. He has sedulously endeavored to introduce in it all new preparations and combinations deserving of confidence, besides adding two new classes, Antemetics and Disinfectants, with brief references to the inhalation of atomized fluids, the nasal douche of Thudichum, suggestions upon the method of hypodermic injection, the administration of anæsthetics, &c. &c. To accommodate these numerous additions, he has omitted much which the advance of science has rendered obsolete or of minor importance, notwithstanding which the volume has been increased by more than thirty pages. A new feature will be found in a copious Index of Diseases and their remedies, which cannot but increase the value of the work as a suggestive book of reference for the working practitioner. Every precaution has been taken to secure the typographical accuracy so necessary in a work of this nature, and it is hoped that the new edition will fully maintain the position which "ELLIS' FORMULARY" has long occupied.

CARSON (JOSEPH), M.D.,
Professor of Materia Medica and Pharmacy in the University of Pennsylvania, &c.

SYNOPSIS OF THE COURSE OF LECTURES ON MATERIA MEDICA AND PHARMACY, delivered in the University of Pennsylvania. With three Lectures on the Modus Operandi of Medicines. Fourth and revised edition, extra cloth, $3 00. (*Just Issued.*)

ROYLE'S MATERIA MEDICA AND THERAPEUTICS; including the Preparations of the Pharmacopœias of London, Edinburgh, Dublin, and of the United States. With many new medicines. Edited by JOSEPH CARSON, M.D. With ninety-eight illustrations. In one large octavo volume of about 700 pages, extra cloth. $3 00.

CHRISTISON'S DISPENSATORY; OR, COMMENTARY on the Pharmacopœias of Great Britain and the United States. With copious additions, and 213 large wood-engravings. By R. EGLESFELD GRIFFITH, M.D. In one very handsome octavo volume of over 1000 pages, extra cloth. $4 00.

CARPENTER'S PRIZE ESSAY ON THE USE OF ALCOHOLIC LIQUORS IN HEALTH AND DISEASE. New edition, with a Preface by D. F. CONDIE, M.D., and explanations of scientific words. In one neat 12mo. volume, pp. 178, extra cloth. 60 cents.

DE JONGH ON THE THREE KINDS OF COD-LIVER OIL, with their Chemical and Therapeutic Properties. 1 vol. 12mo., cloth. 75 cents.

MAYNE'S DISPENSATORY AND THERAPEUTICAL REMEMBRANCER. With every Practical Formula contained in the three British Pharmacopœias. Edited, with the addition of the Formulæ of the U.S. Pharmacopœia, by R. E. GRIFFITH, M.D. In one 12mo. volume, 300 pp., extra cloth. 75 cents.

GROSS (SAMUEL D.), M. D.,
Professor of Surgery in the Jefferson Medical College of Philadelphia.

ELEMENTS OF PATHOLOGICAL ANATOMY. Third edition,
thoroughly revised and greatly improved. In one large and very handsome octavo volume of nearly 800 pages, with about three hundred and fifty beautiful illustrations, of which a large number are from original drawings; extra cloth. $4 00.

The very beautiful execution of this valuable work, and the exceedingly low price at which it is offered, should command for it a place in the library of every practitioner.

To the student of medicine we would say that we know of no work which we can more heartily commend than Gross's Pathological Anatomy.—*Southern Med. and Surg. Journal.*

The volume commends itself to the medical student; it will repay a careful perusal, and should be upon the book-shelf of every American physician.—*Charleston Med. Journal.*

It contains much new matter, and brings down our knowledge of pathology to the latest period.—*London Lancet.*

JONES (C. HANDFIELD), F.R.S., and SIEVEKING (ED. H.), M. D.,
Assistant Physicians and Lecturers in St. Mary's Hospital.

A MANUAL OF PATHOLOGICAL ANATOMY. First American
edition, revised. With three hundred and ninety-seven handsome wood engravings. In one large and beautifully printed octavo volume of nearly 750 pages, extra cloth, $3 50.

Our limited space alone restrains us from noticing more at length the various subjects treated of in this interesting work; presenting, as it does, an excellent summary of the existing state of knowledge in relation to pathological anatomy, we cannot too strongly urge upon the student the necessity of a thorough acquaintance with its contents.—*Medical Examiner.*

We have long had need of a hand-book of pathological anatomy which should thoroughly reflect the present state of that science. In the treatise before us this desideratum is supplied. Within the limits of a moderate octavo, we have the outlines of this great department of medical science accurately defined, and the most recent investigations presented in sufficient detail for the student of pathology. We cannot at this time undertake a formal analysis of this treatise, as it would involve a separate and lengthy consideration of nearly every subject discussed; nor would such analysis be advantageous to the medical reader. The work is of such a character that every physician ought to obtain it, both for reference and study.—*N. Y. Journal of Medicine.*

Its importance to the physician cannot be too highly estimated, and we would recommend our readers to add it to their library as soon as they conveniently can.—*Montreal Med. Chronicle.*

GLUGE'S ATLAS OF PATHOLOGICAL HISTOLOGY. Translated, with Notes and Additions, by JOSEPH LEIDY, M. D. In one volume, very large imperial quarto, with 320 copper-plate figures, plain and colored, extra cloth. $4 00.

SIMON'S GENERAL PATHOLOGY, as conducive to the Establishment of Rational Principles for the Prevention and Cure of Disease. In one octavo volume of 212 pages, extra cloth. $1 25.

WILLIAMS (CHARLES J. B.), M. D.,
Professor of Clinical Medicine in University College, London.

PRINCIPLES OF MEDICINE. An Elementary View of the Causes,
Nature, Treatment, Diagnosis, and Prognosis of Disease; with brief remarks on Hygienics, or the preservation of health. A new American, from the third and revised London edition. In one octavo volume of about 500 pages, extra cloth. $3 50.

The unequivocal favor with which this work has been received by the profession, both in Europe and America, is one among the many gratifying evidences which might be adduced as going to show that there is a steady progress taking place in the science as well as in the art of medicine.—*St. Louis Med. and Surg. Journal.*

No work has ever achieved or maintained a more deserved reputation.—*Virginia Med. and Surg. Journal.*

One of the best works on the subject of which it treats in our language.

It has already commended itself to the high regard of the profession; and we may well say that we know of no single volume that will afford the source of so thorough a drilling in the principles of practice as this. Students and practitioners should make themselves intimately familiar with its teachings— they will find their labor and study most amply repaid.—*Cincinnati Med. Observer.*

There is no work in medical literature which can fill the place of this one. It is the *Primer* of the young practitioner, the *Koran* of the scientific one.—*Stethoscope.*

A text-book to which no other in our language is comparable.—*Charleston Med. Journal.*

The absolute necessity of such a work must be evident to all who pretend to more than mere empiricism. We must conclude by again expressing our high sense of the immense benefit which Dr. Williams has conferred on medicine by the publication of this work. We are certain that in the present state of our knowledge his Principles of Medicine could not possibly be surpassed.—*London Jour. of Medicine.*

HARRISON'S ESSAY TOWARDS A CORRECT THEORY OF THE NERVOUS SYSTEM. In one octavo volume of 292 pp. $1 50.
SOLLY ON THE HUMAN BRAIN; its Structure, Physiology, and Diseases. From the Second and much enlarged London edition. In one octavo volume of 500 pages, with 120 wood-cuts; extra cloth. $2 50.
LA ROCHE ON YELLOW FEVER, considered in its Historical, Pathological, Etiological, and Therapeutical Relations. In two large and handsome octavo volumes, of nearly 1500 pages, extra cloth, $7 00.
LA ROCHE ON PNEUMONIA; its Supposed Connection, Pathological, and Etiological, with Autumnal Fevers, including an Inquiry into the Existence and Morbid Agency of Malaria. In one handsome octavo volume, extra cloth, of 500 pages. Price $3 00.
BUCKLER ON FIBRO-BRONCHITIS AND RHEUMATIC PNEUMONIA. In one octavo vol., extra cloth, pp. 150. $1 25.
FISKE FUND PRIZE ESSAYS,—LEE ON THE EFFECTS OF CLIMATE ON TUBERCULOUS DISEASE. AND WARREN ON THE INFLUENCE OF PREGNANCY ON THE DEVELOPMENT OF TUBERCLES. Together in one neat octavo volume extra cloth, $1 00.

FLINT (AUSTIN), M. D.,
Professor of the Principles and Practice of Medicine in Bellevue Med. College, N. Y.

A TREATISE ON THE PRINCIPLES AND PRACTICE OF MEDICINE; designed for the use of Students and Practitioners of Medicine. Third edition, revised and enlarged. In one large and closely printed octavo volume of 1002 pages; handsome extra cloth, $6 00; or strongly bound in leather, with raised bands, $7 00. (*Just Issued.*)

From the Preface to the Third Edition.

Since the publication, in December, 1866, of the second edition of this treatise, much time has been devoted to its revision. Recognizing in the favor with which it has been received a proportionate obligation to strive constantly to increase its worthiness, the author has introduced in the present edition additions, derived from his clinical studies, and from the latest contributions in medical literature, which, it is believed, will enhance considerably the practical utility of the work. A slight modification in the typographical arrangement has accommodated these additions without materially increasing the bulk of the volume.

NEW YORK, October, 1868.

At the very low price affixed, the profession will find this to be one of the cheapest volumes within their reach.

This work, which stands pre-eminently as the advance standard of medical science up to the present time in the practice of medicine, has for its author one who is well and widely known as one of the leading practitioners of this continent. In fact, it is seldom that any work is ever issued from the press more deserving of universal recommendation.—*Dominion Med. Journal*, May, 1869.

The third edition of this most excellent book scarcely needs any commendation from us. The volume, as it stands now, is really a marvel; first of all, it is excellently printed and bound — and we encounter that luxury of America, the ready-cut pages, which the Yankees are 'cute enough to insist upon—nor are these by any means trifles; but the contents of the book are astonishing. Not only is it wonderful that any one man can have grasped in his mind the whole scope of medicine with that vigor which Dr Flint shows, but the condensed yet clear way in which this is done is a perfect literary triumph Dr. Flint is pre-eminently one of the strong men, whose right to do this kind of thing is well admitted; and we say no more than the truth when we affirm that he is very nearly the only living man that could do it with such results as the volume before us.—*The London Practitioner*, March, 1869.

This is in some respects the best text-book of medicine in our language, and it is highly appreciated on the other side of the Atlantic, inasmuch as the first edition was exhausted in a few months. The second edition was little more than a reprint, but the present has, as the author says, been thoroughly revised Much valuable matter has been added, and by making the type smaller, the bulk of the volume is not much increased. The weak point in many American works is pathology, but Dr. Flint has taken peculiar pains on this point, greatly to the value of the book.—*London Med. Times and Gazette*, Feb. 6, 1869.

Published in 1866, this valuable book of Dr. Flint's has in two years exhausted two editions, and now we gladly announce a third. We say we gladly announce it, because we are proud of it as a national representative work of not only American, but of cosmopolitan medicine. In it the practice of medicine is young and philosophical, based on reason and common sense, and as such, we hope it will be at the right hand of every practitioner of this vast continent. —*California Medical Gazette*, March, 1869.

Considering the large number of valuable works in the practice of medicine, already before the profession, the marked favor with which this has been received, necessitating a third edition in the short space of two years, indicates unmistakably that it is a work of more than ordinary excellence, and must be accepted as evidence that it has largely fulfilled the object for which the author intended it. A marked feature in the work, and one which particularly adapts it for the use of students as a text-book, and certainly renders it none the less valuable to the busy practitioner as a work of reference, is brevity and simplicity. The present edition has been thoroughly revised, and much new matter incorporated, derived, as the author informs us, both from his own clinical studies, and from the latest contributions to medical literature, thus bringing it fully up with the most recent advances of the science, and greatly enhancing its practical utility; while, by a slight modification of its typographical arrangement, the additions have been accommodated without materially increasing its bulk.—*St Louis Med. Archives*, Feb. 1869.

If there be among our readers any who are not familiar with the treatise before us, we shall do them a service in persuading them to repair their omission forthwith. Combining to a rare degree the highest scientific attainments with the most practical common sense, and the closest habits of observation, the author has given us a volume which not only sets forth the results of the latest investigations of other laborers, but contains more original views than any other single work upon this well-worn theme within our knowledge.—*N. Y. Med. Gazette*, Feb. 27, 1869.

Practical medicine was at sea when this book appeared above the horizon as a safe and capacious harbor It came opportunely and was greeted with pleasurable emotions throughout the land.—*Nashville Med. and Surg. Journal*, May, 1869.

DUNGLISON, FORBES, TWEEDIE, AND CONOLLY.
THE CYCLOPÆDIA OF PRACTICAL MEDICINE: comprising Treatises on the Nature and Treatment of Diseases, Materia Medica and Therapeutics, Diseases of Women and Children, Medical Jurisprudence, &c. &c. In four large super-royal octavo volumes, of 3254 double-columned pages, strongly and handsomely bound in leather, $15; extra cloth, $11.

*** This work contains no less than four hundred and eighteen distinct treatises, contributed by sixty-eight distinguished physicians.

The most complete work on practical medicine extant, or at least in our language.—*Buffalo Medical and Surgical Journal.*

For reference, it is above all price to every practitioner.—*Western Lancet.*

One of the most valuable medical publications of the day. As a work of reference it is invaluable.— *Western Journal of Medicine and Surgery.*

It has been to us, both as learner and teacher, a work for ready and frequent reference, one in which modern English medicine is exhibited in the most advantageous light.—*Medical Examiner.*

BARLOW'S MANUAL OF THE PRACTICE OF MEDICINE. With Additions by D. F. CONDIE, M. D. 1 vol. 8vo., pp. 600, cloth. $2 50.

HOLLAND'S MEDICAL NOTES AND REFLECTIONS. From the third and enlarged English edition. In one handsome octavo volume of about 500 pages, extra cloth. $3 50.

HARTSHORNE (HENRY), M.D.,
Professor of Hygiene in the University of Pennsylvania.

ESSENTIALS OF THE PRINCIPLES AND PRACTICE OF MEDICINE. A handy-book for Students and Practitioners. Second edition, revised and improved. In one handsome royal 12mo. volume of 450 pages, clearly printed on small type, cloth, $2 38; half bound, $2 63. (*Now Ready.*)

The very cordial reception with which this work has met shows that the author has fully succeeded in his attempt to condense within a convenient compass the essential points of scientific and practical medicine, so as to meet the wants not only of the student, but also of the practitioner who desires to acquaint himself with the results of recent advances in medical science.

As a strikingly terse, full, and comprehensive embodiment in a condensed form of the essentials in medical science and art, we hazard nothing in saying that it is incomparably in advance of any work of the kind of the past, and will stand long in the future without a rival. A mere glance will, we think, impress others with the correctness of our estimate. Nor do we believe there will be found many who, after the most cursory examination, will fail to possess it. How one could be able to crowd so much that is valuable, especially to the student and young practitioner, within the limits of so small a book, and yet embrace and present all that is important in a well-arranged, clear form, convenient, satisfactory for reference, with so full a table of contents, and extended general index, with nearly three hundred formulas and recipes, is a marvel.—*Western Journal of Medicine*, Aug. 1867.

The little book before us has this quality, and we can therefore say that all students will find it an invaluable guide in their pursuit of clinical medicine. Dr. Hartshorne speaks of it as "an unambitious effort to make useful the experience of twenty years of private and hospital medical practice, with its attendant study and reflection." That the effort will prove successful we have no doubt, and in his study, and at the bedside, the student will find Dr. Hartshorne a safe and accomplished companion. We speak thus highly of the volume, because it approaches more nearly than any similar manual lately before us the standard at which all such books should aim—of teaching much, and suggesting more. To the student we can heartily recommend the work of our transatlantic colleague, and the busy practitioner, we are sure, will find in it the means of solving many a doubt, and will rise from the perusal of its pages, having gained clearer views to guide him in his daily struggle with disease.—*Dub. Med. Press*, Oct. 2, 1867.

Pocket handbooks of medicine are not desirable, even when they are as carefully and elaborately compiled as this, the latest, most complete, and most accurate which we have seen.—*British Med. Journal*, Sept. 21, 1867.

This work of Dr. Hartshorne must not be confounded with the medical manuals so generally to be found in the hands of students, serving them at best but as blind guides, better adapted to lead them astray than to any useful and reliable knowledge. The work before us presents a careful synopsis of the essential elements of the theory of diseased action, its causes, phenomena, and results, and of the art of healing, as recognized by the most authoritative of our professional writers and teachers. A very careful and candid examination of the volume has convinced us that it will be generally recognized as one of the best manuals for the use of the student that has yet appeared.—*American Journal Med. Sciences*, Oct. 1867.

WATSON (THOMAS), M.D., &c.

LECTURES ON THE PRINCIPLES AND PRACTICE OF PHYSIC. Delivered at King's College, London. A new American, from the last revised and enlarged English edition, with Additions, by D. FRANCIS CONDIE, M. D., author of "A Practical Treatise on the Diseases of Children," &c. With one hundred and eighty-five illustrations on wood. In one very large and handsome volume, imperial octavo, of over 1200 closely printed pages in small type; extra cloth, $6 50; strongly bound in leather, with raised bands, $7 50.

Believing this to be a work which should lie on the table of every physician, and be in the hands of every student, every effort has been made to condense the vast amount of matter which it contains within a convenient compass, and at a very reasonable price, to place it within reach of all. In its present enlarged form, the work contains the matter of at least three ordinary octavos, rendering it one of the cheapest works now offered to the American profession, while its mechanical execution makes it an exceedingly attractive volume.

DICKSON'S ELEMENTS OF MEDICINE; a Compendious View of Pathology and Therapeutics, or the History and Treatment of Diseases. Second edition, revised. 1 vol. 8vo. of 750 pages, extra cloth. $4 00.

WHAT TO OBSERVE AT THE BEDSIDE AND AFTER DEATH IN MEDICAL CASES. Published under the authority of the London Society for Medical Observation. From the second London edition. 1 vol. royal 12mo., extra cloth, $1 00.

LAYCOCK'S LECTURES ON THE PRINCIPLES AND METHODS OF MEDICAL OBSERVATION AND RESEARCH. For the use of advanced students and junior practitioners. In one very neat royal 12mo. volume, extra cloth. $1 00.

BARCLAY (A. W.), M.D.

A MANUAL OF MEDICAL DIAGNOSIS; being an Analysis of the Signs and Symptoms of Disease. Third American from the second and revised London edition. In one neat octavo volume of 451 pages, extra cloth. $3 50.

A work of immense practical utility.—*London Med. Times and Gazette.*

The book should be in the hands of every practical man.—*Dublin Med. Press.*

FULLER (HENRY WILLIAM), M.D.,
Physician to St. George's Hospital, London.

ON DISEASES OF THE LUNGS AND AIR-PASSAGES. Their Pathology, Physical Diagnosis, Symptoms, and Treatment. From the second and revised English edition. In one handsome octavo volume of about 500 pages, extra cloth, $3 50. (*Just Issued.*)

Dr. Fuller's work on diseases of the chest was so favorably received, that to many who did not know the extent of his engagements, it was a matter of wonder that it should be allowed to remain three years out of print. Determined, however, to improve it, Dr. Fuller would not consent to a mere reprint, and accordingly we have what might be with perfect justice styled an entirely new work from his pen, the portion of the work treating of the heart and great vessels being excluded. Nevertheless, this volume is of almost equal size with the first.—*London Medical Times and Gazette*, July 20, 1867.

FLINT (AUSTIN), M. D.,
Professor of the Principles and Practice of Medicine in Bellevue Hospital Med. College, N. Y.

A PRACTICAL TREATISE ON THE PHYSICAL EXPLORATION OF THE CHEST AND THE DIAGNOSIS OF DISEASES AFFECTING THE RESPIRATORY ORGANS. Second and revised edition. In one handsome octavo volume of 595 pages, extra cloth, $4 50. (*Just Issued.*)

Premising this observation of the necessity of each student and practitioner making himself acquainted with auscultation and percussion, we may state our honest opinion that Dr. Flint's treatise is one of the most trustworthy guides which he can consult. The style is clear and distinct, and is also concise, being free from that tendency to over-refinement and unnecessary minuteness which characterizes many works on the same subject.—*Dublin Medical Press*, Feb. 6, 1867.

In the invaluable work before us, we have a book of *facts* of nearly 600 pages, admirably arranged, clear, thorough, and lucid on all points, without prolixity; exhausting every point and topic touched; a monument of patient and long-continued observation, which does credit to its author, and reflects honor on American medicine.—*Atlanta Med. and Surg. Journal*, Feb. 1867.

The chapter on Phthisis is replete with interest; and his remarks on the diagnosis, especially in the early stages, are remarkable for their acumen and great practical value. Dr. Flint's style is clear and elegant, and the tone of freshness and originality which pervades his whole work lend an additional force to its thoroughly practical character, which cannot fail to obtain for it a place as a standard work on diseases of the respiratory system.—*London Lancet*, Jan. 19, 1867.

This is an admirable book. Excellent in detail and execution, nothing better could be desired by the practitioner. Dr. Flint enriches his subject with much solid and not a little original observation.—*Ranking's Abstract*, Jan. 1867.

BY THE SAME AUTHOR. (*Now Ready.*)

A PRACTICAL TREATISE ON THE DIAGNOSIS, PATHOLOGY, AND TREATMENT OF DISEASES OF THE HEART. Second revised and enlarged edition. In one neat octavo volume of 550 pages, with a plate, extra cloth, $4.

The author has sedulously improved the opportunity afforded him of revising this work. Portions of it have been rewritten, and the whole brought up to a level with the most advanced condition of science. It must therefore continue to maintain its position as the standard treatise on the subject.

Dr. Flint chose a difficult subject for his researches, and has shown remarkable powers of observation and reflection, as well as great industry, in his treatment of it. His book must be considered the fullest and clearest practical treatise on those subjects, and should be in the hands of all practitioners and students. It is a credit to American medical literature.—*Amer. Journ. of the Med. Sciences*, July, 1860.

We question the fact of any recent American author in our profession being more extensively known, or more deservedly esteemed in this country than Dr. Flint. We willingly acknowledge his success, more particularly in the volume on diseases of the heart, in making an extended personal clinical study available for purposes of illustration, in connection with cases which have been reported by other trustworthy observers.—*Brit. and For. Med.-Chirurg. Review.*

In regard to the merits of the work, we have no hesitation in pronouncing it full, accurate, and judicious. Considering the present state of science, such a work was much needed. It should be in the hands of every practitioner.—*Chicago Med. Journ.*

With more than pleasure do we hail the advent of this work, for it fills a wide gap on the list of textbooks for our schools, and is, for the practitioner, the most valuable practical work of its kind.—*N. O. Med. News.*

PAVY (F. W.), M. D., F. R. S.
Senior Asst. Physician to and Lecturer on Physiology, at Guy's Hospital, &c.

A TREATISE ON THE FUNCTION OF DIGESTION; its Disorders and their Treatment. From the second London edition. In one handsome volume, small octavo, extra cloth, $2 00. (*Just Ready.*)

A thoroughly good book, being a careful systematic treatise, and sufficiently exhaustive for all practical purposes.—*Leavenworth Med. Herald*, July, 1869.

A very valuable work on the subject of which it treats. Small, yet it is full of valuable information.—*Cincinnati Med. Repertory*, June, 1869.

It presents the reader with a good summary of what is at present known concerning the physiological processes concerned in digestion, the pathological changes these processes are capable of undergoing, and the treatment they require. It is a convenient and practical work for the library of the practitioner.—*Chicago Med. Examiner*, July, 1869.

The work before us is one which deserves a wide circulation. We know of no better guide to the study of digestion and its disorders.—*St. Louis Med. and Surg. Journal*, July 10, 1869.

CHAMBERS (T. K.), M. D.,
Consulting Physician to St. Mary's Hospital, London, &c.

THE INDIGESTIONS; or, Diseases of the Digestive Organs Functionally Treated. Third and revised Edition. In one handsome octavo volume of over 300 pages, extra cloth. (*Nearly Ready.*)

BRINTON (WILLIAM), M. D., F. R. S.

LECTURES ON THE DISEASES OF THE STOMACH; with an Introduction on its Anatomy and Physiology. From the second and enlarged London edition. With illustrations on wood. In one handsome octavo volume of about 300 pages, extra cloth. $3 25. (*Just issued.*)

Nowhere can be found a more full, accurate, plain, and instructive history of these diseases, or more rational views respecting their pathology and therapeutics.—*Am. Journ. of the Med. Sciences*, April, 1865.

The most complete work in our language upon the diagnosis and treatment of these puzzling and important diseases.—*Boston Med. and Surg. Journal*, Nov. 1865.

HABERSHON ON DISEASES OF THE ALIMENTARY CANAL, ŒSOPHAGUS, STOMACH, CÆCUM, AND INTESTINES. With illustrations on wood. One vol. 8vo., 312 pages, extra cloth. $2 50.
CLYMER ON FEVERS; THEIR DIAGNOSIS, PATHOLOGY AND TREATMENT. In one octavo volume of 600 pages, leather. $1 75.
TODD'S CLINICAL LECTURES ON CERTAIN ACUTE DISEASES. In one neat octavo volume, of 320 pages, extra cloth. $2 50.

ROBERTS (WILLIAM), M. D.,
Lecturer on Medicine in the Manchester School of Medicine, &c.

A PRACTICAL TREATISE ON URINARY AND RENAL DISEASES, including Urinary Deposits. Illustrated by numerous cases and engravings. In one very handsome octavo volume of 516 pp., extra cloth. $4 50. (*Just Issued.*)

In carrying out this design, he has not only made good use of his own practical knowledge, but has brought together from various sources a vast amount of information, some of which is not generally possessed by the profession in this country. We must now bring our notice of this book to a close, regretting only that we are obliged to resist the temptation of giving further extracts from it. Dr. Roberts has already on several occasions placed before the profession the results of researches made by him on various points connected with the urine, and had thus led us to expect from him something good—in which expectation we have been by no means disappointed. The book is, beyond question, the most comprehensive work on urinary and renal diseases, considered in their strictly practical aspect, that we possess in the English language.—*British Medical Journal*, Dec. 9, 1865.

We have read this book with much satisfaction. It will take its place beside the best treatises in our language upon urinary pathology and therapeutics. Not the least of its merits is that the author, unlike some other book-makers, is contented to withhold much that he is well qualified to discuss in order to impart to his volume such a strictly practical character as cannot fail to render it popular among British readers.—*London Med. Times and Gazette*, March 17, 1866.

BASHAM (W. R.), M. D.,
Senior Physician to the Westminster Hospital, &c.

RENAL DISEASES: a Clinical Guide to their Diagnosis and Treatment. With illustrations. In one neat royal 12mo. volume of about 300 pages. (*Just Ready.*)

It is with the view of promoting a practical and clinical knowledge of a class of diseases which are not without their difficulties in diagnosis that the present work has been prepared, with the hope that both student and young practitioner may by it be assisted in their clinical observations.
—*Author's Preface.*

MORLAND ON RETENTION IN THE BLOOD OF THE ELEMENTS OF THE URINARY SECRETION.
1 vol. 8vo., extra cloth. 75 cents.

JONES (C. HANDFIELD). M. D.,
Physician to St. Mary's Hospital, &c.

CLINICAL OBSERVATIONS ON FUNCTIONAL NERVOUS DISORDERS. Second American Edition. In one handsome octavo volume of 348 pages, extra cloth, $3 25. (*Just Issued.*)

Taken as a whole, the work before us furnishes a short but reliable account of the pathology and treatment of a class of very common but certainly highly obscure disorders. The advanced student will find it a rich mine of valuable facts, while the medical practitioner will derive from it many a suggestive hint to aid him in the diagnosis of "nervous cases," and in determining the true indications for their amelioration or cure.—*Amer. Journ. Med. Sci.*, Jan. 1867.

We must cordially recommend it to the profession of this country as supplying, in a great measure, a deficiency which exists in the medical literature of the English language.—*New York Med. Journ.*, April, 1867.

The volume is a most admirable one—full of hints and practical suggestions.—*Canada Med. Journal*, April, 1867.

SLADE (D. D.), M. D.

DIPHTHERIA; its Nature and Treatment, with an account of the History of its Prevalence in various Countries. Second and revised edition. In one neat royal 12mo. volume, extra cloth. $1 25. (*Just issued.*)

SMITH ON CONSUMPTION; ITS EARLY AND REMEDIABLE STAGES. In one neat octavo volume of 254 pages, extra cloth. $2 25.
SALTER ON ASTHMA; its Pathology, Causes, Consequences, and Treatment. In one volume octavo, extra cloth. $2 50.

WALSHE'S PRACTICAL TREATISE ON THE DISEASES OF THE HEART AND GREAT VESSELS. Third American, from the third revised and much enlarged London edition. In one handsome octavo volume of 420 pages, extra cloth. $3 00.

HUDSON (A.), M. D., M. R. I. A.,
Physician to the Meath Hospital.

LECTURES ON THE STUDY OF FEVER. In one vol. 8vo., extra Cloth, $2 50. (*Now Ready.*)

As an admirable summary of the present state of our knowledge concerning fever, the work will be as welcome to the medical man in active practice as to the student. To the hard-worked practitioner who wishes to refresh his notions concerning fever, the book will prove most valuable. . . . We heartily commend his excellent volume to students and the profession at large.—*London Lancet*, June 22, 1867

The truly philosophical lectures of Dr. Hudson add much to our previous knowledge, all of which they, moreover, analyze and condense. This well-conceived task has been admirably executed in the lectures, illustrative cases and quotations being arranged in an appendix to each. We regret that space forbids our quotation from the lectures on treatment, which are, in regard to research and judgment, most masterly, and evidently the result of extended and mature experience.—*British Medical Journal*, Feb. 22, 1868.

LYONS (ROBERT D.), K. C. C.

A TREATISE ON FEVER; or, Selections from a Course of Lectures on Fever. Being part of a Course of Theory and Practice of Medicine. In one neat octavo volume, of 362 pages, extra cloth. $2 25.

BUMSTEAD (FREEMAN J.), M. D.,
Professor of Venereal Diseases at the Col. of Phys and Surg., New York, &c.

THE PATHOLOGY AND TREATMENT OF VENEREAL DISEASES. Including the results of recent investigations upon the subject. A new and revised edition, with illustrations. In one large and handsome octavo volume of 640 pages, extra cloth, $5 00. (*Lately Issued*.)

Well known as one of the best authorities of the present day on the subject.—*British and For. Med. Chirurg. Review*, April, 1866.

A regular store-house of special information.—*London Lancet*, Feb. 24, 1866.

A remarkably clear and full systematic treatise on the whole subject.—*Lond. Med. Times and Gazette.*

The best, completest, fullest monograph on this subject in our language.—*British American Journal.*

Indispensable in a medical library.—*Pacific Med. and Surg. Journal.*

We have no doubt that it will supersede in America every other treatise on Venereal.—*San Francisco Med. Press*, Oct. 1864.

A perfect compilation of all that is worth knowing on venereal diseases in general. It fills up a gap which has long been felt in English medical literature.—*Brit. and Foreign Med.-Chirurg. Review*, Jan., '65.

We have not met with any which so highly merits our approval and praise as the second edition of Dr. Bumstead's work.—*Glasgow Med. Journal*, Oct. 1864.

We know of no treatise in any language which is its equal in point of completeness and practical simplicity.—*Boston Medical and Surgical Journal*, Jan. 30, 1864.

CULLERIER (A.), and BUMSTEAD (FREEMAN J.),
Surgeon to the Hôpital du Midi.   Professor of Venereal Diseases in the College of Physicians and Surgeons, N. Y.

AN ATLAS OF VENEREAL DISEASES. Translated and Edited by FREEMAN J. BUMSTEAD. In one large imperial 4to. volume of 328 pages, double-columns, with 26 plates, containing about 150 figures, beautifully colored, many of them the size of life; strongly bound in extra cloth, $17 00; also, in five parts, stout wrappers for mailing, at $3 per part. (*Just Ready*.)

Anticipating a very large sale for this work, it is offered at the very low price of THREE DOLLARS a Part, thus placing it within the reach of all who are interested in this department of practice. Gentlemen desiring early impressions of the plates would do well to order it without delay.
A specimen of the plates and text sent free by mail, on receipt of 25 cents.

We wish for once that our province was not restricted to methods of treatment, that we might say something of the exquisite colored plates in this volume.—*London Practitioner*, May, 1869.

As a whole, it teaches all that can be taught by means of plates and print.—*London Lancet*, March 13, 1869.

Superior to anything of the kind ever before issued on this continent.—*Canada Med. Journal*, March, '69.

The practitioner who desires to understand this branch of medicine thoroughly should obtain this, the most complete and best work ever published.—*Dominion Med. Journal*, May, 1869.

This is a work of master hands on both sides. M. Cullerier is scarcely second to, we think we may truly say is a peer of the illustrious and venerable Ricord, while in this country we do not hesitate to say that Dr. Bumstead, as an authority, is without a rival. Assuring our readers that these illustrations tell the whole history of venereal disease, from its inception to its end, we do not know a single medical work, which for its kind is more *necessary* for them to have.—*California Med. Gazette*, March, 1869.

The most splendidly illustrated work in the language, and in our opinion far more useful than the French original.—*Am. Journ. Med. Sciences*, Jan. '69.

The fifth and concluding number of this magnificent work has reached us, and we have no hesitation in saying that its illustrations surpass those of previous numbers.—*Boston Med. and Surg. Journal*, Jan. 14, 1869.

Other writers besides M. Cullerier have given us a good account of the diseases of which he treats, but no one has furnished us with such a complete series of illustrations of the venereal diseases. There is, however, an additional interest and value possessed by the volume before us; for it is an American reprint and translation of M. Cullerier's work, with incidental remarks by one of the most eminent American syphilographers, Mr. Bumstead. The letter-press is chiefly M. Cullerier's, but every here and there a few lines or sentences are introduced by Mr. Bumstead; and, as M. Cullerier is a unicist, while Mr. Bumstead is a dualist, this method of treating the subject adds very much to its interest. By this means a liveliness is imparted to the volume which many other treatises sorely lack. It is like reading the report of a conversation or debate; for Mr. Bumstead often finds occasion to question M. Cullerier's statements or inferences, and this he does in a short and forcible way which helps to keep up the attention, and to make the book a very readable one.—*Brit. and For. Medico-Chir. Review*, July, 1869.

HILL (BERKELEY),
Surgeon to the Lock Hospital, London.

ON SYPHILIS AND LOCAL CONTAGIOUS DISORDERS. In one handsome octavo volume: extra cloth, $3 25. (*Just Issued*.)

Bringing, as it does, the entire literature of the disease down to the present day, and giving with great ability the results of modern research, it is in every respect a most desirable work, and one which should find a place in the library of every surgeon.—*California Med. Gazette*, June, 1869.

Considering the scope of the book and the careful attention to the manifold aspects and details of its subject, it is wonderfully concise. All these qualities render it an especially valuable book to the beginner, to whom we would most earnestly recommend its study; while it is no less useful to the practitioner.—*St. Louis Med. and Surg. Journal*, May, 1869.

The author, from a vast amount of material, with all of which he was perfectly familiar, has undertaken to construct a new book, and has really succeeded in producing a capital volume upon this subject.—*Nashville Med. and Surg. Journal*, May, 1869.

The most convenient and ready book of reference we have met with.—*N. Y. Med. Record*, May 1, 1869.

Most admirably arranged for both student and practitioner, no other work on the subject equals it; it is more simple, more easily studied.—*Buffalo Med. and Surg. Journal*, March, 1869.

LALLEMAND AND WILSON.

A PRACTICAL TREATISE ON THE CAUSES, SYMPTOMS AND TREATMENT OF SPERMATORRHŒA. By M. LALLEMAND. Fifth American edition. To which is added ———— ON DISEASES OF THE VESICULÆ SEMINALES. By MARRIS WILSON, M.D. In one neat octavo volume, of about 400 pp., extra cloth, $2 75.

WILSON (ERASMUS), F. R. S.,
ON DISEASES OF THE SKIN. With Illustrations on wood. Seventh American, from the sixth and enlarged English edition. In one large octavo volume of over 800 pages, $5. (*Just Issued.*)

A SERIES OF PLATES ILLUSTRATING "WILSON ON DISEASES OF THE SKIN;" consisting of twenty beautifully executed plates, of which thirteen are exquisitely colored, presenting the Normal Anatomy and Pathology of the Skin, and embracing accurate representations of about one hundred varieties of disease, most of them the size of nature. Price, in extra cloth, $5 50.

Also, the Text and Plates, bound in one handsome volume. Extra cloth, $10.

From the Preface to the Sixth English Edition.

The present edition has been carefully revised, in many parts rewritten, and our attention has been specially directed to the practical application and improvements of treatment. And, in conclusion, we venture to remark that if an acute and friendly critic should discover any difference between our present opinions and those announced in former editions, we have only to observe that science and knowledge are progressive, and that we have done our best to move onward with the times.

The industry and care with which the author has revised the present edition are shown by the fact that the volume has been enlarged by more than a hundred pages. In its present improved form it will therefore doubtless retain the position which it has acquired as a standard and classical authority, while at the same time it has additional claims on the attention of the profession as the latest and most complete work on the subject in the English language.

Such a work as the one before us is a most capital and acceptable help. Mr. Wilson has long been held as high authority in this department of medicine, and his book on diseases of the skin has long been regarded as one of the best text-books extant on the subject. The present edition is carefully prepared, and brought up in its revision to the present time In this edition we have also included the beautiful series of plates illustrative of the text, and in the last edition published separately. There are twenty of these plates, nearly all of them colored to nature, and exhibiting with great fidelity the various groups of diseases treated of in the body of the work.—*Cincinnati Lancet,* June, 1863.

No one treating skin diseases should be without a copy of this standard work.—*Canada Lancet,* August, 1863.

We can safely recommend it to the profession as the best work on the subject now in existence in the English language.—*Medical Times and Gazette.*

Mr. Wilson's volume is an excellent digest of the actual amount of knowledge of cutaneous diseases; it includes almost every fact or opinion of importance connected with the anatomy and pathology of the skin.—*British and Foreign Medical Review.*

These plates are very accurate, and are executed with an elegance and taste which are highly creditable to the artistic skill of the American artist who executed them.—*St. Louis Med. Journal.*

The drawings are very perfect, and the finish and coloring artistic and correct; the volume is an indispensable companion to the book it illustrates and completes.—*Charleston Medical Journal.*

BY THE SAME AUTHOR.

THE STUDENT'S BOOK OF CUTANEOUS MEDICINE and DISEASES OF THE SKIN. In one very handsome royal 12mo. volume. $3 50. (*Lately Issued.*)

NELIGAN (J. MOORE), M.D., M.R.I.A.,
A PRACTICAL TREATISE ON DISEASES OF THE SKIN Fifth American, from the second and enlarged Dublin edition by T. W. Belcher, M. D. In one neat royal 12mo. volume of 462 pages, extra cloth. $2 25. (*Just Issued.*)

Fully equal to all the requirements of students and young practitioners. It is a work that has stood its ground, that was worthy the reputation of the author, and the high position of which has been maintained by its learned editor.—*Dublin Med. Press and Circular,* Nov. 17, 1869.

Of the remainder of the work we have nothing beyond unqualified commendation to offer. It is so far the most complete one of its size that has appeared, and for the student there can be none which can compare with it in practical value. All the late discoveries in Dermatology have been duly noticed, and their value justly estimated; in a word, the work is fully up to the times, and is thoroughly stocked with most valuable information.—*New York Med. Record,* Jan. 15, 1867.

This instructive little volume appears once more. Since the death of its distinguished author, the study of skin diseases has been considerably advanced, and the results of these investigations have been added by the present editor to the original work of Dr. Neligan. This, however, has not so far increased its bulk as to destroy its reputation as the most convenient manual of diseases of the skin that can be procured by the student.—*Chicago Med. Journal,* Dec. 1866.

BY THE SAME AUTHOR.

ATLAS OF CUTANEOUS DISEASES. In one beautiful quarto volume, with exquisitely colored plates, &c., presenting about one hundred varieties of disease. Extra cloth, $5 50.

The diagnosis of eruptive disease, however, under all circumstances, is very difficult. Nevertheless, Dr. Neligan has certainly, "as far as possible," given a faithful and accurate representation of this class of diseases, and there can be no doubt that these plates will be of great use to the student and practitioner in drawing a diagnosis as to the class, order, and species to which the particular case may belong While looking over the "Atlas" we have been induced to examine also the "Practical Treatise," and we are inclined to consider it a very superior work, combining accurate verbal description with sound views of the pathology and treatment of eruptive diseases. —*Glasgow Med. Journal.*

A compend which will very much aid the practitioner in this difficult branch of diagnosis. Taken with the beautiful plates of the Atlas, which are remarkable for their accuracy and beauty of coloring, it constitutes a very valuable addition to the library of a practical man.—*Buffalo Med. Journal.*

HILLIER (THOMAS), M.D.,
Physician to the Skin Department of University College Hospital, &c.

HAND-BOOK OF SKIN DISEASES, for Students and Practitioners. (*New edition in preparation.*)

SMITH (J. LEWIS), M. D.,
Professor of Morbid Anatomy in the Bellevue Hospital Med. College, N. Y.
A COMPLETE PRACTICAL TREATISE ON THE DISEASES OF
CHILDREN. In one handsome octavo volume of 620 pages, extra cloth, $4 75; leather, $5 75. (*Now Ready.*)

We have no work upon the Diseases of Infancy and Childhood which can compare with it.—*Buffalo Med. and Surg. Journal*, March, 1869.

The description of the pathology, symptoms, and treatment of the different diseases is excellent.—*Am. Med. Journal*, April, 1869.

So full, satisfactory, and complete is the information to be derived from this work, that at no time have we examined the pages of any book with more pleasure. The diseases incident to childhood are treated with a clearness, precision, and understanding that is not often met with, and which must call forth the approval of all who consult its pages.—*Cincinnati Med. Repertory*, May, 1869.

This work is complete on the subject of which it treats, and enters more fully, with clearness and precision, into the diseases of childhood than most other works which we have seen. Physicians or students who wish to obtain a work containing the latest views on the treatment of children will find this one of the best.—*Dominion Med. Journal*, April, 1869.

The author of this volume is well known as a valued contributor to the literature of his specialty. The faithful manner in which he has worked in the public institutions with which he has been connected, the conscientious regard for truth which has for years characterized all his researches, the great amount of experience which he has been enabled to acquire in the treatment of infantile diseases, and the care which he has accustomed himself to take in the study of the significant facts relating to the pathological anatomy of the diseases of childhood, eminently fit him for the task which he has taken upon himself. The remarkable faculty of bringing out salient points and stating concisely other less important facts, enables him to crowd within a small compass a vast amount of practical information. The attention given to the treatment of the various maladies, as well as the presentation of all the recently accepted pathological views, make it one of the most valuable treatises, within its present compass, that can be placed in the hands of any seeker after truth. The volume as a whole will still further establish for the writer a permanent and enviable reputation as a careful observer, an impartial interpreter, a safe and trustworthy adviser, and a modest and untiring student.—*N. Y. Med. Record*, March 15, 1869.

We have perused Dr. Smith's book with not a little satisfaction; it is indeed an excellent work; well and correctly written; thoroughly up to the modern ideas; concise, yet complete in its material. We cannot help welcoming a work which will be worthy of reliance as a text-book for medical students and younger physicians in their investigation of disease in children.—*Boston Med. and Surg. Journal*, March 4, 1869.

CONDIE (D. FRANCIS), M. D.
A PRACTICAL TREATISE ON THE DISEASES OF CHILDREN.
Sixth edition, revised and augmented. In one large octavo volume of nearly 800 closely-printed pages, extra cloth, $5 25; leather, $6 25. (*Lately Issued.*)

Dr. Condie has been one of those who have performed such a service satisfactorily, and, as a result, his popular, comprehensive, and practical work has received that high compliment of approval on the part of his brethren, which several editions incontestably set forth. The present edition, which is the sixth, is fully up to the times in the discussion of all those points in the pathology and treatment of infantile diseases which have been brought forward by the German and French teachers. As a whole, however, the work is the best American one that we have, and in its special adaptation to American practitioners it certainly has no equal.—*New York Med. Record*, March 2, 1868.

No other treatise on this subject is better adapted to the American physician. Dr. Condie has long stood before his countrymen as one peculiarly pre-eminent in this department of medicine. His work has been so long a standard for practitioners and medical students that we do no more now than refer to the fact that it has reached its sixth edition. We are glad once more to refresh the impressions of our earlier days by wandering through its pages, and at the same time to be able to recommend it to the youngest members of the profession, as well as to those who have the older editions on their shelves.—*St. Louis Med. Reporter*, Feb. 15, 1868.

We pronounced the first edition to be the best work on the diseases of children in the English language, and, notwithstanding all that has been published, we still regard it in that light.—*Medical Examiner*.

WEST (CHARLES), M. D.,
Physician to the Hospital for Sick Children, &c.
LECTURES ON THE DISEASES OF INFANCY AND CHILDHOOD.
Fourth American from the fifth revised and enlarged English edition. In one large and handsome octavo volume of 656 closely-printed pages. Extra cloth, $4 50; leather, $5 50. (*Lately issued.*)

Of all the English writers on the diseases of children, there is no one so entirely satisfactory to us as Dr. West. For years we have held his opinion as judicial, and have regarded him as one of the highest living authorities in the difficult department of medical science in which he is most widely known. His writings are characterized by a sound, practical common sense, at the same time that they bear the marks of the most laborious study and investigation. We commend it to all as a most reliable adviser on many occasions when many treatises on the same subjects will utterly fail to help us.—*Boston Med. and Surg. Journal*, April 26, 1866.

Dr. West's volume is, in our opinion, incomparably the best authority upon the maladies of children that the practitioner can consult. Withal, too—a minor matter, truly, but still not one that should be neglected—Dr. West's composition possesses a peculiar charm, beauty and clearness of expression, thus affording the reader much pleasure, even independent of that which arises from the acquisition of valuable truths.—*Cincinnati Jour. of Medicine*, March, 1866.

We have long regarded it as the most scientific and practical book on diseases of children which has yet appeared in this country.—*Buffalo Medical Journal*.

SMITH (EUSTACE), M. D.,
Physician to the Northwest London Free Dispensary for Sick Children.
A PRACTICAL TREATISE ON THE WASTING DISEASES OF
INFANCY AND CHILDHOOD. 1 vol. 8vo., pp. 195, extra cloth, $1 50. (*Just Ready.*)

DEWEES (WILLIAM P.), M. D.,
Late Professor of Midwifery, &c., in the University of Pennsylvania, &c.
A TREATISE ON THE PHYSICAL AND MEDICAL TREATMENT OF CHILDREN.
Eleventh edition, with the author's last improvements and corrections. In one octavo volume of 548 pages. $2 80.

THOMAS (T. GAILLARD), M. D.,
Professor of Obstetrics, &c in the College of Physicians and Surgeons, N. Y., &c.

A PRACTICAL TREATISE ON THE DISEASES OF WOMEN. Second edition, revised and improved In one large and handsome octavo volume of 650 pages, with 225 illustrations, extra cloth, $5; leather, $6. (*Now Ready.*)

From the Preface to the Second Edition.

In a science so rapidly progressive as that of medicine, the profession has a right to expect that, when its approbation of a work is manifested by a call for a new edition, the author should respond by giving to his book whatever of additional value may be derivable from more extended experience, maturer thought, and the opportunity for correction. Fully sensible of this, the author of the present volume has sought by a careful revision of the whole, and by the addition of a chapter on Chlorosis, to render his work more worthy of the favor with which it has been received.—NEW YORK, March, 1869.

If the excellence of a work is to be judged by its rapid sale, this one must take precedence of all others upon the same, or kindred subjects, as evidenced in the short time from its first appearance, in which a new edition is called for, resulting, as we are informed, from the exhaustion of the previous large edition. We deem it scarcely necessary to recommend this work to physicians as it is now widely known, and most of them already possess it, or will certainly do so. To students we unhesitatingly recommend it as the best text-book on diseases of females extant.—*St. Louis Med. Reporter*, June, 1869.

Of all the army of books that have appeared of late years, on the diseases of the uterus and its appendages, we know of none that is so clear, comprehensive, and practical as this of Dr. Thomas', or one that we should more emphatically recommend to the young practitioner, as his guide.—*California Med. Gazette*, June, 1869.

If not the best work extant on the subject of which it treats, it is certainly second to none other. So short a time has elapsed since the medical press teemed with commendatory notices of the first edition, that it would be superfluous to give an extended review of what is now firmly established as *the* American text-book of Gynæcology.—*N. Y. Med. Gazette*, July 17, 1869.

This is a new and revised edition of a work which we recently noticed at some length, and earnestly commended to the favorable attention of our readers. The fact that, in the short space of one year, this second edition makes its appearance, shows that the general judgment of the profession has largely confirmed the opinion we gave at that time.—*Cincinnati Lancet*, Aug. 1869.

It is so short a time since we gave a full review of the first edition of this book, that we deem it only necessary now to call attention to the second appearance of the work. Its success has been remarkable, and we can only congratulate the author on the brilliant reception his book has received.—*N. Y. Med. Journal*, April, 1869.

We regard this treatise as the one best adapted to serve as a text-book on gynæcology.—*St. Louis Med. and Surg. Journal*, May 10, 1869.

The whole work as it now stands is an absolute indispensable to any physician aspiring to treat the diseases of females with success, and according to the most fully accepted views of their ætiology and pathology.—*Leavenworth Medical Herald*, May, 1869.

We have seldom read a medical book in which we found so much to praise, and so little—we can hardly say to object to—to mention with qualified commendation. We had proposed a somewhat extended review with copious extracts, but we hardly know where we should have space for it. We therefore content ourselves with expressing the belief that every practitioner of medicine would do well to possess himself of the work.—*Boston Med. and Surg. Journal*, April 29, 1869.

The number of works published on diseases of women is large, not a few of which are very valuable. But of those which are the most valuable we do not regard the work of Dr. Thomas as second to any. Without being prolix, it treats of the disorders to which it is devoted fully, perspicuously, and satisfactorily. It will be found a treasury of knowledge to every physician who turns to its pages. We would like to make a number of quotations from the work of a practical bearing, but our space will not permit. The work should find a place in the libraries of all physicians.—*Cincinnati Med. Repertory*, May, 1869.

No one will be surprised to learn that the valuable, readable, and thoroughly practical book of Professor Thomas has so soon advanced to a second edition. Although very little time has necessarily been allowed our author for revision and improvement of the work, he has performed it exceedingly well. Aside from the numerous corrections which he has found necessary to make, he has added an admirable chapter on chlorosis, which of itself is worth the cost of the volume.—*N. Y. Med. Record*, May 15, 1869.

CHURCHILL (FLEETWOOD), M. D., M. R. I. A.

ON THE DISEASES OF WOMEN; including those of Pregnancy and Childbed. A new American edition, revised by the Author. With Notes and Additions, by D. FRANCIS CONDIE, M. D., author of "A Practical Treatise on the Diseases of Children." With numerous illustrations. In one large and handsome octavo volume of 768 pages, extra cloth, $4 00; leather, $5 00.

BY THE SAME AUTHOR.

ESSAYS ON THE PUERPERAL FEVER, AND OTHER DISEASES PECULIAR TO WOMEN. Selected from the writings of British Authors previous to the close of the Eighteenth Century. In one neat octavo volume of about 450 pages, extra cloth. $2 50.

BROWN ON SOME DISEASES OF WOMEN ADMITTING OF SURGICAL TREATMENT. With handsome illustrations. One volume 8vo., extra cloth, pp. 276. $1 60.

ASHWELL'S PRACTICAL TREATISE ON THE DISEASES PECULIAR TO WOMEN. Illustrated by Cases derived from Hospital and Private Practice. Third American, from the Third and revised London edition. In one octavo volume, extra cloth, of 528 pages. $3 50.

RIGBY ON THE CONSTITUTIONAL TREATMENT OF FEMALE DISEASES. In one neat royal 12mo. volume, extra cloth, of about 250 pages. $1 00.

DEWEES'S TREATISE ON THE DISEASES OF FEMALES. With illustrations. Eleventh Edition, with the Author's last improvements and corrections. In one octavo volume of 536 pages, with plates, extra cloth, $3 00.

COLOMBAT DE L'ISÈRE ON THE DISEASES OF FEMALES. Translated by C. D. MEIGS, M. D. Second edition. In one vol. 8vo, extra cloth, with numerous wood-cuts. pp. 720. $3 75.

BENNETT'S PRACTICAL TREATISE ON INFLAMMATION OF THE UTERUS, ITS CERVIX AND APPENDAGES, and on its connection with Uterine Disease. Sixth American, from the fourth and revised English edition. 1 vol. 8vo., of about 500 pages, extra cloth. $3 75.

HODGE (HUGH L.), M.D.
 Emeritus Professor of Obstetrics, &c., in the University of Pennsylvania.
ON DISEASES PECULIAR TO WOMEN; including Displacements of the Uterus. With original illustrations. Second edition, revised and enlarged. In one beautifully printed octavo volume of 531 pages, extra cloth. $4 50. (*Just Issued.*)

In the preparation of this edition the author has spared no pains to improve it with the results of his observation and study during the interval which has elapsed since the first appearance of the work. Considerable additions have thus been made to it, which have been partially accommodated by an enlargement in the size of the page, to avoid increasing unduly the bulk of the volume.

From PROF. W. H. BYFORD, *of the Rush Medical College, Chicago.*

The book bears the impress of a master hand, and must, as its predecessor, prove acceptable to the profession. In diseases of women Dr. Hodge has established a school of treatment that has become world-wide in fame.

Professor Hodge's work is truly an original one from beginning to end, consequently no one can peruse its pages without learning something new. The book, which is by no means a large one, is divided into two grand sections, so to speak: first, that treating of the nervous sympathies of the uterus, and, secondly, that which speaks of the mechanical treatment of displacements of that organ. He is disposed, as a nonbeliever in the frequency of inflammations of the uterus, to take strong ground against many of the highest authorities in this branch of medicine, and the arguments which he offers in support of his position are, to say the least, well put. Numerous woodcuts adorn this portion of the work, and add incalculably to the proper appreciation of the variously shaped instruments referred to by our author. As a contribution to the study of women's diseases, it is of great value, and is abundantly able to stand on its own merits.—*N. Y. Medical Record*, Sept. 15, 1868.

In this point of view, the treatise of Professor Hodge will be indispensable to every student in its department. The large, fair type and general perfection of workmanship will render it doubly welcome. —*Pacific Med. and Surg. Journal,* Oct. 1868.

WEST (CHARLES), M.D.
LECTURES ON THE DISEASES OF WOMEN. Third American, from the Third London edition. In one neat octavo volume of about 550 pages, extra cloth. $3 75; leather, $4 75. (*Just Issued.*)

The reputation which this volume has acquired as a standard book of reference in its department, renders it only necessary to say that the present edition has received a careful revision at the hands of the author, resulting in a considerable increase of size. A few notices of previous editions are subjoined.

The manner of the author is excellent, his descriptions graphic and perspicuous, and his treatment up to the level of the time—clear, precise, definite, and marked by strong common sense.—*Chicago Med. Journal,* Dec. 1861.

We cannot too highly recommend this, the second edition of Dr. West's excellent lectures on the diseases of females. We know of no other book on this subject from which we have derived as much pleasure and instruction. Every page gives evidence of the honest, earnest, and diligent searcher after truth. He is not the mere compiler of other men's ideas, but his lectures are the result of ten years' patient investigation in one of the widest fields for women's diseases—St. Bartholomew's Hospital. As a teacher, Dr. West is simple and earnest in his language, clear and comprehensive in his perceptions, and logical in his deductions.—*Cincinnati Lancet,* Jan. 1862.

We return the author our grateful thanks for the vast amount of instruction he has afforded us. His valuable treatise needs no eulogy on our part. His graphic diction and truthful pictures of disease all speak for themselves.—*Medico-Chirurg. Review.*

Most justly esteemed a standard work. . . . . It bears evidence of having been carefully revised, and is well worthy of the fame it has already obtained. —*Dub. Med. Quar. Jour.*

As a writer, Dr. West stands, in our opinion, second only to Watson, the "Macaulay of Medicine;" he possesses that happy faculty of clothing instruction in easy garments; combining pleasure with profit, he leads his pupils, in spite of the ancient proverb, along a royal road to learning. His work is one which will not satisfy the extreme on either side, but it is one that will please the great majority who are seeking truth, and one that will convince the student that he has committed himself to a candid, safe, and valuable guide.—*N. A. Med.-Chirurg Review.*

We must now conclude this hastily written sketch with the confident assurance to our readers that the work will well repay perusal. The conscientious, painstaking, practical physician is apparent on every page.—*N. Y. Journal of Medicine.*

We have to say of it, briefly and decidedly, that it is the best work on the subject in any language, and that it stamps Dr. West as the *facile princeps* of British obstetric authors.—*Edinburgh Med. Journal.*

We gladly recommend his lectures as in the highest degree instructive to all who are interested in obstetric practice.—*London. Lancet.*

We know of no treatise of the kind so complete, and yet so compact.—*Chicago Med. Journal.*

BY THE SAME AUTHOR.
AN ENQUIRY INTO THE PATHOLOGICAL IMPORTANCE OF ULCERATION OF THE OS UTERI. In one neat octavo volume, extra cloth. $1 25.

MEIGS (CHARLES D.), M.D.,
 Late Professor of Obstetrics, &c. in Jefferson Medical College, Philadelphia.
WOMAN: HER DISEASES AND THEIR REMEDIES. A Series of Lectures to his Class. Fourth and Improved edition. In one large and beautifully printed octavo volume of over 700 pages, extra cloth, $5 00; leather, $6 00.

BY THE SAME AUTHOR.
ON THE NATURE, SIGNS, AND TREATMENT OF CHILDBED FEVER. In a Series of Letters addressed to the Students of his Class. In one handsome octavo volume of 365 pages, extra cloth. $2 00.

SIMPSON (SIR JAMES Y.), M.D.
CLINICAL LECTURES ON THE DISEASES OF WOMEN. With numerous illustrations. In one octavo volume of over 500 pages. Second edition, *preparing.*

HODGE (HUGH L.), M. D.,
Emeritus Professor of Midwifery, &c. in the University of Pennsylvania, &c.

THE PRINCIPLES AND PRACTICE OF OBSTETRICS. Illustrated with large lithographic plates containing one hundred and fifty-nine figures from original photographs, and with numerous wood-cuts. In one large and beautifully printed quarto volume of 550 double-columned pages, strongly bound in extra cloth, $14. (*Lately published.*)

The work of Dr. Hodge is something more than a simple presentation of his particular views in the department of Obstetrics; it is something more than an ordinary treatise on midwifery; it is, in fact, a cyclopædia of midwifery. He has aimed to embody in a single volume the whole science and art of Obstetrics. An elaborate text is combined with accurate and varied pictorial illustrations, so that no fact or principle is left unstated or unexplained.—*Am. Med. Times*, Sept. 3, 1864.

We should like to analyze the remainder of this excellent work, but already has this review extended beyond our limited space. We cannot conclude this notice without referring to the excellent finish of the work. In typography it is not to be excelled; the paper is superior to what is usually afforded by our American cousins, quite equal to the best of English books. The engravings and lithographs are most beautifully executed. The work recommends itself for its originality, and is in every way a most valuable addition to those on the subject of obstetrics.—*Canada Med. Journal*, Oct. 1864.

It is very large, profusely and elegantly illustrated, and is fitted to take its place near the works of great obstetricians. Of the American works on the subject it is decidedly the best.—*Edinb. Med. Jour.*, Dec. '64.

We have examined Professor Hodge's work with great satisfaction; every topic is elaborated most fully. The views of the author are comprehensive, and concisely stated. The rules of practice are judicious, and will enable the practitioner to meet every emergency of obstetric complication with confidence.—*Chicago Med. Journal*, Aug. 1864.

More time than we have had at our disposal since we received the great work of Dr. Hodge is necessary to do it justice. It is undoubtedly by far the most original, complete, and carefully composed treatise on the principles and practice of Obstetrics which has ever been issued from the American press.—*Pacific Med. and Surg. Journal*, July, 1864.

We have read Dr. Hodge's book with great pleasure, and have much satisfaction in expressing our commendation of it as a whole. It is certainly highly instructive, and in the main, we believe, correct. The great attention which the author has devoted to the mechanism of parturition, taken along with the conclusions at which he has arrived, point, we think, conclusively to the fact that, in Britain at least, the doctrines of Naegele have been too blindly received.—*Glasgow Med. Journal*, Oct. 1864.

*** Specimens of the plates and letter-press will be forwarded to any address, free by mail, on receipt of six cents in postage stamps.

TANNER (THOMAS H.), M. D.,

ON THE SIGNS AND DISEASES OF PREGNANCY. First American from the Second and Enlarged English Edition. With four colored plates and illustrations on wood. In one handsome octavo volume of about 500 pages, extra cloth, $4 25. (*Just Issued.*)

The very thorough revision the work has undergone has added greatly to its practical value, and increased materially its efficiency as a guide to the student and to the young practitioner.—*Am. Journ. Med. Sci.*, April, 1868.

With the immense variety of subjects treated of and the ground which they are made to cover, the impossibility of giving an extended review of this truly remarkable work must be apparent. We have not a single fault to find with it, and most heartily commend it to the careful study of every physician who would not only always be sure of his diagnosis of pregnancy, but always ready to treat all the numerous ailments that are, unfortunately for the civilized women of to-day, so commonly associated with the function.—*N. Y. Med. Record*, March 16, 1868.

We have much pleasure in calling the attention of our readers to the volume produced by Dr. Tanner, the second edition of a work that was, in its original state even, acceptable to the profession. We recommend obstetrical students, young and old, to have this volume in their collections. It contains not only a fair statement of the signs, symptoms, and diseases of pregnancy, but comprises in addition much interesting relative matter that is not to be found in any other work that we can name.—*Edinburgh Med. Journal*, Jan. 1868.

In its treatment of the signs and diseases of pregnancy it is the most complete book we know of, abounding on every page with matter valuable to the general practitioner.—*Cincinnati Med. Repertory*, March, 1868.

This is a most excellent work, and should be on the table or in the library of every practitioner.—*Humboldt Med. Archives*, Feb. 1868.

A valuable compendium, enriched by his own labors, of all that is known on the signs and diseases of pregnancy.—*St. Louis Med. Reporter*, Feb. 15, 1868.

MONTGOMERY (W. F.), M. D.,
Professor of Midwifery in the King's and Queen's College of Physicians in Ireland.

AN EXPOSITION OF THE SIGNS AND SYMPTOMS OF PREGNANCY. With some other Papers on Subjects connected with Midwifery. From the second and enlarged English edition. With two exquisite colored plates, and numerous wood-cuts. In one very handsome octavo volume of nearly 600 pages, extra cloth. $3 75.

MILLER (HENRY), M. D.,
Professor of Obstetrics and Diseases of Women and Children in the University of Louisville.

PRINCIPLES AND PRACTICE OF OBSTETRICS, &c.; including the Treatment of Chronic Inflammation of the Cervix and Body of the Uterus considered as a frequent cause of Abortion. With about one hundred illustrations on wood. In one very handsome octavo volume of over 600 pages, extra cloth. $3 75.

RIGBY'S SYSTEM OF MIDWIFERY. With Notes and Additional Illustrations. Second American edition. One volume octavo, extra cloth, 422 pages. $2 50.

DEWEES'S COMPREHENSIVE SYSTEM OF MIDWIFERY. Twelfth edition, with the author's last improvements and corrections. In one octavo volume, extra cloth, of 600 pages. $3 50.

MEIGS (CHARLES D.), M. D.,
Lately Professor of Obstetrics, &c., in the Jefferson Medical College, Philadelphia.
OBSTETRICS: THE SCIENCE AND THE ART. Fifth edition, revised. With one hundred and thirty illustrations. In one beautifully printed octavo volume of 760 large pages. Extra cloth, $5 50; leather, $6 50. (*Just Issued.*)

The original edition is already so extensively and favorably known to the profession that no recommendation is necessary; it is sufficient to say, the present edition is very much extended, improved, and perfected. Whilst the great practical talents and unlimited experience of the author render it a most valuable acquisition to the practitioner, it is so condensed as to constitute a most eligible and excellent text-book for the student.—*Southern Med. and Surg. Journal,* July, 1867.

It is to the student that our author has more particularly addressed himself; but to the practitioner we believe it would be equally serviceable as a book of reference. No work that we have met with so thoroughly details everything that falls to the lot of the accoucheur to perform. Every detail, no matter how minute or how trivial, has found a place.—*Canada Medical Journal,* July, 1867.

This very excellent work on the science and art of obstetrics should be in the hands of every student and practitioner. The rapidity with which the very large editions have been exhausted is the best test of its true merit. Besides, it is the production of an American who has probably had more experience in this branch than any other living practitioner of the country.—*St. Louis Med. and Surg. Journal,* Sept. 1867.

He has also carefully endeavored to be minute and clear in his details, with as little reiteration as possible, and beautifully combines the relations of science to art, as far as the different classifications will admit.—*Detroit Review of Med. and Pharm.,* Aug. 1867.

RAMSBOTHAM (FRANCIS H.), M. D.
THE PRINCIPLES AND PRACTICE OF OBSTETRIC MEDICINE AND SURGERY, in reference to the Process of Parturition. A new and enlarged edition, thoroughly revised by the author. With additions by W. V. KEATING, M. D., Professor of Obstetrics, &c., in the Jefferson Medical College, Philadelphia. In one large and handsome imperial octavo volume of 650 pages, strongly bound in leather, with raised bands; with sixty-four beautiful plates, and numerous wood-cuts in the text, containing in all nearly 200 large and beautiful figures. $7 00.

We will only add that the student will learn from it all he need to know, and the practitioner will find it, as a book of reference, surpassed by none other.—*Stethoscope.*

The character and merits of Dr. Ramsbotham's work are so well known and thoroughly established, that comment is unnecessary and praise superfluous. The illustrations, which are numerous and accurate, are executed in the highest style of art. We cannot too highly recommend the work to our readers.—*St. Louis Med. and Surg. Journal.*

To the physician's library it is indispensable, while to the student, as a text-book, from which to extract the material for laying the foundation of an education on obstetrical science, it has no superior.—*Ohio Med. and Surg. Journal.*

When we call to mind the toil we underwent in acquiring a knowledge of this subject, we cannot but envy the student of the present day the aid which this work will afford him.—*Am. Jour. of the Med. Sciences.*

CHURCHILL (FLEETWOOD), M. D., M. R. I. A.
ON THE THEORY AND PRACTICE OF MIDWIFERY. A new American from the fourth revised and enlarged London edition. With notes and additions by D. FRANCIS CONDIE, M. D., author of a "Practical Treatise on the Diseases of Children," &c. With one hundred and ninety-four illustrations. In one very handsome octavo volume of nearly 700 large pages. Extra cloth, $4 00; leather, $5 00.

In adapting this standard favorite to the wants of the profession in the United States, the editor has endeavored to insert everything that his experience has shown him would be desirable for the American student, including a large number of illustrations. With the sanction of the author, he has added, in the form of an appendix, some chapters from a little "Manual for Midwives and Nurses," recently issued by Dr. Churchill, believing that the details there presented can hardly fail to prove of advantage to the junior practitioner. The result of all these additions is that the work now contains fully one-half more matter than the last American edition, with nearly one-half more illustrations; so that, notwithstanding the use of a smaller type, the volume contains almost two hundred pages more than before.

These additions render the work still more complete and acceptable than ever; and with the excellent style in which the publishers have presented this edition of Churchill, we can commend it to the profession with great cordiality and pleasure.—*Cincinnati Lancet.*

Few works on this branch of medical science are equal to it, certainly none excel it, whether in regard to theory or practice, and in one respect it is superior to all others, viz., in its statistical information, and therefore, on these grounds a most valuable work for the physician, student, or lecturer, all of whom will find in it the information which they are seeking.—*Brit. Am. Journal.*

The present treatise is very much enlarged and amplified beyond the previous editions but nothing has been added which could be well dispensed with. An examination of the table of contents shows how thoroughly the author has gone over the ground, and the care he has taken in the text to present the subjects in all their bearings, will render this new edition even more necessary to the obstetric student than were either of the former editions at the date of their appearance. No treatise on obstetrics with which we are acquainted can compare favorably with this, in respect to the amount of material which has been gathered from every source.—*Boston Med. and Surg. Journal.*

There is no better text-book for students, or work of reference and study for the practising physician than this. It should adorn and enrich every medical library.—*Chicago Med. Journal.*

SWAYNE (JOSEPH GRIFFITHS), M. D.,
Physician-Accoucheur to the British General Hospital, &c.
OBSTETRIC APHORISMS FOR THE USE OF STUDENTS COMMENCING MIDWIFERY PRACTICE. From the Fourth and Revised London Edition, with Additions by E. R. HUTCHINS, M. D. With Illustrations. In one neat 12mo. volume. Extra cloth, $1 25. (*Just Ready.*)

GROSS (SAMUEL D.), M.D.,
Professor of Surgery in the Jefferson Medical College of Philadelphia.

A SYSTEM OF SURGERY: Pathological, Diagnostic, Therapeutic, and Operative. Illustrated by upwards of Thirteen Hundred Engravings. Fourth edition, carefully revised, and improved. In two large and beautifully printed royal octavo volumes of 2200 pages, strongly bound in leather, with raised bands. $15 00.

The continued favor, shown by the exhaustion of successive large editions of this great work, proves that it has successfully supplied a want felt by American practitioners and students. Though but little over six years have elapsed since its first publication, it has already reached its fourth edition, while the care of the author in its revision and correction has kept it in a constantly improved shape. By the use of a close, though very legible type, an unusually large amount of matter is condensed in its pages, the two volumes containing as much as four or five ordinary octavos. This, combined with the most careful mechanical execution, and its very durable binding, renders it one of the cheapest works accessible to the profession. Every subject properly belonging to the domain of surgery is treated in detail, so that the student who possesses this work may be said to have in it a surgical library.

It must long remain the most comprehensive work on this important part of medicine.—*Boston Medical and Surgical Journal*, March 23, 1865.

We have compared it with most of our standard works, such as those of Erichsen, Miller, Fergusson, Syme, and others, and we must, in justice to our author, award it the pre-eminence. As a work, complete in almost every detail, no matter how minute or trifling, and embracing every subject known in the principles and practice of surgery, we believe it stands without a rival. Dr Gross, in his preface, remarks "my aim has been to embrace the whole domain of surgery, and to allot to every subject its legitimate claim to notice;" and, we assure our readers, he has kept his word. It is a work which we can most confidently recommend to our brethren, for its utility is becoming the more evident the longer it is upon the shelves of our library.—*Canada Med. Journal*, September, 1865.

The first two editions of Professor Gross' System of Surgery are so well known to the profession, and so highly prized, that it would be idle for us to speak in praise of this work.—*Chicago Medical Journal*, September, 1865.

We gladly indorse the favorable recommendation of the work, both as regards matter and style, which we made when noticing its first appearance.—*British and Foreign Medico-Chirurgical Review*, Oct. 1865.

The most complete work that has yet issued from the press on the science and practice of surgery.—*London Lancet.*

This system of surgery is, we predict, destined to take a commanding position in our surgical literature, and be the crowning glory of the author's well earned fame. As an authority on general surgical subjects, this work is long to occupy a pre-eminent place, not only at home, but abroad. We have no hesitation in pronouncing it without a rival in our language, and equal to the best systems of surgery in any language.—*N. Y. Med. Journal.*

Not only by far the best text-book on the subject, as a whole, within the reach of American students, but one which will be much more than ever likely to be resorted to and regarded as a high authority abroad.—*Am. Journal Med. Sciences*, Jan. 1865.

The work contains everything, minor and major, operative and diagnostic, including mensuration and examination, venereal diseases, and uterine manipulations and operations. It is a complete Thesaurus of modern surgery, where the student and practitioner shall not seek in vain for what they desire.—*San Francisco Med. Press*, Jan. 1865.

Open it where we may, we find sound practical information conveyed in plain language. This book is no mere provincial or even national system of surgery, but a work which, while very largely indebted to the past, has a strong claim on the gratitude of the future of surgical science.—*Edinburgh Med. Journal*, Jan. 1865.

A glance at the work is sufficient to show that the author and publisher have spared no labor in making it the most complete "System of Surgery" ever published in any country.—*St. Louis Med. and Surg. Journal*, April, 1865.

The third opportunity is now offered during our editorial life to review, or rather to indorse and recommend this great American work on Surgery. Upon this last edition a great amount of labor has been expended, though to all others except the author the work was regarded in its previous editions as so full and complete as to be hardly capable of improvement. Every chapter has been revised; the text augmented by nearly two hundred pages, and a considerable number of wood-cuts have been introduced. Many portions have been entirely re-written, and the additions made to the text are principally of a practical character. This comprehensive treatise upon surgery has undergone revisions and enlargements, keeping pace with the progress of the art and science of surgery, so that whoever is in possession of this work may consult its pages upon any topic embraced within the scope of its department, and rest satisfied that its teaching is fully up to the present standard of surgical knowledge. It is also so comprehensive that it may truthfully be said to embrace all that is actually known, that is really of any value in the diagnosis and treatment of surgical diseases and accidents. Wherever illustration will add clearness to the subject, or make better or more lasting impression, it is not wanting; in this respect the work is eminently superior.—*Buffalo Med. Journal*, Dec. 1864.

A system of surgery which we think unrivalled in our language, and which will indelibly associate his name with surgical science. And what, in our opinion, enhances the value of the work is that, while the practising surgeon will find all that he requires in it, it is at the same time one of the most valuable treatises which can be put into the hands of the student seeking to know the principles and practice of this branch of the profession which he designs subsequently to follow.—*The Brit. Am. Journ.*, Montreal.

BY THE SAME AUTHOR.

A PRACTICAL TREATISE ON THE DISEASES, INJURIES, AND MALFORMATIONS OF THE URINARY BLADDER, THE PROSTATE GLAND, AND THE URETHRA. Second edition, revised and much enlarged, with one hundred and eighty-four illustrations. In one large and very handsome octavo volume of over nine hundred pages, extra cloth. $4 00.

BY THE SAME AUTHOR.

A PRACTICAL TREATISE ON FOREIGN BODIES IN THE AIR-PASSAGES. In one handsome octavo volume, extra cloth, with illustrations. pp. 468. $2 75.

MALGAIGNE'S OPERATIVE SURGERY. With numerous illustrations on wood. In one handsome octavo volume, extra cloth, of nearly 600 pp. $2 50.

SKEY'S OPERATIVE SURGERY. In one very handsome octavo volume, extra cloth, of over 650 pages, with about 100 wood-cuts. $3 25.

ERICHSEN (JOHN),
Senior Surgeon to University College Hospital.

THE SCIENCE AND ART OF SURGERY; being a Treatise on Surgical Injuries, Diseases, and Operations. From the Fifth enlarged and carefully revised London Edition. With Additions by JOHN ASHHURST, Jr., M. D., Surgeon to the Episcopal Hospital, &c. Illustrated by over six hundred Engravings on wood. In one very large and beautifully printed imperial octavo volume, containing over twelve hundred closely printed pages: cloth, $7 50; leather, raised bands, $8 50.

This volume having enjoyed repeated revisions at the hands of the author has been greatly enlarged, and the present edition will thus be found to contain at least one-half more matter than the last American impression. On the latest London edition, just issued, especial care has been bestowed. Besides the most minute attention on the part of the author to bring every portion of it thoroughly on a level with the existing condition of science, he called to his aid gentlemen of distinction in special departments. Thus a chapter on the Surgery of the Eye and its Appendages has been contributed by Mr. Streatfeild; the section devoted to Syphilis has been rearranged under the supervision of Mr. Berkeley Hill; the subjects of General Surgical Diseases, including Pyæmia, Scrofula, and Tumors, have been revised by Mr. Alexander Bruce; and other professional men of eminence have assisted in other branches. The work may thus be regarded as embodying a complete and comprehensive view of the most advanced condition of British surgery; while such omissions of practical details in American surgery as were found have been supplied by the editor, Dr. Ashhurst.

Thus complete in every respect, thoroughly illustrated, and containing in one beautifully printed volume the matter of two or three ordinary octavos, it is presented at a price which renders it one of the cheapest works now accessible to the profession. A continuance of the very remarkable favor which it has thus far enjoyed is therefore confidently expected.

The high position which Mr. Erichsen's Science and Art of Surgery has for some time attained, not only in this country, but on the Continent and in America, almost limits the task of the reviewer, on the appearance of a new edition, to the mere announcement. Elaborate analysis and criticism would be out of place; and nothing remains to be done except to state in general terms that the author has bestowed on it that labor which such a work required in order to be made a representative of the existing state of surgical science and practice. Of the merits of the book as a guide to the "Science and Art of Surgery" it is not necessary for us to say much. Mr. Erichsen is one of those enlightened surgeons of the present day, who regard an acquaintance with the manual part of surgery as only a portion of that knowledge which a surgeon should possess.—*British Medical Journal*, Jan. 2, 1869.

Thus the work bears in every feature a stamp of novelty and freshness which will commend it to those who are making its acquaintance for the first time, whilst those who have found it a safe guide and friend in former years will be able to refer to the new edition for the latest information upon any point of surgical controversy.—*London Lancet*, Jan. 23, 1869.

BY THE SAME AUTHOR. *(Just Issued.)*

ON RAILWAY, AND OTHER INJURIES OF THE NERVOUS SYSTEM. In small octavo volume. Extra cloth, $1 00.

MILLER (JAMES),
Late Professor of Surgery in the University of Edinburgh, &c.

PRINCIPLES OF SURGERY. Fourth American, from the third and revised Edinburgh edition. In one large and very beautiful volume of 700 pages, with two hundred and forty illustrations on wood, extra cloth. $3 75.

BY THE SAME AUTHOR.

THE PRACTICE OF SURGERY. Fourth American, from the last Edinburgh edition. Revised by the American editor. Illustrated by three hundred and sixty-four engravings on wood. In one large octavo volume of nearly 700 pages, extra cloth. $3 75.

It is seldom that two volumes have ever made so profound an impression in so short a time as the "Principles" and the "Practice" of Surgery by Mr. Miller, or so richly merited the reputation they have acquired. The author is an eminently sensible, practical, and well-informed man, who knows exactly what he is talking about and exactly how to talk it.—*Kentucky Medical Recorder.*

PIRRIE (WILLIAM), F. R. S. E.,
Professor of Surgery in the University of Aberdeen.

THE PRINCIPLES AND PRACTICE OF SURGERY. Edited by JOHN NEILL, M. D., Professor of Surgery in the Penna. Medical College, Surgeon to the Pennsylvania Hospital, &c. In one very handsome octavo volume of 780 pages, with 316 illustrations, extra cloth. $3 75.

SARGENT (F. W.), M. D.

ON BANDAGING AND OTHER OPERATIONS OF MINOR SURGERY. New edition, with an additional chapter on Military Surgery. One handsome royal 12mo. volume, of nearly 400 pages, with 184 wood-cuts. Extra cloth, $1 75.

Exceedingly convenient and valuable to all members of the profession.—*Chicago Medical Examiner*, May, 1862.

The very best manual of Minor Surgery we have seen.—*Buffalo Medical Journal.*

We cordially commend this volume as one which the medical student should most closely study; and to the surgeon in practice it must prove itself instructive on many points which he may have forgotten.—*Brit. Am. Journal*, May, 1862.

DRUITT (ROBERT), M.R.C.S., &c.

THE PRINCIPLES AND PRACTICE OF MODERN SURGERY. A new and revised American, from the eighth enlarged and improved London edition. Illustrated with four hundred and thirty-two wood-engravings. In one very handsome octavo volume, of nearly 700 large and closely printed pages. Extra cloth, $4 00; leather, $5 00.

All that the surgical student or practitioner could desire.—*Dublin Quarterly Journal.*

It is a most admirable book. We do not know when we have examined one with more pleasure.—*Boston Med. and Surg. Journal.*

In Mr. Druitt's book, though containing only some seven hundred pages, both the principles and the practice of surgery are treated, and so clearly and perspicuously, as to elucidate every important topic. The fact that twelve editions have already been called for, in these days of active competition, would of itself show it to possess marked superiority. We have examined the book most thoroughly, and can say that this success is well merited. His book, moreover, possesses the inestimable advantages of having the subjects perfectly well arranged and classified, and of being written in a style at once clear and succinct.—*Am. Journal of Med. Sciences.*

Whether we view Druitt's Surgery as a guide to operative procedures, or as representing the latest theoretical surgical opinions, no work that we are at present acquainted with can at all compare with it. It is a compendium of surgical theory (if we may use the word) and practice in itself, and well deserves the estimate placed upon it.—*Brit. Am. Journal.*

Thus enlarged and improved, it will continue to rank among our best text-books on elementary surgery.—*Columbus Rev. of Med. and Surg.*

We must close this brief notice of an admirable work by recommending it to the earnest attention of every medical student.—*Charleston Medical Journal and Review.*

A text-book which the general voice of the profession in both England and America has commended as one of the most admirable "manuals," or, "*vade mecum*," as its English title runs, which can be placed in the hands of the student. The merits of Druitt's Surgery are too well known to every one to need any further eulogium from us.—*Nashville Med. Journal.*

HAMILTON (FRANK H.), M.D.,
Professor of Fractures and Dislocations, &c. in Bellevue Hosp. Med. College, New York.

A PRACTICAL TREATISE ON FRACTURES AND DISLOCATIONS. Third edition, thoroughly revised. In one large and handsome octavo volume of 777 pages, with 294 illustrations, extra cloth, $5 75. (*Just Issued.*)

In fulness of detail, simplicity of arrangement, and accuracy of description, this work stands unrivalled. So far as we know, no other work on the subject in the English language can be compared with it. While congratulating our trans-Atlantic brethren on the European reputation which Dr. Hamilton, along with many other American surgeons, has attained, we also may be proud that, in the *mother tongue*, a classical work has been produced which need not fear comparison with the standard treatises of any other nation.—*Edinburgh Med. Journal,* Dec. 1866.

The credit of giving to the profession the only complete practical treatise on fractures and dislocations in our language during the present century, belongs to the author of the work before us, a distinguished American professor of surgery; and his book adds one more to the list of excellent practical works which have emanated from his country, notices of which have appeared from time to time in our columns during the last few months.—*London Lancet,* Dec. 15, 1866.

These additions make the work much more valuable, and it must be accepted as the most complete monograph on the subject, certainly in our own, if not even in any other language.—*American Journal Med. Sciences,* Jan. 1867.

This is the most complete treatise on the subject in the English language.—*Ranking's Abstract,* Jan.1867.

A mirror of all that is valuable in modern surgery.—*Richmond Med. Journal,* Nov. 1866.

CURLING (T. B.), F.R.S.,
Surgeon to the London Hospital, President of the Hunterian Society, &c.

A PRACTICAL TREATISE ON DISEASES OF THE TESTIS, SPERMATIC CORD, AND SCROTUM. Second American, from the second and enlarged English edition. In one handsome octavo volume, extra cloth, with numerous illustrations. pp. 420. $2 00.

BRODIE'S CLINICAL LECTURES ON SURGERY. 1 vol. 8vo., 350 pp.; cloth, $1 25.

COOPER'S LECTURES ON THE PRINCIPLES AND PRACTICE OF SURGERY. In one very large octavo volume, extra cloth, of 750 pages. $2 00.

GIBSON'S INSTITUTES AND PRACTICE OF SURGERY. Eighth edition, improved and altered. With thirty-four plates. In two handsome octavo volumes, about 1000 pp., leather, raised bands. $6 50.

MACKENZIE ON DISEASES AND INJURIES OF THE EYE. 1 vol. 8vo., 1027 pp., extra cloth. $6.

ASHTON (T. J.)

ON THE DISEASES, INJURIES, AND MALFORMATIONS OF THE RECTUM AND ANUS; with remarks on Habitual Constipation. Second American, from the fourth and enlarged London edition. With handsome illustrations. In one very beautifully printed octavo volume of about 300 pages. $3 25. (*Just Issued.*)

We can recommend this volume of Mr Ashton's in the strongest terms, as containing all the latest details of the pathology and treatment of diseases connected with the rectum.—*Canada Med. Journ.,* March, 1866.

One of the most valuable special treatises that the physician and surgeon can have in his library.—*Chicago Medical Examiner,* Jan. 1866.

The short period which has elapsed since the appearance of the former American reprint, and the numerous editions published in England, are the best arguments we can offer of the merits, and of the uselessness of any commendation on our part of a book already so favorably known to our readers.—*Boston Med. and Surg. Journal,* Jan. 25, 1866.

MORLAND (W. W.), M.D.

DISEASES OF THE URINARY ORGANS; a Compendium of their Diagnosis, Pathology, and Treatment. With illustrations. In one large and handsome octavo volume of about 600 pages, extra cloth. $3 50.

WELLS (J. SOELBERG),
Professor of Ophthalmology in King's College Hospital, &c.

A TREATISE ON DISEASES OF THE EYE. First American Edition, with additions; illustrated with 216 engravings on wood, and six colored plates. Together with selections from the Test-types of Jaeger and Snellen. In one large and very handsome octavo volume of about 750 pages: extra cloth, $5 00; leather, $6 00. (*Just Ready.*)

A work has long been wanting which should represent adequately and completely the present aspect of British Ophthalmology, and this want it has been the aim of Mr. Wells to supply. The favorable reception of his volume by the medical press is a guarantee that he has succeeded in his undertaking, and in reproducing the work in this country every effort has been made to render it in every way suited to the wants of the American practitioner. Such additions as seemed desirable have been introduced by the editor, Dr. I. Minis Hays, and the number of illustrations has been more than doubled. The importance of test-types as an aid to diagnosis is so universally acknowledged at the present day that it seemed essential to the completeness of the work that they should be added, and as the author recommends the use of those both of Jaeger and of Snellen for different purposes, selections have been made from each, so that the practitioner may have at command all the assistance necessary. The work is thus presented as in every way fitted to merit the confidence of the American profession..

His chapters are eminently readable. His style is clear and flowing. He can be short without over-condensing, and accurate without hair splitting. These merits appear in a remarkable degree when he comes to treat of the more abstruse departments of his subject, and contrast favorably with the labored obscurity which mars the writings of some greater authorities in the same line. We congratulate Mr. Wells upon the success with which he has fulfilled his ideal, as represented in the preface, in producing "an English treatise on the diseases of the eye, which should embrace the modern doctrines and practice of the British and Foreign Schools of Ophthalmology." The new school of Ophthalmology may also be congratulated in having found an exponent who is neither a bigoted partisan of everything new, nor a scoffer at everything old.—*Glasgow Med. Journal*, May, 1869.

TOYNBEE (JOSEPH), F. R. S.,
Aural Surgeon to and Lecturer on Surgery at St. Mary's Hospital.

THE DISEASES OF THE EAR: their Nature, Diagnosis, and Treatment. With one hundred engravings on wood. Second American edition. In one very handsomely printed octavo volume of 440 pages; extra cloth, $4.

The appearance of a volume of Mr. Toynbee's, therefore, in which the subject of aural disease is treated in the most scientific manner, and our knowledge in respect to it placed fully on a par with that which we possess respecting most other organs of the body, is a matter for sincere congratulation. We may reasonably hope that henceforth the subject of this treatise will cease to be among the *opprobria* of medical science.—*London Medical Review.*

The work, as was stated at the outset of our notice, is a model of its kind, and every page and paragraph of it are worthy of the most thorough study. Considered all in all—as an original work, well written, philosophically elaborated, and happily illustrated with cases and drawings—it is by far the ablest monograph that has ever appeared on the anatomy and diseases of the ear, and one of the most valuable contributions to the art and science of surgery in the nineteenth century.—*N. Am. Med.-Chirurg. Review.*

LAURENCE (JOHN Z.), F. R. C. S.,
Editor of the Ophthalmic Review, &c.

A HANDY-BOOK OF OPHTHALMIC SURGERY, for the use of Practitioners. Second Edition, revised and enlarged. With numerous illustrations. In one very handsome octavo volume. (*Nearly Ready.*)

No book on ophthalmic surgery was more needed. Designed, as it is, for the wants of the busy practitioner, it is the *ne plus ultra* of perfection. It epitomizes all the diseases incidental to the eye in a clear and masterly manner, not only enabling the practitioner readily to diagnose each variety of disease, but affording him the more important assistance of proper treatment. Altogether this is a work which ought certainly to be in the hands of every general practitioner.—*Dublin Med. Press and Circular*, Sept. 12, '66.

We cordially recommend this book to the notice of our readers, as containing an excellent outline of modern ophthalmic surgery.—*British Med. Journal*, October 13, 1866.

Not only, as its modest title suggests, a "Handy-Book" of Ophthalmic Surgery, but an excellent and well-digested *résumé* of all that is of practical value in the specialty.—*New York Medical Journal*, November, 1866.

This object the authors have accomplished in a highly satisfactory manner, and we know no work we can more highly recommend to the "busy practitioner" who wishes to make himself acquainted with the recent improvements in ophthalmic science. Such a work as this was much wanted at this time, and this want Messrs. Laurence and Moon have now well supplied.—*Am. Journal Med. Sciences*, Jan. 1867.

LAWSON (GEORGE), F. R. C. S., Engl.
Assistant Surgeon to the Royal London Ophthalmic Hospital, Moorfields, &c.

INJURIES OF THE EYE, ORBIT, AND EYELIDS: their Immediate and Remote Effects. With about one hundred illustrations. In one very handsome octavo volume, extra cloth, $3 50. (*Now Ready.*)

This work will be found eminently fitted for the general practitioner. In cases of functional or structural diseases of the eye, the physician who has not made ophthalmic surgery a special study can, in most instances, refer a patient to some competent practitioner. Cases of injury, however, supervene suddenly and usually require prompt assistance, and a work devoted especially to them cannot but prove essentially useful to those who may at any moment be called upon to treat such accidents. The present volume, as the work of a gentleman of large experience, may be considered as eminently worthy of confidence for reference in all such emergencies.

It is an admirable practical book in the highest and best sense of the phrase.—*London Medical Times and Gazette*, May 18, 1867.

WALES (PHILIP S.), M. D., Surgeon U. S. N.

MECHANICAL THERAPEUTICS: a Practical Treatise on Surgical Apparatus, Appliances, and Elementary Operations: embracing Minor Surgery, Bandaging, Orthopraxy, and the Treatment of Fractures and Dislocations. With six hundred and forty-two illustrations on wood. In one large and handsome octavo volume of about 700 pages: extra cloth, $5 75; leather, $6 75. *(Just Issued.)*

A Naval Medical Board directed to examine and report upon the merits of this volume, officially states that "it should in our opinion become a standard work in the hands of every naval surgeon;" and its adoption for use in both the Army and Navy of the United States is sufficient guarantee of its adaptation to the needs of every-day practice.

The title of this book will give a reasonably good idea of its scope, but its merits can only be appreciated by a careful perusal of its text. No one who undertakes such a task will have any reason to complain that the author has not performed his duty, and has not taken every pains to present every subject in a clear, common-sense, and practical light. It is a unique specimen of literature in its way, in that, treating upon a variety of subjects, it is as a whole so completely up to the wants of the student and the general practitioner. We have never seen any work of its kind that can compete with it in real utility and extensive adaptability. Dr Wales perfectly understands what may naturally be required of him in the premises, and in the work before us has bridged over a very wide gap which has always heretofore existed between the first rudiments of surgery and practical surgery proper. He has emphatically given us a comprehensive work for the beginner; and when we say of his labors, that in their particular sphere they leave nothing to be desired, we assert a great deal to recommend the book to the attention of those specially concerned. In conclusion, we would state, at the risk of reiteration, that this is the most comprehensive book on the subject that we have seen; is the best that can be placed in the hands of the student in need of a first book on surgery, and the most useful that can be named for such general practitioners who, without any special pretensions to surgery, are occasionally liable to treat surgical cases.—*N. Y. Med. Record,* March 2, 1868.

It is certainly the most complete and thorough work of its kind in the English language. Students and young practitioners of surgery will find it invaluable. It will prove especially useful to inexperienced country practitioners, who are continually required to take charge of surgical cases, under circumstances precluding them from the aid of experienced surgeons.—*Pacific Med. and Surg. Journal,* Feb. 1868.

This is a most complete and elegant work of 673 pages, and is certainly well deserving of the commendation of every American surgeon. This work, besides its usefulness as a reference for practitioners, is most admirably adapted as a text-book for students. Its 642 illustrations in wood-cuts, represent every manner of surgical appliance, together with a minute description of each, the name of its inventor, and its practical utility in mechanical surgery. There is, perhaps, no work in the English language so complete in the description and detail of surgical apparatus and appliances as this one. The entire work entitles the author to great credit for his clear and distinct style as a writer, as well as for his accuracy of observation and great research in the field of surgery. We earnestly recommend every member of the profession to add a copy of it to his library, with the assurance that he will find some useful suggestion in the treatment of almost every surgical case that may come under his observation.—*Humboldt Med. Archives,* Feb. 1868.

The title of the above work is sufficiently indicative of its contents. We have not seen for a long time (in the English language) a treatise equal to this in extent, nor one which is better adapted to the wants of the general student and practitioner. It is not to the surgeon alone that this book belongs; the physician has frequent opportunities to fill an emergency by such knowledge as is here given. Every practitioner should make purchase of such a book—it will last him his lifetime.—*St. Louis Med. Reporter,* Feb. 1868.

BIGELOW (HENRY J.), M. D.,
Professor of Surgery in the Massachusetts Med. College.

ON THE MECHANISM OF DISLOCATION AND FRACTURE OF THE HIP. With the Reduction of the Dislocation by the Flexion Method. With numerous original illustrations. In one very handsome octavo volume. Cloth. $2 50. *(Now Ready.)*

The reputation of the author and the importance of the subject cannot fail to attract to this volume the attention which it deserves.

THOMPSON (SIR HENRY).
Surgeon and Professor of Clinical Surgery to University College Hospital.

LECTURES ON DISEASES OF THE URINARY ORGANS. With illustrations on wood. In one neat octavo volume, extra cloth. $2 25. *(Now Ready.)*

These lectures stand the severe test. They are instructive without being tedious, and simple without being diffuse; and they include many of those practical hints so useful for the student, and even more valuable to the young practitioner.—*Edinburgh Med. Journal,* April, 1869.

Very few words of ours are necessary to recommend these lectures to the profession. There is no subject on which Sir Henry Thompson speaks with more authority than that in which he has specially gathered his laurels; in addition to this, the conversational style of instruction, which is retained in these printed lectures, gives them an attractiveness which a systematic treatise can never possess.—*London Medical Times and Gazette,* April 24, 1869.

BY THE SAME AUTHOR. *(Nearly Ready.)*

ON THE PATHOLOGY AND TREATMENT OF STRICTURE OF THE URETHRA AND URINARY FISTULÆ. With plates and wood-cuts. From the third and revised English edition. In one very handsome octavo volume, extra cloth, $3 50. *(Just Ready.)*

This classical work has so long been recognized as a standard authority on its perplexing subjects that it should be rendered accessible to the American profession. Having enjoyed the advantage of a revision at the hands of the author within a few months, it will be found to present his latest views and to be on level with the most recent advances of surgical science.

TAYLOR (ALFRED S.), M.D.,
Lecturer on Med. Jurisp. and Chemistry in Guy's Hospital.

MEDICAL JURISPRUDENCE. Sixth American, from the eighth and revised London edition. With Notes and References to American Decisions, by CLEMENT B. PENROSE, of the Philadelphia Bar. In one large octavo volume of 776 pages, extra cloth, $4 50; leather, $5 50. (*Just Issued.*)

Considerable additions have been made by the editor to this edition, comprising some important sections from the author's larger work, "The Principles and Practice of Medical Jurisprudence," as well as references to American law and practice. The notes of the former editor, Dr. Hartshorne, have likewise been retained, and the whole is presented as fully worthy to maintain the distinguished position which the work has acquired as a leading text-book and authority on the subject.

A new edition of a work acknowledged as a standard authority everywhere within the range of the English language. Considering the new matter introduced, on trichiniasis and other subjects, and the plates representing the crystals of poisons, etc., it may fairly be regarded as the most compact, comprehensive, and practical work on medical jurisprudence which has issued from the press, and the one best fitted for students.—*Pacific Med. and Surg. Journal,* Feb. 1867.

The sixth edition of this popular work comes to us in charge of a new editor, Mr. Penrose, of the Philadelphia bar, who has done much to render it useful, not only to the medical practitioners of this country, but to those of his own profession. Wisely retaining the references of the former American editor, Dr. Hartshorne, he has added many valuable notes of his own. The reputation of Dr. Taylor's work is so well established, that it needs no recommendation. He is now the highest living authority on all matters connected with forensic medicine, and every successive edition of his valuable work gives fresh assurance to his many admirers that he will continue to maintain his well-earned position. No one should, in fact, be without a text-book on the subject, as he does not know but that his next case may create for him an emergency for its use. To those who are not the fortunate possessors of a reliable, readable, interesting, and thoroughly practical work upon the subject, we would earnestly recommend this, as forming the best groundwork for all their future studies of the more elaborate treatises.—*New York Medical Record,* Feb. 15, 1867.

The present edition of this valuable manual is a great improvement on those which have preceded it. Some admirable instruction on the subject of evidence and the duties and responsibilities of medical witnesses has been added by the distinguished author, and some fifty cuts, illustrating chiefly the crystalline forms and microscopic structure of substances used as poisons, inserted. The American editor has also introduced several chapters from Dr. Taylor's larger work, "The Principles and Practice of Medical Jurisprudence," relating to trichiniasis, sexual malformation, insanity as affecting civil responsibility, suicidal mania, and life insurance, &c., which add considerably to its value. Besides this, he has introduced numerous references to cases which have occurred in this country. It makes thus by far the best guide-book in this department of medicine for students and the general practitioner in our language.—*Boston Med. and Surg. Journal,* Dec. 27, 1866.

WINSLOW (FORBES), M.D., D.C.L., &c.
ON OBSCURE DISEASES OF THE BRAIN AND DISORDERS OF THE MIND; their incipient Symptoms, Pathology, Diagnosis, Treatment, and Prophylaxis. Second American, from the third and revised English edition. In one handsome octavo volume of nearly 600 pages, extra cloth. $4 25. (*Just Issued.*)

Of the merits of Dr. Winslow's treatise the profession has sufficiently judged. It has taken its place in the front rank of the works upon the special department of practical medicine to which it pertains.—*Cincinnati Journal of Medicine,* March, 1866.

It is an interesting volume that will amply repay for a careful perusal by all intelligent readers.—*Chicago Med Examiner* Feb. 1866.

A work which, like the present, will largely aid the practitioner in recognizing and arresting the first insidious advances of cerebral and mental disease, is one of immense practical value, and demands earnest attention and diligent study on the part of all who have embraced the medical profession, and have thereby undertaken responsibilities in which the welfare and happiness of individuals and families are largely involved. We shall therefore close this brief and necessarily very imperfect notice of Dr. Winslow's great and classical work by expressing our conviction that it is long since so important and beautifully written a volume has issued from the British medical press.—*Dublin Medical Press.*

It is the most interesting as well as valuable book that we have seen for a long time. It is truly fascinating.—*Am. Jour. Med. Sciences.*

Dr. Winslow's work will undoubtedly occupy an unique position in the medico-psychological literature of this country.—*London Med. Review.*

LEA (HENRY C.)
SUPERSTITION AND FORCE: ESSAYS ON THE WAGER OF LAW, THE WAGER OF BATTLE, THE ORDEAL, AND TORTURE. Second Edition. In one handsome volume royal 12mo. (*Nearly Ready.*)

The copious collection of facts by which Mr. Lea has illustrated his subject shows in the fullest manner the constant conflict and varying success, the advances and defeats, by which the progress of humane legislation has been and is still marked. This work fills up with the fullest exemplification and detail the wise remarks which we have quoted above. As a book of ready reference on the subject it is of the highest value.—*Westminster Review,* Oct. 1867.

When—half in spite of himself, as it appears—he sketches a scene or character in the history of legalized error and cruelty, he betrays so artistic a feeling, and a humor so fine and good, that he makes us regret it was not within his intent, as it was certainly within his power, to render the whole of his thorough work more popular in manner.—*Atlantic Monthly,* Feb. '67.

This is a book of extraordinary research. Mr. Lea has entered into his subject *con amore;* and a more striking record of the cruel superstitions of our unhappy Middle Ages could not possibly have been compiled. . . . As a work of curious inquiry on certain outlying points of obsolete law, "Superstition and Force" is one of the most remarkable books we have met with.—*London Athenæum,* Nov. 3, 1866.

BY THE SAME AUTHOR. (*Now Ready.*)
STUDIES IN CHURCH HISTORY—THE RISE OF THE TEMPORAL POWER—BENEFIT OF CLERGY—EXCOMMUNICATION. In one large royal 12mo. volume of 516 pp. extra cloth. $2 75.

There are few problems in history more interesting than the rise of the Christian Church from the humblest beginnings to the possession of a theocratic despotism throughout Europe. The object of the present volume is to trace this progress, to analyze its causes, and to describe some of the results springing from the power thus intrusted to the church.

INDEX TO CATALOGUE.

	PAGE		PAGE
Allen's Dissector and Practical Anatomist	6	Knapp's Chemical Technology	11
American Journal of the Medical Sciences	1	Lea's Superstition and Force	31
Abstract, Half-Yearly, of the Med. Sciences	3	Lea's Studies in Church History	31
Anatomical Atlas, by Smith and Horner	6	Lallemand and Wilson on Spermatorrhœa	19
Ashton on the Rectum and Anus	28	La Roche on Yellow Fever	14
Ashwell on Diseases of Females	22	La Roche on Pneumonia, &c.	14
Basham on Renal Diseases	18	Laurence and Moon's Ophthalmic Surgery	29
Brinton on the Stomach	17	Lawson on the Eye	29
Bigelow on the Hip	30	Laycock on Medical Observation	16
Barclay's Medical Diagnosis	16	Lehmann's Physiological Chemistry, 2 vols.	9
Barlow's Practice of Medicine	15	Lehmann's Chemical Physiology	9
Bennet (Henry) on Diseases of the Uterus	22	Ludlow's Manual of Examinations	5
Bowman's (John E.) Practical Chemistry	10	Lyons on Fever	18
Bowman's (John E.) Medical Chemistry	10	Maclise's Surgical Anatomy	7
Brande & Taylor's Chemistry	10	Malgaigne's Operative Surgery, by Brittan	26
Brodie's Clinical Lectures on Surgery	28	Marshall's Physiology	8
Brown on the Surgical Diseases of Women	22	Mayne's Dispensatory and Formulary	13
Buckler on Bronchitis	14	Mackenzie on Diseases of the Eye	28
Bucknill and Tuke on Insanity	14	Medical News and Library	2
Bumstead on Venereal	19	Meigs' Obstetrics, the Science and the Art	25
Bumstead and Cullerier's Atlas of Venereal	19	Meigs's Lectures on Diseases of Women	23
Carpenter's Human Physiology	8	Meigs on Puerperal Fever	23
Carpenter's Comparative Physiology	8	Miller's System of Obstetrics	24
Carpenter on the Microscope	8	Miller's Practice of Surgery	27
Carpenter on the Use and Abuse of Alcohol	13	Miller's Principles of Surgery	27
Carson's Synopsis of Materia Medica	13	Montgomery on Pregnancy	24
Chambers on the Indigestions	17	Morland on Urinary Organs	23
Christison and Griffith's Dispensatory	13	Morland on Uræmia	18
Churchill's System of Midwifery	25	Neill and Smith's Compendium of Med. Science	5
Churchill on Diseases of Females	22	Neligan's Atlas of Diseases of the Skin	20
Churchill on Puerperal Fever	22	Neligan on Diseases of the Skin	20
Clymer on Fevers	17	Odling's Practical Chemistry	10
Colombat de l'Isère on Females, by Meigs	22	Pavy on Digestion	17
Condie on Diseases of Children	21	Prize Essays on Consumption	14
Cooper's (B. B.) Lectures on Surgery	28	Parrish's Practical Pharmacy	11
Cullerier's Atlas of Venereal Diseases	19	Pirrie's System of Surgery	27
Curling on Diseases of the Testis	29	Pereira's Mat. Medica and Therapeutics, abridged	13
Cyclopedia of Practical Medicine	15	Quain and Sharpey's Anatomy, by Leidy	6
Dalton's Human Physiology	9	Ranking's Abstract	3
De Jongh on Cod-Liver Oil	13	Roberts on Urinary Diseases	18
Dewees's System of Midwifery	24	Ramsbotham on Parturition	25
Dewees on Diseases of Females	22	Rigby on Female Diseases	22
Dewees on Diseases of Children	21	Rigby's Midwifery	24
Dickson's Practice of Medicine	16	Rokitansky's Pathological Anatomy	14
Druitt's Modern Surgery	28	Royle's Materia Medica and Therapeutics	13
Dunglison's Medical Dictionary	4	Salter on Asthma	18
Dunglison's Human Physiology	9	Swayne's Obstetric Aphorisms	25
Dunglison on New Remedies	10	Sargent's Minor Surgery	27
Ellis's Medical Formulary, by Smith	13	Sharpey and Quain's Anatomy, by Leidy	6
Erichsen's System of Surgery	27	Simon's General Pathology	14
Erichsen on Nervous Injuries	27	Simpson on Females	23
Flint on Respiratory Organs	17	Skey's Operative Surgery	26
Flint on the Heart	17	Slade on Diphtheria	18
Flint's Practice of Medicine	15	Smith (J. L.) on Children	21
Fownes's Elementary Chemistry	11	Smith (H. H.) and Horner's Anatomical Atlas	6
Fuller on the Lungs, &c.	16	Smith (Edward) on Consumption	18
Gibson's Surgery	28	Smith on Wasting Diseases of Children	21
Gluge's Pathological Histology, by Leidy	14	Solly on Anatomy and Diseases of the Brain	14
Graham's Elements of Chemistry	10	Stillé's Therapeutics	12
Gray's Anatomy	6	Tanner's Manual of Clinical Medicine	5
Griffith's (R. E.) Universal Formulary	12	Tanner on Pregnancy	24
Gross on Urinary Organs	26	Taylor's Medical Jurisprudence	31
Gross on Foreign Bodies in Air-Passages	26	Thomas on Diseases of Females	22
Gross's Principles and Practice of Surgery	26	Thompson on Urinary Organs	30
Gross's Pathological Anatomy	14	Thompson on Stricture	30
Hartshorne's Essentials of Medicine	16	Todd and Bowman's Physiological Anatomy	9
Hartshorne's Conspectus of the Medical Sciences	5	Todd on Acute Diseases	17
Hartshorne's Anatomy and Physiology	6	Toynbee on the Ear	29
Habershon on Alimentary Canal	17	Wales on Surgical Operations	30
Hamilton on Dislocations and Fractures	28	Walshe on the Heart	18
Harrison on the Nervous System	14	Watson's Practice of Physic	16
Heath's Practical Anatomy	7	Wells on the Eye	29
Hoblyn's Medical Dictionary	4	West on Diseases of Females	23
Hodge on Women	23	West on Diseases of Children	21
Hodge's Obstetrics	24	West on Ulceration of Os Uteri	23
Hodge's Practical Dissections	7	What to Observe in Medical Cases	16
Holland's Medical Notes and Reflections	15	Williams's Principles of Medicine	14
Horner's Anatomy and Histology	7	Wilson's Human Anatomy	7
Hudson on Fevers	18	Wilson's Dissector	7
Hill on Venereal Diseases	19	Wilson on Diseases of the Skin	20
Hillier's Handbook of Skin Diseases	20	Wilson's Plates on Diseases of the Skin	20
Jones and Sieveking's Pathological Anatomy	14	Wilson's Handbook of Cutaneous Medicine	20
Jones (C. Handfield) on Nervous Disorders	18	Wilson on Spermatorrhœa	19
Kirkes' Physiology	8	Winslow on Brain and Mind	31

www.ingramcontent.com/pod-product-compliance
Lightning Source LLC
Chambersburg PA
CBHW020306240426
43673CB00039B/716